KU-358-324

THE POETICAL WORKS OF WILLIAM COWPER

Edited by

H. S. MILFORD

FOURTH EDITION

LONDON
OXFORD UNIVERSITY PRESS
NEW YORK TORONTO

Oxford University Press, Amen House, London E.C.4
GLASGOW NEW YORK TORONTO MELBOURNE WELLINGTON
BOMBAY CALCUTTA MADRAS KARACHI LAHORE DACCA
CAPE TOWN SALISBURY NAIROBI IBADAN ACCRA
KUALA LUMPUR HONG KONG

WILLIAM COWPER

Born: Great Berkhampstead Rectory, 15 November 1731
Died: East Dereham, 25 April 1800

'The Poetical Works of William Cowper' were first included in the Oxford Series of Standard Authors in 1905, *and reprinted in* 1907. *A second edition, with additions, was published in* 1913, *a third, enlarged, in* 1926, *a fourth, much enlarged, was published in* 1934 *and reprinted in* 1947, 1950, 1959 *and* 1963

PRINTED IN GREAT BRITAIN
O.S.A.

PREFACE

In the thirty-five years that have elapsed since Canon Benham published the last one-volume edition of Cowper's poems, a certain number of new poems have appeared in various books, much new light has been thrown on Cowper's life, but little or no work has been done on the actual text of the poems. It seemed worth while therefore to collect these scattered poems and print them with the rest conveniently in one volume; to utilize the new facts by carefully testing thereby the dates hitherto accepted for the composition of the poems; and to examine the text afresh and if possible constitute it on scientific principles.

The poems first here collected do not, with two or three exceptions, add much to Cowper's poetic reputation; but the aim of this series is to provide complete texts, and readers of the Oxford Cowper have before them every poem of his hitherto printed (besides a few from MS.), except the translations of Homer and *Adamo*. No modern edition has reprinted these; the translation of Homer is dead, that of *Adamo* was never alive.

The dates at which most of the poems were composed are fairly certain; nor have the new facts displayed by Mr. Wright in his *Life of Cowper* (1892) and *Correspondence of Cowper* (1904) much disturbed the traditional order. But a search through various magazines and periodicals of the time, especially *The Gentleman's Magazine*, has enabled me to give earlier dates than have hitherto been known for the first publication of many of the miscellaneous poems; and the first published version often shows a large number of variations from later versions. I cannot hope to have traced all these early versions; an exhaustive search through the files of the *Northampton Mercury*, *General Evening Post*, and other papers not easily accessible, would be necessary for this. But the copies disinterred by previous editors and by myself supply ample evidence of the constant minute alterations made by Cowper in his least important poems; and this is the main interest of the early versions and the variants they supply; for the various readings are often intrinsically of equal value: the alteration has produced no improvement.

Consideration of this point leads naturally to the question of the text. It is in the constitution and presentation of the text that I hope to have made some advance on my predecessors. I have not, of course, attempted to chronicle all the misprints of all the early editions, or all the aberrations of Hayley and other editors; such a chronicle would serve no useful purpose and would take up an intolerable deal of space. But in the editions of the poems printed in Cowper's lifetime all variants which indicate a difference of reading have been noted: where two editors—Croft and Hayley, or Johnson and Hayley—of equal or nearly equal authority, print different versions of posthumous poems, one version has been followed throughout the poem, the variants from the other being placed in the notes: and, as already stated, readings involving verbal changes from early printed or MS. copies are given either in the footnotes or at the end of the volume. Thus an attempt has for the first time been made to supply a sufficiently full critical apparatus[1].

For the text of the poems contained in the two volumes published by Cowper himself I have followed the royal 8vo edition dated 1800. There were eleven editions of each volume before 1801: namely, 1782 and 1785 (first edition of each volume separately), 1786 (first two-volume edition), 1787, 1788, 1793, 1794-5, 1798 (2), 1799, 1800 (2)[2]. These fall into two main groups, those from 1782 (1785) to 1788 forming the first group, the remainder the second.

The second group differs from the first mainly by its adoption of a slightly more consistent and more modern spelling and a less haphazard punctuation; actual differences of text are very few, as may be seen by inspection of the critical notes. No doubt changes of spelling and punctuation were not definitely adopted by Cowper himself or even by his friends; at any rate there is no direct evidence that Cowper saw the proofs of any but the first edition of each volume, and we know that he gave away his copyright in them to Johnson the publisher[3], who doubtless produced editions as they were wanted, on his own responsibility. But the fresh poems added to several later editions (see pp. xx–xxii) can only have been obtained from one or other of Cowper's friends, probably Newton, Lady Hesketh, or John Johnson; and the list

[1] Bruce gave a considerable number of variants; his notes, though incomplete and not always accurate, are valuable.
[2] See p. xx–xxii for a further description of these editions.
[3] See *Letters* (ed. Wright), ii. 419.

of books in the possession of Cowper at his death includes two copies of a 1798 edition[1]. So we may conclude that Cowper's friends and perhaps Cowper himself had no objection to the newer style; and we are therefore not compelled to give the text an American air with 'favor,' 'honor,' 'labor,' &c., nor to print 'satyr' (= satire), 'sieze,' 'cloathes,' and other spellings which check the reader, when nine-tenths of the text is spelt according to modern usage[2]. In punctuation the second group, especially in *Table Talk*, &c., tends to be more 'logical,' less 'rhetorical' (a word which nowadays covers some vagueness about a difficult subject); and Cowper's heroic couplets are even improved by a frequent use of stops. His blank verse is less heavily stopped, as is natural; and the second group, if somewhat inclined to insert unnecessary commas, marks out the boundaries of the comma and the semi-colon far more clearly, to the benefit of sense and rhythm[3].

The royal 8vo edition of 1800 has been chosen rather than any other in the second group for several reasons. A comparison of it with the rest showed clearly that special pains had been taken in printing it, and points of detail, such as the elision of 'e' in preterite forms[4], carefully attended to. It has a far more handsome appearance than any previous edition. Its freedom from misprints is shown by my notes, where I have attempted to report all verbal errors that occur; absolutely, there is no doubt a fair number, but comparatively, there are few; the 1786 edition especially bristles with misprints, and the 1782 volume too has many, in spite of the list of errata which gives a false air of accuracy to the edition. The earlier editions of the second group correct most of the misprints of the first group, but introduce many of their own; these are not worth specifying, any more than those of the first group. A single instance will show the carelessness with which Cowper's proofs were read: the gross mis-

[1] See Mr. Wright's *Life*, p. 664.

[2] But where an antiquated spelling persists throughout all editions up to and beyond 1800, I have felt bound to retain it; this accounts for 'scite,' 'gulph,' and a few others.

[3] Cowper's own views on the punctuation of blank verse are expressed in a letter to Unwin of Oct. 2, 1784 (*Letters*, ii. p. 245).

[4] Cowper theoretically held strong views on this point, which he did not carry out in print; see his letter to Lady Hesketh, April 3, 1786 (*Letters*, iii. 6), where he mentions Madan's criticism on his retention of the silent 'e' in words like 'placed,' and defends himself on the ground that elision might lead foreigners into mispronunciation. But the first two editions of the poems retain or elide the 'e' inconsistently with any supposed requirements of prosody, pronunciation, or typographic beauty.

print 'umber' (*The Task*, Bk. I, l. 58) was not altered to 'lumber' until the 1800 editions, and then only in an errata slip.

Moreover, the 1800 editions contain more poems than any previous issue (see p. xxi); and I conjecture from this fact and from the edition being dated in the year of Cowper's death, that the publisher, on hearing of the author's death, wished to produce as complete and perfect an edition of his poems as possible; and with this object secured from Newton, Lady Hesketh, and other friends of Cowper, some additional poems that either had not been printed before or had not appeared in a uniform manner with the rest. This is of course mere conjecture; for Johnson, with a modesty rare in publishers and annoying to bibliographers, says nothing of these additional poems on the title page or in a preface, and even omits from the list of contents the titles of those printed in vol. I as an Appendix, apparently because the title-sheet was already printed when he determined to add the Appendix.

For poems printed in Cowper's lifetime but not included in his collected poems until after 1800—viz. two translations of Horace, Olney Hymns, *Anti-Thelyphthora*, and a few other poems—I have gone back to the first editions, never consciously deviating from their readings without a note, and altering punctuation and spelling very rarely. There is no other authority for the two translations of Horace's Satires and *Anti-Thelyphthora* than the first edition; but there were many editions of the Olney Hymns from which to choose, and I chose the first because there can be little doubt that Cowper saw proofs of that edition, if any: and further, some of the few alterations in later editions seem to have been made—perhaps by Newton—from a doctrinal point of view, and therefore do not concern us[1].

I have followed the same plan in dealing with the poems first printed by Bull, Hayley, Johnson, Croft, Southey, and others; but it did not seem necessary to record every variation, whether misprint or 'improvement,' due to Hayley's insatiable love of tinkering, that appears in the successive editions of Hayley's *Life*; nor every reading silently introduced by Southey or later editors, apparently without authority and often without reason. For there

[1] Cp. Mr. Willis's reprint of Cowper's Olney Hymns, which was issued when most of this book was already printed. He sees the necessity of returning to what Cowper probably wrote, but goes too far in keeping some impossible readings (for instance 'The' for 'Though' in xlix. 25), and does not apparently realize that many of the alterations of which he justly complains were made in later editions of the Olney Hymns, not by mere compilers of Hymnals.

are few incurable passages in Cowper; Southey, while emending too freely, corrected most of the obvious mistakes in Bull's and Croft's ill-printed volumes; and I have only admitted one emendation of my own into the text (see p. 284 and *note*), where the accepted reading is hardly possible.

The three great didactic poems have in this edition been placed first, a position to which they are I think entitled; then come the Miscellaneous Poems in chronological order; then the Hymns, followed by the Translations. An Appendix—in the same type as the rest of the poems—contains some juvenile, fragmentary, or impromptu verses which on various grounds do not fit well into their chronological order. Doubtless several of the poems included in the body of the book might, with almost equal justice, have been printed in the Appendix; no two critics will agree when the impromptus of an interesting but generally pedestrian poet like Cowper fall markedly below the bulk of his work in merit. But most of the contents of the Appendix are trifles, sometimes hardly intelligible without the context of the letters in which they were written. Mere scraps, however, which are not intelligible at all without their context have been omitted; they can be found in an edition of Cowper's letters. As it is, perhaps too many of such scraps have been inserted.

A few notes, dealing entirely with textual or chronological difficulties, and relieving the footnotes of some lengthy or unimportant variants, follow the Appendix.

A list of editions consulted, and explanations of such abbreviations as do not explain themselves, are given on pp. xx–xxiii.

Biographies or critical appreciations do not form part of the plan of this series; nor is Cowper one of the neglected poets whose lives have still to be written and their position in the poetic hierarchy determined: Southey, Bruce, Mr. Goldwin Smith, Canon Benham, and Mr. Wright supply the necessary facts and critical estimates. But as students have found useful the chronological summary of Wordsworth's life printed in Mr. Hutchinson's Oxford Wordsworth, I hope that the similar summary of Cowper's life printed on pp. xxiv–xxx may be convenient for reference.

It is a pleasure to acknowledge the help that I have received from many sources; my thanks are due to Mr. Thomas Wright for permitting the inclusion of several poems hitherto printed by him alone, and for examining on my behalf the MSS. preserved in the museum at Olney;

to Mr. E. P. Ash, who lent me his valuable MSS. of the Translations from Madame Guion and other poems; to Canon Cowper Johnson for his loan of a collection of Cowper's letters to Joseph Hill, from which I print for the first time the rhyming letter on pp. 624–5; to Miss D. Horace Smith for collating several poems at the British Museum; to Mr. J. C. Bailey—whose edition of Cowper we have long anxiously awaited—for some interchange of views on disputed textual points; and to Messrs. Macmillan and Messrs. Hodder & Stoughton for permission to include the verses *To a Lady* (p. 352), and a few interesting impromptus taken from letters first printed in Mr. Wright's complete edition of Cowper's Letters.

Lastly, I thank most heartily the collaborator whose accurate collations and ungrudging labour have made this task possible and pleasant.

H. S. M.

Oxford,
July, 1905.

NOTE TO FOURTH EDITION.

In this edition I have been able by the kindness of Mr. Falconer Madan to add no less than twenty-three new pieces: the answer to Miss Catherine Fanshawe's Stanzas, six miscellaneous poems from Bodleian Library MSS. (see p. 671) and one from a broadside, twelve more epigrams from the Latin of John Owen, two more from the Greek, and one of uncertain derivation. I am also able to include three poems from unpublished MSS. which have turned up in the auction-rooms, (*a*) a Latin translation from Gay's *Fables*, (*b*) a Sonnet to Sir Richard Phillips, (*c*) a poem in ten heroic couplets. From the MSS. of published poems I have added a few variant readings, and, more importantly, I have followed Mr. J. C. Bailey in including translations of two of Milton's Greek poems. To his admirable edition, also, I am indebted for corrections and improvements. All the above additions (apart from the few variant readings) are made in the Notes at the end of the volume. By the kindness of Mr. Thomas Wright I have been able to see copies of the ninth and tenth editions of the *Poems* in two volumes, which have enabled me to correct my List of Editions.

H. S. M.

London,
November 1934.

CONTENTS

LIST OF CHIEF EDITIONS CONSULTED

1 Olney Hymns, in 3 books, 1779, 12mo. Further editions followed in 1781, 1783, 1787, 1792, 1795, and 1797. See pp. 433, 659.

2 Anti-Thelyphthora, 1781, 4to. Published anonymously; first claimed as Cowper's by Southey. References in his letters (e.g. *Letters* i. 282) clearly prove Cowper's authorship.

3 Poems, 1782, 8vo [see facsimile title-page on p. xxxi]. Pp. [4] + 367 + [1] (Errata). Contents: Table Talk. Progress of Error. Truth. Expostulation. Hope. Charity. Conversation. Retirement. The Doves. A Fable. A Comparison. Verses, supposed to be written by Alexander Selkirk, during his solitary Abode in the Island of Juan Fernandes. On the Promotion of Edward Thurlow, Esq. to the Lord High Chancellorship of England. Ode to Peace. Human Frailty. The Modern Patriot. On observing some Names of little Note recorded in the *Biographia Britannica*. Report of an adjudged Case not to be found in any of the Books. On the burning of Lord Mansfield's Library, together with his MSS. by the Mob, in June 1780. On the same. The Love of the World reproved; or, Hypocrisy detected. The Lily and the Rose. Idem Latine Redditum. The Nightingale and Glowworm. Votum. On a Goldfinch starved to Death in a Cage. Horace, Book the 2nd, Ode the 10th. A Reflection on the foregoing Ode. Translations from Vincent Bourn. The Shrubbery. The Winter Nosegay. Mutual Forbearance. To the Rev. Mr. Newton. Translation of Prior's Chloe and Euphelia. Boadicea. Heroism. The Poet, the Oyster, and the Sensitive Plant. To the Rev. Mr. William Cawthorne Unwin.

4 Poems, 1785, 8vo [see facsimile title-page on p. 127]. Pp. [8] + 359 + [1] (advertisement of 1782 volume). Contents: The Task. An Epistle to Joseph Hill, Esq. Tirocinium, or a Review of Schools. The History of John Gilpin.

5 Poems, 1786, 2 vols. 8vo. The second edition. Reprint of 1782 and 1785.

6 Poems, 1787, 2 vols. 8vo. The third edition. Reprint.

7 Poems, 1788, 2 vols. 8vo. The fourth edition. Reprint.

8 Poems, 1793, 2 vols. 8vo. The fifth edition. Vol. i. adds Newton's preface (see p. 637); otherwise a reprint.

9 Poems, 1794–5, 2 vols. 8vo. The sixth edition. Vol. i. reprint of 1793; vol. ii. adds, between *Tirocinium* and *John Gilpin*, the following poems: On the Death of Mrs. Throckmorton's Bulfinch. The Rose. The Poet's New Year's Gift. Ode to Apollo. Catharina. The Moralizer corrected. The Faithful Friend. Pairing Time anticipated. The Needless Alarm.

10 On the Receipt of my Mother's Picture and The Dog and the Water-lily, 1798, 8vo. Published as a pamphlet before incorporation in the two collected editions of this year.

11 Poems, 1798, 2 vols. 16mo. A new edition (? the seventh edition; called *1798*[1] in my notes). Vol. i. adds, between *The Poet, the Oyster, and the Sensitive Plant* and *Epistle to Unwin*, the two poems, On the receipt of my mother's picture, and The Dog and the Water-lily (not mentioned in Contents): vol. ii. reprint of 6th edition, with different paging. This is a badly-printed edition[a]; the other edition of the same date (see below) is much better produced.

12 Poems, 1798, 2 vols. 16mo. A new edition (? the eighth edition; called *1798*[2] in my notes). Vol. i. omits *The Dog and the Water-lily*, otherwise following 1798[1]: vol. ii. inserts it after *The Needless Alarm.* In one copy of this edition I have found an Appendix (not noted in the Contents) containing Lines printed on the Bills of Mortality for 1793 [92], [1788] and [1793]. The Negro's Complaint. Pity for poor Africans. Probably therefore some copies of this edition were still on hand when the 1800 editions were being set up.

13 Poems, 1799, 2 vols. 12mo. The ninth edition.
Reprint of 1798[1], except that *The Dog and the Water-lily* precedes *On the receipt of my mother's picture.* This is the first edition to have a printer's imprint (T. Bensley, Bolt Court, Fleet Street: in vol. ii.).

14 Poems, 1800, 2 vols. 16mo. The tenth edition.
Vol. i. follows 1798[2] page for page; vol. ii. follows 1798[2] page for page to the end of *John Gilpin*, and then adds the following poems (noted in Contents): The Yearly Distress, or Tithing Time at Stock in Essex. Lines addressed to Dr. Darwin. On Mrs. Montague's Feather Hangings. Sonnet addressed to H. Cowper, Esq. The Morning Dream. Verses printed at the Bottom of the Yearly Bill of Mortality of the Town of Northampton, Dec. 21, 1787. On a Similar Occasion, for the year [1788]. Inscription for the Tomb of Mr. Hamilton. The Poplar Field. Idem Latine Redditum. Epitaph on a Hare. Epitaphium Alterum. Note to line 8, p. 109[b]. [Note on Cowper's treatment of his hares.] The two errata noted are the same as in the other 1800 edition (see below).

15 Poems, 1800, 2 vols. royal 8vo. The eleventh edition.
Vol. i. follows 1798[2] to the end of *On the receipt, &c.* then adds The Poplar Field (called Visit to a Favourite Field, in Contents). Idem Latine Redditum (not in Contents). From the Annual Bill of Mortality, Northampton [1789] before *To Unwin.* Then follows an Appendix (not in Contents) containing Yearly Bill of Mortality, 1793 [92]. On a similar occasion for the year [1788]. On a similar occasion for the year [1793]. The Negro's Complaint. Pity for poor Africans. An Epistle to a Protestant lady in France. Friendship. From the Annual Bill of Mortality, 1790. Four Latin poems by Bourne, viz. Cicindela, Cornicula, Ad Grillum, Simile agit in simile. Vol. ii. follows 1800 (16mo)

[a] My copy has a double set of Contents for vol. ii. bound up in vol. i., and no Contents in vol. ii.

[b] This should be line 7, page 94: the mistake showing that this 16mo was set up from the royal 8vo, where the reference to the line and page is right.

to the end of the 1787 *Bill of Mortality* verses, then omits those for 1788, The *Poplar Field* and *Translation* (all of which are in vol. i.), ending with Epitaph on a Hare. Epitaphium Alterum (not in Contents). Note.

Bensley's imprint is in both volumes. This edition has been followed generally as far as it goes; see preface, pp. iv–vi.

After 1800, editions followed at frequent intervals; I have seen copies of editions dated 1803, 1805, 1806 (2), 1808, 1810, 1811, 1812, 1815 (ed. John Johnson: see No. 19, below), 1817, and later. Of these one of the most important is that of 1808, which apparently received some editorial attention; the following poems were added: On a mischievous bull. Hymn for the Sunday school at Olney. Annus Memorabilis, 1789. In 1806 (the 4to edition) the Olney Hymns and the translations from Madame Guion were for the first time printed uniformly with the rest of Cowper's poems.

16 Translations from Madame Guion, 12mo, 1801. [For title-page and dedication see p. 478; for preface see p. 662.] Quoted as *Bull*.

17 The Life and Letters of William Cowper, by William Hayley, 4 vols. 4to, 1803–6. (The first two volumes are dated 1803, the third 1804; and a supplement at the end of the third volume—with 'Vol. iv' in the signature line—is dated 1806: it has a preface explaining that Hayley, while reprinting the whole Life in 8vo with additions, is at the same time reprinting in 4to for purchasers of the first edition the supplement containing *The Colubriad* and some new letters.) Further editions in 8vo followed in 1806, 1809, 1812 and later. Different readings appear from time to time in these editions; see preface, p. vi. I have generally followed the 1803 edition. Quoted as *Hayley*.

18 Translation of Milton's Latin and Italian Poems, 4to, 1808; edited by Hayley. [See p. 579.]

19 Poems, 3 vols. 12mo, 1815; edited by John Johnson. The third volume contains a certain number of new poems, and versions of others slightly differing from those that had already appeared in Hayley's *Life*. Quoted as *1815*.

20 Private Correspondence of William Cowper, Esq., with several of his most intimate friends, 2 vols. 8vo, 1824; edited by John Johnson. This includes a few new poems. Quoted as *1824*.

21 Poems, the early productions of William Cowper, 16mo, 1825; edited by James Croft. [For Croft's preface, see p. 643.] The poems contained in this interesting volume were almost all hitherto unpublished; they will be found mainly on pp. 264–283 of this volume. Quoted as *Croft*.

22 The Life and Works of William Cowper, by Robert Southey; 15 vols. foolscap 8vo, 1835–1837. Vols. i–vii. contain the life and letters, with a few poems interspersed; vols. viii–x. the bulk of the poems and the translation of *Adamo*; vols. xi–xiv. the translations of Homer; vol. xv. additional letters, Cowper's papers in the *Connoisseur*, and his fragmentary commentary on *Paradise Lost*. Southey reprinted everything written by Cowper that was then accessible, and

produced what will probably long remain the most complete edition of his works. Quoted as *Southey*.

23 POEMS, 3 vols. foolscap 8vo [1863]; edited by John Bruce. This contains some valuable notes of variant readings. Quoted as *Bruce*.

24 THE POETICAL WORKS OF WILLIAM COWPER, 8vo, 1870; edited by Canon Benham.

25 THE LIFE OF WILLIAM COWPER, by Thomas Wright, 8vo. 1892; containing new facts which help to date Cowper's poems more accurately, and a few more poems.

26 THE UNPUBLISHED AND UNCOLLECTED POEMS OF WILLIAM COWPER, 8vo, 1900; edited by Thomas Wright. The new poems were printed mainly from the Ash MSS. and from MSS. in the Cowper museum at Olney.

27 THE CORRESPONDENCE OF WILLIAM COWPER, 4 vols. 8vo, 1904; edited by Thomas Wright. Mr. Wright gives the letters for the first time in chronological order, including more than 100 new letters, some of which contain impromptu poems.

Cowper's autobiographic MEMOIR (1816) contained one unpublished poem (see p. 289), and Grimshawe in his unnecessary eight-volume edition (1836) printed one (see p. 421) not till then included in any edition of Cowper's poems, but which had appeared in *Cowper, illustrated by a series of views* (1804). ADELPHI (1802) is of purely biographical interest. Corry in his *Life of Cowper* printed four of the lines given on p. 428 of this edition.

This list of works consulted has of course no pretensions to be a bibliography of Cowper; it professes to mention only those works which supply material of especial value to an editor whose object is to give a complete and correct text of the poems, and may prevent him from wasting much time and labour on the innumerable textually worthless editions which appeared between 1800 and 1870.

The signs used in the footnotes for the editions explain themselves (*1782*, etc.). The Ash MSS. are quoted as *A.*, the British Museum MSS. (Add. MSS. 24,155-6, consisting of letters mostly addressed to Unwin) as *BM*.

[The Norfolk MS. (Sotheby's Catalogue 16 Nov. 1925, No. 215), is so inscribed in a neat hand of the 18th or early 19th century upon the wrapper. Inside the front cover it is stated that these poems were written at Dereham in Norfolk, and that the book formerly belonged to William Hayley, and afterwards to Joseph Mayer of Liverpool. The MS. consists almost entirely of translations: from the Greek (see p. 564), from Vincent Bourne (see p. 546), from Virgil (see p. 540), from Gay's *Fables* (see pp. 575, 665).

In addition, there are the poems on the Ice Islands in Cowper's Latin and English (see pp. 428, 430), an English poem, hitherto unpublished (see p. 669), and a Latin version of *The Castaway* (see p. 431) beginning: 'Totum velabat nox obscurissima cælum.' This last I regret I have not been able to include.

Apr. 1926.]

CHRONOLOGICAL TABLE

containing the chief events of Cowper's life, and some important dates in the lives of contemporary writers.

A. D.	ÆT.	
1715–18	—	[Pope's translation of Homer's *Iliad.*]
1716	—	[Gray born.]
1726	—	[Pope's translation of Homer's *Odyssey.* Thomson's *Winter*. Martin Madan born.]
1727	—	[Thomson's *Summer.*]
1727–38	—	[Gay's *Fables.*]
1728	—	John Cowper, D.D., Rector of Great Berkhamstead, Chaplain to George II, married Ann Donne. (1) (2) (3) Their children were:—three who died in infancy (Spencer born 1729, Ann and John 1730). [Pope's *Dunciad.* Thomson's *Spring*. Gay's *Beggar's Opera*. Goldsmith born.]
1730	—	[Thomson's *Autumn.*]
1731	—	(4) WILLIAM COWPER, born November 15. [Charles Churchill born.]
1732	1	[Pope's *Essay on Man*, Part I. Gay died.]
1733	2	(5) Theodore C. (died young). [R. Lloyd born. Pope's *Epistle to Lord Cobham.*]
1734	3	(6) Thomas C. (died young).
1735	4	[Somerville's *The Chase*. Beattie born (died 1803).]
1737	6	(7) John C., born November 7. (Ann Cowper died November 12.) [Glover's *Leonidas.*]
1738	7	C. at Dr. Pitman's school at Market Street, where he is bullied. [Johnson's *London.*]
1739	8	During this year and 1740 C. at the house of Mr. Disney the oculist: holidays sometimes spent with cousins, children of Rev. Roger Donne, at Catfield.
1740	9	[Richardson's *Pamela.*]
1741	10	C. goes to Westminster (Dr. Nicholls Headmaster) where he remains till 1748. (See *Tirocinium*, ll. 296–345, *Table Talk*, ll. 506–19, and under year 1747 below.)
1742	11	[Fielding's *Joseph Andrews*. Collins' *Persian Eclogues.*]
1743	12	[Blair's *Grave.*]
1744	13	[Akenside's *Pleasures of Imagination.* Young's *Night Thoughts* completed. W. C. Unwin born. Pope died.]
1745	14	C. has smallpox, which cures his affection of the eyes; he translates an elegy of Tibullus. [Hayley born. Swift died.]
1746	15	[Thomson's *Castle of Indolence.* Blair died.]

A.D.	ÆT.	
1747	16	C's. last year at Westminster. While there he formed friendships with two of the masters, Vincent Bourne, 'slovenly, dirty, and good-natured', fifth form master (1695–1747, see pp. 546–561), and Pierson Lloyd (see p. 561); and with several of his schoolfellows, especially (1) Robert Lloyd, author of *The Actor* (see p. 266); (2) Charles Churchill the satirist (see p. 15); (3) Colman the elder (1732–1794), author of *The Jealous Wife*; (4) Bonnell Thornton (1724–1768), translator of Plautus; (5) most intimate of all, Sir William Russell, (see p. 284). Other schoolfellows were Warren Hastings, Elijah Impey, and Cumberland. C's. chief reading was in Homer, Milton, and Cowley. [Collins' *Odes*.]
1748	17	C. leaves Westminster, spends nine months at Berkhamstead. Entered at Middle Temple, writes *On the Heel of a Shoe*, first extant poem, in imitation of Philips' *Splendid Shilling*. [Richardson's *Clarissa Harlowe*. Smollett's *Roderick Random*. Thomson died.]
1749	18	During this and the two following years, C. is articled to Mr. Chapman, solicitor, of Ely Place, Holborn: leisure spent with his uncle, Ashley Cowper, Southampton Row, where he falls in love with his cousin Theodora Cowper (died 1825; see pp. 269–283). Fellow-clerk is Edward Thurlow, afterwards Lord Chancellor (born 1731, died 1806). [Fielding's *Tom Jones*. Johnson's *Irene* and *Vanity of Human Wishes*. Ambrose Philips died.]
1750	19	[Johnson's *Rambler* begun.]
1751	20	[Gray's *Elegy*. Fielding's *Amelia*. Smollett's *Peregrine Pickle*.]
1752	21	C. visits Catfield (see *This ev'ning, Delia*, p. 272) and Mundesley. In residence in the Middle Temple. Loneliness, and first attack of melancholy; dispersed by visit to Southampton with Thomas Hesketh, engaged to Harriet Cowper (died 1807). [Chatterton born.]
1753	22	C. in Middle Temple. Richardson's *Sir Charles Grandison* published, on which C. writes an Ode (see p. 283).
1754	23	C. called to the bar, Jan. 14. During this period is member of the Nonsense Club, consisting besides C., of Thornton, Colman, Lloyd, Joseph Hill, Bensley, and De Grey. [Crabbe born (died 1832).]
1755	24	C. in Middle Temple. [Johnson's *Dictionary*.]
1756	25	C. in Middle Temple; contributes five papers to Thornton and Colman's *Connoisseur*. He gives up any idea of marrying Theodora Cowper. (His father dies.) [Burke's *Essay on the Sublime and Beautiful*.]

A.D.	ÆT.	
1757	26	C. in Middle Temple; translates two Satires of Horace in Duncombe's Horace (see pp. 521–9). [Gray's *Pindaric Odes*. Dyer's *Fleece*. Blake born (died 1827).]
1758	27	C. in Middle Temple; translates Voltaire's *Henriade* (translation not extant) with his brother John. Friendship with Clotworthy Rowley. [Dyer died.]
1759	28	C. removes to Inner Temple; is made Commissioner of Bankrupts, at £60 a year. Strong patriot. [Reynolds' *Discourses on Painting* begun. Johnson's *Rasselas*. Sterne's *Tristram Shandy*, i. and ii. Collins died. Burns born.]
1760	29	C. in Inner Temple. During this and the next two years his means became straitened; he seems never to have had a brief, and made no income but that of his commissionership. Reads much, but writes very little. Thurlow's jesting promise to 'provide for' C. when he is Lord Chancellor.
1761	30	C. in Inner Temple. [Churchill's *Rosciad*. Colman's *Jealous Wife*.]
1762	31	C. in Inner Temple. [Falconer's *Shipwreck*. Bowles born (died 1850).]
1763	32	C. in Inner Temple: is offered Clerkship of Journals of House of Lords by Major Cowper; breaks down under strain of approaching examination, and, after a two months' visit to Margate, on his return to London has a second and far more serious attack of melancholy, which, after three attempts at suicide, ends in actual insanity. (See *Sapphics*, p. 289, written after his attempted suicide.) Removed by his brother to Dr. Cotton's asylum at St. Albans. [Smart's *David*. Rogers born (died 1855).]
1764	33	C. at St. Albans. [Goldsmith's *Traveller*. Walpole's *Castle of Otranto*. Churchill died.]
1765	34	C. at St. Albans till June 27; adopts Dick Coleman; visits his brother at Cambridge (see *Adelphi*); resigns his commissionership, thus becoming entirely dependent on his friends for an income; moves to lodgings at Huntingdon. Correspondence with Lady Hesketh (Harriet Cowper) and Hill shows returning health. In Nov. moves from lodgings to the Unwins' house; begins to write the *Memoir*. [Percy's *Reliques*. Young died.]
1766	35	C. at Huntingdon with Unwins; financial help—continued for many years—from Major Cowper, Theodora, and the Hesketh; begins to interest himself in gardening. [Goldsmith's *Vicar of Wakefield*.]
1767	36	C. at Huntingdon with Unwins. (Death of Morley Unwin, July 2.) Moves Sept. 14, with

A.D.	ÆT.	
		Mrs. and Miss Unwin to Orchard Side, Olney, where Rev. John Newton (born 1726, died 1807) is curate.
1768	37	C. at Olney; visit to St. Albans; increasing intimacy with Newton. [Sterne's *Sentimental Journey.*]
1769	38	C. at Olney; visits his brother who is ill, at Cambridge. (William Unwin leaves Olney for Stock.) [Burke's *Present State of the Nation. Letters of Junius* begun.]
1770	39	C. at Olney; pays another visit to John Cowper, who dies in March, leaving C. a small legacy. C. writes *Adelphi.* [Burke's *Thoughts on the Present Discontents.* Goldsmith's *Deserted Village.* Beattie's *Minstrel.* Akenside, Smart, Falconer, Chatterton died. Wordsworth born (died 1850).]
1771	40	C. at Olney; begins to write the Olney Hymns, at Newton's suggestion. [Beattie's *Minstrel.* Smollett's *Humphrey Clinker.* Gray died. Scott born (died 1832).]
1772	41	C. at Olney; engaged to be married to Mrs. Unwin, but engagement is broken off by third attack of madness beginning on
1773	42	Jan. 24; his fatal dream 'before the recollection of which all consolation vanishes, and it seems to me must always vanish' (letter to Newton, Oct. 16. 1785); is moved to Newton's house, the Vicarage, in April (Miss Unwin married to Rev. Matthew Powley in May); again treated by Dr. Cotton; attempts suicide. [Coleridge born, 1772 (died 1834).]
1774	43	C. at the Vicarage, Olney, till May 23; there recovers, and returns to Orchard Side; begins to keep hares as pets (see pp. 352, 353, 652); writes *Heu! quam remotus.* [Goldsmith died. Southey born (died 1843).]
1775	44	C. at Olney. [Lamb born (died 1834). Landor born (died 1864).]
1776	45	C. at Olney; tries in vain to get pupils through Hill; again begins correspondence with friends, discontinued for some years. [Adam Smith's *Wealth of Nations.* Gibbon's *Decline and Fall*, vol. I.]
1777	46	C. at Olney. Fire at Olney. [Chatterton's *Rowley Poems.* T. Warton's *Poems.* Cook's *Voyages.* Campbell born (died 1844).]
1778	47	C. at Olney; Sir T. Hesketh dies, leaving C. a legacy; (Thurlow becomes Chancellor); C. makes acquaintance of Rev. T. Scott, curate of Weston, author of *The Force of Truth.* [Miss Burney's *Evelina.*]
1779	48	C. at Olney; Olney Hymns published in Feb.; *Yearly Distress* written. [Johnson's *English*

A.D.	ÆT.	
		Poets, first four volumes. T. Moore born (died 1852).]
1780	49	C. at Olney; Newton goes to London (June); C. introduced to Rev. William Bull, Independent minister of Newport Pagnell (born 1738, died 1814). C. takes up drawing and carpentering, writes *Nightingale and Glowworm, A Fable, Verses on a Goldfinch, Report on an Adjudged Case.* (Mr. and Mrs. Powley at Olney.) Begins to write *Progress of Error* and *Truth.* [Crabbe's *Candidate.* Martin Madan's *Thelyphthora.*]
1781	50	C. at Olney; publishes *Anti-Thelyphthora* anonymously; writes *Table Talk, Expostulation*, etc. Newton visits Olney (June). C's. first meeting with Lady Austen (died 1802). [Johnson's *Lives of the Poets*, vols. v–x. Crabbe's *Library.* Hayley's *Triumphs of Temper.* Newton's *Cardiphonia.*]
1782	51	C. at Olney; quarrels with Lady Austen; publishes first volume of poems (Feb.) with Joseph Johnson, favourably received on the whole; lines to Unwin hastily added to preserve friendship. Reconciled with Lady Austen (June). Begins to translate Madame Guion; writes *John Gilpin*, which is published in Nov. anonymously in *Public Advertiser*; writes *Colubriad.* [Miss Burney's *Cecilia.*]
1783	52	C. at Olney; begins *The Task* in July, at inspiration of Lady Austen. Disgust at indifference of Thurlow and Colman. [Crabbe's *Village.* Blake's *Poetical Sketches.*]
1784	53	C. at Olney; continues *The Task*; (general election). C's. letter to Lady Austen, which breaks off relations between them. Beginning of friendship with Throckmortons. First part of *The Task* sent to Unwin in Oct.; Johnson agrees to publish it. Newton hurt at not being consulted. C. finishes *Tirocinium* (Nov.) and begins translation of Homer. [Charlotte Smith's *Elegiac Sonnets.* Leigh Hunt born (died 1859). Dr. Johnson died.]
1785	54	C. at Olney; continues translation of Homer; publishes *Poplar Field* and other poems in *Gentleman's Magazine.* Second volume, containing *The Task*, published in July; well received. Writes letter to *Gentleman's Magazine* (August) criticising Pope's Homer. Renews correspondence with Lady Hesketh, who supplies him with money. Visit of Walter Bagot (born 1731, died 1806) to Olney. 'Anonymous' (probably Theodora) settles annuity of £50 on C. [Peacock born (died 1866). Glover died.]

A.D.	ÆT.	
1786	55	C. at Olney; continues Homer, and sends portion of MS. to Fuseli and Maty. Lady Hesketh becomes tenant of Olney Vicarage (June). Newton's anxiety about C's. 'dissipation.' C. removes to Weston in Nov. (Death of W. C. Unwin, Nov. 29.) [*Kilmarnock Poems.*]
1787	56	C. at Weston. First visit of Samuel Rose (born 1767, died 1804). C's. fourth attack of madness, Jan. to June.
1788	57	C. at Weston. Correspondence with Mrs. King; continues revision of Iliad; writes ballads on Slavery. Visit of Mr. and Mrs. Newton (July, Aug.). C. begins Odyssey in Sept. [Byron born (died 1824). Charles Wesley died.]
1789	58	C. at Weston. Writes review of Glover's *Athenaid*; finishes rough draft of Odyssey. [Bowles' *Sonnets.* Darwin's *Loves of the Plants.* Blake's *Songs of Innocence.*]
1790	59	C. at Weston. First visit of John Johnson, C's. young cousin. C. writes *Sonnet* to Mrs. Unwin (Feb.?), *Lines on receipt of my Mother's Picture* (Spring). (Samuel Rose's marriage.) Suggestion that C. should have laureateship, vacant by Warton's death. Translates Van Lier's autobiography; finishes Odyssey, which is conveyed to his publisher on Sept. 8. [Burke's *Reflections on the French Revolution.* Madan died.]
1791	60	C. at Weston. Homer published (July); C. receives £1,000 for it. Corresponds with Thurlow on merits of blank verse and rhyme. Joseph Johnson offers him editorship of Milton; C. accepts (Sept.). Mrs. Unwin paralyzed (Dec.). [Boswell's *Life of Johnson.* John Wesley died.]
1792	61	C. at Weston. Throckmortons leave Weston (March). C. translating Milton; begins friendship with Hayley, who is also engaged on an edition of Milton. Hayley's first visit (May). Mrs. Unwin's second stroke of paralysis. Abbott and Romney paint C's. portrait. Visit to Hayley at Eartham. C. at Eartham, Aug., Sept.; translates with Hayley Andreini's *Adamo.* C. much under the influence of the half-educated Olney schoolmaster, Teedon, who sees and interprets visions. [Rogers' *Pleasures of Memory.* Shelley born (died 1822).]
1793	62	C. at Weston. Engaged on second edition of Homer. (Death of Mrs. King (Feb. 6).) Lawrence paints C's. portrait. C. writes *To Mary.* His melancholy increases. Hayley's second visit to Weston (Nov.).

A.D.	ÆT.	
		Lady Hesketh's visit (end of Nov.). [Wordsworth's *Evening Walk* and *Descriptive Sketches*.]
1794	63	C. at Weston. Fifth attack of melancholy, never to be wholly thrown off. Hayley's third visit (April). Pension of £300 a year granted to C., mainly through Hayley's exertions. Lady Hesketh at Weston all the year, and till July 1795. [Blake's *Songs of Experience*. Hayley's *Life of Milton*.]
1795	64	C. at Weston till July; leaves Weston with Mrs. Unwin and John Johnson; at North Tuddenham and Mundesley, July–Oct.; at Dunham Lodge, Oct. [Keats born (died 1821).]
1796	65	C. at Dunham Lodge till Sept., afterwards at East Dereham. Death of Mrs. Unwin (Dec.). [Coleridge's *Poems*. Burke's *Letters on a Regicide Peace*. Southey's *Joan of Arc*. Burns died.]
1797	66	C. at East Dereham; continues revision of Homer. [Southey's *Poems*. *Poems* by Coleridge, Lamb, and Lloyd. H. Walpole died.]
1798	67	C. at East Dereham. Visit from Throckmorton. Johnson reads C's. own poems aloud to him. [Landor's *Gebir*. Wordsworth and Coleridge's *Lyrical Ballads*.]
1799	68	C. at East Dereham; completes revision of Homer (March); writes *Montes Glaciales*, and *The Castaway*; translates Latin and Greek epigrams. [Campbell's *Pleasures of Hope*.]
1800	69	C. at East Dereham; translates some of Gay's *Fables*; is seized with dropsy; dies April 25; buried at East Dereham.

P O E M S

B Y

WILLIAM COWPER,

Of the INNER TEMPLE, Esq.

Sicut aquæ tremulum labris ubi lumen ahenis
Sole repercuſſum, aut radiantis imagine lunæ,
Omnia pervolitat laté loca, jamque ſub auras
Erigitur, ſummique ferit laquearia tecti. ·VIRG. ÆN. VIII.

So water trembling in a poliſh'd vaſe,
Reflects the beam that plays upon its face,
The ſportive light, uncertain where it falls,
Now ſtrikes the roof, now flaſhes on the walls.

Nous ſommes nés pour la vérité, et nous ne pouvons ſouffrir ſon abord. les figures, les paraboles, les emblémes, ſont toujours des ornements néceſſaires pour qu'elle puiſſe s'annoncer. et ſoit quon craigne qu'elle ne découvre trop brûſquement le défaut qu'on voudroit cacher, ou qu'enfin elle n'inſtruiſe avec trop peu de ménagement, ou veut, en la recevant, qu'elle ſoit déguiſée.

CARACCIOLI.

L O N D O N:
Printed for J. JOHNSON, No. 72, St. Paul's Church Yard.
1782.

POEMS

BY

WILLIAM COWPER,

Of the INNER TEMPLE, Esq.

Sicut aquæ tremulum labris ubi lumen ahenis
Sole repercussum, aut radiantis imagine lunæ,
Omnia pervolitat latè loca, jamque sub auras
Erigitur, summique ferit laquearia tecti. VIRG. Æn. viii.

So water trembling in a polish'd vase,
Reflects the beam that plays upon its face,
The sportive light, uncertain where it falls,
Now strikes the roof, now flashes on the walls.

Nous sommes nés pour la vérité, et nous ne pouvons souffrir son abord. Les figures, les paraboles, les emblêmes, sont toujours des ornements nécessaires pour qu'elle puisse s'annoncer. et soit qu'on craigne qu'elle ne découvre trop brusquement le défaut qu'on voudroit cacher, ou qu'enfin elle n'instruise avec trop peu de ménagement, ou veut, en la recevant, qu'elle soit déguisée.

CARACCIOLI.

LONDON:
Printed for J. JOHNSON, No. 72, St. Paul's Church Yard.
1782.

TABLE TALK

[Written Jan. 1781. Published 1782.]

Si te forte meæ gravis uret sarcina chartæ,
Abjicito.—Hor. Lib. i. Epist. 13.

A. You told me, I remember, glory, built
On selfish principles, is shame and guilt;
The deeds that men admire as half divine,
Stark naught, because corrupt in their design.
Strange doctrine this! that without scruple tears
The laurel that the very lightning spares;
Brings down the warrior's trophy to the dust,
And eats into his bloody sword like rust.
B. I grant that, men continuing what they are,
Fierce, avaricious, proud, there must be war; 10
And never meant the rule should be applied
To him that fights with justice on his side.
Let laurels, drench'd in pure Parnassian dews,
Reward his mem'ry, dear to ev'ry muse,
Who, with a courage of unshaken root,
In honour's field advancing his firm foot,
Plants it upon the line that justice draws,
And will prevail or perish in her cause.
'Tis to the virtues of such men, man owes
His portion in the good that heav'n bestows. 20
And, when recording history displays
Feats of renown, though wrought in ancient days,
Tells of a few stout hearts that fought and died
Where duty plac'd them, at their country's side;—
The man that is not mov'd with what he reads,
That takes not fire at their heroic deeds,
Unworthy of the blessings of the brave,
Is base in kind, and born to be a slave.
But let eternal infamy pursue
The wretch to nought but his ambition true, 30
Who, for the sake of filling with one blast
The post-horns of all Europe, lays her waste.
Think yourself station'd on a tow'ring rock,
To see a people scatter'd like a flock,
Some royal mastiff panting at their heels,
With all the savage thirst a tyger feels;
Then view him, self-proclaim'd in a gazette
Chief monster that has plagu'd the nations yet:
The globe and sceptre in such hands misplac'd,
Those ensigns of dominion, how disgrac'd! 40

The glass that bids man mark the fleeting hour,
And Death's own scythe, would better speak his
Then grace the bony phantom in their stead [pow'r;
With the king's shoulder-knot and gay cockade;
Clothe the twin brethren in each other's dress,
The same their occupation and success.

A. 'Tis your belief the world was made for man;
Kings do but reason on the self-same plan:
Maintaining your's, you cannot their's condemn,
Who think, or seem to think, man made for them.

B. Seldom, alas! the pow'r of logic reigns 51
With much sufficiency in royal brains;
Such reas'ning falls like an inverted cone,
Wanting its proper base to stand upon.
Man made for kings! those optics are but dim
That tell you so—say, rather, they for him.
That were indeed a king-ennobling thought,
Could they, or would they, reason as they ought.
The diadem, with mighty projects lin'd,
To catch renown by ruining mankind, 60
Is worth, with all its gold and glitt'ring store,
Just what the toy will sell for, and no more.

Oh! bright occasions of dispensing good,
How seldom us'd, how little understood!
To pour in virtue's lap her just reward;
Keep vice restrain'd behind a double guard;
To quell the faction that affronts the throne
By silent magnanimity alone;
To nurse with tender care the thriving arts,
Watch every beam philosophy imparts; 70
To give religion her unbridled scope,
Nor judge by statute a believer's hope;
With close fidelity and love unfeign'd,
To keep the matrimonial bond unstain'd;
Covetous only of a virtuous praise,
His life a lesson to the land he sways;
To touch the sword with conscientious awe,
Nor draw it but when duty bids him draw;
To sheath it in the peace-restoring close
With joy beyond what victory bestows; 80
Blest country, where these kingly glories shine;
Blest England, if this happiness be thine!

A. Guard what you say; the patriotic tribe
Will sneer, and charge you with a bribe.—*B.* A bribe?
The worth of his three kingdoms I defy,
To lure me to the baseness of a lie.
And, of all lies (be that one poet's boast)
The lie that flatters I abhor the most.

Those arts be their's who hate his gentle reign,
But he that loves him has no need to feign. 90
A. Your smooth eulogium, to one crown address'd,
Seems to imply a censure on the rest.
B. Quevedo, as he tells his sober tale,
Ask'd, when in hell, to see the royal jail;
Approv'd their method in all other things;
But where, good sir, do you confine your kings?
There—said his guide—the group is full in view.
Indeed?—replied the Don—there are but few.
His black interpreter the charge disdain'd—
Few, fellow?—there are all that ever reign'd. 100
Wit, undistinguishing, is apt to strike
The guilty and not guilty, both alike.
I grant the sarcasm is too severe,
And we can readily refute it here;
While Alfred's name, the father of his age,
And the Sixth Edward's grace th' historic page.
A. Kings then at last have but the lot of all.
By their own conduct they must stand or fall.
B. True. While they live, the courtly laureat pays
His quit-rent ode, his pepper-corn of praise; 110
And many a dunce, whose fingers itch to write,
Adds, as he can, his tributary mite:
A subject's faults a subject may proclaim,
A monarch's errors are forbidden game!
Thus, free from censure (overaw'd by fear)
And prais'd for virtues that they scorn to wear,
The fleeting forms of majesty engage
Respect, while stalking o'er life's narrow stage;
Then leave their crimes for history to scan,
And ask with busy scorn, Was this the man? 120
I pity kings whom worship waits upon,
Obsequious, from the cradle to the throne;
Before whose infant eyes the flatt'rer bows,
And binds a wreath about their baby brows;
Whom education stiffens into state,
And death awakens from that dream too late.
Oh! if servility with supple knees,
Whose trade it is to smile, to crouch, to please;
If smooth dissimulation, skill'd to grace
A devil's purpose with an angel's face; 130
If smiling peeresses and simp'ring peers,
Encompassing his throne a few short years;
If the gilt carriage and the pamper'd steed,
That wants no driving, and disdains the lead;

89 who] that *1782, 1786*. 115 *See notes*.

If guards, mechanically form'd in ranks,
Playing, at beat of drum, their martial pranks,
Should'ring and standing as if stuck to stone,
While condescending majesty looks on;
If monarchy consist in such base things,
Sighing, I say again, I pity kings! 140
To be suspected, thwarted, and withstood,
E'en when he labours for his country's good;
To see a band, call'd patriot, for no cause,
But that they catch at popular applause,
Careless of all th' anxiety he feels,
Hook disappointment on the public wheels;
With all their flippant fluency of tongue,
Most confident, when palpably most wrong;
If this be kingly, then farewell for me
All kingship; and may I be poor and free! 150
To be the Table Talk of clubs up stairs,
To which th' unwash'd artificer repairs,
T' indulge his genius after long fatigue,
By diving into cabinet intrigue;
(For what kings deem a toil, as well they may,
To him is relaxation and mere play)
To win no praise when well-wrought plans prevail,
But to be rudely censur'd when they fail;
To doubt the love his fav'rites may pretend,
And in reality to find no friend; 160
If he indulge a cultivated taste,
His gall'ries with the works of art well grac'd,
To hear it call'd extravagance and waste;
If these attendants, and if such as these,
Must follow royalty, then welcome ease;
However humble and confin'd the sphere,
Happy the state that has not these to fear.
A. Thus men, whose thoughts contemplative have dwelt
On situations that they never felt,
Start up sagacious, cover'd with the dust 170
Of dreaming study and pedantic rust,
And prate and preach about what others prove,
As if the world and they were hand and glove.
Leave kingly backs to cope with kingly cares;
They have their weight to carry, subjects their's;
Poets, of all men, ever least regret
Increasing taxes and the nation's debt.
Could you contrive the payment, and rehearse
The mighty plan, oracular, in verse,

137 stuck] struck *1782*, *1786*. 143 patriotic *1786*.

No bard, howe'er majestic, old or new, 180
Should claim my fixt attention more than you.
B. Not Brindley nor Bridgewater would essay
To turn the course of Helicon that way;
Nor would the nine consent the sacred tide
Should purl amidst the traffic of Cheapside,
Or tinkle in 'Change Alley, to amuse
The leathern ears of stock-jobbers and jews.
A. Vouchsafe, at least, to pitch the key of rhime
To themes more pertinent, if less sublime.
When ministers and ministerial arts; 190
Patriots, who love good places at their hearts;
When admirals, extoll'd for standing still,
Or doing nothing with a deal of skill;
Gen'rals, who will not conquer when they may,
Firm friends to peace, to pleasure, and good pay;
When freedom, wounded almost to despair,
Though discontent alone can find out where;
When themes like these employ the poet's tongue,
I hear as mute as if a syren sung.
Or tell me, if you can, what pow'r maintains 200
A Briton's scorn of arbitrary chains?
That were a theme might animate the dead,
And move the lips of poets cast in lead. [elude
B. The cause, though worth the search, may yet
Conjecture and remark, however shrewd.
They take, perhaps, a well-directed aim,
Who seek it in his climate and his frame.
Lib'ral in all things else, yet nature here
With stern severity deals out the year.
Winter invades the spring, and often pours 210
A chilling flood on summer's drooping flow'rs;
Unwelcome vapours quench autumnal beams,
Ungenial blasts attending, curl the streams;
The peasants urge their harvest, ply the fork
With double toil, and shiver at their work;
Thus with a rigour, for his good design'd,
She rears her fav'rite man of all mankind.
His form robust and of elastic tone,
Proportion'd well, half muscle and half bone,
Supplies with warm activity and force 220
A mind well-lodg'd, and masculine of course.
Hence liberty, sweet liberty inspires,
And keeps alive his fierce but noble fires.
Patient of constitutional controul,
He bears it with meek manliness of soul;
But, if authority grow wanton, woe
To him that treads upon his free-born toe;

One step beyond the bound'ry of the laws
Fires him at once in freedom's glorious cause.
Thus proud prerogative, not much rever'd, 230
Is seldom felt, though sometimes seen and heard;
And in his cage, like parrot fine and gay,
Is kept, to strut, look big, and talk away.
Born in a climate softer far than our's,
Not form'd like us, with such Herculean pow'rs,
The Frenchman, easy, debonair, and brisk,
Give him his lass, his fiddle, and his frisk,
Is always happy, reign whoever may,
And laughs the sense of mis'ry far away:
He drinks his simple bev'rage with a gust; 240
And, feasting on an onion and a crust,
We never feel th' alacrity and joy
With which he shouts and carols, *Vive le Roy*,
Fill'd with as much true merriment and glee,
As if he heard his king say—Slave, be free.
Thus happiness depends, as nature shows,
Less on exterior things than most suppose.
Vigilant over all that he has made,
Kind Providence attends with gracious aid;
Bids equity throughout his works prevail, 250
And weighs the nations in an even scale;
He can encourage slav'ry to a smile,
And fill with discontent a British isle.
A. Freeman and slave, then, if the case be such,
Stand on a level; and you prove too much:
If all men indiscriminately share
His fost'ring pow'r, and tutelary care,
As well be yok'd by despotism's hand,
As dwell at large in Britain's charter'd land.
B. No. Freedom has a thousand charms to show,
That slaves, howe'er contented, never know. 261
The mind attains, beneath her happy reign,
The growth that nature meant she should attain;
The varied fields of science, ever new,
Op'ning and wider op'ning on her view,
She ventures onward with a prosp'rous force,
While no base fear impedes her in her course:
Religion, richest favour of the skies,
Stands most reveal'd before the freeman's eyes;
No shades of superstition blot the day, 270
Liberty chases all that gloom away;
The soul, emancipated, unoppress'd,
Free to prove all things and hold fast the best,
Learns much; and, to a thousand list'ning minds,
Communicates with joy the good she finds.

Courage, in arms, and ever prompt to show
His manly forehead to the fiercest foe;
Glorious in war, but for the sake of peace,
His spirits rising as his toils increase,
Guards well what arts and industry have won, 280
And freedom claims him for her first-born son.
Slaves fight for what were better cast away—
The chain that binds them, and a tyrant's sway;
But they, that fight for freedom, undertake
The noblest cause mankind can have at stake:—
Religion, virtue, truth, whate'er we call
A blessing—freedom is the pledge of all.
Oh liberty! the pris'ner's pleasing dream,
The poet's muse, his passion and his theme;
Genius is thine, and thou art fancy's nurse; 290
Lost without thee th' ennobling pow'rs of verse;
Heroic song from thy free touch acquires
Its clearest tone, the rapture it inspires;
Place me where winter breathes his keenest air,
And I will sing, if liberty be there;
And I will sing, at liberty's dear feet,
In Afric's torrid clime, or India's fiercest heat.

A. Sing where you please, in such a cause I grant
An English poet's privilege to rant;
But is not freedom—at least, is not our's, 300
Too apt to play the wanton with her pow'rs,
Grow freakish, and, o'erleaping ev'ry mound,
Spread anarchy and terror all around?

B. Agreed. But would you sell or slay your horse
For bounding and curvetting in his course;
Or if, when ridden with a careless rein,
He break away, and seek the distant plain?
No. His high mettle, under good controul,
Gives him Olympic speed, and shoots him to the goal.

Let discipline employ her wholesome arts; 310
Let magistrates alert perform their parts,
Not skulk or put on a prudential mask,
As if their duty were a desp'rate task;
Let active laws apply the needful curb
To guard the peace that riot would disturb;
And liberty, preserv'd from wild excess,
Shall raise no feuds for armies to suppress.
When tumult lately burst his prison door,
And set plebeian thousands in a roar;
When he usurp'd authority's just place, 320
And dar'd to look his master in the face;
When the rude rabble's watch-word was—destroy,
And blazing London seem'd a second Troy:

Liberty blush'd, and hung her drooping head,
Beheld their progress with the deepest dread;
Blush'd, that effects like these she should produce,
Worse than the deeds of galley-slaves broke loose.
She loses in such storms her very name,
And fierce licentiousness should bear the blame.
  Incomparable gem! thy worth untold; 330
Cheap, though blood-bought; and thrown away when [sold;
May no foes ravish thee, and no false friend
Betray thee, while professing to defend;
Prize it, ye ministers; ye monarchs, spare;
Ye patriots, guard it with a miser's care.
  A. Patriots, alas! the few that have been found,
Where most they flourish, upon English ground,
The country's need have scantily supplied,
And the last left the scene when Chatham died.
  B. Not so—the virtue still adorns our age, 340
Though the chief actor died upon the stage.
In him Demosthenes was heard again;
Liberty taught him her Athenian strain;
She cloth'd him with authority and awe,
Spoke from his lips, and in his looks gave law.
His speech, his form, his action, full of grace,
And all his country beaming in his face,
He stood, as some inimitable hand
Would strive to make a Paul or Tully stand.
No sycophant or slave, that dar'd oppose 350
Her sacred cause, but trembled when he rose;
And ev'ry venal stickler for the yoke
Felt himself crush'd at the first word he spoke.
  Such men are rais'd to station and command,
When Providence means mercy to a land.
He speaks, and they appear; to him they owe
Skill to direct, and strength to strike the blow;
To manage with address, to seize with pow'r,
The crisis of a dark decisive hour.
So Gideon earn'd a vict'ry not his own; 360
Subserviency his praise, and that alone.
  Poor England! thou art a devoted deer,
Beset with ev'ry ill but that of fear.
The nations hunt; all mark thee for a prey;
They swarm around thee, and thou stand'st at bay.
Undaunted still, though wearied and perplex'd,
Once Chatham sav'd thee; but who saves thee next?
Alas! the tide of pleasure sweeps along
All that should be the boast of British song.
'Tis not the wreath that once adorn'd thy brow, 370
The prize of happier times, will serve thee now.

Our ancestry, a gallant christian race,
Patterns of ev'ry virtue, ev'ry grace,
Confess'd a God; they kneel'd before they fought,
And prais'd him in the victories he wrought.
Now from the dust of ancient days bring forth
Their sober zeal, integrity, and worth;
Courage, ungrac'd by these, affronts the skies,
Is but the fire without the sacrifice.
The stream that feeds the well-spring of the heart
Not more invigorates life's noblest part, 381
Than virtue quickens, with a warmth divine,
The pow'rs that sin has brought to a decline.
A. Th' inestimable estimate of Brown
Rose like a paper-kite, and charm'd the town;
But measures, plann'd and executed well,
Shifted the wind that rais'd it, and it fell.
He trod the very self-same ground you tread,
And victory refuted all he said.
B. And yet his judgment was not fram'd amiss;
Its error, if it err'd, was merely this— 391
He thought the dying hour already come,
And a complete recov'ry struck him dumb.
But that effeminacy, folly, lust,
Enervate and enfeeble, and needs must,
And that a nation shamefully debas'd,
Will be despis'd and trampled on at last,
Unless sweet penitence her pow'rs renew,
Is truth, if history itself be true.
There is a time, and justice marks the date, 400
For long-forbearing clemency to wait;
That hour elaps'd, th' incurable revolt
Is punish'd, and down comes the thunder-bolt.
If mercy *then* put by the threat'ning blow,
Must she perform the same kind office *now*?
May she! and, if offended heav'n be still
Accessible, and pray'r prevail, she will.
'Tis not, however, insolence and noise,
The tempest of tumultuary joys,
Nor is it, yet, despondence and dismay, 410
Will win her visits or engage her stay;
Pray'r only, and the penitential tear,
Can call her smiling down, and fix her here.
But, when a country (one that I could name)
In prostitution sinks the sense of shame;
When infamous venality, grown bold,
Writes on his bosom, *to be let or sold*:
When perjury, that heav'n defying vice,
Sells oaths by tale, and at the lowest price,

Stamps God's own name upon a lie just made, 420
To turn a penny in the way of trade;
When av'rice starves (and never hides his face)
Two or three millions of the human race,
And not a tongue inquires, how, where, or when,
Though conscience will have twinges now and then;
When profanation of the sacred cause
In all its parts, times, ministry, and laws,
Bespeaks a land, once christian, fall'n, and lost
In all that wars against that title most;
What follows next let cities of great name, 430
And regions long since desolate, proclaim.
Nineveh, Babylon, and ancient Rome,
Speak to the present times, and times to come;
They cry aloud, in ev'ry careless ear,
Stop, while ye may; suspend your mad career;
O learn, from our example and our fate,
Learn wisdom and repentance ere too late.
Not only vice disposes and prepares
The mind, that slumbers sweetly in her snares,
To stoop to tyranny's usurp'd command, 440
And bend her polish'd neck beneath his hand
(A dire effect, by one of nature's laws
Unchangeably connected with its cause);
But Providence himself will intervene
To throw his dark displeasure o'er the scene.
All are his instruments; each form of war,
What burns at home, or threatens from afar,
Nature in arms, her elements at strife,
The storms that overset the joys of life,
Are but his rods to scourge a guilty land, 450
And waste it at the bidding of his hand.
He gives the word, and mutiny soon roars
In all her gates, and shakes her distant shores;
The standards of all nations are unfurl'd;
She has one foe, and that one foe the world.
And, if he doom that people with a frown,
And mark them with the seal of wrath press'd down,
Obduracy takes place; callous and tough,
The reprobated race grows judgment proof: 459
Earth shakes beneath them, and heav'n roars above;
But nothing scares them from the course they love:
To the lascivious pipe and wanton song,
That charm down fear, they frolic it along,
With mad rapidity and unconcern,
Down to the gulf from which is no return.
They trust in navies, and their navies fail—
God's curse can cast away ten thousand sail!

They trust in armies, and their courage dies;
In wisdom, wealth, in fortune, and in lies;
But all they trust in withers, as it must, 470
When He commands, in whom they place no trust.
Vengeance at last pours down upon their coast,
A long despis'd, but now victorious, host;
Tyranny sends the chain that must abridge
The noble sweep of all their privilege;
Gives liberty the last, the mortal shock;
Slips the slave's collar on, and snaps the lock.
A. Such lofty strains embellish what you teach,
Mean you to prophesy, or but to preach?
B. I know the mind that feels indeed the fire 480
The muse imparts, and can command the lyre,
Acts with a force, and kindles with a zeal,
Whate'er the theme, that others never feel.
If human woes her soft attention claim,
A tender sympathy pervades the frame,
She pours a sensibility divine
Along the nerve of ev'ry feeling line.
But, if a deed not tamely to be borne
Fire indignation and a sense of scorn, 489
The strings are swept with such a pow'r, so loud,
The storm of music shakes th' astonish'd crowd.
So, when remote futurity is brought
Before the keen inquiry of her thought,
A terrible sagacity informs
The poet's heart; he looks to distant storms;
He hears the thunder ere the tempest low'rs;
And, arm'd with strength surpassing human pow'rs,
Seizes events as yet unknown to man,
And darts his soul into the dawning plan.
Hence, in a Roman mouth, the graceful name 500
Of prophet and of poet was the same;
Hence British poets, too, the priesthood shar'd,
And ev'ry hallow'd druid was a bard.
But no prophetic fires to me belong;
I play with syllables, and sport in song.
A. At Westminster, where little poets strive
To set a distich upon six and five,
Where discipline helps op'ning buds of sense,
And makes his pupils proud with silver pence,
I was a poet too: but modern taste 510
Is so refin'd, and delicate, and chaste,
That verse, whatever fire the fancy warms,
Without a creamy smoothness has no charms.
Thus, all success depending on an ear,
And thinking I might purchase it too dear,

If sentiment were sacrific'd to sound,
And truth cut short to make a period round,
I judg'd a man of sense could scarce do worse
Than caper in the morris-dance of verse.
B. Thus reputation is a spur to wit, 520
And some wits flag through fear of losing it.
Give me the line that plows its stately course
Like a proud swan, conq'ring the stream by force;
That, like some cottage beauty, strikes the heart,
Quite unindebted to the tricks of art.
When labour and when dullness, club in hand,
Like the two figures at St. Dunstan's, stand,
Beating alternately, in measur'd time,
The clockwork tintinabulum of rhime,
Exact and regular the sounds will be; 530
But such mere quarter-strokes are not for me.
From him who rears a poem lank and long,
To him who strains his all into a song;
Perhaps some bonny Caledonian air,
All birks and braes, though he was never there;
Or, having whelp'd a prologue with great pains,
Feels himself spent, and fumbles for his brains;
A prologue interdash'd with many a stroke—
An art contriv'd to advertise a joke,
So that the jest is clearly to be seen, 540
Not in the words—but in the gap between:
Manner is all in all, whate'er is writ,
The substitute for genius, sense, and wit.
To dally much with subjects mean and low
Proves that the mind is weak, or makes it so.
Neglected talents rust into decay,
And ev'ry effort ends in push-pin play.
The man that means success should soar above
A soldier's feather, or a lady's glove;
Else, summoning the muse to such a theme, 550
The fruit of all her labour is whipt-cream.
As if an eagle flew aloft, and then—
Stoop'd from his highest pitch to pounce a wren.
As if the poet, purposing to wed,
Should carve himself a wife in gingerbread.
Ages elaps'd ere Homer's lamp appear'd,
And ages ere the Mantuan swan was heard:
To carry nature lengths unknown before,
To give a Milton birth, ask'd ages more.
Thus genius rose and set at order'd times, 560
And shot a day-spring into distant climes,
Ennobling ev'ry region that he chose;
He sunk in Greece, in Italy he rose;

And, tedious years of Gothic darkness pass'd,
Emerg'd all splendour in our isle at last.
Thus lovely halcyons dive into the main,
Then show far off their shining plumes again.
A. Is genius only found in epic lays?
Prove this, and forfeit all pretence to praise.
Make their heroic pow'rs your own at once, 570
Or candidly confess yourself a dunce.
B. These were the chief: each interval of night
Was grac'd with many an undulating light.
In less illustrious bards his beauty shone
A meteor, or a star; in these, the sun.
The nightingale may claim the topmost bough,
While the poor grasshopper must chirp below:
Like him, unnotic'd, I, and such as I,
Spread little wings, and rather skip than fly;
Perch'd on the meagre produce of the land, 580
An ell or two of prospect we command;
But never peep beyond the thorny bound,
Or oaken fence, that hems the paddoc round.
In Eden, ere yet innocence of heart
Had faded, poetry was not an art;
Language, above all teaching, or, if taught,
Only by gratitude and glowing thought,
Elegant as simplicity, and warm
As ecstasy, unmanacled by form,
Not prompted, as in our degen'rate days, 590
By low ambition and the thirst of praise,
Was natural as is the flowing stream,
And yet magnificent—a God the theme!
That theme on earth exhausted, though above
'Tis found as everlasting as his love,
Man lavish'd all his thoughts on human things—
The feats of heroes, and the wrath of kings:
But still, while virtue kindled his delight,
The song was moral, and so far was right.
'Twas thus till luxury seduc'd the mind 600
To joys less innocent, as less refin'd;
Then genius danc'd a bacchanal; he crown'd
The brimming goblet, seiz'd the thyrsus, bound
His brows with ivy, rush'd into the field
Of wild imagination, and there reel'd,
The victim of his own lascivious fires,
And, dizzy with delight, profan'd the sacred wires.
Anacreon, Horace, play'd in Greece and Rome
This Bedlam part; and others nearer home. 609
When Cromwell fought for pow'r, and while he reign'd
The proud protector of the pow'r he gain'd,

Religion, harsh, intolerant, austere,
Parent of manners like herself severe,
Drew a rough copy of the Christian face
Without the smile, the sweetness, or the grace;
The dark and sullen humour of the time
Judg'd ev'ry effort of the muse a crime;
Verse, in the finest mould of fancy cast,
Was lumber in an age so void of taste:
But, when the second Charles assum'd the sway, 620
And arts reviv'd beneath a softer day,
Then, like a bow long forc'd into a curve,
The mind, releas'd from too constrain'd a nerve,
Flew to its first position with a spring
That made the vaulted roofs of pleasure ring.
His court, the dissolute and hateful school
Of wantonness, where vice was taught by rule,
Swarm'd with a scribbling herd, as deep inlaid
With brutal lust as ever Circe made.
From these a long succession, in the rage 630
Of rank obscenity, debauch'd their age;
Nor ceas'd, till, ever anxious to redress
Th' abuses of her sacred charge, the press,
The muse instructed a well-nurtur'd train
Of abler votaries to cleanse the stain,
And claim the palm for purity of song,
That lewdness had usurp'd and worn so long.
Then decent pleasantry and sterling sense,
That neither gave nor would endure offence,
Whipp'd out of sight, with satire just and keen, 640
The puppy pack that had defil'd the scene.
In front of these came Addison. In him
Humour in holiday and sightly trim,
Sublimity and Attic taste, combin'd,
To polish, furnish, and delight, the mind.
Then Pope, as harmony itself exact,
In verse well disciplin'd, complete, compact,
Gave virtue and morality a grace,
That, quite eclipsing pleasure's painted face,
Levied a tax of wonder and applause, 650
Ev'n on the fools that trampled on their laws.
But he (his musical finesse was such,
So nice his ear, so delicate his touch)
Made poetry a mere mechanic art;
And ev'ry warbler has his tune by heart.
Nature imparting her satiric gift,
Her serious mirth, to Arbuthnot and Swift,
With droll sobriety they rais'd a smile
At folly's cost, themselves unmov'd the while.

That constellation set, the world in vain 660
Must hope to look upon their like again.
A. Are we then left—*B*. Not wholly in the dark;
Wit now and then, struck smartly, shows a spark,
Sufficient to redeem the modern race
From total night and absolute disgrace.
While servile trick and imitative knack
Confine the million in the beaten track,
Perhaps some courser, who disdains the road,
Snuffs up the wind, and flings himself abroad.
Contemporaries all surpass'd, see one, 670
Short his career, indeed, but ably run;
Churchill; himself unconscious of his pow'rs,
In penury consum'd his idle hours;
And, like a scatter'd seed at random sown,
Was left to spring by vigour of his own.
Lifted at length, by dignity of thought
And dint of genius, to an affluent lot,
He laid his head in luxury's soft lap,
And took, too often, there his easy nap.
If brighter beams than all he threw not forth, 680
'Twas negligence in him, not want of worth.
Surly and slovenly, and bold and coarse,
Too proud for art, and trusting in mere force,
Spendthrift alike of money and of wit,
Always at speed, and never drawing bit,
He struck the lyre in such a careless mood,
And so disdain'd the rules he understood,
The laurel seem'd to wait on his command;
He snatch'd it rudely from the muses' hand.
Nature, exerting an unwearied pow'r, 690
Forms, opens, and gives scent to, ev'ry flow'r;
Spreads the fresh verdure of the field, and leads
The dancing Naiads through the dewy meads:
She fills profuse ten thousand little throats
With music, modulating all their notes; [known,
And charms the woodland scenes, and wilds un-
With artless airs and concerts of her own:
But seldom (as if fearful of expense)
Vouchsafes to man a poet's just pretence—
Fervency, freedom, fluency of thought, 700
Harmony, strength, words exquisitely sought;
Fancy, that from the bow that spans the sky
Brings colours, dipt in heav'n, that never die;
A soul exalted above earth, a mind
Skill'd in the characters that form mankind;
And, as the sun in rising beauty dress'd,
Looks to the westward from the dappled east,

And marks, whatever clouds may interpose,
Ere yet his race begins, its glorious close;
An eye like his to catch the distant goal, 710
Or ere the wheels of verse begin to roll;
Like his to shed illuminating rays
On ev'ry scene and subject it surveys:
Thus grac'd, the man asserts a poet's name,
And the world cheerfully admits the claim.
  Pity religion has so seldom found
A skilful guide into poetic ground!
The flow'rs would spring where'er she deign'd to [stray,
And ev'ry muse attend her in her way.
Virtue indeed meets many a rhiming friend, 720
And many a compliment politely penn'd;
But, unattir'd in that becoming vest
Religion weaves for her, and half undress'd,
Stands in the desert, shiv'ring and forlorn,
A wintry figure, like a wither'd thorn.
The shelves are full, all other themes are sped;
Hackney'd and worn to the last flimsy thread,
Satire has long since done his best; and curst
And loathsome ribaldry has done his worst;
Fancy has sported all her pow'rs away 730
In tales, in trifles, and in children's play;
And 'tis the sad complaint, and almost true,
Whate'er we write, we bring forth nothing new.
'Twere new indeed to see a bard all fire,
Touch'd with a coal from heav'n, assume the lyre,
And tell the world, still kindling as he sung,
With more than mortal music on his tongue,
That He, who died below, and reigns above,
Inspires the song, and that his name is love.
  For, after all, if merely to beguile, 740
By flowing numbers and a flow'ry style,
The tædium that the lazy rich endure,
Which now and then sweet poetry may cure;
Or, if to see the name of idol self,
Stamp'd on the well-bound quarto, grace the shelf,
To float a bubble on the breath of fame,
Prompt his endeavour, and engage his aim,
Debas'd to servile purposes of pride,
How are the pow'rs of genius misapplied!
The gift, whose office is the Giver's praise, 750
To trace him in his word, his works, his ways,
Then spread the rich discov'ry, and invite
Mankind to share in the divine delight,

744 idle *1793–1800*.

Distorted from its use and just design,
To make the pitiful possessor shine,
To purchase, at the fool-frequented fair
Of vanity, a wreath for self to wear,
Is profanation of the basest kind—
Proof of a trifling and a worthless mind.
A. Hail Sternhold, then; and Hopkins, hail!
B. Amen. 760
If flatt'ry, folly, lust, employ the pen;
If acrimony, slander, and abuse,
Give it a charge to blacken and traduce;
Though Butler's wit, Pope's numbers, Prior's ease,
With all that fancy can invent to please,
Adorn the polish'd periods as they fall,
One madrigal of their's is worth them all.
A. 'Twould thin the ranks of the poetic tribe,
To dash the pen through all that you proscribe.
B. No matter—we could shift when they were not; 770
And should, no doubt, if they were all forgot.

THE PROGRESS OF ERROR

[Written Dec. 1780. Published 1782.]

Si quid loquar audiendum.—Hor. Lib. iv. Od. 2.

Sing, muse, (if such a theme, so dark, so long,
May find a muse to grace it with a song)
By what unseen and unsuspected arts
The serpent error twines round human hearts;
Tell where she lurks, beneath what flow'ry shades,
That not a glimpse of genuine light pervades,
The pois'nous, black, insinuating worm
Successfully conceals her loathsome form.
Take, if ye can, ye careless and supine,
Counsel and caution from a voice like mine! 10
Truths, that the theorist could never reach,
And observation taught me, I would teach.
Not all, whose eloquence the fancy fills,
Musical as the chime of tinkling rills,
Weak to perform, though mighty to pretend,
Can trace her mazy windings to their end;
Discern the fraud beneath the specious lure,
Prevent the danger, or prescribe the cure.
The clear harangue, and cold as it is clear,
Falls soporific on the listless ear; 20

11 theorists *1800*.

Like quicksilver, the rhet'ric they display
Shines as it runs, but, grasp'd at, slips away.
  Plac'd for his trial on this bustling stage,
From thoughtless youth to ruminating age,
Free in his will to choose or to refuse,
Man may improve the crisis, or abuse;
Else, on the fatalist's unrighteous plan,
Say, to what bar amenable were man?
With nought in charge, he could betray no trust;
And, if he fell, would fall because he must; 30
If love reward him, or if vengeance strike,
His recompense in both unjust alike.
Divine authority within his breast
Brings ev'ry thought, word, action, to the test;
Warns him or prompts, approves him or restrains,
As reason, or as passion, takes the reins.
Heav'n from above, and conscience from within,
Cries in his startled ear—Abstain from sin!
The world around solicits his desire,
And kindles in his soul a treach'rous fire; 40
While, all his purposes and steps to guard,
Peace follows virtue as its sure reward;
And pleasure brings as surely in her train
Remorse, and sorrow, and vindictive pain.
  Man, thus endued with an elective voice,
Must be supplied with objects of his choice.
Where'er he turns, enjoyment and delight,
Or present, or in prospect, meet his sight;
Those open on the spot their honey'd store;
These call him loudly to pursuit of more. 50
His unexhausted mine the sordid vice
Avarice shows, and virtue is the price.
Here various motives his ambition raise—
Pow'r, pomp, and splendour, and the thirst of praise;
There beauty wooes him with expanded arms;
E'en Bacchanalian madness has its charms.
  Nor these alone, whose pleasures, less refin'd,
Might well alarm the most unguarded mind,
Seek to supplant his inexperienc'd youth,
Or lead him devious from the path of truth; 60
Hourly allurements on his passions press,
Safe in themselves, but dang'rous in th' excess.
  Hark! how it floats upon the dewy air!
O what a dying, dying close was there!
'Tis harmony from yon sequester'd bow'r,
Sweet harmony, that sooths the midnight hour!

32 is *1794–1800.* 38 Cry *1782–1787.* 43 as] us *1800.*
49, 50 Those . . . These *transposed in edd. 1782–1788.*

Long ere the charioteer of day had run
His morning course, th' enchantment was begun;
And he shall gild yon mountain's height again,
Ere yet the pleasing toil becomes a pain. 70
Is this the rugged path, the steep ascent,
That virtue points to? Can a life thus spent
Lead to the bliss she promises the wise,
Detach the soul from earth, and speed her to the skies?
Ye devotees to your ador'd employ,
Enthusiasts, drunk with an unreal joy,
Love makes the music of the blest above,
Heav'n's harmony is universal love;
And earthly sounds, though sweet and well combin'd,
And lenient as soft opiates to the mind, 80
Leave vice and folly unsubdu'd behind.
Grey dawn appears; the sportsman and his train
Speckle the bosom of the distant plain;
'Tis he, the Nimrod of the neighb'ring lairs;
Save that his scent is less acute than their's,
For persevering chase, and headlong leaps,
True beagle as the staunchest hound he keeps.
Charg'd with the folly of his life's mad scene,
He takes offence, and wonders what you mean;
The joy the danger and the toil o'erpays— 90
'Tis exercise, and health, and length of days.
Again impetuous to the field he flies;
Leaps ev'ry fence but one, there falls and dies;
Like a slain deer, the tumbrel brings him home,
Unmiss'd but by his dogs and by his groom.
Ye clergy; while your orbit is your place,
Lights of the world, and stars of human race;
But, if eccentric ye forsake your sphere,
Prodigies ominous, and view'd with fear.
The comet's baneful influence is a dream; 100
Your's real, and pernicious in th' extreme.
What then!—are appetites and lusts laid down
With the same ease that man puts on his gown?
Will av'rice and concupiscence give place,
Charm'd by the sounds—Your Rev'rence, or Your
Grace?
No. But his own engagement binds him fast;
Or, if it does not, brands him to the last,
What atheists call him—a designing knave,
A mere church juggler, hypocrite, and slave.
Oh, laugh or mourn with me the rueful jest, 110
A cassock'd huntsman and a fiddling priest!

99 Prodigies] Prodigious, *1782–1787*.
103 that] the *1782*, *1786*.

He from Italian songsters takes his cue:
Set Paul to music, he shall quote him too.
He takes the field. The master of the pack
Cries—Well done, saint! and claps him on the back.
Is this the path of sanctity? Is this
To stand a way-mark in the road to bliss?
Himself a wand'rer from the narrow way,
His silly sheep, what wonder if they stray?
Go, cast your orders at your bishop's feet, 120
Send your dishonour'd gown to Monmouth-street!
The sacred function in your hands is made—
Sad sacrilege! no function, but a trade!
Occiduus is a pastor of renown,
When he has pray'd and preach'd the sabbath down,
With wire and catgut he concludes the day,
Quav'ring and semiquav'ring care away.
The full concerto swells upon your ear;
All elbows shake. Look in, and you would swear
The Babylonian tyrant with a nod 130
Had summon'd them to serve his golden god.
So well that thought th' employment seems to suit,
Psalt'ry and sackbut, dulcimer, and flute.
Oh fie! 'tis evangelical and pure!
Observe each face, how sober and demure!
Ecstasy sets her stamp on ev'ry mien;
Chins fall'n, and not an eye-ball to be seen.
Still I insist, though music heretofore
Has charm'd me much, (not e'en Occiduus more)
Love, joy, and peace, make harmony more meet 140
For sabbath ev'nings, and perhaps as sweet.
Will not the sickliest sheep of every flock
Resort to this example as a rock;
There stand, and justify the foul abuse
Of sabbath hours with plausible excuse?
If apostolic gravity be free
To play the fool on Sundays, why not we?
If he the tinkling harpsichord regards
As inoffensive, what offence in cards?
Strike up the fiddles, let us all be gay! 150
Laymen have leave to dance, if parsons play.
Oh Italy!—thy sabbaths will be soon
Our sabbaths, clos'd with mumm'ry and buffoon.
Preaching and pranks will share the motley scene:
Our's parcell'd out, as thine have ever been,
God's worship and the mountebank between.
What says the prophet? Let that day be blest
With holiness and consecrated rest.

Pastime and bus'ness both it should exclude,
And bar the door the moment they intrude; 160
Nobly distinguish'd above all the six,
By deeds in which the world must never mix.
Hear him again. He calls it a delight,
A day of luxury, observ'd aright,
When the glad soul is made heav'n's welcome guest,
Sits banqueting, and God provides the feast.
But triflers are engag'd and cannot come;
Their answer to the call is—*Not at home.*
  Oh the dear pleasures of the velvet plain,
The painted tablets, dealt and dealt again. 170
Cards, with what rapture, and the polish'd die,
The yawning chasm of indolence supply!
Then to the dance, and make the sober moon
Witness of joys that shun the sight of noon.
Blame, cynic, if you can, quadrille or ball,
The snug close party, or the splendid hall,
Where night, down-stooping from her ebon throne,
Views constellations brighter than her own.
'Tis innocent, and harmless, and refin'd;
The balm of care, elysium of the mind. 180
Innocent! Oh, if venerable time
Slain at the foot of pleasure be no crime,
Then, with his silver beard and magic wand,
Let Comus rise archbishop of the land;
Let him your rubric and your feasts prescribe,
Grand metropolitan of all the tribe.
  Of manners rough, and coarse athletic cast,
The rank debauch suits Clodio's filthy taste.
Rufillus, exquisitely form'd by rule,
Not of the moral, but the dancing school, 190
Wonders at Clodio's follies, in a tone
As tragical, as others at his own.
He cannot drink five bottles, bilk the score,
Then kill a constable, and drink five more;
But he can draw a pattern, make a tart,
And has the ladies' etiquette by heart.
Go, fool; and, arm in arm with Clodio, plead
Your cause before a bar you little dread;
But know, the law that bids the drunkard die
Is far too just to pass the trifler by. 200
Both baby-featur'd, and of infant size,
View'd from a distance, and with heedless eyes,
Folly and innocence are so alike,
The diff'rence, though essential, fails to strike.
Yet folly ever has a vacant stare,
A simp'ring count'nance, and a trifling air;

But innocence, sedate, serene, erect,
Delights us, by engaging our respect.
 Man, nature's guest by invitation sweet,
Receives from her both appetite and treat; 210
But, if he play the glutton and exceed,
His benefactress blushes at the deed.
For nature, nice, as lib'ral to dispense,
Made nothing but a brute the slave of sense.
Daniel ate pulse by choice—example rare! [fair.
Heav'n bless'd the youth, and made him fresh and
Gorgonius sits, abdominous and wan,
Like a fat squab upon a Chinese fan:
He snuffs far off th' anticipated joy;
Turtle and ven'son all his thoughts employ; 220
Prepares for meals as jockies take a sweat,
Oh, nauseous!—an emetic for a whet!
Will Providence o'erlook the wasted good?
Temperance were no virtue if he could.
 That pleasures, therefore, or what such we call,
Are hurtful, is a truth confess'd by all;
And some, that seem to threaten virtue less,
Still hurtful, in th' abuse, or by th' excess.
 Is man then only for his torment plac'd
The centre of delights he may not taste? 230
Like fabled Tantalus, condemn'd to hear
The precious stream still purling in his ear,
Lip-deep in what he longs for, and yet curst
With prohibition, and perpetual thirst?
No, wrangler—destitute of shame and sense,
The precept, that enjoins him abstinence,
Forbids him none but the licentious joy,
Whose fruit, though fair, tempts only to destroy.
Remorse, the fatal egg by pleasure laid
In every bosom where her nest is made, 240
Hatch'd by the beams of truth, denies him rest,
And proves a raging scorpion in his breast.
No pleasure? Are domestic comforts dead?
Are all the nameless sweets of friendship fled?
Has time worn out, or fashion put to shame,
Good sense, good health, good conscience, and good
 fame?
All these belong to virtue, and all prove
That virtue has a title to your love.
Have you no touch of pity, that the poor
Stand starv'd at your inhospitable door? 250
Or, if yourself, too scantily supplied,
Need help, let honest industry provide.

230 I' the *1786*.

Earn, if you want; if you abound, impart:
These both are pleasures to the feeling heart.
No pleasure? Has some sickly eastern waste
Sent us a wind to parch us at a blast?
Can British paradise no scenes afford
To please her sated and indiff'rent lord?
Are sweet philosophy's enjoyments run
Quite to the lees? And has religion none? 260
Brutes capable, would tell you 'tis a lie,
And judge you from the kennel and the stye.
Delights like these, ye sensual and profane,
Ye are bid, begg'd, besought to entertain;
Call'd to these crystal streams, do ye turn off,
Obscene, to swill and swallow at a trough?
Envy the beast, then, on whom heav'n bestows
Your pleasures, with no curses in the close.
Pleasure admitted in undue degree,
Enslaves the will, nor leaves the judgment free. 270
'Tis not alone the grape's enticing juice
Unnerves the moral pow'rs, and mars their use;
Ambition, av'rice, and the lust of fame,
And woman, lovely woman, does the same.
The heart, surrender'd to the ruling pow'r
Of some ungovern'd passion ev'ry hour,
Finds, by degrees, the truths that once bore sway,
And all their deep impressions, wear away.
So coin grows smooth, in traffic current pass'd,
Till Cæsar's image is effac'd at last. 280
The breach, though small at first, soon op'ning [wide,
In rushes folly with a full-moon tide.
Then welcome errors, of whatever size,
To justify it by a thousand lies.
As creeping ivy clings to wood or stone,
And hides the ruin that it feeds upon;
So sophistry cleaves close to, and protects,
Sin's rotten trunk, concealing its defects.
Mortals, whose pleasures are their only care,
First wish to be impos'd on, and then are. 290
And, lest the fulsome artifice should fail,
Themselves will hide its coarseness with a veil.
Not more industrious are the just and true
To give to virtue what is virtue's due—
The praise of wisdom, comeliness, and worth;
And call her charms to public notice forth—
Than vice's mean and disingenuous race
To hide the shocking features of her face.

261 should *1782, 1786.* 278 impression *1782–1788.*

Her form with dress and lotion they repair;
Then kiss their idol, and pronounce her fair. 300
The sacred implement I now employ
Might prove a mischief, or at best a toy;
A trifle, if it move but to amuse:
But, if to wrong the judgment and abuse,
Worse than a poignard in the basest hand,
It stabs at once the morals of a land.
Ye writers of what none with safety reads,
Footing it in the dance that fancy leads:
Ye novelists, who mar what ye would mend,
Sniv'ling and driv'ling folly without end, 310
Whose corresponding misses fill the ream
With sentimental frippery and dream,
Caught in a delicate soft silken net
By some lewd earl or rake-hell baronet:
Ye pimps, who, under virtue's fair pretence,
Steal to the closet of young innocence,
And teach her, inexperienc'd yet and green,
To scribble as you scribbled at fifteen;
Who, kindling a combustion of desire,
With some cold moral think to quench the fire; 320
Though all your engineering proves in vain,
The dribbling stream ne'er puts it out again:
Oh that a verse had pow'r, and could command
Far, far away, these flesh-flies of the land;
Who fasten without mercy on the fair,
And suck, and leave a craving maggot there.
Howe'er disguis'd th' inflammatory tale,
And covered with a fine-spun specious veil;
Such writers, and such readers, owe the gust
And relish of their pleasure all to lust. 330
But the muse, eagle-pinion'd, has in view
A quarry more important still than you;
Down, down the wind she swims, and sails away;
Now stoops upon it, and now grasps the prey.
Petronius! all the muses weep for thee;
But ev'ry tear shall scald thy memory:
The graces too, while virtue at their shrine
Lay bleeding under that soft hand of thine,
Felt each a mortal stab in her own breast,
Abhorr'd the sacrifice, and curst the priest. 340
Thou polish'd and high-finish'd foe to truth,
Grey-beard corrupter of our list'ning youth,
To purge and skim away the filth of vice,
That, so refin'd, it might the more entice,

318 scribbled] scribble *1782*, *1786*.

Then pour it on the morals of thy son,
To taint *his* heart, was worthy of *thine own*!
Now, while the poison all high life pervades,
Write, if thou canst, one letter from the shades;
One, and one only, charg'd with deep regret
That thy worst part, thy principles, live yet; 350
One sad epistle thence may cure mankind
Of the plague spread by bundles left behind.
'Tis granted, and no plainer truth appears,
Our most important are our earliest years;
The mind, impressible and soft, with ease
Imbibes and copies what she hears and sees,
And through life's labyrinth holds fast the clue
That education gives her, false or true.
Plants rais'd with tenderness are seldom strong;
Man's coltish disposition asks the thong; 360
And, without discipline, the fav'rite child,
Like a neglected forester, runs wild.
But we, as if good qualities would grow
Spontaneous, take but little pains to sow;
We give some Latin, and a smatch of Greek;
Teach him to fence and figure twice a week;
And, having done, we think, the best we can,
Praise his proficiency, and dub him man.
From school to Cam or Isis, and thence home;
And thence, with all convenient speed, to Rome, 370
With rev'rend tutor, clad in habit lay,
To tease for cash, and quarrel with, all day;
With memorandum-book for ev'ry town,
And ev'ry post, and where the chaise broke down;
His stock, a few French phrases got by heart;
With much to learn, but nothing to impart,
The youth, obedient to his sire's commands,
Sets off a wand'rer into foreign lands.
Surpris'd at all they meet, the gosling pair,
With awkward gait, stretch'd neck, and silly stare,
Discover huge cathedrals, built with stone, 381
And steeples tow'ring high, much like our own;
But show peculiar light by many a grin
At popish practices observ'd within.
Ere long, some bowing, smirking, smart abbé,
Remarks two loit'rers that have lost their way;
And, being always prim'd with *politesse*
For men of their appearance and address,

373, 4 *Orig. printed*:
With memorandum-book to minute down
The sev'ral posts, and where the chaise broke down:
cancel inserted in 1782.

With much compassion undertakes the task
To tell them—more than they have wit to ask: 390
Points to inscriptions wheresoe'er they tread,
Such as, when legible, were never read,
But, being canker'd now, and half worn out,
Craze antiquarian brains with endless doubt;
Some headless hero, or some Cæsar shows—
Defective only in his Roman nose;
Exhibits elevations, drawings, plans,
Models of Herculanean pots and pans;
And sells them medals, which, if neither rare
Nor ancient, will be so, preserv'd with care. 400
Strange the recital! from whatever cause
His great improvement and new lights he draws,
The squire, once bashful, is shame-fac'd no more,
But teems with powers he never felt before;
Whether increas'd momentum, and the force
With which from clime to clime he sped his course,
(As axles sometimes kindle as they go)
Chaf'd him, and brought dull nature to a glow;
Or whether clearer skies and softer air,
That make Italian flow'rs so sweet and fair, 410
Fresh'ning his lazy spirits as he ran,
Unfolded genially, and spread the man;
Returning, he proclaims, by many a grace,
By shrugs, and strange contortions of his face,
How much a dunce that has been sent to roam
Excels a dunce that has been kept at home.
Accomplishments have taken virtue's place,
And wisdom falls before exterior grace;
We slight the precious kernel of the stone,
And toil to polish its rough coat alone. 420
A just deportment, manners grac'd with ease,
Elegant phrase, and figure form'd to please,
Are qualities that seem to comprehend
Whatever parents, guardians, schools, intend.
Hence an unfurnish'd and a listless mind,
Though busy, trifling; empty, though refin'd;
Hence all that interferes, and dares to clash
With indolence and luxury, is trash;
While learning, once the man's exclusive pride,
Seems verging fast towards the female side. 430
Learning itself, receiv'd into a mind
By nature weak, or viciously inclin'd,
Serves but to lead philosophers astray,
Where children would with ease discern the way.
And, of all arts sagacious dupes invent,
To cheat themselves and gain the world's assent,

The worst is—scripture warp'd from its intent.
  The carriage bowls along, and all are pleas'd
If Tom be sober, and the wheels well greas'd;
But, if the rogue have gone a cup too far, 440
Left out his linch-pin, or forgot his tar,
It suffers interruption and delay,
And meets with hindrance in the smoothest way.
When some hypothesis absurd and vain
Has fill'd with all its fumes a critic's brain,
The text that sorts not with his darling whim,
Though plain to others, is obscure to him.
The will made subject to a lawless force,
All is irregular, and out of course;
And judgment drunk, and brib'd to lose his way, 450
Winks hard, and talks of darkness at noon-day.
  A critic on the sacred book should be
Candid and learn'd, dispassionate and free;
Free from the wayward bias bigots feel,
From fancy's influence, and intemp'rate zeal:
But, above all, (or let the wretch refrain,
Nor touch the page he cannot but profane)
Free from the domineering pow'r of lust;
A lewd interpreter is never just.
  How shall I speak thee, or thy pow'r address, 460
Thou god of our idolatry, the press?
By thee, religion, liberty, and laws,
Exert their influence, and advance their cause;
By thee, worse plagues than Pharaoh's land befel,
Diffus'd, make earth the vestibule of hell;
Thou fountain, at which drink the good and wise;
Thou ever-bubbling spring of endless lies;
Like Eden's dread probationary tree,
Knowledge of good and evil is from thee.
  No wild enthusiast ever yet could rest 470
Till half mankind were like himself possess'd.
Philosophers, who darken and put out
Eternal truth by everlasting doubt;
Church quacks, with passions under no command,
Who fill the world with doctrines contraband,
Discov'rers of they know not what, confin'd
Within no bounds—the blind that lead the blind;
To streams of popular opinion drawn,
Deposit in those shallows all their spawn.
The wriggling fry soon fill the creeks around, 480
Pois'ning the waters where their swarms abound.
Scorn'd by the nobler tenants of the flood,
Minnows and gudgeons gorge th' unwholesome
    food.

The propagated myriads spread so fast,
E'en Leuwenhoeck himself would stand aghast,
Employ'd to calculate th' enormous sum,
And own his crab-computing pow'rs o'ercome.
Is this hyperbole? The world well known,
Your sober thoughts will hardly find it one.
  Fresh confidence the speculatist takes 490
From ev'ry hair-brain'd proselyte he makes;
And therefore prints: himself but half deceiv'd,
Till others have the soothing tale believ'd.
Hence comment after comment, spun as fine
As bloated spiders draw the flimsy line:
Hence the same word, that bids our lusts obey,
Is misapplied to sanctify their sway.
If stubborn Greek refuse to be his friend,
Hebrew or Syriac shall be forc'd to bend:
If languages and copies all cry, No— 500
Somebody prov'd it centuries ago.
Like trout pursued, the critic, in despair,
Darts to the mud, and finds his safety there.
Women, whom custom has forbid to fly
The scholar's pitch, (the scholar best knows why)
With all the simple and unletter'd poor,
Admire his learning, and almost adore.
Whoever errs, the priest can ne'er be wrong,
With such fine words familiar to his tongue.
  Ye ladies! (for, indiff'rent in your cause, 510
I should deserve to forfeit all applause)
Whatever shocks, or gives the least offence
To virtue, delicacy, truth, or sense,
(Try the criterion, 'tis a faithful guide)
Nor has, nor can have, scripture on its side.
  None but an author knows an author's cares,
Or fancy's fondness for the child she bears.
Committed once into the public arms,
The baby seems to smile with added charms.
Like something precious ventur'd far from shore,
'Tis valued for the danger's sake the more. 521
He views it with complacency supreme,
Solicits kind attention to his dream;
And daily, more enamour'd of the cheat,
Kneels, and asks heav'n to bless the dear deceit.
So one, whose story serves at least to show
Men lov'd their own productions long ago,
Woo'd an unfeeling statue for his wife,
Nor rested till the gods had given it life.
If some mere driv'ler suck the sugar'd fib, 530
One that still needs his leading-string and bib,

And praise his genius, he is soon repaid
In praise applied to the same part—his head:
For 'tis a rule, that holds for ever true,
Grant me discernment, and I grant it you.
  Patient of contradiction as a child,
Affable, humble, diffident, and mild;
Such was sir Isaac, and such Boyle and Locke:
Your blund'rer is as sturdy as a rock.
The creature is so sure to kick and bite, 540
A muleteer's the man to set him right.
First appetite enlists him truth's sworn foe,
Then obstinate self-will confirms him so.
Tell him he wanders; that his error leads
To fatal ills; that, though the path he treads
Be flow'ry, and he see no cause of fear,
Death and the pains of hell attend him there;
In vain; the slave of arrogance and pride,
He has no hearing on the prudent side.
His still refuted quirks he still repeats; 550
New-rais'd objections with new quibbles meets;
Till, sinking in the quicksand he defends,
He dies disputing, and the contest ends—
But not the mischiefs; they, still left behind,
Like thistle-seeds, are sown by ev'ry wind.
  Thus men go wrong with an ingenious skill;
Bend the straight rule to their own crooked will;
And, with a clear and shining lamp supplied,
First put it out, then take it for a guide.
Halting on crutches of unequal size; 560
One leg by truth supported, one by lies;
They sidle to the goal with awkward pace,
Secure of nothing—but to lose the race.
  Faults in the life breed errors in the brain;
And these, reciprocally, those again.
The mind and conduct mutually imprint
And stamp their image in each other's mint:
Each, sire and dam of an infernal race,
Begetting and conceiving all that's base.
  None sends his arrow to the mark in view, 570
Whose hand is feeble, or his aim untrue.
For though, ere yet the shaft is on the wing,
Or when it first forsakes th' elastic string,
It err but little from th' intended line,
It falls at last far wide of his design:
So he, who seeks a mansion in the sky,
Must watch his purpose with a stedfast eye;

576 who] that *1782*, *1786*.

That prize belongs to none but the sincere,
The least obliquity is fatal here.
  With caution taste the sweet Circean cup: 580
He that sips often, at last drinks it up.
Habits are soon assum'd; but, when we strive
To strip them off, 'tis being flay'd alive.
Call'd to the temple of impure delight,
He that abstains, and he alone, does right.
If a wish wander that way, call it home;
He cannot long be safe whose wishes roam.
But, if you pass the threshold, you are caught;
Die then, if pow'r Almighty save you not.
There, hard'ning by degrees, till double steel'd, 590
Take leave of nature's God, and God reveal'd;
Then laugh at all you trembled at before;
And, joining the free-thinkers' brutal roar,
Swallow the two grand nostrums they dispense—
That scripture lies, and blasphemy is sense:
If clemency revolted by abuse
Be damnable, then damn'd without excuse.
  Some dream that they can silence when they will
The storm of passion, and say, *Peace, be still*;
But "*Thus far and no farther*," when address'd 600
To the wild wave, or wilder human breast,
Implies authority that never can,
That never ought to be the lot of man.
  But, muse, forbear; long flights forebode a fall;
Strike on the deep-ton'd chord the sum of all.
  Hear the just law—the judgment of the skies!
He that hates truth shall be the dupe of lies:
And he that *will* be cheated to the last,
Delusions, strong as hell, shall bind him fast.
But, if the wand'rer his mistake discern, 610
Judge his own ways, and sigh for a return,
Bewilder'd once, must he bewail his loss
For ever and for ever? No—the cross!
There, and there only (though the deist rave,
And atheist, if earth bear so base a slave);
There, and there only, is the pow'r to save.
There no delusive hope invites despair;
No mock'ry meets you, no deception, there.
The spells and charms, that blinded you before,
All vanish there, and fascinate no more. 620
  I am no preacher, let this hint suffice—
The cross, once seen, is death to ev'ry vice:
Else he that hung there suffer'd all his pain,
Bled, groan'd, and agoniz'd, and died, in vain.

TRUTH

[Written Jan. 1781. Published 1782.]

Pensantur trutina.—Hor. Lib. ii. Epist. i.

MAN, on the dubious waves of error toss'd,
His ship half founder'd, and his compass lost,
Sees, far as human optics may command,
A sleeping fog, and fancies it dry land:
Spreads all his canvass, ev'ry sinew plies;
Pants for 't, aims at it, enters it, and dies!
Then farewell all self-satisfying schemes,
His well-built systems, philosophic dreams;
Deceitful views of future bliss, farewell!
He reads his sentence at the flames of hell. 10
Hard lot of man—to toil for the reward
Of virtue, and yet lose it! Wherefore hard?—
He that would win the race must guide his horse
Obedient to the customs of the course;
Else, though unequall'd to the goal he flies,
A meaner than himself shall gain the prize.
Grace leads the right way: if you choose the wrong,
Take it, and perish; but restrain your tongue.
Charge not, with light sufficient, and left free,
Your wilful suicide on God's decree. 20
Oh how unlike the complex works of man,
Heav'n's easy, artless, unincumber'd, plan!
No meretricious graces to beguile,
No clust'ring ornaments to clog the pile;
From ostentation, as from weakness, free,
It stands like the cerulean arch we see,
Majestic in its own simplicity.
Inscrib'd above the portal, from afar
Conspicuous as the brightness of a star,
Legible only by the light they give, 30
Stand the soul-quick'ning words—BELIEVE, AND LIVE!
Too many, shock'd at what should charm them most,
Despise the plain direction, and are lost.
Heav'n on such terms! (they cry, with proud disdain)
Incredible, impossible, and vain!—
Rebel, because 'tis easy to obey;
And scorn, for its own sake, the gracious way.

27 its] his *1800*.

These are the sober, in whose cooler brains
Some thought of immortality remains;
The rest, too busy, or too gay, to wait 40
On the sad theme, their everlasting state,
Sport for a day, and perish in a night;
The foam upon the waters not so light.
Who judg'd the pharisee? What odious cause
Expos'd him to the vengeance of the laws?
Had he seduc'd a virgin, wrong'd a friend,
Or stabb'd a man to serve some private end?
Was blasphemy his sin? Or did he stray
From the strict duties of the sacred day?
Sit long and late at the carousing board? 50
(Such were the sins with which he charg'd his
Lord.)
No—the man's morals were exact. What then?
'Twas his ambition to be seen of men;
His virtues were his pride, and that one vice
Made all his virtues gewgaws of no price;
He wore them, as fine trappings, for a show;
A praying, synagogue-frequenting, beau.
The self-applauding bird, the peacock, see—
Mark what a sumptuous pharisee is he!
Meridian sun-beams tempt him to unfold 60
His radiant glories; azure, green, and gold:
He treads as if, some solemn music near,
His measur'd step were govern'd by his ear;
And seems to say—Ye meaner fowl, give place;
I am all splendour, dignity, and grace!
Not so the pheasant on his charms presumes;
Though he, too, has a glory in his plumes.
He, christian like, retreats with modest mien
To the close copse, or far-sequester'd green,
And shines, without desiring to be seen. 70
The plea of works, as arrogant and vain,
Heav'n turns from with abhorrence and disdain:
Not more affronted by avow'd neglect
Than by the mere dissembler's feign'd respect.
What is all righteousness that men devise?
What—but a sordid bargain for the skies?
But Christ as soon would abdicate his own,
As stoop from heav'n to sell the proud a throne.
His dwelling a recess in some rude rock;
Book, beads, and maple-dish, his meagre stock; 80
In shirt of hair and weeds of canvass dress'd,
Girt with a bell-rope that the pope has bless'd;
Adust with stripes told out for ev'ry crime,
And sore tormented, long before his time;

His pray'r preferr'd to saints that cannot aid;
His praise postpon'd, and never to be paid;
See the sage hermit, by mankind admir'd,
With all that bigotry adopts inspir'd,
Wearing out life in his religious whim,
Till his religious whimsy wears out him. 90
His works, his abstinence, his zeal, allow'd,
You think him humble—God accounts him proud.
High in demand though lowly in pretence,
Of all his conduct this the genuine sense—
My penitential stripes, my streaming blood,
Have purchas'd heav'n, and prove my title good.
Turn eastward now, and fancy shall apply
To your weak sight her telescopic eye.
The bramin kindles on his own bare head
The sacred fire—self-torturing his trade! 100
His voluntary pains, severe and long,
Would give a barb'rous air to British song;
No grand inquisitor could worse invent,
Than he contrives, to suffer, well content.
Which is the saintlier worthy of the two?
Past all dispute, yon anchorite, say you.
Your sentence and mine differ. What's a name?
I say the bramin has the fairer claim.
If suff'rings, scripture no where recommends,
Devis'd by self, to answer selfish ends, 110
Give saintship, then all Europe must agree
Ten starvling hermits suffer less than he.
The truth is (if the truth may suit your ear,
And prejudice have left a passage clear)
Pride has attain'd its most luxuriant growth,
And poison'd ev'ry virtue in them both.
Pride may be pamper'd while the flesh grows lean;
Humility may clothe an English dean;
That grace was Cowper's—his, confess'd by all—
Though plac'd in golden Durham's second stall. 120
Not all the plenty of a bishop's board,
His palace, and his lacqueys, and "My Lord,"
More nourish pride, that condescending vice,
Than abstinence, and beggary, and lice;
It thrives in mis'ry, and abundant grows
In mis'ry fools upon themselves impose.
But why before us protestants produce
An Indian mystic, or a French recluse?
Their sin is plain; but what have we to fear,
Reform'd, and well instructed? You shall hear. 130
Yon ancient prude, whose wither'd features show
She might be young some forty years ago,

Her elbows pinion'd close upon her hips,
Her head erect, her fan upon her lips,
Her eye-brows arch'd, her eyes both gone astray
To watch yon am'rous couple in their play,
With bony and unkerchief'd neck, defies
The rude inclemency of wintry skies,
And sails, with lappet-head and mincing airs,
Duly, at clink of bell, to morning pray'rs. 140
To thrift and parsimony much inclin'd,
She yet allows herself that boy behind.
The shiv'ring urchin, bending as he goes,
With slip-shod heels, and dew-drop at his nose;
His predecessor's coat advanc'd to wear,
Which future pages yet are doom'd to share;
Carries her bible, tuck'd beneath his arm,
And hides his hands, to keep his fingers warm.
She, half an angel in her own account,
Doubts not hereafter with the saints to mount, 150
Though not a grace appears, on strictest search,
But that she fasts, and, *item*, goes to church.
Conscious of age, she recollects her youth,
And tells, not always with an eye to truth,
Who spann'd her waist, and who, where'er he came,
Scrawl'd upon glass miss Bridget's lovely name;
Who stole her slipper, fill'd it with tokay,
And drank the little bumper ev'ry day.
Of temper as envenom'd as an asp;
Censorious, and her ev'ry word a wasp; 160
In faithful mem'ry she records the crimes,
Or real, or fictitious, of the times;
Laughs at the reputations she has torn,
And holds them, dangling at arm's length, in scorn.
Such are the fruits of sanctimonious pride,
Of malice fed while flesh is mortified:
Take, Madam, the reward of all your pray'rs,
Where hermits and where bramins meet with theirs:
Your portion is with them.—Nay, never frown;
But, if you please, some fathoms lower down. 170
Artist, attend! your brushes and your paint—
Produce them—take a chair—now draw a saint.
Oh, sorrowful and sad! the streaming tears
Channel her cheeks—a Niobe appears!
Is this a saint? Throw tints and all away—
True piety is cheerful as the day;
Will weep, indeed, and heave a pitying groan,
For others' woes, but smiles upon her own.

146 yet are] are yet *1782-1788.*

What purpose has the King of saints in view?
Why falls the gospel like a gracious dew? 180
To call up plenty from the teeming earth,
Or curse the desert with a tenfold dearth?
Is it that Adam's offspring may be sav'd
From servile fear, or be the more enslav'd?
To loose the links that gall'd mankind before,
Or bind them faster on, and add still more?
The freeborn Christian has no chains to prove;
Or, if a chain, the golden one of love:
No fear attends to quench his glowing fires,
What fear he feels his gratitude inspires. 190
Shall he for such deliv'rance, freely wrought,
Recompense ill? He trembles at the thought.
His master's int'rest and his own, combin'd,
Prompt ev'ry movement of his heart and mind:
Thought, word, and deed, his liberty evince;
His freedom is the freedom of a prince.
Man's obligations infinite, of course
His life should prove that he perceives their force:
His utmost he can render is but small—
The principle and motive all in all. 200
You have two servants—Tom, an arch, sly rogue,
From top to toe the Geta now in vogue,
Genteel in figure, easy in address,
Moves without noise, and swift as an express,
Reports a message with a pleasing grace,
Expert in all the duties of his place:
Say, on what hinge does his obedience move?
Has he a world of gratitude and love?
No, not a spark—'tis all mere sharper's play;
He likes your house, your housemaid, and your pay;
Reduce his wages, or get rid of her, 211
Tom quits you, with—Your most obedient, Sir.
The dinner serv'd, Charles takes his usual stand,
Watches your eye, anticipates command;
Sighs, if perhaps your appetite should fail;
And, if he but suspects a frown, turns pale;
Consults all day your int'rest and your ease,
Richly rewarded if he can but please;
And, proud to make his firm attachment known,
To save your life would nobly risk his own. 220
Now which stands highest in your serious thought?
Charles, without doubt, say you—and so he ought;
One act, that from a thankful heart proceeds,
Excels ten thousand mercenary deeds.
Thus heav'n approves, as honest and sincere,
The work of gen'rous love, and filial fear;

But, with averted eyes, th' omniscient Judge
Scorns the base hireling, and the slavish drudge.
  Where dwell these matchless saints?—old Curio
Ev'n at your side, Sir, and before your eyes, [cries.
The favour'd few—th' enthusiasts you despise; 231
And, pleas'd at heart, because on holy ground
Sometimes a canting hypocrite is found,
Reproach a people with his single fall,
And cast his filthy raiment at them all.
Attend!—an apt similitude shall show
Whence springs the conduct that offends you so.
  See where it smokes along the sounding plain,
Blown all aslant, a driving, dashing rain,
Peal upon peal redoubling all around, 240
Shakes it again, and faster to the ground;
Now flashing wide, now glancing as in play,
Swift beyond thought the lightnings dart away.
Ere yet it came, the trav'ler urg'd his steed,
And hurried, but with unsuccessful speed;
Now, drench'd throughout, and hopeless of his case,
He drops the rein, and leaves him to his pace.
Suppose, unlook'd for in a scene so rude,
Long hid by interposing hill or wood,
Some mansion, neat and elegantly dress'd, 250
By some kind hospitable heart possess'd,
Offer him warmth, security, and rest;
Think with what pleasure, safe, and at his ease,
He hears the tempest howling in the trees;
What glowing thanks his lips and heart employ,
While danger past is turn'd to present joy.
So fares it with the sinner, when he feels
A growing dread of vengeance at his heels:
His conscience, like a glassy lake before,
Lash'd into foaming waves, begins to roar; 260
The law, grown clamorous, though silent long,
Arraigns him—charges him with ev'ry wrong—
Asserts the rights of his offended Lord;
And death, or restitution, is the word:
The last impossible, he fears the first,
And, having well deserv'd, expects the worst.
Then welcome refuge and a peaceful home;
Oh for a shelter from the wrath to come!
Crush me, ye rocks; ye falling mountains, hide
Or bury me in ocean's angry tide.— 270
The scrutiny of those all-seeing eyes
I dare not—And you need not, God replies;
The remedy you want I freely give:
The book shall teach you—read, believe, and live!

'Tis done—the raging storm is heard no more,
Mercy receives him on her peaceful shore;
And Justice, guardian of the dread command,
Drops the red vengeance from his willing hand.
A soul redeem'd demands a life of praise;
Hence the complexion of his future days, 280
Hence a demeanour holy and unspeck'd,
And the world's hatred, as its sure effect.
  Some lead a life unblameable and just,
Their own dear virtue their unshaken trust:
They never sin—or, if (as all offend)
Some trivial slips their daily walk attend,
The poor are near at hand, the charge is small,
A slight gratuity atones for all!
For, though the pope has lost his int'rest here,
And pardons are not sold as once they were, 290
No papist more desirous to compound,
Than some grave sinners upon English ground.
That plea refuted, other quirks they seek—
Mercy is infinite, and man is weak;
The future shall obliterate the past,
And heav'n, no doubt, shall be their home at last.
  Come, then—a still, small whisper in your ear—
He has no hope who never had a fear;
And he that never doubted of his state,
He may, perhaps—perhaps he may—too late. 300
  The path to bliss abounds with many a snare;
Learning is one, and wit, however rare.
The Frenchman, first in literary fame,
(Mention him, if you please. Voltaire?—The same.)
With spirit, genius, eloquence, supplied,
Liv'd long, wrote much, laugh'd heartily, and died.
The scripture was his jest-book, whence he drew
Bon mots to gall the Christian and the Jew.
An infidel in health, but what when sick?
Oh—then a text would touch him at the quick. 310
View him at Paris, in his last career:
Surrounding throngs the demi-god revere;
Exalted on his pedestal of pride,
And fum'd with frankincense on ev'ry side,
He begs their flatt'ry with his latest breath;
And, smother'd in't at last, is prais'd to death!
  Yon cottager, who weaves at her own door,
Pillow and bobbins all her little store;
Content, though mean; and cheerful, if not gay;
Shuffling her threads about the live-long day, 320

298 who] that *1782*, *1786*.

Just earns a scanty pittance; and at night
Lies down secure, her heart and pocket light:
She, for her humble sphere by nature fit,
Has little understanding, and no wit,
Receives no praise; but though her lot be such,
(Toilsome and indigent) she renders much;
Just knows, and knows no more, her Bible true—
A truth the brilliant Frenchman never knew;
And in that charter reads, with sparkling eyes,
Her title to a treasure in the skies. 330

Oh, happy peasant! Oh, unhappy bard!
His the mere tinsel, her's the rich reward;
He prais'd, perhaps, for ages yet to come;
She never heard of half a mile from home;
He, lost in errors, his vain heart prefers;
She, safe in the simplicity of her's.

Not many wise, rich, noble, or profound
In science, win one inch of heav'nly ground.
And is it not a mortifying thought
The poor should gain it, and the rich should not?
No—the volupt'aries, who ne'er forget 341
One pleasure lost, lose heav'n without regret;
Regret would rouse them, and give birth to pray'r;
Pray'r would add faith, and faith would fix them there.

Not that the Former of us all in this,
Or aught he does, is govern'd by caprice;
The supposition is replete with sin,
And bears the brand of blasphemy burnt in.
Not so—the silver trumpet's heav'nly call
Sounds for the poor, but sounds alike for all: 350
Kings are invited; and, would kings obey,
No slaves on earth more welcome were than they:
But royalty, nobility, and state,
Are such a dead preponderating weight,
That endless bliss, (how strange soe'er it seem)
In counterpoise, flies up and kicks the beam.
'Tis open, and ye cannot enter—why?
Because ye will not, Conyers would reply—
And he says much that many may dispute
And cavil at with ease, but none refute. 360
Oh, bless'd effect of penury and want,
The seed sown there, how vig'rous is the plant!
No soil like poverty for growth divine,
As leanest land supplies the richest wine.
Earth gives too little, giving only bread,
To nourish pride, or turn the weakest head:
To them the sounding jargon of the schools
Seems what it is—a cap and bells for fools:

The light they walk by, kindled from above,
Shows them the shortest way to life and love: 370
They, strangers to the controversial field,
Where deists, always foil'd, yet scorn to yield,
And never check'd by what impedes the wise,
Believe, rush forward, and possess the prize.
Envy, ye great, the dull unletter'd small:
Ye have much cause for envy—but not all.
We boast some rich ones whom the gospel sways;
And one who wears a coronet, and prays;
Like gleanings of an olive-tree, they show
Here and there one upon the topmost bough. 380
How readily, upon the gospel plan
That question has its answer—What is man?
Sinful and weak, in ev'ry sense a wretch;
An instrument, whose cords, upon the stretch,
And strain'd to the last screw that he can bear,
Yield only discord in his Maker's ear:
Once the blest residence of truth divine,
Glorious as Solyma's interior shrine,
Where, in his own oracular abode,
Dwelt visibly the light-creating God; 390
But made long since, like Babylon of old,
A den of mischiefs never to be told:
And she, once mistress of the realms around,
Now scatter'd wide, and no where to be found,
As soon shall rise and reascend the throne,
By native pow'r and energy her own,
As nature, at her own peculiar cost,
Restore to man the glories he has lost.
Go—bid the winter cease to chill the year;
Replace the wand'ring comet in his sphere; 400
Then boast (but wait for that unhop'd for hour)
The self-restoring arm of human pow'r.
But what is man in his own proud esteem?
Hear him—himself the poet and the theme:
A monarch, cloth'd with majesty and awe;
His mind his kingdom, and his will his law;
Grace in his mien, and glory in his eyes,
Supreme on earth, and worthy of the skies,
Strength in his heart, dominion in his nod,
And, thunderbolts excepted, quite a God! 410
So sings he, charm'd with his own mind and form,
The song magnificent—the theme a worm!
Himself so much the source of his delight,
His Maker has no beauty in his sight.

378 who] that *1782*, *1786*.

See where he sits, contemplative and fix'd,
Pleasure and wonder in his features mix'd;
His passions tam'd, and all at his controul,
How perfect the composure of his soul!
Complacency has breath'd a gentle gale
O'er all his thoughts, and swell'd his easy sail: 420
His books well trimm'd, and in the gayest style,
Like regimented coxcombs, rank and file,
Adorn his intellects as well as shelves,
And teach him notions splendid as themselves:
The Bible only stands neglected there—
Though that of all most worthy of his care;
And, like an infant, troublesome awake,
Is left to sleep, for peace and quiet sake.
What shall the man deserve of human kind,
Whose happy skill and industry, combin'd, 430
Shall prove (what argument could never yet)
The Bible an imposture and a cheat?
The praises of the libertine profess'd,
The worst of men, and curses of the best.
Where should the living, weeping o'er his woes;
The dying, trembling at the awful close;
Where the betray'd, forsaken, and oppress'd,
The thousands whom the world forbids to rest;
Where should they find, (those comforts at an end
The scripture yields) or hope to find, a friend? 440
Sorrow might muse herself to madness then;
And, seeking exile from the sight of men,
Bury herself in solitude profound,
Grow frantic with her pangs, and bite the ground.
Thus often unbelief, grown sick of life,
Flies to the tempting pool, or felon knife.
The jury meet, the coroner is short,
And lunacy the verdict of the court.
Reverse the sentence, let the truth be known,
Such lunacy is ignorance alone. 450
They knew not, what some bishops may not know,
That scripture is the only cure of woe.
That field of promise, how it flings abroad
Its odour o'er the Christian's thorny road!
The soul, reposing on assur'd relief,
Feels herself happy amidst all her grief,
Forgets her labour as she toils along,
Weeps tears of joy, and bursts into a song.
But the same word, that, like the polish'd share,
Ploughs up the roots of a believer's care, 460

422 regimental *1808 and some later edd.*

Kills too the flow'ry weeds, where'er they grow,
That bind the sinner's Bacchanalian brow.
Oh, that unwelcome voice of heav'nly love,
Sad messenger of mercy from above!
How does it grate upon his thankless ear,
Crippling his pleasures with the cramp of fear!
His will and judgment at continual strife,
That civil war imbitters all his life:
In vain he points his pow'rs against the skies,
In vain he closes or averts his eyes, 470
Truth will intrude—she bids him yet beware;
And shakes the sceptic in the scorner's chair.
  Though various foes against the truth combine,
Pride above all opposes her design;
Pride, of a growth superior to the rest,
The subtlest serpent, with the loftiest crest,
Swells at the thought, and, kindling into rage,
Would hiss the cherub mercy from the stage.
  And is the soul, indeed, so lost?—she cries;
Fall'n from her glory, and too weak to rise? 480
Torpid and dull, beneath a frozen zone,
Has she no spark that may be deem'd her own?
Grant her indebted to what zealots call
Grace undeserv'd—yet, surely, not for all!
Some beams of rectitude she yet displays,
Some love of virtue, and some pow'r to praise;
Can lift herself above corporeal things,
And, soaring on her own unborrow'd wings,
Possess herself of all that's good or true,
Assert the skies, and vindicate her due. 490
Past indiscretion is a venial crime;
And, if the youth, unmellow'd yet by time,
Bore on his branch, luxuriant then and rude,
Fruits of a blighted size, austere and crude,
Maturer years shall happier stores produce,
And meliorate the well concocted juice.
Then, conscious of her meritorious zeal,
To justice she may make her bold appeal;
And leave to mercy, with a tranquil mind,
The worthless and unfruitful of mankind. 500
Hear, then, how mercy, slighted and defied,
Retorts th' affront against the crown of pride.
  Perish the virtue, as it ought, abhorr'd,
And the fool with it, who insults his Lord.
Th' atonement a Redeemer's love has wrought
Is not for you—the righteous need it not.

482 doom'd *1794-1800*. 504 who] that *1782*, *1786*.

Seest thou yon harlot, wooing all she meets,
The worn-out nuisance of the public streets;
Herself, from morn to night, from night to morn,
Her own abhorrence, and as much your scorn! 510
The gracious show'r, unlimited and free,
Shall fall on her, when heav'n denies it thee.
Of all that wisdom dictates, this the drift—
That man is dead in sin, and life a gift.

Is virtue, then, unless of Christian growth,
Mere fallacy, or foolishness, or both?
Ten thousand sages lost in endless woe,
For ignorance of what they could not know?
That speech betrays at once a bigot's tongue—
Charge not a God with such outrageous wrong! 520
Truly, not I—the partial light men have,
My creed persuades me, well employ'd, may save;
While he that scorns the noon-day beam, perverse,
Shall find the blessing, unimprov'd, a curse.
Let heathen worthies, whose exalted mind
Left sensuality and dross behind,
Possess, for me, their undisputed lot,
And take, unenvied, the reward they sought:
But still in virtue of a Saviour's plea,
Not blind by choice, but destin'd not to see. 530
Their fortitude and wisdom were a flame
Celestial, though they knew not whence it came,
Deriv'd from the same source of light and grace
That guides the Christian in his swifter race.
Their judge was conscience, and her rule their law:
That rule, pursued with rev'rence and with awe,
Led them, however falt'ring, faint, and slow,
From what they knew to what they wish'd to know.
But let not him that shares a brighter day
Traduce the splendour of a noon-tide ray, 540
Prefer the twilight of a darker time,
And deem his base stupidity no crime;
The wretch, who slights the bounty of the skies,
And sinks, while favour'd with the means to rise,
Shall find them rated at their full amount,
The good he scorn'd all carried to account.

Marshalling all his terrors as he came;
Thunder, and earthquake, and devouring flame;
From Sinai's top Jehovah gave the law—
Life for obedience—death for ev'ry flaw. 550
When the great Sov'reign would his will express,
He gives a perfect rule; what can he less?

543 who] that *1782*, *1786*.

And guards it with a sanction as severe
As vengeance can inflict, or sinners fear:
Else his own glorious rights he would disclaim,
And man might safely trifle with his name.
He bids him glow with unremitting love
To all on earth, and to himself above;
Condemns th' injurious deed, the sland'rous tongue,
The thought that meditates a brother's wrong: 560
Brings not alone the more conspicuous part—
His conduct—to the test, but tries his heart.
Hark! universal nature shook and groan'd,
'Twas the last trumpet—see the Judge enthron'd:
Rouse all your courage at your utmost need;
Now summon ev'ry virtue—stand, and plead.
What! silent? Is your boasting heard no more?
That self-renouncing wisdom, learn'd before,
Had shed immortal glories on your brow,
That all your virtues cannot purchase now. 570
All joy to the believer! He can speak—
Trembling, yet happy; confident, yet meek.
Since the dear hour that brought me to thy foot,
And cut up all my follies by the root,
I never trusted in an arm but thine,
Nor hop'd, but in thy righteousness divine:
My pray'rs and alms, imperfect, and defil'd,
Were but the feeble efforts of a child;
Howe'er perform'd, it was their brightest part
That they proceeded from a grateful heart: 580
Cleans'd in thine own all purifying blood,
Forgive their evil, and accept their good.
I cast them at thy feet—my only plea
Is what it was—dependence upon thee:
While struggling in the vale of tears below,
That never fail'd, nor shall it fail me now.
Angelic gratulations rend the skies:
Pride falls unpitied, never more to rise;
Humility is crown'd; and faith receives the prize.

EXPOSTULATION

[Written March 1781. Published 1782.]

Tantane, tam patiens, nullo certamine tolli
Dona sines?—VIRGIL.

WHY weeps the muse for England? What appears
In England's case to move the muse to tears?
From side to side of her delightful isle,
Is she not cloth'd with a perpetual smile?

Can nature add a charm, or art confer
A new-found luxury, not seen in her?
Where under heav'n is pleasure more pursued?
Or where does cold reflection less intrude?
Her fields a rich expanse of wavy corn,
Pour'd out from plenty's overflowing horn; 10
Ambrosial gardens, in which art supplies
The fervour and the force of Indian skies;
Her peaceful shores, where busy commerce waits
To pour his golden tide through all her gates;
Whom fiery suns, that scorch the russet spice
Of eastern groves, and oceans floor'd with ice,
Forbid in vain to push his daring way
To darker climes, or climes of brighter day;
Whom the winds waft where'er the billows roll,
From the world's girdle to the frozen pole; 20
The chariots, bounding in her wheel-worn streets;
Her vaults below, where ev'ry vintage meets;
Her theatres, her revels, and her sports;
The scenes to which not youth alone resorts,
But age, in spite of weakness and of pain,
Still haunts, in hope to dream of youth again;
All speak her happy: let the muse look round
From East to West, no sorrow can be found;
Or only what, in cottages confin'd,
Sighs unregarded to the passing wind. 30
Then wherefore weep for England? What appears
In England's case to move the muse to tears?
The prophet wept for Israel; wish'd his eyes
Were fountains fed with infinite supplies:
For Israel dealt in robbery and wrong;
There were the scorner's and the sland'rer's tongue;
Oaths, us'd as playthings or convenient tools,
As int'rest bias'd knaves, or fashion fools;
Adult'ry, neighing at his neighbour's door;
Oppression, labouring hard to grind the poor; 40
The partial balance, and deceitful weight;
The treach'rous smile, a mask for secret hate;
Hypocrisy, formality in pray'r,
And the dull service of the lip, were there.
Her women, insolent and self-caress'd,
By vanity's unwearied finger dress'd,
Forgot the blush that virgin fears impart
To modest cheeks, and borrow'd one from art;
Were just such trifles, without worth or use,
As silly pride and idleness produce; 50
Curl'd, scented, furbelow'd and flounc'd around,
With feet too delicate to touch the ground,

They stretch'd the neck, and roll'd the wanton eye,
And sigh'd for ev'ry fool that flutter'd by.
He saw his people slaves to ev'ry lust,
Lewd, avaricious, arrogant, unjust;
He heard the wheels of an avenging God
Groan heavily along the distant road;
Saw Babylon set wide her two-leav'd brass
To let the military deluge pass; 60
Jerusalem a prey, her glory soil'd,
Her princes captive, and her treasures spoil'd;
Wept till all Israel heard his bitter cry;
Stamped with his foot; and smote upon his thigh:
But wept, and stamp'd, and smote his thigh, in vain—
Pleasure is deaf when told of future pain,
And sounds prophetic are too rough to suit
Ears long accustom'd to the pleasing lute—
They scorn'd his inspiration and his theme;
Pronounc'd him frantic, and his fears a dream; 70
With self-indulgence wing'd the fleeting hours,
Till the foe found them, and down fell the tow'rs.
Long time Assyria bound them in her chain;
Till penitence had purg'd the public stain,
And Cyrus, with relenting pity mov'd,
Return'd them happy to the land they lov'd;
There, proof against prosperity, awhile
They stood the test of her ensnaring smile;
And had the grace, in scenes of peace, to show
The virtue they had learn'd in scenes of woe. 80
But man is frail, and can but ill sustain
A long immunity from grief and pain;
And, after all the joys that plenty leads,
With tip-toe step vice silently succeeds.
When he that rul'd them with a shepherd's rod,
In form a man, in dignity a God,
Came, not expected in that humble guise,
To sift and search them with unerring eyes,
He found, conceal'd beneath a fair outside,
The filth of rottenness and worm of pride; 90
Their piety a system of deceit,
Scripture employ'd to sanctify the cheat;
The pharisee the dupe of his own art,
Self-idoliz'd, and yet a knave at heart!
When nations are to perish in their sins,
'Tis in the church the leprosy begins.
The priest, whose office is, with zeal sincere,
To watch the fountain, and preserve it clear,
Carelessly nods and sleeps upon the brink,
While others poison what the flock must drink; 100

Or, waking at the call of lust alone,
Infuses lies and errors of his own.
His unsuspecting sheep believe it pure;
And, tainted by the very means of cure,
Catch from each other a contagious spot,
The foul forerunner of a gen'ral rot.
Then truth is hush'd, that heresy may preach;
And all is trash that reason cannot reach:
Then God's own image on the soul impress'd
Becomes a mock'ry, and a standing jest; 110
And faith, the root whence only can arise
The graces of a life that wins the skies,
Loses at once all value and esteem,
Pronounced by gray-beards a pernicious dream:
Then ceremony leads her bigots forth,
Prepar'd to fight for shadows of no worth;
While truths, on which eternal things depend,
Find not, or hardly find, a single friend:
As soldiers watch the signal of command,
They learn to bow, to kneel, to sit, to stand; 120
Happy to fill religion's vacant place
With hollow form, and gesture, and grimace.
  Such, when the teacher of his church was there,
People and priest, the sons of Israel were;
Stiff in the letter, lax in the design
And import, of their oracles divine;
Their learning legendary, false, absurd,
And yet exalted above God's own word;
They drew a curse from an intended good,
Puff'd up with gifts they never understood. 130
He judg'd them with as terrible a frown
As if not love, but wrath, had brought him down:
Yet he was gentle as soft summer airs;
Had grace for others' sins, but none for theirs.
Through all he spoke a noble plainness ran—
Rhet'ric is artifice, the work of man;
And tricks and turns, that fancy may devise,
Are far too mean for him that rules the skies.
Th' astonish'd vulgar trembled while he tore
The mask from faces never seen before; 140
He stripp'd th' impostors in the noon-day sun;
Show'd that they follow'd all they seem'd to shun;
Their pray'rs made public, their excesses kept
As private as the chambers where they slept;
The temple and its holy rites profan'd
By mumm'ries he that dwelt in it disdain'd;

108 reach] teach *1798, 1800.*

Uplifted hands, that at convenient times
Could act extortion and the worst of crimes,
Wash'd with a neatness scrupulously nice,
And free from ev'ry taint but that of vice. 150
Judgment, however tardy, mends her pace
When obstinacy once has conquer'd grace.
They saw distemper heal'd, and life restor'd,
In answer to the fiat of his word;
Confess'd the wonder, and, with daring tongue,
Blasphem'd th' authority from which it sprung.
They knew, by sure prognostics seen on high,
The future tone and temper of the sky;
But, grave dissemblers! could not understand
That sin let loose speaks punishment at hand. 160
Ask now of history's authentic page,
And call up evidence from ev'ry age;
Display with busy and laborious hand
The blessings of the most indebted land;
What nation will you find, whose annals prove
So rich an int'rest in almighty love?
Where dwell they now, where dwelt in ancient day,
A people planted, water'd, blest, as they?
Let Egypt's plagues, and Canaan's woes proclaim
The favours pour'd upon the Jewish name— 170
Their freedom, purchas'd for them at the cost
Of all their hard oppressors valued most;
Their title to a country not their own
Made sure by prodigies till then unknown;
For them, the state they left made waste and void;
For them, the states to which they went destroy'd;
A cloud to measure out their march by day,
By night a fire to cheer the gloomy way;
That moving signal summoning, when best,
Their host to move; and, when it stay'd, to rest.
For them the rocks dissolv'd into a flood, 181
The dews condens'd into angelic food;
Their very garments sacred—old, yet new,
And Time forbid to touch them as he flew;
Streams, swell'd above the bank, enjoin'd to stand,
While they pass'd through to their appointed land;
Their leader arm'd with meekness, zeal, and love,
And grac'd with clear credentials from above;
Themselves secur'd beneath th' Almighty wing;
Their God their captain [1], lawgiver, and king; 190
Crown'd with a thousand vict'ries, and at last
Lords of the conquer'd soil, there rooted fast,

[1] Vide Joshua v. 14 [C.].

In peace possessing what they won by war,
Their name far publish'd, and rever'd as far;
Where will you find a race like their's, endow'd
With all that man e'er wish'd, or heav'n bestow'd?
They, and they only, amongst all mankind,
Receiv'd the transcript of th' eternal mind;
Were trusted with his own engraven laws,
And constituted guardians of his cause; 200
Theirs were the prophets, theirs the priestly call,
And theirs, by birth, the Saviour of us all.
In vain the nations, that had seen them rise
With fierce and envious, yet admiring, eyes,
Had sought to crush them, guarded as they were
By pow'r divine, and skill that could not err.
Had they maintain'd allegiance firm and sure,
And kept the faith immaculate and pure,
Then the proud eagles of all conqu'ring Rome
Had found one city not to be o'ercome; 210
And the twelve standards of the tribes unfurl'd,
Had bid defiance to the warring world.
But grace abus'd brings forth the foulest deeds,
As richest soil the most luxuriant weeds.
Cur'd of the golden calves, their fathers' sin,
They set up self, that idol god within;
View'd a Deliv'rer with disdain and hate
Who left them still a tributary state;
Seiz'd fast his hand, held out to set them free
From a worse yoke, and nail'd it to the tree: 220
There was the consummation and the crown,
The flow'r of Israel's infamy full blown;
Thence date their sad declension, and their fall;
Their woes, not yet repealed—thence date them all!
Thus fell the best instructed in her day,
And the most favour'd land, look where we may.
Philosophy, indeed, on Grecian eyes
Had pour'd the day, and clear'd the Roman skies;
In other climes, perhaps, creative art,
With pow'r surpassing their's, perform'd her part;
Might give more life to marble, or might fill 231
The glowing tablets with a juster skill,
Might shine in fable, and grace idle themes
With all th' embroid'ry of poetic dreams:
'Twas their's alone to dive into the plan
That truth and mercy had reveal'd to man;
And, while the world beside, that plan unknown,
Deified useless wood, or senseless stone,
They breath'd in faith their well directed pray'rs,
And the true God—the God of truth—was their's.

Their glory faded, and their race dispers'd; 241
The last of nations now, though once the first;
They warn and teach the proudest, would they
learn,
Keep wisdom, or meet vengeance in your turn:
If we escap'd not, if Heav'n spar'd not us,
Peel'd, scatter'd, and exterminated, thus;
If vice receiv'd her retribution due
When we were visited, what hope for you?
When God arises, with an awful frown,
To punish lust, or pluck presumption down; 250
When gifts perverted, or not duly priz'd,
Pleasure o'ervalued, and his grace despis'd,
Provoke the vengeance of his righteous hand
To pour down wrath upon a thankless land;
He will be found impartially severe;
Too just to wink, or speak the guilty clear.
Oh, Israel, of all nations most undone!
Thy diadem displac'd, thy sceptre gone;
Thy temple, once thy glory, fall'n and ras'd,
And thou a worshipper e'en where thou may'st;
Thy services, once holy without spot, 261
Mere shadows now, their ancient pomp forgot;
Thy Levites, once a consecrated host,
No longer Levites, and their lineage lost,
And thou thyself o'er ev'ry country sown,
With none on earth that thou canst call thine own;
Cry aloud, thou that sittest in the dust,
Cry to the proud, the cruel, and unjust;
Knock at the gates of nations, rouse their fears;
Say wrath is coming, and the storm appears; 270
But raise the shrillest cry in British ears.
What ails thee, restless as the waves that roar,
And fling their foam against thy chalky shore?
Mistress, at least while Providence shall please,
And trident-bearing queen of the wide seas—
Why, having kept good faith, and often shown
Friendship and truth to others, find'st thou none?
Thou that hast set the persecuted free,
None interposes now to succour thee.
Countries, indebted to thy pow'r, that shine 280
With light deriv'd from thee, would smother thine:
Thy very children watch for thy disgrace—
A lawless brood! and curse thee to thy face.
Thy rulers load thy credit, year by year,
With sums Peruvian mines could never clear;
As if, like arches built with skilful hand,
The more 'twere prest the firmer it would stand.

The cry in all thy ships is still the same—
Speed us away to battle and to fame.
Thy mariners explore the wild expanse, 290
Impatient to descry the flags of France;
But, though they fight as thine have ever fought,
Return, asham'd, without the wreaths they sought.
Thy senate is a scene of civil jar,
Chaos of contrarieties at war;
Where sharp and solid, phlegmatic and light,
Discordant atoms meet, ferment, and fight;
Where obstinacy takes his sturdy stand,
To disconcert what policy has plann'd;
Where policy is busied all night long 300
In setting right what faction has set wrong;
Where flails of oratory thresh the floor,
That yields them chaff and dust, and nothing more.
Thy rack'd inhabitants repine, complain,
Tax'd till the brow of labour sweats in vain;
War lays a burden on the reeling state,
And peace does nothing to relieve the weight;
Successive loads succeeding broils impose,
And sighing millions prophesy the close.

Is adverse providence, when ponder'd well, 310
So dimly writ, or difficult to spell,
Thou canst not read with readiness and ease
Providence adverse in events like these?
Know, then, that heav'nly wisdom on this ball
Creates, gives birth to, guides, consummates, all;
That, while laborious and quick-thoughted man
Snuffs up the praise of what he seems to plan,
He first conceives, then perfects his design,
As a mere instrument in hands divine.
Blind to the working of that secret pow'r 320
That balances the wings of ev'ry hour,
The busy trifler dreams himself alone,
Frames many a purpose, and God works his own.
States thrive or wither, as moons wax and wane,
Ev'n as his will and his decrees ordain.
While honour, virtue, piety, bear sway,
They flourish; and, as these decline, decay.
In just resentment of his injur'd laws,
He pours contempt on them, and on their cause;
Strikes the rough thread of error right athwart
The web of ev'ry scheme they have at heart; 331
Bids rottenness invade and bring to dust
The pillars of support, in which they trust,
And do his errand of disgrace and shame
On the chief strength and glory of the frame.

None ever yet impeded what he wrought;
None bars him out from his most secret thought:
Darkness itself before his eye is light,
And hell's close mischief naked in his sight.
  Stand now, and judge thyself.—Hast thou incurr'd
His anger, who can waste thee with a word, 341
Who poises and proportions sea and land,
Weighing them in the hollow of his hand,
And in whose awful sight all nations seem
As grasshoppers, as dust, a drop, a dream?
Hast thou (a sacrilege his soul abhors)
Claim'd all the glory of thy prosp'rous wars?
Proud of thy fleets and armies, stol'n the gem
Of his just praise, to lavish it on them?
Hast thou not learn'd, what thou art often told, 350
A truth still sacred, and believ'd of old,
That no success attends on spears and swords
Unblest, and that the battle is the Lord's?
That courage is his creature, and dismay
The post that at his bidding speeds away,
Ghastly in feature, and his stamm'ring tongue
With doleful rumour and sad presage hung,
To quell the valour of the stoutest heart,
And teach the combatant a woman's part?
That he bids thousands fly when none pursue, 360
Saves as he will, by many or by few,
And claims for ever, as his royal right,
Th' event and sure decision of the fight?
  Hast thou, though suckled at fair freedom's breast,
Exported slav'ry to the conquer'd East,
Pull'd down the tyrants India serv'd with dread,
And rais'd thyself, a greater, in their stead?
Gone thither arm'd and hungry, return'd full,
Fed from the richest veins of the Mogul,
A despot big with pow'r obtain'd by wealth, 370
And that obtain'd by rapine and by stealth?
With Asiatic vices stor'd thy mind,
But left their virtues and thine own behind;
And, having truck'd thy soul, brought home the fee,
To tempt the poor to sell himself to thee?
  Hast thou by statute shov'd from its design
The Saviour's feast, his own blest bread and wine,
And made the symbols of atoning grace
An office-key, a pick-lock to a place,
That infidels may prove their title good 380
By an oath dipp'd in sacramental blood?

357 humour *1794-1800*. 376 mov'd *1799*. 380 make *1799*, *1800*.

A blot that will be still a blot, in spite
Of all that grave apologists may write;
And, though a bishop toil to cleanse the stain,
He wipes and scours the silver cup in vain.
And hast thou sworn, on ev'ry slight pretence,
Till perjuries are common as bad pence,
While thousands, careless of the damning sin,
Kiss the book's outside who ne'er look within?

Hast thou, when heav'n has cloth'd thee with dis-
And, long provok'd, repaid thee to thy face, [grace,
(For thou hast known eclipses, and endur'd 392
Dimness and anguish, all thy beams obscur'd,
When sin has shed dishonour on thy brow;
And never of a sabler hue than now)
Hast thou, with heart perverse and conscience sear'd,
Despising all rebuke, still persever'd,
And, having chosen evil, scorn'd the voice
That cried, Repent!—and gloried in thy choice?
Thy fastings, when calamity at last 400
Suggests th' expedient of a yearly fast,
What mean they? Canst thou dream there is a pow'r
In lighter diet, at a later hour,
To charm to sleep the threat'ning of the skies,
And hide past folly from all-seeing eyes?
The fast that wins deliv'rance, and suspends
The stroke that a vindictive God intends,
Is to renounce hypocrisy; to draw
Thy life upon the pattern of the law;
To war with pleasure, idoliz'd before; 410
To vanquish lust, and wear its yoke no more.
All fasting else, whate'er be the pretence,
Is wooing mercy by renew'd offence.

Hast thou within thee sin, that in old time
Brought fire from heav'n, the sex-abusing crime,
Whose horrid perpetration stamps disgrace
Baboons are free from upon human race?
Think on the fruitful and well water'd spot
That fed the flocks and herds of wealthy Lot,
Where Paradise seem'd still vouchsaf'd on earth, 420
Burning and scorch'd into perpetual dearth,
Or, in his words who damn'd the base desire,
Suff'ring the vengeance of eternal fire:
Then nature, injur'd, scandaliz'd, defil'd,
Unveil'd her blushing cheek, look'd on, and smil'd;
Beheld with joy the lovely scene defac'd,
And prais'd the wrath that laid her beauties waste.

390–413 *for cancelled passage see notes.* 414 sins *1786*.

Far be the thought from any verse of mine,
And farther still the form'd and fix'd design,
To thrust the charge of deeds that I detest 430
Against an innocent unconscious breast:
The man that dares traduce, because he can
With safety to himself, is not a man:
An individual is a sacred mark,
Not to be pierc'd in play, or in the dark;
But public censure speaks a public foe,
Unless a zeal for virtue guide the blow.
The priestly brotherhood, devout, sincere,
From mean self int'rest and ambition clear,
Their hope in Heav'n, servility their scorn, 440
Prompt to persuade, expostulate, and warn,
Their wisdom pure, and giv'n them from above,
Their usefulness insur'd by zeal and love,
As meek as the man Moses, and withal
As bold as in Agrippa's presence Paul,
Should fly the world's contaminating touch,
Holy and unpolluted:—are thine such?
Except a few with Eli's spirit blest,
Hophni and Phineas may describe the rest.
Where shall a teacher look in days like these, 450
For ears and hearts that he can hope to please?
Look to the poor—the simple and the plain
Will hear, perhaps, thy salutary strain:
Humility is gentle, apt to learn,
Speak but the word, will listen and return.
Alas, not so! the poorest of the flock
Are proud, and set their faces as a rock;
Denied that earthly opulence they choose,
God's better gift they scoff at, and refuse.
The rich, the produce of a nobler stem, 460
Are more intelligent, at least—try them.
Oh, vain inquiry! they, without remorse,
Are altogether gone a devious course;
Where beck'ning pleasure leads them, wildly stray;
Have burst the bands, and cast the yoke away.
Now, borne upon the wings of truth sublime,
Review thy dim original and prime.
This island, spot of unreclaim'd rude earth,
The cradle that receiv'd thee at thy birth,
Was rock'd by many a rough Norwegian blast, 470
And Danish howlings scar'd thee as they pass'd;
For thou wast born amid the din of arms,
And suck'd a breast that panted with alarms.

468 island spot *1782–1788*: island-spot *Southey*.

While yet thou wast a grov'ling, puling chit,
Thy bones not fashion'd, and thy joints not knit,
The Roman taught thy stubborn knee to bow,
Though twice a Cæsar could not bend thee now:
His victory was that of orient light,
When the sun's shafts disperse the gloom of night.
Thy language at this distant moment shows 480
How much the country to the conqu'ror owes;
Expressive, energetic, and refin'd,
It sparkles with the gems he left behind:
He brought thy land a blessing when he came;
He found thee savage, and he left thee tame;
Taught thee to clothe thy pink'd and painted hide,
And grace thy figure with a soldier's pride;
He sow'd the seeds of order where he went,
Improv'd thee far beyond his own intent,
And, while he rul'd thee by the sword alone, 490
Made thee at last a warrior like his own.
Religion, if in heav'nly truths attir'd,
Needs only to be seen to be admir'd;
But thine, as dark as witch'ries of the night,
Was form'd to harden hearts and shock the sight.
Thy Druids struck the well-strung harps they bore
With fingers deeply dy'd in human gore;
And, while the victim slowly bled to death,
Upon the rolling chords rung out his dying breath.
Who brought the lamp, that with awaking beams
Dispell'd thy gloom, and broke away thy dreams,
Tradition, now decrepid and worn out, 502
Babbler of ancient fables, leaves a doubt:
But still light reach'd thee; and those gods of thine,
Woden and Thor, each tott'ring in his shrine,
Fell, broken, and defac'd, at their own door,
As Dagon in Philistia long before.
But Rome, with sorceries and magic wand,
Soon rais'd a cloud that darken'd ev'ry land;
And thine was smother'd in the stench and fog 510
Of Tiber's marshes and the papal bog.
Then priests, with bulls and briefs, and shaven crowns,
And griping fists, and unrelenting frowns,
Legates and delegates, with pow'rs from hell,
Though heavenly in pretension, fleec'd thee well;
And to this hour, to keep it fresh in mind,
Some twigs of that old scourge are left[1] behind.

[1] Which may be found at Doctors' Commons [C.].

496 well-hung *1794–1800*. 499 tolling *1782–1787*. 500 awak'ning *1782–1787*. 506 their] his *1782–1794, and edd. after 1800.*

Thy soldiery, the pope's well manag'd pack,
Were train'd beneath his lash, and knew the smack,
And, when he laid them on the scent of blood, 520
Would hunt a Saracen through fire and flood.
Lavish of life, to win an empty tomb,
That prov'd a mint of wealth, a mine, to Rome,
They left their bones beneath unfriendly skies,
His worthless absolution all the prize!
Thou wast the veriest slave, in days of yore,
That ever dragg'd a chain, or tugg'd an oar.
Thy monarchs, arbitrary, fierce, unjust,
Themselves the slaves of bigotry or lust,
Disdain'd thy counsels; only in distress 530
Found thee a goodly spunge for pow'r to press.
Thy chiefs, the lords of many a petty fee,
Provok'd and harass'd, in return plagu'd thee;
Call'd thee away from peaceable employ,
Domestic happiness and rural joy,
To waste thy life in arms, or lay it down
In causeless feuds and bick'rings of their own.
Thy parliaments ador'd, on bended knees,
The sov'reignty they were conven'd to please;
Whate'er was ask'd, too timid to resist, 540
Comply'd with, and were graciously dismiss'd;
And, if some Spartan soul a doubt express'd,
And, blushing at the tameness of the rest,
Dar'd to suppose the subject had a choice,
He was a traitor by the gen'ral voice.
Oh, slave! with pow'rs thou didst not dare exert,
Verse cannot stoop so low as thy desert;
It shakes the sides of splenetic disdain,
Thou self-entitled ruler of the main,
To trace thee to the date when yon fair sea, 550
That clips thy shores, had no such charms for thee;
When other nations flew from coast to coast,
And thou hadst neither fleet nor flag to boast.
  Kneel now, and lay thy forehead in the dust;
Blush, if thou canst; not petrified, thou must;
Act but an honest and a faithful part;
Compare what then thou wast with what thou art;
And, God's disposing providence confess'd,
Obduracy itself must yield the rest.—
Then thou art bound to serve him, and to prove,
Hour after hour, thy gratitude and love. 561
  Has he not hid thee, and thy favour'd land,
For ages safe beneath his shelt'ring hand,
Giv'n thee his blessing on the clearest proof,
Bid nations leagu'd against thee stand aloof,

And charg'd hostility and hate to roar
Where else they would, but not upon thy shore?
His pow'r secur'd thee when presumptuous Spain
Baptiz'd her fleet invincible in vain.
Her gloomy monarch, doubtful and resign'd 570
To ev'ry pang that racks an anxious mind,
Ask'd of the waves that broke upon his coast,
What tidings? and the surge replied—All lost!
And, when the Stuart, leaning on the Scot,
Then too much fear'd, and now too much forgot,
Pierc'd to the very centre of the realm,
And hop'd to seize his abdicated helm,
'Twas but to prove how quickly, with a frown,
He that had rais'd thee could have pluck'd thee down.
Peculiar is the grace by thee possess'd, 580
Thy foes implacable, thy land at rest;
Thy thunders travel over earth and seas,
And all at home is pleasure, wealth, and ease.
'Tis thus, extending his tempestuous arm,
Thy Maker fills the nations with alarm,
While his own heav'n surveys the troubled scene,
And feels no change, unshaken and serene.
Freedom, in other lands scarce known to shine,
Pours out a flood of splendour upon thine;
Thou hast as bright an int'rest in her rays 590
As ever Roman had in Rome's best days.
True freedom is where no restraint is known
That scripture, justice, and good sense, disown,
Where only vice and injury are tied,
And all from shore to shore is free beside.
Such freedom is—and Windsor's hoary tow'rs
Stood trembling at the boldness of thy pow'rs,
That won a nymph on that immortal plain,
Like her the fabled Phœbus woo'd in vain:
He found the laurel only—happier you 600
Th' unfading laurel, and the virgin[1] too!
Now think, if pleasure have a thought to spare,
If God himself be not beneath her care;
If bus'ness, constant as the wheels of time,
Can pause an hour to read a serious rhyme;
If the new mail thy merchants now receive,
Or expectation of the next, give leave;
Oh think, if chargeable with deep arrears
For such indulgence gilding all thy years,
How much, though long neglected, shining yet, 610
The beams of heav'nly truth have swell'd the debt!

[1] Alluding to the grant of Magna Charta, which was extorted from king John by the Barons at Runnymede near Windsor [C.].

When persecuting zeal made royal sport
With tortur'd innocence in Mary's court,
And Bonner, blithe as shepherd at a wake,
Enjoy'd the show, and danc'd about the stake;
The sacred book, its value understood,
Receiv'd the seal of martyrdom in blood.
Those holy men, so full of truth and grace,
Seem, to reflection, of a diff'rent race;
Meek, modest, venerable, wise, sincere, 620
In such a cause they could not dare to fear;
They could not purchase earth with such a prize,
Or spare a life too short to reach the skies.
From them to thee convey'd along the tide,
Their streaming hearts pour'd freely when they died;
Those truths, which neither use nor years impair,
Invite thee, woo thee, to the bliss they share.
What dotage will not vanity maintain?
What web too weak to catch a modern brain?
The moles and bats in full assembly find, 630
On special search, the keen-ey'd eagle blind.
And did they dream, and art thou wiser now?
Prove it—if better, I submit and bow.
Wisdom and goodness are twin-born, one heart
Must hold both sisters, never seen apart.
So then—as darkness overspread the deep,
Ere nature rose from her eternal sleep,
And this delightful earth, and that fair sky,
Leap'd out of nothing, call'd by the Most High;
By such a change thy darkness is made light, 640
Thy chaos order, and thy weakness might;
And He, whose pow'r mere nullity obeys,
Who found thee nothing, form'd thee for his praise.
To praise him is to serve him, and fulfil,
Doing and suff'ring, his unquestion'd will;
'Tis to believe what men inspir'd of old,
Faithful, and faithfully inform'd, unfold:
Candid and just, with no false aim in view,
To take for truth what cannot but be true;
To learn in God's own school the Christian part, 650
And bind the task assign'd thee to thine heart:
Happy the man there seeking and there found,
Happy the nation where such men abound!
How shall a verse impress thee? by what name
Shall I adjure thee not to court thy shame?
By their's whose bright example, unimpeach'd,
Directs thee to that eminence they reach'd—

623 Or] Nor *1782–1788*.

Heroes and worthies of days past, thy sires?
Or his, who touch'd their heart with hallow'd fires?
Their names, alas! in vain reproach an age, 660
Whom all the vanities they scorn'd engage;
And his, that seraphs tremble at, is hung
Disgracefully on ev'ry trifler's tongue,
Or serves the champion in forensic war
To flourish and parade with at the bar.
Pleasure herself, perhaps, suggests a plea,
If int'rest move thee, to persuade e'en thee;
By ev'ry charm that smiles upon her face,
By joys possess'd, and joys still held in chase.
If dear society be worth a thought, 670
And if the feast of freedom cloy thee not,
Reflect that these, and all that seems thine own,
Held by the tenure of his will alone,
Like angels in the service of their Lord,
Remain with thee, or leave thee at his word;
That gratitude and temp'rance in our use
Of what he gives, unsparing and profuse,
Secure the favour, and enhance the joy,
That thankless waste and wild abuse destroy.
  But, above all, reflect—how cheap soe'er 680
Those rights that millions envy thee appear,
And, though resolv'd to risk them, and swim down
The tide of pleasure, heedless of his frown—
That blessings truly sacred, and when giv'n
Mark'd with the signature and stamp of heav'n,
The word of prophesy, those truths divine
Which make that heav'n if thou desire it thine,
(Awful alternative! believ'd, belov'd,
Thy glory; and thy shame, if unimprov'd)
Are never long vouchsaf'd, if push'd aside 690
With cold disgust or philosophic pride;
And that, judicially withdrawn, disgrace,
Error, and darkness, occupy their place.
  A world is up in arms, and thou, a spot
Not quickly found if negligently sought,
Thy soul as ample as thy bounds are small,
Endur'st the brunt, and dar'st defy them all:
And wilt thou join to this bold enterprize
A bolder still, a contest with the skies?
Remember, if he guard thee and secure, 700
Whoe'er assails thee, thy success is sure;
But, if he leave thee, though the skill and pow'r
Of nations, sworn to spoil thee and devour,
Were all collected in thy single arm,
And thou could'st laugh away the fear of harm,

That strength would fail, oppos'd against the push
And feeble onset of a pigmy rush.
Say not (and, if the thought of such defence
Should spring within thy bosom, drive it thence)
What nation amongst all my foes is free 710
From crimes as base as any charg'd on me?
Their measure fill'd, they too shall pay the debt
Which God, though long forborn, will not forget.
But know that wrath divine, when most severe,
Makes justice still the guide of his career,
And will not punish, in one mingled crowd,
Them without light, and thee without a cloud.
Muse, hang this harp upon yon aged beech,
Still murm'ring with the solemn truths I teach;
And, while, at intervals, a cold blast sings 720
Through the dry leaves, and pants upon the strings,
My soul shall sigh in secret, and lament
A nation scourg'd, yet tardy to repent.
I know the warning song is sung in vain,
That few will hear, and fewer heed the strain:
But, if a sweeter voice, and one design'd
A blessing to my country and mankind,
Reclaim the wand'ring thousands, and bring home
A flock, so scatter'd and so wont to roam,
Then place it once again between my knees; 730
The sound of truth will then be sure to please:
And truth alone, where'er my life be cast,
In scenes of plenty or the pining waste,
Shall be my chosen theme, my glory to the last.

HOPE

[Written May or June, 1781. Published 1782.]

—— doceas iter, et sacra ostia pandas.
VIRG. En. 6.

ASK what is human life — the sage replies,
With disappointment low'ring in his eyes,
A painful passage o'er a restless flood,
A vain pursuit of fugitive false good,
A scene of fancied bliss and heart-felt care,
Closing at last in darkness and despair.
The poor, inur'd to drudg'ry and distress,
Act without aim, think little, and feel less,
And no where, but in feign'd Arcadian scenes,
Taste happiness, or know what pleasure means. 10
Riches are pass'd away from hand to hand,
As fortune, vice, or folly, may command.

As in a dance the pair that take the lead
Turn downward, and the lowest pair succeed,
So shifting and so various is the plan
By which Heav'n rules the mixt affairs of man:
Vicissitude wheels round the motley crowd,
The rich grow poor, the poor become purse-proud;
Bus'ness is labour, and man's weakness such,
Pleasure is labour too, and tires as much, 20
The very sense of it foregoes its use,
By repetition pall'd, by age obtuse.
Youth lost in dissipation, we deplore,
Through life's sad remnant, what no sighs restore;
Our years, a fruitless race without a prize,
Too many, yet too few to make us wise.
  Dangling his cane about, and taking snuff,
Lothario cries, What philosophic stuff—
Oh, querulous and weak!—whose useless brain
Once thought of nothing, and now thinks in vain;
Whose eye, reverted, weeps o'er all the past, 31
Whose prospect shows thee a disheart'ning waste;
Would age in thee resign his wintry reign,
And youth invigorate that frame again,
Renew'd desire would grace with other speech
Joys always priz'd—when plac'd within our reach.
  For lift thy palsied head, shake off the gloom
That overhangs the borders of thy tomb,
See nature, gay as when she first began,
With smiles alluring her admirer man; 40
She spreads the morning over eastern hills;
Earth glitters with the drops the night distils;
The sun, obedient, at her call appears
To fling his glories o'er the robe she wears;
Banks cloth'd with flow'rs, groves fill'd with sprightly sounds,
The yellow tilth, green meads, rocks, rising grounds,
Streams edg'd with osiers, fatt'ning ev'ry field
Where'er they flow, now seen and now conceal'd;
From the blue rim where skies and mountains meet,
Down to the very turf beneath thy feet, 50
Ten thousand charms, that only fools despise,
Or pride can look at with indiff'rent eyes,
All speak one language, all with one sweet voice
Cry to her universal realm, Rejoice!
Man feels the spur of passions and desires,
And she gives largely more than he requires;
Not that, his hours devoted all to care,
Hollow-ey'd abstinence, and lean despair,

The wretch may pine, while to his smell, taste, sight,
She holds a paradise of rich delight; 60
But gently to rebuke his awkward fear,
To prove that what she gives she gives sincere,
To banish hesitation, and proclaim
His happiness, her dear, her only aim.
'Tis grave philosophy's absurdest dream,
That heav'n's intentions are not what they seem,
That only shadows are dispens'd below,
And earth has no reality but woe.
Thus things terrestrial wear a diff'rent hue,
As youth or age persuades; and neither true: 70
So Flora's wreath through colour'd crystal seen,
The rose or lily appears blue or green,
But still th' imputed tints are those alone
The medium represents, and not their own.
To rise at noon, sit slipshod and undress'd,
To read the news, or fiddle, as seems best,
Till half the world comes rattling at his door,
To fill the dull vacuity till four;
And, just when ev'ning turns the blue vault grey,
To spend two hours in dressing for the day; 80
To make the sun a bauble without use,
Save for the fruits his heav'nly beams produce;
Quite to forget, or deem it worth no thought,
Who bids him shine, or if he shine or not;
Through mere necessity to close his eyes
Just when the larks and when the shepherds rise;
Is such a life, so tediously the same,
So void of all utility or aim,
That poor JONQUIL, with almost ev'ry breath,
Sighs for his exit, vulgarly call'd death: 90
For he, with all his follies, has a mind
Not yet so blank, or fashionably blind,
But now and then, perhaps, a feeble ray
Of distant wisdom shoots across his way,
By which he reads, that life without a plan,
As useless as the moment it began,
Serves merely as a soil for discontent
To thrive in; an incumbrance, ere half spent.
Oh! weariness beyond what asses feel,
That tread the circuit of the cistern wheel; 100
A dull rotation, never at a stay,
Yesterday's face twin image of to-day;
While conversation, an exhausted stock,
Grows drowsy as the clicking of a clock.
No need, he cries, of gravity stuff'd out
With academic dignity devout,

To read wise lectures—vanity the text!
Proclaim the remedy, ye learned, next;
For truth, self-evident, with pomp impress'd,
Is vanity surpassing all the rest. 110
  That remedy, not hid in deeps profound,
Yet seldom sought where only to be found,
While passion turns aside from its due scope
Th' inquirer's aim—that remedy is hope.
Life is his gift, from whom whate'er life needs,
With every good and perfect gift, proceeds;
Bestow'd on man, like all that we partake,
Royally, freely, for his bounty sake;
Transient indeed, as is the fleeting hour,
And yet the seed of an immortal flow'r; 120
Design'd, in honour of his endless love,
To fill with fragrance his abode above;
No trifle, howsoever short it seem,
And, howsoever shadowy, no dream;
Its value, what no thought can ascertain,
Nor all an angel's eloquence explain.
  Men deal with life as children with their play,
Who first misuse, then cast their toys away;
Live to no sober purpose, and contend
That their Creator had no serious end. 130
When God and man stand opposite in view,
Man's disappointment must of course ensue.
The just Creator condescends to write,
In beams of inextinguishable light,
His names of wisdom, goodness, pow'r, and love,
On all that blooms below or shines above;
To catch the wand'ring notice of mankind,
And teach the world, if not perversely blind,
His gracious attributes, and prove the share
His offspring hold in his paternal care. 140
If, led from earthly things to things divine,
His creature thwart not his august design,
Then praise is heard instead of reas'ning pride,
And captious cavil and complaint subside.
Nature, employ'd in her allotted place,
Is handmaid to the purposes of grace;
By good vouchsaf'd, makes known superior good,
And bliss not seen, by blessings understood:
That bliss, reveal'd in scripture, with a glow
Bright as the covenant-ensuring bow, 150
Fires all his feelings with a noble scorn
Of sensual evil, and thus Hope is born.

116 With] And *1782-1788.*

Hope sets the stamp of vanity on all
That men have deem'd substantial since the fall,
Yet has the wondrous virtue to educe
From emptiness itself a real use;
And, while she takes, as at a father's hand,
What health and sober appetite demand,
From fading good derives, with chemic art,
That lasting happiness, a thankful heart. 160
Hope, with uplifted foot set free from earth,
Pants for the place of her ethereal birth,
On steady wings sails through th' immense abyss,
Plucks amaranthine joys from bow'rs of bliss,
And crowns the soul, while yet a mourner here,
With wreaths like those triumphant spirits wear.
Hope, as an anchor firm and sure, holds fast
The Christian vessel, and defies the blast.
Hope! nothing else can nourish and secure
His new-born virtues, and preserve him pure. 170
Hope! let the wretch, once conscious of the joy,
Whom now despairing agonies destroy,
Speak, for he can, and none so well as he,
What treasures centre, what delights, in thee.
Had he the gems, the spices, and the land
That boasts the treasure, all at his command;
The fragrant grove, th' inestimable mine,
Were light when weigh'd against one smile of thine.
Though clasp'd and cradled in his nurse's arms,
He shine with all a cherub's artless charms, 180
Man is the genuine offspring of revolt,
Stubborn and sturdy—a wild ass's colt;
His passions, like the wat'ry stores that sleep
Beneath the smiling surface of the deep,
Wait but the lashes of a wintry storm,
To frown and roar, and shake his feeble form.
From infancy, through childhood's giddy maze,
Froward at school, and fretful in his plays,
The puny tyrant burns to subjugate
The free republic of the whip-gig state. 190
If one, his equal in athletic frame,
Or, more provoking still, of nobler name,
Dare step across his arbitrary views,
An Iliad, only not in verse, ensues:
The little Greeks look trembling at the scales,
Till the best tongue, or heaviest hand, prevails.
Now see him launch'd into the world at large:
If priest, supinely droning o'er his charge,

163 wings] wing *1782–1793.*

Their fleece his pillow, and his weekly drawl,
Though short, too long, the price he pays for all.
If lawyer, loud whatever cause he plead, 201
But proudest of the worst, if that succeed;
Perhaps a grave physician, gath'ring fees,
Punctu'lly paid for length'ning out disease;
No COTTON, whose humanity sheds rays
That make superior skill his second praise;
If arms engage him, he devotes to sport
His date of life, so likely to be short.
A soldier may be any thing, if brave;
So may a tradesman, if not quite a knave. 210
Such stuff the world is made of; and mankind,
To passion, int'rest, pleasure, whim, resign'd,
Insist on, as if each were his own pope,
Forgiveness, and the privilege of hope.
But conscience, in some awful silent hour,
When captivating lusts have lost their pow'r—
Perhaps when sickness, or some fearful dream,
Reminds him of religion, hated theme!—
Starts from the down on which she lately slept,
And tells of laws despis'd, at least not kept; 220
Shows, with a pointing finger but no noise,
A pale procession of past sinful joys,
All witnesses of blessings foully scorn'd,
And life abus'd, and not to be suborn'd.
Mark these, she says; these, summon'd from afar,
Begin their march, to meet thee at the bar;
There find a Judge inexorably just,
And perish there, as all presumption must.

Peace be to those (such peace as earth can give)
Who live in pleasure, dead ev'n while they live;
Born capable, indeed, of heav'nly truth; 231
But down to latest age, from earliest youth,
Their mind a wilderness, through want of care,
The plough of wisdom never ent'ring there.
Peace (if insensibility may claim
A right to the meek honours of her name)
To men of pedigree, their noble race
Emulous always of the nearest place
To any throne except the throne of grace.
(Let cottagers and unenlighten'd swains 240
Revere the laws they dream that heav'n ordains;
Resort on Sundays to the house of pray'r,
And ask, and fancy they find, blessings there.)

221 but] and *1782*, *1786*.

Themselves, perhaps, when weary they retreat
T' enjoy cool nature in a country seat,
T' exchange the centre of a thousand trades,
For clumps, and lawns, and temples, and cascades,
May now and then their velvet cushions take.
And seem to pray, for good example sake;
Judging, in charity, no doubt, the town 250
Pious enough, and having need of none.
Kind souls! to teach their tenantry to prize
What they themselves, without remorse, despise:
Nor hope have they, nor fear, of aught to come—
As well for them had prophecy been dumb.
They could have held the conduct they pursue,
Had Paul of Tarsus liv'd and died a Jew;
And truth, propos'd to reas'ners wise as they,
Is a pearl cast—completely cast away.

They die.—Death lends them, pleas'd, and as in sport, 260
All the grim honours of his ghastly court.
Far other paintings grace the chamber now,
Where late we saw the mimic landscape glow:
The busy heralds hang the sable scene
With mournful 'scutcheons, and dim lamps between;
Proclaim their titles to the crowd around,
But they that wore them move not at the sound;
The coronet, plac'd idly at their head,
Adds nothing now to the degraded dead;
And ev'n the star that glitters on the bier 270
Can only say—Nobility lies here.
Peace to all such—'twere pity to offend,
By useless censure, whom we cannot mend;
Life without hope can close but in despair—
'Twas there we found them, and must leave them there.

As, when two pilgrims in a forest stray,
Both may be lost, yet each in his own way;
So fares it with the multitudes beguil'd
In vain opinion's waste and dang'rous wild. 279
Ten thousand rove the brakes and thorns among,
Some eastward, and some westward, and all wrong.
But here, alas! the fatal diff'rence lies,
Each man's belief is right in his own eyes;
And he that blames what they have blindly chose,
Incurs resentment for the love he shows.

Say, botanist, within whose province fall
The cedar and the hyssop on the wall,
Of all that deck the lanes, the fields, the bow'rs,
What parts the kindred tribes of weeds and flow'rs?

Sweet scent, or lovely form, or both combin'd, 290
Distinguish ev'ry cultivated kind;
The want of both denotes a meaner breed,
And Chloe from her garland picks the weed.
Thus hopes of ev'ry sort, whatever sect
Esteem them, sow them, rear them, and protect,
If wild in nature, and not duly found,
Gethsemane, in thy dear hallow'd ground,
That cannot bear the blaze of scripture light,
Nor cheer the spirit, nor refresh the sight,
Nor animate the soul to Christian deeds, 300
(Oh cast them from thee!) are weeds, arrant weeds.
Ethelred's house, the centre of six ways,
Diverging each from each, like equal rays,
Himself as bountiful as April rains,
Lord paramount of the surrounding plains,
Would give relief of bed and board to none,
But guests that sought it in th' appointed ONE.
And they might enter at his open door,
Ev'n till his spacious hall would hold no more.
He sent a servant forth by ev'ry road, 310
To sound his horn and publish it abroad,
That all might mark—knight, menial, high, and low—
An ord'nance it concern'd them much to know.
If, after all, some headstrong hardy lout
Would disobey, though sure to be shut out,
Could he with reason murmur at his case,
Himself sole author of his own disgrace?
No! the decree was just and without flaw;
And he that made, had right to make, the law;
His sov'reign pow'r and pleasure unrestrain'd, 320
The wrong was his who wrongfully complain'd.
Yet half mankind maintain a churlish strife
With him the Donor of eternal life,
Because the deed, by which his love confirms
The largess he bestows, prescribes the terms.
Compliance with his will your lot ensures—
Accept it only, and the boon is yours.
And sure it is as kind to smile and give,
As with a frown to say—Do this, and live!
Love is not pedlar's trump'ry, bought and sold; 330
He *will* give freely, or he *will* withhold;
His soul abhors a mercenary thought,
And him as deeply who abhors it not;
He stipulates, indeed, but merely this—
That man will freely take an unbought bliss,
Will trust him for a faithful gen'rous part,
Nor set a price upon a willing heart.

Of all the ways that seem to promise fair,
To place you where his saints his presence share,
This only can ; for this plain cause, express'd 340
In terms as plain—himself has shut the rest.
But oh the strife, the bick'ring, and debate,
The tidings of unpurchas'd heav'n create !
The flirted fan, the bridle, and the toss,
All speakers, yet all language at a loss.
From stucco'd walls smart arguments rebound ;
And beaus, adepts in ev'ry thing profound,
Die of disdain, or whistle off the sound.
Such is the clamour of rooks, daws, and kites,
Th' explosion of the levell'd tube excites, 350
Where mould'ring abbey walls o'erhang the glade,
And oaks coeval spread a mournful shade.
The screaming nations, hov'ring in mid air,
Loudly resent the stranger's freedom there,
And seem to warn him never to repeat
His bold intrusion on their dark retreat.
  Adieu, Vinoso cries, ere yet he sips
The purple bumper, trembling at his lips,
Adieu to all morality—if grace
Make works a vain ingredient in the case ! 360
The Christian hope is—Waiter, draw the cork—
If I mistake not—Blockhead! with a fork !—
Without good works, whatever some may boast,
Mere folly and delusion—Sir, your toast !—
My firm persuasion is, at least sometimes,
That heav'n will weigh man's virtues and his crimes
With nice attention, in a righteous scale,
And save or damn as these or those prevail.
I plant my foot upon this ground of trust,
And silence ev'ry fear with—God is just. 370
But if perchance, on some dull drizzling day,
A thought intrude that says, or seems to say,
If thus th' important cause is to be tried,
Suppose the beam should dip on the wrong side ;
I soon recover from these needless frights,
And, God is merciful—sets all to rights.
Thus, between justice, as my prime support,
And mercy, fled to as the last resort,
I glide and steal along with heav'n in view,
And—pardon me—the bottle stands with you. 380
  I never will believe, the col'nel cries,
The sanguinary schemes that some devise,

338 seem'd *1798*[1], *1799*, *1800*. 357 Vinosa *1787-1800*.

Who make the good Creator, on their plan,
A being of less equity than man.
If appetite, or what divines call lust,
Which men comply with, e'en because they must,
Be punish'd with perdition, who is pure?
Then their's, no doubt, as well as mine, is sure.
If sentence of eternal pain belong
To ev'ry sudden slip and transient wrong, 390
Then heav'n enjoins the fallible and frail
An hopeless task, and damns them if they fail!
My creed (whatever some creed-makers mean
By Athanasian nonsense, or Nicene)
My creed is—he is safe that does his best,
And death's a doom sufficient for the rest.
Right, says an ensign; and, for aught I see,
Your faith and mine substantially agree;
The best of ev'ry man's performance here
Is to discharge the duties of his sphere. 400
A lawyer's dealings should be just and fair—
Honesty shines with great advantage there.
Fasting and pray'r sit well upon a priest—
A decent caution and reserve at least.
A soldier's best is courage in the field,
With nothing here that wants to be conceal'd:
Manly deportment, gallant, easy, gay;
An hand as lib'ral as the light of day.
The soldier thus endow'd, who never shrinks,
Nor closets up his thought, whate'er he thinks, 410
Who scorns to do an injury by stealth,
Must go to heav'n—and I must drink his health.
Sir Smug, he cries, (for lowest at the board—
Just made fifth chaplain of his patron lord,
His shoulders witnessing by many a shrug
How much his feelings suffer'd—sat Sir Smug)
Your office is to winnow false from true;
Come, prophet, drink, and tell us—What think you?
Sighing and smiling as he takes his glass,
Which they that woo preferment rarely pass, 420
Fallible man, the church-bred youth replies,
Is still found fallible, however wise;
And diff'ring judgments serve but to declare
That truth lies somewhere, if we knew but where.
Of all it ever was my lot to read,
Of critics now alive, or long since dead,
The book of all the world that charm'd me most
Was—well-a-day, the title page was lost!

401 dealing *1782–1788.*

The writer well remarks, an heart that knows
To take with gratitude what heav'n bestows, 430
With prudence always ready at our call
To guide our use of it, is all in all.
Doubtless it is.—To which, of my own store,
I superadd a few essentials more;
But these, excuse the liberty I take,
I wave just now, for conversation sake.—
Spoke like an oracle, they all exclaim,
And add Right Rev'rend to Smug's honour'd name!
And yet our lot is giv'n us in a land
Where busy arts are never at a stand; 440
Where science points her telescopic eye,
Familiar with the wonders of the sky;
Where bold inquiry, diving out of sight,
Brings many a precious pearl of truth to light;
Where nought eludes the persevering quest,
That fashion, taste, or luxury, suggest.
But, above all, in her own light array'd,
See mercy's grand apocalypse display'd!
The sacred book no longer suffers wrong,
Bound in the fetters of an unknown tongue; 450
But speaks with plainness, art could never mend,
What simplest minds can soonest comprehend.
God gives the word—the preachers throng around,
Live from his lips, and spread the glorious sound:
That sound bespeaks salvation on her way,
The trumpet of a life-restoring day!
'Tis heard where England's eastern glory shines,
And in the gulphs of her Cornubian mines.
And still it spreads. See Germany send forth
Her sons[1] to pour it on the farthest north: 460
Fir'd with a zeal peculiar, *they* defy
The rage and rigour of a polar sky,
And plant successfully sweet Sharon's rose
On icy plains, and in eternal snows.
Oh, blest within th' inclosure of your rocks,
Nor herds have ye to boast, nor bleating flocks;
No fertilizing streams your fields divide,
That show, revers'd, the villas on their side;
No groves have ye; no cheerful sound of bird,
Or voice of turtle, in your land is heard; 470
Nor grateful eglantine regales the smell
Of those that walk at ev'ning where ye dwell:
But winter, arm'd with terrors here unknown,
Sits absolute on his unshaken throne;

[1] The Moravian missionaries in Greenland. Vide Krantz [C.].

Piles up his stores amidst the frozen waste,
And bids the mountains he has built stand fast;
Beckons the legions of his storms away
From happier scenes, to make your land a prey;
Proclaims the soil a conquest he has won,
And scorns to share it with the distant sun. 480
—Yet truth is your's, remote, unenvied isle!
And peace, the genuine offspring of her smile;
The pride of letter'd ignorance, that binds
In chains of errour our accomplish'd minds,
That decks, with all the splendour of the true,
A false religion, is unknown to you.
Nature indeed vouchsafes, for our delight,
The sweet vicissitudes of day and night;
Soft airs and genial moisture feed and cheer
Field, fruit, and flow'r, and ev'ry creature here; 490
But brighter beams, than his who fires the skies,
Have ris'n at length on your admiring eyes,
That shoot into your darkest caves the day,
From which our nicer optics turn away.

Here see th' encouragement grace gives to vice,
The dire effect of mercy without price!
What were they? what some fools are made by art,
They were by nature—atheists, head and heart.
The gross idolatry blind heathens teach
Was too refin'd for them, beyond their reach. 500
Not ev'n the glorious sun—though men revere
The monarch most that seldom will appear,
And tho' his beams, that quicken where they shine,
May claim some right to be esteem'd divine—
Not e'en the sun, desirable as rare,
Could bend one knee, engage one vot'ry there!
They were, what base credulity believes
True Christians are, dissemblers, drunkards, thieves.
The full-gorg'd savage, at his nauseous feast
Spent half the darkness, and snor'd out the rest,
Was one whom justice, on an equal plan, 511
Denouncing death upon the sins of man,
Might almost have indulg'd with an escape,
Chargeable only with a human shape.

What are they now?—Morality may spare
Her grave concern, her kind suspicions, there:
The wretch, who once sang wildly, danc'd and laugh'd,
And suck'd in dizzy madness with his draught,
Has wept a silent flood, revers'd his ways,
Is sober, meek, benevolent, and prays, 520
Feeds sparingly, communicates his store,

Abhors the craft he boasted of before—
And he that stole has learn'd to steal no more.
Well spake the prophet, Let the desert sing,
Where sprang the thorn the spiry fir shall spring,
And where unsightly and rank thistles grew
Shall grow the myrtle and luxuriant yew.
  Go now, and with important tone demand
On what foundation virtue is to stand,
If self-exalting claims be turn'd adrift, 530
And grace be grace indeed, and life a gift.
The poor reclaim'd inhabitant, his eyes
Glist'ning at once with pity and surprise,
Amaz'd that shadows should obscure the sight
Of one whose birth was in a land of light,
Shall answer, Hope, sweet hope, has set me free,
And made all pleasures else mere dross to me.
  These, amidst scenes as waste as if denied
The common care that waits on all beside,
Wild as if nature there, void of all good, 540
Play'd only gambols in a frantic mood,
(Yet charge not heav'nly skill with having plann'd
A play-thing world, unworthy of his hand!)
Can see his love, though secret evil lurks
In all we touch, stamp'd plainly on his works;
Deem life a blessing with its numerous woes,
Nor spurn away a gift a God bestows.
  Hard task, indeed, o'er arctic seas to roam!
Is hope exotic? grows it not at home?
Yes, but an object, bright as orient morn, 550
May press the eye too closely to be born;
A distant virtue we can all confess,
It hurts our pride, and moves our envy, less.
  Leuconomus (beneath well-sounding Greek
I slur a name a poet must not speak)
Stood pilloried on infamy's high stage,
And bore the pelting scorn of half an age;
The very butt of slander, and the blot
For ev'ry dart that malice ever shot.
The man that mention'd *him* at once dismiss'd 560
All mercy from his lips, and sneer'd and hiss'd;
His crimes were such as Sodom never knew,
And perjury stood up to swear all true;
His aim was mischief, and his zeal pretence,
His speech rebellion against common sense;
A knave, when tried on honesty's plain rule,
And, when by that of reason, a mere fool;
The world's best comfort was, his doom was pass'd;
Die when he might, he must be damn'd at last.

Now, truth, perform thine office; waft aside 570
The curtain drawn by prejudice and pride,
Reveal (the man is dead) to wond'ring eyes
This more than monster in his proper guise.
He lov'd the world that hated him: the tear
That dropp'd upon his Bible was sincere:
Assail'd by scandal and the tongue of strife,
His only answer was, a blameless life;
And he that forg'd, and he that threw, the dart,
Had each a brother's int'rest in his heart!
Paul's love of Christ, and steadiness unbrib'd, 580
Were copied close in him, and well transcrib'd.
He followed Paul—his zeal a kindred flame,
His apostolic charity the same.
Like him, cross'd cheerfully tempestuous seas,
Forsaking country, kindred, friends, and ease;
Like him he labour'd, and, like him, content
To bear it, suffer'd shame where'er he went.
Blush, calumny! and write upon his tomb,
If honest eulogy can spare thee room,
Thy deep repentance of thy thousand lies, 590
Which, aim'd at him, have pierc'd th' offended skies;
And say, Blot out my sin, confess'd, deplor'd,
Against thine image in thy saint, oh Lord!
No blinder bigot, I maintain it still,
Than he who must have pleasure, come what will:
He laughs, whatever weapon truth may draw,
And deems her sharp artillery mere straw.
Scripture, indeed, is plain; but God and he,
On scripture-ground, are sure to disagree;
Some wiser rule must teach him how to live, 600
Than this his Maker has seen fit to give;
Supple and flexible as Indian cane,
To take the bend his appetites ordain;
Contriv'd to suit frail nature's crazy case,
And reconcile his lusts with saving grace.
By this, with nice precision of design,
He draws upon life's map a zig-zag line,
That shows how far 'tis safe to follow sin,
And where his danger and God's wrath begin.
By this he forms, as pleas'd he sports along, 610
His well-pois'd estimate of right and wrong;
And finds the modish manners of the day,
Though loose, as harmless as an infant's play.
Build by whatever plan caprice decrees,
With what materials, on what ground, you please;

601 this] that *1782*, *1786*.

Your hope shall stand unblam'd, perhaps admir'd,
If not that hope the scripture has requir'd.
The strange conceits, vain projects, and wild
dreams,
With which hypocrisy for ever teems,
(Though other follies strike the public eye, 620
And raise a laugh) pass unmolested by;
But if, unblameable in word and thought,
A *man* arise—a man whom God has taught,
With all Elijah's dignity of tone,
And all the love of the beloved John—
To storm the citadels they build in air,
And smite th' untemper'd wall, 'tis death to spare;
To sweep away all refuges of lies,
And place, instead of quirks themselves devise,
Lama sabacthani before their eyes; 630
To prove that without Christ all gain is loss,
All hope despair, that stands not on his cross;
Except the few his God may have impress'd,
A tenfold frenzy seizes all the rest.
Throughout mankind, the Christian kind at least,
There dwells a consciousness in ev'ry breast,
That folly ends where genuine hope begins,
And he that finds his heav'n must lose his sins.
Nature opposes, with her utmost force,
This riving stroke, this ultimate divorce; 640
And, while religion seems to be her view,
Hates with a deep sincerity *the true*:
For this—of all that ever influenc'd man,
Since Abel worshipp'd, or the world began—
This only spares no lust; admits no plea;
But makes him, if at all, completely free;
Sounds forth the signal, as she mounts her car,
Of an eternal, universal war;
Rejects all treaty; penetrates all wiles; 649
Scorns with the same indiff'rence frowns and smiles;
Drives through the realms of sin, where riot reels,
And grinds his crown beneath her burning wheels!
Hence all that is in man—pride, passion, art,
Pow'rs of the mind, and feelings of the heart—
Insensible of truth's almighty charms,
Starts at her first approach, and sounds, To arms!
While bigotry, with well dissembled fears,
His eyes shut fast, his fingers in his ears,
Mighty to parry and push by God's word
With senseless noise, his argument the sword, 660
Pretends a zeal for godliness and grace,
And spits abhorrence in the Christian's face.

Parent of hope, immortal truth! make known
Thy deathless wreaths and triumphs, all thine own:
The silent progress of thy pow'r is such,
Thy means so feeble, and despis'd so much,
That few believe the wonders thou hast wrought,
And none can teach them but whom thou hast taught.
Oh, see me sworn to serve thee, and command
A painter's skill into a poet's hand! 670
That, while I, trembling, trace a work divine,
Fancy may stand aloof from the design,
And light, and shade, and ev'ry stroke, be thine.

If ever thou hast felt another's pain,
If ever when he sigh'd hast sigh'd again,
If ever on thine eye-lid stood the tear
That pity had engender'd, drop one here!
This man was happy—had the world's good word,
And with it ev'ry joy it can afford;
Friendship and love seem'd tenderly at strife, 680
Which most should sweeten his untroubled life;
Politely learn'd, and of a gentle race,
Good-breeding and good sense gave all a grace,
And, whether at the toilette of the fair
He laugh'd and trifled, made him welcome there,
Or, if in masculine debate he shar'd,
Ensur'd him mute attention and regard.
Alas, how chang'd!—Expressive of his mind,
His eyes are sunk, arms folded, head reclin'd;
Those awful syllables, hell, death, and sin, 690
Though whisper'd, plainly tell what works within;
That conscience there performs her proper part,
And writes a doomsday sentence on his heart!
Forsaking, and forsaken of all friends,
He now perceives where earthly pleasure ends;
Hard task—for one who lately knew no care,
And harder still, as learnt beneath despair!
His hours no longer pass unmark'd away,
A dark importance saddens every day;
He hears the notice of the clock, perplex'd, 700
And cries—perhaps eternity strikes next!
Sweet music is no longer music here,
And laughter sounds like madness in his ear:
His grief the world of all her pow'r disarms;
Wine has no taste, and beauty has no charms:
God's holy word, once trivial in his view,
Now by the voice of his experience true,
Seems, as it is, the fountain whence alone
Must spring that hope he pants to make his own.

676 thy *1794–1800*. 680 seem *1800*.

Now let the bright reverse be known abroad; 710
Say man's a worm, and pow'r belongs to God.
As when a felon, whom his country's laws
Have justly doom'd for some atrocious cause,
Expects, in darkness and heart-chilling fears,
The shameful close of all his mispent years;
If chance, on heavy pinions slowly born,
A tempest usher in the dreaded morn,
Upon his dungeon walls the lightning play,
The thunder seems to summon him away,
The warder at the door his key applies, 720
Shoots back the bolt, and all his courage dies:
If then, just then, all thoughts of mercy lost,
When hope, long ling'ring, at last yields the ghost,
The sound of pardon pierce his startled ear,
He drops at once his fetters and his fear;
A transport glows in all he looks and speaks,
And the first thankful tears bedew his cheeks.
Joy, far superior joy, that much outweighs
The comfort of a few poor added days,
Invades, possesses, and o'erwhelms, the soul 730
Of him, whom hope has with a touch made whole.
'Tis heav'n, all heav'n, descending on the wings
Of the glad legions of the King of kings;
'Tis more—'tis God diffus'd through ev'ry part,
'Tis God himself triumphant in his heart!
Oh, welcome now the sun's once hated light,
His noon-day beams were never half so bright.
Not kindred minds alone are call'd t' employ
Their hours, their days, in list'ning to his joy;
Unconscious nature, all that he surveys, 740
Rocks, groves, and streams, must join him in his praise.
These are thy glorious works, eternal truth,
The scoff of wither'd age and beardless youth;
These move the censure and illib'ral grin
Of fools that hate thee and delight in sin:
But these shall last when night has quench'd the pole,
And heav'n is all departed as a scroll:
And when, as justice has long since decreed,
This earth shall blaze, and a new world succeed,
Then these thy glorious works, and they who share
That hope which can alone exclude despair, 751
Shall live exempt from weakness and decay,
The brightest wonders of an endless day.
Happy the bard (if that fair name belong
To him that blends no fable with his song)

718 lightnings *1782, 1786.* 750 who] that *1782, 1786.*

Whose lines, uniting, by an honest art,
The faithful monitor's and poet's part,
Seek to delight, that they may mend mankind,
And, while they captivate, inform the mind:
Still happier, if he till a thankful soil, 760
And fruit reward his honourable toil:
But happier far, who comfort those that wait
To hear plain truth at Judah's hallow'd gate.
Their language simple, as their manners meek,
No shining ornaments have they to seek;
Nor labour they, nor time, nor talents, waste,
In sorting flow'rs to suit a fickle taste;
But, while they speak the wisdom of the skies,
Which art can only darken and disguise,
Th' abundant harvest, recompense divine, 770
Repays their work—the gleaning only mine.

CHARITY

[Written June and July, 1781. Published 1782.]

Quo nihil majus meliusve terris
Fata donavere, bonique divi,
Nec dabunt, quamvis redeant in aurum
Tempora priscum.—Hor. Lib. iv. Ode 2.

Fairest and foremost of the train, that wait
On man's most dignified and happiest state,
Whether we name thee Charity or love,
Chief grace below, and all in all above,
Prosper (I press thee with a powr'ful plea)
A task I venture on, impell'd by thee:
Oh, never seen but in thy blest effects,
Or felt but in the soul that heav'n selects;
Who seeks to praise thee, and to make thee known
To other hearts, must have thee in his own. 10
Come, prompt me with benevolent desires,
Teach me to kindle at thy gentle fires,
And, though disgrac'd and slighted, to redeem
A poet's name, by making thee the theme.
God, working ever on a social plan,
By various ties attaches man to man:
He made at first, though free and unconfin'd,
One man the common father of the kind;
That ev'ry tribe, though plac'd as he sees best,
Where seas or deserts part them from the rest, 20
Diff'ring in language, manners, or in face,
Might feel themselves allied to all the race.

8 Or] Nor *1782–1788*.

When Cook—lamented, and with tears as just
As ever mingled with heroic dust—
Steer'd Britain's oak into a world unknown,
And in his country's glory sought his own,
Wherever he found man, to nature true,
The rights of man were sacred in his view.
He sooth'd with gifts, and greeted with a smile,
The simple native of the new-found isle; 30
He spurn'd the wretch that slighted or withstood
The tender argument of kindred blood,
Nor would endure that any should controul
His free-born brethren of the southern pole.
But, though some nobler minds a law respect,
That none shall with impunity neglect,
In baser souls unnumber'd evils meet,
To thwart its influence, and its end defeat.
While Cook is lov'd for savage lives he sav'd,
See Cortez odious for a world enslav'd! 40
Where wast thou then, sweet Charity? where then,
Thou tutelary friend of helpless men?
Wast thou in monkish cells and nunn'ries found,
Or building hospitals on English ground?
No.—Mammon makes the world his legatee
Through fear, not love; and heav'n abhors the fee.
Wherever found, (and all men need thy care)
Nor age nor infancy could find thee there.
The hand that slew, till it could slay no more,
Was glu'd to the sword-hilt with Indian gore. 50
Their prince, as justly seated on his throne
As vain imperial Philip on his own,
Trick'd out of all his royalty by art,
That stripp'd him bare, and broke his honest heart,
Died, by the sentence of a shaven priest,
For scorning what they taught him to detest.
How dark the veil that intercepts the blaze
Of heav'n's mysterious purposes and ways!
God stood not, though he seem'd to stand, aloof;
And at this hour the conqu'ror feels the proof: 60
The wreath he won drew down an instant curse,
The fretting plague is in the public purse,
The canker'd spoil corrodes the pining state,
Starv'd by that indolence their mines create.
Oh, could their ancient Incas rise again,
How would they take up Israel's taunting strain!
Art thou too fall'n, Iberia? Do we see
The robber and the murd'rer weak as we?
Thou that hast wasted earth, and dar'd despise
Alike the wrath and mercy of the skies, 70

Thy pomp is in the grave, thy glory laid
Low in the pits thine avarice has made!
We come with joy from our eternal rest,
To see th' oppressor in his turn oppress'd.
Art thou the god, the thunder of whose hand
Roll'd over all our desolated land,
Shook principalities and kingdoms down,
And made the mountains tremble at his frown?
The sword shall light upon thy boasted pow'rs,
And waste them, as thy sword has wasted our's. 80
'Tis thus Omnipotence his law fulfils,
And vengeance executes what justice wills.

Again—the band of commerce was design'd
T' associate all the branches of mankind;
And, if a boundless plenty be the robe,
Trade is the golden girdle of the globe.
Wise to promote whatever end he means,
God opens fruitful nature's various scenes:
Each climate needs what other climes produce,
And offers something to the gen'ral use; 90
No land but listens to the common call,
And in return receives supply from all.
This genial intercourse, and mutual aid,
Cheers what were else an universal shade,
Calls nature from her ivy mantled den,
And softens human rock-work into men.
Ingenious Art, with her expressive face,
Steps forth to fashion and refine the race;
Not only fills necessity's demand,
But overcharges her capacious hand: 100
Capricious taste itself can crave no more
Than she supplies from her abounding store;
She strikes out all that luxury can ask,
And gains new vigour at her endless task.
Her's is the spacious arch, the shapely spire,
The painter's pencil, and the poet's lyre;
From her the canvass borrows light and shade,
And verse, more lasting, hues that never fade.
She guides the finger o'er the dancing keys,
Gives difficulty all the grace of ease, 110
And pours a torrent of sweet notes around,
Fast as the thirsting ear can drink the sound.

These are the gifts of art; and art thrives most
Where commerce has enrich'd the busy coast;
He catches all improvements in his flight,
Spreads foreign wonders in his country's sight,
Imports what others have invented well,
And stirs his own to match them, or excel.

'Tis thus, reciprocating each with each,
Alternately the nations learn and teach; 120
While providence enjoins to ev'ry soul
An union with the vast terraqueous whole.
Heav'n speed the canvass, gallantly unfurl'd
To furnish and accommodate a world,
To give the pole the produce of the sun,
And knit th' unsocial climates into one.
Soft airs and gentle heavings of the wave
Impel the fleet whose errand is to save,
To succour, wasted regions, and replace
The smile of opulence in sorrow's face.— 130
Let nothing adverse, nothing unforeseen,
Impede the bark that plows the deep serene,
Charg'd with a freight transcending in its worth
The gems of India, nature's rarest birth,
That flies, like Gabriel on his Lord's commands,
An herald of God's love to pagan lands.
But, ah! what wish can prosper, or what pray'r,
For merchants, rich in cargoes of despair,
Who drive a loathsome traffic, gage, and span,
And buy, the muscles and the bones of man? 140
The tender ties of father, husband, friend,
All bonds of nature, in that moment end;
And each endures, while yet he draws his breath,
A stroke as fatal as the scythe of death.
The sable warrior, frantic with regret
Of her he loves, and never can forget,
Loses in tears the far receding shore,
But not the thought that they must meet no more;
Depriv'd of her and freedom at a blow,
What has he left that he can yet forego? 150
Yes, to deep sadness sullenly resign'd,
He feels his body's bondage in his mind;
Puts off his gen'rous nature; and, to suit
His manners with his fate, puts on the brute.
Oh, most degrading of all ills, that wait
On man, a mourner in his best estate!
All other sorrows virtue may endure,
And find submission more than half a cure;
Grief is itself a med'cine, and bestow'd
T' improve the fortitude that bears the load, 160
To teach the wand'rer, as his woes increase,
The path of wisdom, all whose paths are peace;
But slav'ry!—virtue dreads it as her grave:
Patience itself is meanness in a slave.
Or, if the will and sov'reignty of God
Bid suffer it awhile, and kiss the rod,

Wait for the dawning of a brighter day,
And snap the chain the moment when you may.
Nature imprints upon whate'er we see
That has a heart and life in it—Be free! 170
The beasts are charter'd—neither age nor force
Can quell the love of freedom in a horse:
He breaks the cord that held him at the rack;
And, conscious of an unincumber'd back,
Snuffs up the morning air, forgets the rein,
Loose fly his forelock and his ample mane;
Responsive to the distant neigh he neighs;
Nor stops, till, overleaping all delays,
He finds the pasture where his fellows graze.
Canst thou, and honour'd with a Christian name, 180
Buy what is woman-born, and feel no shame?
Trade in the blood of innocence, and plead
Expedience as a warrant for the deed?
So may the wolf, whom famine has made bold
To quit the forest and invade the fold:
So may the ruffian, who with ghostly glide,
Dagger in hand, steals close to your bedside;
Not he, but his emergence forc'd the door,
He found it inconvenient to be poor.
Has God then giv'n its sweetness to the cane— 190
Unless his laws be trampled on—in vain?
Built a brave world, which cannot yet subsist,
Unless his right to rule it be dismiss'd?
Impudent blasphemy!—So folly pleads,
And, av'rice being judge, with ease succeeds.
But grant the plea—and let it stand for just,
That man make man his prey because he *must*;
Still there is room for pity to abate,
And soothe, the sorrows of so sad a state.
A Briton knows—or, if he knows it not, 200
The Scripture plac'd within his reach, he ought—
That souls have no discriminating hue,
Alike important in their Maker's view;
That none are free from blemish since the fall,
And love divine has paid one price for all.
The wretch that works and weeps without relief,
Has one that notices his silent grief.
He, from whose hands alone all pow'r proceeds,
Ranks its abuse among the foulest deeds,
Considers *all* injustice with a frown; 210
But *marks* the man that treads his fellow down.
Begone!—the whip and bell in that hard hand
Are hateful ensigns of usurp'd command.

Not Mexico could purchase kings a claim
To scourge him, weariness his only blame.
Remember, heav'n has an avenging rod—
To smite the poor is treason against God!
  Trouble is grudgingly and hardly brook'd,
While life's sublimest joys are overlook'd:
We wander o'er a sun-burnt thirsty soil, 220
Murm'ring and weary of our daily toil,
Forget t' enjoy the palm-tree's offer'd shade,
Or taste the fountain in the neighb'ring glade:
Else who would lose, that had the pow'r t' improve,
Th' occasion of transmuting fear to love?
Oh, 'tis a godlike privilege to save!
And he that scorns it is himself a slave.
Inform his mind; one flash of heav'nly day
Would heal his heart and melt his chains away.
"Beauty for ashes" is a gift indeed! 230
And slaves, by truth enlarg'd, are doubly freed.
Then would he say, submissive at thy feet,
While gratitude and love made service sweet,
My dear deliv'rer out of hopeless night,
Whose bounty bought me but to give me light,
I was a bondman on my native plain;
Sin forg'd, and ignorance made fast, the chain;
Thy lips have shed instruction as the dew,
Taught me what path to shun and what pursue;
Farewell, my former joys! I sigh no more 240
For Africa's once lov'd, benighted shore;
Serving a benefactor, I am free—
At my best home, if not exil'd from thee.
  Some men make gain a fountain, whence proceeds
A stream of lib'ral and heroic deeds.
The swell of pity, not to be confin'd
Within the scanty limits of the mind,
Disdains the bank, and throws the golden sands,
A rich deposit, on the bord'ring lands:
These have an ear for his paternal call, 250
Who makes some rich for the supply of all;
God's gift with pleasure in his praise employ,
And THORNTON is familiar with the joy.
  Oh, could I worship aught beneath the skies,
That earth hath seen, or fancy can devise,
Thine altar, sacred liberty, should stand,
Built, by no mercenary vulgar hand,
With fragrant turf, and flow'rs as wild and fair
As ever dress'd a bank, or scented summer air!
Duly, as ever on the mountain's height 260
The peep of morning shed a dawning light,

Again, when ev'ning in her sober vest
Drew the grey curtain of the fading west,
My soul should yield thee willing thanks and
praise
For the chief blessings of my fairest days:
But that were sacrilege—praise is not thine,
But his who gave thee, and preserves thee mine:
Else I would say, and as I spake bid fly
A captive bird into the boundless sky,
This triple realm adores thee—thou art come 270
From Sparta hither, and art here at home.
We feel thy force still active, at this hour
Enjoy immunity from priestly pow'r,
While conscience, happier than in ancient years,
Owns no superior but the God she fears.
Propitious spirit! yet expunge a wrong
Thy rights have suffer'd, and our land, too long.
Teach mercy to ten thousand hearts, that share
The fears and hopes of a commercial care.
Prisons expect the wicked, and were built 280
To bind the lawless, and to punish guilt;
But shipwreck, earthquake, battle, fire, and flood,
Are mighty mischiefs, not to be withstood;
And honest merit stands on slipp'ry ground,
Where covert guile and artifice abound.
Let just restraint, for public peace design'd,
Chain up the wolves and tigers of mankind;
The foe of virtue has no claim to thee—
But let insolvent innocence go free.
Patron of else the most despis'd of men, 290
Accept the tribute of a stranger's pen;
Verse, like the laurel, its immortal meed,
Should be the guerdon of a noble deed;
I may alarm thee, but I fear the shame
(Charity chosen as my theme and aim)
I must incur, forgetting HOWARD's name.
Blest with all wealth can give thee, to resign
Joys doubly sweet to feelings quick as thine,
To quit the bliss thy rural scenes bestow
To seek a nobler amidst scenes of woe, 300
To traverse seas, range kingdoms, and bring home,
Not the proud monuments of Greece or Rome,
But knowledge such as only dungeons teach,
And only sympathy like thine could reach;
That grief, sequester'd from the public stage,
Might smooth her feathers, and enjoy her cage;
Speaks a divine ambition, and a zeal,
The boldest patriot might be proud to feel.

Oh that the voice of clamour and debate,
That pleads for peace till it disturbs the state, 310
Were hush'd in favour of thy gen'rous plea—
The poor thy clients, and heav'n's smile thy fee!
Philosophy, that does not dream or stray,
Walks arm in arm with nature all his way;
Compasses earth, dives into it, ascends
Whatever steep inquiry recommends,
Sees planetary wonders smoothly roll
Round other systems under her control,
Drinks wisdom at the milky stream of light
That cheers the silent journey of the night, 320
And brings, at his return, a bosom charg'd
With rich instruction, and a soul enlarg'd.
The treasur'd sweets of the capacious plan
That heav'n spreads wide before the view of man,
All prompt his pleas'd pursuit, and to pursue
Still prompt him, with a pleasure always new;
He, too, has a connecting pow'r, and draws
Man to the centre of the common cause;
Aiding a dubious and deficient sight
With a new medium, and a purer light. 330
All truth is precious, if not all divine;
And what dilates the pow'rs must needs refine.
He reads the skies, and, watching ev'ry change,
Provides the faculties an ampler range;
And wins mankind, as his attempts prevail,
A prouder station on the gen'ral scale.
But reason still, unless divinely taught,
Whate'er she learns, learns nothing as she ought;
The lamp of revelation only shows—
What human wisdom cannot but oppose— 340
That man, in nature's richest mantle clad,
And grac'd with all philosophy can add,
Though fair without, and luminous within,
Is still the progeny and heir of sin.
Thus taught, down falls the plumage of his pride;
He feels his need of an unerring guide,
And knows that, falling, he shall rise no more,
Unless the pow'r that bade him stand restore.
This is indeed philosophy; this, known,
Makes wisdom, worthy of the name, his own; 350
And, without this—whatever he discuss;
Whether the space between the stars and us,
Whether he measure earth, compute the sea,
Weigh sun-beams, carve a fly, or spit a flea—
The solemn trifler, with his boasted skill,
Toils much, and is a solemn trifler still:

Blind was he born, and, his misguided eyes
Grown dim in trifling studies, blind he dies.
Self-knowledge, truly learn'd, of course implies
The rich possession of a nobler prize; 360
For self to self, and God to man, reveal'd,
(Two themes to nature's eye for ever seal'd)
Are taught by rays that fly with equal pace
From the same centre of enlight'ning grace.
Here stay thy foot;—how copious and how clear
Th' o'erflowing well of Charity springs here!
Hark! 'tis the music of a thousand rills!
Some thro' the groves, some down the sloping hills,
Winding a secret or an open course,
And all supplied from an eternal source. 370
The ties of nature do but feebly bind,
And commerce partially reclaims, mankind;
Philosophy, without his heav'nly guide,
May blow up self-conceit, and nourish pride;
But, while his province is the reas'ning part,
Has still a veil of midnight on his heart;
'Tis truth divine, exhibited on earth,
Gives Charity her being and her birth.
Suppose (when thought is warm, and fancy flows,
What will not argument sometimes suppose?) 380
An isle possess'd by creatures of our kind,
Endu'd with reason, yet by nature blind.
Let supposition lend her aid once more,
And land some grave optician on the shore:
He claps his lens, if haply they may see,
Close to the part where vision ought to be;
But finds that, though his tubes assist the sight,
They cannot give it, or make darkness light.
He reads wise lectures, and describes aloud
A sense they know not, to the wond'ring crowd;
He talks of light and the prismatic hues, 391
As men of depth in erudition use;
But all he gains for his harangue is—Well,
What monstrous lies some travellers will tell!
The soul, whose sight all-quick'ning grace renews,
Takes the resemblance of the good she views,
As di'monds, stript of their opaque disguise,
Reflect the noon-day glory of the skies.
She speaks of him, her author, guardian, friend,
Whose love knew no beginning, knows no end, 400
In language warm as all that love inspires;
And, in the glow of her intense desires,
Pants to communicate her noble fires.

She sees a world stark blind to what employs
Her eager thought, and feeds her flowing joys;
Though wisdom hail them, heedless of her call,
Flies to save some, and feels a pang for all:
Herself as weak as her support is strong,
She feels that frailty she denied so long;
And, from a knowledge of her own disease, 410
Learns to compassionate the sick she sees.
Here see, acquitted of all vain pretence,
The reign of genuine Charity commence.
Though scorn repay her sympathetic tears,
She still is kind, and still she perseveres;
The truth she loves a sightless world blaspheme—
'Tis childish dotage, a delirious dream!
The danger they discern not they deny;
Laugh at their only remedy, and die.
But still a soul thus touch'd can never cease, 420
Whoever threatens war, to speak of peace:
Pure in her aim, and in her temper mild,
Her wisdom seems the weakness of a child.
She makes excuses where she might condemn;
Reviled by those that hate her, prays for them;
Suspicion lurks not in her artless breast;
The worst suggested, she believes the best;
Not soon provok'd, however stung and teas'd;
And, if perhaps made angry, soon appeas'd;
She rather waves than will dispute her right; 430
And, injur'd, makes forgiveness her delight.
 Such was the portrait an apostle drew;
The bright original was one he knew;
Heav'n held his hand—the likeness must be true.
 When one, that holds communion with the skies,
Has fill'd his urn where these pure waters rise,
And once more mingles with us meaner things,
'Tis ev'n as if an angel shook his wings;
Immortal fragrance fills the circuit wide,
That tells us whence his treasures are supplied. 440
So, when a ship, well freighted with the stores
The sun matures on India's spicy shores,
Has dropt her anchor and her canvass furl'd
In some safe haven of our western world,
'Twere vain inquiry to what port she went;
The gale informs us, laden with the scent.
 Some seek, when queasy conscience has its qualms,
To lull the painful malady with alms;
But charity, not feign'd, intends alone
Another's good—their's centres in their own; 450

And, too short liv'd to reach the realms of peace,
Must cease for ever when the poor shall cease.
Flavia, most tender of her own good name,
Is rather careless of her sister's fame:
Her superfluity the poor supplies,
But, if she touch a character, it dies.
The seeming virtue weigh'd against the vice,
She deems all safe, for she has paid the price:
No charity but alms aught values she,
Except in porcelain on her mantle-tree. 460
How many deeds, with which the world has rung,
From pride, in league with ignorance, have sprung!
But God o'errules all human follies still,
And bends the tough materials to his will.
A conflagration, or a wintry flood,
Has left some hundreds without home or food;
Extravagance and av'rice shall subscribe,
While fame and self-complacence are the bribe.
The brief proclaim'd, it visits ev'ry pew,
But first the squire's—a compliment but due: 470
With slow deliberation he unties
His glitt'ring purse—that envy of all eyes!
And, while the clerk just puzzles out the psalm,
Slides guinea behind guinea in his palm;
Till, finding (what he might have found before)
A smaller piece amidst the precious store,
Pinch'd close between his finger and his thumb,
He half exhibits, and then drops the sum.
Gold, to be sure!—Throughout the town 'tis told
How the good squire gives never less than gold.
From motives such as his, though not the best, 481
Springs in due time supply for the distress'd;
Not less effectual than what love bestows—
Except that office clips it as it goes.
  But, lest I seem to sin against a friend,
And wound the grace I mean to recommend,
(Though vice derided with a just design
Implies no trespass against love divine)
Once more I would adopt the graver style—
A teacher should be sparing of his smile. 490
  Unless a love of virtue light the flame,
Satire is, more than those he brands, to blame;
He hides behind a magisterial air
His own offences, and strips others bare;
Affects, indeed a most humane concern,
That men, if gently tutor'd, will not learn;
That mulish folly, not to be reclaim'd
By softer methods, must be made asham'd;

454 her] a *1782–1788.*

But (I might instance in St. Patrick's dean)
Too often rails to gratify his spleen. 500
Most sat'rists are indeed a public scourge;
Their mildest physic is a farrier's purge;
Their acrid temper turns, as soon as stirr'd,
The milk of their good purpose all to curd.
Their zeal begotten, as their works rehearse,
By lean despair upon an empty purse,
The wild assassins start into the street,
Prepar'd to poignard whomsoe'er they meet.
No skill in swordmanship, however just,
Can be secure against a madman's thrust; 510
And even virtue, so unfairly match'd,
Although immortal, may be prick'd or scratch'd.
When scandal has new minted an old lie,
Or tax'd invention for a fresh supply,
'Tis call'd a satire, and the world appears
Gath'ring around it with erected ears:
A thousand names are toss'd into the crowd;
Some whisper'd softly, and some twang'd aloud;
Just as the sapience of an author's brain
Suggests it safe or dang'rous to be plain. 520
Strange! how the frequent interjected dash
Quickens a market, and helps off the trash;
Th' important letters, that include the rest
Serve as a key to those that are suppress'd;
Conjecture gripes the victims in his paw,
The world is charm'd, and Scrib. escapes the law.
So, when the cold damp shades of night prevail,
Worms may be caught by either head or tail;
Forcibly drawn from many a close recess,
They meet with little pity, no redress; 530
Plung'd in the stream, they lodge upon the mud,
Food for the famish'd rovers of the flood.
All zeal for a reform, that gives offence
To peace and charity, is mere pretence:
A bold remark; but which, if well applied,
Would humble many a tow'ring poet's pride.
Perhaps the man was in a sportive fit,
And had no other play-place for his wit;
Perhaps, enchanted with the love of fame,
He sought the jewel in his neighbour's shame; 540
Perhaps—whatever end he might pursue,
The cause of virtue could not be his view.
At ev'ry stroke wit flashes in our eyes;
The turns are quick, the polish'd points surprise,
But shine with cruel and tremendous charms,
That, while they please, possess us with alarms:

So have I seen, (and hasten'd to the sight
On all the wings of holiday delight)
Where stands that monument of ancient pow'r,
Nam'd with emphatic dignity—the tow'r, 550
Guns, halberts, swords, and pistols, great and small,
In starry forms dispos'd upon the wall.
We wonder, as we gazing stand below,
That brass and steel should make so fine a show;
But, though we praise th' exact designer's skill,
Account them implements of mischief still.
No works shall find acceptance, in that day
When all disguises shall be rent away,
That square not truly with the scripture plan,
Nor spring from love to God, or love to man. 560
As he ordains things, sordid in their birth,
To be resolv'd into their parent earth;
And, though the soul shall seek superior orbs,
Whate'er this world produces, it absorbs;
So self starts nothing but what tends apace
Home to the goal where it began the race.
Such as our motive is our aim must be;
If this be servile, that can ne'er be free:
If self employ us, whatsoe'er is wrought,
We glorify that self, not him we ought. 570
Such virtues had need prove their own reward,
The judge of all men owes them no regard.
True charity, a plant divinely nurs'd,
Fed by the love from which it rose at first,
Thrives against hope; and, in the rudest scene,
Storms but enliven its unfading green;
Exub'rant is the shadow it supplies;
Its fruit on earth, its growth above the skies.
To look at him, who form'd us and redeem'd;
So glorious now, though once so disesteem'd; 580
To see a God stretch forth his human hand,
T' uphold the boundless scenes of his command;
To recollect that, in a form like our's,
He bruis'd beneath his feet th' infernal pow'rs,
Captivity led captive, rose to claim
The wreath he won so dearly in our name;
That, thron'd above all height, he condescends
To call the few that trust in him his friends;
That, in the heav'n of heav'ns, that space he deems
Too scanty for th' exertion of his beams, 590
And shines, as if impatient to bestow
Life and a kingdom upon worms below;
That sight imparts a never-dying flame,
Though feeble in degree, in kind the same.

Like him, the soul, thus kindled from above,
Spreads wide her arms of universal love;
And, still enlarg'd as she receives the grace,
Includes creation in her close embrace.
Behold a Christian!—and, without the fires
The founder of that name alone inspires, 600
Though all accomplishment, all knowledge meet,
To make the shining prodigy complete,
Whoever boasts that name—behold a cheat!
Were love, in these the world's last doting years,
As frequent as the want of it appears,
The churches warm'd, they would no longer hold
Such frozen figures, stiff as they are cold;
Relenting forms would lose their pow'r, or cease;
And ev'n the dipt and sprinkled live in peace:
Each heart would quit its prison in the breast, 610
And flow in free communion with the rest.
The statesman, skill'd in projects dark and deep,
Might burn his useless Machiavel, and sleep;
His budget, often fill'd, yet always poor,
Might swing at ease behind his study door,
No longer prey upon our annual rents,
Or scare the nation with its big contents:
Disbanded legions freely might depart,
And slaying man would cease to be an art.
No learned disputants would take the field, 620
Sure not to conquer, and sure not to yield;
Both sides deceiv'd, if rightly understood,
Pelting each other for the public good.
Did charity prevail, the press would prove
A vehicle of virtue, truth, and love;
And I might spare myself the pains to show
What few can learn, and all suppose they know.
Thus have I sought to grace a serious lay
With many a wild, indeed, but flow'ry spray,
In hopes to gain, what else I must have lost, 630
Th' attention pleasure has so much engross'd.
But if, unhappily deceiv'd, I dream,
And prove too weak for so divine a theme,
Let Charity forgive me a mistake,
That zeal, not vanity, has chanc'd to make,
And spare the poet for his subject's sake.

601 accomplishments *1782, 1786.* 617 Or] Nor *1782–1788.*
636 subject *1782–1788.*

CONVERSATION

[Written July and August, 1781. Published 1782.]

Nam neque me tantum venientis sibilus austri,
Nec percussa juvant fluctû tam litora, nec quæ
Saxosas inter decurrunt flumina valles.
VIRG. Ecl. 5.

THOUGH nature weigh our talents, and dispense
To ev'ry man his modicum of sense,
And Conversation, in its better part,
May be esteem'd a gift and not an art,
Yet much depends, as in the tiller's toil,
On culture, and the sowing of the soil.
Words learn'd by rote a parrot may rehearse,
But talking is not always to converse;
Not more distinct from harmony divine,
The constant creaking of a country sign. 10
As alphabets in ivory employ,
Hour after hour, the yet unletter'd boy,
Sorting and puzzling with a deal of glee
Those seeds of science call'd his A B C;
So language in the mouths of the adult,
Witness its insignificant result,
Too often proves an implement of play,
A toy to sport with and pass time away.
Collect at ev'ning what the day brought forth,
Compress the sum into its solid worth, 20
And, if it weigh th' importance of a fly,
The scales are false, or Algebra a lie.
Sacred interpreter of human thought,
How few respect or use thee as they ought!
But all shall give account of ev'ry wrong,
Who dare dishonour or defile the tongue;
Who prostitute it in the cause of vice,
Or sell their glory at a market-price;
Who vote for hire, or point it with lampoon—
The dear-bought placeman, and the cheap buffoon.
There is a prurience in the speech of some, 31
Wrath stays him, or else God would strike them dumb:
His wise forbearance has their end in view;
They fill their measure, and receive their due.
The heathen law-givers of ancient days,
Names almost worthy of a Christian's praise,

36 Christian *1782–1787.*

Would drive them forth from the resort of men,
And shut up ev'ry satyr in his den.
Oh, come not ye near innocence and truth,
Ye worms that eat into the bud of youth! 40
Infectious as impure, your blighting pow'r
Taints in its rudiments the promis'd flow'r;
Its odour perish'd and its charming hue,
Thenceforth 'tis hateful, for it smells of you.
Not ev'n the vigorous and headlong rage
Of adolescence, or a firmer age,
Affords a plea allowable or just
For making speech the pamperer of lust;
But, when the breath of age commits the fault,
'Tis nauseous as the vapour of a vault. 50
So wither'd stumps disgrace the sylvan scene,
No longer fruitful, and no longer green;
The sapless wood, divested of the bark,
Grows fungous, and takes fire at ev'ry spark.
  Oaths terminate, as Paul observes, all strife—
Some men have surely then a peaceful life!
Whatever subject occupy discourse,
The feats of Vestris, or the naval force,
Asseveration, blust'ring in your face,
Makes contradiction such an hopeless case: 60
In ev'ry tale they tell, or false or true,
Well known, or such as no man ever knew,
They fix attention, heedless of your pain,
With oaths, like rivets, forc'd into the brain;
And ev'n when sober truth prevails throughout,
They swear it, till affirmance breeds a doubt.
A Persian, humble servant of the sun,
Who, though devout, yet bigotry had none,
Hearing a lawyer, grave in his address,
With adjurations ev'ry word impress, 70
Suppos'd the man a bishop, or at least,
God's name so much upon his lips, a priest;
Bow'd at the close with all his graceful airs,
And begg'd an int'rest in his frequent pray'rs.
  Go, quit the rank to which ye stood preferr'd,
Henceforth associate in one common herd;
Religion, virtue, reason, common sense,
Pronounce your human form a false pretence;
A mere disguise, in which a devil lurks,
Who yet betrays his secret by his works. 80
  Ye pow'rs who rule the tongue, if such there are,
And make colloquial happiness your care,
Preserve me from the thing I dread and hate—
A duel in the form of a debate.

The clash of arguments and jar of words,
Worse than the mortal brunt of rival swords,
Decide no question with their tedious length,
(For opposition gives opinion strength)
Divert the champions, prodigal of breath,
And put the peaceably disposed to death. 90
Oh, thwart me not, sir Soph, at ev'ry turn,
Nor carp at ev'ry flaw you may discern;
Though syllogisms hang not on my tongue,
I am not surely always in the wrong!
'Tis hard if all is false that I advance—
A fool must now and then be right, by chance.
Not that all freedom of dissent I blame;
No—there I grant the privilege I claim.
A disputable point is no man's ground;
Rove where you please, 'tis common all around. 100
Discourse may want an animated—No,
To brush the surface and to make it flow;
But still remember, if you mean to please,
To press your point with modesty and ease.
The mark, at which my juster aim I take,
Is contradiction for its own dear sake.
Set your opinion at whatever pitch,
Knots and impediments make something hitch;
Adopt his own, 'tis equally in vain,
Your thread of argument is snapt again; 110
The wrangler, rather than accord with you,
Will judge himself deceiv'd, and prove it too.
Vociferated logic kills me quite;
A noisy man is always in the right—
I twirl my thumbs, fall back into my chair,
Fix on the wainscot a distressful stare,
And, when I hope his blunders are all out,
Reply discreetly—To be sure—no doubt!
 DUBIUS is such a scrupulous good man—
Yes—you may catch him tripping if you can. 120
He would not with a peremptory tone,
Assert the nose upon his face his own;
With hesitation admirably slow,
He humbly hopes—presumes—it may be so.
His evidence, if he were call'd by law
To swear to some enormity he saw,
For want of prominence and just relief,
Would hang an honest man, and save a thief.
Through constant dread of giving truth offence,
He ties up all his hearers in suspense; 130

127 prominent *1800*.

Knows what he knows as if he knew it not,
What he remembers seems to have forgot;
His sole opinion, whatsoe'er befall,
Cent'ring at last in having none at all.
Yet, though he tease and baulk your list'ning ear,
He makes one useful point exceeding clear;
Howe'er ingenious on his darling theme
A sceptic in philosophy may seem,
Reduc'd to practice, his beloved rule
Would only prove him a consummate fool; 140
Useless in him alike both brain and speech,
Fate having plac'd all truth above his reach,
His ambiguities his total sum,
He might as well be blind, and deaf, and dumb.
Where men of judgment creep and feel their way,
The positive pronounce without dismay;
Their want of light and intellect supplied
By sparks absurdity strikes out of pride:
Without the means of knowing right from wrong,
They always are decisive, clear, and strong. 150
Where others toil with philosophic force,
Their nimble nonsense takes a shorter course;
Flings at your head conviction in the lump,
And gains remote conclusions at a jump:
Their own defect, invisible to them,
Seen in another, they at once condemn;
And, though self-idoliz'd in ev'ry case,
Hate their own likeness in a brother's face.
The cause is plain, and not to be denied,
The proud are always most provok'd by pride. 160
Few competitions but engender spite;
And those the most, where neither has a right.
The point of honour has been deem'd of use,
To teach good manners, and to curb abuse:
Admit it true, the consequence is clear,
Our polish'd manners are a mask we wear,
And at the bottom barb'rous still and rude;
We are restrain'd, indeed, but not subdued.
The very remedy, however sure,
Springs from the mischief it intends to cure, 170
And savage in its principle appears,
Tried, as it should be, by the fruit it bears.
'Tis hard, indeed, if nothing will defend
Mankind from quarrels but their fatal end;
That now and then an hero must decease,
That the surviving world may live in peace.
Perhaps at last close scrutiny may show
The practice dastardly, and mean, and low;

That men engage in it compell'd by force;
And fear, not courage, is its proper source: 180
The fear of tyrant custom, and the fear
Lest fops should censure us, and fools should sneer.
At least to trample on our Maker's laws,
And hazard life for any or no cause,
To rush into a fixt eternal state
Out of the very flames of rage and hate,
Or send another shiv'ring to the bar
With all the guilt of such unnat'ral war,
Whatever use may urge, or honour plead,
On reason's verdict is a madman's deed. 190
Am I to set my life upon a throw,
Because a bear is rude and surly? No—
A moral, sensible, and well-bred man
Will not affront me, and no other can.
Were I empow'r'd to regulate the lists,
They should encounter with well-loaded fists;
A Trojan combat would be something new,
Let DARES beat ENTELLUS black and blue;
Then each might show, to his admiring friends,
In honourable bumps his rich amends, 200
And carry, in contusions of his skull,
A satisfactory receipt in full.
  A story, in which native humour reigns,
Is often useful, always entertains:
A graver fact, enlisted on your side,
May furnish illustration, well applied;
But sedentary weavers of long tales
Give me the fidgets, and my patience fails.
'Tis the most asinine employ on earth,
To hear them tell of parentage and birth, 210
And echo conversations, dull and dry,
Embellish'd with—*He said*, and *So said I*.
At ev'ry interview their route the same,
The repetition makes attention lame;
We bustle up with unsuccessful speed,
And in the saddest part cry—*Droll indeed!*
The path of narrative with care pursue,
Still making probability your clue;
On all the vestiges of truth attend,
And let *them* guide you to a decent end. 220
Of all ambitions man may entertain,
The worst that can invade a sickly brain
Is that which angles hourly for surprise,
And baits its hook with prodigies and lies.
Credulous infancy, or age as weak,
Are fittest auditors for such to seek,

Who to please others will themselves disgrace;
Yet please not, but affront you to your face.
A great retailer of this curious ware,
Having unloaded and made many stare, 230
Can this be true?—an arch observer cries.
Yes, (rather mov'd) I saw it with these eyes!
Sir! I believe it on that ground alone;
I could not, had I seen it with my own.

A tale should be judicious, clear, succinct;
The language plain, and incidents well link'd;
Tell not as new what ev'ry body knows;
And, new or old, still hasten to a close;
There, cent'ring in a focus round and neat,
Let all your rays of information meet. 240
What neither yields us profit nor delight
Is like a nurse's lullaby at night;
Guy Earl of Warwick and fair Eleanore,
Or giant killing Jack, would please me more.

The pipe, with solemn interposing puff,
Makes half a sentence at a time enough;
The dozing sages drop the drowsy strain,
Then pause, and puff—and speak, and pause again.
Such often, like the tube they so admire,
Important triflers! have more smoke than fire! 250
Pernicious weed! whose scent the fair annoys,
Unfriendly to society's chief joys,
Thy worst effect is banishing for hours
The sex whose presence civilizes our's:
Thou art, indeed, the drug a gard'ner wants,
To poison vermin that infest his plants;
But are we so to wit and beauty blind,
As to despise the glory of our kind,
And show the softest minds and fairest forms
As little mercy as the grubs and worms? 260
They dare not wait the riotous abuse,
Thy thirst-creating steams at length produce,
When wine has giv'n indecent language birth,
And forc'd the flood-gates of licentious mirth;
For sea-born Venus her attachment shows,
Still to that element from which she rose,
And, with a quiet which no fumes disturb,
Sips meek infusions of a milder herb.

Th' emphatic speaker dearly loves t' oppose,
In contact inconvenient, nose to nose, 270
As if the gnomon on his neighbour's phiz,
Touch'd with a magnet, had attracted his.

250 trifles *1782-1787*.

His whisper'd theme, dilated and at large,
Proves after all a wind-gun's airy charge,
An extract of his diary—no more,
A tasteless journal of the day before.
He walk'd abroad, o'ertaken in the rain
Call'd on a friend, drank tea, stept home again,
Resum'd his purpose, had a world of talk
With one he stumbled on, and lost his walk. 280
I interrupt him with a sudden bow,
Adieu, dear Sir! lest you should lose it now.
I cannot talk with civet in the room,
A fine puss-gentleman that's all perfume;
The sight's enough—no need to smell a beau—
Who thrusts his nose into a raree-show?
His odoriferous attempts to please,
Perhaps might prosper with a swarm of bees;
But we that make no honey, though we sting,
Poets, are sometimes apt to maul the thing. 290
'Tis wrong to bring into a mixt resort
What makes some sick, and others *a-la-mort;*
An argument of cogence, we may say,
Why such an one should keep himself away.
A graver coxcomb we may sometimes see,
Quite as absurd, though not so light as he:
A shallow brain behind a serious mask,
An oracle within an empty cask,
The solemn fop; significant and budge;
A fool with judges, amongst fools a judge; 300
He says but little, and that little said
Owes all its weight, like loaded dice, to lead.
His wit invites you by his looks to come,
But when you knock it never is at home:
'Tis like a parcel sent you by the stage,
Some handsome present, as your hopes presage;
'Tis heavy, bulky, and bids fair to prove
An absent friend's fidelity and love,
But when unpack'd your disappointment groans
To find it stuff'd with brickbats, earth, and stones.
Some men employ their health, an ugly trick, 311
In making known how oft they have been sick,
And give us, in recitals of disease,
A doctor's trouble, but without the fees;
Relate how many weeks they kept their bed,
How an emetic or cathartic sped;
Nothing is slightly touch'd, much less forgot,
Nose, ears, and eyes, seem present on the spot.
Now the distemper, spite of draught or pill,
Victorious seem'd, and now the doctor's skill; 320

And now—alas for unforeseen mishaps!
They put on a damp night-cap and relapse;
They thought they must have died they were so bad—
Their peevish hearers almost wish they had.
  Some fretful tempers wince at ev'ry touch,
You always do too little or too much:
You speak with life, in hopes to entertain,
Your elevated voice goes through the brain;
You fall at once into a lower key,
That's worse—the drone-pipe of an humble bee. 330
The southern sash admits too strong a light,
You rise and drop the curtain—now it's night.
He shakes with cold—you stir the fire and strive
To make a blaze—that's roasting him alive.
Serve him with ven'son, and he chooses fish;
With soal—that's just the sort he would not wish.
He takes what he at first profess'd to loath,
And in due time feeds heartily on both;
Yet still, o'erclouded with a constant frown,
He does not swallow, but he gulps it down. 340
Your hope to please him, vain on ev'ry plan,
Himself should work that wonder, if he can—
Alas! his efforts double his distress,
He likes your's little, and his own still less.
Thus always teasing others, always teas'd,
His only pleasure is—to be displeas'd.
  I pity bashful men who feel the pain
Of fancied scorn and undeserv'd disdain,
And bear the marks, upon a blushing face,
Of needless shame, and self-impos'd disgrace. 350
Our sensibilities are so acute,
The fear of being silent makes us mute.
We sometimes think we could a speech produce,
Much to the purpose, if our tongues were loose;
But, being tried, it dies upon the lip,
Faint as a chicken's note that has the pip:
Our wasted oil unprofitably burns,
Like hidden lamps in old sepulchral urns.
Few Frenchmen of this evil have complain'd;
It seems as if we Britons were ordain'd, 360
By way of wholesome curb upon our pride,
To fear each other, fearing none beside.
The cause perhaps inquiry may descry,
Self-searching with an introverted eye,
Conceal'd within an unsuspected part,
The vainest corner of our own vain heart:

355 tried] tied *1782–1788*.

For ever aiming at the world's esteem,
Our self importance ruins its own scheme;
In other eyes our talents rarely shown,
Become at length so splendid in our own, 370
We dare not risque them into public view,
Lest they miscarry of what seems their due.
True modesty is a discerning grace,
And only blushes in the proper place;
But counterfeit is blind, and skulks through fear,
Where 'tis a shame to be asham'd t' appear:
Humility the parent of the first;
The last by vanity produc'd and nurst.
The circle form'd, we sit in silent state,
Like figures drawn upon a dial-plate; 380
Yes ma'am, and no ma'am, utter'd softly, show
Ev'ry five minutes how the minutes go;
Each individual suffering a constraint
Poetry may, but colours cannot paint;
As if in close committee on the sky,
Reports it hot or cold, or wet or dry;
And finds a changing clime an happy source
Of wise reflection and well-tim'd discourse.
We next inquire, but softly and by stealth,
Like conservators of the public health, 390
Of epidemic throats, if such there are,
And coughs, and rheums, and phthisic, and catarrh.
That theme exhausted, a wide chasm ensues,
Fill'd up at last with interesting news;
Who danc'd with whom, and who are like to wed,
And who is hang'd, and who is brought to bed;
But fear to call a more important cause,
As if 'twere treason against English laws.
The visit paid, with ecstasy we come,
As from a seven years transportation, home, 400
And there resume an unembarrass'd brow,
Recov'ring what we lost we know not how,
The faculties that seem'd reduc'd to nought,
Expression and the privilege of thought.
The reeking, roaring hero of the chase,
I give him over as a desp'rate case.
Physicians write in hopes to work a cure,
Never, if honest ones, when death is sure;
And though the fox he follows may be tam'd,
A mere fox-follower never is reclaim'd. 410
Some farrier should prescribe his proper course,
Whose only fit companion is his horse,

385 As *1782–1788*, *1803*: And, *1793–1800*.

Or if, deserving of a better doom,
The noble beast judge otherwise, his groom.
Yet ev'n the rogue that serves him, though he stand
To take his honour's orders, cap in hand,
Prefers his fellow-grooms, with much good sense,
Their skill a truth, his master's a pretence.
If neither horse nor groom affect the squire,
Where can at last his jockeyship retire? 420
Oh to the club, the scene of savage joys,
The school of coarse good fellowship and noise;
There, in the sweet society of those
Whose friendship from his boyish years he chose,
Let him improve his talent, if he can,
Till none but beasts acknowledge him a man.
  Man's heart had been impenetrably seal'd,
Like their's that cleave the flood or graze the field,
Had not his Maker's all-bestowing hand
Giv'n him a soul, and bade him understand; 430
The reas'ning pow'r vouchsaf'd of course inferr'd
The pow'r to clothe that reason with his word;
For all is perfect that God works on earth,
And he that gives conception, aids the birth.
If this be plain, 'tis plainly understood,
What uses of his boon the giver would.
The mind, dispatch'd upon her busy toil,
Should range where Providence has blest the soil;
Visiting ev'ry flow'r with labour meet,
And gathering all her treasures sweet by sweet, 440
She should imbue the tongue with what she sips,
And shed the balmy blessing on the lips,
That good diffus'd may more abundant grow,
And speech may praise the pow'r that bids it flow.
Will the sweet warbler of the live-long night,
That fills the list'ning lover with delight,
Forget his harmony, with rapture heard,
To learn the twitt'ring of a meaner bird,
Or make the parrot's mimicry his choice,
That odious libel on an human voice? 450
No—nature unsophisticate by man,
Starts not aside from her Creator's plan;
The melody that was at first design'd
To cheer the rude forefathers of mankind,
Is note for note deliver'd in our ears,
In the last scene of her six thousand years:
Yet fashion, leader of a chatt'ring train,
Whom man for his own hurt permits to reign,

434 aids] adds *1782*, *1786*.

Who shifts and changes all things but his shape,
And would degrade her vot'ry to an ape, 460
The fruitful parent of abuse and wrong,
Holds an usurp'd dominion o'er his tongue;
There sits and prompts him with his own disgrace,
Prescribes the theme, the tone and the grimace,
And, when accomplish'd in her wayward school,
Calls gentleman whom she has made a fool.
'Tis an unalterable fix'd decree,
That none could frame or ratify but she,
That heav'n and hell, and righteousness and sin,
Snares in his path and foes that lurk within, 470
God and his attributes (a field of day
Where 'tis an angel's happiness to stray),
Fruits of his love and wonders of his might,
Be never nam'd in ears esteem'd polite;
That he who dares, when she forbids, be grave,
Shall stand proscrib'd, a madman or a knave,
A close designer not to be believ'd,
Or, if excus'd that charge, at least deceiv'd.
Oh folly worthy of the nurse's lap,
Give it the breast, or stop its mouth with pap! 480
Is it incredible, or can it seem
A dream to any except those that dream,
That man should love his Maker, and *that* fire,
Warming his heart, should at his lips transpire?
Know then, and modestly let fall your eyes,
And veil your daring crest that braves the skies;
That air of insolence affronts your God,
You need his pardon, and provoke his rod:
Now, in a posture that becomes you more
Than that heroic strut assum'd before, 490
Know, your arrears with ev'ry hour accrue,
For mercy shown, while wrath is justly due.
The time is short, and there are souls on earth,
Though future pain may serve for present mirth,
Acquainted with the woes that fear or shame,
By fashion taught, forbade them once to name,
And, having felt the pangs you deem a jest,
Have prov'd them truths too big to be express'd:
Go, seek on revelation's hallow'd ground,
Sure to succeed, the remedy they found; 500
Touch'd by that pow'r that you have dar'd to mock,
That makes seas stable, and dissolves the rock,
Your heart shall yield a life-renewing stream,
That fools, as you have done, shall call a dream.
It happen'd, on a solemn even-tide,
Soon after He that was our Surety died,

Two bosom friends, each pensively inclin'd,
The scene of all those sorrows left behind,
Sought their own village, busied as they went,
In musings worthy of the great event: 510
They spake of him they lov'd, of him whose life,
Though blameless, had incurr'd perpetual strife,
Whose deeds had left, in spite of hostile arts,
A deep memorial graven on their hearts.
The recollection, like a vein of ore,
The farther trac'd, enrich'd them still the more;
They thought him, and they justly thought him, one
Sent to do more than he appear'd t' have done;
T' exalt a people, and to place them high
Above all else, and wonder'd he should die. 520
Ere yet they brought their journey to an end,
A stranger join'd them, courteous as a friend,
And ask'd them, with a kind engaging air,
What their affliction was, and begg'd a share.
Inform'd, he gather'd up the broken thread,
And, truth and wisdom gracing all he said,
Explain'd, illustrated, and search'd so well,
The tender theme, on which they chose to dwell,
That reaching home, the night, they said, is near,
We must not now be parted, sojourn here— 530
The new acquaintance soon became a guest,
And made so welcome at their simple feast,
He bless'd the bread, but vanish'd at the word,
And left them both exclaiming, 'Twas the Lord!
Did not our hearts feel all he deign'd to say,
Did they not burn within us by the way?
Now their's was converse such as it behoves
Man to maintain, and such as God approves:
Their views indeed were indistinct and dim,
But yet successful, being aim'd at him. 540
Christ and his character their only scope,
Their object, and their subject, and their hope,
They felt what it became them much to feel,
And, wanting him to loose the sacred seal,
Found him as prompt as their desire was true
To spread the new-born glories in their view.
Well—what are ages and the lapse of time,
Match'd against truths, as lasting as sublime?
Can length of years on God himself exact,
Or make that fiction which was once a fact? 550
No—marble and recording brass decay,
And like the graver's mem'ry pass away;
The works of man inherit, as is just,
Their author's frailty, and return to dust;

But truth divine for ever stands secure,
Its head is guarded as its base is sure;
Fix'd in the rolling flood of endless years,
The pillar of th' eternal plan appears,
The raving storm and dashing wave defies,
Built by that architect who built the skies. 560
Hearts may be found, that harbour at this hour
That love of Christ in all its quick'ning power,
And lips unstain'd by folly or by strife,
Whose wisdom, drawn from the deep well of life,
Tastes of its healthful origin, and flows
A Jordan for th' ablution of our woes.
Oh days of heav'n, and nights of equal praise,
Serene and peaceful as those heav'nly days,
When souls drawn upwards, in communion sweet,
Enjoy the stillness of some close retreat, 570
Discourse, as if releas'd and safe at home,
Of dangers past and wonders yet to come,
And spread the sacred treasures of the breast
Upon the lap of covenanted rest.
What, always dreaming over heav'nly things,
Like angel heads in stone with pigeon-wings?
Canting and whining out all day the word,
And half the night? fanatic and absurd!
Mine be the friend less frequent in his pray'rs,
Who makes no bustle with his soul's affairs, 580
Whose wit can brighten up a wintry day,
And chase the splenetic dull hours away;
Content on earth in earthly things to shine,
Who waits for heav'n ere he becomes divine,
Leaves saints t' enjoy those altitudes they teach,
And plucks the fruit plac'd more within his reach.
Well spoken, Advocate of sin and shame,
Known by thy bleating—Ignorance thy name.
Is sparkling wit the world's exclusive right,
The fixt fee-simple of the vain and light? 590
Can hopes of heav'n, bright prospects of an hour,
That come to waft us out of sorrow's pow'r,
Obscure or quench a faculty, that finds
Its happiest soil in the serenest minds?
Religion curbs indeed its wanton play,
And brings the trifler under rig'rous sway,
But gives it usefulness unknown before,
And, purifying, makes it shine the more.
A Christian's wit is inoffensive light,
A beam that aids, but never grieves the sight; 600

556 is guarded] as guarded *1782–1788*. 569 upward *1782–1787*.
592 comes *1782 errata, 1786, 1787*.

Vig'rous in age as in the flush of youth,
'Tis always active on the side of truth;
Temp'rance and peace insure its healthful state,
And make it brightest at its latest date.
Oh I have seen (nor hope perhaps in vain,
Ere life go down, to see such sights again)
A vet'ran warrior in the Christian field,
Who never saw the sword he could not wield;
Grave without dullness, learned without pride,
Exact, yet not precise, though meek, keen-ey'd;
A man that would have foiled, at their own play,
A dozen would-be's of the modern day; 612
Who, when occasion justified its use,
Had wit as bright as ready to produce,
Could fetch from records of an earlier age,
Or from philosophy's enlighten'd page,
His rich materials, and regale your ear
With strains it was a privilege to hear:
Yet, above all, his luxury supreme,
And his chief glory, was the gospel theme; 620
There he was copious as old Greece or Rome,
His happy eloquence seem'd there at home,
Ambitious not to shine or to excel,
But to treat justly what he lov'd so well.

It moves me more perhaps than folly ought,
When some green heads, as void of wit as thought,
Suppose *themselves* monopolists of sense,
And wiser men's ability pretence.
Though time will wear us, and we must grow old,
Such men are not forgot as soon as cold, 630
Their fragrant mem'ry will out-last their tomb,
Embalm'd for ever in its own perfume:
And, to say truth, though in its early prime,
And when unstain'd with any grosser crime,
Youth has a sprightliness and fire to boast,
That in the valley of decline are lost,
And virtue with peculiar charms appears,
Crown'd with the garland of life's blooming years;
Yet age, by long experience well inform'd,
Well read, well temper'd, with religion warm'd, 640
That fire abated which impels rash youth,
Proud of his speed, to overshoot the truth,
As time improves the grape's authentic juice,
Mellows and makes the speech more fit for use,
And claims a rev'rence in its short'ning day,
That 'tis an honour and a joy to pay.
The fruits of age, less fair, are yet more sound,
Than those a brighter season pours around;

And, like the stores autumnal suns mature,
Through wintry rigours unimpair'd endure. 650
What is fanatic frenzy, scorn'd so much,
And dreaded more than a contagious touch?
I grant it dang'rous, and approve your fear,
That fire is catching if you draw too near;
But sage observers oft mistake the flame,
And give true piety that odious name.
To tremble (as the creature of an hour
Ought at the view of an almighty power)
Before his presence, at whose awful throne,
All tremble, in all worlds, except our own, 660
To supplicate his mercy, love his ways,
And prize them above pleasure, wealth, or praise,
Though common sense allow'd a casting voice,
And free from bias, must approve the choice,
Convicts a man fanatic in th' extreme,
And wild as madness in the world's esteem.
But that disease, when soberly defin'd,
Is the false fire of an o'erheated mind;
It views the truth with a distorted eye,
And either warps or lays it useless by; 670
'Tis narrow, selfish, arrogant, and draws
Its sordid nourishment from man's applause;
And, while at heart sin unrelinquish'd lies,
Presumes itself chief fav'rite of the skies.
'Tis such a light as putrefaction breeds
In fly-blown flesh whereon the maggot feeds,
Shines in the dark, but, usher'd into day,
The stench remains, the lustre dies away.
True bliss, if man may reach it, is compos'd
Of hearts in union mutually disclos'd; 680
And, farewell else all hope of pure delight,
Those hearts should be reclaim'd, renew'd, upright.
Bad men, profaning friendship's hallow'd name,
Form, in its stead, a covenant of shame,
A dark confed'racy against the laws
Of virtue, and religion's glorious cause:
They build each other up with dreadful skill,
As bastions set point blank against God's will;
Enlarge and fortify the dread redoubt,
Deeply resolv'd to shut a Saviour out; 690
Call legions up from hell to back the deed;
And, curst with conquest, finally succeed.
But souls that carry on a blest exchange
Of joys they meet with in their heav'nly range,

660 our *1782–1788, 1803*: your *1793–1800*.

And with a fearless confidence make known
The sorrows sympathy esteems its own,
Daily derive increasing light and force
From such communion in their pleasant course,
Feel less the journey's roughness and its length,
Meet their opposers with united strength, 700
And, one in heart, in int'rest and design,
Gird up each other to the race divine.

But Conversation, choose what theme we may,
And chiefly when religion leads the way,
Should flow, like waters after summer show'rs,
Not as if rais'd by mere mechanic pow'rs.
The Christian, in whose soul, though now distress'd,
Lives the dear thought of joys he once possess'd,
When all his glowing language issued forth
With God's deep stamp upon its current worth, 710
Will speak without disguise, and must impart,
Sad as it is, his undissembling heart,
Abhors constraint, and dares not feign a zeal,
Or seem to boast a fire, he does not feel.
The song of Sion is a tasteless thing,
Unless, when rising on a joyful wing,
The soul can mix with the celestial bands,
And give the strain the compass it demands.

Strange tidings these to tell a world who treat
All but their own experience as deceit! 720
Will they believe, though credulous enough
To swallow much upon much weaker proof,
That there are blest inhabitants of earth,
Partakers of a new ethereal birth,
Their hopes, desires, and purposes estrang'd
From things terrestrial, and divinely chang'd,
Their very language of a kind that speaks
The soul's sure int'rest in the good she seeks,
Who deal with scripture, its importance felt,
As Tully with philosophy once dealt, 730
And in the silent watches of the night,
And through the scenes of toil-renewing light,
The social walk, or solitary ride,
Keep still the dear companion at their side?
No—shame upon a self-disgracing age,
God's work may serve an ape upon a stage
With such a jest as fill'd with hellish glee
Certain invisibles as shrewd as he;
But veneration or respect finds none,
Save from the subjects of that work alone. 740
The world grown old, her deep discernment shows,
Claps spectacles on her sagacious nose,

Peruses closely the true Christian's face,
And finds it a mere mask of sly grimace,
Usurps God's office, lays his bosom bare,
And finds hypocrisy close lurking there,
And, serving God herself, through mere constraint,
Concludes his unfeign'd love of him, a feint.
And yet, God knows, look human nature through,
(And in due time the world shall know it too) 750
That since the flow'rs of Eden felt the blast,
That after man's defection laid all waste,
Sincerity towards th' heart-searching God
Has made the new-born creature her abode,
Nor shall be found in unregen'rate souls,
Till the last fire burn all between the poles.
Sincerity! Why 'tis his only pride,
Weak and imperfect in all grace beside,
He knows that God demands his heart entire,
And gives him all his just demands require. 760
Without it, his pretensions were as vain,
As, having it, he deems the world's disdain;
That great defect would cost him not alone
Man's favourable judgment, but his own;
His birthright shaken, and no longer clear,
Than while his conduct proves his heart sincere.
Retort the charge, and let the world be told
She boasts a confidence she does not hold;
That, conscious of her crimes, she feels instead
A cold misgiving, and a killing dread; 770
That, while in health, the ground of her support
Is madly to forget that life is short;
That sick she trembles knowing she must die,
Her hope presumption, and her faith a lie;
That while she dotes, and dreams that she believes,
She mocks her Maker, and herself deceives,
Her utmost reach, historical assent,
The doctrines warpt to what they never meant;
That truth itself is in her head as dull,
And useless, as a candle in a scull, 780
And all her love of God a groundless claim,
A trick upon the canvass, painted flame.
Tell her again, the sneer upon her face,
And all her censures of the work of grace,
Are insincere, meant only to conceal
A dread she would not, yet is forc'd to feel;
That in her heart the Christian she reveres,
And while she seems to scorn him, only fears.
A poet does not work by square or line,
As smiths and joiners perfect a design; 790

At least we moderns, our attention less,
Beyond th' example of our sires, digress,
And claim a right to scamper and run wide,
Wherever chance, caprice, or fancy guide.
The world and I fortuitously met;
I ow'd a trifle, and have paid the debt;
She did me wrong, I recompens'd the deed,
And, having struck the balance, now proceed.
Perhaps, however, as some years have pass'd,
Since she and I convers'd together last, 800
And I have liv'd recluse in rural shades,
Which seldom a distinct report pervades,
Great changes and new manners have occurr'd,
And blest reforms that I have never heard,
And she may now be as discreet and wise,
As once absurd in all discerning eyes.
Sobriety, perhaps, may now be found,
Where once intoxication press'd the ground;
The subtle and injurious may be just, 809
And he grown chaste that was the slave of lust;
Arts once esteem'd may be with shame dismiss'd;
Charity may relax the miser's fist;
The gamester may have cast his cards away,
Forgot to curse, and only kneel to pray.
It has indeed been told me (with what weight,
How credible, 'tis hard for me to state)
That fables old, that seem'd for ever mute,
Reviv'd, are hast'ning into fresh repute,
And gods and goddesses discarded long,
Like useless lumber, or a stroller's song, 820
Are bringing into vogue their heathen train,
And Jupiter bids fair to rule again;
That certain feasts are instituted now,
Where Venus hears the lover's tender vow;
That all Olympus through the country roves,
To consecrate our few remaining groves,
And echo learns politely to repeat
The praise of names for ages obsolete;
That having prov'd the weakness, it should seem,
Of revelation's ineffectual beam, 830
To bring the passions under sober sway,
And give the moral springs their proper play,
They mean to try what may at last be done,
By stout substantial gods of wood and stone,
And whether Roman rites may not produce
The virtues of old Rome for English use.
May such success attend the pious plan,
May Mercury once more embellish man,

837 such] much *1782*, *1786*.

Grace him again with long forgotten arts,
Reclaim his taste and brighten up his parts, 840
Make him athletic as in days of old,
Learn'd at the bar, in the palæstra bold,
Divest the rougher sex of female airs,
And teach the softer not to copy their's:
The change shall please, nor shall it matter aught
Who works the wonder, if it be but wrought.
'Tis time, however, if the case stand thus,
For us plain folks, and all who side with us,
To build our altar, confident and bold,
And say as stern Elijah said of old— 850
The strife now stands upon a fair award,
If Isr'el's Lord be God, then serve the Lord;
If he be silent, faith is all a whim,
Then Baal is the God, and worship him.
  Digression is so much in modern use,
Thought is so rare, and fancy so profuse,
Some never seem so wide of their intent,
As when returning to the theme they meant;
As mendicants, whose business is to roam,
Make ev'ry parish, but their own, their home. 860
Though such continual zigzags in a book,
Such drunken reelings, have an awkward look,
And I had rather creep to what is true,
Than rove and stagger with no mark in view;
Yet to consult a little, seem'd no crime,
The freakish humour of the present time:
But now to gather up what seems dispers'd,
And touch the subject I design'd at first,
May prove, though much beside the rules of art,
Best for the public, and my wisest part. 870
And first, let no man charge me that I mean
To clothe in sable every social scene,
And give good company a face severe,
As if they met around a father's bier;
For tell some men, that pleasure all their bent,
And laughter all their work, is life mispent,
Their wisdom bursts into this sage reply,
Then mirth is sin, and we should always cry.
To find the medium asks some share of wit,
And therefore 'tis a mark fools never hit. 880
But though life's valley be a vale of tears,
A brighter scene beyond that vale appears,
Whose glory, with a light that never fades,
Shoots between scatter'd rocks and op'ning shades,

872 sables *1782–1787*.

And, while it shows the land the soul desires,
The language of the land she seeks, inspires.
Thus touch'd, the tongue receives a sacred cure,
Of all that was absurd, profane, impure;
Held within modest bounds, the tide of speech
Pursues the course that truth and nature teach;
No longer labours merely to produce 891
The pomp of sound, or tinkle without use:
Where'er it winds, the salutary stream,
Sprightly and fresh, enriches ev'ry theme,
While all the happy man possess'd before,
The gift of nature, or the classic store,
Is made subservient to the grand design,
For which heav'n form'd the faculty divine.
So, should an idiot, while at large he strays,
Find the sweet lyre on which an artist plays, 900
With rash and awkward force the chords he shakes,
And grins with wonder at the jar he makes;
But let the wise and well-instructed hand
Once take the shell beneath his just command,
In gentle sounds it seems as it complain'd
Of the rude injuries it late sustain'd,
Till, tun'd at length to some immortal song,
It sounds Jehovah's name, and pours his praise along.

RETIREMENT

[Written Aug. to Oct., 1781. Published 1782.]

——— studiis florens ignobilis oti.
VIRG. Georg. Lib. 4.

HACKNEY'D in business, wearied at that oar
Which thousands, once fast chain'd to, quit no more,
But which, when life at ebb runs weak and low,
All wish, or seem to wish, they could forego;
The statesman, lawyer, merchant, man of trade,
Pants for the refuge of some rural shade,
Where, all his long anxieties forgot
Amid the charms of a sequester'd spot,
Or recollected only to gild o'er
And add a smile to what was sweet before, 10
He may possess the joys he thinks he sees,
Lay his old age upon the lap of ease,
Improve the remnant of his wasted span,
And, having liv'd a trifler, die a man.
Thus conscience pleads her cause within the breast,
Though long rebell'd against, not yet suppress'd,

And calls a creature form'd for God alone,
For heav'n's high purposes, and not his own;
Calls him away from selfish ends and aims,
From what debilitates and what inflames, 20
From cities, humming with a restless crowd,
Sordid as active, ignorant as loud,
Whose highest praise is that they live in vain,
The dupes of pleasure, or the slaves of gain,
Where works of man are cluster'd close around,
And works of God are hardly to be found,
To regions where, in spite of sin and woe,
Traces of Eden are still seen below,
Where mountain, river, forest, field, and grove,
Remind him of his Maker's power and love. 30
'Tis well if, look'd for at so late a day,
In the last scene of such a senseless play,
True wisdom will attend his feeble call,
And grace his action ere the curtain fall.
Souls that have long despis'd their heav'nly birth,
Their wishes all impregnated with earth,
For threescore years employ'd with ceaseless care
In catching smoke and feeding upon air,
Conversant only with the ways of men,
Rarely redeem the short remaining ten. 40
Invet'rate habits choke th' unfruitful heart,
Their fibres penetrate its tend'rest part,
And, draining its nutritious pow'rs to feed
Their noxious growth, starve ev'ry better seed.

Happy, if full of days—but happier far,
If, ere we yet discern life's ev'ning star,
Sick of the service of a world that feeds
Its patient drudges with dry chaff and weeds,
We can escape from custom's idiot sway,
To serve the Sov'reign we were born t' obey. 50
Then sweet to muse upon his skill display'd
(Infinite skill) in all that he has made!
To trace, in nature's most minute design,
The signature and stamp of pow'r divine,
Contrivance intricate, express'd with ease,
Where unassisted sight no beauty sees,
The shapely limb and lubricated joint,
Within the small dimensions of a point,
Muscle and nerve miraculously spun,
His mighty work, who speaks and it is done, 60
Th' invisible in things scarce seen reveal'd,
To whom an atom is an ample field;
To wonder at a thousand insect forms,
These hatch'd, and those resuscitated worms,

New life ordain'd and brighter scenes to share,
Once prone on earth, now buoyant upon air,
Whose shape would make them, had they bulk
and size,
More hideous foes than fancy can devise;
With helmet heads and dragon scales adorn'd,
The mighty myriads, now securely scorn'd, 70
Would mock the majesty of man's high birth,
Despise his bulwarks, and unpeople earth:
Then with a glance of fancy to survey,
Far as the faculty can stretch away,
Ten thousand rivers pour'd at his command
From urns that never fail through every land;
These like a deluge with impetuous force,
Those winding modestly a silent course;
The cloud-surmounting alps, the fruitful vales;
Seas on which ev'ry nation spreads her sails; 80
The sun, a world whence other worlds drink light;
The crescent moon, the diadem of night;
Stars countless, each in his appointed place,
Fast-anchor'd in the deep abyss of space—
At such a sight to catch the poet's flame,
And with a rapture like his own exclaim,
These are thy glorious works, thou source of good,
How dimly seen, how faintly understood!
Thine, and upheld by thy paternal care,
This universal frame, thus wondrous fair; 90
Thy pow'r divine, and bounty beyond thought,
Ador'd and prais'd in all that thou hast wrought.
Absorb'd in that immensity I see,
I shrink abas'd, and yet aspire to thee;
Instruct me, guide me, to that heav'nly day
Thy words more clearly than thy works display,
That, while thy truths my grosser thoughts refine,
I may resemble thee and call thee mine.
Oh blest proficiency! surpassing all
That men erroneously their glory call, 100
The recompense that arts or arms can yield,
The bar, the senate, or the tented field.
Compar'd with this sublimest life below,
Ye kings and rulers, what have courts to show?
Thus studied, us'd and consecrated thus,
On earth what is, seems form'd indeed for us;
Not as the plaything of a froward child,
Fretful unless diverted and beguil'd,

69 helmed *1782*, *1786*. 106 On earth what is] Whatever *is* *1782*, *1786*: What *is* *1787*: What is *1788*.

Much less to feed and fan the fatal fires
Of pride, ambition, or impure desires, 110
But as a scale by which the soul ascends
From mighty means to more important ends,
Securely, though by steps but rarely trod,
Mounts from inferior beings up to God,
And sees, by no fallacious light or dim,
Earth made for man, and man himself for him.
  Not that I mean t' approve, or would enforce,
A superstitious and monastic course:
Truth is not local, God alike pervades
And fills the world of traffic and the shades, 120
And may be fear'd amidst the busiest scenes,
Or scorn'd where business never intervenes.
But 'tis not easy with a mind like our's,
Conscious of weakness in its noblest pow'rs,
And in a world where, other ills apart,
The roving eye misleads the careless heart,
To limit thought, by nature prone to stray
Wherever freakish fancy points the way;
To bid the pleadings of self-love be still,
Resign our own and seek our Maker's will; 130
To spread the page of scripture, and compare
Our conduct with the laws engraven there;
To measure all that passes in the breast,
Faithfully, fairly, by that sacred test;
To dive into the secret deeps within,
To spare no passion and no fav'rite sin,
And search the themes, important above all,
Ourselves and our recov'ry from our fall.
But leisure, silence, and a mind releas'd
From anxious thoughts how wealth may be increas'd,
How to secure in some propitious hour 141
The point of int'rest or the post of pow'r,
A soul serene, and equally retir'd
From objects too much dreaded or desir'd,
Safe from the clamours of perverse dispute,
At least are friendly to the great pursuit.
  Op'ning the map of God's extensive plan,
We find a little isle, this life of man;
Eternity's unknown expanse appears
Circling around and limiting his years; 150
The busy race examine and explore
Each creek and cavern of the dang'rous shore,
With care collect what in their eyes excels,
Some shining pebbles, and some weeds and shells;
Thus laden, dream that they are rich and great,
And happiest he that groans beneath his weight:

The waves o'ertake them in their serious play,
And ev'ry hour sweeps multitudes away;
They shriek and sink, survivors start and weep,
Pursue their sport, and follow to the deep. 160
A few forsake the throng; with lifted eyes
Ask wealth of heav'n, and gain a real prize—
Truth, wisdom, grace, and peace like that above,
Seal'd with his signet whom they serve and love;
Scorn'd by the rest, with patient hope they wait
A kind release from their imperfect state,
And, unregretted, are soon snatch'd away
From scenes of sorrow into glorious day.
  Nor these alone prefer a life recluse,
Who seek retirement for its proper use; 170
The love of change that lives in ev'ry breast,
Genius, and temper, and desire of rest,
Discordant motives in one centre meet,
And each inclines its vot'ry to retreat.
Some minds by nature are averse to noise,
And hate the tumult half the world enjoys,
The lure of av'rice, or the pompous prize
That courts display before ambitious eyes;
The fruits that hang on pleasure's flow'ry stem,
Whate'er enchants them, are no snares to them.
To them the deep recess of dusky groves, 181
Or forest where the deer securely roves,
The fall of waters, and the song of birds,
And hills that echo to the distant herds,
Are luxuries excelling all the glare
The world can boast, and her chief fav'rites share.
With eager step, and carelessly array'd,
For such a cause the poet seeks the shade,
From all he sees he catches new delight,
Pleas'd fancy claps her pinions at the sight, 190
The rising or the setting orb of day,
The clouds that flit, or slowly float away,
Nature in all the various shapes she wears,
Frowning in storms, or breathing gentle airs,
The snowy robe her wintry state assumes,
Her summer heats, her fruits, and her perfumes—
All, all alike transport the glowing bard,
Success in rhyme his glory and reward.
Oh nature! whose Elysian scenes disclose
His bright perfections at whose word they rose, 200
Next to that pow'r who form'd thee and sustains,
Be thou the great inspirer of my strains.
Still, as I touch the lyre, do thou expand
Thy genuine charms, and guide an artless hand,

That I may catch a fire but rarely known,
Give useful light though I should miss renown,
And, poring on thy page, whose ev'ry line
Bears proof of an intelligence divine,
May feel an heart enrich'd by what it pays,
That builds its glory on its Maker's praise. 210
Woe to the man whose wit disclaims its use,
Glitt'ring in vain, or only to seduce,
Who studies nature with a wanton eye,
Admires the work, but slips the lesson by;
His hours of leisure and recess employs
In drawing pictures of forbidden joys,
Retires to blazon his own worthless name,
Or shoot the careless with a surer aim.
The lover too shuns business and alarms,
Tender idolater of absent charms. 220
Saints offer nothing in their warmest pray'rs,
That he devotes not with a zeal like their's;
'Tis consecration of his heart, soul, time,
And ev'ry thought that wanders, is a crime.
In sighs he worships his supremely fair,
And weeps a sad libation in despair,
Adores a creature, and, devout in vain,
Wins in return an answer of disdain.
As woodbine weds the plant within her reach,
Rough elm, or smooth-grain'd ash, or glossy beech,
In spiral rings ascends the trunk, and lays 231
Her golden tassels on the leafy sprays,
But does a mischief while she lends a grace,
Strait'ning its growth by such a strict embrace—
So love, that clings around the noblest minds,
Forbids th' advancement of the soul he binds;
The suitor's air indeed he soon improves,
And forms it to the taste of her he loves,
Teaches his eyes a language, and no less
Refines his speech, and fashions his address: 240
But farewell promises of happier fruits,
Manly designs, and learning's grave pursuits;
Girt with a chain he cannot wish to break,
His only bliss is sorrow for her sake;
Who will may pant for glory and excel,
Her smile his aim, all higher aims farewell!
Thyrsis, Alexis, or whatever name
May least offend against so pure a flame,
Though sage advice of friends the most sincere
Sounds harshly in so delicate an ear, 250
And lovers of all creatures, tame or wild,
Can least brook management, however mild,

Yet let a poet (poetry disarms
The fiercest animals with magic charms)
Risque an intrusion on thy pensive mood,
And woo and win thee to thy proper good.
Pastoral images and still retreats,
Umbrageous walks and solitary seats,
Sweet birds in concert with harmonious streams,
Soft airs, nocturnal vigils, and day dreams, 260
Are all enchantments in a case like thine,
Conspire against thy peace with one design,
Sooth thee to make thee but a surer prey,
And feed the fire that wastes thy pow'rs away.
Up—God has form'd thee with a wiser view,
Not to be led in chains, but to subdue;
Calls thee to cope with enemies, and first
Points out a conflict with thyself, the worst.
Woman indeed, a gift he would bestow
When he design'd a paradise below, 270
The richest earthly boon his hands afford,
Deserves to be belov'd, but not ador'd.
Post away swiftly to more active scenes,
Collect the scatter'd truths that study gleans,
Mix with the world, but with its wiser part,
No longer give an image all thine heart;
Its empire is not her's, nor is it thine,
'Tis God's just claim, prerogative divine.
  Virtuous and faithful HEBERDEN! whose skill
Attempts no task it cannot well fulfil, 280
Gives melancholy up to nature's care,
And sends the patient into purer air.
Look where he comes—in this embow'r'd alcove—
Stand close conceal'd, and see a statue move:
Lips busy, and eyes fixt, foot falling slow,
Arms hanging idly down, hands clasp'd below,
Interpret to the marking eye distress,
Such as its symptoms can alone express.
That tongue is silent now; that silent tongue
Could argue once, could jest or join the song, 290
Could give advice, could censure or commend,
Or charm the sorrows of a drooping friend.
Renounc'd alike its office and its sport,
Its brisker and its graver strains fall short;
Both fail beneath a fever's secret sway,
And, like a summer-brook, are past away.
This is a sight for pity to peruse,
Till she resemble faintly what she views,
Till sympathy contract a kindred pain,
Pierc'd with the woes that she laments in vain. 300

This, of all maladies that man infest,
Claims most compassion, and receives the least:
Job felt it, when he groan'd beneath the rod
And the barb'd arrows of a frowning God;
And such emollients as his friends could spare,
Friends such as his for modern Jobs prepare.
Blest, rather curst, with hearts that never feel,
Kept snug in caskets of close-hammer'd steel,
With mouths made only to grin wide and eat,
And minds that deem derided pain a treat, 310
With limbs of British oak, and nerves of wire,
And wit that puppet-prompters might inspire,
Their sov'reign nostrum is a clumsy joke,
On pangs enforc'd with God's severest stroke.
But, with a soul that ever felt the sting
Of sorrow, sorrow is a sacred thing:
Not to molest, or irritate, or raise
A laugh at his expence, is slender praise;
He that has not usurp'd the name of man
Does all, and deems too little all, he can, 320
T' assuage the throbbings of the fester'd part,
And staunch the bleedings of a broken heart.
'Tis not, as heads that never ache suppose,
Forg'ry of fancy, and a dream of woes;
Man is an harp whose chords elude the sight,
Each yielding harmony dispos'd aright;
The screws revers'd (a task which if he please
God in a moment executes with ease),
Ten thousand thousand strings at once go loose,
Lost, till he tune them, all their pow'r and use. 330
Then neither heathy wilds, nor scenes as fair
As ever recompens'd the peasant's care,
Nor soft declivities with tufted hills,
Nor view of waters turning busy mills,
Parks in which art preceptress nature weds,
Nor gardens interspers'd with flow'ry beds,
Nor gales that catch the scent of blooming groves,
And waft it to the mourner as he roves,
Can call up life into his faded eye,
That passes all he sees unheeded by: 340
No wounds like those a wounded spirit feels,
No cure for such, till God who makes them, heals.
And thou, sad suff'rer under nameless ill,
That yields not to the touch of human skill,
Improve the kind occasion, understand
A Father's frown, and kiss his chast'ning hand:

318 his] its *1782*, *1786*.

To thee the day-spring, and the blaze of noon,
The purple ev'ning and resplendent moon,
The stars that, sprinkled o'er the vault of night,
Seem drops descending in a show'r of light, 350
Shine not, or undesir'd and hated shine,
Seen through the medium of a cloud like thine:
Yet seek him, in his favour life is found,
All bliss beside—a shadow or a sound:
Then heav'n, eclips'd so long, and this dull earth,
Shall seem to start into a second birth;
Nature, assuming a more lovely face,
Borrowing a beauty from the works of grace,
Shall be despis'd and overlook'd no more,
Shall fill thee with delights unfelt before, 360
Impart to things inanimate a voice,
And bid her mountains and her hills rejoice;
The sound shall run along the winding vales,
And thou enjoy an Eden ere it fails.
Ye groves (the statesman at his desk exclaims,
Sick of a thousand disappointed aims,)
My patrimonial treasure and my pride,
Beneath your shades your grey possessor hide,
Receive me languishing for that repose
The servant of the public never knows. 370
Ye saw me once (ah, those regretted days
When boyish innocence was all my praise!)
Hour after hour delightfully allot
To studies then familiar, since forgot,
And cultivate a taste for ancient song,
Catching its ardour as I mus'd along;
Nor seldom, as propitious heav'n might send,
What once I valued and could boast, a friend,
Were witnesses how cordially I press'd
His undissembling virtue to my breast; 380
Receive me now, not uncorrupt as then,
Nor guiltless of corrupting other men,
But vers'd in arts that, while they seem to stay
A falling empire, hasten its decay.
To the fair haven of my native home,
The wreck of what I was, fatigu'd, I come;
For once I can approve the patriot's voice,
And make the course he recommends my choice;
We meet at last in one sincere desire,
His wish and mine both prompt me to retire. 390
'Tis done—he steps into the welcome chaise,
Lolls at his ease behind four handsome bays,
That whirl away from business and debate
The disincumber'd Atlas of the state.

384 fallen *1786.*

Ask not the boy, who when the breeze of morn
First shakes the glitt'ring drops from every thorn
Unfolds his flock, then under bank or bush
Sits linking cherry stones, or platting rush,
How fair is freedom?—he was always free:
To carve his rustic name upon a tree, 400
To snare the mole, or with ill-fashion'd hook,
To draw th' incautious minnow from the brook,
Are life's prime pleasures in his simple view,
His flock the chief concern he ever knew—
She shines but little in his heedless eyes,
The good we never miss we rarely prize:
But ask the noble drudge in state affairs,
Escap'd from office and its constant cares,
What charms he sees in freedom's smile express'd,
In freedom lost so long, now repossess'd; 410
The tongue whose strains were cogent as commands,
Rever'd at home, and felt in foreign lands,
Shall own itself a stamm'rer in that cause,
Or plead its silence as its best applause.
He knows indeed that, whether dress'd or rude,
Wild without art, or artfully subdu'd,
Nature in ev'ry form inspires delight,
But never mark'd her with so just a sight.
Her hedge-row shrubs, a variegated store,
With woodbine and wild roses mantled o'er, 420
Green balks and furrow'd lands, the stream that spreads
Its cooling vapour o'er the dewy meads,
Downs that almost escape th' inquiring eye,
That melt and fade into the distant sky,
Beauties he lately slighted as he pass'd,
Seem all created since he travell'd last.
Master of all th' enjoyments he design'd,
No rough annoyance rankling in his mind,
What early philosophic hours he keeps,
How regular his meals, how sound he sleeps! 430
Not sounder he that on the mainmast head,
While morning kindles with a windy red,
Begins a long look-out for distant land,
Nor quits, till ev'ning watch, his giddy stand,
Then swift descending with a seaman's haste,
Slips to his hammock, and forgets the blast.
He chooses company, but not the squire's,
Whose wit is rudeness, whose good breeding tires;
Nor yet the parson's, who would gladly come,
Obsequious when abroad, though proud at home; 440
Nor can he much affect the neighb'ring peer,
Whose toe of emulation treads too near;

But wisely seeks a more convenient friend,
With whom, dismissing forms, he may unbend!
A man whom marks of condescending grace
Teach, while they flatter him, his proper place:
Who comes when call'd, and at a word withdraws,
Speaks with reserve, and listens with applause;
Some plain mechanic, who, without pretence
To birth or wit, nor gives nor takes offence; 450
On whom he rests well-pleas'd his weary pow'rs,
And talks and laughs away his vacant hours.
The tide of life, swift always in its course,
May run in cities with a brisker force,
But no where with a current so serene,
Or half so clear, as in the rural scene.
Yet how fallacious is all earthly bliss,
What obvious truths the wisest heads may miss;
Some pleasures live a month, and some a year,
But short the date of all we gather here; 460
No happiness is felt, except the true,
That does not charm the more for being new.
This observation, as it chanc'd, not made,
Or if the thought occurr'd, not duly weigh'd,
He sighs—for, after all, by slow degrees,
The spot he lov'd has lost the pow'r to please;
To cross his ambling pony day by day,
Seems at the best but dreaming life away;
The prospect, such as might enchant despair,
He views it not, or sees no beauty there; 470
With aching heart, and discontented looks,
Returns at noon to billiards or to books,
But feels, while grasping at his faded joys,
A secret thirst of his renounc'd employs.
He chides the tardiness of ev'ry post,
Pants to be told of battles won or lost,
Blames his own indolence, observes, though late,
'Tis criminal to leave a sinking state,
Flies to the levee, and, receiv'd with grace,
Kneels, kisses hands, and shines again in place. 480
  Suburban villas, highway-side retreats,
That dread th' encroachment of our growing streets,
Tight boxes, neatly sash'd, and in a blaze
With all a July sun's collected rays,
Delight the citizen, who, gasping there,
Breathes clouds of dust, and calls it country air.
Oh sweet retirement, who would balk the thought,
That could afford retirement, or could not?

461 No] Nor *1782–1788.* 462 the] thee *1793–1798, 1800, 1803.*
484 July's *1800.*

'Tis such an easy walk, so smooth and straight,
The second milestone fronts the garden gate; 490
A step if fair, and, if a shower approach,
You find safe shelter in the next stage-coach.
There, prison'd in a parlour snug and small,
Like bottled wasps upon a southern wall,
The man of bus'ness and his friends compress'd,
Forget their labours, and yet find no rest;
But still 'tis rural—trees are to be seen
From ev'ry window, and the fields are green;
Ducks paddle in the pond before the door,
And what could a remoter scene show more? 500
A sense of elegance we rarely find
The portion of a mean or vulgar mind,
And ignorance of better things makes man,
Who cannot much, rejoice in what he can;
And he that deems his leisure well bestow'd
In contemplation of a turnpike road,
Is occupied as well, employs his hours
As wisely, and as much improves his pow'rs,
As he that slumbers in pavilions grac'd
With all the charms of an accomplish'd taste. 510
Yet hence, alas! insolvencies; and hence
The unpitied victim of ill-judg'd expence,
From all his wearisome engagements freed,
Shakes hands with business, and retires indeed.
Your prudent grand-mammas, ye modern belles,
Content with Bristol, Bath, and Tunbridge-wells,
When health requir'd it would consent to roam,
Else more attach'd to pleasures found at home.
But now alike, gay widow, virgin, wife,
Ingenious to diversify dull life, 520
In coaches, chaises, caravans, and hoys,
Fly to the coast for daily, nightly joys,
And all, impatient of dry land, agree
With one consent, to rush into the sea.—
Ocean exhibits, fathomless and broad,
Much of the power and majesty of God.
He swathes about the swelling of the deep,
That shines and rests, as infants smile and sleep;
Vast as it is, it answers as it flows
The breathings of the lightest air that blows; 530
Curling and whit'ning over all the waste,
The rising waves obey th' increasing blast,
Abrupt and horrid as the tempest roars,
Thunder and flash upon the stedfast shores,
Till he that rides the whirlwind checks the rein,
Then, all the world of waters sleeps again.—

Nereids or Dryads, as the fashion leads,
Now in the floods, now panting in the meads,
Vot'ries of pleasure still, where'er she dwells,
Near barren rocks, in palaces, or cells, 540
Oh grant a poet leave to recommend
(A poet fond of nature, and your friend)
Her slighted works to your admiring view;
Her works must needs excel, who fashion'd you.
Would ye, when rambling in your morning ride,
With some unmeaning coxcomb at your side,
Condemn the prattler for his idle pains,
To waste unheard the music of his strains,
And, deaf to all th' impertinence of tongue,
That, while it courts, affronts and does you wrong,
Mark well the finish'd plan without a fault, 551
The seas globose and huge, th' o'erarching vault,
Earth's millions daily fed, a world employ'd
In gath'ring plenty yet to be enjoy'd,
Till gratitude grew vocal in the praise
Of God, beneficent in all his ways;
Grac'd with such wisdom, how would beauty shine!
Ye want but that to seem indeed divine.

Anticipated rents, and bills unpaid,
Force many a shining youth into the shade, 560
Not to redeem his time, but his estate,
And play the fool, but at a cheaper rate:
There, hid in loath'd obscurity, remov'd
From pleasures left, but never more belov'd,
He just endures, and with a sickly spleen
Sighs o'er the beauties of the charming scene.
Nature indeed looks prettily in rhyme;
Streams tinkle sweetly in poetic chime;
The warblings of the blackbird, clear and strong,
Are musical enough in Thomson's song; 570
And Cobham's groves, and Windsor's green retreats,
When Pope describes them, have a thousand sweets;
He likes the country, but in truth must own,
Most likes it, when he studies it in town.

Poor Jack—no matter who—for when I blame
I pity, and must therefore sink the name,
Liv'd in his saddle, lov'd the chase, the course,
And always, ere he mounted, kiss'd his horse.
Th' estate his sires had own'd in ancient years
Was quickly distanc'd, match'd against a peer's.
Jack vanish'd, was regretted and forgot; 581
'Tis wild good-nature's never-failing lot.
At length, when all had long suppos'd him dead,
By cold submersion, razor, rope, or lead,

My lord, alighting at his usual place,
The Crown, took notice of an ostler's face.
Jack knew his friend, but hop'd in that disguise
He might escape the most observing eyes,
And whistling, as if unconcern'd and gay,
Curried his nag, and look'd another way. 590
Convinc'd at last, upon a nearer view,
'Twas he, the same, the very Jack he knew,
O'erwhelm'd at once with wonder, grief, and joy,
He press'd him much to quit his base employ;
His countenance, his purse, his heart, his hand,
Infl'ence and pow'r, were all at his command:
Peers are not always gen'rous as well-bred,
But Granby was, meant truly what he said.
Jack bow'd, and was oblig'd—confess'd 'twas strange
That so retir'd he should not wish a change, 600
But knew no medium between guzzling beer,
And his old stint—three thousand pounds a year.
  Thus some retire to nourish hopeless woe;
Some seeking happiness not found below;
Some to comply with humour, and a mind
To social scenes by nature disinclin'd;
Some sway'd by fashion, some by deep disgust;
Some self-impoverish'd, and because they must;
But few that court Retirement are aware
Of half the toils they must encounter there. 610
  Lucrative offices are seldom lost
For want of pow'rs proportion'd to the post:
Give e'en a dunce th' employment he desires,
And he soon finds the talents it requires;
A business with an income at its heels
Furnishes always oil for its own wheels.
But in his arduous enterprise to close
His active years with indolent repose,
He finds the labours of that state exceed
His utmost faculties, severe indeed. 620
'Tis easy to resign a toilsome place,
But not to manage leisure with a grace;
Absence of occupation is not rest,
A mind quite vacant is a mind distress'd.
The vet'ran steed, excus'd his task at length,
In kind compassion of his failing strength,
And turn'd into the park or mead to graze,
Exempt from future service all his days,
There feels a pleasure perfect in its kind,
Ranges at liberty, and snuffs the wind: 630
But when his lord would quit the busy road,
To taste a joy like that he has bestow'd,

He proves, less happy than his favour'd brute,
A life of ease a difficult pursuit.
Thought, to the man that never thinks, may seem
As natural as, when asleep, to dream;
But reveries (for human minds will act)
Specious in show, impossible in fact,
Those flimsy webs that break as soon as wrought,
Attain not to the dignity of thought: 640
Nor yet the swarms that occupy the brain,
Where dreams of dress, intrigue, and pleasure reign;
Nor such as useless conversation breeds,
Or lust engenders, and indulgence feeds.
Whence, and what are we? to what end ordain'd?
What means the drama by the world sustain'd?
Business or vain amusement, care or mirth,
Divide the frail inhabitants of earth.
Is duty a mere sport, or an employ?
Life an intrusted talent, or a toy? 650
Is there, as reason, conscience, scripture, say,
Cause to provide for a great future day,
When, earth's assign'd duration at an end,
Man shall be summon'd and the dead attend?
The trumpet—will it sound? the curtain rise?
And show th' august tribunal of the skies,
Where no prevarication shall avail,
Where eloquence and artifice shall fail,
The pride of arrogant distinctions fall,
And conscience and our conduct judge us all? 660
Pardon me, ye that give the midnight oil
To learned cares or philosophic toil,
Though I revere your honourable names,
Your useful labours and important aims,
And hold the world indebted to your aid,
Enrich'd with the discoveries ye have made;
Yet let me stand excus'd, if I esteem
A mind employ'd on so sublime a theme,
Pushing her bold inquiry to the date
And outline of the present transient state, 670
And, after poising her advent'rous wings,
Settling at last upon eternal things,
Far more intelligent, and better taught
The strenuous use of profitable thought,
Than ye, when happiest, and enlighten'd most,
And highest in renown, can justly boast.

A mind unnerv'd, or indispos'd to bear
The weight of subjects worthiest of her care,
Whatever hopes a change of scene inspires,
Must change her nature, or in vain retires. 680

An idler is a watch that wants both hands,
As useless if it goes as when it stands.
Books therefore, not the scandal of the shelves,
In which lewd sensualists print out themselves;
Nor those in which the stage gives vice a blow,
With what success let modern manners show;
Nor his who, for the bane of thousands born,
Built God a church, and laugh'd his word to scorn,
Skilful alike to seem devout and just,
And stab religion with a sly side-thrust; 690
Nor those of learn'd philologists, who chase
A panting syllable through time and space,
Start it at home, and hunt it in the dark,
To Gaul, to Greece, and into Noah's ark;
But such as learning without false pretence,
The friend of truth, th' associate of sound sense,
And such as, in the zeal of good design,
Strong judgment lab'ring in the scripture mine,
All such as manly and great souls produce,
Worthy to live, and of eternal use: 700
Behold in these what leisure hours demand,
Amusement and true knowledge hand in hand.
Luxury gives the mind a childish cast,
And while she polishes, perverts the taste;
Habits of close attention, thinking heads,
Become more rare as dissipation spreads,
Till authors hear at length, one gen'ral cry,
Tickle and entertain us, or we die.
The loud demand, from year to year the same,
Beggars invention and makes fancy lame, 710
Till farce itself, most mournfully jejune,
Calls for the kind assistance of a tune;
And novels (witness ev'ry month's review)
Belie their name, and offer nothing new.
The mind, relaxing into needful sport,
Should turn to writers of an abler sort,
Whose wit well manag'd, and whose classic style,
Give truth a lustre, and make wisdom smile.
Friends (for I cannot stint, as some have done,
Too rigid in my view, that name to one; 720
Though one, I grant it, in the gen'rous breast,
Will stand advanc'd a step above the rest:
Flow'rs by that name promiscuously we call,
But one, the rose, the regent of them all)—
Friends, not adopted with a school-boy's haste,
But chosen with a nice discerning taste,
Well-born, well-disciplin'd, who, plac'd apart
From vulgar minds, have honour much at heart,

And, though the world may think th' ingredients odd,
The love of virtue, and the fear of God! 730
Such friends prevent what else would soon succeed,
A temper rustic as the life we lead,
And keep the polish of the manners clean,
As their's who bustle in the busiest scene;
For solitude, however some may rave,
Seeming a sanctuary, proves a grave,
A sepulchre in which the living lie,
Where all good qualities grow sick and die.
I praise the Frenchman[1], his remark was shrewd—
How sweet, how passing sweet, is solitude! 740
But grant me still a friend in my retreat,
Whom I may whisper—solitude is sweet.
Yet neither these delights, nor aught beside
That appetite can ask, or wealth provide,
Can save us always from a tedious day,
Or shine the dulness of still life away:
Divine communion, carefully enjoy'd,
Or sought with energy, must fill the void.
Oh sacred art, to which alone life owes
Its happiest seasons, and a peaceful close, 750
Scorn'd in a world, indebted to that scorn
For evils daily felt and hardly born,
Not knowing thee, we reap, with bleeding hands,
Flow'rs of rank odour upon thorny lands,
And, while experience cautions us in vain,
Grasp seeming happiness, and find it pain.
Despondence, self-deserted in her grief,
Lost by abandoning her own relief,
Murmuring and ungrateful discontent,
That scorns afflictions mercifully meant, 760
Those humours tart as wines upon the fret,
Which idleness and weariness beget;
These, and a thousand plagues that haunt the breast,
Fond of the phantom of an earthly rest,
Divine communion chases, as the day
Drives to their dens th' obedient beasts of prey.
See Judah's promis'd king, bereft of all,
Driv'n out an exile from the face of Saul,
To distant caves the lonely wand'rer flies,
To seek that peace a tyrant's frown denies. 770
Hear the sweet accents of his tuneful voice,
Hear him, o'erwhelm'd with sorrow, yet rejoice;
No womanish or wailing grief has part,
No, not a moment, in his royal heart;

[1] Bruyere [C.].

'Tis manly music, such as martyrs make,
Suff'ring with gladness for a Saviour's sake;
His soul exults, hope animates his lays,
The sense of mercy kindles into praise,
And wilds, familiar with the lion's roar,
Ring with ecstatic sounds unheard before: 780
'Tis love like his that can alone defeat
The foes of man, or make a desert sweet.

Religion does not censure or exclude
Unnumber'd pleasures harmlessly pursu'd;
To study culture, and with artful toil
To meliorate and tame the stubborn soil;
To give dissimilar yet fruitful lands
The grain, or herb, or plant, that each demands;
To cherish virtue in an humble state,
And share the joys your bounty may create; 790
To mark the matchless workings of the pow'r
That shuts within its seed the future flow'r,
Bids these in elegance of form excel,
In colour these, and those delight the smell,
Sends nature forth the daughter of the skies,
To dance on earth, and charm all human eyes;
To teach the canvass innocent deceit,
Or lay the landscape on the snowy sheet—
These, these are arts pursu'd without a crime,
That leave no stain upon the wing of time. 800

Me poetry (or, rather, notes that aim
Feebly and vainly at poetic fame)
Employs, shut out from more important views,
Fast by the banks of the slow winding Ouse;
Content if, thus sequester'd, I may raise
A monitor's, though not a poet's praise,
And while I teach an art too little known,
To close life wisely, may not waste my own.

779 a *1798*[2], *1800*. 793 bids *1782*, *1786*, *1803*; bid *1787-1800*.

THE TASK, A POEM, IN SIX BOOKS.

BY WILLIAM COWPER, OF THE INNER TEMPLE, ESQ.

Fit surculus arbor.

ANONYM.

To which are added,

BY THE SAME AUTHOR,

An EPISTLE to JOSEPH HILL, Esq. TIROCINIUM, or a REVIEW of SCHOOLS, and the HISTORY of JOHN GILPIN.

LONDON:

PRINTED FOR J. JOHNSON, N° 72, ST PAULS CHURCH-YARD

1785.

ADVERTISEMENT

The history of the following production is briefly this:—A lady, fond of blank verse, demanded a poem of that kind from the author, and gave him the Sofa for a subject. He obeyed; and, having much leisure, connected another subject with it; and, pursuing the train of thought to which his situation and turn of mind led him, brought forth at length, instead of the trifle which he at first intended, a serious affair—a Volume!

In the Poem on the subject of Education, he would be very sorry to stand suspected of having aimed his censure at any particular school. His objections are such as naturally apply themselves to schools in general. If there were not, as for the most part there is, wilful neglect in those who manage them, and an omission even of such discipline as they are susceptible of, the objects are yet too numerous for minute attention; and the aching hearts of ten thousand parents, mourning under the bitterest of all disappointments, attest the truth of the allegation. His quarrel, therefore, is with the mischief at large, and not with any particular instance of it.

THE TASK

[Written July (?), 1783, to Sept., 1784. Published 1785.]

BOOK I

THE SOFA

ARGUMENT OF THE FIRST BOOK.—Historical deduction of seats, from the stool to the Sofa—A School-boy's ramble—A walk in the country—The scene described—Rural sounds as well as sights delightful—Another walk—Mistake concerning the charms of solitude corrected—Colonnades commended—Alcove, and the view from it—The wilderness—The grove—The thresher—The necessity and the benefits of exercise—The works of nature superior to, and in some instances inimitable by, art—The wearisomeness of what is commonly called a life of pleasure—Change of scene sometimes expedient—A common described, and the character of crazy Kate introduced—Gipsies—The blessings of civilized life—That state most favourable to virtue—The South Sea islanders compassionated, but chiefly Omai—His present state of mind supposed—Civilized life friendly to virtue, but not great cities—Great cities, and London in particular, allowed their due praise, but censured—Fete champetre—The book concludes with a reflection on the fatal effects of dissipation and effeminacy upon our public measures.

I SING the SOFA. I, who lately sang
Truth, Hope, and Charity[1], and touch'd with awe
The solemn chords, and with a trembling hand,
Escap'd with pain from that advent'rous flight,
Now seek repose upon an humbler theme;
The theme though humble, yet august and proud
Th' occasion—for the Fair commands the song.
 Time was, when clothing sumptuous or for use,
Save their own painted skins, our sires had none.
As yet black breeches were not; satin smooth, 10
Or velvet soft, or plush with shaggy pile:
The hardy chief upon the rugged rock
Wash'd by the sea, or on the grav'ly bank
Thrown up by wintry torrents roaring loud,
Fearless of wrong, repos'd his weary strength.
Those barb'rous ages past, succeeded next
The birth-day of invention; weak at first,
Dull in design, and clumsy to perform.
Joint-stools were then created; on three legs
Upborn they stood. Three legs upholding firm 20
A massy slab, in fashion square or round.
On such a stool immortal Alfred sat,

[1] See Poems, vol. i. [C.]

Argument 11 *after* introduced *1785, 1786 have* upon it.

And sway'd the sceptre of his infant realms:
And such in ancient halls and mansions drear
May still be seen; but perforated sore,
And drill'd in holes, the solid oak is found,
By worms voracious eating through and through.
At length a generation more refin'd
Improv'd the simple plan; made three legs four,
Gave them a twisted form vermicular, 30
And o'er the seat, with plenteous wadding stuff'd,
Induc'd a splendid cover, green and blue,
Yellow and red, of tap'stry richly wrought,
And woven close, or needle-work sublime.
There might ye see the piony spread wide,
The full-blown rose, the shepherd and his lass,
Lap-dog and lambkin with black staring eyes,
And parrots with twin cherries in their beak.
Now came the cane from India, smooth and bright
With Nature's varnish; sever'd into stripes 40
That interlac'd each other, these supplied
Of texture firm a lattice-work, that brac'd
The new machine, and it became a chair.
But restless was the chair; the back erect
Distress'd the weary loins, that felt no ease;
The slipp'ry seat betray'd the sliding part
That press'd it, and the feet hung dangling down,
Anxious in vain to find the distant floor.
These for the rich: the rest, whom fate had plac'd
In modest mediocrity, content 50
With base materials, sat on well-tann'd hides,
Obdurate and unyielding, glassy smooth,
With here and there a tuft of crimson yarn,
Or scarlet crewel, in the cushion fixt;
If cushion might be call'd, what harder seem'd
Than the firm oak of which the frame was form'd.
No want of timber then was felt or fear'd
In Albion's happy isle. The lumber stood
Pond'rous and fixt by its own massy weight.
But elbows still were wanting; these, some say, 60
An alderman of Cripplegate contriv'd:
And some ascribe th' invention to a priest
Burly and big, and studious of his ease.
But, rude at first, and not with easy slope
Receding wide, they press'd against the ribs,
And bruis'd the side; and, elevated high,
Taught the rais'd shoulders to invade the ears.
Long time elaps'd or e'er our rugged sires
Complain'd, though incommodiously pent in,

58 lumber *1800 errata*: umber *all previous edd.*

And ill at ease behind. The ladies first 70
'Gan murmur, as became the softer sex.
Ingenious fancy, never better pleas'd
Than when employ'd t' accommodate the fair,
Heard the sweet moan with pity, and devis'd
The soft settee; one elbow at each end,
And in the midst an elbow it receiv'd,
United yet divided, twain at once.
So sit two kings of Brentford on one throne;
And so two citizens who take the air,
Close pack'd, and smiling, in a chaise and one. 80
But relaxation of the languid frame,
By soft recumbency of outstretch'd limbs,
Was bliss reserv'd for happier days. So slow
The growth of what is excellent; so hard
T' attain perfection in this nether world.
Thus first necessity invented stools,
Convenience next suggested elbow-chairs,
And luxury th' accomplish'd SOFA last.

The nurse sleeps sweetly, hir'd to watch the sick,
Whom snoring she disturbs. As sweetly he, 90
Who quits the coach-box at the midnight hour
To sleep within the carriage more secure,
His legs depending at the open door.
Sweet sleep enjoys the curate in his desk,
The tedious rector drawling o'er his head;
And sweet the clerk below. But neither sleep
Of lazy nurse, who snores the sick man dead,
Nor his who quits the box at midnight hour
To slumber in the carriage more secure,
Nor sleep enjoy'd by curate in his desk, 100
Nor yet the dozings of the clerk, are sweet,
Compar'd with the repose the SOFA yields.

Oh may I live exempted (while I live
Guiltless of pamper'd appetite obscene)
From pangs arthritic, that infest the toe
Of libertine excess. The SOFA suits
The gouty limb, 'tis true; but gouty limb,
Though on a SOFA, may I never feel:
For I have lov'd the rural walk through lanes
Of grassy swarth, close cropt by nibbling sheep,
And skirted thick with intertexture firm 111
Of thorny boughs; have lov'd the rural walk
O'er hills, through valleys, and by rivers' brink,
E'er since a truant boy I pass'd my bounds
T' enjoy a ramble on the banks of Thames;
And still remember, nor without regret
Of hours that sorrow since has much endear'd,

How oft, my slice of pocket store consum'd,
Still hung'ring, pennyless and far from home,
I fed on scarlet hips and stony haws, 120
Or blushing crabs, or berries, that emboss
The bramble, black as jet, or sloes austere.
Hard fare! but such as boyish appetite
Disdains not; nor the palate, undeprav'd
By culinary arts, unsav'ry deems.
No SOFA then awaited my return;
Nor SOFA then I needed. Youth repairs
His wasted spirits quickly, by long toil
Incurring short fatigue; and, though our years
As life declines speed rapidly away, 130
And not a year but pilfers as he goes
Some youthful grace that age would gladly keep;
A tooth or auburn lock, and by degrees
Their length and colour from the locks they spare;
Th' elastic spring of an unwearied foot
That mounts the stile with ease, or leaps the fence,
That play of lungs, inhaling and again
Respiring freely the fresh air, that makes
Swift pace or steep ascent no toil to me,
Mine have not pilfer'd yet; nor yet impair'd 140
My relish of fair prospect; scenes that sooth'd
Or charm'd me young, no longer young, I find
Still soothing and of pow'r to charm me still.
And witness, dear companion of my walks,
Whose arm this twentieth winter I perceive
Fast lock'd in mine, with pleasure such as love,
Confirm'd by long experience of thy worth
And well-tried virtues, could alone inspire—
Witness a joy that thou hast doubled long.
Thou know'st my praise of nature most sincere, 150
And that my raptures are not conjur'd up
To serve occasions of poetic pomp,
But genuine, and art partner of them all.
How oft upon yon eminence our pace
Has slacken'd to a pause, and we have born
The ruffling wind, scarce conscious that it blew,
While admiration, feeding at the eye,
And still unsated, dwelt upon the scene.
Thence with what pleasure have we just discern'd
The distant plough slow moving, and beside 160
His lab'ring team, that swerv'd not from the track,
The sturdy swain diminish'd to a boy!
Here Ouse, slow winding through a level plain
Of spacious meads with cattle sprinkled o'er,
Conducts the eye along its sinuous course

Delighted. There, fast rooted in their bank,
Stand, never overlook'd, our fav'rite elms,
That screen the herdsman's solitary hut;
While far beyond, and overthwart the stream
That, as with molten glass, inlays the vale, 170
The sloping land recedes into the clouds;
Displaying on its varied side the grace
Of hedge-row beauties numberless, square tow'r,
Tall spire, from which the sound of cheerful bells
Just undulates upon the list'ning ear,
Groves, heaths, and smoking villages, remote.
Scenes must be beautiful, which, daily view'd,
Please daily, and whose novelty survives
Long knowledge and the scrutiny of years.
Praise justly due to those that I describe. 180
  Nor rural sights alone, but rural sounds,
Exhilarate the spirit, and restore
The tone of languid Nature. Mighty winds,
That sweep the skirt of some far-spreading wood
Of ancient growth, make music not unlike
The dash of ocean on his winding shore,
And lull the spirit while they fill the mind;
Unnumber'd branches waving in the blast,
And all their leaves fast flutt'ring, all at once.
Nor less composure waits upon the roar 190
Of distant floods, or on the softer voice
Of neighb'ring fountain, or of rills that slip
Through the cleft rock, and, chiming as they fall
Upon loose pebbles, lose themselves at length
In matted grass, that with a livelier green
Betrays the secret of their silent course.
Nature inanimate employs sweet sounds,
But animated nature sweeter still,
To sooth and satisfy the human ear.
Ten thousand warblers cheer the day, and one 200
The live-long night: nor these alone, whose notes
Nice finger'd art must emulate in vain,
But cawing rooks, and kites that swim sublime
In still repeated circles, screaming loud,
The jay, the pie, and ev'n the boding owl
That hails the rising moon, have charms for me.
Sounds inharmonious in themselves and harsh,
Yet heard in scenes where peace for ever reigns,
And only there, please highly for their sake.
  Peace to the artist, whose ingenious thought 210
Devis'd the weather-house, that useful toy!
Fearless of humid air and gathering rains,
Forth steps the man—an emblem of myself!

166 their] his *1785*, *1786*.

More delicate, his tim'rous mate retires.
When Winter soaks the fields, and female feet,
Too weak to struggle with tenacious clay,
Or ford the rivulets, are best at home,
The task of new discov'ries falls on me.
At such a season, and with such a charge,
Once went I forth; and found, till then unknown,
A cottage, whither oft we since repair: 221
'Tis perch'd upon the green-hill top, but close
Environ'd with a ring of branching elms
That overhang the thatch, itself unseen
Peeps at the vale below; so thick beset
With foliage of such dark redundant growth,
I call'd the low-roof'd lodge the *peasant's nest*.
And, hidden as it is, and far remote
From such unpleasing sounds as haunt the ear
In village or in town, the bay of curs 230
Incessant, clinking hammers, grinding wheels,
And infants clam'rous whether pleas'd or pain'd,
Oft have I wish'd the peaceful covert mine.
Here, I have said, at least I should possess
The poet's treasure, silence, and indulge
The dreams of fancy, tranquil and secure.
Vain thought! the dweller in that still retreat
Dearly obtains the refuge it affords.
Its elevated scite forbids the wretch
To drink sweet waters of the crystal well; 240
He dips his bowl into the weedy ditch,
And, heavy-laden, brings his bev'rage home,
Far-fetch'd and little worth; nor seldom waits,
Dependant on the baker's punctual call,
To hear his creaking panniers at the door,
Angry and sad, and his last crust consum'd.
So farewell envy of the *peasant's nest!*
If solitude make scant the means of life,
Society for me!—thou seeming sweet,
Be still a pleasing object in my view; 250
My visit still, but never mine abode.
  Not distant far, a length of colonnade
Invites us. Monument of ancient taste,
Now scorn'd, but worthy of a better fate.
Our fathers knew the value of a screen
From sultry suns; and, in their shaded walks
And long protracted bow'rs, enjoy'd at noon
The gloom and coolness of declining day.
We bear our shades about us; self-depriv'd
Of other screen, the thin umbrella spread, 260
And range an Indian waste without a tree.

Thanks to Benevolus[1]—he spares me yet
These chesnuts rang'd in corresponding lines;
And, though himself so polish'd, still reprieves
The obsolete prolixity of shade.
  Descending now (but cautious, lest too fast)
A sudden steep, upon a rustic bridge
We pass a gulph, in which the willows dip
Their pendent boughs, stooping as if to drink.
Hence, ancle-deep in moss and flow'ry thyme, 270
We mount again, and feel at ev'ry step
Our foot half sunk in hillocks green and soft,
Raised by the mole, the miner of the soil.
He, not unlike the great ones of mankind,
Disfigures earth; and, plotting in the dark,
Toils much to earn a monumental pile,
That may record the mischiefs he has done.
  The summit gain'd, behold the proud alcove
That crowns it! yet not all its pride secures
The grand retreat from injuries impress'd 280
By rural carvers, who with knives deface
The pannels, leaving an obscure, rude name,
In characters uncouth, and spelt amiss.
So strong the zeal t' immortalize himself
Beats in the breast of man, that ev'n a few
Few transient years, won from th' abyss abhorr'd
Of blank oblivion, seem a glorious prize,
And even to a clown. Now roves the eye;
And, posted on this speculative height,
Exults in its command. The sheep-fold here 290
Pours out its fleecy tenants o'er the glebe.
At first, progressive as a stream, they seek
The middle field; but, scatter'd by degrees,
Each to his choice, soon whiten all the land.
There from the sun-burnt hay-field, homeward
    creeps
The loaded wain; while, lighten'd of its charge,
The wain that meets it passes swiftly by;
The boorish driver leaning o'er his team
Vocif'rous, and impatient of delay.
Nor less attractive is the woodland scene, 300
Diversified with trees of ev'ry growth,
Alike, yet various. Here the gray smooth trunks
Of ash, or lime, or beech, distinctly shine,
Within the twilight of their distant shades;
There, lost behind a rising ground, the wood
Seems sunk, and shorten'd to its topmost boughs.

[1] John Courtney Throckmorton, Esq., of Weston Underwood [C.]

No tree in all the grove but has its charms,
Though each its hue peculiar; paler some,
And of a wannish gray; the willow such,
And poplar, that with silver lines his leaf, 310
And ash far-stretching his umbrageous arm;
Of deeper green the elm; and deeper still,
Lord of the woods, the long-surviving oak.
Some glossy-leav'd, and shining in the sun,
The maple, and the beech of oily nuts
Prolific, and the lime at dewy eve
Diffusing odours: nor unnoted pass
The sycamore, capricious in attire,
Now green, now tawny, and, ere autumn yet
Have chang'd the woods, in scarlet honours
bright. 320
O'er these, but far beyond (a spacious map
Of hill and valley interpos'd between),
The Ouse, dividing the well-water'd land,
Now glitters in the sun, and now retires,
As bashful, yet impatient to be seen.
Hence the declivity is sharp and short,
And such the re-ascent; between them weeps
A little naiad her impov'rish'd urn
All summer long, which winter fills again.
The folded gates would bar my progress now, 330
But that the lord[1] of this enclos'd demesne,
Communicative of the good he owns,
Admits me to a share; the guiltless eye
Commits no wrong, nor wastes what it enjoys.
Refreshing change! where now the blazing sun?
By short transition we have lost his glare,
And stepp'd at once into a cooler clime.
Ye fallen avenues! once more I mourn
Your fate unmerited, once more rejoice
That yet a remnant of your race survives. 340
How airy and how light the graceful arch,
Yet awful as the consecrated roof
Re-echoing pious anthems! while beneath
The chequer'd earth seems restless as a flood
Brush'd by the wind. So sportive is the light
Shot through the boughs, it dances as they dance,
Shadow and sunshine intermingling quick,
And dark'ning and enlight'ning, as the leaves
Play wanton, ev'ry moment, ev'ry spot.
And now, with nerves new-brac'd and spirits
cheer'd, 350

[1] See the foregoing note [C.]

We tread the wilderness, whose well-roll'd walks,
With curvature of slow and easy sweep—
Deception innocent—give ample space
To narrow bounds. The grove receives us next;
Between the upright shafts of whose tall elms
We may discern the thresher at his task.
Thump after thump resounds the constant flail,
That seems to swing uncertain, and yet falls
Full on the destin'd ear. Wide flies the chaff.
The rustling straw sends up a frequent mist 360
Of atoms, sparkling in the noon-day beam.
Come hither, ye that press your beds of down
And sleep not: see him sweating o'er his bread
Before he eats it.—'Tis the primal curse,
But soften'd into mercy; made the pledge
Of cheerful days, and nights without a groan.

By ceaseless action all that is subsists.
Constant rotation of th' unwearied wheel
That nature rides upon maintains her health,
Her beauty, her fertility. She dreads 370
An instant's pause, and lives but while she moves.
Its own revolvency upholds the world.
Winds from all quarters agitate the air,
And fit the limpid element for use,
Else noxious: oceans, rivers, lakes, and streams,
All feel the fresh'ning impulse, and are cleans'd
By restless undulation: ev'n the oak
Thrives by the rude concussion of the storm:
He seems indeed indignant, and to feel
Th' impression of the blast with proud disdain, 380
Frowning as if in his unconscious arm
He held the thunder: but the monarch owes
His firm stability to what he scorns—
More fixt below, the more disturb'd above.
The law, by which all creatures else are bound,
Binds man the lord of all. Himself derives
No mean advantage from a kindred cause,
From strenuous toil his hours of sweetest ease.
The sedentary stretch their lazy length
When custom bids, but no refreshment find, 390
For none they need: the languid eye, the cheek
Deserted of its bloom, the flaccid, shrunk,
And wither'd muscle, and the vapid soul,
Reproach their owner with that love of rest
To which he forfeits ev'n the rest he loves.
Not such th' alert and active. Measure life
By its true worth, the comforts it affords,
And their's alone seems worthy of the name.

Good health, and, its associate in most,
Good temper; spirits prompt to undertake, 400
And not soon spent, though in an arduous task;
The pow'rs of fancy and strong thought are their's;
Ev'n age itself seems privileg'd in them
With clear exemption from its own defects.
A sparkling eye beneath a wrinkled front
The vet'ran shows, and, gracing a gray beard
With youthful smiles, descends toward the grave
Sprightly, and old almost without decay.
 Like a coy maiden, ease, when courted most,
Farthest retires—an idol, at whose shrine 410
Who oft'nest sacrifice are favour'd least.
The love of Nature, and the scene she draws,
Is Nature's dictate. Strange! there should be found,
Who, self-imprison'd in their proud saloons,
Renounce the odours of the open field
For the unscented fictions of the loom;
Who, satisfied with only pencil'd scenes,
Prefer to the performance of a God
Th' inferior wonders of an artist's hand!
Lovely indeed the mimic works of art; 420
But Nature's works far lovelier. I admire—
None more admires—the painter's magic skill,
Who shows me that which I shall never see,
Conveys a distant country into mine,
And throws Italian light on English walls:
But imitative strokes can do no more
Than please the eye—sweet Nature ev'ry sense.
The air salubrious of her lofty hills,
The cheering fragrance of her dewy vales,
And music of her woods—no works of man 430
May rival these; these all bespeak a pow'r
Peculiar, and exclusively her own.
Beneath the open sky she spreads the feast;
'Tis free to all—'tis ev'ry day renew'd;
Who scorns it starves deservedly at home.
He does not scorn it, who, imprison'd long
In some unwholesome dungeon, and a prey
To sallow sickness, which the vapours, dank
And clammy, of his dark abode have bred,
Escapes at last to liberty and light: 440
His cheek recovers soon its healthful hue;
His eye relumines its extinguish'd fires;
He walks, he leaps, he runs—is wing'd with joy,
And riots in the sweets of ev'ry breeze.

399 the most *1785–1788, 1803.*

He does not scorn it, who has long endur'd
A fever's agonies, and fed on drugs.
Nor yet the mariner, his blood inflam'd
With acrid salts; his very heart athirst
To gaze at Nature in her green array,
Upon the ship's tall side he stands, possess'd 450
With visions prompted by intense desire:
Fair fields appear below, such as he left,
Far distant, such as he would die to find—
He seeks them headlong, and is seen no more.
The spleen is seldom felt where Flora reigns;
The low'ring eye, the petulance, the frown,
And sullen sadness, that o'ershade, distort,
And mar the face of beauty, when no cause
For such immeasurable woe appears,
These Flora banishes, and gives the fair 460
Sweet smiles, and bloom less transient than her own.
It is the constant revolution, stale
And tasteless, of the same repeated joys,
That palls and satiates, and makes languid life
A pedlar's pack, that bows the bearer down.
Health suffers, and the spirits ebb; the heart
Recoils from its own choice—at the full feast
Is famish'd—finds no music in the song,
No smartness in the jest; and wonders why.
Yet thousands still desire to journey on, 470
Though halt, and weary of the path they tread.
The paralytic, who can hold her cards,
But cannot play them, borrows a friend's hand
To deal and shuffle, to divide and sort,
Her mingled suits and sequences; and sits,
Spectatress both and spectacle, a sad
And silent cypher, while her proxy plays.
Others are dragg'd into the crowded room
Between supporters; and, once seated, sit,
Through downright inability to rise, 480
Till the stout bearers lift the corpse again.
These speak a loud memento. Yet ev'n these
Themselves love life, and cling to it, as he
That overhangs a torrent to a twig.
They love it, and yet loath it; fear to die,
Yet scorn the purposes for which they live.
Then wherefore not renounce them? No—the dread,
The slavish dread of solitude, that breeds
Reflection and remorse, the fear of shame,
And their invet'rate habits, all forbid. 490
Whom call we gay? That honour has been long
The boast of mere pretenders to the name.

The innocent are gay—the lark is gay,
That dries his feathers, saturate with dew,
Beneath the rosy cloud, while yet the beams
Of day-spring overshoot his humble nest.
The peasant too, a witness of his song,
Himself a songster, is as gay as he.
But save me from the gaiety of those
Whose head-aches nail them to a noon-day bed: 500
And save me too from their's whose haggard eyes
Flash desperation, and betray their pangs
For property stripp'd off by cruel chance;
From gaiety that fills the bones with pain,
The mouth with blasphemy, the heart with woe.
  The earth was made so various, that the mind
Of desultory man, studious of change,
And pleas'd with novelty, might be indulg'd.
Prospects, however lovely, may be seen
Till half their beauties fade; the weary sight, 510
Too well acquainted with their smiles, slides off,
Fastidious, seeking less familiar scenes.
Then snug enclosures in the shelter'd vale,
Where frequent hedges intercept the eye,
Delight us; happy to renounce awhile,
Not senseless of its charms, what still we love,
That such short absence may endear it more.
Then forests, or the savage rock, may please,
That hides the sea-mew in his hollow clefts
Above the reach of man. His hoary head, 520
Conspicuous many a league, the mariner
Bound homeward, and in hope already there,
Greets with three cheers exulting. At his waist
A girdle of half-wither'd shrubs he shows,
And at his feet the baffled billows die.
The common, overgrown with fern, and rough
With prickly gorse, that, shapeless and deform'd,
And dang'rous to the touch, has yet its bloom,
And decks itself with ornaments of gold,
Yields no unpleasing ramble; there the turf 530
Smells fresh, and, rich in odorif'rous herbs
And fungous fruits of earth, regales the sense
With luxury of unexpected sweets.
  There often wanders one, whom better days
Saw better clad, in cloak of satin trimm'd
With lace, and hat with splendid ribband bound.
A serving maid was she, and fell in love
With one who left her, went to sea, and died.

527 goss *1785, 1786*   deform *1785, 1786.*

Her fancy follow'd him through foaming waves
To distant shores; and she would sit and weep 540
At what a sailor suffers; fancy, too,
Delusive most where warmest wishes are,
Would oft anticipate his glad return,
And dream of transports she was not to know.
She heard the doleful tidings of his death
And never smil'd again! And now she roams
The dreary waste; there spends the livelong day,
And there, unless when charity forbids,
The livelong night. A tatter'd apron hides,
Worn as a cloak, and hardly hides, a gown 550
More tatter'd still; and both but ill conceal
A bosom heav'd with never-ceasing sighs.
She begs an idle pin of all she meets,
And hoards them in her sleeve; but needful food,
Though press'd with hunger oft, or comelier clothes,
Though pinch'd with cold, asks never.—Kate is
craz'd!

I see a column of slow rising smoke
O'ertop the lofty wood that skirts the wild.
A vagabond and useless tribe there eat
Their miserable meal. A kettle, slung 560
Between two poles upon a stick transverse,
Receives the morsel—flesh obscene of dog,
Or vermin, or, at best, of cock purloin'd
From his accustom'd perch. Hard faring race!
They pick their fuel out of ev'ry hedge,
Which, kindled with dry leaves, just saves un-
quench'd
The spark of life. The sportive wind blows wide
Their flutt'ring rags, and shows a tawny skin,
The vellum of the pedigree they claim.
Great skill have they in palmistry, and more 570
To conjure clean away the gold they touch,
Conveying worthless dross into its place;
Loud when they beg, dumb only when they steal.
Strange! that a creature rational, and cast
In human mould, should brutalize by choice
His nature; and, though capable of arts
By which the world might profit, and himself,
Self-banish'd from society, prefer
Such squalid sloth to honourable toil!
Yet even these, though, feigning sickness oft, 580
They swathe the forehead, drag the limping limb,
And vex their flesh with artificial sores,
Can change their whine into a mirthful note
When safe occasion offers; and, with dance,

And music of the bladder and the bag,
Beguile their woes, and make the woods resound.
Such health and gaiety of heart enjoy
The houseless rovers of the sylvan world;
And, breathing wholesome air, and wand'ring much,
Need other physic none to heal th' effects 590
Of loathsome diet, penury, and cold.
Blest he, though undistinguish'd from the crowd
By wealth or dignity, who dwells secure,
Where man, by nature fierce, has laid aside
His fierceness, having learnt, though slow to learn,
The manners and the arts of civil life.
His wants, indeed, are many; but supply
Is obvious, plac'd within the easy reach
Of temp'rate wishes and industrious hands.
Here virtue thrives as in her proper soil; 600
Not rude and surly, and beset with thorns,
And terrible to sight, as when she springs
(If e'er she spring spontaneous) in remote
And barb'rous climes, where violence prevails,
And strength is lord of all; but gentle, kind,
By culture tam'd, by liberty refresh'd,
And all her fruits by radiant truth matur'd.
War and the chase engross the savage whole;
War follow'd for revenge, or to supplant
The envied tenants of some happier spot, 610
The chase for sustenance, precarious trust!
His hard condition with severe constraint
Binds all his faculties, forbids all growth
Of wisdom, proves a school in which he learns
Sly circumvention, unrelenting hate,
Mean self-attachment, and scarce aught beside.
Thus fare the shiv'ring natives of the north,
And thus the rangers of the western world,
Where it advances far into the deep,
Towards th' antarctic. Ev'n the favour'd isles, 620
So lately found, although the constant sun
Cheer all their seasons with a grateful smile,
Can boast but little virtue; and, inert
Through plenty, lose in morals what they gain
In manners—victims of luxurious ease.
These therefore I can pity, plac'd remote
From all that science traces, art invents,
Or inspiration teaches; and enclosed
In boundless oceans, never to be pass'd
By navigators uninform'd as they, 630
Or plough'd perhaps by British bark again:
But, far beyond the rest, and with most cause,

Thee, gentle savage[1]! whom no love of thee
Or thine, but curiosity perhaps,
Or else vain glory, prompted us to draw
Forth from thy native bow'rs, to show thee here
With what superior skill we can abuse
The gifts of Providence, and squander life.
The dream is past; and thou hast found again 639
Thy cocoas and bananas, palms and yams,
And homestall thatch'd with leaves. But hast thou [found
Their former charms? And, having seen our state,
Our palaces, our ladies, and our pomp
Of equipage, our gardens, and our sports,
And heard our music; are thy simple friends,
Thy simple fare, and all thy plain delights,
As dear to thee as once? And have thy joys
Lost nothing by comparison with our's?
Rude as thou art, (for we return'd thee rude
And ignorant, except of outward show) 650
I cannot think thee yet so dull of heart
And spiritless, as never to regret
Sweets tasted here, and left as soon as known.
Methinks I see thee straying on the beach,
And asking of the surge that bathes thy foot
If ever it has wash'd our distant shore.
I see thee weep, and thine are honest tears,
A patriot's for his country: thou art sad
At thought of her forlorn and abject state,
From which no pow'r of thine can raise her up. 660
Thus fancy paints thee, and, though apt to err,
Perhaps errs little when she paints thee thus.
She tells me, too, that duly ev'ry morn
Thou climb'st the mountain top, with eager eye
Exploring far and wide the wat'ry waste
For sight of ship from England. Ev'ry speck
Seen in the dim horizon turns thee pale
With conflict of contending hopes and fears.
But comes at last the dull and dusky eve,
And sends thee to thy cabin, well-prepar'd 670
To dream all night of what the day denied.
Alas! expect it not. We found no bait
To tempt us in thy country. Doing good,
Disinterested good, is not our trade.
We travel far, 'tis true, but not for nought;
And must be brib'd, to compass earth again,
By other hopes and richer fruits than your's.
  But, though true worth and virtue in the mild
And genial soil of cultivated life

[1] Omai [C.].

Thrive most, and may perhaps thrive only there, 680
Yet not in cities oft: in proud and gay
And gain-devoted cities. Thither flow,
As to a common and most noisome sew'r,
The dregs and feculence of ev'ry land.
In cities foul example on most minds
Begets its likeness. Rank abundance breeds
In gross and pamper'd cities sloth and lust,
And wantonness and gluttonous excess.
In cities vice is hidden with most ease,
Or seen with least reproach; and virtue, taught 690
By frequent lapse, can hope no triumph there
Beyond th' achievement of successful flight.
I do confess them nurs'ries of the arts,
In which they flourish most; where, in the beams
Of warm encouragement, and in the eye
Of public note, they reach their perfect size.
Such London is, by taste and wealth proclaim'd
The fairest capital of all the world,
By riot and incontinence the worst.
There, touch'd by Reynolds, a dull blank becomes
A lucid mirror, in which Nature sees 701
All her reflected features. Bacon there
Gives more than female beauty to a stone,
And Chatham's eloquence to marble lips.
Nor does the chissel occupy alone
The pow'rs of sculpture, but the style as much;
Each province of her art her equal care.
With nice incision of her guided steel
She ploughs a brazen field, and clothes a soil
So sterile with what charms soe'er she will, 710
The richest scen'ry and the loveliest forms.
Where finds philosophy her eagle eye,
With which she gazes at yon burning disk
Undazzled, and detects and counts his spots?
In London: where her implements exact,
With which she calculates, computes, and scans,
All distance, motion, magnitude, and now
Measures an atom, and now girds a world?
In London. Where has commerce such a mart,
So rich, so throng'd, so drain'd, and so supplied, 720
As London—opulent, enlarg'd, and still
Increasing, London? Babylon of old
Not more the glory of the earth than she,
A more accomplish'd world's chief glory now.
She has her praise. Now mark a spot or two,
That so much beauty would do well to purge;
And show this queen of cities, that so fair

May yet be foul; so witty, yet not wise.
It is not seemly, nor of good report,
That she is slack in discipline; more prompt 730
T' avenge than to prevent the breach of law:
That she is rigid in denouncing death
On petty robbers, and indulges life
And liberty, and oft-times honour too,
To peculators of the public gold:
That thieves at home must hang; but he, that puts
Into his overgorg'd and bloated purse
The wealth of Indian provinces, escapes.
Nor is it well, nor can it come to good,
That, through profane and infidel contempt 740
Of holy writ, she has presum'd t' annul
And abrogate, as roundly as she may,
The total ordinance and will of God;
Advancing fashion to the post of truth,
And cent'ring all authority in modes
And customs of her own, till sabbath rites
Have dwindled into unrespected forms,
And knees and hassocks are well-nigh divorc'd.

God made the country, and man made the town.
What wonder then that health and virtue, gifts 750
That can alone make sweet the bitter draught
That life holds out to all, should most abound
And least be threaten'd in the fields and groves?
Possess ye, therefore, ye, who, borne about
In chariots and sedans, know no fatigue
But that of idleness, and taste no scenes
But such as art contrives, possess ye still
Your element; there only can ye shine,
There only minds like your's can do no harm.
Our groves were planted to console at noon 760
The pensive wand'rer in their shades. At eve
The moon-beam, sliding softly in between
The sleeping leaves, is all the light they wish,
Birds warbling all the music. We can spare
The splendour of your lamps; they but eclipse
Our softer satellite. Your songs confound
Our more harmonious notes: the thrush departs
Scar'd, and th' offended nightingale is mute.
There is a public mischief in your mirth;
It plagues your country. Folly such as your's, 770
Grac'd with a sword, and worthier of a fan,
Has made, what enemies could ne'er have done,
Our arch of empire, stedfast but for you,
A mutilated structure, soon to fall.

758 ye can *1785-1788.* 772 what] which *1785*, *1786*.

BOOK II

THE TIME-PIECE

ARGUMENT OF THE SECOND BOOK.—Reflections suggested by the conclusion of the former book—Peace among the nations recommended, on the ground of their common fellowship in sorrow—Prodigies enumerated—Sicilian earthquakes—Man rendered obnoxious to these calamities by sin—God the agent in them—The philosophy that stops at secondary causes reproved—Our own late miscarriages accounted for—Satirical notice taken of our trips to Fontainbleau—But the pulpit, not satire, the proper engine of reformation—The reverend Advertiser of engraved sermons—Petit-maitre parson—The good preacher—Pictures of a theatrical clerical coxcomb—Story-tellers and jesters in the pulpit reproved—Apostrophe to popular applause—Retailers of ancient philosophy expostulated with—Sum of the whole matter—Effects of sacerdotal mismanagement on the laity—Their folly and extravagance—The mischiefs of profusion—Profusion itself, with all its consequent evils, ascribed, as to its principal cause, to the want of discipline in the universities.

OH for a lodge in some vast wilderness,
Some boundless contiguity of shade,
Where rumour of oppression and deceit,
Of unsuccessful or successful war,
Might never reach me more. My ear is pain'd,
My soul is sick, with ev'ry day's report
Of wrong and outrage with which earth is fill'd.
There is no flesh in man's obdurate heart,
It does not feel for man; the nat'ral bond
Of brotherhood is sever'd as the flax 10
That falls asunder at the touch of fire.
He finds his fellow guilty of a skin
Not colour'd like his own; and, having pow'r
T' enforce the wrong, for such a worthy cause
Dooms and devotes him as his lawful prey.
Lands intersected by a narrow frith
Abhor each other. Mountains interpos'd
Make enemies of nations, who had else,
Like kindred drops, been mingled into one.
Thus man devotes his brother, and destroys; 20
And, worse than all, and most to be deplor'd,
As human nature's broadest, foulest blot,
Chains him, and tasks him, and exacts his sweat
With stripes, that mercy, with a bleeding heart,
Weeps when she sees inflicted on a beast.
Then what is man? And what man, seeing this,
And having human feelings, does not blush,
And hang his head, to think himself a man?
I would not have a slave to till my ground,

Argument 11 Picture *1785-1788.*

To carry me, to fan me while I sleep, 30
And tremble when I wake, for all the wealth
That sinews bought and sold have ever earn'd.
No: dear as freedom is, and in my heart's
Just estimation priz'd above all price,
I had much rather be myself the slave,
And wear the bonds, than fasten them on him.
We have no slaves at home.—Then why abroad?
And they themselves, once ferried o'er the wave
That parts us, are emancipate and loos'd.
Slaves cannot breathe in England; if their lungs 40
Receive our air, that moment they are free;
They touch our country, and their shackles fall.
That's noble, and bespeaks a nation proud
And jealous of the blessing. Spread it then,
And let it circulate through ev'ry vein
Of all your empire; that where Britain's pow'r
Is felt, mankind may feel her mercy too.
  Sure there is need of social intercourse,
Benevolence, and peace, and mutual aid,
Between the nations, in a world that seems 50
To toll the death-bell of its own decease,
And by the voice of all its elements
To preach the gen'ral doom[1]. When were the winds
Let slip with such a warrant to destroy?
When did the waves so haughtily o'erleap
Their ancient barriers, deluging the dry?
Fires from beneath, and meteors[2] from above,
Portentous, unexampled, unexplain'd,
Have kindled beacons in the skies; and th' old
And crazy earth has had her shaking fits 60
More frequent, and forgone her usual rest.
Is it a time to wrangle, when the props
And pillars of our planet seem to fail,
And Nature[3] with a dim and sickly eye
To wait the close of all? But grant her end
More distant, and that prophecy demands
A longer respite, unaccomplish'd yet;
Still they are frowning signals, and bespeak
Displeasure in his breast who smites the earth
Or heals it, makes it languish or rejoice. 70
And 'tis but seemly, that where all deserve
And stand expos'd by common peccancy
To what no few have felt, there should be peace,
And brethren in calamity should love.

[1] Alluding to the calamities at Jamaica [C.].
[2] August 18, 1783 [C.]. [3] Alluding to the fog that covered both Europe and Asia during the summer of 1783 [C.].

Alas for Sicily! rude fragments now
Lie scatter'd where the shapely column stood.
Her palaces are dust. In all her streets
The voice of singing and the sprightly chord
Are silent. Revelry, and dance, and show,
Suffer a syncope and solemn pause; 80
While God performs upon the trembling stage
Of his own works his dreadful part alone.
How does the earth receive him?—With what signs
Of gratulation and delight, her king?
Pours she not all her choicest fruits abroad,
Her sweetest flow'rs, her aromatic gums,
Disclosing paradise where'er he treads?
She quakes at his approach. Her hollow womb,
Conceiving thunders, through a thousand deeps
And fiery caverns roars beneath his foot. 90
The hills move lightly, and the mountains smoke,
For he has touch'd them. From th' extremest point
Of elevation down into th' abyss,
His wrath is busy, and his frown is felt.
The rocks fall headlong, and the vallies rise,
The rivers die into offensive pools,
And, charg'd with putrid verdure, breathe a gross
And mortal nuisance into all the air.
What solid was, by transformation strange,
Grows fluid; and the fixt and rooted earth, 100
Tormented into billows, heaves and swells,
Or with vortiginous and hideous whirl
Sucks down its prey insatiable. Immense
The tumult and the overthrow, the pangs
And agonies of human and of brute
Multitudes, fugitive on ev'ry side,
And fugitive in vain. The sylvan scene
Migrates uplifted; and, with all its soil
Alighting in far distant fields, finds out
A new possessor, and survives the change. 110
Ocean has caught the frenzy, and, upwrought
To an enormous and o'erbearing height,
Not by a mighty wind, but by that voice
Which winds and waves obey, invades the shore
Resistless. Never such a sudden flood,
Upridg'd so high, and sent on such a charge,
Possess'd an inland scene. Where now the throng
That press'd the beach, and, hasty to depart,
Look'd to the sea for safety? They are gone,
Gone with the refluent wave into the deep— 120
A prince with half his people! Ancient tow'rs,

And roofs embattled high, the gloomy scenes
Where beauty oft and letter'd worth consume
Life in the unproductive shades of death,
Fall prone: the pale inhabitants come forth,
And, happy in their unforeseen release
From all the rigours of restraint, enjoy
The terrors of the day that sets them free.
Who then, that has thee, would not hold thee fast,
Freedom! whom they that lose thee so regret, 130
That ev'n a judgment, making way for thee,
Seems in their eyes a mercy for thy sake.

Such evil sin hath wrought; and such a flame
Kindled in heav'n, that it burns down to earth,
And, in the furious inquest that it makes
On God's behalf, lays waste his fairest works.
The very elements, though each be meant
The minister of man, to serve his wants,
Conspire against him. With his breath he draws
A plague into his blood; and cannot use 140
Life's necessary means, but he must die.
Storms rise t' o'erwhelm him: or, if stormy winds
Rise not, the waters of the deep shall rise,
And, needing none assistance of the storm,
Shall roll themselves ashore, and reach him there.
The earth shall shake him out of all his holds,
Or make his house his grave: nor so content,
Shall counterfeit the motions of the flood,
And drown him in her dry and dusty gulphs.
What then!—were they the wicked above all, 150
And we the righteous, whose fast anchor'd isle
Mov'd not, while their's was rock'd, like a light skiff,
The sport of ev'ry wave? No: none are clear,
And none than we more guilty. But, where all
Stand chargeable with guilt, and to the shafts
Of wrath obnoxious, God may choose his mark:
May punish, if he please, the less, to warn
The more malignant. If he spar'd not them,
Tremble and be amaz'd at thine escape,
Far guiltier England, lest he spare not thee! 160

Happy the man who sees a God employ'd
In all the good and ill that chequer life!
Resolving all events, with their effects
And manifold results, into the will
And arbitration wise of the Supreme.
Did not his eye rule all things, and intend
The least of our concerns (since from the least
The greatest oft originate); could chance
Find place in his dominion, or dispose

One lawless particle to thwart his plan; 170
Then God might be surpris'd, and unforeseen
Contingence might alarm him, and disturb
The smooth and equal course of his affairs.
This truth philosophy, though eagle-ey'd
In nature's tendencies, oft overlooks;
And, having found his instrument, forgets
Or disregards, or, more presumptuous still,
Denies the pow'r that wields it. God proclaims
His hot displeasure against foolish men,
That live an atheist life: involves the heav'n 180
In tempests; quits his grasp upon the winds,
And gives them all their fury; bids a plague
Kindle a fiery boil upon the skin,
And putrefy the breath of blooming health.
He calls for famine, and the meagre fiend
Blows mildew from between his shrivel'd lips,
And taints the golden ear. He springs his mines,
And desolates a nation at a blast.
Forth steps the spruce philosopher, and tells
Of homogeneal and discordant springs 190
And principles; of causes, how they work
By necessary laws their sure effects;
Of action and re-action. He has found
The source of the disease that nature feels,
And bids the world take heart and banish fear.
Thou fool! will thy discovery of the cause
Suspend th' effect, or heal it? Has not God
Still wrought by means since first he made the world?
And did he not of old employ his means
To drown it? What is his creation less 200
Than a capacious reservoir of means
Form'd for his use, and ready at his will?
Go, dress thine eyes with eye-salve; ask of him,
Or ask of whomsoever he has taught;
And learn, though late, the genuine cause of all.

England, with all thy faults, I love thee still—
My country! and, while yet a nook is left
Where English minds and manners may be found,
Shall be constrain'd to love thee. Though thy clime
Be fickle, and thy year most part deform'd 210
With dripping rains, or wither'd by a frost,
I would not yet exchange thy sullen skies,
And fields without a flow'r, for warmer France
With all her vines; nor for Ausonia's groves
Of golden fruitage, and her myrtle bow'rs.
To shake thy senate, and from heights sublime

Of patriot eloquence to flash down fire
Upon thy foes, was never meant my task:
But I can feel thy fortunes, and partake
Thy joys and sorrows, with as true a heart 220
As any thund'rer there. And I can feel
Thy follies, too; and with a just disdain
Frown at effeminates, whose very looks
Reflect dishonour on the land I love.
How, in the name of soldiership and sense,
Should England prosper, when such things, as smooth
And tender as a girl, all essenc'd o'er
With odours, and as profligate as sweet;
Who sell their laurel for a myrtle wreath,
And love when they should fight; when such as these
Presume to lay their hand upon the ark 231
Of her magnificent and awful cause?
Time was when it was praise and boast enough
In ev'ry clime, and travel where we might,
That we were born her children. Praise enough
To fill th' ambition of a private man,
That Chatham's language was his mother tongue,
And Wolfe's great name compatriot with his own.
Farewell those honours, and farewell with them
The hope of such hereafter! They have fall'n 240
Each in his field of glory; one in arms,
And one in council—Wolfe upon the lap
Of smiling victory that moment won,
And Chatham heart-sick of his country's shame!
They made us many soldiers. Chatham, still
Consulting England's happiness at home,
Secur'd it by an unforgiving frown,
If any wrong'd her. Wolfe, where'er he fought,
Put so much of his heart into his act,
That his example had a magnet's force, 250
And all were swift to follow whom all lov'd.
Those suns are set. Oh, rise some other such!
Or all that we have left is empty talk
Of old achievements, and despair of new.

Now hoist the sail, and let the streamers float
Upon the wanton breezes. Strew the deck
With lavender, and sprinkle liquid sweets,
That no rude savour maritime invade
The nose of nice nobility! Breathe soft,
Ye clarionets; and softer still, ye flutes; 260
That winds and waters, lull'd by magic sounds,
May bear us smoothly to the Gallic shore!
True, we have lost an empire—let it pass.
True; we may thank the perfidy of France,

That pick'd the jewel out of England's crown,
With all the cunning of an envious shrew.
And let that pass—'twas but a trick of state!
A brave man knows no malice, but at once
Forgets in peace the injuries of war,
And gives his direst foe a friend's embrace. 270
And, sham'd as we have been, to th' very beard
Brav'd and defied, and in our own sea prov'd
Too weak for those decisive blows that once
Ensur'd us mast'ry there, we yet retain
Some small pre-eminence; we justly boast
At least superior jockeyship, and claim
The honours of the turf as all our own!
Go, then, well worthy of the praise ye seek,
And show the shame ye might conceal at home
In foreign eyes!—be grooms, and win the plate 280
Where once your nobler fathers won a crown!—
'Tis gen'rous to communicate your skill
To those that need it. Folly is soon learn'd:
And, under such preceptors, who can fail!

There is a pleasure in poetic pains
Which only poets know. The shifts and turns,
Th' expedients and inventions, multiform,
To which the mind resorts, in chase of terms
Though apt, yet coy, and difficult to win—
T' arrest the fleeting images that fill 290
The mirror of the mind, and hold them fast,
And force them sit till he has pencil'd off
A faithful likeness of the forms he views;
Then to dispose his copies with such art,
That each may find its most propitious light,
And shine by situation, hardly less
Than by the labour and the skill it cost;
Are occupations of the poet's mind
So pleasing, and that steal away the thought
With such address from themes of sad import, 300
That, lost in his own musings, happy man!
He feels th' anxieties of life, denied
Their wonted entertainment, all retire.
Such joys has he that sings. But ah! not such,
Or seldom such, the hearers of his song.
Fastidious, or else listless, or perhaps
Aware of nothing arduous in a task
They never undertook, they little note
His dangers or escapes, and haply find
There least amusement where he found the most.
But is amusement all? Studious of song, 311
And yet ambitious not to sing in vain,

I would not trifle merely, though the world
Be loudest in their praise who do no more.
Yet what can satire, whether grave or gay?
It may correct a foible, may chastise
The freaks of fashion, regulate the dress,
Retrench a sword-blade, or displace a patch;
But where are its sublimer trophies found?
What vice has it subdu'd? whose heart reclaim'd
By rigour, or whom laugh'd into reform? 321
Alas! Leviathan is not so tam'd:
Laugh'd at, he laughs again; and, stricken hard,
Turns to the stroke his adamantine scales,
That fear no discipline of human hands.
The pulpit, therefore (and I name it fill'd
With solemn awe, that bids me well beware
With what intent I touch that holy thing)—
The pulpit (when the sat'rist has at last,
Strutting and vap'ring in an empty school, 330
Spent all his force and made no proselyte)—
I say the pulpit (in the sober use
Of its legitimate, peculiar pow'rs)
Must stand acknowledg'd, while the world shall stand,
The most important and effectual guard,
Support, and ornament, of virtue's cause.
There stands the messenger of truth: there stands
The legate of the skies!—His theme divine,
His office sacred, his credentials clear.
By him the violated law speaks out 340
Its thunders; and by him, in strains as sweet
As angels use, the gospel whispers peace.
He 'stablishes the strong, restores the weak,
Reclaims the wand'rer, binds the broken heart,
And, arm'd himself in panoply complete
Of heav'nly temper, furnishes with arms,
Bright as his own, and trains, by ev'ry rule
Of holy discipline, to glorious war,
The sacramental host of God's elect! 349
Are all such teachers?—would to heav'n all were!
But hark—the doctor's voice!—fast wedg'd between
Two empirics he stands, and with swoln cheeks
Inspires the news, his trumpet. Keener far
Than all invective is his bold harangue,
While through that public organ of report
He hails the clergy; and, defying shame,
Announces to the world his own and their's!
He teaches those to read, whom schools dismiss'd,
And colleges, untaught; sells accent, tone,
And emphasis in score, and gives to pray'r 360

Th' *adagio* and *andante* it demands.
He grinds divinity of other days
Down into modern use; transforms old print
To zig-zag manuscript, and cheats the eyes
Of gall'ry critics by a thousand arts.
Are there who purchase of the doctor's ware?
Oh, name it not in Gath!—it cannot be,
That grave and learned clerks should need such aid.
He doubtless is in sport, and does but droll,
Assuming thus a rank unknown before— 370
Grand caterer and dry-nurse of the church!
  I venerate the man whose heart is warm,
Whose hands are pure, whose doctrine and whose life,
Coincident, exhibit lucid proof
That he is honest in the sacred cause.
To such I render more than mere respect,
Whose actions say that they respect themselves.
But, loose in morals, and in manners vain,
In conversation frivolous, in dress
Extreme, at once rapacious and profuse; 380
Frequent in park with lady at his side,
Ambling and prattling scandal as he goes;
But rare at home, and never at his books,
Or with his pen, save when he scrawls a card;
Constant at routs, familiar with a round
Of ladyships—a stranger to the poor;
Ambitious of preferment for its gold,
And well-prepar'd, by ignorance and sloth,
By infidelity and love of world,
To make God's work a sinecure; a slave 390
To his own pleasures and his patron's pride:
From such apostles, oh, ye mitred heads,
Preserve the church! and lay not careless hands
On sculls that cannot teach, and will not learn.
  Would I describe a preacher, such as Paul,
Were he on earth, would hear, approve, and own—
Paul should himself direct me. I would trace
His master-strokes, and draw from his design.
I would express him simple, grave, sincere;
In doctrine uncorrupt; in language plain, 400
And plain in manner; decent, solemn, chaste,
And natural in gesture; much impress'd
Himself, as conscious of his awful charge,
And anxious mainly that the flock he feeds
May feel it too; affectionate in look,
And tender in address, as well becomes
A messenger of grace to guilty men.

389 of] o' th' *1785, 1786.*

Behold the picture!—Is it like?—Like whom?
The things that mount the rostrum with a skip,
And then skip down again; pronounce a text; 410
Cry—hem: and, reading what they never wrote,
Just fifteen minutes, huddle up their work,
And with a well-bred whisper close the scene!
  In man or woman, but far most in man,
And most of all in man that ministers
And serves the altar, in my soul I loath
All affectation. 'Tis my perfect scorn;
Object of my implacable disgust.
What!—will a man play tricks, will he indulge
A silly fond conceit of his fair form, 420
And just proportion, fashionable mien,
And pretty face, in presence of his God?
Or will he seek to dazzle me with tropes,
As with the di'mond on his lily hand,
And play his brilliant parts before my eyes,
When I am hungry for the bread of life?
He mocks his Maker, prostitutes and shames
His noble office, and, instead of truth,
Displaying his own beauty, starves his flock!
Therefore, avaunt all attitude, and stare, 430
And start theatric, practised at the glass!
I seek divine simplicity in him
Who handles things divine; and all besides,
Tho' learn'd with labour, and tho' much admir'd
By curious eyes and judgments ill-inform'd,
To me is odious as the nasal twang
Heard at conventicle, where worthy men,
Misled by custom, strain celestial themes
Through the prest nostril, spectacle-bestrid.
Some, decent in demeanour while they preach, 440
That task perform'd, relapse into themselves,
And, having spoken wisely, at the close
Grow wanton, and give proof to ev'ry eye—
Whoe'er was edified, themselves were not!
Forth comes the pocket mirror.—First we stroke
An eye-brow; next, compose a straggling lock;
Then with an air, most gracefully perform'd,
Fall back into our seat, extend an arm,
And lay it at its ease with gentle care,
With handkerchief in hand depending low: 450
The better hand, more busy, gives the nose
Its bergamot, or aids th' indebted eye
With op'ra glass, to watch the moving scene,
And recognize the slow-retiring fair.—

433 beside *1785–1788.* 437 At conventicle heard *1785, 1786.*

Now this is fulsome; and offends me more
Than in a churchman slovenly neglect
And rustic coarseness would. An heav'nly mind
May be indiff'rent to her house of clay,
And slight the hovel as beneath her care;
But how a body so fantastic, trim, 460
And quaint, in its deportment and attire,
Can lodge an heav'nly mind—demands a doubt.
He that negociates between God and man,
As God's ambassador, the grand concerns
Of judgment and of mercy, should beware
Of lightness in his speech. 'Tis pitiful
To court a grin, when you should woo a soul;
To break a jest, when pity would inspire
Pathetic exhortation; and t' address
The skittish fancy with facetious tales, 470
When sent with God's commission to the heart!
So did not Paul. Direct me to a quip
Or merry turn in all he ever wrote,
And I consent you take it for your text,
Your only one, till sides and benches fail.
No: he was serious in a serious cause,
And understood too well the weighty terms
That he had ta'en in charge. He would not stoop
To conquer those by jocular exploits,
Whom truth and soberness assail'd in vain. 480
Oh, popular applause! what heart of man
Is proof against thy sweet seducing charms?
The wisest and the best feel urgent need
Of all their caution in thy gentlest gales;
But, swell'd into a gust—who then, alas!
With all his canvass set, and inexpert,
And therefore heedless, can withstand thy pow'r?
Praise from the rivel'd lips of toothless, bald
Decrepitude; and in the looks of lean
And craving poverty; and in the bow 490
Respectful of the smutch'd artificer;
Is oft too welcome, and may much disturb
The bias of the purpose. How much more,
Pour'd forth by beauty splendid and polite,
In language soft as adoration breathes?
Ah, spare your idol! think him human still.
Charms he may have, but he has frailties too!
Dote not too much, nor spoil what ye admire.
All truth is from the sempiternal source
Of light divine. But Egypt, Greece, and Rome, 500
Drew from the stream below. More favour'd, we
Drink, when we choose it, at the fountain head.

To them it flow'd much mingled and defil'd
With hurtful error, prejudice, and dreams
Illusive of philosophy, so call'd,
But falsely. Sages after sages strove
In vain to filter off a crystal draught
Pure from the lees, which often more enhanc'd
The thirst than slak'd it, and not seldom bred
Intoxication and delirium wild. 510
In vain they push'd inquiry to the birth
And spring-time of the world; ask'd, Whence is man?
Why form'd at all? and wherefore as he is?
Where must he find his Maker? with what rites
Adore him? Will he hear, accept, and bless?
Or does he sit regardless of his works?
Has man within him an immortal seed?
Or does the tomb take all? If he survive
His ashes, where? and in what weal or woe?
Knots worthy of solution, which alone 520
A Deity could solve. Their answers, vague,
And all at random, fabulous and dark,
Left them as dark themselves. Their rules of life
Defective and unsanction'd, prov'd too weak
To bind the roving appetite, and lead
Blind nature to a God not yet reveal'd.
'Tis revelation satisfies all doubts,
Explains all mysteries, except her own,
And so illuminates the path of life,
That fools discover it, and stray no more. 530
Now tell me, dignified and sapient sir,
My man of morals, nurtur'd in the shades
Of Academus—is this false or true?
Is Christ the abler teacher, or the schools?
If Christ, then why resort at ev'ry turn
To Athens or to Rome, for wisdom short
Of man's occasions, when in him reside
Grace, knowledge, comfort—an unfathom'd store?
How oft, when Paul has serv'd us with a text,
Has Epictetus, Plato, Tully, preach'd! 540
Men that, if now alive, would sit content
And humble learners of a Saviour's worth,
Preach it who might. Such was their love of truth,
Their thirst of knowledge, and their candour too!
  And thus it is.—The pastor, either vain
By nature, or by flatt'ry made so, taught
To gaze at his own splendour, and t' exalt
Absurdly, not his office, but himself;
Or unenlighten'd, and too proud to learn;
Or vicious, and not therefore apt to teach; 550

Perverting often, by the stress of lewd
And loose example, whom he should instruct;
Exposes, and holds up to broad disgrace
The noblest function, and discredits much
The brightest truths that man has ever seen.
For ghostly counsel; if it either fall
Below the exigence, or be not back'd
With show of love, at least with hopeful proof
Of some sincerity on th' giver's part;
Or be dishonour'd, in th' exterior form 560
And mode of its conveyance, by such tricks
As move derision, or by foppish airs
And histrionic mumm'ry, that let down
The pulpit to the level of the stage;
Drops from the lips a disregarded thing.
The weak perhaps are mov'd, but are not taught,
While prejudice in men of stronger minds
Takes deeper root, confirm'd by what they see.
A relaxation of religion's hold
Upon the roving and untutor'd heart 570
Soon follows, and, the curb of conscience snapt,
The laity run wild.—But do they now?
Note their extravagance, and be convinc'd.
  As nations, ignorant of God, contrive
A wooden one, so we, no longer taught
By monitors that mother church supplies,
Now make our own. Posterity will ask
(If e'er posterity see verse of mine)
Some fifty or an hundred lustrums hence,
What was a monitor in George's days! 580
My very gentle reader, yet unborn,
Of whom I needs must augur better things,
Since heav'n would sure grow weary of a world
Productive only of a race like our's,
A monitor is wood—plank shaven thin.
We wear it at our backs. There, closely brac'd
And neatly fitted, it compresses hard
The prominent and most unsightly bones,
And binds the shoulders flat. We prove its use
Sov'reign and most effectual to secure 590
A form, not now gymnastic as of yore,
From rickets and distortion, else our lot.
But, thus admonish'd, we can walk erect—
One proof at least of manhood! while the friend
Sticks close, a Mentor worthy of his charge.
Our habits, costlier than Lucullus wore,
And by caprice as multiplied as his,

584 our's] us *1785*, *1786*.

Just please us while the fashion is at full,
But change with ev'ry moon. The sycophant,
Who waits to dress us, arbitrates their date; 600
Surveys his fair reversion with keen eye;
Finds one ill made, another obsolete,
This fits not nicely, that is ill conceiv'd;
And, making prize of all that he condemns
With our expenditure defrays his own.
Variety's the very spice of life,
That gives it all its flavour. We have run
Through ev'ry change that fancy at the loom,
Exhausted, has had genius to supply;
And, studious of mutation still, discard 610
A real elegance, a little us'd,
For monstrous novelty and strange disguise.
We sacrifice to dress, till household joys
And comforts cease. Dress drains our cellar dry,
And keeps our larder lean; puts out our fires;
And introduces hunger, frost, and woe,
Where peace and hospitality might reign.
What man that lives, and that knows how to live,
Would fail t' exhibit at the public shows
A form as splendid as the proudest there, 620
Though appetite raise outcries at the cost?
A man o' th' town dines late, but soon enough,
With reasonable forecast and dispatch,
T' ensure a side-box station at half price.
You think, perhaps, so delicate his dress,
His daily fare as delicate. Alas!
He picks clean teeth, and, busy as he seems
With an old tavern quill, is hungry yet!
The rout is folly's circle, which she draws
With magic wand. So potent is the spell, 630
That none, decoy'd into that fatal ring,
Unless by heav'n's peculiar grace, escape.
There we grow early gray, but never wise;
There form connexions, but acquire no friend;
Solicit pleasure, hopeless of success;
Waste youth in occupations only fit
For second childhood, and devote old age
To sports which only childhood could excuse.
There they are happiest who dissemble best
Their weariness; and they the most polite 640
Who squander time and treasure with a smile,
Though at their own destruction. She, that asks
Her dear five hundred friends, contemns them all,
And hates their coming. They (what can they less?)

600 Who] That *1785, 1786*. 633 but] and *1785, 1786*.

Make just reprisals; and, with cringe and shrug,
And bow obsequious, hide their hate of her.
All catch the frenzy, downward from her grace,
Whose flambeaux flash against the morning skies,
And gild our chamber ceilings as they pass
To her who, frugal only that her thrift 650
May feed excesses she can ill afford,
Is hackney'd home unlacquey'd; who, in haste
Alighting, turns the key in her own door,
And, at the watchman's lantern borrowing light,
Finds a cold bed her only comfort left.
Wives beggar husbands, husbands starve their wives,
On fortune's velvet altar off'ring up
Their last poor pittance—fortune, most severe
Of goddesses yet known, and costlier far
Than all that held their routs in Juno's heav'n.—
So fare we in this prison-house the world. 661
And 'tis a fearful spectacle to see
So many maniacs dancing in their chains.
They gaze upon the links that hold them fast
With eyes of anguish, execrate their lot,
Then shake them in despair, and dance again!

Now basket up the family of plagues
That waste our vitals; peculation, sale
Of honour, perjury, corruption, frauds
By forgery, by subterfuge of law, 670
By tricks and lies as num'rous and as keen
As the necessities their authors feel;
Then cast them, closely bundled, ev'ry brat
At the right door. Profusion is the sire.
Profusion unrestrain'd, with all that's base
In character, has litter'd all the land,
And bred, within the mem'ry of no few,
A priesthood such as Baal's was of old,
A people such as never was till now.
It is a hungry vice:—it eats up all 680
That gives society its beauty, strength,
Convenience, and security, and use:
Makes men mere vermin, worthy to be trapp'd
And gibbeted as fast as catchpole claws
Can seize the slipp'ry prey: unties the knot
Of union, and converts the sacred band
That holds mankind together to a scourge.
Profusion, deluging a state with lusts
Of grossest nature and of worst effects,
Prepares it for its ruin: hardens, blinds, 690

660 Juno's] heathen *1785, 1786.* 674 the sire] its sire *1785, 1786.*

And warps, the consciences of public men,
Till they can laugh at virtue; mock the fools
That trust them; and, in th' end, disclose a face
That would have shock'd credulity herself,
Unmask'd, vouchsafing this their sole excuse—
Since all alike are selfish, why not they?
This does profusion, and th' accursed cause
Of such deep mischief has itself a cause.
  In colleges and halls, in ancient days,
When learning, virtue, piety, and truth, 700
Were precious, and inculcated with care,
There dwelt a sage call'd Discipline. His head,
Not yet by time completely silver'd o'er,
Bespoke him past the bounds of freakish youth,
But strong for service still, and unimpair'd.
His eye was meek and gentle, and a smile
Play'd on his lips; and in his speech was heard
Paternal sweetness, dignity, and love.
The occupation dearest to his heart
Was to encourage goodness. He would stroke 710
The head of modest and ingenuous worth,
That blush'd at its own praise; and press the youth
Close to his side that pleas'd him. Learning grew,
Beneath his care, a thriving vig'rous plant;
The mind was well inform'd, the passions held
Subordinate, and diligence was choice.
If e'er it chanc'd, as sometimes chance it must,
That one among so many overleap'd
The limits of controul, his gentle eye
Grew stern, and darted a severe rebuke: 720
His frown was full of terror, and his voice
Shook the delinquent with such fits of awe
As left him not, till penitence had won
Lost favour back again, and clos'd the breach.
But Discipline, a faithful servant long,
Declin'd at length into the vale of years:
A palsy struck his arm; his sparkling eye
Was quench'd in rheums of age; his voice, unstrung,
Grew tremulous, and mov'd derision more
Than rev'rence in perverse rebellious youth. 730
So colleges and halls neglected much
Their good old friend; and Discipline at length,
O'erlook'd and unemploy'd, fell sick and died.
Then study languish'd, emulation slept,
And virtue fled. The schools became a scene
Of solemn farce, where Ignorance in stilts,
His cap well lin'd with logic not his own,
With parrot tongue perform'd the scholar's part,

Proceeding soon a graduated dunce.
Then compromise had place, and scrutiny 740
Became stone-blind; precedence went in truck,
And he was competent whose purse was so.
A dissolution of all bonds ensued;
The curbs, invented for the mulish mouth
Of head-strong youth, were broken; bars and bolts
Grew rusty by disuse; and massy gates
Forgot their office, op'ning with a touch;
Till gowns at length are found mere masquerade;
The tassell'd cap and the spruce band a jest,
A mock'ry of the world! What need of these 750
For gamesters, jockeys, brothellers impure,
Spendthrifts, and booted sportsmen, oft'ner seen
With belted waist and pointers at their heels
Than in the bounds of duty? What was learn'd,
If aught was learn'd in childhood, is forgot;
And such expense as pinches parents blue,
And mortifies the lib'ral hand of love,
Is squander'd in pursuit of idle sports
And vicious pleasures; buys the boy a name,
That sits a stigma on his father's house, 760
And cleaves through life inseparably close
To him that wears it. What can after-games
Of riper joys, and commerce with the world,
The lewd vain world, that must receive him soon,
Add to such erudition, thus acquir'd,
Where science and where virtue are profess'd?
They may confirm his habits, rivet fast
His folly, but to spoil him is a task
That bids defiance to th' united pow'rs
Of fashion, dissipation, taverns, stews. 770
Now, blame we most the nurslings or the nurse?
The children, crook'd, and twisted, and deform'd,
Through want of care; or her, whose winking eye
And slumb'ring oscitancy mars the brood?
The nurse no doubt. Regardless of her charge,
She needs herself correction; needs to learn,
That it is dang'rous sporting with the world,
With things so sacred as a nation's trust,
The nurture of her youth, her dearest pledge.
 All are not such. I had a brother once— 780
Peace to the mem'ry of a man of worth,
A man of letters, and of manners too!
Of manners sweet as virtue always wears,
When gay good-nature dresses her in smiles.
He grac'd a college[1], in which order yet

[1] Ben'et Coll. Cambridge [C.].

Was sacred; and was honour'd, lov'd, and wept,
By more than one, themselves conspicuous there.
Some minds are temper'd happily, and mixt
With such ingredients of good sense and taste
Of what is excellent in man, they thirst 790
With such a zeal to be what they approve,
That no restraints can circumscribe them more
Than they themselves by choice, for wisdom's sake;
Nor can example hurt them: what they see
Of vice in others but enhancing more
The charms of virtue in their just esteem.
If such escape contagion, and emerge
Pure, from so foul a pool, to shine abroad,
And give the world their talents and themselves,
Small thanks to those whose negligence or sloth
Expos'd their inexperience to the snare, 801
And left them to an undirected choice.

See, then, the quiver broken and decay'd,
In which are kept our arrows! Rusting there
In wild disorder, and unfit for use,
What wonder if, discharg'd into the world,
They shame their shooters with a random flight,
Their points obtuse, and feathers drunk with wine!
Well may the church wage unsuccessful war,
With such artill'ry arm'd. Vice parries wide 810
Th' undreaded volley with a sword of straw,
And stands an impudent and fearless mark.

Have we not track'd the felon home, and found
His birth-place and his dam? The country mourns—
Mourns, because ev'ry plague that can infest
Society, and that saps and worms the base
Of th' edifice that policy has rais'd,
Swarms in all quarters; meets the eye, the ear,
And suffocates the breath at ev'ry turn.
Profusion breeds them; and the cause itself 820
Of that calamitous mischief has been found:
Found, too, where most offensive, in the skirts
Of the rob'd pedagogue! Else, let th' arraign'd
Stand up unconscious, and refute the charge.
So, when the Jewish leader stretch'd his arm,
And wav'd his rod divine, a race obscene,
Spawn'd in the muddy beds of Nile, came forth
Polluting Egypt: gardens, fields, and plains,
Were cover'd with the pest; the streets were fill'd;
The croaking nuisance lurk'd in ev'ry nook; 830
Nor palaces, nor even chambers, 'scap'd;
And the land stank—so num'rous was the fry.

BOOK III

THE GARDEN

ARGUMENT OF THE THIRD BOOK.—Self-recollection and reproof—Address to domestic happiness—Some account of myself—The vanity of many of their pursuits who are reputed wise—Justification of my censures—Divine illumination necessary to the most expert philosopher—The question, What is truth? answered by other questions—Domestic happiness addressed again—Few lovers of the country—My tame hare—Occupations of a retired gentleman in his garden—Pruning—Framing—Greenhouse—Sowing of flower-seeds—The country preferable to the town even in the winter—Reasons why it is deserted at that season—Ruinous effects of gaming and of expensive improvement—Book concludes with an apostrophe to the metropolis.

As one who, long in thickets and in brakes
Entangled, winds now this way and now that
His devious course uncertain, seeking home;
Or, having long in miry ways been foil'd
And sore discomfited, from slough to slough
Plunging, and half despairing of escape;
If chance at length he find a greensward smooth
And faithful to the foot, his spirits rise,
He chirrups brisk his ear-erecting steed,
And winds his way with pleasure and with ease;
So I, designing other themes, and call'd 11
T' adorn the Sofa with eulogium due,
To tell its slumbers, and to paint its dreams,
Have rambled wide. In country, city, seat
Of academic fame (howe'er deserv'd),
Long held, and scarcely disengag'd at last.
But now, with pleasant pace, a cleanlier road
I mean to tread. I feel myself at large,
Courageous, and refresh'd for future toil,
If toil await me, or if dangers new. 20

Since pulpits fail, and sounding-boards reflect
Most part an empty ineffectual sound,
What chance that I, to fame so little known,
Nor conversant with men or manners much,
Should speak to purpose, or with better hope
Crack the satiric thong? 'Twere wiser far
For me, enamour'd of sequester'd scenes,
And charm'd with rural beauty, to repose,
Where chance may throw me, beneath elm or vine,
My languid limbs, when summer sears the plains;
Or, when rough winter rages, on the soft 31
And shelter'd Sofa, while the nitrous air
Feeds a blue flame, and makes a cheerful hearth;
There, undisturb'd by folly, and appriz'd

How great the danger of disturbing her,
To muse in silence, or at least confine
Remarks that gall so many to the few
My partners in retreat. Disgust conceal'd
Is oft-times proof of wisdom, when the fault
Is obstinate, and cure beyond our reach. 40
  Domestic happiness, thou only bliss
Of Paradise that has surviv'd the fall!
Though few now taste thee unimpair'd and pure,
Or, tasting, long enjoy thee; too infirm,
Or too incautious, to preserve thy sweets
Unmixt with drops of bitter, which neglect
Or temper sheds into thy crystal cup.
Thou art the nurse of virtue—in thine arms
She smiles, appearing, as in truth she is,
Heav'n-born, and destin'd to the skies again. 50
Thou art not known where pleasure is ador'd,
That reeling goddess with the zoneless waist
And wand'ring eyes, still leaning on the arm
Of novelty, her fickle frail support;
For thou art meek and constant, hating change,
And finding, in the calm of truth-tried love,
Joys that her stormy raptures never yield.
Forsaking thee, what shipwreck have we made
Of honour, dignity, and fair renown!
Till prostitution elbows us aside 60
In all our crowded streets; and senates seem
Conven'd for purposes of empire less
Than to release th' adultress from her bond.
Th' adultress! what a theme for angry verse!
What provocation to th' indignant heart
That feels for injur'd love! but I disdain
The nauseous task to paint her as she is,
Cruel, abandon'd, glorying in her shame!
No:—let her pass, and, chariotted along
In guilty splendour, shake the public ways; 70
The frequency of crimes has wash'd them white!
And verse of mine shall never brand the wretch,
Whom matrons now, of character unsmirch'd,
And chaste themselves, are not asham'd to own.
Virtue and vice had bound'ries in old time,
Not to be pass'd: and she, that had renounc'd
Her sex's honour, was renounc'd herself
By all that priz'd it; not for prud'ry's sake,
But dignity's, resentful of the wrong.
'Twas hard, perhaps, on here and there a waif, 80

52 the] a *1798*[2], *1800*

Desirous to return, and not receiv'd;
But was an wholesome rigour in the main,
And taught th' unblemish'd to preserve with care
That purity, whose loss was loss of all.
Men, too, were nice in honour in those days,
And judg'd offenders well. Then he that sharp'd,
And pocketted a prize by fraud obtain'd,
Was mark'd and shunn'd as odious. He that sold
His country, or was slack when she requir'd
His ev'ry nerve in action and at stretch, 90
Paid, with the blood that he had basely spar'd,
The price of his default. But now—yes, now
We are become so candid and so fair,
So lib'ral in construction, and so rich
In Christian charity, (good-natur'd age!)
That they are safe, sinners of either sex,
Transgress what laws they may. Well dress'd, well
bred,
Well equipag'd, is ticket good enough
To pass us readily through ev'ry door.
Hypocrisy, detest her as we may, 100
(And no man's hatred ever wrong'd her yet)
May claim this merit still—that she admits
The worth of what she mimics with such care,
And thus gives virtue indirect applause;
But she has burnt her mask, not needed here,
Where vice has such allowance, that her shifts
And specious semblances have lost their use.
I was a stricken deer, that left the herd
Long since; with many an arrow deep infixt
My panting side was charg'd, when I withdrew 110
To seek a tranquil death in distant shades.
There was I found by one who had himself
Been hurt by th' archers. In his side he bore,
And in his hands and feet, the cruel scars.
With gentle force soliciting the darts,
He drew them forth, and heal'd, and bade me live.
Since then, with few associates, in remote
And silent woods I wander, far from those
My former partners of the peopled scene;
With few associates, and not wishing more. 120
Here much I ruminate, as much I may,
With other views of men and manners now
Than once, and others of a life to come.
I see that all are wand'rers, gone astray
Each in his own delusions; they are lost

95 (good-natur'd age!)] a good-natur'd age! *1785-1788.*

In chase of fancied happiness, still woo'd
And never won. Dream after dream ensues;
And still they dream that they shall still succeed.
And still are disappointed. Rings the world
With the vain stir. I sum up half mankind, 130
And add two thirds of the remaining half,
And find the total of their hopes and fears
Dreams, empty dreams. The million flit as gay
As if created only like the fly,
That spreads his motley wings in th' eye of noon,
To sport their season, and be seen no more.
The rest are sober dreamers, grave and wise,
And pregnant with discov'ries new and rare.
Some write a narrative of wars, and feats
Of heroes little known; and call the rant 140
An history: describe the man, of whom
His own coevals took but little note;
And paint his person, character, and views,
As they had known him from his mother's womb.
They disentangle from the puzzled skein,
In which obscurity has wrapp'd them up,
The threads of politic and shrewd design,
That ran through all his purposes, and charge
His mind with meanings that he never had,
Or, having, kept conceal'd. Some drill and bore
The solid earth, and from the strata there 151
Extract a register, by which we learn
That he who made it, and reveal'd its date
To Moses, was mistaken in its age.
Some, more acute, and more industrious still,
Contrive creation; travel nature up
To the sharp peak of her sublimest height,
And tell us whence the stars; why some are fix'd,
And planetary some; what gave them first
Rotation, from what fountain flow'd their light. 160
Great contest follows, and much learned dust
Involves the combatants; each claiming truth,
And truth disclaiming both. And thus they spend
The little wick of life's poor shallow lamp,
In playing tricks with nature, giving laws
To distant worlds, and trifling in their own.
Is't not a pity now, that tickling rheums
Should ever tease the lungs and blear the sight
Of oracles like these? Great pity too,
That, having wielded th' elements, and built 170
A thousand systems, each in his own way,

131 remainder *1785, 1786.*

They should go out in fume, and be forgot?
Ah! what is life thus spent? and what are they
But frantic who thus spend it? all for smoke—
Eternity for bubbles, proves at last
A senseless bargain. When I see such games
Play'd by the creatures of a pow'r who swears
That he will judge the earth, and call the fool
To a sharp reck'ning that has liv'd in vain;
And when I weigh this seeming wisdom well, 180
And prove it in th' infallible result
So hollow and so false—I feel my heart
Dissolve in pity, and account the learn'd,
If this be learning, most of all deceiv'd.
Great crimes alarm the conscience, but it sleeps
While thoughtful man is plausibly amus'd.
Defend me, therefore, common sense, say I,
From reveries so airy, from the toil
Of dropping buckets into empty wells,
And growing old in drawing nothing up! 190
'Twere well, says one sage erudite, profound,
Terribly arch'd and aquiline his nose,
And overbuilt with most impending brows,
'Twere well, could you permit the world to live
As the world pleases. What's the world to you?—
Much. I was born of woman, and drew milk,
As sweet as charity, from human breasts.
I think, articulate, I laugh and weep,
And exercise all functions of a man.
How then should I and any man that lives 200
Be strangers to each other? Pierce my vein,
Take of the crimson stream meand'ring there,
And catechise it well; apply thy glass,
Search it, and prove now if it be not blood
Congenial with thine own: and, if it be,
What edge of subtlety canst thou suppose
Keen enough, wise and skilful as thou art,
To cut the link of brotherhood, by which
One common Maker bound me to the kind?
True; I am no proficient, I confess, 210
In arts like your's. I cannot call the swift
And perilous lightnings from the angry clouds,
And bid them hide themselves in earth beneath;
I cannot analyse the air, nor catch
The parallax of yonder luminous point,
That seems half quench'd in the immense abyss:
Such pow'rs I boast not—neither can I rest

203 thy] your *1785–1788*. 213 th' earth *1785*, *1786*.

A silent witness of the headlong rage
Or heedless folly by which thousands die,
Bone of my bone, and kindred souls to mine. 220
  God never meant that man should scale the heav'ns
By strides of human wisdom. In his works
Though wondrous, he commands us in his word
To seek *him* rather, where his mercy shines.
The mind indeed, enlighten'd from above,
Views him in all; ascribes to the grand cause
The grand effect; acknowledges with joy
His manner, and with rapture tastes his style.
But never yet did philosophic tube,
That brings the planets home into the eye 230
Of observation, and discovers, else
Not visible, his family of worlds,
Discover him that rules them; such a veil
Hangs over mortal eyes, blind from the birth,
And dark in things divine. Full often, too,
Our wayward intellect, the more we learn
Of nature, overlooks her author more;
From instrumental causes proud to draw
Conclusions retrograde, and mad mistake.
But if his word once teach us, shoot a ray 240
Through all the heart's dark chambers, and reveal
Truths undiscern'd but by that holy light,
Then all is plain. Philosophy, baptiz'd
In the pure fountain of eternal love,
Has eyes indeed; and, viewing all she sees
As meant to indicate a God to man,
Gives *him* his praise, and forfeits not her own.
Learning has borne such fruit in other days
On all her branches: piety has found
Friends in the friends of science, and true pray'r
Has flow'd from lips wet with Castalian dews. 251
Such was thy wisdom, Newton, childlike sage!
Sagacious reader of the works of God,
And in his word sagacious. Such too thine,
Milton, whose genius had angelic wings,
And fed on manna! And such thine, in whom
Our British Themis gloried with just cause,
Immortal Hale! for deep discernment prais'd
And sound integrity, not more than fam'd
For sanctity of manners undefil'd. 260
  All flesh is grass, and all its glory fades
Like the fair flow'r dishevell'd in the wind;
Riches have wings, and grandeur is a dream:
The man we celebrate must find a tomb,
And we that worship him ignoble graves.

Nothing is proof against the gen'ral curse
Of vanity, that seizes all below.
The only amaranthine flow'r on earth
Is virtue; th' only lasting treasure, truth.
But what is truth? 'twas Pilate's question, put 270
To Truth itself, that deign'd him no reply.
And wherefore? will not God impart his light
To them that ask it?—Freely—'tis his joy,
His glory, and his nature, to impart.
But to the proud, uncandid, insincere,
Or negligent, inquirer not a spark.
What's that which brings contempt upon a book,
And him who writes it; though the style be neat,
The method clear, and argument exact?
That makes a minister in holy things 280
The joy of many, and the dread of more,
His name a theme for praise and for reproach?—
That, while it gives us worth in God's account,
Depreciates and undoes us in our own?
What pearl is it that rich men cannot buy,
That learning is too proud to gather up;
But which the poor, and the despis'd of all,
Seek and obtain, and often find unsought?
Tell me—and I will tell thee what is truth.
O, friendly to the best pursuits of man, 290
Friendly to thought, to virtue, and to peace,
Domestic life in rural leisure pass'd!
Few know thy value, and few taste thy sweets;
Though many boast thy favours, and affect
To understand and choose thee for their own.
But foolish man foregoes his proper bliss,
Ev'n as his first progenitor, and quits,
Though placed in paradise, (for earth has still
Some traces of her youthful beauty left)
Substantial happiness for transient joy. 300
Scenes form'd for contemplation, and to nurse
The growing seeds of wisdom; that suggest,
By ev'ry pleasing image they present,
Reflections such as meliorate the heart,
Compose the passions, and exalt the mind;
Scenes such as these 'tis his supreme delight
To fill with riot, and defile with blood.
Should some contagion, kind to the poor brutes
We persecute, annihilate the tribes
That draw the sportsman over hill and dale, 310
Fearless, and rapt away from all his cares;

278 who] that *1785, 1786.*

Should never game-fowl hatch her eggs again,
Nor baited hook deceive the fish's eye;
Could pageantry and dance, and feast and song,
Be quell'd in all our summer-months' retreat;
How many self-deluded nymphs and swains,
Who dream they have a taste for fields and groves,
Would find them hideous nurs'ries of the spleen,
And crowd the roads, impatient for the town!
They love the country, and none else, who seek   320
For their own sake its silence and its shade.
Delights which who would leave, that has a heart
Susceptible of pity, or a mind
Cultur'd and capable of sober thought,
For all the savage din of the swift pack,
And clamours of the field?—Detested sport,
That owes its pleasures to another's pain;
That feeds upon the sobs and dying shrieks
Of harmless nature, dumb, but yet endu'd
With eloquence, that agonies inspire,   330
Of silent tears and heart-distending sighs!
Vain tears, alas, and sighs, that never find
A corresponding tone in jovial souls!
Well—one at least is safe. One shelter'd hare
Has never heard the sanguinary yell
Of cruel man, exulting in her woes.
Innocent partner of my peaceful home,
Whom ten long years' experience of my care
Has made at last familiar; she has lost
Much of her vigilant instinctive dread,   340
Not needful here, beneath a roof like mine.
Yes—thou may'st eat thy bread, and lick the hand
That feeds thee; thou may'st frolic on the floor
At evening, and at night retire secure
To thy straw couch, and slumber unalarm'd;
For I have gain'd thy confidence, have pledg'd
All that is human in me to protect
Thine unsuspecting gratitude and love.
If I survive thee I will dig thy grave;
And, when I place thee in it, sighing, say,   350
I knew at least one hare that had a friend.

How various his employments, whom the world
Calls idle; and who justly, in return,
Esteems that busy world an idler too!
Friends, books, a garden, and perhaps his pen,
Delightful industry enjoy'd at home,

315 summer-months' retreat *1793-1803*; summer-month retreats *1785*, *1786*; summer-months retreat *1787*, *1788*. *Later edd. read* summer-month's retreat *or* summer-month's retreats.

And nature in her cultivated trim
Dress'd to his taste, inviting him abroad—
Can he want occupation who has these?
Will he be idle who has much t' enjoy? 360
Me, therefore, studious of laborious ease,
Not slothful; happy to deceive the time,
Not waste it; and aware that human life
Is but a loan to be repaid with use,
When he shall call his debtors to account
From whom are all our blessings; bus'ness finds
Ev'n here: while sedulous I seek t' improve,
At least neglect not, or leave unemploy'd,
The mind he gave me; driving it, though slack
Too oft, and much impeded in its work 370
By causes not to be divulg'd in vain,
To its just point—the service of mankind.
He that attends to his interior self,
That has a heart, and keeps it; has a mind
That hungers, and supplies it; and who seeks
A social, not a dissipated life;
Has business; feels himself engag'd t' achieve
No unimportant, though a silent, task.
A life all turbulence and noise may seem
To him that leads it, wise, and to be prais'd; 380
But wisdom is a pearl with most success
Sought in still water, and beneath clear skies.
He that is ever occupied in storms,
Or dives not for it, or brings up instead,
Vainly industrious, a disgraceful prize.
  The morning finds the self-sequester'd man
Fresh for his task, intend what task he may.
Whether inclement seasons recommend
His warm but simple home, where he enjoys,
With her who shares his pleasures and his heart, 390
Sweet converse, sipping calm the fragrant lymph
Which neatly she prepares; then to his book,
Well chosen, and not sullenly perus'd
In selfish silence, but imparted oft
As aught occurs that she may smile to hear,
Or turn to nourishment, digested well.
Or, if the garden with its many cares,
All well repaid, demand him, he attends
The welcome call, conscious how much the hand
Of lubbard labour needs his watchful eye, 400
Oft loit'ring lazily, if not o'erseen,
Or misapplying his unskilful strength.
Nor does he govern only or direct,
But much performs himself. No works indeed

That ask robust tough sinews, bred to toil,
Servile employ; but such as may amuse,
Not tire, demanding rather skill than force.
Proud of his well-spread walls, he views his trees
That meet (no barren interval between) 409
With pleasure more than ev'n their fruits afford,
Which, save himself who trains them, none can feel.
These, therefore, are his own peculiar charge;
No meaner hand may discipline the shoots,
None but his steel approach them. What is weak,
Distemper'd, or has lost prolific pow'rs,
Impair'd by age, his unrelenting hand
Dooms to the knife: nor does he spare the soft
And succulent, that feeds its giant growth,
But barren, at th' expence of neighb'ring twigs
Less ostentatious, and yet studded thick 420
With hopeful gems. The rest, no portion left
That may disgrace his art, or disappoint
Large expectation, he disposes neat
At measur'd distances, that air and sun,
Admitted freely, may afford their aid,
And ventilate and warm the swelling buds.
Hence summer has her riches, autumn hence,
And hence ev'n winter fills his wither'd hand
With blushing fruits, and plenty, not his own[1].
Fair recompense of labour well bestow'd, 430
And wise precaution; which a clime so rude
Makes needful still, whose spring is but the child
Of churlish winter, in her froward moods
Discov'ring much the temper of her sire.
For oft, as if in her the stream of mild
Maternal nature had revers'd its course,
She brings her infants forth with many smiles;
But, once deliver'd, kills them with a frown.
He, therefore, timely warn'd, himself supplies
Her want of care, screening and keeping warm 440
The plenteous bloom, that no rough blast may sweep
His garlands from the boughs. Again, as oft
As the sun peeps and vernal airs breathe mild,
The fence withdrawn, he gives them ev'ry beam,
And spreads his hopes before the blaze of day.

To raise the prickly and green-coated gourd,
So grateful to the palate, and when rare
So coveted, else base and disesteem'd—
Food for the vulgar merely—is an art
That toiling ages have but just matur'd, 450

[1] Miraturque novos fructus et non sua poma. VIRG. [C.]

405 tough] rough *1800*. 432 needed *1798*[1].

And at this moment unassay'd in song.
Yet gnats have had, and frogs and mice, long since,
Their eulogy; those sang the Mantuan bard,
And these the Grecian, in ennobling strains;
And in thy numbers, Phillips, shines for aye
The solitary shilling. Pardon then,
Ye sage dispensers of poetic fame,
Th' ambition of one, meaner far, whose pow'rs,
Presuming an attempt not less sublime,
Pant for the praise of dressing to the taste 460
Of critic appetite, no sordid fare,
A cucumber, while costly yet and scarce.
 The stable yields a stercoraceous heap,
Impregnated with quick fermenting salts,
And potent to resist the freezing blast:
For, ere the beech and elm have cast their leaf
Deciduous, when now November dark
Checks vegetation in the torpid plant
Expos'd to his cold breath, the task begins.
Warily, therefore, and with prudent heed, 470
He seeks a favour'd spot; that where he builds
Th' agglomerated pile his frame may front
The sun's meridian disk, and at the back
Enjoy close shelter, wall, or reeds, or hedge
Impervious to the wind. First he bids spread
Dry fern or litter'd hay, that may imbibe
Th' ascending damps; then leisurely impose,
And lightly, shaking it with agile hand
From the full fork, the saturated straw.
What longest binds the closest forms secure 480
The shapely side, that as it rises takes,
By just degrees, an overhanging breadth,
Shelt'ring the base with its projected eaves:
Th' uplifted frame, compact at ev'ry joint,
And overlaid with clear translucent glass,
He settles next upon the sloping mount,
Whose sharp declivity shoots off secure
From the dash'd pane the deluge as it falls.
He shuts it close, and the first labour ends.
Thrice must the voluble and restless earth 490
Spin round upon her axle, ere the warmth,
Slow gathering in the midst, through the square mass
Diffus'd, attain the surface: when, behold!
A pestilent and most corrosive steam,
Like a gross fog Bœotian, rising fast,
And fast condens'd upon the dewy sash,

463 stercorarious *1785, 1786.* 467 and when *1785, 1786.*

Asks egress; which obtain'd, the overcharg'd
And drench'd conservatory breathes abroad,
In volumes wheeling slow, the vapour dank;
And, purified, rejoices to have lost 500
Its foul inhabitant. But to assuage
Th' impatient fervour which it first conceives
Within its reeking bosom, threat'ning death
To his young hopes, requires discreet delay.
Experience, slow preceptress, teaching oft
The way to glory by miscarriage foul,
Must prompt him, and admonish how to catch
Th' auspicious moment, when the temper'd heat,
Friendly to vital motion, may afford
Soft fomentation, and invite the seed. 510
The seed, selected wisely, plump, and smooth,
And glossy, he commits to pots of size
Diminutive, well fill'd with well-prepar'd
And fruitful soil, that has been treasur'd long,
And drank no moisture from the dripping clouds:
These on the warm and genial earth, that hides
The smoking manure and o'erspreads it all,
He places lightly, and, as time subdues
The rage of fermentation, plunges deep
In the soft medium, till they stand immers'd. 520
Then rise the tender germs, upstarting quick,
And spreading wide their spongy lobes; at first
Pale, wan, and livid; but assuming soon,
If fann'd by balmy and nutritious air,
Strain'd through the friendly mats, a vivid green.
Two leaves produc'd, two rough indented leaves,
Cautious he pinches from the second stalk
A pimple, that portends a future sprout,
And interdicts its growth. Thence straight succeed
The branches, sturdy to his utmost wish; 530
Prolific all, and harbingers of more.
The crowded roots demand enlargement now,
And transplantation in an ampler space.
Indulg'd in what they wish, they soon supply
Large foliage, overshadowing golden flow'rs,
Blown on the summit of th' apparent fruit.
These have their sexes; and, when summer shines,
The bee transports the fertilizing meal
From flow'r to flow'r, and ev'n the breathing air
Wafts the rich prize to its appointed use. 540
Not so when winter scowls. Assistant art
Then acts in nature's office, brings to pass
The glad espousals, and ensures the crop.

510 fermentation *1786*.

Grudge not, ye rich, (since luxury must have
His dainties, and the world's more num'rous half
Lives by contriving delicates for you)
Grudge not the cost. Ye little know the cares,
The vigilance, the labour, and the skill,
That day and night are exercis'd, and hang
Upon the ticklish balance of suspense, 550
That ye may garnish your profuse regales
With summer fruits brought forth by wintry suns.
Ten thousand dangers lie in wait to thwart
The process. Heat and cold, and wind, and steam,
Moisture and drought, mice, worms, and swarming flies,
Minute as dust, and numberless, oft work
Dire disappointment that admits no cure,
And which no care can obviate. It were long,
Too long, to tell th' expedients and the shifts
Which he that fights a season so severe 560
Devises, while he guards his tender trust;
And oft, at last, in vain. The learn'd and wise
Sarcastic would exclaim, and judge the song
Cold as its theme, and, like its theme, the fruit
Of too much labour, worthless when produc'd.

Who loves a garden loves a green-house too.
Unconscious of a less propitious clime,
There blooms exotic beauty, warm and snug,
While the winds whistle and the snows descend.
The spiry myrtle with unwith'ring leaf 570
Shines there, and flourishes. The golden boast
Of Portugal and western India there,
The ruddier orange, and the paler lime,
Peep through their polish'd foliage at the storm,
And seem to smile at what they need not fear.
Th' amomum there with intermingling flow'rs
And cherries hangs her twigs. Geranium boasts
Her crimson honours, and the spangled beau,
Ficoides, glitters bright the winter long.
All plants, of ev'ry leaf, that can endure 580
The winter's frown, if screen'd from his shrewd bite,
Live there, and prosper. Those Ausonia claims,
Levantine regions these; th' Azores send
Their jessamine, her jessamine remote
Caffraia: foreigners from many lands,
They form one social shade, as if conven'd
By magic summons of th' Orphean lyre.
Yet just arrangement, rarely brought to pass

585 Caffraria *Southey, and some edd. after 1800.*

But by a master's hand, disposing well
The gay diversities of leaf and flow'r, 590
Must lend its aid t' illustrate all their charms,
And dress the regular yet various scene.
Plant behind plant aspiring, in the van
The dwarfish, in the rear retir'd, but still
Sublime above the rest, the statelier stand.
So once were rang'd the sons of ancient Rome,
A noble show! while Roscius trod the stage;
And so, while Garrick, as renown'd as he,
The sons of Albion; fearing each to lose
Some note of Nature's music from his lips, 600
And covetous of Shakespeare's beauty, seen
In ev'ry flash of his far-beaming eye.
Nor taste alone and well-contriv'd display
Suffice to give the marshall'd ranks the grace
Of their complete effect. Much yet remains
Unsung, and many cares are yet behind,
And more laborious; cares on which depends
Their vigour, injur'd soon, not soon restor'd.
The soil must be renew'd, which, often wash'd,
Loses its treasure of salubrious salts, 610
And disappoints the roots; the slender roots
Close interwoven, where they meet the vase,
Must smooth be shorn away; the sapless branch
Must fly before the knife; the wither'd leaf
Must be detach'd, and where it strews the floor
Swept with a woman's neatness, breeding else
Contagion, and disseminating death.
Discharge but these kind offices, (and who
Would spare, that loves them, offices like these?)
Well they reward the toil. The sight is pleas'd,
The scent regal'd, each odorif'rous leaf, 621
Each op'ning blossom, freely breathes abroad
Its gratitude, and thanks him with its sweets.
  So manifold, all pleasing in their kind,
All healthful, are th' employs of rural life,
Reiterated as the wheel of time
Runs round; still ending, and beginning still.
Nor are these all. To deck the shapely knoll,
That, softly swell'd and gaily dress'd, appears
A flow'ry island, from the dark green lawn 630
Emerging, must be deem'd a labour due
To no mean hand, and asks the touch of taste.
Here also grateful mixture of well-match'd
And sorted hues (each giving each relief,

607 depend *1787–1800.*

And by contrasted beauty shining more)
Is needful. Strength may wield the pond'rous spade,
May turn the clod, and wheel the compost home;
But elegance, chief grace the garden shows,
And most attractive, is the fair result
Of thought, the creature of a polish'd mind. 640
Without it all is gothic as the scene
To which th' insipid citizen resorts
Near yonder heath; where industry mispent,
But proud of his uncouth ill-chosen task,
Has made a heav'n on earth; with suns and moons
Of close-ramm'd stones has charg'd th' encumber'd
soil,
And fairly laid the zodiac in the dust.
He, therefore, who would see his flow'rs dispos'd
Sightly and in just order, ere he gives
The beds the trusted treasure of their seeds, 650
Forecasts the future whole; that, when the scene
Shall break into its preconceiv'd display,
Each for itself, and all as with one voice
Conspiring, may attest his bright design.
Nor even then, dismissing as perform'd
His pleasant work, may he suppose it done.
Few self-supported flow'rs endure the wind
Uninjur'd, but expect th' upholding aid
Of the smooth-shaven prop, and, neatly tied,
Are wedded thus, like beauty to old age, 660
For int'rest sake, the living to the dead.
Some clothe the soil that feeds them, far diffus'd
And lowly creeping, modest and yet fair,
Like virtue, thriving most where little seen:
Some, more aspiring, catch the neighbour shrub
With clasping tendrils, and invest his branch,
Else unadorn'd, with many a gay festoon
And fragrant chaplet, recompensing well
The strength they borrow with the grace they lend.
All hate the rank society of weeds, 670
Noisome, and ever greedy to exhaust
Th' impov'rish'd earth; an overbearing race,
That, like the multitude made faction-mad,
Disturb good order, and degrade true worth.
Oh, blest seclusion from a jarring world,
Which he, thus occupied, enjoys! Retreat
Cannot indeed to guilty man restore
Lost innocence, or cancel follies past;
But it has peace, and much secures the mind
From all assaults of evil; proving still 680
A faithful barrier, not o'erleap'd with ease

By vicious custom, raging uncontroll'd
Abroad, and desolating public life.
When fierce temptation, seconded within
By traitor appetite, and arm'd with darts
Temper'd in hell, invades the throbbing breast,
To combat may be glorious, and success
Perhaps may crown us; but to fly is safe.
Had I the choice of sublunary good,
What could I wish that I possess not here? 690
Health, leisure, means t' improve it, friendship, peace,
No loose or wanton, though a wand'ring, muse,
And constant occupation without care.
Thus blest, I draw a picture of that bliss;
Hopeless, indeed, that dissipated minds,
And profligate abusers of a world
Created fair so much in vain for them,
Should seek the guiltless joys that I describe,
Allur'd by my report: but sure no less, 699
That, self-condemn'd, they must neglect the prize,
And what they will not taste must yet approve.
What we admire we praise; and, when we praise,
Advance it into notice, that, its worth
Acknowledg'd, others may admire it too.
I therefore recommend, though at the risk
Of popular disgust, yet boldly still,
The cause of piety and sacred truth,
And virtue, and those scenes which God ordain'd
Should best secure them and promote them most;
Scenes that I love, and with regret perceive 710
Forsak'n, or through folly not enjoy'd.
Pure is the nymph, though lib'ral of her smiles,
And chaste, though unconfin'd, whom I extol.
Not as the prince in Shushan, when he call'd,
Vain-glorious of her charms, his Vashti forth
To grace the full pavilion. His design
Was but to boast his own peculiar good,
Which all might view with envy, none partake.
My charmer is not mine alone; my sweets,
And she that sweetens all my bitters too, 720
Nature, enchanting Nature, in whose form
And lineaments divine I trace a hand
That errs not, and find raptures still renew'd,
Is free to all men—universal prize.
Strange that so fair a creature should yet want
Admirers, and be destin'd to divide
With meaner objects ev'n the few she finds!
Stripp'd of her ornaments, her leaves and flow'rs,

She loses all her influence. Cities then
Attract us, and neglected Nature pines, 730
Abandon'd, as unworthy of our love.
But are not wholesome airs, though unperfum'd
By roses; and clear suns, though scarcely felt;
And groves, if unharmonious, yet secure
From clamour, and whose very silence charms;
To be preferr'd to smoke, to the eclipse
That Metropolitan volcanos make,
Whose Stygian throats breathe darkness all day long;
And to the stir of commerce, driving slow,
And thund'ring loud, with his ten thousand wheels?
They would be, were not madness in the head, 741
And folly in the heart; were England now
What England was; plain, hospitable, kind,
And undebauch'd. But we have bid farewell
To all the virtues of those better days,
And all their honest pleasures. Mansions once
Knew their own masters; and laborious hinds
Who had surviv'd the father, serv'd the son.
Now the legitimate and rightful lord
Is but a transient guest, newly arriv'd, 750
And soon to be supplanted. He that saw
His patrimonial timber cast its leaf,
Sells the last scantling, and transfers the price
To some shrewd sharper, ere it buds again.
Estates are landscapes, gaz'd upon a while,
Then advertis'd, and auctioneer'd away.
The country starves, and they that feed th' o'er-
charg'd
And surfeited lewd town with her fair dues,
By a just judgment strip and starve themselves.
The wings that waft our riches out of sight 760
Grow on the gamester's elbows; and th' alert
And nimble motion of those restless joints,
That never tire, soon fans them all away.
Improvement too, the idol of the age,
Is fed with many a victim. Lo, he comes!
Th' omnipotent magician, Brown, appears!
Down falls the venerable pile, th' abode
Of our forefathers—a grave whisker'd race,
But tasteless. Springs a palace in its stead,
But in a distant spot; where, more expos'd, 770
It may enjoy th' advantage of the north,
And aguish east, till time shall have transform'd
Those naked acres to a shelt'ring grove.

748 Who] That *1785*, *1786*.

He speaks. The lake in front becomes a lawn;
Woods vanish, hills subside, and vallies rise:
And streams, as if created for his use,
Pursue the track of his directing wand,
Sinuous or straight, now rapid and now slow,
Now murm'ring soft, now roaring in cascades—
Ev'n as he bids! Th' enraptur'd owner smiles. 780
'Tis finish'd, and yet, finish'd as it seems,
Still wants a grace, the loveliest it could show,
A mine to satisfy th' enormous cost.
Drain'd to the last poor item of his wealth,
He sighs, departs, and leaves th' accomplish'd plan
That he has touch'd, retouch'd, many a long day
Labour'd, and many a night pursu'd in dreams,
Just when it meets his hopes, and proves the heav'n
He wanted, for a wealthier to enjoy!
And now perhaps the glorious hour is come, 790
When, having no stake left, no pledge t' endear
Her int'rests, or that gives her sacred cause
A moment's operation on his love,
He burns with most intense and flagrant zeal
To serve his country. Ministerial grace
Deals him out money from the public chest;
Or, if that mine be shut, some private purse
Supplies his need with an usurious loan,
To be refunded duly when his vote,
Well-manag'd, shall have earn'd its worthy price.
Oh innocent, compar'd with arts like these, 801
Crape, and cock'd pistol, and the whistling ball
Sent through the trav'ller's temples! He that finds
One drop of heav'n's sweet mercy in his cup,
Can dig, beg, rot, and perish, well content,
So he may wrap himself in honest rags
At his last gasp; but could not for a world
Fish up his dirty and dependent bread
From pools and ditches of the commonwealth,
Sordid and sick'ning at his own success. 810
Ambition, av'rice, penury incurr'd
By endless riot, vanity, the lust
Of pleasure and variety, dispatch,
As duly as the swallows disappear,
The world of wand'ring knights and squires to town.
London ingulphs them all! The shark is there,
And the shark's prey; the spendthrift, and the leech
That sucks him. There the sycophant, and he
Who, with bare-headed and obsequious bows,

819 Who] That *1785. 1786.*

Begs a warm office, doom'd to a cold jail 820
And groat per diem, if his patron frown.
The levee swarms, as if, in golden pomp,
Were character'd on ev'ry statesman's door,
"BATTER'D AND BANKRUPT FORTUNES MENDED HERE."
These are the charms that sully and eclipse
The charms of nature. 'Tis the cruel gripe
That lean hard-handed poverty inflicts,
The hope of better things, the chance to win,
The wish to shine, the thirst to be amus'd,
That at the sound of winter's hoary wing 830
Unpeople all our counties of such herds
Of flutt'ring, loit'ring, cringing, begging, loose
And wanton vagrants, as make London, vast
And boundless as it is, a crowded coop.
Oh thou, resort and mart of all the earth,
Chequer'd with all complexions of mankind,
And spotted with all crimes; in whom I see
Much that I love, and more that I admire,
And all that I abhor; thou freckled fair,
That pleasest and yet shock'st me, I can laugh 840
And I can weep, can hope, and can despond,
Feel wrath and pity, when I think on thee!
Ten righteous would have sav'd a city once,
And thou hast many righteous.—Well for thee!
That salt preserves thee; more corrupted else,
And therefore more obnoxious, at this hour
Than Sodom in her day had pow'r to be,
For whom God heard his Abr'am plead in vain.

BOOK IV

THE WINTER EVENING

ARGUMENT OF THE FOURTH BOOK.—The post comes in—The newspaper is read—The world contemplated at a distance—Address to winter—The rural amusements of a winter evening compared with the fashionable ones—Address to evening—A brown study—Fall of snow in the evening—The waggoner—A poor family-piece—The rural thief—Public houses—The multitude of them censured—The farmer's daughter: what she was—what she is—The simplicity of country manners almost lost—Causes of the change—Desertion of the country by the rich—Neglect of magistrates—The militia principally in fault—The new recruit and his transformation—Reflection on bodies corporate—The love of rural objects natural to all, and never to be totally extinguished.

HARK! 'tis the twanging horn o'er yonder bridge,
That with its wearisome but needful length
Bestrides the wintry flood, in which the moon
Sees her unwrinkled face reflected bright;—

831 countries *1798*², *1800*. 840 pleases . . . shocks *1785-1788*.
Argument 3 rural . . . of a] amusements of a rural *1785*, *1786*.
1, 4 *for punctuation, see notes.*

He comes, the herald of a noisy world,
With spatter'd boots, strapp'd waist, and frozen locks;
News from all nations lumb'ring at his back.
True to his charge, the close-pack'd load behind,
Yet careless what he brings, his one concern
Is to conduct it to the destin'd inn: 10
And, having dropp'd th' expected bag, pass on.
He whistles as he goes, light-hearted wretch,
Cold and yet cheerful: messenger of grief
Perhaps to thousands, and of joy to some;
To him indiff'rent whether grief or joy.
Houses in ashes, and the fall of stocks,
Births, deaths, and marriages, epistles wet
With tears, that trickled down the writer's cheeks
Fast as the periods from his fluent quill,
Or charg'd with am'rous sighs of absent swains, 20
Or nymphs responsive, equally affect
His horse and him, unconscious of them all.
But oh th' important budget! usher'd in
With such heart-shaking music, who can say
What are its tidings? have our troops awak'd?
Or do they still, as if with opium drugg'd,
Snore to the murmurs of th' Atlantic wave?
Is India free? and does she wear her plum'd
And jewell'd turban with a smile of peace,
Or do we grind her still? The grand debate, 30
The popular harangue, the tart reply,
The logic, and the wisdom, and the wit,
And the loud laugh—I long to know them all;
I burn to set th' imprison'd wranglers free,
And give them voice and utt'rance once again.
  Now stir the fire, and close the shutters fast,
Let fall the curtains, wheel the sofa round,
And, while the bubbling and loud-hissing urn
Throws up a steamy column, and the cups,
That cheer but not inebriate, wait on each, 40
So let us welcome peaceful ev'ning in.
Not such his ev'ning, who with shining face
Sweats in the crowded theatre, and, squeez'd
And bor'd with elbow-points through both his sides,
Out-scolds the ranting actor on the stage:
Nor his, who patient stands till his feet throb,
And his head thumps, to feed upon the breath
Of patriots, bursting with heroic rage,
Or placemen, all tranquillity and smiles.
This folio of four pages, happy work! 50
Which not ev'n critics criticise; that holds
Inquisitive attention, while I read,

Fast bound in chains of silence, which the fair,
Though eloquent themselves, yet fear to break;
What is it, but a map of busy life,
Its fluctuations, and its vast concerns?
Here runs the mountainous and craggy ridge
That tempts ambition. On the summit see
The seals of office glitter in his eyes;
He climbs, he pants, he grasps them! At his heels, 60
Close at his heels, a demagogue ascends,
And with a dext'rous jerk soon twists him down,
And wins them, but to lose them in his turn.
Here rills of oily eloquence in soft
Meanders lubricate the course they take;
The modest speaker is asham'd and griev'd
T' engross a moment's notice, and yet begs,
Begs a propitious ear for his poor thoughts,
However trivial all that he conceives.
Sweet bashfulness! it claims at least this praise, 70
The dearth of information and good sense
That it foretells us always comes to pass.
Cat'racts of declamation thunder here;
There forests of no meaning spread the page,
In which all comprehension wanders, lost;
While fields of pleasantry amuse us there
With merry descants on a nation's woes.
The rest appears a wilderness of strange
But gay confusion; roses for the cheeks,
And lilies for the brows of faded age, 80
Teeth for the toothless, ringlets for the bald,
Heav'n, earth, and ocean, plunder'd of their sweets,
Nectareous essences, Olympian dews,
Sermons, and city feasts, and fav'rite airs,
Æthereal journies, submarine exploits,
And Katterfelto, with his hair on end
At his own wonders, wond'ring for his bread.
'Tis pleasant through the loop-holes of retreat
To peep at such a world; to see the stir
Of the great Babel, and not feel the crowd; 90
To hear the roar she sends through all her gates
At a safe distance, where the dying sound
Falls a soft murmur on th' uninjur'd ear.
Thus sitting, and surveying thus at ease
The globe and its concerns, I seem advanc'd
To some secure and more than mortal height,
That lib'rates and exempts me from them all.
It turns submitted to my view, turns round
With all its generations; I behold
The tumult, and am still. The sound of war 100

Has lost its terrors ere it reaches me;
Grieves, but alarms me not. I mourn the pride
And av'rice that make man a wolf to man;
Hear the faint echo of those brazen throats
By which he speaks the language of his heart,
And sigh, but never tremble at the sound.
He travels and expatiates, as the bee
From flow'r to flow'r, so he from land to land;
The manners, customs, policy of all
Pay contribution to the store he gleans; 110
He sucks intelligence in ev'ry clime,
And spreads the honey of his deep research
At his return—a rich repast for me.
He travels, and I too. I tread his deck,
Ascend his topmast, through his peering eyes
Discover countries, with a kindred heart
Suffer his woes, and share in his escapes;
While fancy, like the finger of a clock,
Runs the great circuit, and is still at home.
Oh Winter, ruler of th' inverted year, 120
Thy scatter'd hair with sleet like ashes fill'd,
Thy breath congeal'd upon thy lips, thy cheeks
Fring'd with a beard made white with other snows
Than those of age, thy forehead wrapt in clouds,
A leafless branch thy sceptre, and thy throne
A sliding car, indebted to no wheels,
But urg'd by storms along its slipp'ry way,
I love thee, all unlovely as thou seem'st,
And dreaded as thou art! Thou hold'st the sun
A pris'ner in the yet undawning east, 130
Short'ning his journey between morn and noon,
And hurrying him, impatient of his stay,
Down to the rosy west; but kindly still
Compensating his loss with added hours
Of social converse and instructive ease,
And gath'ring, at short notice, in one group
The family dispers'd, and fixing thought,
Not less dispers'd by day-light and its cares.
I crown thee king of intimate delights,
Fire-side enjoyments, home-born happiness, 140
And all the comforts that the lowly roof
Of undisturb'd retirement, and the hours
Of long uninterrupted ev'ning, know.
No rattling wheels stop short before these gates;
No powder'd pert, proficient in the art
Of sounding an alarm, assaults these doors

103 makes *1785*, *1786*.

Till the street rings; no stationary steeds
Cough their own knell, while, heedless of the sound,
The silent circle fan themselves, and quake:
But here the needle plies its busy task, 150
The pattern grows, the well-depicted flow'r,
Wrought patiently into the snowy lawn,
Unfolds its bosom; buds, and leaves, and sprigs,
And curling tendrils, gracefully dispos'd,
Follow the nimble finger of the fair;
A wreath that cannot fade, of flow'rs that blow
With most success when all besides decay.
The poet's or historian's page, by one
Made vocal for th' amusement of the rest;
The sprightly lyre, whose treasure of sweet sounds
The touch from many a trembling chord shakes
out; 161
And the clear voice symphonious, yet distinct,
And in the charming strife triumphant still;
Beguile the night, and set a keener edge
On female industry: the threaded steel
Flies swiftly, and, unfelt, the task proceeds.
The volume clos'd, the customary rites
Of the last meal commence. A Roman meal;
Such as the mistress of the world once found
Delicious, when her patriots of high note, 170
Perhaps by moonlight, at their humble doors,
And under an old oak's domestic shade,
Enjoy'd—spare feast!—a radish and an egg!
Discourse ensues, not trivial, yet not dull,
Nor such as with a frown forbids the play
Of fancy, or proscribes the sound of mirth:
Nor do we madly, like an impious world,
Who deem religion frenzy, and the God
That made them an intruder on their joys,
Start at his awful name, or deem his praise 180
A jarring note. Themes of a graver tone,
Exciting oft our gratitude and love,
While we retrace with mem'ry's pointing wand,
That calls the past to our exact review,
The dangers we have 'scap'd, the broken snare,
The disappointed foe, deliv'rance found
Unlook'd for, life preserv'd and peace restor'd—
Fruits of omnipotent eternal love.
Oh ev'nings worthy of the gods! exclaim'd
The Sabine bard. Oh ev'nings, I reply, 190
More to be priz'd and coveted than yours,
As more illumin'd, and with nobler truths,
That I, and mine, and those we love, enjoy.

Is winter hideous in a garb like this?
Needs he the tragic fur, the smoke of lamps,
The pent-up breath of an unsav'ry throng,
To thaw him into feeling; or the smart
And snappish dialogue, that flippant wits
Call comedy, to prompt him with a smile?
The self-complacent actor, when he views 200
(Stealing a side-long glance at a full house)
The slope of faces, from the floor to th' roof,
(As if one master-spring controul'd them all)
Relax'd into an universal grin,
Sees not a count'nance there that speaks of joy
Half so refin'd or so sincere as our's.
Cards were superfluous here, with all the tricks
That idleness has ever yet contriv'd
To fill the void of an unfurnish'd brain,
To palliate dulness, and give time a shove. 210
Time, as he passes us, has a dove's wing,
Unsoil'd, and swift, and of a silken sound;
But the world's time is time in masquerade!
Their's, should I paint him, has his pinions fledg'd
With motley plumes; and, where the peacock shows
His azure eyes, is finctur'd black and red
With spots quadrangular of di'mond form,
Ensanguin'd hearts, clubs typical of strife,
And spades, the emblem of untimely graves.
What should be and what was an hour-glass once,
Becomes a dice-box, and a billiard mast 221
Well does the work of his destructive scythe.
Thus deck'd, he charms a world whom fashion blinds
To his true worth, most pleas'd when idle most;
Whose only happy are their wasted hours.
Ev'n misses, at whose age their mothers wore
The back-string and the bib, assume the dress
Of womanhood, sit pupils in the school
Of card-devoted time, and, night by night,
Plac'd at some vacant corner of the board, 230
Learn ev'ry trick, and soon play all the game.
But truce with censure. Roving as I rove,
Where shall I find an end, or how proceed?
As he that travels far oft turns aside
To view some rugged rock or mould'ring tow'r,
Which, seen, delights him not; then, coming home,
Describes and prints it, that the world may know
How far he went for what was nothing worth;
So I, with brush in hand and pallet spread,
With colours mix'd for a far diff'rent use, 240

221 mast] mace *1808 and later edd.*

Paint cards and dolls, and ev'ry idle thing
That fancy finds in her excursive flights.
  Come, Ev'ning, once again, season of peace;
Return, sweet Ev'ning, and continue long!
Methinks I see thee in the streaky west,
With matron-step slow-moving, while the night
Treads on thy sweeping train; one hand employ'd
In letting fall the curtain of repose
On bird and beast, the other charg'd for man
With sweet oblivion of the cares of day: 250
Not sumptuously adorn'd, nor needing aid,
Like homely featur'd night, of clust'ring gems;
A star or two, just twinkling on thy brow,
Suffices thee; save that the moon is thine
No less than her's, not worn indeed on high
With ostentatious pageantry, but set
With modest grandeur in thy purple zone,
Resplendent less, but of an ampler round.
Come then, and thou shalt find thy vot'ry calm,
Or make me so. Composure is thy gift: 260
And, whether I devote thy gentle hours
To books, to music, or the poet's toil;
To weaving nets for bird-alluring fruit;
Or twining silken threads round iv'ry reels,
When they command whom man was born to please;
I slight thee not, but make thee welcome still.
  Just when our drawing-rooms begin to blaze
With lights, by clear reflection multiplied
From many a mirror, in which he of Gath,
Goliath, might have seen his giant bulk 270
Whole, without stooping, tow'ring crest and all,
My pleasures, too, begin. But me, perhaps,
The glowing hearth may satisfy awhile
With faint illumination, that uplifts
The shadow to the ceiling, there by fits
Dancing uncouthly to the quiv'ring flame.
Not undelightful is an hour to me
So spent in parlour twilight: such a gloom
Suits well the thoughtful or unthinking mind,
The mind contemplative, with some new theme 280
Pregnant, or indispos'd alike to all.
Laugh ye, who boast your more mercurial pow'rs,
That never feel a stupor, know no pause,
Nor need one; I am conscious, and confess,
Fearless, a soul that does not always think.
Me oft has fancy, ludicrous and wild,
Sooth'd with a waking dream of houses, tow'rs,
Trees, churches, and strange visages, express'd

In the red cinders, while with poring eye
I gaz'd, myself creating what I saw. 290
Nor less amus'd have I quiescent watch'd
The sooty films that play upon the bars,
Pendulous, and foreboding, in the view
Of superstition, prophesying still,
Though still deceiv'd, some stranger's near approach.
'Tis thus the understanding takes repose
In indolent vacuity of thought,
And sleeps and is refresh'd. Meanwhile the face
Conceals the mood lethargic with a mask
Of deep deliberation, as the man 300
Were task'd to his full strength, absorb'd and lost.
Thus oft, reclin'd at ease, I lose an hour
At ev'ning, till at length the freezing blast,
That sweeps the bolted shutter, summons home
The recollected pow'rs; and, snapping short
The glassy threads, with which the fancy weaves
Her brittle toys, restores me to myself.
How calm is my recess; and how the frost,
Raging abroad, and the rough wind, endear
The silence and the warmth enjoy'd within! 310
I saw the woods and fields, at close of day,
A variegated show; the meadows green,
Though faded; and the lands, where lately wav'd
The golden harvest, of a mellow brown,
Upturn'd so lately by the forceful share.
I saw far off the weedy fallows smile
With verdure not unprofitable, graz'd
By flocks, fast feeding, and selecting each
His fav'rite herb; while all the leafless groves,
That skirt th' horizon, wore a sable hue, 320
Scarce notic'd in the kindred dusk of eve.
To-morrow brings a change, a total change!
Which even now, though silently perform'd,
And slowly, and by most unfelt, the face
Of universal nature undergoes.
Fast falls a fleecy show'r: the downy flakes,
Descending, and with never-ceasing lapse,
Softly alighting upon all below,
Assimilate all objects. Earth receives
Gladly the thick'ning mantle; and the green 330
And tender blade, that fear'd the chilling blast,
Escapes unhurt beneath so warm a veil.

In such a world; so thorny, and where none
Finds happiness unblighted; or, if found,

307 toys] toils *1803 and later edd.*

Without some thistly sorrow at its side;
It seems the part of wisdom, and no sin
Against the law of love, to measure lots
With less distinguish'd than ourselves; that thus
We may with patience bear our mod'rate ills,
And sympathise with others, suff'ring more. 340
Ill fares the trav'ller now, and he that stalks
In pond'rous boots beside his reeking team.
The wain goes heavily, impeded sore
By congregated loads adhering close
To the clogg'd wheels; and in its sluggish pace,
Noiseless, appears a moving hill of snow.
The toiling steeds expand the nostril wide,
While ev'ry breath, by respiration strong
Forc'd downward, is consolidated soon
Upon their jutting chests. He, form'd to bear 350
The pelting brunt of the tempestuous night,
With half-shut eyes, and pucker'd cheeks, and teeth
Presented bare against the storm, plods on.
One hand secures his hat, save when with both
He brandishes his pliant length of whip,
Resounding oft, and never heard in vain.
Oh happy; and, in my account, denied
That sensibility of pain with which
Refinement is endued, thrice happy thou!
Thy frame, robust and hardy, feels indeed 360
The piercing cold, but feels it unimpair'd.
The learned finger never need explore
Thy vig'rous pulse; and the unhealthful east,
That breathes the spleen, and searches ev'ry bone
Of the infirm, is wholesome air to thee.
Thy days roll on, exempt from household care;
The waggon is thy wife; and the poor beasts,
That drag the dull companion to and fro,
Thine helpless charge, dependent on thy care.
Ah, treat them kindly! rude as thou appear'st, 370
Yet show that thou hast mercy! which the great,
With needless hurry whirl'd from place to place,
Humane as they would seem, not always show.

Poor, yet industrious, modest, quiet, neat;
Such claim compassion in a night like this,
And have a friend in ev'ry feeling heart.
Warm'd, while it lasts, by labour, all day long
They brave the season, and yet find at eve,
Ill clad and fed but sparely, time to cool.
The frugal housewife trembles when she lights 380
Her scanty stock of brush-wood, blazing clear,
But dying soon, like all terrestrial joys.

The few small embers left she nurses well;
And, while her infant race, with outspread hands
And crowded knees, sit cow'ring o'er the sparks,
Retires, content to quake, so they be warm'd.
The man feels least, as more inur'd than she
To winter, and the current in his veins
More briskly mov'd by his severer toil;
Yet he, too, finds his own distress in their's. 390
The taper soon extinguish'd, which I saw
Dangled along at the cold finger's end
Just when the day declin'd, and the brown loaf
Lodg'd on the shelf, half eaten, without sauce
Of sav'ry cheese, or butter, costlier still;
Sleep seems their only refuge: for, alas,
Where penury is felt the thought is chain'd,
And sweet colloquial pleasures are but few!
With all this thrift they thrive not. All the care
Ingenious parsimony takes but just 400
Saves the small inventory, bed, and stool,
Skillet, and old carv'd chest, from public sale.
They live, and live without extorted alms
From grudging hands; but other boast have none
To sooth their honest pride, that scorns to beg,
Nor comfort else, but in their mutual love.
I praise you much, ye meek and patient pair,
For ye are worthy; choosing rather far
A dry but independent crust, hard earn'd,
And eaten with a sigh, than to endure 410
The rugged frowns and insolent rebuffs
Of knaves in office, partial in the work
Of distribution; lib'ral of their aid
To clam'rous importunity in rags,
But oft-times deaf to suppliants, who would blush
To wear a tatter'd garb however coarse,
Whom famine cannot reconcile to filth:
These ask with painful shyness, and, refus'd
Because deserving, silently retire!
But be ye of good courage! Time itself 420
Shall much befriend you. Time shall give increase;
And all your num'rous progeny, well-train'd,
But helpless, in few years shall find their hands,
And labour too. Meanwhile ye shall not want
What, conscious of your virtues, we can spare,
Nor what a wealthier than ourselves may send.
I mean the man, who, when the distant poor
Need help, denies them nothing but his name.
But poverty, with most who whimper forth
Their long complaints, is self-inflicted woe; 430

Th' effect of laziness or sottish waste.
Now goes the nightly thief prowling abroad
For plunder; much solicitous how best
He may compensate for a day of sloth
By works of darkness and nocturnal wrong.
Woe to the gard'ner's pale, the farmer's hedge,
Plash'd neatly, and secur'd with driven stakes
Deep in the loamy bank. Uptorn by strength,
Resistless in so bad a cause, but lame
To better deeds, he bundles up the spoil— 440
An ass's burden—and, when laden most
And heaviest, light of foot, steals fast away.
Nor does the boarded hovel better guard
The well-stack'd pile of riven logs and roots
From his pernicious force. Nor will he leave
Unwrench'd the door, however well secur'd,
Where Chanticleer amidst his haram sleeps
In unsuspecting pomp. Twitch'd from the perch,
He gives the princely bird, with all his wives,
To his voracious bag, struggling in vain, 450
And loudly wond'ring at the sudden change.—
Nor this to feed his own! 'Twere some excuse
Did pity of their suff'rings warp aside
His principle, and tempt him into sin
For their support, so destitute.—But they
Neglected pine at home; themselves, as more
Expos'd than others, with less scruple made
His victims, robb'd of their defenceless all.
Cruel is all he does. 'Tis quenchless thirst
Of ruinous ebriety that prompts 460
His ev'ry action, and imbrutes the man.
Oh for a law to noose the villain's neck
Who starves his own; who persecutes the blood
He gave them in his children's veins, and hates
And wrongs the woman he has sworn to love!

Pass where we may, through city or through town,
Village, or hamlet, of this merry land,
Though lean and beggar'd, ev'ry twentieth pace
Conducts th' unguarded nose to such a whiff
Of stale debauch, forth-issuing from the styes 470
That law has licens'd, as makes temp'rance reel.
There sit, involv'd and lost in curling clouds
Of Indian fume, and guzzling deep, the boor,
The lackey, and the groom: the craftsman there
Takes a Lethean leave of all his toil;
Smith, cobbler, joiner, he that plies the shears,
And he that kneads the dough; all loud alike,
All learned, and all drunk! The fiddle screams

Plaintive and piteous, as it wept and wail'd
Its wasted tones and harmony unheard: 480
Fierce the dispute, whate'er the theme; while she,
Fell Discord, arbitress of such debate,
Perch'd on the sign-post, holds with even hand
Her undecisive scales. In this she lays
A weight of ignorance; in that, of pride;
And smiles, delighted with th' eternal poise.
Dire is the frequent curse, and its twin sound
The cheek-distending oath, not to be prais'd
As ornamental, musical, polite,
Like those which modern senators employ, 490
Whose oath is rhet'ric, and who swear for fame!
Behold the schools in which plebeian minds,
Once simple, are initiated in arts
Which some may practise with politer grace,
But none with readier skill!—'tis here they learn
The road that leads, from competence and peace,
To indigence and rapine; till at last
Society, grown weary of the load,
Shakes her encumber'd lap, and casts them out.
But censure profits little: vain th' attempt 500
To advertise in verse a public pest,
That, like the filth with which the peasant feeds
His hungry acres, stinks, and is of use.
Th' excise is fatten'd with the rich result
Of all this riot; and ten thousand casks,
For ever dribbling out their base contents,
Touch'd by the Midas finger of the state,
Bleed gold for ministers to sport away.
Drink, and be mad, then; 'tis your country bids!
Gloriously drunk, obey th' important call! 510
Her cause demands th' assistance of your throats;—
Ye all can swallow, and she asks no more.

Would I had fall'n upon those happier days
That poets celebrate; those golden times,
And those Arcadian scenes, that Maro sings,
And Sidney, warbler of poetic prose.
Nymphs were Dianas then, and swains had hearts
That felt their virtues: innocence, it seems,
From courts dismiss'd, found shelter in the groves;
The footsteps of simplicity, impress'd 520
Upon the yielding herbage, (so they sing)
Then were not all effac'd: then speech profane,
And manners profligate, were rarely found;
Observ'd as prodigies, and soon reclaim'd.
Vain wish! those days were never: airy dreams
Sat for the picture; and the poet's hand,

Imparting substance to an empty shade,
Impos'd a gay delirium for a truth.
Grant it:—I still must envy them an age
That favour'd such a dream; in days like these 530
Impossible, when virtue is so scarce,
That to suppose a scene where she presides,
Is tramontane, and stumbles all belief.
No: we are polish'd now! the rural lass,
Whom once her virgin modesty and grace,
Her artless manners, and her neat attire,
So dignified, that she was hardly less
Than the fair shepherdess of old romance,
Is seen no more. The character is lost!
Her head, adorn'd with lappets pinn'd aloft, 540
And ribbands streaming gay, superbly rais'd,
And magnified beyond all human size,
Indebted to some smart wig-weaver's hand
For more than half the tresses it sustains;
Her elbows ruffled, and her tott'ring form
Ill propp'd upon French heels, she might be deem'd
(But that the basket dangling on her arm
Interprets her more truly) of a rank
Too proud for dairy work, or sale of eggs.
Expect her soon with foot-boy at her heels, 550
No longer blushing for her awkward load,
Her train and her umbrella all her care!

The town has ting'd the country; and the stain
Appears a spot upon a vestal's robe,
The worse for what it soils. The fashion runs
Down into scenes still rural; but, alas,
Scenes rarely grac'd with rural manners now!
Time was when, in the pastoral retreat,
Th' unguarded door was safe; men did not watch
T' invade another's right, or guard their own. 560
Then sleep was undisturb'd by fear, unscar'd
By drunken howlings; and the chilling tale
Of midnight murder was a wonder heard
With doubtful credit, told to frighten babes.
But farewell now to unsuspicious nights,
And slumbers unalarm'd! Now, ere you sleep,
See that your polish'd arms be prim'd with care,
And drop the night-bolt;—ruffians are abroad;
And the first larum of the cock's shrill throat
May prove a trumpet, summoning your ear 570
To horrid sounds of hostile feet within.
Ev'n day-light has its dangers; and the walk
Through pathless wastes and woods, unconscious once

Of other tenants than melodious birds,
Or harmless flocks, is hazardous and bold.
Lamented change! to which full many a cause
Invet'rate, hopeless of a cure, conspires.
The course of human things from good to ill,
From ill to worse, is fatal, never fails.
Increase of pow'r begets increase of wealth; 580
Wealth luxury, and luxury excess;
Excess, the scrofulous and itchy plague
That seizes first the opulent, descends
To the next rank contagious, and in time
Taints downward all the graduated scale
Of order, from the chariot to the plough.
The rich, and they that have an arm to check
The license of the lowest in degree,
Desert their office; and themselves, intent
On pleasure, haunt the capital, and thus 590
To all the violence of lawless hands
Resign the scenes their presence might protect.
Authority herself not seldom sleeps,
Though resident, and witness of the wrong.
The plump convivial parson often bears
The magisterial sword in vain, and lays
His rev'rence and his worship both to rest
On the same cushion of habitual sloth.
Perhaps timidity restrains his arm;
When he should strike he trembles, and sets free,
Himself enslav'd by terror of the band, 601
Th' audacious convict, whom he dares not bind.
Perhaps, though by profession ghostly pure,
He too may have his vice, and sometimes prove
Less dainty than becomes his grave outside
In lucrative concerns. Examine well
His milk-white hand; the palm is hardly clean—
But here and there an ugly smutch appears.
Foh! 'twas a bribe that left it: he has touch'd
Corruption! Whoso seeks an audit here 610
Propitious, pays his tribute, game or fish,
Wild-fowl or ven'son; and his errand speeds.
  But faster far, and more than all the rest,
A noble cause, which none who bears a spark
Of public virtue ever wish'd remov'd,
Works the deplor'd and mischievous effect.
'Tis universal soldiership has stabb'd
The heart of merit in the meaner class.
Arms, through the vanity and brainless rage
Of those that bear them, in whatever cause, 620
Seem most at variance with all moral good,

And incompatible with serious thought.
The clown, the child of nature, without guile,
Blest with an infant's ignorance of all
But his own simple pleasures; now and then
A wrestling-match, a foot-race, or a fair;
Is ballotted, and trembles at the news:
Sheepish he doffs his hat, and, mumbling, swears
A bible-oath to be whate'er they please,
To do he knows not what! The task perform'd,
That instant he becomes the serjeant's care, 631
His pupil, and his torment, and his jest.
His awkward gait, his introverted toes,
Bent knees, round shoulders, and dejected looks,
Procure him many a curse. By slow degrees,
Unapt to learn, and form'd of stubborn stuff,
He yet by slow degrees puts off himself,
Grows conscious of a change, and likes it well:
He stands erect; his slouch becomes a walk;
He steps right onward, martial in his air, 640
His form and movement; is as smart above
As meal and larded locks can make him; wears
His hat, or his plum'd helmet, with a grace;
And, his three years of heroship expir'd,
Returns indignant to the slighted plough.
He hates the field, in which no fife or drum
Attends him; drives his cattle to a march;
And sighs for the smart comrades he has left.
'Twere well if his exterior change were all—
But with his clumsy port the wretch has lost 650
His ignorance and harmless manners too!
To swear, to game, to drink; to show at home
By lewdness, idleness, and sabbath-breach,
The great proficiency he made abroad;
T' astonish and to grieve his gazing friends,
To break some maiden's and his mother's heart;
To be a pest where he was useful once;
Are his sole aim, and all his glory, now!

Man in society is like a flow'r
Blown in its native bed: 'tis there alone 660
His faculties, expanded in full bloom,
Shine out; there only reach their proper use.
But man, associated and leagu'd with man
By regal warrant, or self-join'd by bond
For int'rest-sake, or swarming into clans
Beneath one head for purposes of war,
Like flow'rs selected from the rest, and bound
And bundled close to fill some crowded vase,
Fades rapidly, and, by compression marr'd,

Contracts defilement not to be endur'd. 670
Hence charter'd boroughs are such public plagues;
And burghers, men immaculate perhaps
In all their private functions, once combin'd,
Become a loathsome body, only fit
For dissolution, hurtful to the main.
Hence merchants, unimpeachable of sin
Against the charities of domestic life,
Incorporated, seem at once to lose
Their nature; and, disclaiming all regard
For mercy and the common rights of man, 680
Build factories with blood, conducting trade
At the sword's point, and dyeing the white robe
Of innocent commercial justice red.
Hence, too, the field of glory, as the world
Misdeems it, dazzled by its bright array,
With all its majesty of thund'ring pomp,
Enchanting music, and immortal wreaths,
Is but a school where thoughtlessness is taught
On principle, where foppery atones
For folly, gallantry for ev'ry vice. 690

But, slighted as it is, and by the great
Abandon'd, and, which still I more regret,
Infected with the manners and the modes
It knew not once, the country wins me still.
I never fram'd a wish, or form'd a plan,
That flatter'd me with hopes of earthly bliss,
But there I laid the scene. There early stray'd
My fancy, ere yet liberty of choice
Had found me, or the hope of being free.
My very dreams were rural; rural, too, 700
The first-born efforts of my youthful muse,
Sportive, and jingling her poetic bells
Ere yet her ear was mistress of their pow'rs.
No bard could please me but whose lyre was tun'd
To Nature's praises. Heroes and their feats
Fatigued me, never weary of the pipe
Of Tityrus, assembling, as he sang,
The rustic throng beneath his fav'rite beech.
Then Milton had indeed a poet's charms:
New to my taste, his Paradise surpass'd 710
The struggling efforts of my boyish tongue
To speak its excellence. I danced for joy.
I marvell'd much that, at so ripe an age
As twice sev'n years, his beauties had then first
Engag'd my wonder; and, admiring still,
And still admiring, with regret suppos'd
The joy half lost because not sooner found.

Thee too, enamour'd of the life I lov'd,
Pathetic in its praise, in its pursuit
Determin'd, and possessing it at last 720
With transports such as favour'd lovers feel,
I studied, priz'd, and wish'd that I had known,
Ingenious Cowley! and, though now reclaim'd
By modern lights from an erroneous taste,
I cannot but lament thy splendid wit
Entangled in the cobwebs of the schools.
I still revere thee, courtly though retir'd;
Though stretch'd at ease in Chertsey's silent bow'rs,
Not unemploy'd; and finding rich amends
For a lost world in solitude and verse. 730
'Tis born with all: the love of Nature's works
Is an ingredient in the compound man,
Infus'd at the creation of the kind.
And, though th' Almighty Maker has throughout
Discriminated each from each, by strokes
And touches of his hand, with so much art
Diversified, that two were never found
Twins at all points—yet this obtains in all,
That all discern a beauty in his works,
And all can taste them: minds that have been form'd
And tutor'd, with a relish more exact, 741
But none without some relish, none unmov'd.
It is a flame that dies not even there,
Where nothing feeds it: neither business, crowds,
Nor habits of luxurious city-life;
Whatever else they smother of true worth
In human bosoms; quench it, or abate.
The villas with which London stands begirt,
Like a swarth Indian with his belt of beads,
Prove it. A breath of unadult'rate air, 750
The glimpse of a green pasture, how they cheer
The citizen, and brace his languid frame!
Ev'n in the stifling bosom of the town,
A garden, in which nothing thrives, has charms
That soothe the rich possessor; much consol'd,
That here and there some sprigs of mournful mint,
Of nightshade, or valerian, grace the well
He cultivates. These serve him with a hint
That nature lives; that sight-refreshing green
Is still the liv'ry she delights to wear, 760
Though sickly samples of th' exub'rant whole.
What are the casements lin'd with creeping herbs,
The prouder sashes fronted with a range

718 Thee] There *1793–1800*.

Of orange, myrtle, or the fragrant weed,
The Frenchman's darling[1]? are they not all proofs
That man, immur'd in cities, still retains
His inborn inextinguishable thirst
Of rural scenes, compensating his loss
By supplemental shifts, the best he may?
The most unfurnish'd with the means of life, 770
And they that never pass their brick-wall bounds
To range the fields and treat their lungs with air,
Yet feel the burning instinct: over head
Suspend their crazy boxes, planted thick,
And water'd duly. There the pitcher stands
A fragment, and the spoutless tea-pot there;
Sad witnesses how close-pent man regrets
The country, with what ardour he contrives
A peep at nature, when he can no more.
  Hail, therefore, patroness of health, and ease, 780
And contemplation, heart-consoling joys
And harmless pleasures, in the throng'd abode
Of multitudes unknown! hail, rural life!
Address himself who will to the pursuit
Of honours, or emolument, or fame;
I shall not add myself to such a chase,
Thwart his attempts, or envy his success.
Some must be great. Great offices will have
Great talents. And God gives to ev'ry man
The virtue, temper, understanding, taste, 790
That lifts him into life; and lets him fall
Just in the niche he was ordain'd to fill.
To the deliv'rer of an injur'd land
He gives a tongue t' enlarge upon, an heart
To feel, and courage to redress her wrongs;
To monarchs dignity; to judges sense;
To artists ingenuity and skill;
To me an unambitious mind, content
In the low vale of life, that early felt
A wish for ease and leisure, and ere long 800
Found here that leisure and that ease I wish'd.

[1] Mignonette [C.].

771 pass'd *1800* (*8vo*). 785 emolument *1785–1793*, *1803*: emoluments *1795–1800*.

BOOK V

THE WINTER MORNING WALK

ARGUMENT OF THE FIFTH BOOK.—A frosty morning—The foddering of cattle—The woodman and his dog—The poultry—Whimsical effects of frost at a waterfall—The Empress of Russia's palace of ice—Amusements of monarchs—War, one of them—Wars, whence—And whence monarchy—The evils of it—English and French loyalty contrasted—The Bastile, and a prisoner there—Liberty the chief recommendation of this country—Modern patriotism questionable, and why—The perishable nature of the best human institutions—Spiritual liberty not perishable—The slavish state of man by nature—Deliver him, Deist, if you can—Grace must do it—The respective merits of patriots and martyrs stated—Their different treatment—Happy freedom of the man whom grace makes free—His relish of the works of God—Address to the Creator.

'TIS morning; and the sun, with ruddy orb
Ascending, fires th' horizon: while the clouds,
That crowd away before the driving wind,
More ardent as the disk emerges more,
Resemble most some city in a blaze,
Seen through the leafless wood. His slanting ray
Slides ineffectual down the snowy vale,
And, tinging all with his own rosy hue,
From ev'ry herb and ev'ry spiry blade
Stretches a length of shadow o'er the field. 10
Mine, spindling into longitude immense,
In spite of gravity, and sage remark
That I myself am but a fleeting shade,
Provokes me to a smile. With eye askance
I view the muscular proportion'd limb
Transform'd to a lean shank. The shapeless pair,
As they design'd to mock me, at my side
Take step for step; and, as I near approach
The cottage, walk along the plaster'd wall,
Prepost'rous sight! the legs without the man. 20
The verdure of the plain lies buried deep
Beneath the dazzling deluge; and the bents,
And coarser grass, upspearing o'er the rest,
Of late unsightly and unseen, now shine
Conspicuous, and, in bright apparel clad
And fledg'd with icy feathers, nod superb.
The cattle mourn in corners where the fence
Screens them, and seem half petrified to sleep
In unrecumbent sadness. There they wait
Their wonted fodder; not like hung'ring man, 30
Fretful if unsupply'd; but silent, meek,
And patient of the slow-pac'd swain's delay.
He from the stack carves out th' accustom'd load,

Deep-plunging, and again deep-plunging oft,
His broad keen knife into the solid mass:
Smooth as a wall the upright remnant stands,
With such undeviating and even force
He severs it away: no needless care,
Lest storms should overset the leaning pile
Deciduous, or its own unbalanc'd weight. 40
Forth goes the woodman, leaving unconcern'd
The cheerful haunts of man; to wield the axe
And drive the wedge, in yonder forest drear,
From morn to eve his solitary task.
Shaggy, and lean, and shrewd, with pointed ears
And tail cropp'd short, half lurcher and half cur—
His dog attends him. Close behind his heel
Now creeps he slow; and now, with many a frisk
Wide-scamp'ring, snatches up the drifted snow
With iv'ry teeth, or ploughs it with his snout; 50
Then shakes his powder'd coat, and barks for joy.
Heedless of all his pranks, the sturdy churl
Moves right toward the mark; nor stops for aught,
But now and then with pressure of his thumb
T' adjust the fragrant charge of a short tube
That fumes beneath his nose: the trailing cloud
Streams far behind him, scenting all the air.
Now from the roost, or from the neighb'ring pale,
Where, diligent to catch the first faint gleam
Of smiling day, they gossip'd side by side, 60
Come trooping at the housewife's well-known call
The feather'd tribes domestic. Half on wing,
And half on foot, they brush the fleecy flood,
Conscious, and fearful of too deep a plunge.
The sparrows peep, and quit the shelt'ring eaves
To seize the fair occasion. Well they eye
The scatter'd grain; and, thievishly resolv'd
T' escape th' impending famine, often scar'd,
As oft return—a pert voracious kind.
Clean riddance quickly made, one only care 70
Remains to each—the search of sunny nook,
Or shed impervious to the blast. Resign'd
To sad necessity, the cock foregoes
His wonted strut; and, wading at their head
With well-consider'd steps, seems to resent
His alter'd gait and stateliness retrench'd.
How find the myriads, that in summer cheer
The hills and vallies with their ceaseless songs,
Due sustenance, or where subsist they now?
Earth yields them nought: th' imprison'd worm is safe 80

Beneath the frozen clod; all seeds of herbs
Lie cover'd close; and berry-bearing thorns,
That feed the thrush, (whatever some suppose)
Afford the smaller minstrels no supply.
The long protracted rigour of the year
Thins all their num'rous flocks. In chinks and holes
Ten thousand seek an unmolested end,
As instinct prompts; self-buried ere they die.
The very rooks and daws forsake the fields,
Where neither grub, nor root, nor earth-nut, now
Repays their labour more; and, perch'd aloft 91
By the way-side, or stalking in the path,
Lean pensioners upon the trav'ler's track,
Pick up their nauseous dole, though sweet to them,
Of voided pulse or half-digested grain.
The streams are lost amid the splendid blank,
O'erwhelming all distinction. On the flood,
Indurated and fixt, the snowy weight
Lies undissolv'd; while silently beneath,
And unperceiv'd, the current steals away. 100
Not so where, scornful of a check, it leaps
The mill-dam, dashes on the restless wheel,
And wantons in the pebbly gulph below:
No frost can bind it there; its utmost force
Can but arrest the light and smoky mist
That in its fall the liquid sheet throws wide.
And see where it has hung th' embroider'd banks
With forms so various, that no pow'rs of art,
The pencil or the pen, may trace the scene!
Here glitt'ring turrets rise, upbearing high 110
(Fantastic misarrangement!) on the roof
Large growth of what may seem the sparkling trees
And shrubs of fairy land. The crystal drops
That trickle down the branches, fast congeal'd,
Shoot into pillars of pellucid length,
And prop the pile they but adorn'd before.
Here grotto within grotto safe defies
The sun-beam; there, emboss'd and fretted wild,
The growing wonder takes a thousand shapes
Capricious, in which fancy seeks in vain 120
The likeness of some object seen before.
Thus nature works as if to mock at art,
And in defiance of her rival pow'rs;
By these fortuitous and random strokes
Performing such inimitable feats
As she with all her rules can never reach.
Less worthy of applause, though more admir'd,
Because a novelty, the work of man,

Imperial mistress of the fur-clad Russ!
Thy most magnificent and mighty freak, 130
The wonder of the North. No forest fell
When thou wouldst build; no quarry sent its stores
T' enrich thy walls: but thou didst hew the floods,
And make thy marble of the glassy wave.
In such a palace Aristæus found
Cyrene, when he bore the plaintive tale
Of his lost bees to her maternal ear:
In such a palace poetry might place
The armory of winter; where his troops,
The gloomy clouds, find weapons, arrowy sleet, 140
Skin-piercing volley, blossom-bruising hail,
And snow that often blinds the trav'ler's course,
And wraps him in an unexpected tomb.
Silently as a dream the fabric rose;—
No sound of hammer or of saw was there:
Ice upon ice, the well-adjusted parts
Were soon conjoin'd; nor other cement ask'd
Than water interfus'd to make them one.
Lamps gracefully dispos'd, and of all hues,
Illumin'd ev'ry side: a wat'ry light 150
Gleam'd through the clear transparency, that seem'd
Another moon new risen, or meteor fall'n
From heav'n to earth, of lambent flame serene.
So stood the brittle prodigy; though smooth
And slipp'ry the materials, yet frost-bound
Firm as a rock. Nor wanted aught within,
That royal residence might well befit,
For grandeur or for use. Long wavy wreaths
Of flow'rs, that fear'd no enemy but warmth,
Blush'd on the pannels. Mirror needed none 160
Where all was vitreous; but in order due
Convivial table and commodious seat
(What seem'd at least commodious seat) were there;
Sofa, and couch, and high-built throne august.
The same lubricity was found in all,
And all was moist to the warm touch; a scene
Of evanescent glory, once a stream,
And soon to slide into a stream again.
Alas! 'twas but a mortifying stroke
Of undesign'd severity, that glanc'd 170
(Made by a monarch) on her own estate,
On human grandeur and the courts of kings.
'Twas transient in its nature, as in show
'Twas durable: as worthless, as it seem'd
Intrinsically precious; to the foot
Treach'rous and false; it smil'd, and it was cold.

Great princes have great playthings. Some have play'd
At hewing mountains into men, and some
At building human wonders mountain-high.
Some have amus'd the dull, sad years of life 180
(Life spent in indolence, and therefore sad)
With schemes of monumental fame; and sought
By pyramids and mausolean pomp,
Short-lived themselves, t' immortalize their bones.
Some seek diversion in the tented field,
And make the sorrows of mankind their sport.
But war's a game, which, were their subjects wise,
Kings would not play at. Nations would do well
T' extort their truncheons from the puny hands
Of heroes, whose infirm and baby minds 190
Are gratified with mischief; and who spoil,
Because men suffer it, their toy the world.

When Babel was confounded, and the great
Confed'racy of projectors wild and vain
Was split into diversity of tongues,
Then, as a shepherd separates his flock,
These to the upland, to the valley those,
God drave asunder, and assign'd their lot
To all the nations. Ample was the boon
He gave them, in its distribution fair 200
And equal, and he bade them dwell in peace.
Peace was awhile their care: they plough'd, and sow'd,
And reap'd their plenty, without grudge or strife.
But violence can never longer sleep
Than human passions please. In ev'ry heart
Are sown the sparks that kindle fi'ry war;
Occasion needs but fan them, and they blaze.
Cain had already shed a brother's blood:
The deluge wash'd it out; but left unquench'd
The seeds of murder in the breast of man. 210
Soon, by a righteous judgment, in the line
Of his descending progeny was found
The first artificer of death; the shrewd
Contriver who first sweated at the forge,
And forc'd the blunt and yet unbloodied steel
To a keen edge, and made it bright for war.
Him, Tubal nam'd, the Vulcan of old times,
The sword and faulchion their inventor claim;
And the first smith was the first murd'rer's son.
His art surviv'd the waters; and ere long, 220

188 would] should *1785, 1786*. 215 unbloodied *1785, 1786*.

When man was multiplied and spread abroad
In tribes and clans, and had begun to call
These meadows and that range of hills his own,
The tasted sweets of property begat
Desire of more, and industry in some,
T' improve and cultivate their just demesne,
Made others covet what they saw so fair.
Thus war began on earth; these fought for spoil,
And those in self-defence. Savage at first
The onset, and irregular. At length 230
One eminent above the rest, for strength,
For stratagem, or courage, or for all,
Was chosen leader; him they serv'd in war,
And him in peace, for sake of warlike deeds
Rev'renc'd no less. Who could with him compare?
Or who so worthy to control themselves
As he whose prowess had subdu'd their foes?
Thus war, affording field for the display
Of virtue, made one chief, whom times of peace,
Which have their exigencies too, and call 240
For skill in government, at length made king.
King was a name too proud for man to wear
With modesty and meekness; and the crown,
So dazzling in their eyes who set it on,
Was sure t' intoxicate the brows it bound.
It is the abject property of most,
That, being parcel of the common mass,
And destitute of means to raise themselves,
They sink, and settle lower than they need.
They know not what it is to feel within 250
A comprehensive faculty, that grasps
Great purposes with ease, that turns and wields,
Almost without an effort, plans too vast
For their conception, which they cannot move.
Conscious of impotence, they soon grow drunk
With gazing, when they see an able man
Step forth to notice; and, besotted thus,
Build him a pedestal, and say, Stand there,
And be our admiration and our praise.
They roll themselves before him in the dust, 260
Then most deserving in their own account
When most extravagant in his applause,
As if exalting him they rais'd themselves.
Thus by degrees, self-cheated of their sound
And sober judgment, that he is but man,
They demi-deify and fume him so,
That in due season he forgets it too.
Inflated and astrut with self-conceit,

He gulps the windy diet; and ere long,
Adopting their mistake, profoundly thinks 270
The world was made in vain, if not for him.
Thenceforth they are his cattle: drudges born
To bear his burdens; drawing in his gears,
And sweating in his service, his caprice
Becomes the soul that animates them all.
He deems a thousand, or ten thousand lives,
Spent in the purchase of renown for him,
An easy reck'ning; and they think the same.
Thus kings were first invented, and thus kings
Were burnish'd into heroes, and became 280
The arbiters of this terraqueous swamp;
Storks among frogs, that have but croak'd and died.
Strange, that such folly as lifts bloated man
To eminence, fit only for a god,
Should ever drivel out of human lips,
Ev'n in the cradled weakness of the world!
Still stranger much, that, when at length mankind
Had reach'd the sinewy firmness of their youth,
And could discriminate and argue well
On subjects more mysterious, they were yet 290
Babes in the cause of freedom, and should fear
And quake before the gods themselves had made!
But above measure strange, that neither proof
Of sad experience, nor examples set
By some whose patriot virtue has prevail'd,
Can even now, when they are grown mature
In wisdom, and with philosophic deeps
Familiar, serve t' emancipate the rest!
Such dupes are men to custom, and so prone
To rev'rence what is ancient, and can plead 300
A course of long observance for its use,
That even servitude, the worst of ills,
Because deliver'd down from sire to son,
Is kept and guarded as a sacred thing!
But is it fit, or can it bear the shock
Of rational discussion, that a man,
Compounded and made up like other men
Of elements tumultuous, in whom lust
And folly in as ample measure meet
As in the bosoms of the slaves he rules, 310
Should be a despot absolute, and boast
Himself the only freeman of his land?
Should, when he pleases, and on whom he will,
Wage war, with any or with no pretence

297 deeds *1799, 1803.*

Of provocation giv'n, or wrong sustain'd,
And force the beggarly last doit, by means
That his own humour dictates, from the clutch
Of poverty, that thus he may procure
His thousands, weary of penurious life,
A splendid opportunity to die? 320
Say ye, who (with less prudence than of old
Jotham ascrib'd to his assembled trees
In politic convention) put your trust
I' th' shadow of a bramble, and, reclin'd
In fancied peace beneath his dang'rous branch,
Rejoice in him, and celebrate his sway,
Where find ye passive fortitude? Whence springs
Your self-denying zeal, that holds it good
To stroke the prickly grievance, and to hang
His thorns with streamers of continual praise? 330
We, too, are friends to loyalty. We love
The king who loves the law, respects his bounds,
And reigns content within them: him we serve
Freely and with delight, who leaves us free:
But recollecting still that he is man,
We trust him not too far. King though he be,
And king in England too, he may be weak,
And vain enough to be ambitious still;
May exercise amiss his proper pow'rs,
Or covet more than freemen choose to grant: 340
Beyond that mark is treason. He is our's,
T' administer, to guard, t' adorn the state,
But not to warp or change it. We are his
To serve him nobly in the common cause,
True to the death, but not to be his slaves.
Mark now the diff'rence, ye that boast your love
Of kings, between your loyalty and our's.
We love the man; the paltry pageant you.
We the chief patron of the commonwealth;
You the regardless author of its woes. 350
We, for the sake of liberty, a king;
You chains and bondage, for a tyrant's sake.
Our love is principle, and has its root
In reason, is judicious, manly, free;
Your's, a blind instinct, crouches to the rod,
And licks the foot that treads it in the dust.
Were kingship as true treasure as it seems,
Sterling, and worthy of a wise man's wish,
I would not be a king to be belov'd
Causeless, and daub'd with undiscerning praise,
Where love is mere attachment to the throne, 361
Not to the man who fills it as he ought.

Whose freedom is by suff'rance, and at will
Of a superior, he is never free.
Who lives, and is not weary of a life
Expos'd to manacles, deserves them well.
The state that strives for liberty, though foil'd,
And forc'd t' abandon what she bravely sought,
Deserves at least applause for her attempt,
And pity for her loss. But that's a cause 370
Not often unsuccessful: pow'r usurp'd
Is weakness when oppos'd; conscious of wrong,
'Tis pusillanimous and prone to flight.
But slaves, that once conceive the glowing thought
Of freedom, in that hope itself possess
All that the contest calls for; spirit, strength,
The scorn of danger, and united hearts;
The surest presage of the good they seek[1].

Then shame to manhood, and opprobrious more
To France than all her losses and defeats, 380
Old or of later date, by sea or land,
Her house of bondage, worse than that of old
Which God aveng'd on Pharaoh—the Bastile!
Ye horrid tow'rs, th' abode of broken hearts;
Ye dungeons and ye cages of despair,
That monarchs have supplied from age to age
With music such as suits their sov'reign ears—
The sighs and groans of miserable men!
There's not an English heart that would not leap
To hear that ye were fall'n at last; to know 390
That ev'n our enemies, so oft employ'd
In forging chains for us, themselves were free.
For he who values liberty confines
His zeal for her predominance within
No narrow bounds; her cause engages him
Wherever pleaded. 'Tis the cause of man.
There dwell the most forlorn of human kind;
Immur'd though unaccus'd, condemn'd untried,
Cruelly spar'd, and hopeless of escape!
There, like the visionary emblem seen 400
By him of Babylon, life stands a stump,
And, filletted about with hoops of brass,
Still lives, though all its pleasant boughs are gone.
To count the hour-bell and expect no change;

[1] The author hopes that he shall not be censured for unnecessary warmth upon so interesting a subject. He is aware that it is become almost fashionable to stigmatise such sentiments as no better than empty declamation; but it is an ill symptom, and peculiar to modern times [C.].

393 who] that *1785. 1786.* 403 its] his *1803 first.*

And ever, as the sullen sound is heard,
Still to reflect, that, though a joyless note
To him whose moments all have one dull pace,
Ten thousand rovers in the world at large
Account it music; that it summons some
To theatre, or jocund feast or ball: 410
The wearied hireling finds it a release
From labour; and the lover, who has chid
Its long delay, feels ev'ry welcome stroke
Upon his heart-strings, trembling with delight—
To fly for refuge from distracting thought
To such amusements as ingenious woe
Contrives, hard-shifting, and without her tools—
To read engraven on the mouldy walls,
In stagg'ring types, his predecessor's tale,
A sad memorial, and subjoin his own— 420
To turn purveyor to an overgorg'd
And bloated spider, till the pamper'd pest
Is made familiar, watches his approach,
Comes at his call, and serves him for a friend—
To wear out time in numb'ring to and fro
The studs that thick emboss his iron door;
Then downward and then upward, then aslant
And then alternate; with a sickly hope
By dint of change to give his tasteless task
Some relish; till the sum, exactly found 430
In all directions, he begins again—
Oh comfortless existence! hemm'd around
With woes, which who that suffers would not kneel
And beg for exile, or the pangs of death?
That man should thus encroach on fellow man,
Abridge him of his just and native rights,
Eradicate him, tear him from his hold
Upon th' endearments of domestic life
And social, nip his fruitfulness and use,
And doom him for perhaps an heedless word 440
To barrenness, and solitude, and tears,
Moves indignation; makes the name of king
(Of king whom such prerogative can please)
As dreadful as the Manichean god,
Ador'd through fear, strong only to destroy.
'Tis liberty alone that gives the flow'r
Of fleeting life its lustre and perfume;
And we are weeds without it. All constraint,
Except what wisdom lays on evil men,
Is evil; hurts the faculties, impedes 450
Their progress in the road of science; blinds
The eyesight of discov'ry; and begets,

In those that suffer it, a sordid mind
Bestial, a meagre intellect, unfit
To be the tenant of man's noble form.
Thee therefore still, blame-worthy as thou art,
With all thy loss of empire, and though squeez'd
By public exigence till annual food
Fails for the craving hunger of the state,
Thee I account still happy, and the chief 460
Among the nations, seeing thou art free:
My native nook of earth! Thy clime is rude,
Replete with vapours, and disposes much
All hearts to sadness, and none more than mine:
Thine unadult'rate manners are less soft
And plausible than social life requires,
And thou hast need of discipline and art
To give thee what politer France receives
From nature's bounty—that humane address
And sweetness, without which no pleasure is 470
In converse, either starv'd by cold reserve,
Or flush'd with fierce dispute, a senseless brawl:
Yet, being free, I love thee: for the sake
Of that one feature can be well content,
Disgrac'd as thou hast been, poor as thou art,
To seek no sublunary rest beside.
But, once enslav'd, farewell! I could endure
Chains no where patiently; and chains at home,
Where I am free by birthright, not at all.
Then what were left of roughness in the grain 480
Of British natures, wanting its excuse
That it belongs to freemen, would disgust
And shock me. I should then, with double pain,
Feel all the rigour of thy fickle clime;
And, if I must bewail the blessing lost,
For which our Hampdens and our Sidneys bled,
I would at least bewail it under skies
Milder, among a people less austere;
In scenes which, having never known me free,
Would not reproach me with the loss I felt. 490
Do I forebode impossible events,
And tremble at vain dreams? Heav'n grant I may!
But th' age of virtuous politics is past,
And we are deep in that of cold pretence.
Patriots are grown too shrewd to be sincere,
And we too wise to trust them. He that takes
Deep in his soft credulity the stamp
Design'd by loud declaimers on the part
Of liberty, themselves the slaves of lust,
Incurs derision for his easy faith 500

And lack of knowledge, and with cause enough:
For when was public virtue to be found
Where private was not? Can he love the whole
Who loves no part? He be a nation's friend
Who is, in truth, the friend of no man there?
Can he be strenuous in his country's cause
Who slights the charities, for whose dear sake
That country, if at all, must be belov'd?
'Tis therefore sober and good men are sad
For England's glory, seeing it wax pale 510
And sickly, while her champions wear their hearts
So loose to private duty, that no brain,
Healthful and undisturb'd by factious fumes,
Can dream them trusty to the gen'ral weal.
Such were not they of old, whose temper'd blades
Dispers'd the shackles of usurp'd control,
And hew'd them link from link: then Albion's sons
Were sons indeed; they felt a filial heart
Beat high within them at a mother's wrongs;
And, shining each in his domestic sphere, 520
Shone brighter still, once call'd to public view.
'Tis therefore many, whose sequester'd lot
Forbids their interference, looking on,
Anticipate perforce some dire event;
And, seeing the old castle of the state,
That promis'd once more firmness, so assail'd
That all its tempest-beaten turrets shake,
Stand motionless expectants of its fall.
All has its date below; the fatal hour
Was register'd in heav'n ere time began. 530
We turn to dust, and all our mightiest works
Die too: the deep foundations that we lay,
Time ploughs them up, and not a trace remains.
We build with what we deem eternal rock:
A distant age asks where the fabric stood;
And in the dust, sifted and search'd in vain,
The undiscoverable secret sleeps.
But there is yet a liberty, unsung
By poets, and by senators unprais'd,
Which monarchs cannot grant, nor all the pow'rs
Of earth and hell confed'rate take away: 541
A liberty, which persecution, fraud,
Oppression, prisons, have no power to bind;
Which whoso tastes can be enslav'd no more.
'Tis liberty of heart, deriv'd from heav'n;
Bought with HIS blood who gave it to mankind,

515 they not *1798*[2], *1800*.

And seal'd with the same token! It is held
By charter, and that charter sanction'd sure
By th' unimpeachable and awful oath
And promise of a God! His other gifts 550
All bear the royal stamp that speaks them his,
And are august; but this transcends them all.
His other works, the visible display
Of all-creating energy and might,
Are grand, no doubt, and worthy of the word
That, finding an interminable space
Unoccupied, has fill'd the void so well,
And made so sparkling what was dark before.
But these are not his glory. Man, 'tis true,
Smit with the beauty of so fair a scene, 560
Might well suppose th' artificer divine
Meant it eternal, had he not himself
Pronounc'd it transient, glorious as it is,
And, still designing a more glorious far,
Doom'd it as insufficient for his praise.
These, therefore, are occasional, and pass;
Form'd for the confutation of the fool,
Whose lyeing heart disputes against a God;
That office serv'd, they must be swept away.
Not so the labours of his love: they shine 570
In other heav'ns than these that we behold,
And fade not. There is paradise that fears
No forfeiture, and of its fruits he sends
Large prelibation oft to saints below.
Of these the first in order, and the pledge
And confident assurance of the rest,
Is liberty:—a flight into his arms
Ere yet mortality's fine threads give way,
A clear escape from tyrannizing lust,
And full immunity from penal woe. 580

Chains are the portion of revolted man,
Stripes and a dungeon; and his body serves
The triple purpose. In that sickly, foul,
Opprobrious residence, he finds them all.
Propense his heart to idols, he is held
In silly dotage on created things,
Careless of their Creator. And that low
And sordid gravitation of his pow'rs
To a vile clod so draws him, with such force
Resistless from the centre he should seek, 590
That he at last forgets it. All his hopes
Tend downward; his ambition is to sink,
To reach a depth profounder still, and still
Profounder, in the fathomless abyss

Of folly, plunging in pursuit of death.
But, ere he gain the comfortless repose
He seeks, and acquiescence of his soul,
In heav'n-renouncing exile, he endures—
What does he not? from lusts oppos'd in vain,
And self-reproaching conscience. He foresees 600
The fatal issue to his health, fame, peace,
Fortune, and dignity; the loss of all
That can ennoble man, and make frail life,
Short as it is, supportable. Still worse,
Far worse than all the plagues with which his sins
Infect his happiest moments, he forebodes
Ages of hopeless mis'ry. Future death,
And death still future. Not an hasty stroke,
Like that which sends him to the dusty grave;
But unrepealable enduring death! 610
Scripture is still a trumpet to his fears:
What none can prove a forg'ry, may be true;
What none but bad men wish exploded, must.
That scruple checks him. Riot is not loud,
Nor drunk enough to drown it. In the midst
Of laughter his compunctions are sincere;
And he abhors the jest by which he shines.
Remorse begets reform. His master-lust
Falls first before his resolute rebuke,
And seems dethron'd and vanquish'd. Peace ensues,
But spurious and short-liv'd; the puny child 621
Of self-congratulating pride, begot
On fancied innocence. Again he falls,
And fights again; but finds his best essay
A presage ominous, portending still
Its own dishonour by a worse relapse.
Till Nature, unavailing Nature, foil'd
So oft, and wearied in the vain attempt,
Scoffs at her own performance. Reason now
Takes part with appetite, and pleads the cause, 630
Perversely, which of late she so condemn'd;
With shallow shifts and old devices, worn
And tatter'd in the service of debauch,
Cov'ring his shame from his offended sight.
"Hath God indeed giv'n appetites to man,
And stor'd the earth so plenteously with means
To gratify the hunger of his wish;
And doth he reprobate, and will he damn,
The use of his own bounty? making first
So frail a kind, and then enacting laws 640

597 and] an *1785*, *1786*.

So strict, that less than perfect must despair?
Falsehood! which whoso but suspects of truth
Dishonours God, and makes a slave of man.
Do they themselves, who undertake for hire
The teacher's office, and dispense at large
Their weekly dole of edifying strains,
Attend to their own music? have they faith
In what with such solemnity of tone
And gesture they propound to our belief?
Nay—conduct hath the loudest tongue. The voice
Is but an instrument, on which the priest 651
May play what tune he pleases. In the deed,
The unequivocal authentic deed,
We find sound argument, we read the heart."
  Such reas'nings (if that name must need belong
T' excuses in which reason has no part)
Serve to compose a spirit well inclin'd
To live on terms of amity with vice,
And sin without disturbance. Often urg'd,
(As often as, libidinous discourse 660
Exhausted, he resorts to solemn themes
Of theological and grave import)
They gain at last his unreserv'd assent;
Till, harden'd his heart's temper in the forge
Of lust, and on the anvil of despair,
He slights the strokes of conscience. Nothing moves,
Or nothing much, his constancy in ill;
Vain tamp'ring has but foster'd his disease;
'Tis desp'rate, and he sleeps the sleep of death!
Haste now, philosopher, and set him free. 670
Charm the deaf serpent wisely. Make him hear
Of rectitude and fitness, moral truth
How lovely, and the moral sense how sure,
Consulted and obey'd, to guide his steps
Directly to the FIRST AND ONLY FAIR.
Spare not in such a cause. Spend all the pow'rs
Of rant and rhapsody in virtue's praise:
Be most sublimely good, verbosely grand,
And with poetic trappings grace thy prose,
Till it out-mantle all the pride of verse.— 680
Ah, tinkling cymbal, and high sounding brass,
Smitten in vain! such music cannot charm
Th' eclipse that intercepts truth's heav'nly beam,
And chills and darkens a wide-wand'ring soul.
The STILL SMALL VOICE is wanted. He must speak,
Whose word leaps forth at once to its effect;
Who calls for things that are not, and they come.

655 needs *1785-1793*.

Grace makes the slave a freeman. 'Tis a change
That turns to ridicule the turgid speech
And stately tone of moralists, who boast 690
As if, like him of fabulous renown,
They had indeed ability to smooth
The shag of savage nature, and were each
An Orpheus, and omnipotent in song:
But transformation of apostate man
From fool to wise, from earthly to divine,
Is work for Him that made him. He alone,
And he by means in philosophic eyes
Trivial and worthy of disdain, achieves
The wonder; humanizing what is brute 700
In the lost kind, extracting from the lips
Of asps their venom, overpow'ring strength
By weakness, and hostility by love.
Patriots have toil'd, and in their country's cause
Bled nobly; and their deeds, as they deserve,
Receive proud recompense. We give in charge
Their names to the sweet lyre. Th' historic muse,
Proud of the treasure, marches with it down
To latest times; and sculpture, in her turn,
Gives bond in stone and ever-during brass 710
To guard them, and t' immortalize her trust:
But fairer wreaths are due, though never paid,
To those who, posted at the shrine of truth,
Have fall'n in her defence. A patriot's blood,
Well spent in such a strife, may earn indeed,
And for a time ensure, to his lov'd land,
The sweets of liberty and equal laws;
But martyrs struggle for a brighter prize,
And win it with more pain. Their blood is shed
In confirmation of the noblest claim— 720
Our claim to feed upon immortal truth,
To walk with God, to be divinely free,
To soar, and to anticipate the skies!
Yet few remember them. They liv'd unknown
Till persecution dragg'd them into fame,
And chas'd them up to heav'n. Their ashes flew
—No marble tells us whither. With their names
No bard embalms and sanctifies his song:
And history, so warm on meaner themes,
Is cold on this. She execrates indeed 730
The tyranny that doom'd them to the fire,
But gives the glorious suff'rers little praise[1].
He is the freeman whom the truth makes free,
And all are slaves beside. There's not a chain

[1] See Hume [C.].

That hellish foes, confed'rate for his harm,
Can wind around him, but he casts it off
With as much ease as Samson his green wyths.
He looks abroad into the varied field
Of nature, and, though poor perhaps compar'd
With those whose mansions glitter in his sight,
Calls the delightful scen'ry all his own. 741
His are the mountains, and the vallies his,
And the resplendent rivers. His t' enjoy
With a propriety that none can feel,
But who, with filial confidence inspir'd,
Can lift to heaven an unpresumptuous eye,
And smiling say—My Father made them all!
Are they not his by a peculiar right,
And by an emphasis of int'rest his,
Whose eye they fill with tears of holy joy, 750
Whose heart with praise, and whose exalted mind
With worthy thoughts of that unwearied love
That plann'd, and built, and still upholds, a world
So cloth'd with beauty for rebellious man?
Yes—ye may fill your garners, ye that reap
The loaded soil, and ye may waste much good
In senseless riot; but ye will not find,
In feast or in the chase, in song or dance,
A liberty like his, who, unimpeach'd
Of usurpation, and to no man's wrong, 760
Appropriates nature as his father's work,
And has a richer use of your's than you.
He is indeed a freeman. Free by birth
Of no mean city; plann'd or ere the hills
Were built, the fountains open'd, or the sea
With all his roaring multitude of waves.
His freedom is the same in ev'ry state;
And no condition of this changeful life,
So manifold in cares, whose ev'ry day
Brings its own evil with it, makes it less: 770
For he has wings that neither sickness, pain,
Nor penury, can cripple or confine.
No nook so narrow but he spreads them there
With ease, and is at large. Th' oppressor holds
His body bound; but knows not what a range
His spirit takes, unconscious of a chain;
And that to bind him is a vain attempt
Whom God delights in, and in whom he dwells.
  Acquaint thyself with God, if thou would'st taste
His works. Admitted once to his embrace, 780
Thou shalt perceive that thou wast blind before:
Thine eye shall be instructed; and thine heart,

Made pure, shall relish, with divine delight
Till then unfelt, what hands divine have wrought.
Brutes graze the mountain-top, with faces prone
And eyes intent upon the scanty herb
It yields them; or, recumbent on its brow,
Ruminate heedless of the scene outspread
Beneath, beyond, and stretching far away
From inland regions to the distant main. 790
Man views it, and admires; but rests content
With what he views. The landscape has his praise,
But not its author. Unconcern'd who form'd
The paradise he sees, he finds it such,
And such well-pleas'd to find it, asks no more.
Not so the mind that has been touch'd from heav'n,
And in the school of sacred wisdom taught
To read his wonders, in whose thought the world,
Fair as it is, existed ere it was.
Not for its own sake merely, but for his 800
Much more who fashion'd it, he gives it praise;
Praise that, from earth resulting, as it ought,
To earth's acknowledg'd sov'reign, finds at once
Its only just proprietor in Him.
The soul that sees him, or receives sublim'd
New faculties, or learns at least t' employ
More worthily the pow'rs she own'd before;
Discerns in all things, what, with stupid gaze
Of ignorance, till then she overlook'd—
A ray of heav'nly light, gilding all forms 810
Terrestrial in the vast and the minute;
The unambiguous footsteps of the God
Who gives its lustre to an insect's wing,
And wheels his throne upon the rolling worlds.
Much conversant with heav'n, she often holds
With those fair ministers of light to man,
That fill the skies nightly with silent pomp,
Sweet conference: inquires what strains were they
With which heav'n rang, when ev'ry star, in haste
To gratulate the new-created earth, 820
Sent forth a voice, and all the sons of God
Shouted for joy.—"Tell me, ye shining hosts,
That navigate a sea that knows no storms,
Beneath a vault unsullied with a cloud,
If from your elevation, whence ye view
Distinctly scenes invisible to man,
And systems of whose birth no tidings yet
Have reach'd this nether world, ye spy a race
Favour'd as our's; transgressors from the womb,
And hasting to a grave, yet doom'd to rise, 830

And to possess a brighter heav'n than your's?
As one who long detain'd on foreign shores
Pants to return, and when he sees afar
His country's weather-bleach'd and batter'd rocks,
From the green wave emerging, darts an eye
Radiant with joy towards the happy land;
So I with animated hopes behold,
And many an aching wish, your beamy fires,
That show like beacons in the blue abyss,
Ordain'd to guide th' embodied spirit home 840
From toilsome life to never-ending rest.
Love kindles as I gaze. I feel desires
That give assurance of their own success,
And that, infus'd from heav'n, must thither tend."

So reads he nature whom the lamp of truth
Illuminates. Thy lamp, mysterious word!
Which whoso sees no longer wanders lost,
With intellects bemaz'd in endless doubt,
But runs the road of wisdom. Thou hast built,
With means that were not till by thee employ'd, 850
Worlds that had never been hadst thou in strength
Been less, or less benevolent than strong.
They are thy witnesses, who speak thy pow'r
And goodness infinite, but speak in ears
That hear not, or receive not their report.
In vain thy creatures testify of thee
Till thou proclaim thyself. Their's is indeed
A teaching voice; but 'tis the praise of thine
That whom it teaches it makes prompt to learn,
And with the boon gives talents for its use. 860
Till thou art heard, imaginations vain
Possess the heart, and fables false as hell;
Yet, deem'd oracular, lure down to death
The uninform'd and heedless souls of men.
We give to chance, blind chance, ourselves as blind,
The glory of thy work; which yet appears
Perfect and unimpeachable of blame,
Challenging human scrutiny, and prov'd
Then skilful most when most severely judg'd.
But chance is not; or is not where thou reign'st:
Thy providence forbids that fickle pow'r 871
(If power she be that works but to confound)
To mix her wild vagaries with thy laws.
Yet thus we dote, refusing while we can
Instruction, and inventing to ourselves
Gods such as guilt makes welcome; gods that sleep,
Or disregard our follies, or that sit
Amus'd spectators of this bustling stage.

Thee we reject, unable to abide
Thy purity, till pure as thou art pure; 880
Made such by thee, we love thee for that cause
For which we shunn'd and hated thee before.
Then we are free. Then liberty, like day,
Breaks on the soul, and by a flash from heav'n
Fires all the faculties with glorious joy
A voice is heard that mortal ears hear not
Till thou hast touch'd them; 'tis the voice of song—
A loud hosanna sent from all thy works;
Which he that hears it with a shout repeats,
And adds his rapture to the gen'ral praise. 890
In that blest moment Nature, throwing wide
Her veil opaque, discloses with a smile
The author of her beauties, who, retir'd
Behind his own creation, works unseen
By the impure, and hears his power denied.
Thou art the source and centre of all minds,
Their only point of rest, eternal Word!
From thee departing, they are lost, and rove
At random, without honour, hope, or peace.
From thee is all that sooths the life of man, 900
His high endeavour, and his glad success,
His strength to suffer, and his will to serve.
But oh thou bounteous giver of all good,
Thou art of all thy gifts thyself the crown!
Give what thou canst, without thee we are poor;
And with thee rich, take what thou wilt away.

BOOK VI

THE WINTER WALK AT NOON

ARGUMENT OF THE SIXTH BOOK.—Bells at a distance—Their effect—A fine noon in winter—A sheltered walk—Meditation better than books—Our familiarity with the course of nature makes it appear less wonderful than it is—The transformation that spring effects in a shrubbery described—A mistake concerning the course of nature corrected—God maintains it by an unremitted act—The amusements fashionable at this hour of the day reproved—Animals happy, a delightful sight—Origin of cruelty to animals—That it is a great crime proved from scripture—That proof illustrated by a tale—A line drawn between the lawful and unlawful destruction of them—Their good and useful properties insisted on—Apology for the encomiums bestowed by the author upon animals—Instances of man's extravagant praise of man—The groans of the creation shall have an end—A view taken of the restoration of all things—An invocation and an invitation of him who shall bring it to pass—The retired man vindicated from the charge of uselessness—Conclusion.

THERE is in souls a sympathy with sounds;
And, as the mind is pitch'd, the ear is pleas'd
With melting airs, or martial, brisk, or grave:

Some chord in unison with what we hear
Is touch'd within us, and the heart replies.
How soft the music of those village bells,
Falling at intervals upon the ear
In cadence sweet, now dying all away,
Now pealing loud again, and louder still,
Clear and sonorous, as the gale comes on! 10
With easy force it opens all the cells
Where mem'ry slept. Wherever I have heard
A kindred melody, the scene recurs,
And with it all its pleasures and its pains.
Such comprehensive views the spirit takes,
That in a few short moments I retrace
(As in a map the voyager his course)
The windings of my way through many years.
Short as in retrospect the journey seems,
It seem'd not always short; the rugged path, 20
And prospect oft so dreary and forlorn,
Mov'd many a sigh at its disheart'ning length.
Yet, feeling present evils, while the past
Faintly impress the mind, or not at all,
How readily we wish time spent revok'd,
That we might try the ground again, where once
(Through inexperience, as we now perceive)
We miss'd that happiness we might have found!
Some friend is gone, perhaps his son's best friend!
A father, whose authority in show 30
When most severe, and must'ring all its force,
Was but the graver countenance of love;
Whose favour, like the clouds of spring, might low'r,
And utter now and then an awful voice,
But had a blessing in its darkest frown,
Threat'ning at once and nourishing the plant.
We lov'd, but not enough, the gentle hand
That rear'd us. At a thoughtless age, allur'd
By ev'ry gilded folly, we renounc'd
His shelt'ring side, and wilfully forewent 40
That converse which we now in vain regret.
How gladly would the man recall to life
The boy's neglected sire! a mother too,
That softer friend, perhaps more gladly still,
Might he demand them at the gates of death.
Sorrow has, since they went, subdu'd and tam'd
The playful humour; he could now endure,
(Himself grown sober in the vale of tears)
And feel a parent's presence no restraint.
But not to understand a treasure's worth 50
Till time has stol'n away the slighted good,

Is cause of half the poverty we feel,
And makes the world the wilderness it is.
The few that pray at all pray oft amiss,
And, seeking grace t' improve the prize they hold,
Would urge a wiser suit than asking more.
  The night was winter in his roughest mood;
The morning sharp and clear. But now at noon
Upon the southern side of the slant hills,
And where the woods fence off the northern blast,
The season smiles, resigning all its rage, 61
And has the warmth of May. The vault is blue
Without a cloud, and white without a speck
The dazzling splendour of the scene below.
Again the harmony comes o'er the vale;
And through the trees I view th' embattled tow'r
Whence all the music. I again perceive
The soothing influence of the wafted strains,
And settle in soft musings as I tread
The walk, still verdant, under oaks and elms, 70
Whose outspread branches overarch the glade.
The roof, though moveable through all its length
As the wind sways it, has yet well suffic'd,
And, intercepting in their silent fall
The frequent flakes, has kept a path for me.
No noise is here, or none that hinders thought.
The redbreast warbles still, but is content
With slender notes, and more than half suppress'd:
Pleas'd with his solitude, and flitting light
From spray to spray, where'er he rests he shakes
From many a twig the pendent drops of ice, 81
That tinkle in the wither'd leaves below.
Stillness, accompanied with sounds so soft,
Charms more than silence. Meditation here
May think down hours to moments. Here the heart
May give an useful lesson to the head,
And learning wiser grow without his books.
Knowledge and wisdom, far from being one,
Have oft-times no connexion. Knowledge dwells
In heads replete with thoughts of other men; 90
Wisdom in minds attentive to their own.
Knowledge, a rude unprofitable mass,
The mere materials with which wisdom builds,
Till smooth'd and squar'd and fitted to its place,
Does but encumber whom it seems t' enrich.
Knowledge is proud that he has learn'd so much;
Wisdom is humble that he knows no more.

57 his] its *1800* (*8vo*).

Books are not seldom talismans and spells,
By which the magic art of shrewder wits
Holds an unthinking multitude enthrall'd. 100
Some to the fascination of a name
Surrender judgment, hood-wink'd. Some the style
Infatuates, and through labyrinths and wilds
Of error leads them by a tune entranc'd.
While sloth seduces more, too weak to bear
The insupportable fatigue of thought,
And swallowing, therefore, without pause or choice,
The total grist unsifted, husks and all.
But trees, and rivulets whose rapid course
Defies the check of winter, haunts of deer, 110
And sheep-walks populous with bleating lambs,
And lanes in which the primrose ere her time
Peeps through the moss that clothes the hawthorn
root,
Deceive no student. Wisdom there, and truth,
Not shy, as in the world, and to be won
By slow solicitation, seize at once
The roving thought, and fix it on themselves.

What prodigies can pow'r divine perform
More grand than it produces year by year,
And all in sight of inattentive man? 120
Familiar with th' effect we slight the cause,
And, in the constancy of nature's course,
The regular return of genial months,
And renovation of a faded world,
See nought to wonder at. Should God again,
As once in Gibeon, interrupt the race
Of the undeviating and punctual sun,
How would the world admire! but speaks it less
An agency divine, to make him know
His moment when to sink and when to rise, 130
Age after age, than to arrest his course?
All we behold is miracle; but, seen
So duly, all is miracle in vain.
Where now the vital energy that mov'd,
While summer was, the pure and subtile lymph
Through th' imperceptible meand'ring veins
Of leaf and flow'r? It sleeps; and th' icy touch
Of unprolific winter has impress'd
A cold stagnation on th' intestine tide.
But let the months go round, a few short months,
And all shall be restor'd. These naked shoots, 141
Barren as lances, among which the wind
Makes wintry music, sighing as it goes,
Shall put their graceful foliage on again,

And, more aspiring, and with ampler spread,
Shall boast new charms, and more than they have
 lost.
Then, each in its peculiar honours clad,
Shall publish, even to the distant eye,
Its family and tribe. Laburnum, rich
In streaming gold; syringa, iv'ry pure; 150
The scentless and the scented rose; this red
And of an humbler growth, the other tall[1],
And throwing up into the darkest gloom
Of neighb'ring cypress, or more sable yew,
Her silver globes, light as the foamy surf
That the wind severs from the broken wave;
The lilac, various in array, now white,
Now sanguine, and her beauteous head now set
With purple spikes pyramidal, as if,
Studious of ornament, yet unresolv'd 160
Which hue she most approv'd, she chose them all;
Copious of flow'rs the woodbine, pale and wan,
But well compensating her sickly looks
With never-cloying odours, early and late;
Hypericum, all bloom, so thick a swarm
Of flow'rs, like flies clothing her slender rods,
That scarce a leaf appears; mezerion, too,
Though leafless, well attir'd, and thick beset
With blushing wreaths, investing ev'ry spray;
Althæa with the purple eye; the broom, 170
Yellow and bright, as bullion unalloy'd,
Her blossoms; and, luxuriant above all,
The jasmine, throwing wide her elegant sweets,
The deep dark green of whose unvarnish'd leaf
Makes more conspicuous, and illumines more
The bright profusion of her scatter'd stars.—
These have been, and these shall be in their day;
And all this uniform, uncolour'd scene,
Shall be dismantled of its fleecy load,
And flush into variety again. 180
From dearth to plenty, and from death to life,
Is Nature's progress when she lectures man
In heav'nly truth; evincing, as she makes
The grand transition, that there lives and works
A soul in all things, and that soul is God.
The beauties of the wilderness are his,
That make so gay the solitary place
Where no eye sees them. And the fairer forms
That cultivation glories in, are his.

[1] The Guelder-rose [C.]. 181 dearth] death *1798*[1].

He sets the bright procession on its way, 190
And marshals all the order of the year;
He marks the bounds which winter may not pass,
And blunts his pointed fury; in its case,
Russet and rude, folds up the tender germ,
Uninjur'd, with inimitable art;
And, ere one flow'ry season fades and dies,
Designs the blooming wonders of the next.
Some say that, in the origin of things,
When all creation started into birth,
The infant elements receiv'd a law, 200
From which they swerve not since. That under force
Of that controuling ordinance they move,
And need not his immediate hand, who first
Prescrib'd their course, to regulate it now.
Thus dream they, and contrive to save a God
Th' incumbrance of his own concerns, and spare
The great Artificer of all that moves
The stress of a continual act, the pain
Of unremitted vigilance and care,
As too laborious and severe a task. 210
So man, the moth, is not afraid, it seems,
To span omnipotence, and measure might
That knows no measure, by the scanty rule
And standard of his own, that is to-day,
And is not ere to-morrow's sun go down!
But how should matter occupy a charge
Dull as it is, and satisfy a law
So vast in its demands, unless impell'd
To ceaseless service by a ceaseless force,
And under pressure of some conscious cause? 220
The Lord of all, himself through all diffus'd,
Sustains, and is the life of all that lives.
Nature is but a name for an effect,
Whose cause is God. He feeds the secret fire
By which the mighty process is maintain'd,
Who sleeps not, is not weary; in whose sight
Slow circling ages are as transient days;
Whose work is without labour; whose designs
No flaw deforms, no difficulty thwarts;
And whose beneficence no charge exhausts. 230
Him blind antiquity profan'd, not serv'd,
With self-taught rites, and under various names,
Female and male, Pomona, Pales, Pan,
And Flora, and Vertumnus; peopling earth
With tutelary goddesses and gods
That were not; and commending, as they would,
To each some province, garden, field, or grove.

But all are under one. One spirit—His
Who wore the platted thorns with bleeding brows—
Rules universal nature. Not a flow'r 240
But shows some touch, in freckle, streak, or stain,
Of his unrivall'd pencil. He inspires
Their balmy odours, and imparts their hues,
And bathes their eyes with nectar, and includes,
In grains as countless as the sea-side sands,
The forms with which he sprinkles all the earth.
Happy who walks with him! whom what he finds
Of flavour or of scent in fruit or flow'r,
Or what he views of beautiful or grand
In nature, from the broad majestic oak 250
To the green blade that twinkles in the sun,
Prompts with remembrance of a present God!
His presence, who made all so fair, perceiv'd,
Makes all still fairer. As with him no scene
Is dreary, so with him all seasons please.
Though winter had been none, had man been true,
And earth be punish'd for its tenant's sake,
Yet not in vengeance; as this smiling sky,
So soon succeeding such an angry night,
And these dissolving snows, and this clear stream
Recov'ring fast its liquid music, prove. 261
Who then, that has a mind well strung and tun'd
To contemplation, and within his reach
A scene so friendly to his fav'rite task,
Would waste attention at the chequer'd board,
His host of wooden warriors to and fro
Marching and counter-marching, with an eye
As fixt as marble, with a forehead ridg'd
And furrow'd into storms, and with a hand
Trembling, as if eternity were hung 270
In balance on his conduct of a pin?—
Nor envies he aught more their idle sport,
Who pant with application misapplied
To trivial toys, and, pushing iv'ry balls
Across a velvet level, feel a joy
Akin to rapture when the bawble finds
Its destin'd goal, of difficult access.—
Nor deems he wiser him, who gives his noon
To miss, the mercer's plague, from shop to shop
Wand'ring, and litt'ring with unfolded silks 280
The polish'd counter, and approving none,
Or promising with smiles to call again.—
Nor him, who by his vanity seduc'd,

239 wore] bore *1786*. 257 be] been *1800* (*8vo*).

And sooth'd into a dream that he discerns
The diff'rence of a Guido from a daub,
Frequents the crowded auction: station'd there
As duly as the Langford of the show,
With glass at eye, and catalogue in hand,
And tongue accomplish'd in the fulsome cant
And pedantry that coxcombs learn with ease; 290
Oft as the price-deciding hammer falls
He notes it in his book, then raps his box,
Swears 'tis a bargain, rails at his hard fate
That he has let it pass—but never bids!

Here, unmolested, through whatever sign
The sun proceeds, I wander. Neither mist,
Nor freezing sky nor sultry, checking me,
Nor stranger intermeddling with my joy.
Ev'n in the spring and play-time of the year,
That calls th' unwonted villager abroad 300
With all her little ones, a sportive train,
To gather king-cups in the yellow mead,
And prink their hair with daisies, or to pick
A cheap but wholesome sallad from the brook,
These shades are all my own. The tim'rous hare,
Grown so familiar with her frequent guest,
Scarce shuns me; and the stock-dove, unalarm'd,
Sits cooing in the pine-tree, nor suspends
His long love-ditty for my near approach.
Drawn from his refuge in some lonely elm 310
That age or injury has hollow'd deep,
Where, on his bed of wool and matted leaves,
He has outslept the winter, ventures forth
To frisk awhile, and bask in the warm sun,
The squirrel, flippant, pert, and full of play:
He sees me, and at once, swift as a bird,
Ascends the neighb'ring beach; there whisks his brush,
And perks his ears, and stamps and cries aloud,
With all the prettiness of feign'd alarm,
And anger insignificantly fierce. 320

The heart is hard in nature, and unfit
For human fellowship, as being void
Of sympathy, and therefore dead alike
To love and friendship both, that is not pleas'd
With sight of animals enjoying life,
Nor feels their happiness augment his own.
The bounding fawn, that darts across the glade
When none pursues, through mere delight of heart,

318 cries] scolds *1785-1793.*

And spirits buoyant with excess of glee;
The horse as wanton, and almost as fleet, 330
That skims the spacious meadow at full speed,
Then stops and snorts, and, throwing high his heels,
Starts to the voluntary race again;
The very kine that gambol at high noon,
The total herd receiving first from one
That leads the dance a summons to be gay,
Though wild their strange vagaries, and uncouth
Their efforts, yet resolv'd with one consent
To give such act and utt'rance as they may
To ecstasy too big to be suppress'd— 340
These, and a thousand images of bliss,
With which kind nature graces ev'ry scene
Where cruel man defeats not her design,
Impart to the benevolent, who wish
All that are capable of pleasure pleas'd,
A far superior happiness to their's,
The comfort of a reasonable joy.
Man scarce had ris'n, obedient to his call
Who form'd him from the dust, his future grave,
When he was crown'd as never king was since. 350
God set the diadem upon his head,
And angel choirs attended. Wond'ring stood
The new-made monarch, while before him pass'd,
All happy, and all perfect in their kind,
The creatures summon'd from their various haunts
To see their sov'reign, and confess his sway.
Vast was his empire, absolute his pow'r,
Or bounded only by a law, whose force
'Twas his sublimest privilege to feel
And own—the law of universal love. 360
He rul'd with meekness, they obey'd with joy;
No cruel purpose lurk'd within his heart,
And no distrust of his intent in their's.
So Eden was a scene of harmless sport,
Where kindness on his part who rul'd the whole
Begat a tranquil confidence in all,
And fear as yet was not, nor cause for fear.
But sin marr'd all; and the revolt of man,
That source of evils not exhausted yet,
Was punish'd with revolt of his from him. 370
Garden of God, how terrible the change
Thy groves and lawns then witness'd! Ev'ry heart,
Each animal of ev'ry name, conceiv'd
A jealousy and an instinctive fear,
And, conscious of some danger, either fled
Precipitate the loath'd abode of man,

Or growl'd defiance in such angry sort,
As taught him, too, to tremble in his turn.
Thus harmony and family accord
Were driv'n from Paradise; and in that hour 380
The seeds of cruelty, that since have swell'd
To such gigantic and enormous growth,
Were sown in human nature's fruitful soil.
Hence date the persecution and the pain
That man inflicts on all inferior kinds,
Regardless of their plaints. To make him sport,
To gratify the frenzy of his wrath,
Or his base gluttony, are causes good
And just, in his account, why bird and beast
Should suffer torture, and the streams be dyed 390
With blood of their inhabitants impal'd.
Earth groans beneath the burden of a war
Wag'd with defenceless innocence, while he,
Not satisfied to prey on all around,
Adds tenfold bitterness to death by pangs
Needless, and first torments ere he devours.
Now happiest they that occupy the scenes
The most remote from his abhorr'd resort,
Whom once, as delegate of God on earth,
They fear'd, and, as his perfect image, lov'd. 400
The wilderness is their's, with all its caves,
Its hollow glens, its thickets, and its plains,
Unvisited by man. There they are free,
And howl and roar as likes them, uncontrol'd;
Nor ask his leave to slumber or to play.
Wo to the tyrant, if he dare intrude
Within the confines of their wild domain!
The lion tells him—I am monarch here!
And, if he spare him, spares him on the terms
Of royal mercy, and through gen'rous scorn 410
To rend a victim trembling at his foot.
In measure, as by force of instinct drawn,
Or by necessity constrain'd, they live
Dependent upon man; those in his fields,
These at his crib, and some beneath his roof.
They prove too often at how dear a rate
He sells protection.—Witness at his foot,
The spaniel dying, for some venial fault,
Under dissection of the knotted scourge—
Witness the patient ox, with stripes and yells 420
Driv'n to the slaughter, goaded, as he runs,
To madness; while the savage at his heels

409 spare] spares *1786*.

Laughs at the frantic suff'rer's fury, spent
Upon the guiltless passenger o'erthrown.
He, too, is witness, noblest of the train
That wait on man, the flight-performing horse:
With unsuspecting readiness he takes
His murd'rer on his back, and, push'd all day,
With bleeding sides and flanks that heave for life,
To the far-distant goal, arrives and dies. 430
So little mercy shows who needs so much!
Does law, so jealous in the cause of man,
Denounce no doom on the delinquent?—None.
He lives, and o'er his brimming beaker boasts
(As if barbarity were high desert)
Th' inglorious feat, and, clamorous in praise
Of the poor brute, seems wisely to suppose
The honours of his matchless horse his own!
But many a crime, deem'd innocent on earth,
Is registered in heav'n; and these, no doubt, 440
Have each their record, with a curse annex'd.
Man may dismiss compassion from his heart,
But God will never. When he charg'd the Jew
T' assist his foe's down-fallen beast to rise;
And when the bush-exploring boy, that seiz'd
The young, to let the parent bird go free;
Prov'd he not plainly that his meaner works
Are yet his care, and have an int'rest all,
All, in the universal Father's love?
On Noah, and in him on all mankind, 450
The charter was conferr'd, by which we hold
The flesh of animals in fee, and claim
O'er all we feed on pow'r of life and death.
But read the instrument, and mark it well:
Th' oppression of a tyrannous controul
Can find no warrant there. Feed then, and yield
Thanks for thy food. Carnivorous, through sin,
Feed on the slain, but spare the living brute!
  The Governor of all, himself to all
So bountiful, in whose attentive ear 460
The unfledg'd raven and the lion's whelp
Plead not in vain for pity on the pangs
Of hunger unassuag'd, has interpos'd,
Not seldom, his avenging arm, to smite
Th' injurious trampler upon nature's law,
That claims forbearance even for a brute.
He hates the hardness of a Balaam's heart;
And, prophet as he was, he might not strike
The blameless animal, without rebuke,
On which he rode. Her opportune offence 470

Sav'd him, or th' unrelenting seer had died.
He sees that human equity is slack
To interfere, though in so just a cause;
And makes the task his own. Inspiring dumb
And helpless victims with a sense so keen
Of inj'ry, with such knowledge of their strength,
And such sagacity to take revenge,
That oft the beast has seem'd to judge the man.
An ancient, not a legendary tale,
By one of sound intelligence rehears'd, 480
(If such who plead for Providence may seem
In modern eyes) shall make the doctrine clear.—
 Where England, stretch'd towards the setting sun,
Narrow and long, o'erlooks the western wave,
Dwelt young Misagathus; a scorner he
Of God and goodness, atheist in ostent,
Vicious in act, in temper savage-fierce.
He journey'd; and his chance was as he went
To join a trav'ller, of far diff'rent note—
Evander, fam'd for piety, for years 490
Deserving honour, but for wisdom more.
Fame had not left the venerable man
A stranger to the manners of the youth,
Whose face, too, was familiar to his view.
Their way was on the margin of the land,
O'er the green summit of the rocks, whose base
Beats back the roaring surge, scarce heard so high.
The charity that warm'd his heart was mov'd
At sight of the man-monster. With a smile
Gentle, and affable, and full of grace, 500
As fearful of offending whom he wish'd
Much to persuade, he plied his ear with truths
Not harshly thunder'd forth or rudely press'd,
But, like his purpose, gracious, kind, and sweet.
"And dost thou dream," th' impenetrable man
Exclaim'd, "that me the lullabies of age,
And fantasies of dotards, such as thou,
Can cheat, or move a moment's fear in me?
Mark now the proof I give thee, that the brave
Need no such aids as superstition lends 510
To steel their hearts against the dread of death."
He spoke, and to the precipice at hand
Push'd with a madman's fury. Fancy shrinks,
And the blood thrills and curdles, at the thought
Of such a gulph as he design'd his grave.
But, though the felon on his back could dare
The dreadful leap, more rational, his steed
Declin'd the death, and wheeling swiftly round,

Or e'er his hoof had press'd the crumbling verge,
Baffled his rider, sav'd against his will! 520
The frenzy of the brain may be redress'd
By med'cine well applied, but without grace
The heart's insanity admits no cure.
Enrag'd the more, by what might have reform'd
His horrible intent, again he sought
Destruction, with a zeal to be destroy'd,
With sounding whip, and rowels dyed in blood.
But still in vain. The Providence, that meant
A longer date to the far nobler beast,
Spar'd yet again th' ignobler, for his sake. 530
And now, his prowess prov'd, and his sincere
Incurable obduracy evinc'd,
His rage grew cool; and, pleas'd perhaps t' have
earn'd
So cheaply the renown of that attempt,
With looks of some complacence he resum'd
His road, deriding much the blank amaze
Of good Evander, still where he was left
Fixt motionless, and petrified with dread.
So on they far'd. Discourse on other themes
Ensuing, seem'd t' obliterate the past; 540
And, tamer far for so much fury shown,
(As is the course of rash and fiery men)
The rude companion smil'd, as if transform'd.
But 'twas a transient calm. A storm was near,
An unsuspected storm. His hour was come.
The impious challenger of Pow'r divine
Was now to learn that Heav'n, tho' slow to wrath,
Is never with impunity defied.
His horse, as he had caught his master's mood,
Snorting, and starting into sudden rage, 550
Unbidden, and not now to be control'd,
Rush'd to the cliff, and, having reach'd it, stood.
At once the shock unseated him: he flew
Sheer o'er the craggy barrier; and, immers'd
Deep in the flood, found, when he sought it not,
The death he had deserv'd—and died alone!
So God wrought double justice; made the fool
The victim of his own tremendous choice,
And taught a brute the way to safe revenge.
I would not enter on my list of friends 560
(Tho' grac'd with polish'd manners and fine sense,
Yet wanting sensibility) the man
Who needlessly sets foot upon a worm.

527 dyed *1785*, *1786*, *1798*[1], *1803*: dy'd *1787*, *1788*: died *1793*, *1795*, *1798*[2]-*1800*.

An inadvertent step may crush the snail
That crawls at ev'ning in the public path;
But he that has humanity, forewarn'd,
Will tread aside, and let the reptile live.
The creeping vermin, loathsome to the sight,
And charg'd perhaps with venom, that intrudes,
A visitor unwelcome, into scenes 570
Sacred to neatness and repose—th' alcove,
The chamber, or refectory—may die:
A necessary act incurs no blame.
Not so when, held within their proper bounds,
And guiltless of offence, they range the air,
Or take their pastime in the spacious field:
There they are privileg'd; and he that hunts
Or harms them there is guilty of a wrong,
Disturbs th' economy of nature's realm,
Who, when she form'd, design'd them an abode. 580
The sum is this.—If man's convenience, health,
Or safety, interfere, his rights and claims
Are paramount, and must extinguish their's.
Else they are all—the meanest things that are—
As free to live, and to enjoy that life,
As God was free to form them at the first,
Who, in his sov'reign wisdom, made them all.
Ye, therefore, who love mercy, teach your sons
To love it too. The spring-time of our years
Is soon dishonour'd and defil'd in most 590
By budding ills, that ask a prudent hand
To check them. But, alas! none sooner shoots,
If unrestrain'd, into luxuriant growth,
Than cruelty, most dev'lish of them all.
Mercy to him that shows it, is the rule
And righteous limitation of its act,
By which Heav'n moves in pard'ning guilty man;
And he that shows none, being ripe in years,
And conscious of the outrage he commits,
Shall seek it, and not find it, in his turn. 600

Distinguish'd much by reason, and still more
By our capacity of grace divine,
From creatures that exist but for our sake,
Which, having serv'd us, perish, we are held
Accountable; and God, some future day,
Will reckon with us roundly for th' abuse
Of what he deems no mean or trivial trust.
Superior as we are, they yet depend
Not more on human help than we on their's.
Their strength, or speed, or vigilance, were giv'n
In aid of our defects. In some are found 611

Such teachable and apprehensive parts,
That man's attainments in his own concerns,
Match'd with th' expertness of the brutes in their's,
Are oft-times vanquish'd and thrown far behind.
Some show that nice sagacity of smell,
And read with such discernment, in the port
And figure of the man, his secret aim,
That oft we owe our safety to a skill
We could not teach, and must despair to learn. 620
But learn we might, if not too proud to stoop
To quadrupede instructors, many a good
And useful quality, and virtue too,
Rarely exemplified among ourselves.
Attachment never to be wean'd, or chang'd
By any change of fortune; proof alike
Against unkindness, absence, and neglect;
Fidelity, that neither bribe nor threat
Can move or warp; and gratitude for small
And trivial favours, lasting as the life, 630
And glist'ning even in the dying eye.

Man praises man. Desert in arts or arms
Wins public honour; and ten thousand sit
Patiently present at a sacred song,
Commemoration-mad; content to hear
(Oh wonderful effect of music's pow'r!)
Messiah's eulogy for Handel's sake!
But less, methinks, than sacrilege might serve—
(For, was it less, what heathen would have dar'd
To strip Jove's statue of his oaken wreath, 640
And hang it up in honour of a man?)
Much less might serve, when all that we design
Is but to gratify an itching ear,
And give the day to a musician's praise.
Remember Handel? Who, that was not born
Deaf as the dead to harmony, forgets,
Or can, the more than Homer of his age?
Yes—we remember him; and, while we praise
A talent so divine, remember too
That His most holy book from whom it came 650
Was never meant, was never us'd before,
To buckram out the mem'ry of a man.
But hush!—the muse perhaps is too severe;
And, with a gravity beyond the size
And measure of th' offence, rebukes a deed
Less impious than absurd, and owing more
To want of judgment than to wrong design.
So in the chapel of old Ely House,
When wand'ring Charles, who meant to be the third,

Had fled from William, and the news was fresh,
The simple clerk, but loyal, did announce, 661
And eke did rear right merrily, two staves,
Sung to the praise and glory of King George!
—Man praises man; and Garrick's mem'ry next,
When time hath somewhat mellow'd it, and made
The idol of our worship while he liv'd
The god of our idolatry once more,
Shall have its altar; and the world shall go
In pilgrimage to bow before his shrine.
The theatre, too small, shall suffocate 670
Its squeez'd contents, and more than it admits
Shall sigh at their exclusion, and return
Ungratified. For there some noble lord
Shall stuff his shoulders with king Richard's bunch,
Or wrap himself in Hamlet's inky cloak,
And strut, and storm, and straddle, stamp, and stare,
To show the world how Garrick did not act—
For Garrick was a worshipper himself;
He drew the liturgy, and fram'd the rites
And solemn ceremonial of the day, 680
And call'd the world to worship on the banks
Of Avon, fam'd in song. Ah, pleasant proof
That piety has still in human hearts
Some place, a spark or two not yet extinct!
The mulb'ry tree was hung with blooming wreaths;
The mulb'ry tree stood centre of the dance;
The mulb'ry tree was hymn'd with dulcet airs;
And from his touchwood trunk the mulb'ry tree
Supplied such relics as devotion holds
Still sacred, and preserves with pious care. 690
So 'twas an hallow'd time: decorum reign'd,
And mirth without offence. No few return'd,
Doubtless, much edified, and all refresh'd.
—Man praises man. The rabble, all alive,
From tippling-benches, cellars, stalls, and styes,
Swarm in the streets. The statesman of the day,
A pompous and slow-moving pageant, comes.
Some shout him, and some hang upon his car,
To gaze in's eyes, and bless him. Maidens wave
Their 'kerchiefs, and old women weep for joy: 700
While others, not so satisfied, unhorse
The gilded equipage, and, turning loose
His steeds, usurp a place they well deserve.
Why? what has charm'd them? Hath he sav'd the state?
No. Doth he purpose its salvation? No.
Enchanting novelty, that moon at full,

Flows into her; unbounded is her joy,
And endless her increase. Thy rams are there,
Nebaioth[1], and the flocks of Kedar there;
The looms of Ormus, and the mines of Ind,
And Saba's spicy groves, pay tribute there.
Praise is in all her gates: upon her walls,
And in her streets, and in her spacious courts,
Is heard salvation. Eastern Java there 810
Kneels with the native of the farthest west;
And Æthiopia spreads abroad the hand,
And worships. Her report has travell'd forth
Into all lands. From ev'ry clime they come
To see thy beauty and to share thy joy,
O Sion! an assembly such as earth
Saw never, such as heav'n stoops down to see.
Thus heav'n-ward all things tend. For all were once
Perfect, and all must be at length restor'd.
So God has greatly purpos'd; who would else 820
In his dishonour'd works himself endure
Dishonour, and be wrong'd without redress.
Haste, then, and wheel away a shatter'd world,
Ye slow-revolving seasons! we would see
(A sight to which our eyes are strangers yet)
A world that does not dread and hate his laws,
And suffer for its crime; would learn how fair
The creature is that God pronounces good,
How pleasant in itself what pleases him.
Here ev'ry drop of honey hides a sting, 830
Worms wind themselves into our sweetest flow'rs;
And ev'n the joy that haply some poor heart
Derives from heav'n, pure as the fountain is,
Is sullied in the stream, taking a taint
From touch of human lips, at best impure.
Oh for a world in principle as chaste
As this is gross and selfish! over which
Custom and prejudice shall bear no sway,
That govern all things here, should'ring aside
The meek and modest truth, and forcing her 840
To seek a refuge from the tongue of strife
In nooks obscure, far from the ways of men:—
Where violence shall never lift the sword,
Nor cunning justify the proud man's wrong,
Leaving the poor no remedy but tears:—

[1] Nebaioth and Kedar, the sons of Ishmael, and progenitors of the Arabs, in the prophetic scripture here alluded to, may be reasonably considered as representatives of the Gentiles at large [C.].

830 Here] How *1800* (*8vo*).

Where he that fills an office shall esteem
Th' occasion it presents of doing good
More than the perquisite;—where law shall speak
Seldom, and never but as wisdom prompts
And equity; not jealous more to guard 850
A worthless form, than to decide aright:—
Where fashion shall not sanctify abuse,
Nor smooth good-breeding (supplemental grace)
With lean performance ape the work of love!

Come then, and, added to thy many crowns,
Receive yet one, the crown of all the earth,
Thou who alone art worthy! It was thine
By ancient covenant, ere nature's birth;
And thou hast made it thine by purchase since,
And overpaid its value with thy blood. 860
Thy saints proclaim thee king; and in their hearts
Thy title is engraven with a pen
Dipt in the fountain of eternal love.
Thy saints proclaim thee king; and thy delay
Gives courage to their foes, who, could they see
The dawn of thy last advent, long-desir'd,
Would creep into the bowels of the hills,
And flee for safety to the falling rocks.
The very spirit of the world is tir'd
Of its own taunting question, ask'd so long, 870
"Where is the promise of your Lord's approach?"
The infidel has shot his bolts away,
Till, his exhausted quiver yielding none,
He gleans the blunted shafts that have recoil'd,
And aims them at the shield of truth again.
The veil is rent, rent too by priestly hands,
That hides divinity from mortal eyes;
And all the mysteries to faith propos'd,
Insulted and traduc'd, are cast aside,
As useless, to the moles and to the bats. 880
They now are deem'd the faithful, and are prais'd,
Who, constant only in rejecting thee,
Deny thy Godhead with a martyr's zeal,
And quit their office for their error's sake.
Blind, and in love with darkness! yet ev'n these
Worthy, compar'd with sycophants, who knee
Thy name adoring, and then preach thee man!
So fares thy church. But how thy church may fare
The world takes little thought. Who will may preach,
And what they will. All pastors are alike 890
To wand'ring sheep, resolv'd to follow none.
Two gods divide them all—Pleasure and Gain:
For these they live, they sacrifice to these,

And in their service wage perpetual war
With conscience and with thee. Lust in their hearts,
And mischief in their hands, they roam the earth
To prey upon each other; stubborn, fierce,
High-minded, foaming out their own disgrace.
Thy prophets speak of such; and, noting down
The features of the last degen'rate times, 900
Exhibit ev'ry lineament of these.
Come then, and, added to thy many crowns,
Receive yet one, as radiant as the rest,
Due to thy last and most effectual work,
Thy word fulfill'd, the conquest of a world!

He is the happy man, whose life ev'n now
Shows somewhat of that happier life to come;
Who, doom'd to an obscure but tranquil state,
Is pleas'd with it, and, were he free to choose,
Would make his fate his choice; whom peace, the
fruit 910
Of virtue, and whom virtue, fruit of faith,
Prepare for happiness; bespeak him one
Content indeed to sojourn while he must
Below the skies, but having there his home.
The world o'erlooks him in her busy search
Of objects, more illustrious in her view;
And, occupied as earnestly as she,
Though more sublimely, he o'erlooks the world.
She scorns his pleasures, for she knows them not;
He seeks not her's, for he has prov'd them vain. 920
He cannot skim the ground like summer birds
Pursuing gilded flies; and such he deems
Her honours, her emoluments, her joys.
Therefore in contemplation is his bliss,
Whose pow'r is such, that whom she lifts from earth
She makes familiar with a heav'n unseen,
And shows him glories yet to be reveal'd.
Not slothful he, though seeming unemploy'd,
And censur'd oft as useless. Stillest streams
Oft water fairest meadows, and the bird 930
That flutters least is longest on the wing.
Ask him, indeed, what trophies he has rais'd,
Or what achievements of immortal fame
He purposes, and he shall answer—None.
His warfare is within. There unfatigu'd
His fervent spirit labours. There he fights,
And there obtains fresh triumphs o'er himself,
And never with'ring wreaths, compar'd with which
The laurels that a Cæsar reaps are weeds.
Perhaps the self-approving haughty world, 940

That as she sweeps him with her whistling silks
Scarce deigns to notice him, or, if she see,
Deems him a cypher in the works of God,
Receives advantage from his noiseless hours,
Of which she little dreams. Perhaps she owes
Her sunshine and her rain, her blooming spring
And plenteous harvest, to the pray'r he makes,
When, Isaac like, the solitary saint
Walks forth to meditate at even tide,
And think on her, who thinks not for herself. 950
Forgive him, then, thou bustler in concerns
Of little worth, an idler in the best,
If, author of no mischief and some good,
He seek his proper happiness by means
That may advance, but cannot hinder, thine.
Nor, though he tread the secret path of life,
Engage no notice, and enjoy much ease,
Account him an incumbrance on the state,
Receiving benefits, and rend'ring none.
His sphere though humble, if that humble sphere
Shine with his fair example, and though small 961
His influence, if that influence all be spent
In soothing sorrow and in quenching strife,
In aiding helpless indigence, in works
From which at least a grateful few derive
Some taste of comfort in a world of woe,
Then let the supercilious great confess
He serves his country, recompenses well
The state, beneath the shadow of whose vine
He sits secure, and in the scale of life 970
Holds no ignoble, though a slighted, place.
The man, whose virtues are more felt than seen,
Must drop indeed the hope of public praise;
But he may boast what few that win it can—
That if his country stand not by his skill,
At least his follies have not wrought her fall.
Polite refinement offers him in vain
Her golden tube, through which a sensual world
Draws gross impurity, and likes it well,
The neat conveyance hiding all th' offence. 980
Not that he peevishly rejects a mode
Because that world adopts it. If it bear
The stamp and clear impression of good sense,
And be not costly more than of true worth,
He puts it on, and, for decorum sake,
Can wear it e'en as gracefully as she.

952 an] and *1785-1788.*

She judges of refinement by the eye,
He by the test of conscience, and a heart
Not soon deceiv'd; aware that what is base
No polish can make sterling; and that vice, 990
Though well perfum'd and elegantly dress'd,
Like an unburied carcase trick'd with flow'rs,
Is but a garnish'd nuisance, fitter far
For cleanly riddance than for fair attire.
So life glides smoothly and by stealth away,
More golden than that age of fabled gold
Renown'd in ancient song; not vex'd with care
Or stain'd with guilt, beneficent, approv'd
Of God and man, and peaceful in its end.
So glide my life away! and so at last, 1000
My share of duties decently fulfill'd,
May some disease, not tardy to perform
Its destin'd office, yet with gentle stroke,
Dismiss me, weary, to a safe retreat,
Beneath the turf that I have often trod.
It shall not grieve me, then, that once, when call'd
To dress a Sofa with the flow'rs of verse,
I play'd awhile, obedient to the fair, 1008
With that light task; but soon, to please her more,
Whom flow'rs alone I knew would little please,
Let fall th' unfinish'd wreath, and rov'd for fruit;
Rov'd far, and gather'd much: some harsh, 'tis true,
Pick'd from the thorns and briers of reproof,
But wholesome, well-digested; grateful some
To palates that can taste immortal truth;
Insipid else, and sure to be despis'd.
But all is in his hand whose praise I seek.
In vain the poet sings, and the world hears,
If he regard not, though divine the theme.
'Tis not in artful measures, in the chime 1020
And idle tinkling of a minstrel's lyre,
To charm his ear, whose eye is on the heart;
Whose frown can disappoint the proudest strain,
Whose approbation—prosper even mine.

TIROCINIUM:

OR,

A REVIEW OF SCHOOLS.

Κεφαλαιον δη παιδειας ορθη τροφη. PLATO.

Αρχη πολιτειας απασης, νεων τροφα. DIOG. LAERT.

TO THE

REV. WILLIAM CAWTHORNE UNWIN,

RECTOR OF STOCK IN ESSEX,

THE TUTOR OF HIS TWO SONS,

THE FOLLOWING POEM, RECOMMENDING PRIVATE TUITION, IN PREFERENCE TO AN EDUCATION AT SCHOOL, IS INSCRIBED, BY HIS AFFECTIONATE FRIEND,

WILLIAM COWPER.

Olney, Nov. 6, 1784.

[Begun Nov. (?), 1781, and laid aside; finished Nov., 1784. Published 1785.]

IT is not from his form, in which we trace
Strength join'd with beauty, dignity with grace,
That man, the master of this globe, derives
His right of empire over all that lives.
That form, indeed, th' associate of a mind
Vast in its pow'rs, ethereal in its kind,
That form, the labour of almighty skill,
Fram'd for the service of a free-born will,
Asserts precedence, and bespeaks control,
But borrows all its grandeur from the soul. 10
Hers is the state, the splendour, and the throne,
An intellectual kingdom all her own.
For her the mem'ry fills her ample page
With truths pour'd down from ev'ry distant age;
For her amasses an unbounded store,
The wisdom of great nations, now no more:
Though laden, not incumber'd with her spoil;
Laborious, yet unconscious of her toil;
When copiously supplied, then most enlarg'd;
Still to be fed, and not to be surcharg'd. 20
For her the fancy, roving unconfin'd,
The present muse of ev'ry pensive mind,

11 Hers] Here *1795-1800.*

Works magic wonders, adds a brighter hue
To nature's scenes than nature ever knew.
At her command winds rise and waters roar,
Again she lays them slumb'ring on the shore;
With flow'r and fruit the wilderness supplies,
Or bids the rocks in ruder pomp arise.
For her the judgment, umpire in the strife
That grace and nature have to wage through life,
Quick-sighted arbiter of good and ill, 31
Appointed sage preceptor to the will,
Condemns, approves, and with a faithful voice
Guides the decision of a doubtful choice.
Why did the fiat of a God give birth
To yon fair sun and his attendant earth?
And, when descending he resigns the skies,
Why takes the gentler moon her turn to rise,
Whom ocean feels through all his countless waves,
And owns her pow'r on ev'ry shore he laves? 40
Why do the seasons still enrich the year,
Fruitful and young, as in their first career?
Spring hangs her infant blossoms on the trees,
Rock'd in the cradle of the western breeze;
Summer in haste the thriving charge receives
Beneath the shade of her expanded leaves,
Till autumn's fiercer heats and plenteous dews
Dye them at last in all their glowing hues.—
'Twere wild profusion all, and bootless waste,
Pow'r misemploy'd, munificence misplac'd, 50
Had not its author dignified the plan,
And crown'd it with the majesty of man.
Thus form'd, thus plac'd, intelligent, and taught,
Look where he will, the wonders God has wrought,
The wildest scorner of his Maker's laws
Finds in a sober moment time to pause,
To press th' important question on his heart,
"Why form'd at all, and wherefore as thou art?"
If man be what he seems—this hour a slave,
The next mere dust and ashes in the grave; 60
Endu'd with reason only to descry
His crimes and follies with an aching eye;
With passions, just that he may prove, with pain,
The force he spends against their fury vain;
And if, soon after having burnt, by turns,
With ev'ry lust with which frail nature burns,
His being end where death dissolves the bond,
The tomb take all, and all be blank beyond—
Then he, of all that nature has brought forth,
Stands self-impeach'd the creature of least worth,

And, useless while he lives, and when he dies, 71
Brings into doubt the wisdom of the skies.
Truths that the learn'd pursue with eager thought
Are not important always as dear bought,
Proving at last, though told in pompous strains,
A childish waste of philosophic pains;
But truths on which depends our main concern,
That 'tis our shame and mis'ry not to learn,
Shine by the side of ev'ry path we tread
With such a lustre, he that runs may read. 80
'Tis true that, if to trifle life away
Down to the sun-set of their latest day,
Then perish on futurity's wide shore
Like fleeting exhalations, found no more,
Were all that Heav'n requir'd of human kind,
And all the plan their destiny design'd,
What none could rev'rence all might justly blame,
And man would breathe but for his Maker's shame.
But reason heard, and nature well perus'd,
At once the dreaming mind is disabus'd. 90
If all we find possessing earth, sea, air,
Reflect his attributes who plac'd them there,
Fulfil the purpose, and appear design'd
Proofs of the wisdom of th' all-seeing mind;
'Tis plain the creature, whom he chose t' invest
With kingship and dominion o'er the rest,
Receiv'd his nobler nature, and was made
Fit for the pow'r in which he stands array'd,
That first or last, hereafter if not here,
He too might make his author's wisdom clear, 100
Praise him on earth, or, obstinately dumb,
Suffer his justice in a world to come.
This once believ'd, 'twere logic misapplied
To prove a consequence by none denied,
That we are bound to cast the minds of youth
Betimes into the mould of heav'nly truth,
That, taught of God they may indeed be wise,
Nor, ignorantly wand'ring, miss the skies.
In early days the conscience has in most
A quickness, which in later life is lost: 110
Preserv'd from guilt by salutary fears,
Or, guilty, soon relenting into tears.
Too careless often, as our years proceed,
What friends we sort with, or what books we read,
Our parents yet exert a prudent care
To feed our infant minds with proper fare;
And wisely store the nurs'ry by degrees
With wholesome learning, yet acquir'd with ease.

Neatly secur'd from being soil'd or torn
Beneath a pane of thin translucent horn, 120
A book (to please us at a tender age
'Tis call'd a book, though but a single page)
Presents the pray'r the Saviour deign'd to teach,
Which children use, and parsons—when they preach.
Lisping our syllables, we scramble next
Through moral narrative, or sacred text;
And learn with wonder how this world began,
Who made, who marr'd, and who has ransom'd man:
Points which, unless the scripture made them plain,
The wisest heads might agitate in vain. 130
Oh thou, whom, borne on fancy's eager wing
Back to the season of life's happy spring,
I pleas'd remember, and, while mem'ry yet
Holds fast her office here, can ne'er forget;
Ingenious dreamer, in whose well-told tale
Sweet fiction and sweet truth alike prevail;
Whose hum'rous vein, strong sense, and simple style,
May teach the gayest, make the gravest smile;
Witty, and well employ'd, and, like thy Lord,
Speaking in parables his slighted word; 140
I name thee not, lest so despis'd a name
Should move a sneer at thy deserved fame;
Yet e'en in transitory life's late day,
That mingles all my brown with sober gray,
Revere the man, whose PILGRIM marks the road,
And guides the PROGRESS of the soul to God.
'Twere well with most, if books, that could engage
Their childhood, pleas'd them at a riper age;
The man, approving what had charm'd the boy,
Would die at last in comfort, peace, and joy; 150
And not with curses on his art who stole
The gem of truth from his unguarded soul.
The stamp of artless piety, impress'd
By kind tuition on his yielding breast,
The youth now bearded, and yet pert and raw,
Regards with scorn, though once receiv'd with awe;
And, warp'd into the labyrinth of lies,
That babblers, call'd philosophers, devise,
Blasphemes his creed, as founded on a plan
Replete with dreams, unworthy of a man. 160
Touch but his nature in its ailing part,
Assert the native evil of his heart,
His pride resents the charge, although the proof[1]
Rise in his forehead, and seem rank enough:

[1] See 2 Chron. ch. xxvi. ver. 19 [C.].

151 art] heart *1798*[2], *1800*.

Point to the cure, describe a Saviour's cross
As God's expedient to retrieve his loss,
The young apostate sickens at the view,
And hates it with the malice of a Jew.
 How weak the barrier of mere nature proves,
Oppos'd against the pleasures nature loves! 170
While, self-betray'd, and wilfully undone,
She longs to yield, no sooner woo'd than won.
Try now the merits of this blest exchange
Of modest truth for wit's eccentric range.
Time was he clos'd, as he began, the day,
With decent duty, not asham'd to pray;
The practice was a bond upon his heart,
A pledge he gave for a consistent part;
Nor could he dare presumptuously displease
A pow'r, confess'd so lately on his knees. 180
But now farewell all legendary tales—
The shadows fly, philosophy prevails!
Pray'r to the winds, and caution to the waves;
Religion makes the free by nature slaves!
Priests have invented, and the world admir'd
What knavish priests promulgate as inspir'd;
Till reason, now no longer overaw'd,
Resumes her pow'rs, and spurns the clumsy fraud;
And, common-sense diffusing real day,
The meteor of the gospel dies away! 190
Such rhapsodies our shrewd discerning youth
Learn from expert inquirers after truth;
Whose only care, might truth presume to speak,
Is not to find what they profess to seek.
And thus, well-tutor'd only while we share
A mother's lectures and a nurse's care;
And taught at schools much mythologic stuff[1],
But sound religion sparingly enough;
Our early notices of truth, disgrac'd,
Soon lose their credit, and are all effac'd. 200
 Would you your son should be a sot or dunce,
Lascivious, headstrong; or all these at once;
That, in good time, the stripling's finish'd taste
For loose expense and fashionable waste
Should prove your ruin and his own at last;

[1] The author begs leave to explain.—Sensible that, without such knowledge, neither the ancient poets nor historians can be tasted, or indeed understood, he does not mean to censure the pains that are taken to instruct a school-boy in the religion of the heathen, but merely that neglect of Christian culture which leaves him shamefully ignorant of his own [C.].

192 inquiries *1800* (*8vo*).

Train him in public with a mob of boys,
Childish in mischief only and in noise,
Else of a mannish growth, and five in ten
In infidelity and lewdness men.
There shall he learn, ere sixteen winters old, 210
That authors are most useful pawn'd or sold;
That pedantry is all that schools impart,
But taverns teach the knowledge of the heart;
There waiter Dick, with Bacchanalian lays,
Shall win his heart, and have his drunken praise,
His counsellor and bosom-friend shall prove,
And some street-pacing harlot his first love.
Schools, unless discipline were doubly strong,
Detain their adolescent charge too long;
The management of tiros of eighteen 220
Is difficult, their punishment obscene.
The stout tall captain, whose superior size
The minor heroes view with envious eyes,
Becomes their pattern, upon whom they fix
Their whole attention, and ape all his tricks.
His pride, that scorns t' obey or to submit,
With them is courage; his effront'ry wit.
His wild excursions, window-breaking feats,
Robb'ry of gardens, quarrels in the streets,
His hair-breadth 'scapes, and all his daring schemes,
Transport them, and are made their fav'rite themes. 231
In little bosoms such achievements strike
A kindred spark; they burn to do the like.
Thus, half-accomplish'd ere he yet begin
To show the peeping down upon his chin;
And, as maturity of years comes on,
Made just th' adept that you design'd your son;
T' ensure the perseverance of his course,
And give your monstrous project all its force,
Send him to college. If he there be tam'd, 240
Or in one article of vice reclaim'd,
Where no regard of ord'nances is shown
Or look'd for now, the fault must be his own.
Some sneaking virtue lurks in him, no doubt,
Where neither strumpets' charms, nor drinking-bout,
Nor gambling practices, can find it out.
Such youths of spirit, and that spirit too,
Ye nurs'ries of our boys, we owe to you!
Though from ourselves the mischief more proceeds,
For public schools 'tis public folly feeds. 250

245 strumpet's *1785, 1786.*

The slaves of custom and establish'd mode,
With pack-horse constancy we keep the road,
Crooked or straight, through quags or thorny dells,
True to the jingling of our leader's bells.
To follow foolish precedents, and wink
With both our eyes, is easier than to think:
And such an age as our's balks no expense,
Except of caution and of common-sense;
Else, sure, notorious fact and proof so plain
Would turn our steps into a wiser train. 260
I blame not those who with what care they can
O'erwatch the num'rous and unruly clan;
Or, if I blame, 'tis only that they dare
Promise a work of which they must despair.
Have ye, ye sage intendants of the whole,
An ubiquarian presence and control—
Elisha's eye, that, when Gehazi stray'd,
Went with him, and saw all the game he play'd?
Yes—ye are conscious; and on all the shelves
Your pupils strike upon, have struck yourselves.
Or if, by nature sober, ye had then, 271
Boys as ye were, the gravity of men;
Ye knew at least, by constant proofs address'd
To ears and eyes, the vices of the rest.
But ye connive at what ye cannot cure,
And evils not to be endur'd, endure,
Lest pow'r exerted, but without success,
Should make the little ye retain still less.
Ye once were justly fam'd for bringing forth
Undoubted scholarship and genuine worth; 280
And in the firmament of fame still shines
A glory, bright as that of all the signs,
Of poets rais'd by you, and statesmen, and divines.
Peace to them all! those brilliant times are fled,
And no such lights are kindling in their stead.
Our striplings shine, indeed, but with such rays
As set the midnight riot in a blaze;
And seem, if judg'd by their expressive looks,
Deeper in none than in their surgeons' books.
Say, muse (for, education made the song, 290
No muse can hesitate or linger long)
What causes move us, knowing, as we must,
That these *menageries* all fail their trust,
To send our sons to scout and scamper there,
While colts and puppies cost us so much care?
Be it a weakness, it deserves some praise;
We love the play-place of our early days—

The scene is touching, and the heart is stone
That feels not at that sight, and feels at none.
The wall on which we tried our graving skill, 300
The very name we carv'd, subsisting still;
The bench on which we sat while deep employ'd,
Tho' mangled, hack'd, and hew'd, not yet destroy'd:
The little ones, unbutton'd, glowing hot,
Playing our games, and on the very spot;
As happy as we once, to kneel and draw
The chalky ring, and knuckle down at taw;
To pitch the ball into the grounded hat,
Or drive it devious with a dext'rous pat—
The pleasing spectacle at once excites 310
Such recollection of our own delights,
That, viewing it, we seem almost t' obtain
Our innocent sweet simple years again.
This fond attachment to the well-known place,
Whence first we started into life's long race,
Maintains its hold with such unfailing sway,
We feel it ev'n in age, and at our latest day.
Hark! how the sire of chits, whose future share
Of classic food begins to be his care,
With his own likeness plac'd on either knee, 320
Indulges all a father's heart-felt glee;
And tells them, as he strokes their silver locks,
That they must soon learn Latin, and to box;
Then, turning, he regales his list'ning wife
With all th' adventures of his early life;
His skill in coachmanship, or driving chaise,
In bilking tavern bills, and spouting plays;
What shifts he us'd, detected in a scrape,
How he was flogg'd, or had the luck t' escape;
What sums he lost at play, and how he sold 330
Watch, seals, and all—till all his pranks are told.
Retracing thus his *frolics*, ('tis a name
That palliates deeds of folly and of shame)
He gives the local bias all its sway;
Resolves that where he play'd his sons shall play,
And destines their bright genius to be shown
Just in the scene where he display'd his own.
The meek and bashful boy will soon be taught
To be as bold and forward as he ought; 339
The rude will scuffle through with ease enough,
Great schools suit best the sturdy and the rough.
Ah, happy designation, prudent choice,
Th' event is sure; expect it, and rejoice!
Soon see your wish fulfill'd in either child—
The pert made perter, and the tame made wild.

The great, indeed, by titles, riches, birth,
Excus'd th' incumbrance of more solid worth,
Are best dispos'd of where with most success
They may acquire that confident address,
Those habits of profuse and lewd expense, 350
That scorn of all delights but those of sense,
Which, though in plain plebeians we condemn,
With so much reason all expect from them.
But families of less illustrious fame,
Whose chief distinction is their spotless name,
Whose heirs, their honours none, their income
Must shine by true desert, or not at all— [small,
What dream they of, that with so little care
They risk their hopes, their dearest treasure, there?
They dream of little Charles or William grac'd 360
With wig prolix, down-flowing to his waist;
They see th' attentive crowds his talents draw,
They hear him speak—the oracle of law!
The father, who designs his babe a priest,
Dreams him episcopally such at least;
And, while the playful jockey scours the room
Briskly, astride upon the parlour broom,
In fancy sees him more superbly ride
In coach with purple lin'd, and mitres on its side.
Events improbable and strange as these, 370
Which only a parental eye foresees,
A public school shall bring to pass with ease.
But how! resides such virtue in that air
As must create an appetite for pray'r?
And will it breathe into him all the zeal
That candidates for such a prize should feel,
To take the lead and be the foremost still
In all true worth and literary skill?
"Ah, blind to bright futurity, untaught
The knowledge of the world, and dull of thought!
Church-ladders are not always mounted best 381
By learned clerks and Latinists profess'd.
Th' exalted prize demands an upward look,
Not to be found by poring on a book.
Small skill in Latin, and still less in Greek,
Is more than adequate to all I seek.
Let erudition grace him or not grace,
I give the bauble but the second place;
His wealth, fame, honours, all that I intend,
Subsist and centre in one point—a friend! 390
A friend, whate'er he studies or neglects,
Shall give him consequence, heal all defects.

357 not] none *1798*², *1800*.

His intercourse with peers, and sons of peers—
There dawns the splendour of his future years;
In that bright quarter his propitious skies
Shall blush betimes, and there his glory rise.
Your Lordship, and *Your Grace!* what school can teach
A rhet'ric equal to those parts of speech?
What need of Homer's verse or Tully's prose,
Sweet interjections! if he learn but those? 400
Let rev'rend churls his ignorance rebuke,
Who starve upon a dog's-ear'd Pentateuch,
The parson knows enough who knows a duke."—
Egregious purpose! worthily begun
In barb'rous prostitution of your son;
Press'd on *his* part by means that would disgrace
A scriv'ner's clerk or footman out of place,
And ending, if at last its end be gain'd,
In sacrilege, in God's own house profan'd!
It may succeed, and, if his sins should call 410
For more than common punishment, it shall;
The wretch shall rise, and be the thing on earth
Least qualified in honour, learning, worth,
To occupy a sacred, awful post,
In which the best and worthiest tremble most.
The *royal letters* are a thing of course—
A king, that would, might recommend his horse;
And deans, no doubt, and chapters, with one voice,
As bound in duty, would confirm the choice.
Behold your bishop! well he plays his part— 420
Christian in name, and infidel in heart,
Ghostly in office, earthly in his plan,
A slave at court, elsewhere a lady's man!
Dumb as a senator, and, as a priest,
A piece of mere church-furniture at best;
To live estrang'd from God his total scope,
And his end sure, without one glimpse of hope!
But, fair although and feasible it seem,
Depend not much upon your golden dream;
For Providence, that seems concern'd t' exempt
The hallow'd bench from absolute contempt, 431
In spite of all the wrigglers into place,
Still keeps a seat or two for worth and grace;
And therefore 'tis, that, though the sight be rare,
We sometimes see a Lowth or Bagot there.
Besides, school-friendships are not always found,
Though fair in promise, permanent and sound;
The most disint'rested and virtuous minds,
In early years connected, time unbinds;

New situations give a diff'rent cast 440
Of habit, inclination, temper, taste;
And he, that seem'd our counterpart at first,
Soon shows the strong similitude revers'd.
Young heads are giddy, and young hearts are warm,
And make mistakes for manhood to reform.
Boys are at best but pretty buds unblown,
Whose scent and hues are rather guess'd than known;
Each dreams that each is just what he appears,
But learns his error in maturer years,
When disposition, like a sail unfurl'd, 450
Shows all its rents and patches to the world.
If, therefore, ev'n when honest in design,
A boyish friendship may so soon decline,
'Twere wiser sure t' inspire a little heart
With just abhorrence of so mean a part,
Than set your son to work at a vile trade
For wages so unlikely to be paid.

Our public hives of puerile resort,
That are of chief and most approv'd report,
To such base hopes, in many a sordid soul, 460
Owe their repute in part, but not the whole.
A principle, whose proud pretensions pass
Unquestion'd, though the jewel be but glass—
That with a world, not often over-nice,
Ranks as a virtue, and is yet a vice;
Or rather a gross compound, justly tried,
Of envy, hatred, jealousy, and pride—
Contributes most perhaps t' enhance their fame;
And emulation is its specious name.
Boys, once on fire with that contentious zeal, 470
Feel all the rage that female rivals feel;
The prize of beauty in a woman's eyes
Not brighter than in their's the scholar's prize.
The spirit of that competition burns
With all varieties of ill by turns;
Each vainly magnifies his own success,
Resents his fellow's, wishes it were less,
Exults in his miscarriage if he fail,
Deems his reward too great if he prevail,
And labours to surpass him day and night, 480
Less for improvement than to tickle spite.
The spur is powerful, and I grant its force;
It pricks the genius forward in its course,
Allows short time for play, and none for sloth;
And, felt alike by each, advances both:

469 And] An *1795-1800*.

But judge, where so much evil intervenes,
The end, though plausible, not worth the means.
Weigh, for a moment, classical desert
Against an heart deprav'd and temper hurt;
Hurt, too, perhaps for life; for early wrong, 490
Done to the nobler part, affects it long;
And you are staunch indeed in learning's cause,
If you can crown a discipline, that draws
Such mischiefs after it, with much applause.
  Connexion form'd for int'rest, and endear'd
By selfish views, thus censur'd and cashier'd;
And emulation, as engend'ring hate,
Doom'd to a no less ignominious fate;
The props of such proud seminaries fall,
The Jachin and the Boaz of them all. 500
Great schools rejected, then, as those that swell
Beyond a size that can be manag'd well,
Shall royal institutions miss the bays,
And small academies win all the praise?
Force not my drift beyond its just intent,
I praise a school as Pope a government;
So take my judgment in his language dress'd—
"Whate'er is best administer'd is best."
Few boys are born with talents that excel,
But all are capable of living well; 510
Then ask not, Whether limited or large?
But, Watch they strictly, or neglect their charge?
If anxious only that their boys may *learn*,
While *morals* languish, a despis'd concern,
The great and small deserve one common blame,
Diff'rent in size, but in effect the same.
Much zeal in virtue's cause all teachers boast,
Though motives of mere lucre sway the most;
Therefore in towns and cities they abound,
For there the game they seek is easiest found; 520
Though there, in spite of all that care can do,
Traps to catch youth are most abundant too.
If shrewd, and of a well-constructed brain,
Keen in pursuit, and vig'rous to retain,
Your son come forth a prodigy of skill;
As, wheresoever taught, so form'd, he will;
The pedagogue, with self-complacent air,
Claims more than half the praise as his due share.
But, if, with all his genius, he betray,
Not more intelligent than loose and gay, 530
Such vicious habits as disgrace his name,
Threaten his health, his fortune, and his fame;

Though want of due restraint alone have bred
The symptoms that you see with so much dread;
Unenvy'd there, he may sustain alone
The whole reproach—the fault was all his own!
Oh 'tis a sight to be with joy perus'd,
By all whom sentiment has not abus'd;
New-fangled sentiment, the boasted grace
Of those who never feel in the right place; 540
A sight surpass'd by none that we can show,
Though Vestris on one leg still shine below;
A father blest with an ingenuous son—
Father, and friend, and tutor, all in one.
How!—turn again to tales long since forgot,
Æsop, and Phædrus, and the rest?—Why not?
He will not blush that has a father's heart,
To take in childish plays a childish part;
But bends his sturdy back to any toy
That youth takes pleasure in, to please his boy:
Then why resign into a stranger's hand 551
A task as much within your own command,
That God and nature, and your int'rest too,
Seem with one voice to delegate to you?
Why hire a lodging in a house unknown
For one whose tend'rest thoughts all hover round
This second weaning, needless as it is, [your own?
How does it lac'rate both your heart and his!
Th' indented stick, that loses day by day
Notch after notch, till all are smooth'd away, 560
Bears witness, long ere his dismission come,
With what intense desire he wants his home.
But, though the joys he hopes beneath your roof
Bid fair enough to answer in the proof,
Harmless, and safe, and nat'ral, as they are,
A disappointment waits him even there:
Arriv'd, he feels an unexpected change;
He blushes, hangs his head, is shy and strange,
No longer takes, as once, with fearless ease,
His fav'rite stand between his father's knees, 570
But seeks the corner of some distant seat,
And eyes the door, and watches a retreat,
And, least familiar where he should be most,
Feels all his happiest privileges lost.
Alas, poor boy!—the natural effect
Of love by absence chill'd into respect.
Say, what accomplishments, at school acquir'd,
Brings he, to sweeten fruits so undesir'd?
Thou well deserv'st an alienated son,
Unless thy conscious heart acknowledge—none;

None that, in thy domestic snug recess, 581
He had not made his own with more address,
Though some perhaps that shock thy feeling mind,
And better never learn'd, or left behind.
Add too, that, thus estrang'd, thou canst obtain
By no kind arts his confidence again;
That here begins with most that long complaint
Of filial frankness lost, and love grown faint,
Which, oft neglected, in life's waning years
A parent pours into regardless ears. 590
Like caterpillars, dangling under trees
By slender threads, and swinging in the breeze,
Which filthily bewray and sore disgrace
The boughs in which are bred th' unseemly race;
While ev'ry worm industriously weaves
And winds his web about the rivell'd leaves;
So num'rous are the follies that annoy
The mind and heart of every sprightly boy;
Imaginations noxious and perverse,
Which admonition can alone disperse. 600
Th' encroaching nuisance asks a faithful hand,
Patient, affectionate, of high command,
To check the procreation of a breed
Sure to exhaust the plant on which they feed.
'Tis not enough that Greek or Roman page,
At stated hours, his freakish thoughts engage;
Ev'n in his pastimes he requires a friend,
To warn, and teach him safely to unbend,
O'er all his pleasures gently to preside,
Watch his emotions, and control their tide; 610
And, levying thus, and with an easy sway,
A tax of profit from his very play,
T' impress a value, not to be eras'd,
On moments squander'd else, and running all to waste.
And seems it nothing in a father's eye
That unimprov'd those many moments fly?
And is he well content his son should find
No nourishment to feed his growing mind,
But conjugated verbs and nouns declin'd?
For such is all the mental food purvey'd 620
By public hacknies in the schooling trade;
Who feed a pupil's intellect with store
Of syntax, truly, but with little more;
Dismiss their cares when they dismiss their flock—
Machines themselves, and govern'd by a clock.
Perhaps a father, blest with any brains,
Would deem it no abuse, or waste of pains,

T' improve this diet, at no great expense,
With sav'ry truth and wholesome common sense;
To lead his son, for prospects of delight, 630
To some not steep, though philosophic, height,
Thence to exhibit to his wond'ring eyes
Yon circling worlds, their distance, and their size,
The moons of Jove, and Saturn's belted ball,
And the harmonious order of them all;
To show him, in an insect or a flow'r,
Such microscopic proof of skill and pow'r,
As, hid from ages past, God now displays
To combat atheists with in modern days;
To spread the earth before him, and commend, 640
With designation of the finger's end,
Its various parts to his attentive note,
Thus bringing home to him the most remote;
To teach his heart to glow with gen'rous flame,
Caught from the deeds of men of ancient fame;
And, more than all, with commendation due,
To set some living worthy in his view,
Whose fair example may at once inspire
A wish to copy what he must admire.
Such knowledge, gain'd betimes, and which appears,
Though solid, not too weighty for his years, 651
Sweet in itself, and not forbidding sport,
When health demands it, of athletic sort,
Would make him—what some lovely boys have been,
And more than one, perhaps, that I have seen—
An evidence and reprehension both
Of the mere school-boy's lean and tardy growth.
Art thou a man professionally tied,
With all thy faculties elsewhere applied,
Too busy to intend a meaner care 660
Than how t' enrich thyself, and next thine heir;
Or art thou (as, though rich, perhaps thou art)
But poor in knowledge, having none t' impart;—
Behold that figure, neat, though plainly clad;
His sprightly mingled with a shade of sad;
Not of a nimble tongue, though now and then
Heard to articulate like other men;
No jester, and yet lively in discourse,
His phrase well chosen, clear, and full of force;
And his address, if not quite French in ease, 670
Not English stiff, but frank, and form'd to please;
Low in the world, because he scorns its arts;
A man of letters, manners, morals, parts;

637 proofs *1785–1787*.

Unpatroniz'd, and therefore little known;
Wise for himself and his few friends alone—
In him thy well-appointed proxy see,
Arm'd for a work too difficult for thee;
Prepar'd by taste, by learning, and true worth,
To form thy son, to strike his genius forth;
Beneath thy roof, beneath thine eye, to prove 680
The force of discipline when back'd by love;
To double all thy pleasure in thy child,
His mind inform'd, his morals undefil'd.
Safe under such a wing, the boy shall show
No spots contracted among grooms below,
Nor taint his speech with meannesses, design'd
By footman Tom for witty and refin'd.
There, in his commerce with the liv'ried herd,
Lurks the contagion chiefly to be fear'd;
For, since (so fashion dictates) all, who claim 690
An higher than a mere plebeian fame,
Find it expedient, come what mischief may,
To entertain a thief or two in pay,
(And they that can afford th' expense of more,
Some half a dozen, and some half a score)
Great cause occurs to save him from a band
So sure to spoil him, and so near at hand;
A point secur'd, if once he be supplied
With some such Mentor always at his side.
Are such men rare? perhaps they would abound
Were occupation easier to be found, 701
Were education, else so sure to fail,
Conducted on a manageable scale,
And schools, that have out-liv'd all just esteem,
Exchang'd for the secure domestic scheme.—
But, having found him, be thou duke or earl,
Show thou hast sense enough to prize the pearl,
And, as thou would'st th' advancement of thine heir
In all good faculties beneath his care,
Respect, as is but rational and just, 710
A man deem'd worthy of so dear a trust.
Despis'd by thee, what more can he expect
From youthful folly than the same neglect?
A flat and fatal negative obtains,
That instant, upon all his future pains;
His lessons tire, his mild rebukes offend,
And all th' instructions of thy son's best friend
Are a stream choak'd, or trickling to no end.
Doom him not then to solitary meals;
But recollect that he has sense and feels; 720

And that, possessor of a soul refin'd,
An upright heart, and cultivated mind,
His post not mean, his talents not unknown,
He deems it hard to vegetate alone.
And, if admitted at thy board he sit,
Account him no just mark for idle wit;
Offend not him, whom modesty restrains
From repartee, with jokes that he disdains;
Much less transfix his feelings with an oath;
Nor frown, unless he vanish with the cloth.— 730
And, trust me, his utility may reach
To more than he is hir'd or bound to teach;
Much trash unutter'd, and some ills undone,
Through rev'rence of the censor of thy son.
  But, if thy table be indeed unclean,
Foul with excess, and with discourse obscene,
And thou a wretch, whom, following her old plan,
The world accounts an honourable man,
Because forsooth thy courage has been tried
And stood the test, perhaps on the wrong side; 740
Though thou hadst never grace enough to prove
That anything but vice could win thy love;—
Or hast thou a polite, card-playing wife,
Chain'd to the routs that she frequents for life;
Who, just when industry begins to snore,
Flies, wing'd with joy, to some coach-crowded door;
And thrice in ev'ry winter throngs thine own
With half the chariots and sedans in town,
Thyself meanwhile e'en shifting as thou may'st;
Not very sober though, not very chaste;— 750
Or is thine house, though less superb thy rank,
If not a scene of pleasure, a mere blank,
And thou at best, and in thy sob'rest mood,
A trifler vain, and empty of all good;—
Though mercy for thyself thou canst have none,
Hear nature plead, show mercy to thy son.
Sav'd from his home, where ev'ry day brings forth
Some mischief fatal to his future worth,
Find him a better in a distant spot,
Within some pious pastor's humble cot, 760
Where vile example (your's I chiefly mean,
The most seducing and the oft'nest seen)
May never more be stamp'd upon his breast,
Not yet perhaps incurably impress'd:—
Where early rest makes early rising sure,
Disease or comes not, or finds easy cure,

750 not *1795-1800*: nor *1785-1793, 1803*.

Prevented much by diet neat and plain;
Or, if it enter, soon starv'd out again:—
Where all th' attention of his faithful host,
Discreetly limited to two at most, 770
May raise such fruits as shall reward his care,
And not at last evaporate in air:—
Where, stillness aiding study, and his mind
Serene, and to his duties much inclin'd,
Not occupied in day-dreams, as at home,
Of pleasures past, or follies yet to come,
His virtuous toil may terminate at last
In settled habit and decided taste.—
But whom do I advise? the fashion-led,
Th' incorrigibly wrong, the deaf, the dead! 780
Whom care and cool deliberation suit
Not better much than spectacles a brute;
Who, if their sons some slight tuition share,
Deem it of no great moment whose, or where;
Too proud t' adopt the thoughts of one unknown,
And much too gay t' have any of their own.
But, courage, man! methought the muse replied,
Mankind are various, and the world is wide:
The ostrich, silliest of the feather'd kind,
And form'd of God without a parent's mind, 790
Commits her eggs, incautious, to the dust,
Forgetful that the foot may crush the trust;
And, while on public nurs'ries they rely,
Not knowing, and too oft not caring, why,
Irrational in what they thus prefer,
No few, that would seem wise, resemble her.
But all are not alike. Thy warning voice
May here and there prevent erroneous choice;
And some perhaps, who, busy as they are,
Yet make their progeny their dearest care, 800
(Whose hearts will ache, once told what ills may reach
Their offspring, left upon so wild a beach)
Will need no stress of argument t' enforce
Th' expedience of a less advent'rous course:
The rest will slight thy counsel, or condemn;
But *they* have human feelings—turn to *them*.
To you, then, tenants of life's middle state,
Securely plac'd between the small and great,
Whose character, yet undebauch'd, retains
Two thirds of all the virtue that remains, 810
Who, wise yourselves, desire your sons should learn
Your wisdom and your ways—to you I turn.
Look round you on a world perversely blind;
See what contempt is fall'n on human kind;

See wealth abus'd, and dignities misplac'd,
Great titles, offices, and trusts disgrac'd,
Long lines of ancestry, renown'd of old,
Their noble qualities all quench'd and cold;
See Bedlam's closetted and hand-cuff'd charge
Surpass'd in frenzy by the mad at large; 820
See great commanders making war a trade,
Great lawyers, lawyers without study made;
Churchmen, in whose esteem their blest employ
Is odious, and their wages all their joy,
Who, far enough from furnishing their shelves
With gospel lore, turn infidels themselves;
See womanhood despis'd, and manhood sham'd
With infamy too nauseous to be nam'd,
Fops at all corners, lady-like in mien,
Civeted fellows, smelt ere they are seen; 830
Else coarse and rude in manners, and their tongue
On fire with curses, and with nonsense hung,
Now flush'd with drunk'ness, now with whoredom [pale,
Their breath a sample of last night's regale;
See volunteers in all the vilest arts,
Men well endow'd, of honourable parts,
Design'd by nature wise, but self-made fools;
All these, and more like these, were bred at schools!
And, if it chance, as sometimes chance it will,
That, though school-bred, the boy be virtuous still;
Such rare exceptions, shining in the dark, 841
Prove, rather than impeach, the just remark;
As here and there a twinkling star descried
Serves but to show how black is all beside.
Now look on him, whose very voice in tone
Just echoes thine, whose features are thine own,
And stroke his polish'd cheek of purest red,
And lay thine hand upon his flaxen head,
And say—My boy, th' unwelcome hour is come,
When thou, transplanted from thy genial home,
Must find a colder soil and bleaker air, 851
And trust for safety to a stranger's care;
What character, what turn, thou wilt assume
From constant converse with I know not whom;
Who there will court thy friendship, with what views,
And, artless as thou art, whom thou wilt choose;
Though much depends on what thy choice shall be,
Is all chance-medley, and unknown to me.—
Can'st thou, the tear just trembling on thy lids,
And while the dreadful risqué foreseen forbids; 860

823 best *1800* (*8vo*).

Free, too, and under no constraining force,
Unless the sway of custom warp thy course;
Lay such a stake upon the losing side,
Merely to gratify so blind a guide?
Thou can'st not! Nature, pulling at thine heart,
Condemns th' unfatherly, th' imprudent part.
Thou would'st not, deaf to Nature's tend'rest plea,
Turn him adrift upon a rolling sea,
Nor say, *Go thither*, conscious that there lay
A brood of asps, or quicksands in his way; 870
Then, only govern'd by the self-same rule
Of nat'ral pity, send him not to school.
No—guard him better. Is he not thine own,
Thyself in miniature, thy flesh, thy bone?
And hop'st thou not ('tis ev'ry father's hope)
That, since thy strength must with thy years elope,
And thou wilt need some comfort to assuage
Health's last farewell, a staff of thine old age,
That then, in recompense of all thy cares,
Thy child shall show respect to thy gray hairs, 880
Befriend thee, of all other friends bereft,
And give thy life its only cordial left?
Aware then how much danger intervenes,
To compass that good end, forecast the means.
His heart, now passive, yields to thy command;—
Secure it thine, its key is in thine hand.
If thou desert thy charge, and throw it wide,
Nor heed what guests there enter and abide,
Complain not if attachments lewd and base
Supplant thee in it, and usurp thy place. 890
But, if thou guard its sacred chambers sure
From vicious inmates and delights impure,
Either his gratitude shall hold him fast,
And keep him warm and filial to the last;
Or, if he prove unkind (as who can say
But, being man, and therefore frail, he may?)
One comfort yet shall cheer thine aged heart—
Howe'er he slight thee, thou hast done thy part.
Oh barb'rous! would'st thou with a Gothic hand
Pull down the schools—what!—all the schools i' th' land; 900
Or throw them up to liv'ry-nags and grooms,
Or turn them into shops and auction rooms?
A captious question, sir, (and your's is one)
Deserves an answer similar, or none.

886 it] in *1800* (*8vo*).

Would'st thou, possessor of a flock, employ
(Appriz'd that he is such) a careless boy,
And feed him well, and give him handsome pay,
Merely to sleep, and let them run astray?
Survey our schools and colleges, and see
A sight not much unlike my simile. 910
From education, as the leading cause,
The public character its colour draws;
Thence the prevailing manners take their cast,
Extravagant or sober, loose or chaste.
And, though I would not advertise them yet,
Nor write on each—*This Building to be Let*,
Unless the world were all prepar'd t' embrace
A plan well worthy to supply their place;
Yet, backward as they are, and long have been,
To cultivate and keep the MORALS clean, 920
(Forgive the crime) I wish them, I confess,
Or better manag'd, or encourag'd less.

MISCELLANEOUS POEMS

VERSES

WRITTEN AT BATH ON FINDING THE HEEL OF A SHOE

[Written 1748. Published by Hayley, 1803, and by Johnson, 1815.]

FORTUNE ! I thank thee : gentle Goddess ! thanks !
Not that my muse, tho' bashful, shall deny
She would have thank'd thee rather, hadst thou cast
A treasure in her way ; for neither meed
Of early breakfast, to dispel the fumes
And bowel-raking pains of emptiness,
Nor noon-tide feast, nor ev'ning's cool repast,
Hopes she from this—presumptuous,—tho', perhaps,
The cobbler, leather-carving artist, might !
Nathless she thanks thee, and accepts thy boon, 10
Whatever, not as erst the fabled cock,
Vain-glorious fool, unknowing what he found,
Spurn'd the rich gem thou gav'st him. Wherefore ah !
Why not on me that favour, (worthier sure !)
Conferr'dst thou, Goddess ? Thou art blind, thou say'st :
Enough !—Thy blindness shall excuse the deed.
  Nor does my muse no benefit exhale
From this thy scant indulgence,—even here
Hints, worthy sage philosophy, are found ;
Illustrious hints to moralize my song ! 20
This pond'rous Heel of perforated hide
Compact, with pegs indented, many a row,
Haply (for such its massy form bespeaks)
The weighty tread of some rude peasant clown
Upbore : on this supported oft he stretch'd,
With uncouth strides, along the furrow'd glebe,
Flatt'ning the stubborn clod, till cruel time,
(What will not cruel time ?) on a wry step,
Sever'd the strict cohesion ; when, alas !
He, who could erst with even equal pace 30
Pursue his destin'd way with symmetry
And some proportion form'd, now, on one side,
Curtail'd and maim'd, the sport of vagrant boys,
Cursing his frail supporter, treach'rous prop,

With toilsome steps, and difficult, moves on!
Thus fares it oft with other than the feet
Of humble villager:—the statesman thus,
Up the steep road, where proud ambition leads,
Aspiring first uninterrupted winds
His prosp'rous way; nor fears miscarriage foul, 40
While policy prevails, and friends prove true:
But that support soon failing, by him left
On whom he most depended, basely left,
Betray'd, deserted, from his airy height
Head-long he falls; and thro' the rest of life
Drags the dull load of disappointment on.

PSALM CXXXVII

[Written (?). Published by Croft, 1825.]

To Babylon's proud waters brought,
In bondage where we lay,
With tears on Sion's Hill we thought,
And sigh'd our hours away;
Neglected on the willows hung
Our useless harps, while ev'ry tongue
Bewail'd the fatal day. 7

Then did the base insulting foe
Some joyous notes demand,
Such as in Sion used to flow
From Judah's happy band—
Alas! what joyous notes have we,
Our country spoil'd, no longer free,
And in a foreign land? 14

Oh Solyma! if e'er thy praise
Be silent in my song,
Rude and unpleasing be the lays,
And artless be my tongue!
Thy name my fancy still employs;
To thee, great fountain of my joys,
My sweetest airs belong. 21

Remember, Lord! that hostile sound,
When Edom's children cried,
Raz'd be her turrets to the ground,
And humbled be her pride!
Remember, Lord! and let the foe
The terrors of thy vengeance know—
The vengeance they defied. 28

Thou too, great Babylon, shalt fall
  A victim to our God;
Thy monstrous crimes already call
  For Heav'n's chastising rod.
Happy who shall thy little ones
Relentless dash against the stones,
  And spread their limbs abroad. 35

SONG

[Written (?). Published by Croft, 1825.]

No more shall hapless Celia's ears
  Be flatter'd with the cries
Of lovers drown'd in floods of tears,
  Or murder'd by her eyes;
No serenades to break her rest,
Nor songs her slumbers to molest, 6
    With my fa, la, la.

The fragrant flowers that once would bloom
  And flourish in her hair,
Since she no longer breathes perfume
  Their odours to repair,
Must fade, alas! and wither now,
As plac'd on any common brow, 13
    With my fa, la, la.

Her lip, so winning and so meek,
  No longer has its charms;
As well she might by whistling seek
  To lure us to her arms;
Affected once, 'tis real now,
As her forsaken gums may show, 20
    With my fa, la, la.

The down that on her chin so smooth
  So lovely once appear'd,
That, too, has left her with her youth,
  Or sprouts into a beard;
As fields, so green when newly sown,
With stubble stiff are overgrown, 27
    With my fa, la, la.

Then, Celia, leave your apish tricks,
  And change your girlish airs,
For ombre, snuff, and politics,
  Those joys that suit your years;
No patches can lost youth recal,
Nor whitewash prop a tumbling wall, 34
    With my fa, la, la.

Psalm CXXXVII.—29 shalt *Southey*: shall *Croft*. *Song.*—3 Of *Southey*: And *Croft*.

A SONG

[Written (?). Published by Croft, 1825.]

On the green margin of the brook
  Despairing Phyllida reclin'd,
Whilst ev'ry sigh and ev'ry look
  Declar'd the anguish of her mind. 4

Am I less lovely then? (she cries,
  And in the waves her form survey'd;)
Oh yes, I see my languid eyes,
  My faded cheek, my colour fled:
These eyes no more like light'ning pierc'd,
These cheeks grew pale when Damon first
  His Phyllida betray'd. 11

The rose he in his bosom wore,
  How oft upon my breast was seen!
And when I kiss'd the drooping flow'r,
  Behold, he cried, it blooms again!
The wreaths that bound my braided hair,
Himself next day was proud to wear
  At church or on the green. 18

While thus sad Phyllida lamented,
  Chance brought unlucky Thyrsis on;
Unwillingly the nymph consented,
  But Damon first the cheat begun.
She wip'd the fall'n tears away,
Then sigh'd and blush'd, as who should say
  Ah! Thyrsis, I am won. 25

AN EPISTLE TO ROBERT LLOYD, ESQ.

[Written 1754. Published by Hayley, 1803, and by Johnson, 1815.]

'Tis not that I design to rob
Thee of thy birthright, gentle Bob,
For thou art born sole heir, and single,
Of dear Mat Prior's easy jingle;
Nor that I mean, while thus I knit
My thread-bare sentiments together,
To show my genius or my wit,
When God and you know I have neither;
Or such, as might be better shown
By letting poetry alone. 10
'Tis not with either of these views,
That I presume t' address the Muse:

23 She *Southey*: He *Croft*.

But to divert a fierce banditti
(Sworn foes to ev'ry thing that's witty),
That, with a black infernal train,
Make cruel inroads in my brain,
And daily threaten to drive thence
My little garrison of sense:
The fierce banditti, which I mean,
Are gloomy thoughts led on by Spleen. 20
Then there's another reason yet,
Which is, that I may fairly quit
The debt, which justly became due
The moment when I heard from you:
And you might grumble, crony mine,
If paid in any other coin;
Since twenty sheets of lead, God knows,
(I would say twenty sheets of prose,)
Can ne'er be deem'd worth half so much
As one of gold, and yours was such. 30
Thus, the preliminaries settled,
I fairly find myself pitch-kettled[1];
And cannot see, though few see better,
How I shall hammer out a letter.
First, for a thought—since all agree—
A thought—I have it—let me see—
'Tis gone again—plague on't! I thought
I had it—but I have it not.
Dame Gurton thus, and Hodge her son,
That useful thing, her needle, gone, 40
Rake well the cinders—sweep the floor,
And sift the dust behind the door;
While eager Hodge beholds the prize
In old Grimalkin's glaring eyes;
And Gammer finds it on her knees
In every shining straw she sees.
This simile were apt enough;
But I've another, critic-proof!
The virtuoso thus, at noon,
Broiling beneath a July sun, 50
The gilded butterfly pursues
O'er hedge and ditch, through gaps and mews;
And after many a vain essay
To captivate the tempting prey,
Gives him at length the lucky pat,
And has him safe beneath his hat:

[1] Pitch-kettled, a favourite phrase at the time when this epistle was written, expressive of being puzzled, or what in the Spectator's time, would have been called bamboozled [H.].

Then lifts it gently from the ground;
But ah! 'tis lost as soon as found;
Culprit his liberty regains;
Flits out of sight and mocks his pains. 60
The sense was dark; 'twas therefore fit
With simile t' illustrate it;
But as too much obscures the sight,
As often as too little light,
We have our similes cut short,
For matters of more grave import.
That Matthew's numbers run with ease
Each man of common-sense agrees;
All men of common-sense allow,
That Robert's lines are easy too; 70
Where then the preference shall we place,
Or how do justice in this case?
Matthew, (says Fame) with endless pains
Smooth'd and refin'd the meanest strains;
Nor suffer'd one ill-chosen rhyme
T' escape him, at the idlest time;
And thus o'er all a lustre cast,
That, while the language lives, shall last.
An't please your Ladyship, (quoth I,
For 'tis my business to reply;) 80
Sure so much labour, so much toil,
Bespeak at least a stubborn soil.
Theirs be the laurel-wreath decreed,
Who both write well and write full-speed!
Who throw their Helicon about
As freely as a conduit spout!
Friend Robert, thus like *chien sçavant*,
Lets fall a poem *en passant*,
Nor needs his genuine ore refine;
'Tis ready polish'd from the mine. 90

[Written (?). Published by Croft, 1825.]

MORTALS! around your destin'd heads
Thick fly the shafts of death,
And lo! the savage spoiler spreads
A thousand toils beneath.

In vain we trifle with our fate,
Try every art in vain;
At best we but prolong the date,
And lengthen out our pain. 8

2 Thick *Southey*: Which *Croft*.

Fondly we think all danger fled,
For death is ever nigh;
Outstrips our unavailing speed,
Or meets us as we fly.

Thus the wreck'd mariner may strive
Some desert shore to gain,
Secure of life if he survive
The fury of the main: 16

But there, to famine doom'd a prey,
Finds the mistaken wretch!
He but escap'd the troubled sea,
To perish on the beach.

Since then in vain we strive to guard
Our frailty from the foe;
Lord, let me live not unprepar'd
To meet the fatal blow! 24

OF HIMSELF

[Written 1752. Published by Croft, 1825. This and the next eighteen poems are concerned with Cowper's attachment to 'Delia,' his cousin Theodora Cowper.]

WILLIAM was once a bashful youth,
His modesty was such,
That one might say (to say the truth)
He rather had too much.

Some said that it was want of sense,
And others, want of spirit,
(So blest a thing is impudence,)
While others could not bear it. 8

But some a different notion had,
And at each other winking,
Observ'd that though he little said,
He paid it off with thinking.

Howe'er, it happen'd, by degrees,
He mended and grew perter,
In company was more at ease,
And dress'd a little smarter: 16

Nay, now and then would look quite gay,
As other people do;
And sometimes said, or tried to say,
A witty thing or so.

He eyed the women, and made free
To comment on their shapes,
So that there was, or seem'd to be,
No fear of a relapse. 24

Of Himself.—20 so] *Bruce suggests* two.

The women said, who thought him rough,
But now no longer foolish,
The creature may do well enough,
But wants a deal of polish.

At length, improv'd from head to heel,
'Twere scarce too much to say,
No dancing bear was so genteel,
Or half so dégagé. 32

Now, that a miracle so strange
May not in vain be shown,
Let the dear maid who wrought the change
E'er claim him for her own.

THE SYMPTOMS OF LOVE

[Written 1752 (?). Published by Croft, 1825.]

WOULD my Delia know if I love, let her take
My last thought at night, and the first when I wake;
With my prayers and best wishes preferr'd for her sake.

Let her guess what I muse on, when rambling alone
I stride o'er the stubble each day with my gun,
Never ready to shoot till the covey is flown. 6

Let her think what odd whimsies I have in my brain,
When I read one page over and over again,
And discover at last that I read it in vain.

Let her say why so fix'd and so steady my look,
Without ever regarding the person who spoke,
Still affecting to laugh, without hearing the joke. 12

Or why when with pleasure her praises I hear,
(That sweetest of melody sure to my ear)
I attend, and at once inattentive appear.

And lastly, when summon'd to drink to my flame,
Let her guess why I never once mention her name, 17
Though herself and the woman I love are *the same.*

AN APOLOGY

FOR NOT SHOWING HER WHAT I HAD WROTE

[Written at Catfield, July, 1752. Published by Croft, 1825.]

DID not my muse (what can she less?)
Perceive her own unworthiness,
Could she by some well chosen theme,
But hope to merit your esteem,
She would not thus conceal her lays,
Ambitious to deserve your praise.

36 E'er] E'en *sugg. Bruce, adopted by Bailey.*

But should my Delia take offence,
And frown on her impertinence,
In silence, sorrowing and forlorn,
Would the despairing trifler mourn, 10
Curse her ill-tun'd, unpleasing lute,
Then sigh and sit for ever mute.
In secret, therefore, let her play,
Squand'ring her idle notes away;
In secret as she chants along,
Cheerful and careless in her song;
Nor heed she whether harsh or clear,
Free from each terror, ev'ry fear,
From that, of all most dreaded, free,
The terror of offending *Thee*. 20

[Written at the same place, 1752. Published by Croft, 1825.]

DELIA, th' unkindest girl on earth,
When I besought the fair,
That favour of intrinsic worth,
A ringlet of her hair,—

Refus'd that instant to comply
With my absurd request,
For reasons she could specify,
Some twenty score at least. 8

Trust me, my dear, however odd
It may appear to say,
I sought it merely to defraud
Thy spoiler of his prey.

Yet, when its sister locks shall fade,
As quickly fade they must,
When all their beauties are decay'd,
Their gloss, their colour, lost, 16

Ah then! if haply to my share
Some slender pittance fall,
If I but gain one single hair,
Nor age usurp them all;—

When you behold it still as sleek,
As lovely to the view,
As when it left thy snowy neck—
That Eden where it grew— 24

Then shall my Delia's self declare,
That I profess'd the truth,
And have preserv'd my little share
In everlasting youth.

Apology.—17 heed] heeds *Southey*. *Delia.*—13 Yet] Yes *Bruce*.

[Written at the same place, 1752. Published by Croft, 1825.]

THIS ev'ning, Delia, you and I
Have manag'd most delightfully,
  For with a frown we parted;
Having contrived some trifle that
We both may be much troubled at,
  And sadly disconcerted. 6

Yet well as each perform'd their part,
We might perceive it was but art,
  And that we both intended
To sacrifice a little ease;
For all such petty flaws as these
  Are made but to be mended. 12

You knew, Dissembler! all the while,
How sweet it was to reconcile
  After this heavy pelt;
That we should gain by this allay
When next we met, and laugh away
  The care we never felt. 18

Happy! when we but seek t' endure
A little pain, then find a cure
  By double joy requited;
For friendship, like a sever'd bone,
Improves and joins a stronger tone
  When aptly reunited. 24

AN ATTEMPT AT THE MANNER OF WALLER

[Written at Drayton, March 1753. Published by Croft, 1825.]

DID not thy reason and thy sense,
With most persuasive eloquence,
Convince me that obedience due
None may so justly claim as you,
By right of beauty you would be
Mistress o'er my heart and me. 6

Then fear not I should e'er rebel,
My gentle love! I might as well
A forward peevishness put on,
And quarrel with the mid-day sun;
Or question who gave him a right
To be so fiery and so bright. 12

23 joins] gains *Bruce*.

Nay, this were less absurd and vain
Than disobedience to thy reign:
His beams are often too severe;
But thou art mild, as thou art fair;
First from necessity we own your sway, 17
Then scorn our freedom, and by choice obey.

A SONG

[Written (?). Published by Croft, 1825.]

THE sparkling eye, the mantling cheek,
The polish'd front, the snowy neck,
  How seldom we behold in one!
Glossy locks, and brow serene,
Venus' smiles, Diana's mien,
  All meet in you, and you alone. 6

Beauty, like other pow'rs, maintains
Her empire, and by *union* reigns;
  Each single feature faintly warms,
But where at once we view display'd
Unblemish'd grace, the perfect maid
  Our eyes, our ears, our heart alarms. 12

So when on earth the God of day
Obliquely sheds his temper'd ray,
  Through convex orbs the beams transmit,
The beams that gently warm'd before,
Collected, gently warm no more,
  But glow with more prevailing heat. 18

UPON A VENERABLE RIVAL

[Written (?). Published by Croft, 1825.]

FULL thirty frosts since thou wert young
  Have chill'd the wither'd grove,
Thou wretch! and hast thou liv'd so long,
  Nor yet forgot to love?

Ye Sages! spite of your pretences
  To wisdom, you must own
Your folly frequently commences
  When you acknowledge none. 8

Not that I deem it weak to love,
  Or folly to admire,
But ah! the pangs we lovers prove
  Far other years require.

Song—4 Glossy *Southey* : Glassy *Croft*.

Unheeded on the youthful brow
  The beams of Phœbus play,
But unsupported Age stoops low
  Beneath the sultry ray. 16

For once, then, if untutor'd youth,
  Youth unapprov'd by years,
May chance to deviate into truth,
  When your experience errs;

For once attempt not to despise
  What I esteem a rule:
Who early loves, though young, is wise—
  Who old, though grey, a fool. 24

WRITTEN IN A QUARREL,

THE DELIVERY OF IT PREVENTED BY A RECONCILIATION

[Written 1753 (?). Published by Croft, 1825.]

THINK, Delia, with what cruel haste
  Our fleeting pleasures move,
Nor heedless thus in sorrow waste
  The moments due to love.

Be wise, my fair, and gently treat
  These few that are our friends;
Think, thus abus'd, what sad regret
  Their speedy flight attends! 8

Sure in those eyes I lov'd so well,
  And wish'd so long to see,
Anger I thought could never dwell,
  Or anger aim'd at me.

No bold offence of mine I knew
  Should e'er provoke your hate;
And, early taught to think you true,
  Still hop'd a gentler fate. 16

With kindness bless the present hour,
  Or oh! we meet in vain!
What can we do in absence more
  Than suffer and complain?

Fated to ills beyond redress,
  We must endure our woe;
The days allow'd us to possess,
  'Tis madness to forego. 24

[Written 1753 (?). Published by Croft, 1825.]

SEE where the Thames, the purest stream
That wavers to the noon-day beam,
  Divides the vale below:
While like a vein of liquid ore
His waves enrich the happy shore,
  Still shining as they flow. 6

Nor yet, my Delia, to the main
Runs the sweet tide without a stain,
  Unsullied as it seems:
The nymphs of many a sable flood
Deform with streaks of oozy mud
  The bosom of the Thames. 12

Some idle rivulets, that feed
And suckle ev'ry noisome weed,
  A sandy bottom boast:
For ever bright, for ever clear,
The trifling shallow rills appear
  In their own channel lost. 18

Thus fares it with the human soul,
Where copious floods of passion roll,
  By genuine love supplied:
Fair in itself the current shows,
But ah! a thousand anxious woes
  Pollute the noble tide. 24

These are emotions known to few;
For where at most a vap'ry dew
  Surrounds the tranquil heart,
Then, as the triflers never prove
The glad excess of real love,
  They never prove the smart. 30

Oh then, my life, at last relent,
Though cruel the reproach I sent,
  My sorrow was unfeign'd:
Your passion, had I lov'd you not,
You might have scorn'd, renounc'd, forgot,
  And I had ne'er complain'd. 36

While you indulge a groundless fear,
Th' imaginary woes you bear
  Are real woes to me:
But thou art kind, and good thou art,
Nor wilt, by wronging thine own heart,
  Unjustly punish me. 42

11 Deform *Southey*: Deform'd *Croft*.

[Written (?). Published by Croft, 1825.]

How blest the youth whom Fate ordains
A kind relief from all his pains,
  In some admired fair;
Whose tend'rest wishes find express'd
Their own resemblance in her breast
  Exactly copied there. 6

What good soe'er the Gods dispense,
Th' enjoyment of its influence
  Still on her love depends;
Her love the shield that guards his heart,
Or wards the blow, or blunts the dart,
  That peevish Fortune sends. 12

Thus, Delia, while thy love endures,
The flame my happy breast secures
  From Fortune's fickle pow'r;
Change as she list, she may increase,
But not abate my happiness,
  Confirm'd by thee before. 18

Thus while I share her smiles with thee,
Welcome, my love, shall ever be
  The favours she bestows;
Yet not on those I found my bliss,
But in the noble ecstasies
  The faithful bosom knows. 24

And when she prunes her wings for flight,
And flutters nimbly from my sight,
  Contented I resign
Whate'er she gave; thy love alone
I can securely call my own,
  Happy while that is mine. 30

ODE

SUPPOSED TO BE WRITTEN ON THE MARRIAGE OF A FRIEND

[Written (?). Published by Croft, 1825.]

THOU magic lyre, whose fascinating sound
  Seduc'd the savage monsters from their cave,
Drew rocks and trees, and forms uncouth around,
  And bade wild Hebrus hush his list'ning wave;
No more thy undulating warblings flow
O'er Thracian wilds of everlasting snow! 6

Awake to sweeter sounds, thou magic lyre,
  And paint a lover's bliss—a lover's pain!
Far nobler triumphs now thy notes inspire,—

How blest—4 find *Southey*: finds *Croft*. *Ode*—1-6 *see notes.*

For see, Euridice attends thy strain;
Her smile, a prize beyond the conjuror's aim—
Superior to the cancell'd breath of fame. 12

From her sweet brow to chase the gloom of care,
To check that tear that dims the beaming eye,
To bid her heart the rising sigh forbear,
And flush her orient cheek with brighter joy,
In that dear breast soft sympathy to move,
And touch the springs of rapture and of love! 18

Ah me! how long bewilder'd and astray,
Lost and benighted, did my footsteps rove,
Till, sent by heav'n to cheer my pathless way,
A star arose—the radiant star of love.
The God propitious join'd our willing hands,
And Hymen wreath'd us in his rosy bands. 24

Yet not the beaming eye, or placid brow,
Or golden tresses, hid the subtle dart;
To charms superior far than those I bow,
And nobler worth enslaves my vanquish'd heart;
The beauty, elegance, and grace combin'd, 29
Which beam transcendant from that angel mind;
While vulgar passions—meteors of a day,
Expire before the chilling blasts of age,
Our holy flame, with pure and steady ray,
Its glooms shall brighten, and its pangs assuage;
By Virtue (sacred vestal) fed, shall shine, 35
And warm our fainting souls with energy divine.

ON HER ENDEAVOURING TO CONCEAL HER GRIEF AT PARTING

[Written 1754 (?). Published by Croft, 1825.]

Ah! wherefore should my weeping maid suppress
Those gentle signs of undissembled woe?
When from soft love proceeds the deep distress,
Ah! why forbid the willing tears to flow?

Since for my sake each dear translucent drop
Breaks forth, best witness of thy truth sincere,
My lips should drink the precious mixture up,
And, ere it falls, receive the trembling tear. 8

Trust me, these symptoms of thy faithful heart,
In absence, shall my dearest hopes sustain,
Delia! since such thy sorrow that we part,
Such when we meet thy joy shall be again.

21 way *Bruce* : ray *Croft*.

Hard is that heart and unsubdued by love
That feels no pain, nor ever heaves a sigh,
Such hearts the fiercest passions only prove,
Or freeze in cold insensibility. 16

Oh! then indulge thy grief, nor fear to tell
The gentle source from whence thy sorrows flow!
Nor think it weakness when we love to feel,
Nor think it weakness what we feel to show.

[Written at Berkhamstead 1754 (?). Published by Croft, 1825.]

BID adieu, my sad heart, bid adieu to thy peace,
Thy pleasure is past, and thy sorrows increase;
See the shadows of ev'ning how far they extend,
And a long night is coming, that never may end;
For the sun is now set that enliven'd the scene,
And an age must be past ere it rises again. 6

Already depriv'd of its splendour and heat,
I feel thee more slowly, more heavily beat;
Perhaps overstrain'd with the quick pulse of pleasure,
Thou art glad of this respite to beat at thy leisure;
But the sigh of distress shall now weary thee more
Than the flutter and tumult of passion before. 12

The heart of a lover is never at rest,
With joy overwhelm'd, or with sorrow oppress'd:
When Delia is near, all is ecstasy then,
And I even forget I must lose her again:
When absent, as wretched as happy before,
Despairing I cry, I shall see her no more. 18

WRITTEN AFTER LEAVING HER AT NEW BURNS

[Written at Berkhamstead 1754 (?). Published by Croft, 1825.]

How quick the change from joy to woe,
How chequer'd is our lot below!
Seldom we view the prospect fair;
Dark clouds of sorrow, pain, and care,
(Some pleasing intervals between,)
Scowl over more than half the scene.
Last week with Delia, gentle maid!
Far hence in happier fields I stray'd,
While on her dear enchanting tongue
Soft sounds of grateful welcome hung, 10
For absence had withheld it long.

Welcome my long-lost love, she said,
E'er since our adverse fates decreed
That we must part, and I must mourn
Till once more blest by thy return,
Love, on whose influence I relied
For all the transports I enjoy'd,
Has play'd the cruel tyrant's part,
And turn'd tormentor to my heart;
But let me hold thee to my breast, 20
Dear partner of my joy and rest,
And not a pain, and not a fear,
Or anxious doubt, shall enter there.—
Happy, thought I, the favour'd youth,
Blest with such undissembled truth!—
Five suns successive rose and set,
And saw no monarch in his state,
Wrapt in the blaze of majesty,
So free from every care as I.—
Next day the scene was overcast, 30
Such day till then I never pass'd,—
For on that day, relentless fate!
Delia and I must separate.
Yet ere we look'd our last farewell,
From her dear lips this comfort fell:—
"Fear not that time, where'er we rove,
Or absence, shall abate my love."
And can I doubt, my charming maid!
As unsincere what you have said?
Banish'd from thee to what I hate, 40
Dull neighbours and insipid chat,
No joy to cheer me, none in view,
But the dear hope of meeting you;—
And that through passion's optic seen,
With ages interpos'd between,—
Blest with the kind support you give,
'Tis by your promis'd truth I live;
How deep my woes, how fierce my flame,
You best may tell, who feel the same.

R. S. S.

[Written 1755 (?). Published by Croft, 1825.]

ALL-WORSHIPP'D Gold! thou mighty mystery!
Say by what name shall I address thee rather,
Our blessing, or our bane? without thy aid,
The gen'rous pangs of pity but distress

26 set *Southey* : sat *Croft*.

The human heart, that fain would feel the bliss
Of blessing others; and, enslav'd by thee,
Far from relieving woes which others feel,
Misers oppress themselves. Our blessing then
With virtue when possess'd; without, our bane!
If in my bosom unperceiv'd there lurk 10
The deep-sown seeds of av'rice or ambition,
Blame me, ye great ones, (for I scorn your censure)
But let the gen'rous and the good commend me;
That to my Delia I direct them all,
The worthiest object of a virtuous love.
Oh! to some distant scene, a willing exile
From the wild uproar of this busy world,
Were it my fate with Delia to retire;
With her to wander through the sylvan shade,
Each morn, or o'er the moss-imbrowned turf, 20
Where, blest as the prime parents of mankind
In their own Eden, we would envy none;
But, greatly pitying whom the world calls happy,
Gently spin out the silken thread of life;
While from her lips attentive I receive
The tend'rest dictates of the purest flame,
And from her eyes (where soft complacence sits
Illumin'd with the radiant beams of sense)
Tranquillity beyond a monarch's reach!
Forgive me, heav'n! this only avarice 30
My soul indulges; I confess the crime,
(If to esteem, to covet such perfection
Be criminal,) Oh grant me Delia! grant me wealth!
Wealth to alleviate, not increase my wants,
And grant me virtue, without which nor wealth
Nor Delia can avail to make me blest.

R. S. S.

WRITTEN IN A FIT OF ILLNESS

[Written 1755 (?). Published by Croft, 1825.]

In these sad hours, a prey to ceaseless pain,
While feverish pulses leap in ev'ry vein,
When each faint breath the last short effort seems
Of life just parting from my feeble limbs;
How wild soe'er my wand'ring thoughts may be,
Still, gentle Delia, still they turn on thee!
At length if, slumb'ring to a short repose,
A sweet oblivion frees me from my woes,
Thy form appears, thy footsteps I pursue,
Through springy vales, and meadows wash'd in dew;

Thy arm supports me to the fountain's brink, 11
Where, by some secret pow'r forbid to drink,
Gasping with thirst, I view the tempting flood
That flies my touch, or thickens into mud,
Till thine own hand immerg'd the goblet dips,
And bears it streaming to my burning lips;
There borne aloft on Fancy's wing we fly,
Like souls embodied to their native sky;
Now ev'ry rock, each mountain, disappears,
And the round earth an even surface wears; 20
When lo! the force of some resistless weight
Bears me straight down from that pernicious height;
Parting, in vain our struggling arms we close;
Abhorred forms, dire phantoms interpose;
With trembling voice on thy lov'd name I call,
And gulphs yawn ready to receive my fall;
From these fallacious visions of distress
I wake; nor are my real sorrows less.
Thy absence, Delia! heightens every ill,
And gives e'en trivial pains the pow'r to kill. 30
Oh! wert thou near me; yet that wish forbear!
'Twere vain, my love—'twere vain to wish thee near;
Thy tender heart would heave with anguish too,
And by partaking but increase my woe.
Alone I'll grieve, till, gloomy sorrow past,
Health, like the cheerful day-spring, comes at last—
Comes fraught with bliss to banish ev'ry pain,
Hope, joy, and peace, and Delia in her train!

TO DELIA

[Written 1755. Published by Croft, 1825.]

Me to whatever state the Gods assign,
Believe, my love, whatever state be mine,
Ne'er shall my breast one anxious sorrow know,
Ne'er shall my heart confess a real woe;
If to thy share heav'n's choicest blessings fall,
As thou hast virtue to deserve them all.
Yet vain, alas! that idle hope would be
That builds on happiness remote from thee.
Oh! may thy charms, whate'er our fate decrees,
Please, as they must, but let them only please— 10
Not like the sun with equal influence shine,
Nor warm with transport any heart but mine.
Ye who from wealth th' ill-grounded title boast
To claim whatever beauty charms you most;
Ye sons of fortune, who consult alone
Her parents' will, regardless of her own,

17 There] Then *Bailey*.

Know that a love like ours, a gen'rous flame,
No wealth can purchase, and no pow'r reclaim.
The soul's affection can be only given
Free, unextorted, as the grace of heaven. 20
  Is there whose faithful bosom can endure
Pangs fierce as mine, nor ever hope a cure?
Who sighs in absence of the dear-lov'd maid,
Nor summons once indiff'rence to his aid?
Who can, like me, the nice resentment prove,
The thousand soft disquietudes of love;
The trivial strifes that cause a real pain;
The real bliss when reconcil'd again?
Let him alone dispute the real prize,
And read his sentence in my Delia's eyes; 30
There shall he read all gentleness and truth,
But not himself, the dear distinguish'd youth;
Pity for him perhaps they may express—
Pity, that will but heighten his distress.
But, wretched rival! he must sigh to see
The sprightlier rays of love directed all to me.
  And thou, dear antidote of ev'ry pain
Which fortune can inflict, or love ordain,
Since early love has taught thee to despise
What the world's worthless vot'ries only prize, 40
Believe, my love! no less the gen'rous God
Rules in my breast, his ever blest abode;
There has he driven each gross desire away,
Directing ev'ry wish and ev'ry thought to thee!
Then can I ever leave my Delia's arms,
A slave, devoted to inferior charms?
Can e'er my soul her reason so disgrace?
For what blest minister of heav'nly race
Would quit that heav'n to find a happier place?

[Written 1757 (?). Published by Croft, 1825.]

HOPE, like the short-liv'd ray that gleams awhile
  Through wintry skies upon the frozen waste,
Cheers e'en the face of misery to a smile;
  But soon the momentary pleasure's past!
How oft, my Delia! since our last farewell,
  (Years that have roll'd since that distressful hour,)
Griev'd I have said, when most our hopes prevail
  Our promis'd happiness is least secure. 8
Oft I have thought the scene of troubles closed,
  And hop'd once more to gaze upon your charms;
As oft some dire mischance has interposed,
  And snatch'd th' expected blessing from my arms.

The seaman thus, his shatter'd vessel lost,
  Still vainly strives to shun the threat'ning death;
And while he thinks to gain the friendly coast,
  And drops his feet, and feels the sands beneath: 16

Borne by the wave, steep-sloping from the shore,
  Back to th' inclement deep again he beats
The surge aside, and seems to tread secure;
  And now the refluent wave his baffled toil defeats.

Had you, my love, forbade me to pursue
  My fond attempt, disdainfully retired,
And with proud scorn compell'd me to subdue
  Th' ill-fated passion by yourself inspired; 24

Then haply to some distant spot removed,
  Hopeless to gain, unwilling to molest
With fond entreaties whom I dearly loved,
  Despair or absence had redeem'd my rest.

But now, sole partner in my Delia's heart,
  Yet doom'd far off in exile to complain,
Eternal absence cannot ease my smart,
  And hope subsists but to prolong my pain. 32

Oh then! kind heav'n, be this my latest breath;
  Here end my life, or make it worth my care;
Absence from whom we love is worse than death,
  And frustrate hope severer than despair.

AN ODE

ON READING MR. RICHARDSON'S HISTORY OF SIR CHARLES GRANDISON

[Written 1753. Published complete by Croft, 1825; last four stanzas published by Hayley, 1803.]

SAY, ye apostate and profane
Wretches who blush not to disdain
    Allegiance to your God,—
Did e'er your idly-wasted love
Of virtue for her sake remove
    And lift you from the crowd? 6

Would you the race of glory run,
Know, the devout, and they alone,
    Are equal to the task:
The labours of th' illustrious course
Far other than th' unaided force
    Of human vigour ask. 12

To arm against repeated ill
The patient heart too brave to feel
The tortures of despair;
Nor suffer yet high-crested Pride,
When wealth flows in with ev'ry tide,
To gain admittance there; 18

To rescue from the tyrant's sword
Th' oppress'd; unseen, and unimplor'd,
To cheer the face of woe;
From lawless insult to defend
An orphan's right, a fallen friend,
And a forgiven foe; 24

These, these distinguish from the crowd,
And these alone, the great and good,
The guardians of mankind:
Whose bosoms with these virtues heave,
Oh with what matchless speed they leave
The multitude behind! 30

Then ask ye from what source on earth
Virtues like these derive their birth?
Deriv'd from Heaven alone,
Full on that favour'd breast they shine
Where faith and resignation join
To call the blessing down. 36

Such is that heart:—but while the muse
Thy theme, O Richardson, pursues,
Her feebler spirits faint;
She cannot reach, and shall not wrong
That subject for an angel's song,
The hero, and the saint! 42

ON THE DEATH OF SIR W. RUSSELL

[Written in a letter to Harriet Cowper, afterwards Lady Hesketh, 1757. Published by Hayley, 1803.]

Doom'd as I am in solitude to waste
The present moments, and regret the past;
Depriv'd of ev'ry joy I valued most,
My friend torn from me, and my mistress lost;
Call not this gloom I wear, this anxious mien,
The dull effect of humour, or of spleen!
Still, still I mourn, with each returning day,
Him[1] snatch'd by fate, in early youth away,

[1] Sir William Russell, the favourite friend of the young poet [H.].

16 suffer] safer *all previous edd.* 31 source *Croft*: cause *Hayley.* 40 shall *Croft*: would *Hayley.*

And her—through tedious years of doubt and pain,
Fix'd in her choice, and faithful—but in vain. 10
O prone to pity, gen'rous, and sincere,
Whose eye ne'er yet refus'd the wretch a tear;
Whose heart the real claim of friendship knows,
Nor thinks a lover's are but fancied woes;
See me—ere yet my destin'd course half done,
Cast forth a wand'rer on a wild unknown!
See me neglected on the world's rude coast,
Each dear companion of my voyage lost!
Nor ask why clouds of sorrow shade my brow,
And ready tears wait only leave to flow! 20
Why all that soothes a heart from anguish free,
All that delights the happy—palls with me!

ADDRESSED TO MISS MACARTNEY

ON READING THE PRAYER FOR INDIFFERENCE[1]

[Written 1762. Published by Johnson, 1815.]

AND dwells there in a female heart,
By bounteous heav'n design'd
The choicest raptures to impart,
To feel the most refin'd—

Dwells there a wish in such a breast
Its nature to forego,
To smother in ignoble rest
At once both bliss and woe? 8

Far be the thought, and far the strain,
Which breathes the low desire,
How sweet soe'er the verse complain,
Tho' Phœbus string the lyre.

Come then fair maid (in nature wise)
Who, knowing them, can tell
From gen'rous sympathy what joys
The glowing bosom swell: 16

In justice to the various pow'rs
Of pleasing, which you share,
Join me, amid your silent hours,
To form the better pray'r.

[1] For Mrs. Greville's Ode see Annual Register, vol. v. p. 202 [J.]

Death of Sir W. Russell—15 distant *Hayley* (*1812*).
To Miss Macartney—Title blank in 1815.

With lenient balm may *Ob'ron* hence
  To fairy-land be driv'n;
With ev'ry herb that blunts the sense
  Mankind receiv'd from heav'n. 24

"Oh! if my Sov'reign Author please,
  Far be it from my fate,
To live, unblest, in torpid ease,
  And slumber on in state;

Each tender tie of life defied,
  Whence social pleasures spring,
Unmov'd with all the world beside,
  A solitary thing."— 32

Some Alpine mountain, wrapt in snow,
  Thus braves the whirling blast,
Eternal winter doom'd to know,
  No genial spring to taste.

In vain warm suns their influence shed,
  The zephyrs sport in vain,
He rears unchang'd his barren head,
  Whilst beauty decks the plain. 40

What though, in scaly armour drest,
  Indifference may repel
The shafts of woe—in such a breast
  No joy can ever dwell.

'Tis woven in the world's great plan,
  And fix'd by heav'n's decree,
That all the true delights of man
  Should spring from *Sympathy*. 48

'Tis nature bids, and whilst the laws
  Of nature we retain,
Our self-approving bosom draws
  A pleasure from its pain.

Thus grief itself has comforts dear,
  The sordid never know;
And ecstasy attends the tear,
  When virtue bids it flow. 56

For, when it streams from that pure source,
  No bribes the heart can win,
To check, or alter from its course,
  The luxury within.

Peace to the phlegm of sullen elves,
  Who, if from labour eas'd,
Extend no care beyond themselves,
  Unpleasing and unpleas'd. 64

Let no low thought suggest the pray'r,
Oh! grant, kind heav'n, to me,
Long as I draw ethereal air,
Sweet Sensibility.

Where'er the heav'nly nymph is seen,
With lustre-beaming eye,
A train, attendant on their queen,
(Her rosy chorus) fly. 72

The jocund Loves in Hymen's band,
With torches ever bright,
And gen'rous Friendship hand in hand,
With Pity's wat'ry sight;

The gentler Virtues too are join'd,
In youth immortal warm,
The soft relations which, combin'd,
Give life her ev'ry charm. 80

The Arts come smiling in the close,
And lend celestial fire,
The marble breathes, the canvas glows,
The Muses sweep the lyre.

"Still may my melting bosom cleave
To suff'rings not my own;
And still the sigh responsive heave,
Where'er is heard a groan. 88

So Pity shall take Virtue's part,
Her natural ally,
And fashioning my soften'd heart,
Prepare it for the sky."

This artless vow may heav'n receive,
And you, fond maid, approve:
So may your guiding angel give
Whate'er you wish or love. 96

So may the rosy-finger'd hours
Lead on the various year,
And ev'ry joy, which now is yours,
Extend a larger sphere:

And suns to come, as round they wheel,
Your golden moments bless,
With all a tender heart can feel,
Or lively fancy guess. 104

AN ODE

SECUNDUM ARTEM

[Written 1763 (?). Published in the *St. James' Magazine*, edited by Robert Lloyd, Nov., 1763. First claimed, on somewhat doubtful evidence, as probably Cowper's by Southey.]

I

SHALL I begin with *Ah*, or *Oh*?
Be sad? *Oh!* yes. Be glad? *Ah!* no.
Light subjects suit not grave Pindaric ode,
Which walks in metre down the Strophic road.
But let the sober matron wear
Her own mechanic sober air:
Ah me! ill suits, *alas!* the sprightly jig,
Long robes of ermine, or Sir Cloudsley's wig.
Come, placid DULLNESS, gently come,
And all my faculties benumb, 10
Let thought turn exile, while the vacant mind
To trickie words and pretty phrase confin'd,
Pumping for trim description's art,
To win the ear, neglects the heart.
So shall thy sister TASTE's peculiar sons,
Lineal Descendants from the GOTHS and HUNS,
Struck with the true and grand sublime
Of *rythm* converted into *Rime*,
Court the quaint Muse; and con her lessons o'er,
When sleep the sluggish waves by Granta's shore:
There shall each poet pare and trim, 21
Stretch, cramp, or lop the verse's limb,
While rebel WIT beholds them with disdain,
And Fancy flies aloft, nor heeds their servile chain.

II

Oh Fancy, bright aerial maid!
Where have thy vagrant footsteps stray'd?
For *ah!* I miss thee midst thy wonted haunt,
Since silent now th' enthusiastic chaunt,
Which erst like frenzy roll'd along,
Driv'n by th' impetuous tide of song, 30
Rushing secure where native genius bore,
Not Cautious Coasting by the Shelving Shore.
Hail to the sons of modern Rime,
Mechanic dealers in sublime,
Whose lady Muse full wantonly is dress'd,
In light expressions quaint, and tinsel vest,
Where swelling epithets are laid
(Art's ineffectual parade)

As varnish on the cheek of Harlot light;
The rest thin sown with profit or delight, 40
But ill compares with antient song,
Where Genius pour'd its flood along;
Yet such is Art's presumptuous idle claim,
She marshals out the way to modern fame;
From Grecian fables' pompous lore,
Description's studied, glittering store,
Smooth, Soothing Sounds, and sweet alternate rime,
Clinking like change of bells, in tingle tangle chime.

III

The lark shall soar in ev'ry Ode,
With flow'rs of light description strew'd, 50
And sweetly, warbling Philomel, shall flow
Thy Soothing Sadness in mechanic woe.
Trim Epithets shall spread their gloss,
While ev'ry Cell's o'ergrown with moss:
Here Oaks shall rise in chains of ivy bound,
There Smould'ring Stones o'er-spread the rugged ground.
Here forests brown, and azure hills,
There babbling fonts, and prattling rills;
Here some gay river floats in crisped streams,
While the bright Sun now gilds his morning beams,
Or sinking to his Thetis' breast, 61
Drives in description down the west.
—Oh let me boast, with pride becoming skill,
I crown the summit of Parnassus' Hill:
While Taste with Genius shall dispense,
And sound shall triumph over sense;
O'er the gay mead with curious steps I'll stray;
And, like the Bee, steal all its sweets away,
Extract its beauty, and its pow'r,
From every new poetic flow'r, 70
Whose sweets collected may a wreath compose,
To bind the Poet's brow, or please the Critic's nose.

LINES WRITTEN DURING A PERIOD OF INSANITY

[Written 1763. Published in the *Autobiography*, 1816.]

HATRED and vengeance, my eternal portion,
Scarce can endure delay of execution,
Wait, with impatient readiness, to seize my
Soul in a moment.

71 wreath *Southey*: wreathe *1763*

Damn'd below Judas: more abhorr'd than he was,
Who for a few pence sold his holy Master.
Twice betrayed Jesus me, the last delinquent,
Deems the profanest. 8

Man disavows, and Deity disowns me:
Hell might afford my miseries a shelter;
Therefore hell keeps her ever hungry mouths all
Bolted against me.

Hard lot! encompass'd with a thousand dangers;
Weary, faint, trembling with a thousand terrors;
I'm called, if vanquish'd, to receive a sentence
Worse than Abiram's. 16

Him the vindictive rod of angry justice
Sent quick and howling to the centre headlong;
I, fed with judgment, in a fleshly tomb, am
Buried above ground.

A SONG OF MERCY AND JUDGMENT

[Written 1764. Published, from the copy among the Ash MSS., in *The Universal Review*, 1890.]

LORD, I love the habitation
Where the Saviour's honour dwells;
At the sound of thy salvation
With delight my bosom swells.
Grace Divine, how sweet the sound,
Sweet the grace that I have found. 6

Me thro' waves of deep affliction,
Dearest Saviour! thou hast brought,
Fiery deeps of sharp conviction
Hard to bear and passing thought.
Sweet the sound of Grace Divine,
Sweet the grace which makes me thine. 12

From the cheerful beams of morning
Sad I turn'd mine eyes away:
And the shades of night returning
Fill'd my soul with new dismay. 16
Grace Divine, &c.

Food I loath'd nor ever tasted
But by violence constrain'd.
Strength decay'd and body wasted,
Spoke the terrors I sustain'd. 20
Sweet the sound, &c.

Lines—15 if vanquish'd] *Southey suggests* in anguish.

Bound and watch'd, lest life abhorring
  I should my own death procure,
For to me the Pit of Roaring
  Seem'd more easy to endure. 24
      Grace Divine, &c.

Fear of Thee, with gloomy sadness,
  Overwhelm'd thy guilty worm,
Till reduc'd to moping madness
  Reason sank beneath the storm. 28
      Sweet the sound, &c.

Then what soul-distressing noises
  Seem'd to reach me from below,
Visionary scenes and voices,
  Flames of Hell and screams of woe. 32
      Grace Divine, &c.

But at length a word of Healing
  Sweeter than an angel's note,
From the Saviour's lips distilling
  Chas'd despair and chang'd my lot. 36
      Sweet the sound, &c.

'Twas a word well tim'd and suited
  To the need of such an hour,
Sweet to one like me polluted,
  Spoke in love and seal'd with pow'r. 40
      Grace Divine, &c.

I, He said, have seen thee grieving,
  Lov'd thee as I pass'd thee by;
Be not faithless, but believing,
  Look, and live, and never die. 44
      Sweet the sound, &c.

Take the Bloody Seal I give thee,
  Deep impress'd upon thy soul;
God, thy God, will now receive thee,
  Faith hath sav'd thee, thou art whole. 48
      Grace Divine, &c.

All at once my chains were broken,
  From my feet my fetters fell,
And that word in pity spoken,
  Snatch'd me from the gates of Hell. 52
      Grace Divine, &c.

Since that hour, in hope of glory,
  With thy foll'wers I am found,
And relate the wond'rous story
  To thy list'ning saints around. 56
      Sweet the sound of Grace Divine,
      Sweet the grace which makes me thine.

ODE TO PEACE

[Written 1773 (?). Published 1782. There is a copy among the Ash MSS.]

Come, peace of mind, delightful guest!
Return and make thy downy nest
  Once more in this sad heart!—
Nor riches I, nor pow'r, pursue,
Nor hold forbidden joys in view;
  We therefore need not part. 6

Where wilt thou dwell if not with me,
From av'rice and ambition free,
  And pleasure's fatal wiles?
For whom, alas! dost thou prepare
The sweets that I was wont to share,
  The banquet of thy smiles? 12

The great, the gay, shall they partake
The heav'n that thou alone canst make?
  And wilt thou quit the stream
That murmurs through the dewy mead,
The grove and the sequester'd shed,
  To be a guest with them? 18

For thee I panted, thee I priz'd,
For thee I gladly sacrific'd
  Whate'er I lov'd before;
And shall I see thee start away,
And, helpless, hopeless, hear thee say—
  Farewell! we meet no more? 24

THE SHRUBBERY,

WRITTEN IN A TIME OF AFFLICTION

[Written 1773. Published 1782.]

Oh, happy shades—to me unblest!
  Friendly to peace, but not to me!
How ill the scene that offers rest,
  And heart that cannot rest, agree!

This glassy stream, that spreading pine,
  Those alders quiv'ring to the breeze,
Might sooth a soul less hurt than mine,
  And please, if any thing could please. 8

But fix'd unalterable care
  Foregoes not what she feels within,
Shows the same sadness ev'ry where,
  And slights the season and the scene.

Ode to Peace—3 this sad] William's *A*. 9 Whom nothing Base beguiles? *A*.

For all that pleas'd in wood or lawn,
  While peace possess'd these silent bow'rs,
Her animating smile withdrawn,
  Has lost its beauties and its pow'rs. 16

The saint or moralist should tread
  This moss-grown alley, musing, slow;
They seek, like me, the secret shade,
  But not, like me, to nourish woe!

Me fruitful scenes and prospects waste
  Alike admonish not to roam;
These tell me of enjoyments past,
  And those of sorrows yet to come. 24

HEU! QUAM REMOTUS

[Written "die ultimo 1774." Published in the 1835 edition of the *Autobiography*.]

Heu! quam remotus vescor ab omnibus
Quibus fruebar sub lare patrio,
  Quam nescius jucunda quondam
    Arva domum socios reliqui,
Et praeter omnes te mihi flebilem,
Te cariorem luce vel artubus,
  Te vinculo nostram jugali
    Deserui tremulam sub ense;
Sed nec ferocem me genuit pater,
Nec vagientem nutriit ubere 10
  Leaena dumoso sub antro;
    Fata sed haec voluere nostra.
Et fluctuosum ceu mare volvitur,
Dum commovebar mille timoribus,
  Coactus in fauces Averni
    Totus atro perii sub amne.

THE WINTER NOSEGAY

[Written 1777 (?). Published 1782.]

What nature, alas! has denied
  To the delicate growth of our isle,
Art has in a measure supplied,
  And winter is deck'd with a smile.
See, Mary, what beauties I bring
  From the shelter of that sunny shed,
Where the flow'rs have the charms of the spring,
  Though abroad they are frozen and dead. 8

'Tis a bow'r of Arcadian sweets,
  Where Flora is still in her prime,
A fortress, to which she retreats
  From the cruel assaults of the clime.

While earth wears a mantle of snow,
These pinks are as fresh and as gay
As the fairest and sweetest that blow
On the beautiful bosom of May. 16

See how they have safely surviv'd
The frowns of a sky so severe;
Such Mary's true love, that has liv'd
Through many a turbulent year.
The charms of the late blowing rose
Seem grac'd with a livelier hue,
And the winter of sorrow best shows
The truth of a friend such as you. 24

ON THE TRIAL OF ADMIRAL KEPPEL

[Written 1778. Published, from the copy among the Ash MSS., in *The Universal Review*, 1890.]

KEPPEL, returning from afar
With laurels on his brow,
Comes home to wage a sharper war,
And with a fiercer foe.

The blow was rais'd with cruel aim,
And meant to pierce his heart,
But lighting on his well earn'd fame
Struck an immortal part. 8

Slander and Envy strive to tear
His wreath so justly won,
But Truth, who made his cause her care,
Has bound it faster on.

The charge, that was design'd to sound
The signal of disgrace,
Has only call'd a navy round
To praise him to his face. 16

AN ADDRESS TO THE MOB ON OCCASION OF THE LATE RIOT AT THE HOUSE OF SIR HUGH PALLISER

[Written 1778. Published, from the copy among the Ash MSS., in *The Universal Review*, 1890.]

AND is it thus, ye base and blind,
And fickle as the shifting wind,
Ye treat a warrior staunch and true,
Grown old in combating for you?
Can one false step, and made in haste,
Thus cancel every service past?
And have ye all at once forgot,
(As whose deservings have ye not?)

That Palliser, like Keppel brave,
Has baffled France on yonder wave; 10
And when his country ask'd the stake,
Has pledg'd his life for England's sake?
Though now he sink oppress'd with shame,
Forgetful of his former fame,
Yet Keppel with deserv'd applause
Proclaims him bold in Britain's cause,
And to his well known courage pays
The tribute of heroic praise.
Go learn of him whom ye adore,
Whose name now sets you in a roar, 20
Whom ye were more than half prepar'd
To pay with just the same reward,
To render praise where praise is due,
To keep his former deeds in view
Who fought and would have died for you.

A TALE, FOUNDED ON A FACT

WHICH HAPPENED IN JANUARY, 1779

[Written Jan., 1779. Published by Hayley, 1803.]

WHERE Humber pours his rich commercial stream,
There dwelt a wretch, who breath'd but to blaspheme.
In subterraneous caves his life he led,
Black as the mine, in which he wrought for bread.
When on a day, emerging from the deep,
A Sabbath-day! (such sabbaths thousands keep!)
The wages of his weekly toil he bore
To buy a cock—whose blood might win him more;
As if the noblest of the feather'd kind
Were but for battle and for death design'd; 10
As if the consecrated hours were meant
For sport, to minds on cruelty intent;
It chanc'd (such chances Providence obey!)
He met a fellow-lab'rer on the way,
Whose heart the same desires had once inflam'd—
But now the savage temper was reclaim'd;
Persuasion on his lips had taken place;
For all plead well, who plead the cause of grace!
His iron-heart with scripture he assail'd,
Woo'd him to hear a sermon, and prevail'd. 20
His faithful bow the mighty preacher drew,
Swift, as the lightning-glimpse, the arrow flew;
He wept; he trembled; cast his eyes around,
To find a worse than he; but none he found.

6 sabbath *Hayley* (*1806*).

He felt his sins, and wonder'd he should feel.
Grace made the wound, and grace alone could heal!
 Now farewell oaths, and blasphemies, and lies!
He quits the sinner's for the martyr's prize.
That holy day was wash'd with many a tear,
Gilded with hope, yet shaded too by fear. 30
The next, his swarthy brethren of the mine
Learn'd, by his alter'd speech—the change divine!
Laugh'd when they should have wept, and swore
 the day
Was nigh, when he would swear as fast as they.
No, (said the penitent): such words shall share
This breath no more; devoted now to pray'r.
Oh! if thou seest, (thine eye the future sees!)
That I shall yet again blaspheme, like these;
Now strike me to the ground, on which I kneel,
Ere yet this heart relapses into steel; 40
Now take me to that Heav'n, I once defied,
Thy presence, thy embrace!—He spoke, and died!

THE BEE AND THE PINE-APPLE

[Written Sept., 1779. Published, in *Unpublished Poems of Cowper*, 1900, from the copy among the Ash MSS.]

A Bee allur'd by the perfume
Of a rich pine-apple in bloom,
Found it within a frame inclos'd,
And lick'd the glass that interpos'd.
Blossoms of apricot and peach,
The flow'rs that blow'd within his reach,
Were arrant drugs compar'd with that,
He strove so vainly to get at.
No rose could yield so rare a treat,
Nor jessamine were half so sweet. 10
The gard'ner saw this much ado,
(The gard'ner was the master too)
And thus he said—Poor restless bee!
I learn philosophy from thee,
I learn how just it is and wise,
To use what Providence supplies,
To leave fine titles, lordships, graces,
Rich pensions, dignities, and places,
Those gifts of a superior kind,
To those for whom they were design'd. 20
I learn that comfort dwells alone
In that which Heav'n has made our own,
That fools incur no greater pain,
Than pleasure coveted in vain.

THE PINE-APPLE AND THE BEE

[Written Sept., 1779. Published 1782. There is a copy among the Ash MSS.]

THE pine-apples, in triple row,
Were basking hot, and all in blow;
A bee of most discerning taste
Perceiv'd the fragrance as he pass'd,
On eager wing the spoiler came,
And search'd for crannies in the frame,
Urg'd his attempt on ev'ry side,
To ev'ry pane his trunk applied;
But still in vain, the frame was tight,
And only pervious to the light; 10
Thus having wasted half the day,
He trimm'd his flight another way.
Methinks, I said, in thee I find
The sin and madness of mankind.
To joys forbidden man aspires,
Consumes his soul with vain desires,
Folly the spring of his pursuit,
And disappointment all the fruit.
While Cynthio ogles as she passes
The nymph between two chariot glasses, 20
She is the pine-apple, and he
The silly unsuccessful bee.
The maid who views with pensive air
The show-glass fraught with glitt'ring ware,
Sees watches, bracelets, rings, and lockets,
But sighs at thought of empty pockets;
Like thine, her appetite is keen,
But ah, the cruel glass between!
Our dear delights are often such,
Expos'd to view, but not to touch: 30
The sight our foolish heart inflames,
We long for pine-apples in frames:
With hopeless wish one looks and lingers;
One breaks the glass, and cuts his fingers;
But they whom truth and wisdom lead,
Can gather honey from a weed.

ON THE PROMOTION OF EDWARD THURLOW, ESQ. TO THE LORD HIGH CHANCELLORSHIP OF ENGLAND

[Written Nov., 1779. Published 1782.]

ROUND Thurlow's head in early youth,
And in his sportive days,
Fair science pour'd the light of truth,
And genius shed his rays.

7 Urg'd] Push'd *A*. 9 still] all *A*.

See! with united wonder cried
  Th' experienc'd and the sage,
Ambition in a boy supplied
  With all the skill of age! 8

Discernment, eloquence, and grace,
  Proclaim him born to sway
The balance in the highest place,
  And bear the palm away.

The praise bestow'd was just and wise;
  He sprang impetuous forth,
Secure of conquest where the prize
  Attends superior worth. 16

So the best courser on the plain
  Ere yet he starts is known,
And does but at the goal obtain
  What all had deem'd his own.

HUMAN FRAILTY

[Written Nov. (?), 1779. Published 1782. There is a MS. copy in the British Museum.]

Weak and irresolute is man;
  The purpose of to-day,
Woven with pains into his plan,
  To-morrow rends away.

The bow well bent, and smart the spring,
  Vice seems already slain;
But passion rudely snaps the string,
  And it revives again. 8

Some foe to his upright intent
  Finds out his weaker part;
Virtue engages his assent,
  But pleasure wins his heart.

'Tis here the folly of the wise
  Through all his art we view;
And, while his tongue the charge denies,
  His conscience owns it true. 16

Bound on a voyage of awful length
  And dangers little known,
A stranger to superior strength,
  Man vainly trusts his own.

But oars alone can ne'er prevail
  To reach the distant coast,
The breath of heav'n must swell the sail,
  Or all the toil is lost. 24

21 alone can] alas could *BM*.

THE YEARLY DISTRESS

OR, TITHING TIME AT STOCK IN ESSEX

VERSES addressed to a Country Clergyman complaining of the disagreeableness of the day annually appointed for receiving the Dues at the Parsonage.

[Written to Unwin, Dec., 1779 (MS. in British Museum). Published in *The Gentleman's Magazine* Aug., 1783; afterwards in 1800.]

COME, ponder well, for 'tis no jest,
To laugh it would be wrong;
The troubles of a worthy priest
The burthen of my song.

This priest he merry is and blithe
Three quarters of the year,
But oh! it cuts him like a scythe
When tithing time draws near. 8

He then is full of frights and fears,
As one at point to die,
And long before the day appears
He heaves up many a sigh.

For then the farmers come jog, jog,
Along the miry road,
Each heart as heavy as a log,
To make their payments good. 16

In sooth, the sorrow of such days
Is not to be express'd,
When he that takes and he that pays
Are both alike distress'd.

Now all unwelcome, at his gates
The clumsy swains alight,
With rueful faces and bald pates—
He trembles at the sight. 24

And well he may, for well he knows
Each bumpkin of the clan,
Instead of paying what he owes,
Will cheat him if he can.

So in they come—each makes his leg,
And flings his head before,
And looks as if he came to beg,
And not to quit a score. 32

"And how does miss and madam do,
The little boy and all?"
"All tight and well: and how do you,
Good Mr. What-d'ye-call?"

9 frights *BM.*, *1783*: fright *1800*, *1803*.

The dinner comes, and down they sit:
  Were e'er such hungry folk?
There's little talking and no wit;
  It is no time to joke. 40

One wipes his nose upon his sleeve,
  One spits upon the floor,
Yet, not to give offence or grieve,
  Holds up the cloth before.

The punch goes round, and they are dull
  And lumpish still as ever;
Like barrels with their bellies full,
  They only weigh the heavier. 48

At length the busy time begins,
  "Come, neighbours we must wag"—
The money chinks, down drop their chins,
  Each lugging out his bag.

One talks of mildew and of frost,
  And one of storms of hail,
And one, of pigs that he has lost
  By maggots at the tail. 56

Quoth one, A rarer man than you
  In pulpit none shall hear:
But yet, methinks, to tell you true,
  You sell it plaguy dear.

Oh, why are farmers made so coarse,
  Or clergy made so fine!
A kick that scarce would move a horse
  May kill a sound divine. 64

Then let the boobies stay at home;
  'Twould cost him, I dare say,
Less trouble taking twice the sum,
  Without the clowns that pay.

THE MODERN PATRIOT

[Written Feb., 1780. Published 1782.]

Rebellion is my theme all day;
  I only wish 'twould come
(As who knows but perhaps it may?)
  A little nearer home.

Yon roaring boys, who rave and fight
  On t'other side th' Atlantic,
I always held them in the right,
  But most so when most frantic. 8

38 Were] Was *BM*.

When lawless mobs insult the court,
  That man shall be my toast,
If breaking windows be the sport,
  Who bravely breaks the most.

But oh! for him my fancy culls
  The choicest flow'rs she bears,
Who constitutionally pulls
  Your house about your ears. 16

Such civil broils are my delight;
  Though some folks can't endure 'em,
Who say the mob are mad outright,
  And that a rope must cure 'em.

A rope! I wish we patriots had
  Such strings for all who need 'em—
What! hang a man for going mad?
  Then farewell British freedom. 24

THE NIGHTINGALE AND GLOW-WORM

[Written Feb., 1780. Published 1782.]

A NIGHTINGALE, that all day long
Had cheer'd the village with his song,
Nor yet at eve his note suspended,
Nor yet when eventide was ended,
Began to feel, as well he might,
The keen demands of appetite;
When, looking eagerly around,
He spied far off, upon the ground,
A something shining in the dark,
And knew the glow-worm by his spark; 10
So, stooping down from hawthorn top,
He thought to put him in his crop.
The worm, aware of his intent,
Harangu'd him thus, right eloquent—
  Did you admire my lamp, quoth he,
As much as I your minstrelsy,
You would abhor to do me wrong,
As much as I to spoil your song;
For 'twas the self-same pow'r divine
Taught you to sing, and me to shine; 20
That you with music, I with light,
Might beautify and cheer the night.
  The songster heard his short oration,
And, warbling out his approbation,
Releas'd him, as my story tells,
And found a supper somewhere else.

Hence jarring sectaries may learn
Their real int'rest to discern;
That brother should not war with brother,
And worry and devour each other; 30
But sing and shine by sweet consent,
Till life's poor transient night is spent,
Respecting in each other's case
The gifts of nature and of grace.
Those Christians best deserve the name
Who studiously make peace their aim;
Peace, both the duty and the prize
Of him that creeps and him that flies.

A FABLE

[Written May 9, 1780. Published 1782. There is a copy among the Ash MSS.]

A RAVEN, while with glossy breast
Her new-laid eggs she fondly press'd,
And on her wicker-work high mounted
Her chickens prematurely counted,
(A fault philosophers might blame
If quite exempted from the same)
Enjoy'd at ease the genial day;
'Twas April as the bumpkins say,
The legislature call'd it May.
But suddenly a wind as high 10
As ever swept a winter sky
Shook the young leaves about her ears,
And fill'd her with a thousand fears,
Lest the rude blast should snap the bough,
And spread her golden hopes below.
But just at eve the blowing weather
And all her fears were hush'd together:
And now, quoth poor unthinking Ralph,
'Tis over, and the brood is safe;
(For Ravens, though, as birds of omen, 20
They teach both conj'rers and old women
To tell us what is to befall,
Can't prophesy themselves at all.)
The morning came, when neighbour Hodge,
Who long had mark'd her airy lodge,
And destin'd all the treasure there
A gift to his expecting fair,

14, 15 *Instead of these two lines A. has:*
Lest the rude Blast that Threatn'd so,
And Rocked her Cradle to and fro,
Should split the Trunk, or snap the Bough
Then fruitless all her Hopes to see,
A Pretty gaping Progeny.

Climb'd like a squirrel to his dray,
And bore the worthless prize away.

MORAL

'Tis Providence alone secures, 30
In every change, but mine and your's:
Safety consists not in escape
From dangers of a frightful shape;
An earthquake may be bid to spare
The man that's strangled by a hair.
Fate steals along with silent tread,
Found oft'nest in what least we dread,
Frowns in the storm with angry brow,
But in the sunshine strikes the blow.

THE DOVES

[Written May, 1780. Published 1782. There is a copy among the Ash MSS. entitled *Anti-thelyphthora.*]

REAS'NING at every step he treads,
Man yet mistakes his way,
While meaner things, whom instinct leads,
Are rarely known to stray.

One silent eve I wander'd late,
And heard the voice of love;
The turtle thus address'd her mate,
And sooth'd the list'ning dove— 8

Our mutual bond of faith and truth,
No time shall disengage;
Those blessings of our early youth
Shall cheer our latest age:

While innocence without disguise,
And constancy sincere,
Shall fill the circles of those eyes,
And mine can read them there; 16

Those ills that wait on all below
Shall ne'er be felt by me,
Or gently felt, and only so,
As being shar'd with thee.

When lightnings flash among the trees,
Or kites are hov'ring near,
I fear lest thee alone they seize,
And know no other fear. 24

Before verse 1 *A. has:*
Muse, mark the much lamented day,
When, like a tempest fear'd,
Forth issuing on the last of May
Thelyphthora appear'd.
5 One silent] That fatal *A.*

'Tis then I feel myself a wife,
And press thy wedded side,
Resolv'd an union form'd for life
Death never shall divide.

But oh! if, fickle and unchaste,
(Forgive a transient thought)
Thou couldst become unkind at last,
And scorn thy present lot, 32

No need of lightnings from on high,
Or kites with cruel beak;
Denied th' endearments of thine eye,
This widow'd heart would break.

Thus sang the sweet sequester'd bird
Soft as the passing wind,
And I recorded what I heard—
A lesson for mankind. 40

A COMPARISON

[Written (?). Published 1782. MS. copies of this and the next poem are in the British Museum.]

The lapse of time and rivers is the same;
Both speed their journey with a restless stream;
The silent pace with which they steal away
No wealth can bribe, no pray'rs persuade to stay;
Alike irrevocable both when past,
And a wide ocean swallows both at last.
Though each resemble each in ev'ry part,
A difference strikes at length the musing heart;
Streams never flow in vain; where streams abound,
How laughs the land with various plenty crown'd!
But time that should enrich the nobler mind, 11
Neglected, leaves a dreary waste behind.

ANOTHER

ADDRESSED TO A YOUNG LADY

[Written June, 1780. Published 1782.]

Sweet stream that winds thro' yonder glade,
Apt emblem of a virtuous maid—
Silent and chaste she steals along,
Far from the world's gay busy throng,
With gentle, yet prevailing, force
Intent upon her destin'd course;
Graceful and useful all she does,
Blessing and blest where'er she goes,
Pure-bosom'd as that wat'ry glass,
And heav'n reflected in her face. 10

31 could *1787–1800.*

ON A GOLDFINCH STARVED TO DEATH IN HIS CAGE

[Written in the summer of 1780. Published 1782. There is a MS. copy in the British Museum.]

TIME was when I was free as air,
The thistle's downy seed my fare,
  My drink the morning dew;
I perch'd at will on ev'ry spray,
My form genteel, my plumage gay,
  My strains for ever new. 6

But gaudy plumage, sprightly strain,
And form genteel, were all in vain,
  And of a transient date;
For, caught and cag'd, and starv'd to death,
In dying sighs my little breath
  Soon pass'd the wiry grate. 12

Thanks, gentle swain, for all my woes,
And thanks for this effectual close
  And cure of ev'ry ill!
More cruelty could none express;
And I, if you had shown me less,
  Had been your pris'ner still. 18

IN SEDITIONEM HORRENDAM

CORRUPTELIS GALLICIS (UT FERTUR) LONDINI NUPER EXORTAM

[Written in letter to Unwin, June 18, 1780 (MS. in British Museum). Published by Hayley, 1803.]

PERFIDA, crudelis, victa et lymphata furore,
  Non armis laurum Gallia, fraude petit.
Venalem pretio plebem conducit, et urit
  Undique privatas patriciasque domos.
Nequicquam conata sua, fœdissima sperat
  Posse tamen nostra nos superare manu.
Gallia, vana struis—Precibus nunc utere! Vinces,
  Nam mites timidis supplicibusque sumus. 8

TRANSLATION

[Written in letter to Unwin, July 11, 1780 (MS. in British Museum). Published by Hayley, 1803.]

FALSE, cruel, disappointed, stung to th' heart,
France quits the warrior's for th' assassin's part;
To dirty hands a dirty bribe conveys,
Bids the low street and lofty palace blaze.
Her sons too weak to vanquish us alone,
She hires the worst and basest of our own.—
Kneel, France!—a suppliant conquers us with ease,
We always spare a coward on his knees. 8

ON THE BURNING OF LORD MANSFIELD'S LIBRARY

TOGETHER WITH HIS MSS. BY THE MOB, IN THE MONTH OF JUNE 1780

[Written in letter to Unwin, June 22, 1780 (MS. copy in British Museum). Published 1782.]

So then—the Vandals of our isle,
Sworn foes to sense and law,
Have burnt to dust a nobler pile
Than ever Roman saw!
And MURRAY sighs o'er Pope and Swift,
And many a treasure more,
The well-judg'd purchase and the gift
That grac'd his letter'd store. 8
Their pages mangled, burnt, and torn,
The loss was *his alone*;
But ages yet to come shall mourn
The burning of *his own*.

ON THE SAME

[Written June, 1780. Published 1782.]

WHEN wit and genius meet their doom
In all devouring flame,
They tell us of the fate of Rome,
And bid us fear the same.
O'er MURRAY'S loss the muses wept,
They felt the rude alarm,
Yet bless'd the guardian care that kept
His sacred head from harm. 8
There mem'ry, like the bee that's fed
From Flora's balmy store,
The quintessence of all he read
Had treasur'd up before.
The lawless herd, with fury blind,
Have done him cruel wrong;
The flow'rs are gone—but still we find
The honey on his tongue. 16

LOVE ABUSED

[Written in letter to Unwin, July 27, 1780 (MS. in British Museum). Published by Hayley, 1803.]

WHAT is there in the vale of life
Half so delightful as a wife,
When friendship, love, and peace combine
To stamp the marriage bond divine?

On the Burning—Title 3] his own *BM*. 2 to] of *BM*. 7 and] or *BM*.

Love Abused—Sub-title in BM. (The thought suggested by Thelyphthora).

The stream of pure and genuine love
Derives its current from above;
And earth a second Eden shows
Where'er the healing water flows.
But ah! if from the dykes and drains
Of sensual nature's fev'rish veins, 10
Lust like a lawless headstrong flood
Impregnated with ooze and mud,
Descending fast on ev'ry side,
Once mingles with the sacred tide,
Farewell the soul-enliv'ning scene!
The banks, that wore a smiling green,
With rank defilement overspread
Bewail their flow'ry beauties dead;
The stream polluted, dark, and dull,
Diffus'd into a Stygian pool, 20
Thro' life's last melancholy years
Is fed with ever flowing tears:
Complaints supply the zephyr's part,
And sighs that heave a breaking heart.

ON OBSERVING SOME NAMES OF LITTLE NOTE RECORDED IN THE BIOGRAPHIA BRITANNICA

[Written in letter to Unwin, Sept. 3, 1780 (MS. in British Museum). Published 1782.]

Oh, fond attempt to give a deathless lot
To names ignoble, born to be forgot!
In vain, recorded in historic page,
They court the notice of a future age:
Those twinkling tiny lustres of the land
Drop one by one from Fame's neglecting hand:
Lethæan gulphs receive them as they fall,
And dark oblivion soon absorbs them all.
So when a child, as playful children use,
Has burnt to tinder a stale last year's news, 10
The flame extinct, he views the roving fire—
There goes my lady, and there goes the squire.
There goes the parson, oh! illustrious spark,
And there, scarce less illustrious, goes the clerk!

TO THE REVEREND MR. NEWTON ON HIS RETURN FROM RAMSGATE

[Written Oct., 1780. Published by Hayley, 1803, and by Johnson, 1815.]

That ocean you of late survey'd,
Those rocks I too have seen,
But I, afflicted and dismay'd,
You, tranquil and serene.

On Observing—10 cinder *Hayley.*
To Newton—1 of] have *Hayley* (*1812*), *1815.*

You from the flood-controlling steep
Saw stretch'd before your view,
With conscious joy, the threat'ning deep,
No longer such to you. 8

To me, the waves that ceaseless broke
Upon the dang'rous coast,
Hoarsely and ominously spoke
Of all my treasure lost.

Your sea of troubles you have past,
And found the peaceful shore;
I, tempest-toss'd, and wreck'd at last,
Come home to port no more. 16

REPORT OF AN ADJUDGED CASE

NOT TO BE FOUND IN ANY OF THE BOOKS

[Written Dec., 1780. Published 1782. There is a MS. copy in the British Museum in a letter to Unwin, another in the possession of Canon Cowper Johnson.]

BETWEEN Nose and Eyes a strange contest arose,—
The spectacles set them unhappily wrong;
The point in dispute was, as all the world knows,
To which the said spectacles ought to belong.

So Tongue was the lawyer, and argued the cause
With a great deal of skill, and a wig full of learning;
While chief baron Ear sat to balance the laws,
So fam'd for his talent in nicely discerning. 8

In behalf of the Nose, it will quickly appear,
And your lordship, he said, will undoubtedly find,
That the Nose has had spectacles always in wear,
Which amounts to possession time out of mind.

Then holding the spectacles up to the court,—
Your lordship observes they are made with a straddle,
As wide as the ridge of the Nose is; in short,
Design'd to sit close to it, just like a saddle. 16

Again, would your lordship a moment suppose,
('Tis a case that has happen'd, and may be again)
That the visage or countenance had not a Nose!
Pray who would, or who could, wear spectacles then?

On the whole, it appears—and my argument shows
With a reasoning the court will never condemn,
That the spectacles plainly were made for the Nose,
And the Nose was as plainly intended for them.

1 a strange] once a *BM.*: a sad *CJ.* 2 unhappily] egregiously *BM.* 5 the *before* Tongue *BM., CJ., 1782, 1786.* 8 in] at *CJ.*

Then, shifting his side, (as a lawyer knows how)
He pleaded again in behalf of the Eyes: 26
But what were his arguments few people know,
For the court did not think they were equally wise.

So his lordship decreed, with a grave solemn tone,
Decisive and clear, without one if or but—
That whenever the Nose put his spectacles on,
By day-light or candle-light—Eyes should be shut!

THE LOVE OF THE WORLD REPROVED;

OR, HYPOCRISY DETECTED[1]

[Written 1780 (?). Published in *The Gentleman's Magazine* Sept., 1780; afterwards in 1782. There is a copy among the Ash MSS.]

Thus says the prophet of the Turk—
Good mussulman, abstain from pork;
There is a part in ev'ry swine
No friend or follower of mine
May taste, whate'er his inclination,
On pain of excommunication.
Such Mahomet's mysterious charge,
And thus he left the point at large.
[Had he the sinful part express'd,
They might with safety eat the rest; 10
But for one piece they thought it hard
From the whole hog to be debarr'd,
And set their wit at work to find
What joint the prophet had in mind.]
Much controversy straight arose—
These choose the back, the belly those;
By some 'tis confidently said
He meant not to forbid the head;
While others at that doctrine rail,
And piously prefer the tail. 20
Thus, conscience freed from ev'ry clog,
Mahometans eat up the hog.
You laugh—'tis well.—The tale applied
May make you laugh on t'other side.
Renounce the world—the preacher cries.
We do—a multitude replies.
While one as innocent regards
A snug and friendly game at cards;

[1] It may be proper to inform the reader that this piece has already appeared in print, having found its way, though with some unnecessary additions by an unknown hand, into the Leeds Journal, without the author's privity [C.].

Title] Almost a Christian. A Tale *A*. 4 Follower or Friend *A*. 9-14 *by Newton; om. A. See Cowper's footnote, printed in 1782, and in subsequent editions.*

And one, whatever you may say,
Can see no evil in a play; 30
Some love a concert, or a race;
And others—shooting, and the chase.
Revil'd and lov'd, renounc'd and follow'd,
Thus, bit by bit, the world is swallow'd;
Each thinks his neighbour makes too free,
Yet likes a slice as well as he;
With sophistry their sauce they sweeten,
Till quite from tail to snout 'tis eaten.

BOADICEA: AN ODE

[Written 1780. Published 1782.]

When the British warrior queen,
Bleeding from the Roman rods,
Sought, with an indignant mien,
Counsel of her country's gods,

Sage beneath a spreading oak
Sat the Druid, hoary chief;
Ev'ry burning word he spoke
Full of rage, and full of grief. 8

Princess! if our aged eyes
Weep upon thy matchless wrongs,
'Tis because resentment ties
All the terrors of our tongues.

Rome shall perish—write that word
In the blood that she has spilt;
Perish, hopeless and abhorr'd,
Deep in ruin as in guilt. 16

Rome, for empire far renown'd,
Tramples on a thousand states;
Soon her pride shall kiss the ground—
Hark! the Gaul is at her gates!

Other Romans shall arise,
Heedless of a soldier's name;
Sounds, not arms, shall win the prize—
Harmony the path to fame. 24

Then the progeny that springs
From the forests of our land,
Arm'd with thunder, clad with wings,
Shall a wider world command.

Regions Cæsar never knew
Thy posterity shall sway,
Where his eagles never flew,
None invincible as they. 32

Such the bard's prophetic words,
Pregnant with celestial fire,
Bending, as he swept the chords
Of his sweet but awful lyre.

She, with all a monarch's pride,
Felt them in her bosom glow;
Rush'd to battle, fought, and died;
Dying, hurl'd them at the foe. 40

Ruffians, pitiless as proud,
Heav'n awards the vengeance due;
Empire is on us bestow'd,
Shame and ruin wait for you.

VERSES

SUPPOSED TO BE WRITTEN BY ALEXANDER SELKIRK, DURING HIS SOLITARY ABODE IN THE ISLAND OF JUAN FERNANDEZ

[Written (?). Published 1782. There is a MS. copy in the British Museum, not in Cowper's handwriting; another among the Ash MSS.]

I AM monarch of all I survey,
My right there is none to dispute;
From the centre all round to the sea,
I am lord of the fowl and the brute.
Oh, solitude! where are the charms
That sages have seen in thy face?
Better dwell in the midst of alarms,
Than reign in this horrible place. 8

I am out of humanity's reach,
I must finish my journey alone,
Never hear the sweet music of speech;
I start at the sound of my own.
The beasts, that roam over the plain,
My form with indifference see;
They are so unacquainted with man,
Their tameness is shocking to me. 16

Society, friendship, and love,
Divinely bestow'd upon man,
Oh, had I the wings of a dove,
How soon would I taste you again!
My sorrows I then might assuage
In the ways of religion and truth,
Might learn from the wisdom of age,
And be cheer'd by the sallies of youth. 24

20 ye *BM. A.*

Religion! what treasure untold
  Resides in that heavenly word!
More precious than silver and gold,
  Or all that this earth can afford.
But the sound of the church-going bell
  These vallies and rocks never heard,
Ne'er sigh'd at the sound of a knell,
  Or smil'd when a sabbath appear'd. 32

Ye winds, that have made me your sport,
  Convey to this desolate shore
Some cordial endearing report
  Of a land I shall visit no more.
My friends, do they now and then send
  A wish or a thought after me?
O tell me I yet have a friend,
  Though a friend I am never to see. 40

How fleet is a glance of the mind!
  Compar'd with the speed of its flight,
The tempest itself lags behind,
  And the swift wing'd arrows of light.
When I think of my own native land,
  In a moment I seem to be there;
But alas! recollection at hand
  Soon hurries me back to despair. 48

But the sea-fowl is gone to her nest,
  The beast is laid down in his lair,
Ev'n here is a season of rest,
  And I to my cabin repair.
There is mercy in every place;
  And mercy, encouraging thought!
Gives even affliction a grace,
  And reconciles man to his lot. 56

THE LILY AND THE ROSE

[Written 1781 (?). Published 1782. There is an undated MS. copy in the British Museum.]

THE nymph must lose her female friend,
  If more admir'd than she—
But where will fierce contention end
  If flow'rs can disagree?

27 and] or *BM.* 31 Never *BM. A.*
37, 38 My friends do they ever (never *BM.*) attend
To the sad recollection of me, *BM. A.*
40 I . . . see] that I never must see *BM. A.* 45 own native land] native abode *BM. A.*
47, 48 'Tis the Body alas! with its Load,
Still holds me a Prisoner here. *BM. A.*
49 her] his *BM. A.*

Within the garden's peaceful scene
  Appear'd two lovely foes,
Aspiring to the rank of queen—
  The Lily and the Rose. 8

The Rose soon redden'd into rage,
  And, swelling with disdain,
Appeal'd to many a poet's page
  To prove her right to reign.

The Lily's height bespoke command—
  A fair imperial flow'r;
She seem'd design'd for Flora's hand,
  The sceptre of her pow'r. 16

This civil bick'ring and debate
  The goddess chanc'd to hear,
And flew to save, ere yet too late,
  The pride of the parterre.—
Your's is, she said, the nobler hue,
  And your's the statelier mien,
And, till a third surpasses you,
  Let each be deem'd a queen. 24

Thus, sooth'd and reconcil'd, each seeks
  The fairest British fair;
The seat of empire is her cheeks,
  They reign united there.

IDEM LATINE REDDITUM

[Written 1781 (?). Published 1782.]

Heu inimicitias quoties parit æmula forma,
  Quam raro pulchræ pulchra placere potest!
Sed fines ultra solitos discordia tendit,
  Cum flores ipsos bilis et ira movent.

Hortus ubi dulces præbet tacitosque recessus,
  Se rapit in partes gens animosa duas;
Hic sibi regales Amaryllis candida cultus,
  Illic purpureo vindicat ore Rosa. 8

Ira Rosam et meritis quæsita superbia tangunt,
  Multaque ferventi vix cohibenda sinu,
Dum sibi fautorum ciet undique nomina vatum,
  Jusque suum, multo carmine fulta, probat.

Altior emicat illa, et celso vertice nutat,
  Ceu flores inter non habitura parem,
Fastiditque alios, et nata videtur in usus
  Imperii, sceptrum, Flora quod ipsa gerat. 16

Nec Dea non sensit civilis murmura rixæ,
  Cui curæ est pictas pandere ruris opes.
Deliciasque suas nunquam non prompta tueri,
  Dum licet et locus est, ut tueatur, adest.

Et tibi forma datur procerior omnibus, inquit,
  Et tibi, principibus qui solet esse, color,
Et donec vincat quædam formosior ambas,
  Et tibi reginæ nomen, et esto tibi. 24

His ubi sedatus furor est, petit utraque nympham,
  Qualem inter Veneres Anglia sola parit;
Hanc penes imperium est, nihil optant amplius, hujus
  Regnant in nitidis, et sine lite, genis.

VOTUM

[Written (?). Published 1782.]

O MATUTINI rores, auræque salubres,
O nemora, et lætæ rivis felicibus herbæ,
Graminei colles, et amænæ in vallibus umbræ!
Fata modo dederint quas olim in rure paterno
Delicias, procul arte, procul formidine novi,
Quam vellem ignotus, quod mens mea semper avebat,
Ante larem proprium placidam expectare senectam,
Tum demum, exactis non infeliciter annis,
Sortiri tacitum lapidem, aut sub cespite condi! 9

HORACE. BOOK THE 2nd. ODE THE 10th.

[Written (?). Published 1782.]

RECEIVE, dear friend, the truths I teach,
So shalt thou live beyond the reach
  Of adverse Fortune's pow'r;
Not always tempt the distant deep,
Nor always timorously creep
  Along the treach'rous shore. 6

He, that holds fast the golden mean,
And lives contentedly between
  The little and the great,
Feels not the wants that pinch the poor,
Nor plagues that haunt the rich man's door,
  Imbitt'ring all his state. 12

The tallest pines feel most the pow'r
Of wintry blasts; the loftiest tow'r
  Comes heaviest to the ground;
The bolts, that spare the mountain's side,
His cloud-capt eminence divide,
  And spread the ruin round. 18

14 blast *1786.*

The well-inform'd philosopher
Rejoices with an wholesome fear,
And hopes, in spite of pain;
If winter bellow from the north,
Soon the sweet spring comes dancing forth,
And nature laughs again. 24

What if thine heav'n be overcast,
The dark appearance will not last;
Expect a brighter sky;
The God that strings the silver bow
Awakes sometimes the muses too,
And lays his arrows by. 30

If hindrances obstruct thy way,
Thy magnanimity display,
And let thy strength be seen;
But oh! if Fortune fill thy sail
With more than a propitious gale,
Take half thy canvass in. 36

A REFLECTION ON THE FOREGOING ODE

[Written (?). Published 1782.]

AND is this all? Can reason do no more
Than bid me shun the deep and dread the shore?
Sweet moralist! afloat on life's rough sea,
The Christian has an art unknown to thee:
He holds no parley with unmanly fears;
Where duty bids, he confidently steers,
Faces a thousand dangers at her call,
And, trusting in his God, surmounts them all. 8

MUTUAL FORBEARANCE

NECESSARY TO THE HAPPINESS OF THE MARRIED STATE

[Written (?). Published 1782. There is a MS. copy in the British Museum.]

THE lady thus address'd her spouse—
What a mere dungeon is this house!
By no means large enough; and, was it,
Yet this dull room, and that dark closet—
Those hangings, with their worn-out graces,
Long beards, long noses, and pale faces—
Are such an antiquated scene,
They overwhelm me with the spleen!

Mutual Forbearance—Title] Patience recommended to Ladies who have deaf Husbands *BM*. 2, 3 What . . . means] How I detest this odious house! It is not *BM*. 4 dull] low *BM*. 8 overwhelm] almost kill *BM*.

Sir Humphry, shooting in the dark,
Makes answer quite beside the mark: 10
No doubt, my dear—I bade him come,
Engag'd myself to be at home,
And shall expect him at the door
Precisely when the clock strikes four.
You are so deaf, the lady cried,
(And rais'd her voice and frown'd beside,)
You are so sadly deaf, my dear,
What shall I do to make you hear?
Dismiss poor Harry! he replies;
Some people are more nice than wise— 20
For one slight trespass all this stir?
What if he did ride whip and spur,
'Twas but a mile—your fav'rite horse
Will never look one hair the worse.
Well, I protest 'tis past all bearing.—
Child! I am rather hard of hearing.—
Yes, truly—one must scream and bawl—
I tell you, you can't hear at all!
Then, with a voice exceeding low,
No matter if you hear or no. 30
Alas! and is domestic strife,
That sorest ill of human life,
A plague so little to be fear'd,
As to be wantonly incurr'd,
To gratify a fretful passion,
On ev'ry trivial provocation?
The kindest and the happiest pair
Will find occasion to forbear;
And something, ev'ry day they live,
To pity, and, perhaps, forgive. 40
But if infirmities that fall
In common to the lot of all—
A blemish or a sense impair'd—
Are crimes so little to be spar'd,—
Then farewell all that must create
The comfort of the wedded state;
Instead of harmony, 'tis jar
And tumult, and intestine war.
The love that cheers life's latest stage,
Proof against sickness and old age, 50
Preserv'd by virtue from declension,
Becomes not weary of attention;

11 bade] bid *BM.* 19 poor Harry] the coachman *BM.* 20 Some people are] You are by far *BM.* 21 blunder *BM.* *After* 22 *BM. adds* A wiser man than he might err. 23 'Twas . . . mile] Well, I protest *BM.*

But lives, when that exterior grace
Which first inspir'd the flame decays.
'Tis gentle, delicate, and kind,
To faults compassionate or blind,
And will with sympathy endure
Those evils it would gladly cure:
But angry, coarse, and harsh expression
Shows love to be a mere profession; 60
Proves that the heart is none of his,
Or soon expels him if it is.

ANTI-THELYPHTHORA

A TALE, IN VERSE

Ah miser,
Quanta laboras in Charybdi!
HOR. *Od.* i. 27.

[Written Jan. (?), 1781. Published anonymously as a 4to pamphlet, 1781.]

AIRY del Castro was as bold a knight
As ever earn'd a lady's love in fight.
Many he sought, but one above the rest
His tender heart victoriously impress'd:
In Fairy land was born the matchless dame,
The land of Dreams, Hypothesis her name.
There Fancy nurs'd her in ideal bow'rs,
And laid her soft in Amaranthine flow'rs;
Delighted with her babe, th' Inchantress smil'd,
And grac'd with all her gifts the fav'rite child. 10
Her, woo'd Sir Airy, by meandring streams,
In daily musings and in nightly dreams;
With all the flow'rs he found, he wove in haste
Wreaths for her brow, and girdles for her waist;
His time, his talents, and his ceaseless care
All consecrated to adorn the fair:
No pastime but with her he deign'd to take,
And if he studied, studied for her sake.
And, for Hypothesis was somewhat long,
Nor soft enough to suit a lover's tongue, 20
He called her Posy, with an amorous art,
And grav'd it on a gem, and wore it next his heart.
But she, inconstant as the beams that play
On rippling waters in an April day,
With many a freakish trick deceiv'd his pains,
To pathless wilds and unfrequented plains
Entic'd him from his oaths of knighthood far,
Forgetful of the glorious toils of war.
'Tis thus the tenderness that love inspires
Too oft betrays the vot'ries of his fires; 30

Borne far away on elevated wings,
They sport like wanton doves in airy rings,
And laws and duties are neglected things.
  Nor he alone address'd the wayward Fair,
Full many a knight had been entangled there.
But still whoever woo'd her or embrac'd,
On ev'ry mind some mighty spell she cast.
Some she would teach (for she was wondrous wise,
And made her dupes see all things with her eyes)
That forms material, whatsoe'er we dream, 40
Are not at all, or are not what they seem;
That substances and modes of ev'ry kind,
Are mere impressions on the passive mind;
And he that splits his cranium, breaks at most
A fancied head against a fancied post:
Others, that earth, ere sin had drown'd it all,
Was smooth and even as an iv'ry ball;
That all the various beauties we survey,
Hills, valleys, rivers, and the boundless sea,
Are but departures from the first design, 50
Effects of punishment and wrath divine.
She tutor'd some in Dædalus's art,
And promis'd they should act his wildgoose part,
On waxen pinions soar without a fall,
Swift as the proudest gander of them all.
  But fate reserv'd Sir Airy to maintain
The wildest project of her teeming brain;
That wedlock is not rig'rous as suppos'd,
But man, within a wider pale enclos'd,
May rove at will, where appetite shall lead, 60
Free as the lordly bull that ranges o'er the mead;
That forms and rites are tricks of human law,
As idle as the chatt'ring of a daw;
That lewd incontinence and lawless rape,
Are marriage in its true and proper shape;
That man by faith and truth is made a slave,
The ring a bauble, and the priest a knave.
  Fair fall the deed! the Knight exulting cried,
Now is the time to make the maid a bride!
  'Twas on the noon of an autumnal day, 70
October hight, but mild and fair as May,
When scarlet fruits the russet hedge adorn,
And floating films envelope ev'ry thorn,
When gently, as in June, the rivers glide,
And only miss the flow'rs that grac'd their side;
The linnet twitter'd out his parting song,
With many a chorister the woods among;

On southern banks the ruminating sheep
Lay snug and warm, 'twas summer's farewel peep.
Propitious to his fond intent, there grew 80
An arbour near at hand of thickest yew,
With many a boxen bush, close clipt between,
And Philyrea of a gilded green.
But what old Chaucer's merry page befits,
The chaster muse of modern days omits.
Suffice it then in decent terms to say,
She saw,—and turn'd her rosy cheek away.
Small need of pray'r-book or of priest I ween,
Where parties are agreed, retir'd the scene,
Occasion prompt, and appetite so keen. 90
Hypothesis (for with such magic pow'r
Fancy endued her in her natal hour)
From many a steaming lake and reeking bog,
Bade rise in haste a dank and drizzling fog,
That curtain'd round the scene where they repos'd,
And wood and lawn in dusky folds inclos'd.
Fear seiz'd the trembling sex; in every grove
They wept the wrongs of honourable love.
"In vain," they cried, "are hymeneal rites,
Vain our delusive hope of constant knights; 100
The marriage bond has lost its pow'r to bind,
And flutters loose, the sport of every wind;
The bride, while yet her bride's attire is on,
Shall mourn her absent lord, for he is gone,
Satiate of her, and weary of the same,
To distant wilds in quest of other game.
Ye fair Circassians! all your lutes employ,
Seraglios sing, and harams dance for joy,
For British nymphs, whose lords were lately true,
Nymphs quite as fair, and happier once than you,
Honour, esteem, and confidence forgot, 111
Feel all the meanness of your slavish lot.
O curst Hypothesis! your hellish arts
Seduce our husbands, and estrange their hearts.
Will none arise? no knight, who still retains
The blood of ancient worthies in his veins,
T' assert the charter of the chaste and fair,
Find out her treach'rous heart, and plant a dagger there!"
A knight (can he that serves the Fair do less?)
Starts at the call of beauty in distress; 120
And he that does not, whatsoe'er occurs,
Is recreant, and unworthy of his spurs[1].

[1] When a knight was degraded, his spurs were chopp'd off [C.].

Full many a champion, bent on hardy deed,
Call'd for his arms, and for his princely steed.
So swarm'd the Sabine youth, and grasp'd the shield,
When Roman rapine, by no laws withheld,
Lest Rome should end with her first founders' lives,
Made half their maids, *sans* ceremony, wives.
But not the mitred few: the soul their charge,
They left these bodily concerns at large; 130
Forms or no forms, pluralities or pairs,
Right reverend Sirs! was no concern of theirs.
The rest, alert and active as became
A courteous knighthood, caught the gen'rous flame;
One was accoutred when the cry began,
Knight of the silver moon, Sir Marmadan[1].
Oft as his Patroness, who rules the night,
Hangs out her lamp in yon cærulean height,
His vow was (and he well perform'd his vow)
Arm'd at all points, with terror on his brow, 140
To judge the land, to purge atrocious crimes,
And quell the shapeless monsters of the times.
For cedars fam'd, fair Lebanon supplied
The well-pois'd lance that quiver'd at his side;
Truth arm'd it with a point so keen, so just,
No spell or charm was proof against the thrust.
He couch'd it firm upon his puissant thigh,
And darting through his helm an eagle's eye,
On all the wings of chivalry advanc'd
To where the fond Sir Airy lay entranc'd. 150
He dreamt not of a foe, or if his fear
Foretold one, dreamt not of a foe so near.
Far other dreams his fev'rish mind employ'd,
Of rights restor'd, variety enjoy'd;
Of virtue too well fenc'd to fear a flaw,
Vice passing current by the stamp of law;
Large population on a lib'ral plan,
And woman trembling at the foot of man;
How simple wedlock fornication works,
And Christians marrying may convert the Turks.
The trumpet now spoke Marmadan at hand, 161
A trumpet that was heard through all the land.
His high-bred steed expands his nostrils wide,
And snorts aloud to cast the mist aside;
But he, the virtues of his lance to show,
Struck thrice the point upon his saddle-bow;
Three sparks ensued that chas'd it all away,
And set th' unseemly pair in open day.

[1] Monthly Review for October [C.].

To horse! he cried, or by this good right hand
And better spear, I smite you where you stand. 170
  Sir Airy, not a whit dismay'd or scar'd,
Buckled his helm, and to his steed repair'd;
Whose bridle, while he cropp'd the grass below,
Hung not far off upon a myrtle bough.
He mounts at once, such confidence infus'd
Th' insidious witch that had his wits abus'd;
And she, regardless of her softer kind,
Seiz'd fast the saddle and sprang up behind.
Oh shame to knighthood! his assailant cried;
Oh shame! ten thousand echoing nymphs replied.
Plac'd with advantage at his list'ning ear, 181
She whisper'd still that he had nought to fear;
That he was cas'd in such inchanted steel,
So polish'd and compact from head to heel,
Come ten, come twenty, should an army call
Thee to the field, thou shouldst withstand them all.
  By Dian's beams, Sir Marmadan exclaim'd,
The guiltiest still are ever least asham'd!
But guard thee well, expect no feign'd attack;
And guard beside the sorc'ress at thy back. 190
  He spoke indignant, and his spurs applied,
Though little need, to his good palfrey's side;
The barb sprang forward, and his lord, whose force
Was equal to the swiftness of his horse,
Rushed with a whirlwind's fury on the foe,
And, Phineas like, transfix'd them at a blow.
  Then sang the married and the maiden throng,
Love grac'd the theme, and harmony the song;
The Fauns and Satyrs, a lascivious race,
Shriek'd at the sight, and, conscious, fled the place:
And Hymen, trimming his dim torch anew, 201
His snowy mantle o'er his shoulders threw;
He turn'd, and view'd it oft on ev'ry side,
And redd'ning with a just and gen'rous pride,
Bless'd the glad beams of that propitious day,
The spot he loath'd so much for ever cleans'd away.

TO THE REV. MR. NEWTON

AN INVITATION INTO THE COUNTRY

[Written (?). Published 1782.]

THE swallows in their torpid state
  Compose their useless wing,
And bees in hives as idly wait
  The call of early spring.

The keenest frost that binds the stream,
The wildest wind that blows,
Are neither felt nor fear'd by them,
Secure of their repose. 8

But man, all feeling and awake,
The gloomy scene surveys;
With present ills his heart must ache,
And pant for brighter days.

Old winter, halting o'er the mead,
Bids me and Mary mourn;
But lovely spring peeps o'er his head,
And whispers your return. 16

Then April, with her sister May,
Shall chase him from the bow'rs;
And weave fresh garlands ev'ry day,
To crown the smiling hours.

And, if a tear, that speaks regret
Of happier times, appear,
A glimpse of joy, that we have met,
Shall shine, and dry the tear. 24

THE POET, THE OYSTER, AND SENSITIVE PLANT

[Written (?). Published 1782.]

An Oyster, cast upon the shore,
Was heard, though never heard before,
Complaining in a speech well worded,
And worthy thus to be recorded—
Ah, hapless wretch! condemn'd to dwell
For ever in my native shell;
Ordain'd to move when others please,
Not for my own content or ease;
But toss'd and buffeted about,
Now *in* the water and now *out*. 10
'Twere better to be born a stone,
Of ruder shape, and feeling none,
Than with a tenderness like mine,
And sensibilities so fine!
I envy that unfeeling shrub,
Fast rooted against ev'ry rub.
The plant he meant grew not far off,
And felt the sneer with scorn enough;
Was hurt, disgusted, mortified,
And with asperity replied. 20

(When, cry the botanists—and stare—
Did plants call'd sensitive grow there?
No matter when—a poet's muse is
To make them grow just where she chooses.)
You, shapeless nothing in a dish—
You that are but almost a fish—
I scorn your coarse insinuation,
And have most plentiful occasion
To wish myself the rock I view,
Or such another dolt as you: 30
For many a grave and learned clerk,
And many a gay unletter'd spark,
With curious touch examines me,
If I can feel as well as he;
And, when I bend, retire, and shrink,
Says—Well, 'tis more than one would think!
Thus life is spent (oh, fie upon't!)
In being touch'd, and crying—Don't!
A poet, in his ev'ning walk,
O'erheard and check'd this idle talk. 40
And your fine sense, he said, and your's,
Whatever evil it endures,
Deserves not, if so soon offended,
Much to be pitied or commended.
Disputes, though short, are far too long,
Where both alike are in the wrong;
Your feelings, in their full amount,
Are all upon your own account.
You, in your grotto-work enclos'd,
Complain of being thus expos'd; 50
Yet nothing feel in that rough coat,
Save when the knife is at your throat,
Wherever driv'n by wind or tide,
Exempt from ev'ry ill beside.
And, as for you, my Lady Squeamish,
Who reckon ev'ry touch a blemish,
If all the plants that can be found
Embellishing the scene around
Should droop and wither where they grow,
You would not feel at all—not you. 60
The noblest minds their virtue prove
By pity, sympathy, and love;
These, these are feelings truly fine,
And prove their owner half divine.
His censure reach'd them as he dealt it,
And each by shrinking show'd he felt it.

A CARD

[Written Feb., 1781 (MS. in British Museum). Published by Southey, 1836.]

POOR Vestris, griev'd beyond all measure,
To have incurr'd so much displeasure,
Although a Frenchman, disconcerted,
And though lightheeled, yet heavy-hearted,
Begs humbly to inform his friends
Next first of April he intends
To take a boat and row right down
To Cuckold's Point from Richmond town,
And as he goes, alert and gay,
Leap all the bridges in his way. 10
The boat, borne downward with the tide,
Shall catch him safe on t'other side.
He humbly hopes by this expedient
To prove himself their most obedient,
(Which shall be always his endeavour,
And jump into the former favour.

TO SIR JOSHUA REYNOLDS

[Written 1781 (?) (MS. in British Museum). Published by Johnson, 1824.]

DEAR President, whose art sublime
Gives perpetuity to time,
And bids transactions of a day
That fleeting hours would waft away,
To dark Futurity survive,
And in unfading beauty live,
You cannot with a grace decline
A special mandate of the Nine—
Yourself, whatever task you choose,
So much indebted to the Muse. 10
Thus say the sisterhood—We come—
Fix well your pallet on your thumb,
Prepare the pencil and the tints,
We come to furnish you with hints.
French disappointment, British glory
Must be the subject of the story.
First strike a curve, a graceful bow,
Then slope it to a point below;
Your outline easy, airy, light,
Fill'd up becomes a paper kite. 20
Let independence, sanguine, horrid,
Blaze, like a meteor in the forehead;
Beneath, (but lay aside your graces)
Draw *six-and-twenty rueful faces*,

24 The Members of Congress, I suppose, two from each colony—*note in BM.*

Each with a staring stedfast eye,
Fixt on his great and good ally.
France flies the kite—'tis on the wing—
Britannia's lightning cuts the string,
The wind that rais'd it, ere it ceases,
Just rends it into thirteen pieces, 30
Takes charge of ev'ry flutt'ring sheet,
And lays them all at George's feet.
Iberia trembling from afar
Renounces the confed'rate war:
Her efforts and her arts o'ercome,
France calls her shatter'd navies home:
Repenting Holland learns to mourn
The sacred treaties she has torn:
Astonishment and awe profound
Are stamp'd upon the nations round: 40
Without one friend, above all foes,
Britannia gives the world repose.

HEROISM

[Written 1781. Published 1782.]

THERE was a time when Ætna's silent fire
Slept unperceiv'd, the mountain yet entire;
When, conscious of no danger from below,
She tow'r'd a cloud-capt pyramid of snow.
No thunders shook with deep intestine sound
The blooming groves that girdled her around.
Her unctuous olives, and her purple vines,
(Unfelt the fury of those bursting mines)
The peasant's hopes, and not in vain, assur'd,
In peace upon her sloping sides matur'd. 10
When on a day, like that of the last doom,
A conflagration lab'ring in her womb,
She teem'd and heav'd with an infernal birth,
That shook the circling seas and solid earth.
Dark and voluminous the vapours rise,
And hang their horrors in the neighb'ring skies,
While through the stygian veil that blots the day,
In dazzling streaks, the vivid lightnings play.
But, oh! what muse, and in what pow'rs of song,
Can trace the torrent as it burns along? 20
Havoc and devastation in the van,
It marches o'er the prostrate works of man—
Vines, olives, herbage, forests, disappear,
And all the charms of a Sicilian year.
Revolving seasons, fruitless as they pass,
See it an uninform'd and idle mass;

Without a soil t' invite the tiller's care,
Or blade that might redeem it from despair.
Yet time at length (what will not time achieve?)
Clothes it with earth, and bids the produce live. 30
Once more the spiry myrtle crowns the glade,
And ruminating flocks enjoy the shade.
Oh, bliss precarious, and unsafe retreats,
Oh charming paradise of short-liv'd sweets!
The self-same gale that wafts the fragrance round
Brings to the distant ear a sullen sound;
Again the mountain feels th' imprison'd foe,
Again pours ruin on the vale below.
Ten thousand swains the wasted scene deplore,
That only future ages can restore. 40

Ye monarchs, whom the lure of honour draws,
Who write in blood the merits of your cause,
Who strike the blow, then plead your own defence—
Glory your aim, but justice your pretence;
Behold in Ætna's emblematic fires
The mischiefs your ambitious pride inspires!

Fast by the stream that bounds your just domain,
And tells you where ye have a right to reign,
A nation dwells, not envious of your throne,
Studious of peace, their neighbours', and their own.
Ill-fated race! how deeply must they rue 51
Their only crime, vicinity to you!
The trumpet sounds, your legions swarm abroad,
Through the ripe harvest lies their destin'd road;
At ev'ry step beneath their feet they tread
The life of multitudes, a nation's bread!
Earth seems a garden in its loveliest dress
Before them, and behind a wilderness.
Famine, and pestilence, her first-born son,
Attend to finish what the sword begun; 60
And echoing praises such as fiends might earn,
And folly pays, resound at your return;
A calm succeeds—but plenty, with her train
Of heart-felt joys, succeeds not soon again,
And years of pining indigence must show
What scourges are the gods that rule below.

Yet man, laborious man, by slow degrees,
(Such is his thirst of opulence and ease)
Plies all the sinews of industrious toil,
Gleans up the refuse of the gen'ral spoil, 70
Rebuilds the tow'rs that smok'd upon the plain,
And the sun gilds the shining spires again.

Increasing commerce and reviving art
Renew the quarrel on the conq'rors' part;

And the sad lesson must be learn'd once more,
That wealth within is ruin at the door.
What are ye, monarchs, laurel'd heroes, say—
But Ætnas of the suff'ring world ye sway?
Sweet nature, stripp'd of her embroider'd robe,
Deplores the wasted regions of her globe; 80
And stands a witness at truth's awful bar,
To prove you, there, destroyers as ye are.
Oh, place me in some heav'n-protected isle,
Where peace, and equity, and freedom smile;
Where no volcano pours his fiery flood,
No crested warrior dips his plume in blood;
Where pow'r secures what industry has won;
Where to succeed is not to be undone;
A land that distant tyrants hate in vain,
In Britain's isle, beneath a George's reign! 90

AN EPISTLE
TO A PROTESTANT LADY IN FRANCE

[Written in the summer of 1781. Published 1800 (vol. I. Appendix), and, clearly from the same MS. (now in the British Museum), by Bull, in 1801. A slightly different version was published by Hayley in 1803, said by him to be "from a copy corrected by the author."]

MADAM, a stranger's purpose in these lays
Is to congratulate, and not to praise.
To give the creature her Creator's due
Were sin in me, and an offence to you.
From man to man, or ev'n to woman paid,
Praise is the medium of a knavish trade,
A coin by craft for folly's use design'd,
Spurious, and only current with the blind.
The path of sorrow, and that path alone,
Leads to the land where sorrow is unknown; 10
No trav'ller ever reach'd that blest abode
Who found not thorns and briars in his road.
The world may dance along the flow'ry plain,
Cheer'd as they go by many a sprightly strain.
Where Nature has her mossy velvet spread,
With unshod feet they yet securely tread,
Admonish'd, scorn the caution and the friend,
Bent upon pleasure, heedless of its end.
But he, who knew what human hearts would prove,
How slow to learn the dictates of his love, 20

Title in Hayley: Epistle to a Lady in France, a person of great piety, and much afflicted. 3 her] the *Hayley*. 4 sin] guilt *Hayley*. 12 in] on *Hayley*. 15 yielding mosses *Hayley*. 16 they yet securely] and yet unharm'd, they *Hayley*. 18 upon] on all *and* all on *Hayley*.

That hard by nature and of stubborn will,
A life of ease would make them harder still,
In pity to the sinners he design'd
To rescue from the ruins of mankind,
Call'd for a cloud to darken all their years,
And said, "go spend them in the vale of tears."
Oh balmy gales of soul-reviving air,
Oh salutary streams that murmur there,
These flowing from the fount of grace above,
Those breath'd from lips of everlasting love! 30
The flinty soil indeed their feet annoys,
And sudden sorrow nips their springing joys,
An envious world will interpose its frown
To mar delights superior to its own,
And many a pang, experienc'd still within,
Reminds them of their hated inmate, sin;
But ills of ev'ry shape and ev'ry name,
Transform'd to blessings, miss their cruel aim,
And ev'ry moment's calm, that sooths the breast,
Is giv'n in earnest of eternal rest. 40
Ah, be not sad, although thy lot be cast
Far from the flock, and in a distant waste!
No shepherd's tents within thy view appear,
But the chief Shepherd is for ever near;
Thy tender sorrows and thy plaintive strain
Flow in a foreign land, but not in vain;
Thy tears all issue from a source divine,
And ev'ry drop bespeaks a Saviour thine—
'Twas thus in Gideon's fleece the dews were found,
And drought on all the drooping herbs around. 50

TO THE
REV. WILLIAM CAWTHORNE UNWIN

[Written 1781. Published 1782. There is a MS. copy in the British Museum.]

UNWIN, I should but ill repay
The kindness of a friend,
Whose worth deserves as warm a lay
As ever friendship penn'd,
Thy name omitted in a page
That would reclaim a vicious age. 6

23 the sinners he] a chosen few *Hayley*: the souls his Grace *first in 1805 ed. of Poems*. 24 T' escape the common ruin of their kind *Hayley*. 32 Chill blasts of trouble nip *Hayley*. 42 boundless *Hayley*. 43 shepherds' *Hayley*. 44 is for ever] even there is *Hayley*. 49 'Twas thus] So once *Hayley*. 50 herbs] flocks *Hayley* (*1803*).

An union form'd, as mine with thee,
  Not rashly, or in sport,
May be as fervent in degree,
  And faithful in its sort,
And may as rich in comfort prove,
As that of true fraternal love. 12

The bud inserted in the rind,
  The bud of peach or rose,
Adorns, though diff'ring in its kind,
  The stock whereon it grows,
With flow'r as sweet, or fruit as fair,
As if produc'd by nature there. 18

Not rich, I render what I may—
  I seize thy name in haste,
And place it in this first assay,
  Lest this should prove the last.
'Tis where it should be—in a plan
That holds in view the good of man. 24

The poet's lyre, to fix his fame,
  Should be the poet's heart;
Affection lights a brighter flame
  Than ever blaz'd by art.
No muses on these lines attend,
I sink the poet in the friend. 30

FRIENDSHIP

[Written Nov., 1781. Published 1800 (vol. I. Appendix), and by Bull in 1801. There is a MS. copy in the British Museum, whose variant readings are given below. Hayley published a version with many important differences in 1803; this is printed entire among the notes at the end of the volume.]

What virtue or what mental grace,
But men unqualified and base
  Will boast it their possession?
Profusion apes the noble part
Of liberality of heart,
  And dullness of discretion. 6

If ev'ry polish'd gem we find,
Illuminating heart or mind,
  Provoke to imitation;
No wonder friendship does the same,
That jewel of the purest flame,
  Or rather constellation. 12

Friendship—11 purest] brightest *BM*.

No knave but boldly will pretend
The requisites that form a friend,
  A real and a sound one,
Nor any fool he would deceive,
But proves as ready to believe,
  And dreams that he has found one. 18

Candid and generous and just,
Boys care but little whom they trust,
  An error soon corrected—
For who but learns in riper years,
That man, when smoothest he appears,
  Is most to be suspected? 24

But here again a danger lies,
Lest, having misapplied our eyes,
  And taken trash for treasure,
We should unwarily conclude
Friendship a false ideal good,
  A mere Utopian pleasure. 30

An acquisition rather rare
Is yet no subject of despair;
  Nor is it wise complaining,
If either on forbidden ground,
Or where it was not to be found,
  We sought without attaining. 36

No friendship will abide the test,
That stands on sordid interest,
  Or mean self-love erected;
Nor such as may awhile subsist
Between the sot and sensualist,
  For vicious ends connected. 42

Who seeks a friend, should come dispos'd
T' exhibit in full bloom disclos'd
  The graces and the beauties
That form the character he seeks,
For 'tis an union that bespeaks
  Reciprocated duties. 48

Mutual attention is implied,
And equal truth on either side,
  And constantly supported;
'Tis senseless arrogance t' accuse
Another of sinister views,
  Our own as much distorted. 54

17 prove *Bull.* 18 dream *BM.*, *Bull.* has *BM.*: had *1800*, *Bull.* 22 in] with *BM.* 26 misemploy'd *BM.*, *Bull.* 48 Reciprocated] A just exchange of *BM.* 49 Mutual attention] Reciprocation *BM.* 54 Your *BM.*

But will sincerity suffice?
It is indeed above all price,
  And must be made the basis;
But ev'ry virtue of the soul
Must constitute the charming whole,
  All shining in their places. 60

A fretful temper will divide
The closest knot that may be tied,
  By ceaseless sharp corrosion;
A temper passionate and fierce
May suddenly your joys disperse
  At one immense explosion. 66

In vain the talkative unite
In hopes of permanent delight—
  The secret just committed,
Forgetting its important weight,
They drop through mere desire to prate,
  And by themselves outwitted. 72

How bright soe'er the prospect seems,
All thoughts of friendship are but dreams
  If envy chance to creep in;
An envious man, if you succeed,
May prove a dangerous foe indeed,
  But not a friend worth keeping. 78

As envy pines at good possess'd,
So jealousy looks forth distress'd
  On good that seems approaching,
And if success his steps attend,
Discerns a rival in a friend,
  And hates him for encroaching. 84

Hence authors of illustrious name,
Unless belied by common fame,
  Are sadly prone to quarrel,
To deem the wit a friend displays
A tax upon their own just praise,
  And pluck each other's laurel. 90

A man renown'd for repartee
Will seldom scruple to make free
  With friendship's finest feeling,
Will thrust a dagger at your breast,
And say he wounded you in jest,
  By way of balm for healing. 96

Whoever keeps an open ear
For tattlers, will be sure to hear

56 It is indeed] I grant it is *BM*. 62 may] can *BM*. 63 By] With *BM*. 79 goods *1800*.

The trumpet of contention;
Aspersion is the babbler's trade,
To listen is to lend him aid,
And rush into dissension. 102

A friendship, that in frequent fits
Of controversial rage emits
The sparks of disputation,
Like Hand-in-Hand insurance plates
Most unavoidably creates
The thought of conflagration. 108

Some fickle creatures boast a soul
True as a needle to the pole,
Their humour yet so various—
They manifest their whole life through
The needle's deviations too,
Their love is so precarious. 114

The great and small but rarely meet
On terms of amity complete,
Plebeians must surrender
And yield so much to noble folk,
It is combining fire with smoke,
Obscurity with splendour. 120

Some are so placid and serene
(As Irish bogs are always green)
They sleep secure from waking;
And are indeed a bog, that bears
Your unparticipated cares
Unmov'd and without quaking. 126

Courtier and patriot cannot mix
Their het'rogeneous politics
Without an effervescence,
Like that of salts with lemon juice,
Which does not yet like that produce
A friendly coalescence. 132

Religion should extinguish strife,
And make a calm of human life;
But friends that chance to differ
On points, which God has left at large,
How fiercely will they meet and charge,
No combatants are stiffer! 138

102 discussion *wrongly Bull.* 110 a] the *BM.* *Verses* 20 *and* 21 (*ll. 115–126*) *transposed in BM.*
121–3 As Irish bogs are always green,
Some minds are sleepy and serene,
Whose heart soe'er is aching *BM.*
133 should] ought t' *BM.* 136 which] that *BM.* 137 freely *1800.*

To prove at last my main intent
Needs no expence of argument,
No cutting and contriving—
Seeking a real friend we seem
T' adopt the chymists' golden dream,
With still less hope of thriving. 144

Sometimes the fault is all our own,
Some blemish in due time made known
By trespass or omission;
Sometimes occasion brings to light
Our friend's defect long hid from sight
And even from suspicion. 150

Then judge yourself, and prove your man
As circumspectly as you can,
And having made election,
Beware, no negligence of yours,
Such as a friend but ill endures,
Enfeeble his affection. 156

That secrets are a sacred trust,
That friends should be sincere and just,
That constancy befits them,
Are observations on the case,
That savour much of common place,
And all the world admits them. 162

But 'tis not timber, lead, and stone,
An architect requires alone
To finish a fine building—
The palace were but half complete,
If he could possibly forget
The carving and the gilding. 168

The man that hails you Tom or Jack,
And proves by thumps upon your back
How he esteems your merit,
Is such a friend, that one had need
Be very much his friend indeed
To pardon or to bear it. 174

As similarity of mind,
Or something not to be defin'd,
First fixes our attention ;
So manners decent and polite,
The same we practis'd at first sight,
Must save it from declension. 180

139 at last] alas *BM.* 146 in due time] suddenly *BM.* 159 constancy] sympathy *BM.* *Verses* 29 *and* 30 (*ll. 169-181*) *transposed in BM.* 171 he esteems] well he knows *BM.*

Some act upon this prudent plan,
"Say little and hear all you can:"
Safe policy, but hateful—
So barren sands imbibe the show'r,
But render neither fruit nor flow'r,
Unpleasant and ungrateful. 186

The man I trust, if shy to me,
Shall find me as reserv'd as he;
No subterfuge or pleading
Shall win my confidence again,
I will by no means entertain
A spy on my proceeding. 192

These samples—for alas! at last
These are but samples, and a taste
Of evils yet unmention'd—
May prove the task a task indeed,
In which 'tis much if we succeed
However well-intention'd. 198

Pursue the search, and you will find
Good sense and knowledge of mankind
To be at least expedient,
And after summing all the rest,
Religion ruling in the breast
A principal ingredient. 204

The noblest Friendship ever shewn
The Saviour's history makes known,
Though some have turn'd and turn'd it;
And whether being craz'd or blind,
Or seeking with a bias'd mind,
Have not, it seems, discern'd it. 210

Oh Friendship! if my soul forego
Thy dear delights while here below;
To mortify and grieve me,
May I myself at last appear
Unworthy, base, and insincere,
Or may my friend deceive me! 216

189-191 And deaf to all his pleading
I will withdraw my trust again,
Determin'd not to entertain *BM*.

200 Good sense] Wisdom *BM*. *Last two verses omitted in BM., which has instead:*

There is a sober serious grace,
A sanctity in friendship's face,
That proves it heav'n-defended;
The love of woman not so pure,
Nor ev'n when truest so secure
To last 'till life is ended.

A POETICAL EPISTLE TO LADY AUSTEN

[Written Dec. 17, 1781. Published by Hayley, 1803.]

DEAR Anna—between friend and friend,
Prose answers every common end;
Serves, in a plain and homely way,
T' express th' occurrence of the day;
Our health, the weather, and the news;
What walks we take, what books we choose;
And all the floating thoughts we find
Upon the surface of the mind.
  But when a Poet takes the pen,
Far more alive than other men, 10
He feels a gentle tingling come
Down to his finger and his thumb,
Deriv'd from nature's noblest part,
The centre of a glowing heart!
And this is what the world, who knows
No flights above the pitch of prose,
His more sublime vagaries slighting,
Denominates an itch for writing.
No wonder I, who scribble rhyme,
To catch the triflers of the time, 20
And tell them truths divine and clear,
Which, couch'd in prose, they will not hear;
Who labour hard to allure and draw
The loiterers I never saw,
Should feel that itching, and that tingling,
With all my purpose intermingling,
To your intrinsic merit true,
When call'd t' address myself to you.
  Mysterious are his ways, whose power
Brings forth that unexpected hour, 30
When minds, that never met before,
Shall meet, unite, and part no more:
It is th' allotment of the skies,
The hand of the Supremely Wise,
That guides and governs our affections,
And plans and orders our connexions;
Directs us in our distant road,
And marks the bounds of our abode.
Thus we were settled when you found us,
Peasants and children all around us, 40
Not dreaming of so dear a friend,
Deep in the abyss of Silver-End[1].
Thus Martha, e'en against her will,
Perch'd on the top of yonder hill;

[1] An obscure part of Olney, adjoining to the residence of Cowper, which faced the market-place [H.].

And you, though you must needs prefer
The fairer scenes of sweet Sancerre [1],
Are come from distant Loire, to choose
A cottage on the banks of Ouse.
This page of Providence, quite new,
And now just op'ning to our view, 50
Employs our present thoughts and pains,
To guess, and spell, what it contains:
But day by day, and year by year,
Will make the dark ænigma clear;
And furnish us, perhaps, at last,
Like other scenes already past,
With proof, that we, and our affairs
Are part of a Jehovah's cares;
For God unfolds, by slow degrees,
The purport of his deep decrees; 60
Sheds every hour a clearer light
In aid of our defective sight;
And spreads, at length, before the soul,
A beautiful and perfect whole,
Which busy man's inventive brain
Toils to anticipate in vain.

Say, Anna, had you never known
The beauties of a rose full-blown,
Could you, tho' luminous your eye,
By looking on the bud, descry, 70
Or guess, with a prophetic power,
The future splendour of the flower?
Just so th' Omnipotent, who turns
The system of a world's concerns,
From mere minutiæ can educe
Events of most important use;
And bid a dawning sky display
The blaze of a meridian day.
The works of man tend, one and all,
As needs they must, from great to small; 80
And vanity absorbs at length
The monuments of human strength.
But who can tell how vast the plan
Which this day's incident began?
Too small perhaps the slight occasion
For our dim-sighted observation;
It passed unnotic'd, as the bird
That cleaves the yielding air unheard,
And yet may prove, when understood,
A harbinger of endless good. 90

[1] Lady Austen's residence in France [H.].

46 fairest *Hayley* (*1806*).

Not that I deem, or mean to call
Friendship, a blessing cheap, or small:
But merely to remark, that ours,
Like some of nature's sweetest flow'rs,
Rose from a seed of tiny size,
That seem'd to promise no such prize:
A transient visit intervening,
And made almost without a meaning,
(Hardly th' effect of inclination,
Much less of pleasing expectation) 100
Produc'd a friendship, then begun,
That has cemented us in one;
And plac'd it in our power to prove,
By long fidelity and love,
That Solomon has wisely spoken;
"A three-fold cord is not soon broken."

TO MISS CREUZÉ ON HER BIRTHDAY

[Written Nov., 1780 (?); see notes: (MS. in British Museum). Published by Hayley, 1803.]

How many between East and West
Disgrace their parent earth,
Whose deeds constrain us to detest
The day that gave them birth!

Not so, when Stella's natal morn
Revolving months restore,
We can rejoice that *She* was born,
And wish her born *once more.* 8

THE FLATTING MILL

[Written Dec. 20, 1781. Published by Johnson, 1815. There is a copy among the Ash MSS.]

When a bar of pure silver or ingot of gold
Is sent to be flatted or wrought into length,
It is pass'd between cylinders often, and roll'd
In an engine of utmost mechanical strength.

Thus tortur'd and squeezed, at last it appears,
Like a loose heap of ribbon, a glittering show,
Like music it tinkles and rings in your ears,
And warm'd by the pressure is all in a glow. 8

This process achiev'd, it is doom'd to sustain
The thump after thump of a gold-beater's mallet,
And at last is of service in sickness or pain
To cover a pill from a delicate palate.

Alas for the poet! who dares undertake
To urge reformation of national ill,
His head and his heart are both likely to ache 15
With the double employment of mallet and mill.

If he wish to instruct, he must learn to delight,
Smooth ductile and even his fancy must flow,
Must tinkle and glitter, like gold to the sight,
And catch in its progress a sensible glow.

After all, he must beat it as thin and as fine
As the leaf that enfolds what an invalid swallows,
For truth is unwelcome however divine,
And unless you adorn it, a nausea follows. 24

TO THE REV. MR. NEWTON,

RECTOR OF ST. MARY, WOOLNOTH

[Written May 28, 1782. Published by Johnson, 1815.]

SAYS the pipe to the snuff-box, I can't understand
What the ladies and gentlemen see in your face,
That you are in fashion all over the land,
And I am so much fallen into disgrace.

Do but see what a pretty contemplative air
I give to the company—pray do but note 'em—
You would think that the wise men of Greece were all there,
Or, at least, would suppose them the wise men of Gotham. 8

My breath is as sweet as the breath of blown roses,
While you are a nuisance where'er you appear;
There is nothing but sniv'ling and blowing of noses,
Such a noise as turns any man's stomach to hear.

The Flatting Mill—10 thumps and the blows *A*. 14 urge] press *A*. 17 If . . . instruct] Before he can teach *A*.
17–20 *re-written at end of poem in A. thus:*
His thoughts like the gold should be sterling and true,
As ductile and even his fancy should flow,
Should jingle and tinkle, and shine to the view,
And catch in its progress a sensible glow.
19 Must jingle and tinkle and shine to the sight *A*. 21 beat it as thin and] beat it and thump it *and* hammer and work it *A*.
24 adorn] disguise *A*.

Then lifting his lid in a delicate way,
And op'ning his mouth with a smile quite engaging,
The box in reply was heard plainly to say,
What a silly dispute is this we are waging! 16

If you have a little of merit to claim,
You may thank the sweet-smelling Virginian weed,
And I, if I seem to deserve any blame,
The before-mention'd drug in apology plead.

Thus neither the praise nor the blame is our own,
No room for a sneer, much less a cachinnus,
We are vehicles, not of tobacco alone, 23
But of any thing else they may choose to put in us.

TO THE REV. WILLIAM BULL

[Written June 22, 1782. Published by Johnson, 1824.]

MY DEAR FRIEND,
If reading verse be your delight,
'Tis mine as much, or more, to write;
But what we would, so weak is man,
Lies oft remote from what we can.
For instance, at this very time
I feel a wish, by cheerful rhyme
To sooth my friend, and, had I pow'r,
To cheat him of an anxious hour;
Not meaning (for I must confess,
It were but folly to suppress,) 10
His pleasure, or his good alone,
But squinting partly at my own.
But though the sun is flaming high
I' th' centre of yon arch, the sky,
And he had once (and who but he?)
The name for setting genius free,
Yet whether poets of past days
Yielded him undeserved praise,
And he by no uncommon lot
Was fam'd for virtues he had not; 20
Or whether, which is like enough,
His Highness may have taken huff,
So seldom sought with invocation,
Since it has been the reigning fashion
To disregard his inspiration,
I seem no brighter in my wits
For all the radiance he emits,
Than if I saw, through midnight vapour,
The glimm'ring of a farthing taper.
Oh for a succedaneum, then, 30
T' accelerate a creeping pen!

Oh for a ready succedaneum,
Quod caput, cerebrum, et cranium
Pondere liberet exoso,
Et morbo jam caliginoso!
'Tis here; this oval box well fill'd
With best tobacco, finely mill'd,
Beats all Anticyra's pretences
To disengage th' encumber'd senses.
Oh Nymph of Transatlantic fame, 40
Where'er thine haunt, whate'er thy name,
Whether reposing on the side
Of Oroonoquo's spacious tide,
Or list'ning with delight not small
To Niagara's distant fall,
'Tis thine to cherish and to feed
The pungent nose-refreshing weed,
Which, whether pulveriz'd it gain
A speedy passage to the brain,
Or whether, touch'd with fire, it rise 50
In circling eddies to the skies,
Does thought more quicken and refine
Than all the breath of all the Nine—
Forgive the Bard, if Bard he be,
Who once too wantonly made free,
To touch with a satiric wipe
That symbol of thy power, the pipe;
So may no blight infest thy plains,
And no unseasonable rains,
And so may smiling Peace once more 60
Visit America's sad shore;
And thou, secure from all alarms
Of thund'ring drums, and glitt'ring arms,
Rove unconfin'd beneath the shade
Thy wide expanded leaves have made;
So may thy votaries increase,
And fumigation never cease.
May Newton with renew'd delights
Perform thy odorif'rous rites,
While clouds of incense half divine 70
Involve thy disappearing shrine;
And so may smoke-inhaling Bull
Be always filling, never full.

THE COLUBRIAD

[Written Aug., 1782. Published by Hayley, 1806.]

CLOSE by the threshold of a door nail'd fast
Three kittens sat: each kitten look'd aghast.

I, passing swift and inattentive by,
At the three kittens cast a careless eye;
Not much concern'd to know what they did there,
Not deeming kittens worth a poet's care.
But presently a loud and furious hiss
Caused me to stop, and to exclaim—what's this?
When, lo! upon the threshold met my view,
With head erect, and eyes of fiery hue, 10
A viper, long as Count de Grasse's queue.
Forth from his head his forked tongue he throws,
Darting it full against a kitten's nose;
Who having never seen in field or house
The like, sat still and silent, as a mouse:
Only, projecting with attention due
Her whisker'd face, she ask'd him—who are you?
On to the hall went I, with pace not slow,
But swift as lightning, for a long Dutch hoe;
With which well arm'd I hasten'd to the spot, 20
To find the viper. But I found him not,
And, turning up the leaves and shrubs around,
Found only, that he was not to be found.
But still the kittens, sitting as before,
Sat watching close the bottom of the door.
I hope—said I—the villain I would kill
Has slipt between the door and the door's sill;
And if I make despatch, and follow hard,
No doubt but I shall find him in the yard:—
For long ere now it should have been rehears'd, 30
'Twas in the garden that I found him first.
E'en there I found him; there the full-grown cat
His head with velvet paw did gently pat,
As curious as the kittens erst had been
To learn what this phenomenon might mean.
Fill'd with heroic ardour at the sight,
And fearing every moment he would bite,
And rob our household of our only cat
That was of age to combat with a rat,
With out-stretch'd hoe I slew him at the door, 40
And taught him NEVER TO COME THERE NO MORE.

TO LADY AUSTEN,

WRITTEN IN RAINY WEATHER

[Written Aug. 12, 1782. Published by Hayley, 1803.]

To watch the storms, and hear the sky
Give all our almanacks the lie;
To shake with cold, and see the plains
In autumn drown'd with wintry rains;

'Tis thus I spend my moments here,
And wish myself a Dutch mynheer;
I then should have no need of wit;
For lumpish Hollander unfit!
Nor should I then repine at mud,
Or meadows delug'd with a flood; 10
But in a bog live well content,
And find it just my element:
Should be a clod, and not a man,
Nor wish in vain for Sister Ann,
With charitable aid to drag
My mind out of its proper quag;
Should have the genius of a boor,
And no ambition to have more.

THE DISTRESSED TRAVELLERS

OR, LABOUR IN VAIN

An excellent New Song to a Tune never sung before.

[Written Aug., 1782 (?). Published in *The Monthly Magazine*, Jan., 1808].

I SING of a journey to Clifton [1]
We would have perform'd if we could,
Without cart or barrow to lift on
Poor Mary [2] and me thro' the mud.
Sle sla slud,
Stuck in the mud;
Oh it is pretty to wade through a flood! 7

So away we went, slipping and sliding,
Hop, hop, *à la mode de deux* frogs,
'Tis near as good walking as riding,
When ladies are dress'd in their clogs.
Wheels, no doubt,
Go briskly about,
But they clatter and rattle, and make such a rout!

She. "Well! now I protest it is charming; 15
How finely the weather improves!
That cloud, though, is rather alarming,
How slowly and stately it moves!"
He. "Pshaw! never mind,
'Tis not in the wind,
We are travelling south and shall leave it behind."

She. "I am glad we are come for an airing, 22
For folks may be pounded and penn'd,
Until they grow rusty, not caring
To stir half a mile to an end."

[1] A village near Olney [1808]. [2] Mrs. Unwin [1808].

He. "The longer we stay,
The longer we may;
It's a folly to think about weather or way." 28

She. "But now I begin to be frighted;
If I fall, what a way I should roll!
I am glad that the bridge was indicted,—
Stop! stop! I am sunk in a hole!"

He. "Nay, never care!
'Tis a common affair;
You'll not be the last that will set a foot there." 35

She. "Let me breathe now a little, and ponder
On what it were better to do;
That terrible lane I see yonder,
I think we shall never get through."

He. "So think I:—
But, by the bye,
We never shall know, if we never should try." 42

She. "But should we get there, how shall we get home?
What a terrible deal of bad road we have past!
Slipping and sliding; and if we should come
To a difficult stile, I am ruin'd at last!
Oh this lane!
Now it is plain
That struggling and striving is labour in vain." 49

He. "Stick fast there while I go and look—"

She. "Don't go away, for fear I should fall!"

He. "I have examin'd it every nook,
And what you have here is a sample of all.
Come, wheel round,
The dirt we have found
Would be an estate at a farthing a pound." 56

Now, sister Anne[1], the guitar you must take,
Set it, and sing it, and make it a song;
I have varied the verse for variety's sake,
And cut it off short—because it was long.
'Tis hobbling and lame,
Which critics won't blame,
For the sense and the sound, they say, should be the same. 63

[1] The late Lady Austen [1808].

ON THE LOSS OF THE ROYAL GEORGE

WRITTEN WHEN THE NEWS ARRIVED,

by desire of Lady Austen, who wanted words to the March in Scipio.

[Written Sept. (?), 1782. Published by Hayley, 1803. The MSS. of both the English and the Latin poems are in the British Museum.]

TOLL for the brave—
The brave! that are no more:
All sunk beneath the wave,
Fast by their native shore.
Eight hundred of the brave,
Whose courage well was tried,
Had made the vessel heel
And laid her on her side;
A land-breeze shook the shrouds,
And she was overset;
Down went the Royal George,
With all her crew complete. 12

Toll for the brave—
Brave Kempenfelt is gone,
His last sea-fight is fought,
His work of glory done.
It was not in the battle,
No tempest gave the shock,
She sprang no fatal leak,
She ran upon no rock;
His sword was in the sheath,
His fingers held the pen,
When Kempenfelt went down
With twice four hundred men. 24

Weigh the vessel up,
Once dreaded by our foes,
And mingle with your cup
The tears that England owes;
Her timbers yet are sound,
And she may float again,
Full charg'd with England's thunder,
And plough the distant main;
But Kempenfelt is gone,
His victories are o'er;
And he and his Eight hundred
Must plough the wave no more. 36

21 the] its *Hayley*. 27 your] our *Hayley*. 36 Must] Shall *Hayley*.

IN SUBMERSIONEM NAVIGII CUI GEORGIUS REGALE NOMEN INDITUM

[Written 1782. Published by Hayley, 1803.]

PLANGIMUS fortes—periere fortes—
Patrium propter periere littus,
Bis quater centum subito sub alto
Æquore mersi.

Navis innitens lateri jacebat,
Malus ad summas trepidabat undas,
Cum levis, funes quatiens, ad imum
Depulit aura. 8

Plangimus fortes—nimis, heu, caducam
Fortibus vitam voluere Parcæ,
Nec sinunt ultra tibi nos recentes
Nectere laurus,

Magne, qui nomen licet incanorum
Traditum ex multis atavis tulisti—
At tuos olim memorabit ævum
Omne triumphos. 16

Non hyems illos furibunda mersit,
Non mari in clauso scopuli latentes,
Non fissa rimis abies, nec atrox
Abstulit ensis.

Navitæ sed tum nimium jocosi
Voce fallebant hilari laborem,
Et quiescebat, calamoque dextram im-
pleverat Heros. 24

Vos quibus cordi est grave opus piumque,
Humidum ex alto spolium levate,
Et putrescentes sub aquis amicos
Reddite amicis.

Hi quidem (sic Dis placuit) fuere;
Sed ratis nondum putris ire possit
Rursus in bellum, Britonumque nomen
Tollere ad astra. 32

19 Fissa non *Hayley, to mend the metre.*

THE DIVERTING HISTORY OF JOHN GILPIN,

SHOWING HOW HE WENT FARTHER THAN HE INTENDED, AND CAME SAFE HOME AGAIN

[Written Oct., 1782. Published anonymously in *The Public Advertiser*, Nov. 14, 1782; afterwards in 1785. The manuscript copy in the British Museum is obviously an early version, before Cowper had finally revised the poem for publication among his Poems: the variant readings taken from it are given in the notes at the end of the volume.]

JOHN GILPIN was a citizen
  Of credit and renown,
A train-band captain eke was he
  Of famous London town.

John Gilpin's spouse said to her dear—
  Though wedded we have been
These twice ten tedious years, yet we
  No holiday have seen. 8

To-morrow is our wedding-day,
  And we will then repair
Unto the Bell at Edmonton
  All in a chaise and pair.

My sister, and my sister's child,
  Myself, and children three,
Will fill the chaise; so you must ride
  On horseback after we. 16

He soon replied—I do admire
  Of womankind but one,
And you are she, my dearest dear,
  Therefore it shall be done.

I am a linen-draper bold,
  As all the world doth know,
And my good friend the calender
  Will lend his horse to go. 24

Quoth Mrs. Gilpin—That's well said;
  And, for that wine is dear,
We will be furnish'd with our own,
  Which is both bright and clear.

John Gilpin kiss'd his loving wife;
  O'erjoy'd was he to find
That, though on pleasure she was bent,
  She had a frugal mind. 32

The morning came, the chaise was brought,
  But yet was not allow'd
To drive up to the door, lest all
  Should say that she was proud.

So three doors off the chaise was stay'd,
  Where they did all get in;
Six precious souls, and all agog
  To dash through thick and thin! 40

Smack went the whip, round went the wheels,
  Were never folk so glad,
The stones did rattle underneath,
  As if Cheapside were mad.

John Gilpin at his horse's side
  Seiz'd fast the flowing mane,
And up he got, in haste to ride,
  But soon came down again; 48

For saddle-tree scarce reach'd had he,
  His journey to begin,
When, turning round his head, he saw
  Three customers come in.

So down he came; for loss of time,
  Although it griev'd him sore,
Yet loss of pence, full well he knew,
  Would trouble him much more. 56

'Twas long before the customers
  Were suited to their mind,
When Betty screaming came down stairs—
  "The wine is left behind!"

Good lack! quoth he—yet bring it me,
  My leathern belt likewise,
In which I bear my trusty sword
  When I do exercise. 64

Now mistress Gilpin (careful soul!)
  Had two stone bottles found,
To hold the liquor that she lov'd,
  And keep it safe and sound.

Each bottle had a curling ear,
  Through which the belt he drew,
And hung a bottle on each side,
  To make his balance true. 72

Then, over all, that he might be
  Equipp'd from top to toe,
His long red cloak, well brush'd and neat,
  He manfully did throw.

Now see him mounted once again
Upon his nimble steed,
Full slowly pacing o'er the stones,
With caution and good heed! 80

But, finding soon a smoother road
Beneath his well-shod feet,
The snorting beast began to trot,
Which gall'd him in his seat.

So, Fair and softly, John he cried,
But John he cried in vain;
That trot became a gallop soon,
In spite of curb and rein. 88

So stooping down, as needs he must
Who cannot sit upright,
He grasp'd the mane with both his hands,
And eke with all his might.

His horse, who never in that sort
Had handled been before,
What thing upon his back had got
Did wonder more and more. 96

Away went Gilpin, neck or nought;
Away went hat and wig!—
He little dreamt, when he set out,
Of running such a rig!

The wind did blow, the cloak did fly,
Like streamer long and gay,
Till, loop and button failing both,
At last it flew away. 104

Then might all people well discern
The bottles he had slung;
A bottle swinging at each side,
As hath been said or sung.

The dogs did bark, the children scream'd,
Up flew the windows all;
And ev'ry soul cried out—Well done!
As loud as he could bawl. 112

Away went Gilpin—who but he?
His fame soon spread around—
He carries weight! he rides a race!
'Tis for a thousand pound!

And still, as fast as he drew near,
'Twas wonderful to view
How in a trice the turnpike-men
Their gates wide open threw. 120

And now, as he went bowing down
  His reeking head full low,
The bottles twain behind his back
  Were shatter'd at a blow.

Down ran the wine into the road,
  Most piteous to be seen,
Which made his horse's flanks to smoke
  As they had basted been. 128

But still he seem'd to carry weight,
  With leathern girdle brac'd;
For all might see the bottle-necks
  Still dangling at his waist.

Thus all through merry Islington
  These gambols he did play,
And till he came unto the Wash
  Of Edmonton so gay. 136

And there he threw the wash about
  On both sides of the way,
Just like unto a trundling mop,
  Or a wild goose at play.

At Edmonton his loving wife
  From the balcony spied
Her tender husband, wond'ring much
  To see how he did ride. 144

Stop, stop, John Gilpin!—Here's the house—
  They all at once did cry;
The dinner waits, and we are tir'd:
  Said Gilpin—So am I!

But yet his horse was not a whit
  Inclin'd to tarry there;
For why?—his owner had a house
  Full ten miles off, at Ware. 152

So like an arrow swift he flew,
  Shot by an archer strong;
So did he fly—which brings me to
  The middle of my song.

Away went Gilpin, out of breath,
  And sore against his will,
Till at his friend the calender's
  His horse at last stood still. 160

The calender, amaz'd to see
  His neighbour in such trim,
Laid down his pipe, flew to the gate,
  And thus accosted him:—

What news? what news? your tidings tell;
  Tell me you must and shall—
Say why bare-headed you are come,
  Or why you come at all? 168

Now Gilpin had a pleasant wit,
  And lov'd a timely joke;
And thus unto the calender
  In merry guise he spoke:—

I came because your horse would come;
  And, if I well forebode,
My hat and wig will soon be here—
  They are upon the road. 176

The calender, right glad to find
  His friend in merry pin,
Return'd him not a single word,
  But to the house went in;

Whence straight he came with hat and wig;
  A wig that flow'd behind,
A hat not much the worse for wear,
  Each comely in its kind. 184

He held them up, and, in his turn,
  Thus show'd his ready wit—
My head is twice as big as your's,
  They therefore needs must fit.

But let me scrape the dirt away
  That hangs upon your face;
And stop and eat, for well you may
  Be in a hungry case. 192

Said John—It is my wedding-day,
  And all the world would stare,
If wife should dine at Edmonton
  And I should dine at Ware!

So, turning to his horse, he said—
  I am in haste to dine;
'Twas for your pleasure you came here,
  You shall go back for mine. 200

Ah, luckless speech, and bootless boast!
  For which he paid full dear;
For, while he spake, a braying ass
  Did sing most loud and clear;

Whereat his horse did snort, as he
  Had heard a lion roar,
And gallop'd off with all his might,
  As he had done before. 208

Away went Gilpin, and away
  Went Gilpin's hat and wig!
He lost them sooner than at first—
  For why?—they were too big!

Now, mistress Gilpin, when she saw
  Her husband posting down
Into the country far away,
  She pull'd out half a crown; 216

And thus unto the youth she said
  That drove them to the Bell—
This shall be yours when you bring back
  My husband safe and well.

The youth did ride, and soon did meet
  John coming back amain;
Whom in a trice he tried to stop,
  By catching at his rein; 224

But, not performing what he meant,
  And gladly would have done,
The frighted steed he frighted more,
  And made him faster run.

Away went Gilpin, and away
  Went post-boy at his heels!—
The post-boy's horse right glad to miss
  The lumb'ring of the wheels. 232

Six gentlemen upon the road,
  Thus seeing Gilpin fly,
With post-boy scamp'ring in the rear,
  They rais'd the hue and cry:

Stop thief! stop thief!—a highwayman!
  Not one of them was mute;
And all and each that pass'd that way
  Did join in the pursuit. 240

And now the turnpike gates again
  Flew open in short space;
The toll-men thinking, as before,
  That Gilpin rode a race.

And so he did—and won it too!—
  For he got first to town;
Nor stopp'd till where he had got up
  He did again get down. 248

Now let us sing—Long live the king,
  And Gilpin long live he;
And, when he next doth ride abroad,
  May I be there to see!

TO A LADY

WHO WORE A LOCK OF HIS HAIR SET WITH DIAMONDS

[Written 1782 (?). Published by Benham, 1870.]

THE star that beams on Anna's breast
  Conceals her William's hair,
'Twas lately sever'd from the rest
  To be promoted there.
The heart that beats beneath that breast
  Is William's, well I know;
A nobler prize and richer far
  Than India could bestow.
She thus his favour'd lock prefers,
  To make her William shine; 10
The ornament indeed is hers,
  But all the honour mine.

EPITAPH ON A HARE

[Written March, 1783. Published in *The Gentleman's Magazine*, Dec., 1784; afterwards in 1800. A MS. copy is in the British Museum.]

HERE lies, whom hound did ne'er pursue,
  Nor swifter greyhound follow,
Whose foot ne'er tainted morning dew,
  Nor ear heard huntsman's hallo',

Old Tiney, surliest of his kind,
  Who, nurs'd with tender care,
And to domestic bounds confin'd,
  Was still a wild Jack-hare. 8

Though duly from my hand he took
  His pittance ev'ry night,
He did it with a jealous look,
  And, when he could, would bite.

His diet was of wheaten bread,
  And milk, and oats, and straw,
Thistles, or lettuces instead,
  With sand to scour his maw. 16

On twigs of hawthorn he regal'd,
  On pippins' russet peel;
And, when his juicy salads fail'd,
  Slic'd carrot pleas'd him well.

To a Lady—9 lock *suggested by Benham*: lot *1870*.
On a Hare—4 hallo'] hollow *BM*. 5 Old Tiney] Tiney, the *BM*., *1784*. 16 scour] cleanse *1784*.

A Turkey carpet was his lawn,
Whereon he lov'd to bound,
To skip and gambol like a fawn,
And swing his rump around. 24

His frisking was at evening hours,
For then he lost his fear;
But most before approaching show'rs,
Or when a storm drew near.

Eight years and five round-rolling moons
He thus saw steal away,
Dozing out all his idle noons,
And ev'ry night at play. 32

I kept him for his humour' sake,
For he would oft beguile
My heart of thoughts that made it ache,
And force me to a smile.

But now, beneath this walnut-shade
He finds his long, last home,
And waits in snug concealment laid,
'Till gentler Puss shall come. 40

He, still more aged, feels the shocks
From which no care can save,
And, partner once of Tiney's box,
Must soon partake his grave.

EPITAPHIUM ALTERUM

[Written 1786. Published 1800.]

Hic etiam jacet
Qui totum novennium vixit
Puss.
Siste paulisper
Qui præteriturus es
Et tecum sic reputa—
Hunc neque canis venaticus
Nec plumbum missile
Nec laqueus
Nec imbres nimii 10
Confecere
Tamen mortuus est—
Et moriar ego.

22 Whereon] On which *BM.* 24 his rump] himself *1784.* 31 Dozing] Slumb'ring *BM.* 33 his humour'] old service *BM.*, *1784.* 41 He] She *BM.* still more aged] still more antient *BM.*: in his turn *1784.* feels] must feel *1784.* 44 Must soon partake] Be partner of *1784.*

SONG ON PEACE

WRITTEN AT THE REQUEST OF LADY AUSTEN

[Written May (?), 1783. Published by Hayley, 1803.]

AIR—*My fond Shepherds of late.*

No longer I follow a sound;
  No longer a dream I pursue;
Oh happiness, not to be found,
  Unattainable treasure, adieu!

I have sought thee in splendour and dress;
  In the regions of pleasure and taste;
I have sought thee, and seem'd to possess,
  But have prov'd thee a vision at last. 8

An humble ambition and hope
  The voice of true wisdom inspires;
'Tis sufficient, if peace be the scope,
  And the summit of all our desires.

Peace may be the lot of the mind,
  That seeks it in meekness and love;
But rapture and bliss are confin'd
  To the glorified spirits above. 16

SONG

ALSO WRITTEN AT THE REQUEST OF LADY AUSTEN

[Written in the summer of 1783. Published by Hayley, 1803.]

AIR—*The Lass of Pattie's Mill.*

WHEN all within is peace,
  How nature seems to smile!
Delights that never cease,
  The live-long day beguile.
From morn to dewy eve,
  With open hand she showers
Fresh blessings, to deceive
  And sooth the silent hours. 8

It is content of heart,
  Gives nature pow'r to please;
The mind that feels no smart
  Enlivens all it sees;
Can make a wintry sky
  Seem bright as smiling May,
And evening's closing eye
  As peep of early day. 16

The vast majestic globe,
So beauteously array'd
In nature's various robe,
With wondrous skill display'd,
Is, to a mourner's heart,
A dreary wild at best:
It flutters to depart,
And longs to be at rest. 24

THE ROSE

[Written June, 1783. Published in *The Gentleman's Magazine*, June, 1785; afterwards in 1795. A MS. copy is in the British Museum.]

THE rose had been wash'd, just wash'd in a shower,
Which Mary to Anna convey'd,
The plentiful moisture incumber'd the flower,
And weigh'd down its beautiful head.

The cup was all fill'd, and the leaves were all wet,
And it seem'd to a fanciful view,
To weep for the buds it had left with regret,
On the flourishing bush where it grew. 8

I hastily seiz'd it, unfit as it was,
For a nosegay, so dripping and drown'd,
And swinging it rudely, too rudely, alas!
I snapp'd it, it fell to the ground.

And such, I exclaim'd, is the pitiless part
Some act by the delicate mind,
Regardless of wringing and breaking a heart
Already to sorrow resign'd. 16

This elegant rose, had I shaken it less,
Might have bloom'd with its owner awhile,
And the tear that is wip'd with a little address,
May be follow'd perhaps by a smile.

THE FAITHFUL FRIEND

[Written Aug. (?), 1783. Published 1795.]

THE green-house is my summer seat;
My shrubs displac'd from that retreat
Enjoy'd the open air;
Two goldfinches, whose sprightly song
Had been their mutual solace long,
Liv'd happy pris'ners there. 6

They sang, as blithe as finches sing
That flutter loose on golden wing,

The Faithful Friend—Title Friend] Bird *first in 1808.*

And frolic where they list;
Strangers to liberty, 'tis true,
But that delight they never knew,
And, therefore, never miss'd. 12

But nature works in ev'ry breast;
Instinct is never quite suppress'd;
And Dick felt some desires,
Which, after many an effort vain,
Instructed him at length to gain
A pass between his wires. 18

The open windows seem'd to invite
The freeman to a farewell flight;
But Tom was still confin'd;
And Dick, although his way was clear,
Was much too gen'rous and sincere
To leave his friend behind. 24

For, settling on his grated roof,
He chirp'd and kiss'd him, giving proof
That he desir'd no more;
Nor would forsake his cage at last,
Till gently seiz'd I shut him fast,
A pris'ner as before. 30

Oh ye, who never knew the joys
Of Friendship, satisfied with noise,
Fandango, ball and rout!
Blush, when I tell you how a bird,
A prison, with a friend, preferr'd
To liberty without. 36

ODE TO APOLLO

ON AN INK-GLASS ALMOST DRIED IN THE SUN

[Written Sept., 1783. Published 1795. A MS. copy is in the British Museum.]

Patron of all those luckless brains,
That, to the wrong side leaning,
Indite much metre with much pains,
And little or no meaning,

14 With force not easily suppress'd *first in 1808.*
25-30 *altered first in 1808 to:*
So settling on his cage, by play,
And chirp, and kiss, he seemed to say,
"You must not live alone;"—
Nor would he quit that chosen stand
Till I, with slow and cautious hand,
Returned him to his own.
31 knew] taste *first in 1808.*
Ode to Apollo—1 those] such *BM.* 2 That] As *BM.*

Ah why, since oceans, rivers, streams
  That water all the nations,
Pay tribute to thy glorious beams,
  In constant exhalations, 8

Why, stooping from the noon of day,
  Too covetous of drink,
Apollo, hast thou stol'n away
  A poet's drop of ink?

Upborne into the viewless air
  It floats a vapour now,
Impell'd through regions dense and rare,
  By all the winds that blow. 16

Ordain'd, perhaps, ere summer flies,
  Combin'd with millions more,
To form an Iris in the skies,
  Though black and foul before.

Illustrious drop! and happy then
  Beyond the happiest lot,
Of all that ever pass'd my pen,
  So soon to be forgot! 24

Phœbus, if such be thy design,
  To place it in thy bow,
Give wit, that what is left may shine
  With equal grace below.

THE VALEDICTION

[Written Nov., 1783 (MS. in British Museum). First published complete by Southey, 1836; ll. 49 to end published by Hayley, 1803.]

FAREWELL, false hearts! whose best affections fail
Like shallow brooks which summer suns exhale,
Forgetful of the man whom once ye chose,
Cold in his cause, and careless of his woes,
I bid you both a long and last adieu,
Cold in my turn and unconcern'd like you.
  First—farewell Niger whom, now duly prov'd,
I disregard as much as once I lov'd.
Your brain well furnish'd, and your tongue well taught
To press with energy your ardent thought, 10
Your senatorial dignity of face,
Sound sense, intrepid spirit, manly grace,
Have rais'd you high as talents can ascend,
Made you a peer, but spoilt you for a friend.

Ode to Apollo—13 into] upon *BM*.

Pretend to all that parts have e'er acquir'd,
Be great, be fear'd, be envied, be admir'd,
To fame as lasting as the earth pretend,
But not, hereafter, to the name of friend.
I sent you verse, and, as your Lordship knows,
Back'd with a modest sheet of humble prose, 20
Not to recall a promise to your mind,
Fulfill'd with ease had you been so inclin'd,
But to comply with feelings, and to give
Proof of an old affection still alive.—
Your sullen silence serves at least to tell
Your alter'd heart—and so, my Lord—farewell!
Next, busy Actor on a meaner stage,
Amusement-monger of a trifling age,
Illustrious histrionic patentee,
Terentius, once my friend, farewell to thee. 30
In thee some virtuous qualities combine
To fit thee for a nobler post than thine,
Who, born a gentleman, hast stoop'd too low
To live by buskin, sock, and raree-show.
Thy schoolfellow, and partner of thy plays
Where Nicol swung the birch and twin'd the bays,
And having known thee bearded and full grown,
The weekly censor of a laughing town,
I thought the volume I presum'd to send,
Grac'd with the name of a long absent friend, 40
Might prove a welcome gift, and touch thine heart,
Not hard by nature, in a feeling part.
But thou, it seems (what cannot grandeur do,
Though but a dream?) art grown disdainful too,
And strutting in thy school of Queens and Kings,
Who fret their hour and are forgotten things,
Hast caught the cold distemper of the day,
And, like his Lordship, cast thy friend away.
Oh, Friendship, cordial of the human breast,
So little felt, so fervently profess'd, 50
Thy blossoms deck our unsuspecting years,
The promise of delicious fruit appears;
We hug the hopes of constancy and truth,
Such is the folly of our dreaming youth;
But soon, alas! detect the rash mistake
That sanguine inexperience loves to make,
And view with tears th' expected harvest lost,
Decay'd by time or wither'd by a frost.
Whoever undertakes a friend's great part
Should be renew'd in nature, pure in heart, 60
Prepar'd for martyrdom, and strong to prove
A thousand ways the force of genuine love.

He may be call'd to give up health and gain,
T' exchange content for trouble, ease for pain,
To echo sigh for sigh, and groan for groan,
And wet his cheeks with sorrows not his own.
The heart of man for such a task too frail,
When most relied on is most sure to fail,
And, summon'd to partake its fellow's woe,
Starts from its office like a broken bow. 70
Vot'ries of bus'ness and of pleasure prove
Faithless alike in friendship and in love.
Retir'd from all the circles of the gay,
And all the crowds that bustle life away,
To scenes where competition, envy, strife,
Beget no thunder-clouds to trouble life,
Let me, the charge of some good angel, find
One who has known and has escap'd mankind,
Polite yet virtuous, who has brought away
The manners, not the morals of the day. 80
With Him, perhaps with Her (for men have known
No firmer friendships than the fair have shown)
Let me enjoy in some unthought-of spot,
All former friends forgiven and forgot,
Down to the close of life's fast-fading scene,
Union of hearts, without a flaw between.
'Tis grace, 'tis bounty, and it calls for praise,
If God give health, that sunshine of our days—
And if he add, a blessing shar'd by few,
Content of heart, more praises still are due— 90
But if he grant a friend, that boon possess'd
Indeed is treasure, and crowns all the rest;
And giving one whose heart is in the skies,
Born from above and made divinely wise,
He gives what bankrupt Nature never can,
Whose noblest coin is light and brittle man,
Gold purer far than Ophir ever knew,
A soul an image of Himself, and therefore true.

TO THE IMMORTAL MEMORY OF THE HALIBUT

ON WHICH I DINED THIS DAY

[Written in letter to Unwin April 25, 1784. Published by Johnson, 1824. There is a copy among the Ash MSS.]

WHERE hast thou floated, in what seas pursued
Thy pastime? when wast thou an egg new-spawn'd,
Lost in th' immensity of ocean's waste?
Roar as they might, the overbearing winds
That rock'd the deep, thy cradle, thou wast safe—

And in thy minikin and embryo state,
Attach'd to the firm leaf of some salt weed,
Didst outlive tempests, such as wrung and rack'd
The joints of many a stout and gallant bark,
And whelm'd them in the unexplor'd abyss. 10
Indebted to no magnet and no chart,
Nor under guidance of the polar fire,
Thou wast a voyager on many coasts,
Grazing at large in meadows submarine,
Where flat Batavia just emerging peeps
Above the brine,—where Caledonia's rocks
Beat back the surge,—and where Hibernia shoots
Her wondrous causeway far into the main.
—Wherever thou hast fed, thou little thought'st,
And I not more, that I should feed on thee. 20
Peace therefore, and good health, and much good
fish,
To him who sent thee! and success, as oft
As it descends into the billowy gulph,
To the same drag that caught thee!—Fare thee
well!
Thy lot thy brethren of the slimy fin
Would envy, could they know that thou wast doom'd
To feed a bard, and to be prais'd in verse.

AN EPISTLE TO JOSEPH HILL, Esq.

[Written Nov., 1784. Published 1785.]

Dear Joseph—five and twenty years ago—
Alas, how time escapes!—'tis even so—
With frequent intercourse, and always sweet,
And always friendly, we were wont to cheat
A tedious hour—and now we never meet!
As some grave gentleman in Terence says,
('Twas therefore much the same in ancient days)
Good lack, we know not what to-morrow brings—
Strange fluctuation of all human things!
True. Changes will befall, and friends may part,
But distance only cannot change the heart: 11
And, were I call'd to prove th' assertion true,
One proof should serve—a reference to you.
Whence comes it then, that in the wane of life,
Though nothing have occurr'd to kindle strife,
We find the friends we fancied we had won,
Though num'rous once, reduc'd to few or none?
Can gold grow worthless that has stood the touch?
No—gold they seem'd, but they were never such.

To the Halibut—9 gallant] noble *A*. 20 I . . . I] me . . . we *A*.

Horatio's servant once, with bow and cringe, 20
Swinging the parlour-door upon its hinge,
Dreading a negative, and overaw'd
Lest he should trespass, begg'd to go abroad.
Go, fellow!—whither?—turning short about—
Nay—stay at home—you're always going out.
'Tis but a step, sir, just at the street's end.—
For what?—An please you, sir, to see a friend.
A friend! Horatio cry'd, and seem'd to start—
Yea, marry shalt thou, and with all my heart.—
And fetch my cloak: for, though the night be raw, 30
I'll see him too—the first I ever saw.

I knew the man, and knew his nature mild,
And was his plaything often when a child;
But somewhat at that moment pinch'd him close,
Else he was seldom bitter or morose.
Perhaps, his confidence just then betray'd,
His grief might prompt him with the speech he made;
Perhaps 'twas mere good-humour gave it birth,
The harmless play of pleasantry and mirth.
Howe'er it was, his language, in my mind, 40
Bespoke at least a man that knew mankind.

But, not to moralize too much, and strain
To prove an evil of which all complain,
(I hate long arguments, verbosely spun)
One story more, dear Hill, and I have done.
Once on a time an emp'ror, a wise man—
No matter where, in China or Japan—
Decreed that whosoever should offend
Against the well-known duties of a friend,
Convicted once, should ever after wear 50
But half a coat, and show his bosom bare.
The punishment importing this, no doubt,
That all was naught within, and all found out.

Oh, happy Britain! we have not to fear
Such hard and arbitrary measure here;
Else, could a law like that which I relate
Once have the sanction of our triple state,
Some few that I have known in days of old,
Would run most dreadful risk of catching cold;
While you, my friend, whatever wind should blow,
Might traverse England safely to and fro, 61
An honest man, close-button'd to the chin,
Broad-cloth without, and a warm heart within.

THE POPLAR-FIELD

[Written 1784. Published in *The Gentleman's Magazine*, **Jan.,** 1785; afterwards in 1800.]

THE poplars are fell'd, farewell to the shade
And the whispering sound of the cool colonnade,
The winds play no longer, and sing in the leaves,
Nor Ouse on his bosom their image receives.

Twelve years have elaps'd since I first took a view
Of my favourite field and the bank where they grew,
And now in the grass behold they are laid,
And the tree is my seat that once lent me a shade. 8

The blackbird has fled to another retreat
Where the hazels afford him a screen from the heat,
And the scene where his melody charm'd me before,
Resounds with his sweet-flowing ditty no more.

My fugitive years are all hasting away,
And I must ere long lie as lowly as they,
With a turf on my breast, and a stone at my head,
Ere another such grove shall arise in its stead. 16

'Tis a sight to engage me, if any thing can,
To muse on the perishing pleasures of man;
Though his life be a dream, his enjoyments, I see,
Have a being less durable even than he.

IDEM LATINE REDDITUM

[Written Jan. (?), 1785. Published in *The Gentleman's Magazine*, Aug., 1785; afterwards in 1800.]

POPULEÆ cecidit gratissima copia silvæ,
Conticuere susurri, omnisque evanuit umbra.
Nullæ jam levibus se miscent frondibus auræ
Et nulla in fluvio ramorum ludit imago.

The Poplar-Field—1 farewell] and adieu *1785*. 3 the] their *1785*. 4 on his] in its *1785*. 5 have] had *1785*. first] last *1785*.

7, 8 When behold on their sides in the grass they were laid,
And I sat on the trees under which I had stray'd *1785*.

9 fled to] sought out *1785*. 11 melody] notes have oft *1785*. 12 Resounds] Shall resound *1785*. 13 hast'ning *1785*. 14 ere long] alas! *1785*. 16 shall arise] rises up *1785*.

17–20 Mr. Cowper afterwards altered this last stanza in the following manner:

The change both my heart and my fancy employs,
I reflect on the frailty of man, and his joys;
Short-lived as we are, yet our pleasures, we see,
Have a still shorter date, and die sooner than we.

Note to 1803 edition: but this is the text of 1785.

Hei mihi! bis senos dum luctu torqueor annos,
His cogor silvis suetoque carere recessu,
Cum sero rediens stratasque in gramine cernens
Insedi arboribus sub queis errare solebam. 8

Ah ubi nunc merulæ cantus? Felicior illum
Silva tegit, duræ nondum permissa bipenni;
Scilicet exustos colles camposque patentes
Odit, et indignans et non rediturus abivit.

Sed qui succisas doleo succidar et ipse,
Et prius huic parilis quam creverit altera silva
Flebor, et, exequiis parvis donatus, habebo
Defixum lapidem tumulique cubantis acervum. 16

Tam subito periisse videns tam digna manere
Agnosco humanas sortes et tristia fata—
Sit licet ipse brevis, volucrique simillimus umbræ,
Est homini brevior citiusque obitura voluptas.

LINES

SENT WITH TWO COCKSCOMBS TO MISS GREEN

[Written 1784 (?). Published by Bruce, 1863. A slightly different version was first printed by Canon Benham in 1870.]

Two powder'd coxcombs wait at your command,
And, what is strange, both dress'd by Nature's hand.
Like other fops, they dread a sudden shower,
And seek a shelter in your closest bower.
Showy like them, like them they yield no fruit,
But then, to make amends, they both are mute. 6

EPITAPH ON DR. JOHNSON

[Written Jan., 1785. Published from letter to Unwin, dated Jan. 15 (MS. in British Museum), by Hayley, 1803.]

Here Johnson lies—a sage, by all allow'd,
Whom to have bred may well make England proud;
Whose prose was eloquence by wisdom taught,
The graceful vehicle of virtuous thought;
Whose verse may claim—grave, masculine, and strong,
Superior praise to the mere poet's song;
Who many a noble gift from heav'n possess'd,
And faith at last—alone worth all the rest.
Oh man immortal by a double prize!
By Fame on earth—by Glory in the skies! 10

Idem Latine Redditum—10 Silva] Umbra *1785.* 13 Sed] Et *1785.* 19 licet] licat *1800, 1803.* volucrique . . . umbræ] præceps devectus ad umbras *1785.*

Lines—1 Madam,—Two Cockscombs *1870.* 3 sudden] hasty *1870.* 4 beg a refuge *1870.*

Epitaph—10 *so BM., Hayley*: On earth by fame, by favour in the skies! *Southey, from letter to Newton, dated Jan. 5,*

ON THE AUTHOR OF LETTERS ON LITERATURE

[Written Nov., 1785. Published by Johnson, 1824.]

THE Genius of th' Augustan age
His head among Rome's ruins rear'd,
And bursting with heroic rage,
When literary Heron appear'd,

Thou hast, he cried, like him of old
Who set th' Ephesian dome on fire,
By being scandalously bold,
Attain'd the mark of thy desire ; 8

And for traducing Virgil's name
Shalt share his merited reward ;
A perpetuity of fame,
That rots, and stinks, and is abhorr'd.

THE POET'S NEW-YEAR'S GIFT

TO MRS. THROCKMORTON

[Written Dec., 1787. Published in *The Gentleman's Magazine*, Dec., 1788 ; afterwards in 1795.]

MARIA ! I have ev'ry good
For thee wish'd many a time,
Both sad, and in a cheerful mood,
But never yet in rhime.

To wish thee fairer is no need,
More prudent, or more sprightly,
Or more ingenious, or more freed
From temper-flaws unsightly. 8

What favour, then, not yet possess'd,
Can I for thee require,
In wedded love already blest,
To thy whole heart's desire ?

None here is happy but in part ;
Full bliss is bliss divine ;
There dwells some wish in ev'ry heart,
And, doubtless, one in thine. 16

That wish, on some fair future day,
Which fate shall brightly gild,
('Tis blameless, be it what it may)
I wish it all fulfill'd.

The Gift—5 is] were *1788.* 7 ingenuous *1788.* 12 whole] full *1788.* 13 is] are *1788.* 15 some] a *1788.*

STANZAS

PRINTED AT THE BOTTOM OF THE YEARLY BILL OF MORTALITY OF THE TOWN OF NORTHAMPTON; DEC. 21, 1787

[Written Nov., 1787. Published in *The Gentleman's Magazine*, June, 1788; afterwards in 1800, and by Bull in 1801.]

Pallida Mors æquo pulsat pede pauperum tabernas
Regumque turres.—HORACE.

Pale Death with equal foot strikes wide the door
Of royal halls and hovels of the poor.

WHILE thirteen moons saw smoothly run
  The Nen's barge-laden wave,
All *these*, life's rambling journey done,
  Have found their home—the grave.

Was man (frail always) made more frail
  Than in foregoing years?
Did famine, or did plague prevail,
  That so much death appears? 8

No; these were vigorous as their sires,
  Nor plague nor famine came;
This annual tribute Death requires,
  And never waves his claim.

Like crowded forest-trees we stand,
  And some are mark'd to fall;
The axe will smite at God's command,
  And soon shall smite us all. 16

Green as the bay-tree, ever green,
  With its new foliage on,
The gay, the thoughtless, have I seen;
  I pass'd—and they were gone.

Read, ye that run, the awful truth
  With which I charge my page;
A worm is in the bud of youth,
  And at the root of age. 24

No present health can health insure
  For yet an hour to come;
No med'cine, though it often cure,
  Can always balk the tomb.

And oh! that (humble as my lot,
  And scorn'd as is my strain)[1]
These truths, though known, too much forgot,
  I may not teach in vain. 32

[1] John Cox, Parish Clerk of Northampton [1788, 1800].

19 have I] I have *Bull*. 21 awful] solemn *Bull, 1803*.

So prays your Clerk, with all his heart;
And, ere he quits the pen,
Begs *you* for once to take *his* part,
And answer all—Amen!

ON A SIMILAR OCCASION

FOR THE YEAR 1788

[Written 1788. Published 1800 (vol. I. Appendix), and by Bull, 1801.]

Quod adest, memento
Componere æquus; cætera fluminis
Ritu feruntur.—HORACE.

Improve the present hour, for all beside
Is a mere feather on the torrent's tide.

COULD I, from heav'n inspir'd, as sure presage
To whom the rising year shall prove the last,
As I can number in my punctual page,
And item down the victims of the past;

How each would trembling wait the mournful sheet
On which the press might stamp him next to die;
And, reading here his sentence, how replete
With anxious meaning, heav'nward cast his eye. 8

Time then would seem more precious than the joys
In which he sports away the treasure now,
And prayer more seasonable than the noise
Of drunkards or the music-drawing bow.

Then, doubtless, many a trifler, on the brink
Of this world's hazardous and headlong shore,
Forc'd to a pause, would feel it good to think,
Told that his setting sun would rise no more. 16

Ah! self-deceiv'd! could I prophetic say
Who next is fated, and who next shall fall,
The rest might then seem privileg'd to play;
But, naming none, the voice now speaks to all.

Observe the dappled foresters, how light
They bound, and airy, o'er the sunny glade:
One falls—the rest, wide scatter'd with affright,
Vanish at once into the thickest shade. 24

Had we their wisdom, should we, often warn'd,
Still need repeated warnings; and at last,
A thousand awful admonitions scorn'd,
Die self-accus'd of life all run to waste?

35 for] at *1788*.

1788—Title] *date blank in 1800*. Motto 5 the] a *Bull*. 2 the last] his last *Bull*. 8 cast] turn *Bull*. 16 would] must *Bull*. 18 shall] to *Bull*. 24 darkest *Bull*.

Sad waste! for which no after-thrift atones:
The grave admits no cure of guilt or sin;
Dew-drops may deck the turf that hides the bones,
But tears of godly grief ne'er flow within. 32

Learn then, ye living! by the mouths be taught
Of all these sepulchres instruction true,
That, soon or late, death also is your lot;
And the next op'ning grave may yawn for you.

ON A SIMILAR OCCASION

FOR THE YEAR 1789

[Written 1789. Published in *Public Characters* 1799, afterwards in 1800, and by Bull, 1801.]

Placidaque ibi demum morte quievit.—VIRG.
There calm at length he breath'd his soul away.

"Oh most delightful hour by man
Experienc'd here below;
The hour that terminates his span,
His folly and his woe.

"Worlds should not bribe me back to tread
Again life's dreary waste;
To see my days again o'erspread
With all the gloomy past. 8

"My home, henceforth, is in the skies,
Earth, seas, and sun adieu;
All heav'n unfolded to my eyes,
I have no sight for you."

Thus spake Aspatio, firm possest
Of faith's supporting rod;
Then breath'd his soul into its rest,
The bosom of his God. 16

He was a man among the few
Sincere on Virtue's side,
And all his strength from Scripture drew,
To hourly use applied.

That rule he priz'd, by that he fear'd,
He hated, hop'd, and lov'd,
Nor ever frown'd, or sad appear'd,
But when his heart had rov'd. 24

32 of] for *Bull*. 34 instruction] instructors *Bull*.
1789—Title] *no date in 1800*. Motto There] Then *1800*.
7 again my day *Bull*. 13, 29 Aspasio *Bull*. 21 by that] by what *Bull*.

For he was frail as thou or I,
  And evil felt within,
But when he felt it, heav'd a sigh,
  And loath'd the thought of sin.

Such liv'd Aspatio, and at last,
  Call'd up from earth to heaven,
The gulph of death triumphant pass'd,
  By gales of blessing driven. 32

His joys be *mine*, each reader cries,
  When my last hour arrives:
They shall be yours, my verse replies,
  Such ONLY be your lives.

ON A SIMILAR OCCASION

FOR THE YEAR 1790

[Written 1790. Published 1800 (vol. I. Appendix), and by Bull, 1801.]

Ne commonentem recta sperne.—BUCHANAN.

Despise not my good counsel.

HE who sits from day to day,
  Where the prison'd lark is hung,
Heedless of his loudest lay,
  Hardly knows that he has sung.

Where the watchman in his round
  Nightly lifts his voice on high,
None, accustom'd to the sound,
  Wakes the sooner for his cry. 8

So your verse-man I, and clerk,
  Yearly in my song proclaim
Death at hand—yourselves his mark—
  And the foe's unerring aim.

Duly at my time I come,
  Publishing to all aloud—
Soon the grave must be your home,
  And your only suit a shroud. 16

But the monitory strain,
  Oft repeated in your ears,
Seems to sound too much in vain,
  Wins no notice, wakes no fears.

Can a truth, by all confess'd
  Of such magnitude and weight,
Grow, by being oft express'd,
  Trivial as a parrot's prate? 24

23 compress'd *Bull*: impress'd *first in 1808.*

Pleasure's call attention wins,
  Hear it often as we may;
New as ever seem our sins,
  Though committed ev'ry day.

Death and Judgment, Heav'n and Hell—
  These alone, so often heard,
No more move us than the bell
  When some stranger is interr'd. **32**

Oh then, ere the turf or tomb
  Cover us from ev'ry eye,
Spirit of instruction come;
  Make us learn that we must die.

ON A SIMILAR OCCASION

FOR THE YEAR 1792

[Written 1792. Published 1800 (vol. I. Appendix), and by Bull, 1801.]

Felix, qui potuit rerum cognoscere causas,
Atque metus omnes et inexorabile fatum
Subjecit pedibus, strepitumque Acherontis avari!—VIRG.

Happy the mortal, who has trac'd effects
To their First Cause; cast fear beneath his feet;
And death, and roaring hell's voracious fires.

THANKLESS for favours from on high,
  Man thinks he fades too soon;
Though 'tis his privilege to die,
  Would he improve the boon:

But he, not wise enough to scan
  His *best* concerns aright,
Would gladly stretch life's little span
  To ages, if he might— **8**

To ages, in a world of pain,
  To ages, where he goes
Gall'd by Affliction's heavy chain,
  And hopeless of repose.

Strange fondness of the human heart,
  Enamour'd of its harm!
Strange world, that costs it so much smart,
  And still has pow'r to charm! **16**

Whence has the world her magic pow'r?
  Why deem we death a foe?
Recoil from weary life's best hour,
  And covet longer woe?

Title] *1800 gives date* November 5, 1793.

The cause is Conscience—Conscience oft
Her tale of guilt renews:
Her voice is terrible though soft,
And dread of death ensues. 24

Then, anxious to be longer spar'd,
Man mourns his fleeting breath:
All evils then seem light, compar'd
With the approach of death.

'Tis judgment shakes him; there's the fear,
That prompts the wish to stay:
He has incurr'd a long arrear,
And must despair to pay. 32

Pay!—Follow CHRIST, and all is paid:
His death your peace ensures:
Think on the grave where he was laid,
And calm descend to yours.

ON A SIMILAR OCCASION

FOR THE YEAR 1793

[Written 1793. Published 1800 (vol. I. Appendix), and by Bull, 1801.]

De sacris autem hæc sit una sententia, ut conserventur.—CIC. *de Leg.*

But let us all concur in this one sentiment, that things sacred be inviolate.

HE lives who lives to God alone,
And all are dead beside;
For other source than God is none
Whence life can be supplied.

To live to God, is to requite
His love as best we may;
To make his precepts our delight,
His promises our stay. 8

But life, within a narrow ring
Of giddy joys compriz'd,
Is falsely nam'd, and no such thing,
But rather death disguis'd.

Can life in them deserve the name,
Who only live to prove
For what poor toys they can disclaim
An endless life above? 16

Title] *date blank in 1800.* 13 the] a *1800.* 15 joys *1800.*

Who, much diseas'd, yet nothing feel,
  Much menac'd, nothing dread;
Have wounds which only God can heal,
  Yet never ask his aid?

Who deem his house an useless place,
  Faith, want of common sense;
And ardour in the Christian race
  An hypocrite's pretence? 24

Who trample order, and the day
  Which God asserts his own,
Dishonour with unhallow'd play,
  And worship chance alone?

If scorn of God's commands, impress'd
  On word and deed, imply
The better part of man unbless'd
  With life that cannot die, 32

Such want it; and that want, uncur'd
  Till man resigns his breath,
Speaks him a criminal, assur'd
  Of everlasting death.

Sad period to a pleasant course!
  Yet so will God repay
Sabbaths profan'd without remorse,
  And mercy cast away. 40

THE NEGRO'S COMPLAINT

[Written Feb. (?), 1788. Published in *The Gentleman's Magazine* Dec., 1793; afterwards in 1800 (vol. I. Appendix).]

Forc'd from home, and all its pleasures,
  Afric's coast I left forlorn;
To increase a stranger's treasures,
  O'er the raging billows borne.
Men from England bought and sold me,
  Paid my price in paltry gold;
But, though theirs they have enroll'd me,
  Minds are never to be sold. 8

Still in thought as free as ever,
  What are England's rights, I ask,
Me from my delights to sever,
  Me to torture, me to task?
Fleecy locks, and black complexion
  Cannot forfeit nature's claim;
Skins may differ, but affection
  Dwells in white and black the same. 16

30 employ *1800*. 33 incurr'd *1800*. 34 resign *1800*.
The Negro's Complaint—7 theirs] slave *first in 1808*.

Why did all-creating Nature
  Make the plant for which we toil?
Sighs must fan it, tears must water,
  Sweat of ours must dress the soil.
Think, ye masters, iron-hearted,
  Lolling at your jovial boards;
Think how many backs have smarted
  For the sweets your cane affords. 24

Is there, as ye sometimes tell us,
  Is there one who reigns on high?
Has he bid you buy and sell us,
  Speaking from his throne the sky?
Ask him, if your knotted scourges,
  Matches, blood-extorting screws,
Are the means which duty urges
  Agents of his will to use? 32

Hark! he answers—Wild tornadoes,
  Strewing yonder sea with wrecks;
Wasting towns, plantations, meadows,
  Are the voice with which he speaks.
He, foreseeing what vexations
  Afric's sons should undergo,
Fix'd their tyrants' habitations
  Where his whirlwinds answer—No. 40

By our blood in Afric wasted,
  Ere our necks receiv'd the chain;
By the mis'ries we have tasted,
  Crossing in your barks the main;
By our suff'rings since ye brought us
  To the man-degrading mart;
All sustain'd by patience, taught us
  Only by a broken heart: 48

Deem our nation brutes no longer
  Till some reason ye shall find
Worthier of regard and stronger
  Than the colour of our kind.
Slaves of gold, whose sordid dealings
  Tarnish all your boasted pow'rs,
Prove that you have human feelings,
  Ere you proudly question ours! 56

30 Matches] Fetters *1793, and quoted by T. Wright from a MS.* 37, 39 vexation . . . habitation *1793.* 40 whirlwind *1793.* 43 we have] which we *1793.*

THE MORNING DREAM

[Written March (?), 1788. Published in *The Gentleman's Magazine* Nov., 1788; afterwards in 1800.]

'TWAS in the glad season of spring,
  Asleep at the dawn of the day,
I dream'd what I cannot but sing,
  So pleasant it seem'd as I lay.
I dream'd that on ocean afloat,
  Far hence to the westward I sail'd,
While the billows high lifted the boat,
  And the fresh-blowing breeze never fail'd. 8

In the steerage a woman I saw,
  Such at least was the form that she wore,
Whose beauty impress'd me with awe,
  Ne'er taught me by woman before.
She sat, and a shield at her side
  Shed light like a sun on the waves,
And smiling divinely, she cried—
  I go to make Freemen of Slaves.— 16

Then raising her voice to a strain
  The sweetest that ear ever heard,
She sang of the slave's broken chain,
  Wherever her glory appear'd.
Some clouds which had over us hung
  Fled, chas'd by her melody clear,
And methought while she Liberty sung,
  'Twas Liberty only to hear. 24

Thus swiftly dividing the flood,
  To a slave-cultur'd island we came,
Where a Demon, her enemy, stood—
  Oppression his terrible name.
In his hand, as the sign of his sway,
  A scourge hung with lashes he bore,
And stood looking out for his prey
  From Africa's sorrowful shore. 32

But soon as approaching the land
  That goddess-like woman he view'd,
The scourge he let fall from his hand,
  With blood of his subjects imbrued.
I saw him both sicken and die,
  And the moment the monster expir'd
Heard shouts that ascended the sky
  From thousands with rapture inspir'd. 40

1 glad] sweet *1788*. 6 hence . . . westward] West from fair Albion *1788*. 19 slave-broken *1788*. 29 the] a *1788*. 34 That] This *1788*.

Awaking, how could I but muse
  At what such a dream should betide?
But soon my ear caught the glad news
  Which serv'd my weak thought for a guide—
That Britannia, renown'd o'er the waves
  For the hatred she ever has shown
To the black-sceptred rulers of slaves,
  Resolves to have none of her own. 48

SWEET MEAT HAS SOUR SAUCE

OR, THE SLAVE-TRADER IN THE DUMPS

[Written early in 1788. Published by Southey, 1836.]

A TRADER I am to the African shore,
But since that my trading is like to be o'er,
I'll sing you a song that you ne'er heard before,
    Which nobody can deny, deny,
    Which nobody can deny. 5

When I first heard the news it gave me a shock,
Much like what they call an electrical knock,
And now I am going to sell off my stock,
    Which nobody, &c.

'Tis a curious assortment of dainty regales,
To tickle the negroes with when the ship sails,
Fine chains for the neck, and a cat with nine
  tails, 11
    Which nobody, &c.

Here's supple-jack plenty, and store of rat-tan,
That will wind itself round the sides of a man,
As close as a hoop round a bucket or can,
    Which nobody, &c.

Here's padlocks and bolts, and screws for the
  thumbs,
That squeeze them so lovingly till the blood comes,
They sweeten the temper like comfits or plums, 17
    Which nobody, &c.

When a negro his head from his victuals withdraws,
And clenches his teeth and thrusts out his paws,
Here's a notable engine to open his jaws,
    Which nobody, &c.

Thus going to market, we kindly prepare
A pretty black cargo of African ware,
For what they must meet with when they get
  there, 23
    Which nobody, &c.

42 should] might *1788*. 44 thoughts *1788*. 47 Ruler *1788*.

'Twould do your heart good to see 'em below
Lie flat on their backs all the way as we go,
Like sprats on a gridiron, scores in a row,
Which nobody, &c.

But ah! if in vain I have studied an art
So gainful to me, all boasting apart,
I think it will break my compassionate heart, 29
Which nobody, &c.

For oh! how it enters my soul like an awl!
This pity, which some people self-pity call,
Is sure the most heart-piercing pity of all,
Which nobody, &c.

So this is my song, as I told you before;
Come buy off my stock, for I must no more
Carry Cæsars and Pompeys to Sugar-cane shore, 35
Which nobody can deny, deny,
Which nobody can deny.

PITY FOR POOR AFRICANS

Video meliora proboque
Deteriora sequor——

[Written early in 1788. Published 1800 (vol. I. Appendix).]

I OWN I am shock'd at the purchase of slaves,
And fear those who buy them and sell them are knaves;
What I hear of their hardships, their tortures, and groans,
Is almost enough to draw pity from stones.

I pity them greatly, but I must be mum,
For how could we do without sugar and rum?
Especially sugar, so needful we see?
What? give up our desserts, our coffee, and tea! 8

Besides, if we do, the French, Dutch, and Danes,
Will heartily thank us, no doubt, for our pains;
If we do not buy the poor creatures, they will,
And tortures and groans will be multiplied still.

If foreigners likewise would give up the trade,
Much more in behalf of your wish might be said;
But while they get riches by purchasing blacks,
Pray tell me why we may not also go snacks? 16

Your scruples and arguments bring to my mind
A story so pat, you may think it is coin'd,
On purpose to answer you, out of my mint;
But, I can assure you, I saw it in print.

A youngster at school, more sedate than the rest,
Had once his integrity put to the test;
His comrades had plotted an orchard to rob,
And ask'd him to go and assist in the job. 24

He was shock'd, sir, like you, and answer'd—"Oh, no!
What! rob our good neighbour! I pray you, don't go;
Besides, the man's poor, his orchard's his bread,
Then think of his children, for they must be fed."

"You speak very fine, and you look very grave,
But apples we want, and apples we'll have;
If you will go with us, you shall have a share,
If not, you shall have neither apple nor pear." 32

They spoke, and Tom ponder'd—"I see they will go:
Poor man! what a pity to injure him so!
Poor man! I would save him his fruit if I could,
But staying behind will do him no good.

"If the matter depended alone upon me,
His apples might hang till they dropt from the tree;
But, since they will take them, I think I'll go too,
He will lose none by me, though I get a few." 40

His scruples thus silenc'd, Tom felt more at ease,
And went with his comrades the apples to seize;
He blam'd and protested, but join'd in the plan;
He shar'd in the plunder, but pitied the man.

EPIGRAM

(PRINTED IN THE NORTHAMPTON MERCURY)

[Written (?). Published by Johnson, 1815.]

To purify their wine some people bleed
A *lamb* into the barrel, and succeed;
No nostrum, planters say, is half so good
To make fine sugar, as a *negro's* blood.
Now *lambs* and *negroes* both are harmless things,
And thence perhaps this wond'rous virtue springs,
'Tis in the blood of innocence alone—
Good cause why planters never try *their own*. 8

SONNET

ADDRESSED TO HENRY COWPER, ESQ., CLERK ASSISTANT TO THE HOUSE OF LORDS

On his emphatical and interesting delivery of the Defence of WARREN HASTINGS, Esq.

[Written Feb., 1788. Published April, 1788, in *The Gentleman's Magazine*, with the signature T. H.; afterwards in 1800.]

COWPER, whose silver voice, task'd sometimes hard,
  Legends prolix delivers in the ears
  (Attentive when thou read'st) of England's Peers,
Let verse at length yield thee thy just reward.
Thou wast not heard with drowsy disregard,
  Expending late on all that length of plea
  Thy gen'rous pow'rs, but silence honour'd thee,
Mute as e'er gaz'd on Orator or Bard.
Thou art not voice alone, but hast beside
  Both heart and head; and could'st with music sweet
    Of Attic phrase and senatorial tone, 11
Like thy renown'd Forefathers, far and wide
  Thy fame diffuse, prais'd not for utt'rance meet
    Of others' speech, but magic of thy own.

GRATITUDE

ADDRESSED TO LADY HESKETH

[Written April, 1788. Published by Hayley, 1803. Southey, in 1836, printed the poem in its original form as sent to Lady Hesketh. This version differs very largely from that given in the text, and is therefore here printed entire in the notes at the end of the volume.]

THIS cap, that so stately appears,
  With ribbon-bound tassel on high,
Which seems, by the crest that it rears,
  Ambitious of brushing the sky:
This cap to my cousin I owe,
  She gave it, and gave me beside,
Wreath'd into an elegant bow,
  The ribbon with which it is tied. 8

This wheel-footed studying chair,
  Contriv'd both for toil and repose,
Wide-elbow'd, and wadded with hair,
  In which I both scribble and doze,
Bright-studded to dazzle the eyes,
  And rival in lustre of that,
In which, or astronomy lies,
  Fair Cassiopeia sat: 16

Sonnet—4 yield] give *1788*.

These carpets, so soft to the foot,
  Caledonia's traffic and pride!
Oh spare them, ye Knights of the Boot!
  Escap'd from a cross-country ride!
This table and mirror within,
  Secure from collision and dust,
At which I oft shave cheek and chin,
  And periwig nicely adjust: 24

This moveable structure of shelves,
  For its beauty admir'd and its use,
And charg'd with octavos and twelves,
  The gayest I had to produce,
Where, flaming in scarlet and gold,
  My Poems enchanted I view,
And hope, in due time, to behold
  My Iliad and Odyssey too: 32

This china, that decks the alcove,
  Which here people call a beaufette,
But what the Gods call it above,
  Has ne'er been reveal'd to us yet:
These curtains, that keep the room warm
  Or cool, as the season demands,
These stoves, that for pattern and form
  Seem the labour of Mulciber's hands: 40

All these are not half that I owe
  To one, from our earliest youth
To me ever ready to show
  Benignity, friendship, and truth,
For Time, the destroyer declar'd
  And foe of our perishing kind,
If even her face he has spar'd,
  Much less could he alter her mind. 48

Thus compass'd about with the goods
  And chattels of leisure and ease,
I indulge my poetical moods
  In many such fancies as these;
And fancies I fear they will seem,
  Poets' goods are not often so fine;
The poets will swear that I dream,
  When I sing of the splendour of mine. 56

PAIRING TIME ANTICIPATED

A FABLE

[Written (?). Published 1795.]

I SHALL not ask Jean Jacques Rousseau[1],
If birds confabulate or no;
'Tis clear that they were always able
To hold discourse, at least, in fable;
And ev'n the child who knows no better,
Than to interpret by the letter,
A story of a cock and bull,
Must have a most uncommon skull.
It chanc'd then, on a winter's day,
But warm and bright, and calm as May, 10
The birds, conceiving a design
To forestal sweet St. Valentine,
In many an orchard, copse, and grove,
Assembled on affairs of love,
And with much twitter and much chatter,
Began to agitate the matter.
At length a Bulfinch, who could boast
More years and wisdom than the most,
Entreated, op'ning wide his beak,
A moment's liberty to speak; 20
And, silence publicly enjoin'd,
Deliver'd briefly thus his mind.
My friends! be cautious how ye treat
The subject upon which we meet;
I fear we shall have winter yet.
A Finch, whose tongue knew no control,
With golden wing and satin pole,
A last year's bird, who ne'er had tried
What marriage means, thus pert replied.
Methinks the gentleman, quoth she, 30
Opposite in the apple-tree,
By his good will, would keep us single
Till yonder heav'n and earth shall mingle,
Or (which is likelier to befall)
Till death exterminate us all.
I marry without more ado;
My dear Dick Redcap, what say you?
Dick heard, and tweedling, ogling, bridling,
Turning short round, strutting and sideling,

[1] It was one of the whimsical speculations of this philosopher, that all fables which ascribe reason and speech to animals, should be withheld from children, as being only vehicles of deception. But what child was ever deceived by them, or can be, against the evidence of his senses? [C.]

Attested, glad, his approbation 40
Of an immediate conjugation.
Their sentiments so well express'd,
Influenc'd mightily the rest,
All pair'd, and each pair built a nest.
But though the birds were thus in haste,
The leaves came on not quite so fast,
And destiny, that sometimes bears
An aspect stern on man's affairs,
Not altogether smil'd on theirs.
The wind, of late breath'd gently forth, 50
Now shifted east and east by north;
Bare trees and shrubs but ill, you know,
Could shelter them from rain or snow;
Stepping into their nests, they paddled,
Themselves were chill'd, their eggs were addled;
Soon ev'ry father bird and mother
Grew quarrelsome, and peck'd each other,
Parted without the least regret,
Except that they had ever met,
And learn'd, in future, to be wiser, 60
Than to neglect a good adviser.

INSTRUCTION

Misses! the tale that I relate
This lesson seems to carry—
Choose not alone a proper mate,
But proper time to marry.

ON MRS. MONTAGU'S FEATHER-HANGINGS

[Written May, 1788. Published June, 1788, in *The Gentleman's Magazine*; afterwards in 1800.]

THE birds put off their ev'ry hue
To dress a room for Montagu.
The Peacock sends his heav'nly dyes,
His *rainbows* and his *starry eyes*;
The Pheasant, plumes which round infold
His mantling neck with downy gold;
The Cock his arch'd tail's azure show,
And, river-blanch'd, the Swan his snow.
All tribes beside of Indian name,
That glossy shine or vivid flame, 10
Where rises, and where sets the day,
Whate'er they boast of rich or gay,

Heading in 1788: On the beautiful Feather-hangings, designed by Mrs. Montagu, at her house at Portman Square. By the author of the Task. Title] Montague *1800*, *1803* (*and throughout poem*). 12 or] and *1800*.

Contribute to the gorgeous plan,
Proud to advance it all they can.
This plumage, neither dashing show'r,
Nor blasts that shake the dripping bow'r,
Shall drench again or discompose,
But, screen'd from ev'ry storm that blows,
It wears a splendour ever new,
Safe with protecting Montagu. 20
To the same Patroness resort,
(Secure of favour at her court)
Strong Genius, from whose forge of thought
Forms rise, to quick perfection wrought,
Which, though new-born, with vigour move,
Like Pallas springing arm'd from Jove—
Imagination, scatt'ring round
Wild roses over furrow'd ground,
Which Labour of his frowns beguile,
And teach Philosophy a smile— 30
Wit, flashing on Religion's side,
Whose fires to sacred Truth applied,
The gem, though luminous before,
Commend to human notice more,
Like sun-beams on the golden height
Of some tall temple playing bright—
Well-tutor'd Learning, from his books
Dismiss'd with grave, not haughty looks,
Their order on his shelves exact,
Nor more harmonious or compact 40
Than that to which he keeps confin'd
The various treasures of his mind—
All these to MONTAGU's repair,
Ambitious of a shelter there.
There Genius, Learning, Fancy, Wit,
Their ruffled plumage calm refit,
(For stormy troubles loudest roar
Around their flight who highest soar)
And in her eye, and by her aid,
Shine safe, without a fear to fade. 50
She thus maintains divided sway
With yon bright regent of the day;
The plume and poet both, we know,
Their lustre to his influence owe,
And she, the work of Phœbus aiding,
Both poet saves and plume from fading.

19 wears] boasts *1800*. 29 frown *1800*. 34 Commend to] Obtrude on *1800*. 38 not] nor *1788*. 40 Nor] Not *1800* (*with no comma after* exact *line* 39). 55 works *1800*.

LINES COMPOSED FOR A MEMORIAL OF ASHLEY COWPER, ESQ.

IMMEDIATELY AFTER HIS DEATH, BY HIS NEPHEW WILLIAM OF WESTON

[Written June, 1788. Published by Hayley, 1803.]

FAREWELL! endued with all that could engage
All hearts to love thee, both in youth and age!
In prime of life, for sprightliness enroll'd
Among the gay, yet virtuous as the old;
In life's last stage, (Oh blessing rarely found!)
Pleasant as youth, with all its blossoms crown'd;
Through every period of this changeful state
Unchang'd thyself! wise, good, affectionate!
Marble may flatter, and lest this should seem
O'ercharg'd with praises on so dear a theme, 10
Although thy worth be more than half supprest,
Love shall be satisfied, and veil the rest.

THE DOG AND THE WATER-LILY

NO FABLE

[Written Aug., 1788. Published in *The Gentleman's Magazine*, Dec., 1791; then in pamphlet with *On Receipt of my Mother's Picture*, 1798; afterwards in Poems, 1798.]

THE noon was shady, and soft airs
Swept Ouse's silent tide,
When, 'scap'd from literary cares,
I wander'd on his side.

My spaniel, prettiest of his race,
And high in pedigree,
(Two nymphs[1], adorn'd with ev'ry grace,
That spaniel found for me) 8

Now wanton'd lost in flags and reeds,
Now starting into sight
Pursued the swallow o'er the meads
With scarce a slower flight.

It was the time when Ouse display'd
His lilies newly blown;
Their beauties I intent survey'd;
And one I wish'd my own. 16

With cane extended far I sought
To steer it close to land;
But still the prize, though nearly caught,
Escap'd my eager hand.

[1] Sir Robert Gunning's daughters [C.].

The Dog and the Water-Lily—9 and] in *1791.*

Beau marked my unsuccessful pains
With fixt consid'rate face,
And puzzling set his puppy brains
To comprehend the case. 24

But with a chirrup clear and strong,
Dispersing all his dream,
I thence withdrew, and follow'd long
The windings of the stream.

My ramble finish'd, I return'd.
Beau trotting far before
The floating wreath again discern'd,
And plunging left the shore. 32

I saw him with that lily cropp'd
Impatient swim to meet
My quick approach, and soon he dropp'd
The treasure at my feet.

Charm'd with the sight, the world, I cried,
Shall hear of this thy deed,
My dog shall mortify the pride
Of man's superior breed; 40

But, chief, myself I will enjoin,
Awake at duty's call,
To show a love as prompt as thine
To Him who gives me all.

MOTTO ON THE KING'S CLOCK

[Written Aug. 9, 1788. Published by Hayley, 1803.]

QUÆ lenta accedit, quam velox præterit hora!
Ut capias, patiens esto, sed esto vigil!

ON THE DEATH OF MRS. THROCKMORTON'S BULFINCH

[Written Nov. (?), 1788. Published in *The Gentleman's Magazine*, Feb., 1789; afterwards in 1795.]

YE nymphs! if e'er your eyes were red
With tears o'er hapless fav'rites shed,
O share Maria's grief!
Her fav'rite, even in his cage,
(What will not hunger's cruel rage?)
Assassin'd by a thief. 6

Where Rhenus strays his vines among,
The egg was laid from which he sprung,
And though by nature mute,
Or only with a whistle blest,
Well-taught, he all the sounds express'd
Of flagelet or flute. 12

23 set *first in 1808*: sat *1791, 1798–1803.* 29 ended *first in 1808.*
Title Mrs.] Lady *1800, errata.* 3 O] Now *1789.*

The honours of his ebon poll
Were brighter than the sleekest mole;
His bosom of the hue
With which Aurora decks the skies,
When piping winds shall soon arise
To sweep up all the dew. 18

Above, below, in all the house,
Dire foe, alike to bird and mouse,
No cat had leave to dwell;
And Bully's cage supported stood,
On props of smoothest-shaven wood,
Large-built and lattic'd well. 24

Well-lattic'd—but the grate, alas!
Not rough with wire of steel or brass,
For Bully's plumage sake,
But smooth with wands from Ouse's side,
With which, when neatly peel'd and dried,
The swains their baskets make. 30

Night veil'd the pole—all seem'd secure—
When led by instinct sharp and sure,
Subsistence to provide,
A beast forth-sallied on the scout,
Long-back'd, long-tail'd, with whisker'd snout,
And badger-colour'd hide. 36

He, ent'ring at the study-door,
Its ample area 'gan explore;
And something in the wind
Conjectur'd, sniffing round and round,
Better than all the books he found,
Food, chiefly, for the mind. 42

Just then, by adverse fate impress'd,
A dream disturb'd poor Bully's rest;
In sleep he seem'd to view
A rat, fast-clinging to the cage,
And, screaming at the sad presage,
Awoke and found it true. 48

For, aided both by ear and scent,
Right to his mark the monster went—
Ah, Muse! forbear to speak
Minute the horrors that ensued;
His teeth were strong, the cage was wood—
He left poor Bully's beak. 54

18 up all] away *first in 1808.*

He left it—but he should have ta'en
That beak, whence issued many a strain
Of such mellifluous tone,
Might have repaid him well, I wote,
For silencing so sweet a throat,
Fast set within his own. 60

Maria weeps—The Muses mourn—
So, when by Bacchanalians torn,
On Thracian Hebrus' side
The tree-enchanter Orpheus fell;
His head alone remain'd to tell
The cruel death he died. 66

ON A MISCHIEVOUS BULL,

WHICH THE OWNER OF HIM SOLD AT THE AUTHOR'S INSTANCE

[Written 1788 (?). Published 1808.]

Go—thou art all unfit to share
The pleasures of this place
With such as its old tenants are,
Creatures of gentler race.

The squirrel here his hoard provides,
Aware of wintry storms;
And wood-peckers explore the sides
Of rugged oaks for worms; 8

The sheep here smooths the knotted thorn
With frictions of her fleece;
And here I wander eve and morn,
Like her, a friend to peace.

Ah!—I could pity thee exil'd
From this secure retreat—
I would not lose it to be styl'd
The happiest of the great. 16

But thou canst taste no calm delight;
Thy pleasure is to show
Thy magnanimity in fight,
Thy prowess—therefore go—

I care not whether east or north,
So I no more may find thee,
The angry Muse thus sings thee forth,
And claps the gate behind thee. 24

55, 6 Oh, had he made that too his prey! . . . lay *1789*, *1808*.
60 set] stuck *1789*, *1808*.

INSCRIPTION FOR THE TOMB OF MR. HAMILTON

[Written 1788. Published 1800.]

PAUSE here, and think: a monitory rhime
Demands one moment of thy fleeting time.
Consult Life's silent clock, thy bounding vein;
Seems it to say—Health, here, has long to reign?
Hast thou the vigour of thy youth? an eye
That beams delight? an heart untaught to sigh?—
Yet fear. Youth, ofttimes healthful and at ease,
Anticipates a day it never sees,
And many a tomb, like Hamilton's, aloud
Exclaims, "Prepare thee for an early shroud!" 10

ANNUS MEMORABILIS, 1789

WRITTEN IN COMMEMORATION OF HIS MAJESTY'S HAPPY RECOVERY

[Written March, 1789. Published 1808.]

I RANSACK'D, for a theme of song,
Much ancient chronicle, and long;
I read of bright embattled fields,
Of trophied helmets, spears, and shields,
Of chiefs, whose single arm could boast
Prowess to dissipate a host;
Through tomes of fable and of dream
I sought an eligible theme,
But none I found, or found them shar'd
Already by some happier bard. 10
To modern times, with Truth to guide
My busy search, I next applied;
Here cities won, and fleets dispers'd,
Urg'd loud a claim to be rehears'd,
Deeds of unperishing renown,
Our fathers' triumphs, and our own.
Thus, as the bee, from bank to bow'r,
Assiduous sips at ev'ry flow'r,
But rests on none, till that be found
Where most nectareous sweets abound, 20
So I from theme to theme display'd
In many a page historic stray'd,
Siege after siege, fight after fight,
Contemplating with small delight,

Annus Memorabilis—7 tomes] times *1808*.

(For feats of sanguinary hue
Not always glitter in my view;)
Till, settling on the current year,
I found the far-sought treasure near;
A theme for poetry divine,
A theme t' ennoble even mine, 30
In memorable eighty-nine.

The spring of eighty-nine shall be
An æra cherish'd long by me,
Which joyful I will oft record,
And thankful at my frugal board;
For then the clouds of eighty-eight,
That threaten'd England's trembling state
With loss of what she least could spare,
Her sov'reign's tutelary care,
One breath of Heav'n, that cry'd—Restore! 40
Chas'd, never to assemble more,
And far the richest crown on Earth,
If valued by its wearer's worth,
The symbol of a righteous reign,
Sat fast on George's brows again.

Then peace and joy again possess'd
Our Queen's long-agitated breast,
Such joy and peace as can be known
By suff'rers like herself alone,
Who losing, or supposing lost, 50
The good on Earth they valued most,
For that dear sorrow's sake forego
All hope of happiness below,
Then suddenly regain the prize,
And flash thanksgivings to the skies!

O Queen of Albion, queen of isles!
Since all thy tears were chang'd to smiles,
The eyes that never saw thee, shine
With joy not unallied to thine,
Transports not chargeable with art 60
Illume the land's remotest part,
And strangers to the air of courts,
Both in their toils and at their sports,
The happiness of answer'd pray'rs,
That gilds thy features, show in theirs.

If they, who on thy state attend,
Awe-struck before thy presence bend,
'Tis but the natural effect
Of grandeur that ensures respect;
But she is something more than Queen, 70
Who is belov'd where never seen.

ON THE QUEEN'S VISIT TO LONDON

THE NIGHT OF THE 17TH MARCH, 1789

[Written March, 1789. Published by Hayley, 1803.]

WHEN long sequester'd from his throne
George took his seat again,
By right of worth, not blood alone,
Entitled here to reign!

Then Loyalty, with all her lamps
New trimm'd, a gallant show!
Chasing the darkness, and the damps,
Set London in a glow. 8

'Twas hard to tell, of streets or squares,
Which form'd the chief display,
These most resembling cluster'd stars,
Those the long milky way.

Bright shone the roofs, the domes, the spires,
And rockets flew, self-driven,
To hang their momentary fires
Amid the vault of Heaven. 16

So, fire with water to compare,
The ocean serves on high,
Up-spouted by a whale in air,
T' express unwieldy joy.

Had all the pageants of the world
In one procession join'd,
And all the banners been unfurl'd
That heralds e'er design'd, 24

For no such sight had England's Queen
Forsaken her retreat,
Where George recover'd made a scene
Sweet always, doubly sweet.

Yet glad she came that night to prove,
A witness undescried,
How much the object of her love
Was lov'd by all beside. 32

Darkness the skies had mantled o'er
In aid of her design—
Darkness O Queen! ne'er called before
To veil a deed of thine!

On borrow'd wheels away she flies,
Resolv'd to be unknown,
And gratify no curious eyes
That night, except her own. 40

5 her] his *MS.*, *1815*. 9 or *1815*: of *Hayley*.
20 express] attest *MS.*

Arriv'd, a night like noon she sees,
  And hears the million hum;
As all by instinct, like the bees,
  Had known their sov'reign come.

Pleas'd she beheld aloft pourtray'd
  On many a splendid wall,
Emblems of health, and heav'nly aid,
  And George the theme of all. 48

Unlike the ænigmatic line,
  So difficult to spell!
Which shook Belshazzar at his wine,
  The night his city fell.

Soon watery grew her eyes and dim,
  But with a joyful tear!
None else, except in pray'r for him,
  George ever drew from her. 56

It was a scene in ev'ry part
  Like that in fable feign'd,
And seem'd by some magician's art
  Created, and sustain'd.

But other magic there, she knew,
  Had been exerted none,
To raise such wonders in her view,
  Save love of George alone! 64

That cordial thought her spirit cheer'd,
  And through the cumb'rous throng,
Not else unworthy to be fear'd,
  Convey'd her calm along.

So, ancient poets say, serene
  The sea-maid rides the waves,
And fearless of the billowy scene,
  Her peaceful bosom laves. 72

With more than astronomic eyes
  She view'd the sparkling show;
One Georgian star adorns the skies,
  She myriads found below.

Yet let the glories of a night
  Like that, once seen, suffice!
Heav'n grant us no such future sight,
  Such previous woe the price! 80

42 millions *Hayley* (*1803*). 58 that] those *MS.*, *1815*. 61 But] Yet *MS.* 65 spirits *Hayley* (*1803*). 80 precious *Hayley* (*1806*).

ON THE BENEFIT RECEIVED BY HIS MAJESTY FROM SEA-BATHING

IN THE YEAR 1789

[Written 1789. Published by Johnson, 1815.]

O SOV'REIGN of an isle renown'd
  For undisputed sway
Wherever o'er yon gulph profound
  Her navies wing their way,

With juster claim she builds at length
  Her empire on the sea,
And well may boast the waves her strength,
  Which strength restor'd to Thee. 8

CATHARINA

ADDRESSED TO MISS STAPLETON

[Written May 1789. Published 1795.]

SHE came—she is gone—we have met—
  And meet perhaps never again;
The sun of that moment is set,
  And seems to have risen in vain.
Catharina has fled like a dream—
  (So vanishes pleasure, alas!)
But has left a regret and esteem
  That will not so suddenly pass. 8

The last evening ramble we made,
  Catharina, Maria, and I,
Our progress was often delay'd
  By the nightingale warbling nigh.
We paus'd under many a tree,
  And much she was charm'd with a tone
Less sweet to Maria and me,
  Who had witness'd so lately her own. 16

My numbers that day she had sung,
  And gave them a grace so divine,
As only her musical tongue
  Could infuse into numbers of mine.
The longer I heard, I esteem'd
  The work of my fancy the more,
And e'en to myself never seem'd
  So tuneful a poet before. 24

Catharina—Title] now Mrs. Courtney *added after* Stapleton *in 1803.*

Though the pleasures of London exceed
  In number the days of the year,
Catharina, did nothing impede,
  Would feel herself happier here;
For the close-woven arches of limes,
  On the banks of our river, I know,
Are sweeter to her many times
  Than all that the city can show. 32

So it is, when the mind is endued
  With a well-judging taste from above,
Then, whether embellish'd or rude,
  'Tis nature alone that we love.
The achievements of art may amuse,
  May even our wonder excite,
But groves, hills, and vallies, diffuse
  A lasting, a sacred delight. 40

Since then in the rural recess
  Catharina alone can rejoice,
May it still be her lot to possess
  The scene of her sensible choice!
To inhabit a mansion remote
  From the clatter of street-pacing steeds,
And by Philomel's annual note
  To measure the life that she leads. 48

With her book, and her voice, and her lyre,
  To wing all her moments at home,
And with scenes that new rapture inspire
  As oft as it suits her to roam,
She will have just the life she prefers,
  With little to wish or to fear,
And ours will be pleasant as hers,
  Might we view her enjoying it here. 56

THE COCK-FIGHTER'S GARLAND

[Written May, 1789. Published by Johnson, 1815.]

Muse—Hide his name of whom I sing,
Lest his surviving house thou bring
  For his sake, into scorn,
Nor speak the school from which he drew
The much or little that he knew,
  Nor place where he was born. 6

32 all] aught *first in 1808*. 54 wish] hope *first in 1808*.

That such a man once was, may seem
Worthy of record (if the theme
Perchance may credit win)
For proof to man, what man may prove,
If grace depart, and demons move
The source of guilt within. 12

This man (for since the howling wild
Disclaims him, man he must be styl'd)
Wanted no good below,
Gentle he was, if gentle birth
Could make him such, and he had worth,
If wealth can worth bestow. 18

In social talk and ready jest
He shone superior at the feast,
And qualities of mind
Illustrious in the eyes of those
Whose gay society he chose
Possess'd of ev'ry kind. 24

Methinks I see him powder'd red,
With bushy locks his well-dress'd head
Wing'd broad on either side,
The mossy rose-bud not so sweet;
His steeds superb, his carriage neat
As lux'ry could provide. 30

Can such be cruel?—Such can be
Cruel as hell, and so was he;
A tyrant entertain'd
With barb'rous sports, whose fell delight
Was to encourage mortal fight
'Twixt birds to battle train'd. 36

One feather'd champion he possess'd,
His darling far beyond the rest,
Which never knew disgrace,
Nor e'er had fought, but he made flow
The life-blood of his fiercest foe,
The Cæsar of his race. 42

It chanc'd, at last, when on a day
He push'd him to the desp'rate fray,
His courage droop'd, he fled.
The master storm'd, the prize was lost,
And, instant, frantic at the cost,
He doom'd his fav'rite dead. 48

He seiz'd him fast, and from the pit
Flew to the kitchen, snatch'd the spit,
And, Bring me cord, he cried—
The cord was brought, and, at his word,
To that dire implement the bird
Alive and struggling, tied. 54

The horrid sequel asks a veil,
And all the terrors of the tale
That can be, shall be, sunk—
Led by the suff'rer's screams aright
His shock'd companions view the sight
And him with fury drunk. 60

All, suppliant, beg a milder fate
For the old warrior at the grate:
He, deaf to pity's call,
Whirl'd round him rapid as a wheel
His culinary club of steel,
Death menacing on all. 66

But vengeance hung not far remote,
For while he stretch'd his clam'rous throat
And heav'n and earth defied,
Big with the curse too closely pent
That struggled vainly for a vent
He totter'd, reel'd, and died. 72

'Tis not for us, with rash surmise,
To point the judgments of the skies,
But judgments plain as this,
That, sent for man's instruction, bring
A written label on their wing,
'Tis hard to read amiss. 78

TO MRS. THROCKMORTON

ON HER BEAUTIFUL TRANSCRIPT OF HORACE'S ODE, AD LIBRUM SUUM

[Written Feb., 1790. Published by Hayley, 1803.]

Maria, could Horace have guess'd
What honour awaited his ode
To his own little volume address'd,
The honour which you have bestow'd,
Who have trac'd it in characters here,
So elegant, even, and neat;
He had laugh'd at the critical sneer,
Which he seems to have trembled to meet. 8

And sneer, if you please, he had said,
  Hereafter a nymph shall arise,
Who shall give me, when you are all dead,
  The glory your malice denies;
Shall dignity give to my lay,
  Although but a mere bagatelle;
And even a poet shall say,
  Nothing ever was written so well. 16

ON THE RECEIPT OF MY MOTHER'S PICTURE OUT OF NORFOLK

THE GIFT OF MY COUSIN ANN BODHAM

[Written Feb., 1790. Published in pamphlet with *Dog and Water-Lily*, 1798; afterwards in Poems, 1798.]

OH that those lips had language! Life has pass'd
With me but roughly since I heard thee last.
Those lips are thine—thy own sweet smiles I see,
The same that oft in childhood solaced me;
Voice only fails, else, how distinct they say,
"Grieve not, my child, chase all thy fears away!"
The meek intelligence of those dear eyes
(Blest be the art that can immortalize,
The art that baffles time's tyrannic claim
To quench it) here shines on me still the same. 10
  Faithful remembrancer of one so dear,
Oh welcome guest, though unexpected, here!
Who bidd'st me honour with an artless song,
Affectionate, a mother lost so long,
I will obey, not willingly alone,
But gladly, as the precept were her own;
And, while that face renews my filial grief,
Fancy shall weave a charm for my relief—
Shall steep me in Elysian reverie,
A momentary dream, that thou art she. 20
  My mother! when I learn'd that thou wast dead,
Say, wast thou conscious of the tears I shed?
Hover'd thy spirit o'er thy sorrowing son,
Wretch even then, life's journey just begun?
Perhaps thou gav'st me, though unseen, a kiss;
Perhaps a tear, if souls can weep in bliss—
Ah that maternal smile! it answers—Yes.
I heard the bell toll'd on thy burial day,
I saw the hearse that bore thee slow away,
And, turning from my nurs'ry window, drew 30
A long, long sigh, and wept a last adieu!

3 smile *first in 1808*. 25 unfelt *first in 1808*.

But was it such?—It was.—Where thou art gone
Adieus and farewells are a sound unknown.
May I but meet thee on that peaceful shore,
The parting sound shall pass my lips no more!
Thy maidens griev'd themselves at my concern,
Oft gave me promise of a quick return.
What ardently I wish'd, I long believ'd,
And, disappointed still, was still deceiv'd;
By disappointment every day beguil'd, 40
Dupe of *to-morrow* even from a child.
Thus many a sad to-morrow came and went,
Till, all my stock of infant sorrow spent,
I learn'd at last submission to my lot;
But, though I less deplor'd thee, ne'er forgot.
Where once we dwelt our name is heard no more,
Children not thine have trod my nurs'ry floor;
And where the gard'ner Robin, day by day,
Drew me to school along the public way,
Delighted with my bauble coach, and wrapt 50
In scarlet mantle warm, and velvet capt,
'Tis now become a history little known,
That once we call'd the past'ral house our own.
Short-liv'd possession! but the record fair
That mem'ry keeps of all thy kindness there,
Still outlives many a storm that has effac'd
A thousand other themes less deeply trac'd.
Thy nightly visits to my chamber made,
That thou might'st know me safe and warmly laid;
Thy morning bounties ere I left my home, 60
The biscuit, or confectionary plum;
The fragrant waters on my cheeks bestow'd
By thy own hand, till fresh they shone and glow'd;
All this, and more endearing still than all,
Thy constant flow of love, that knew no fall,
Ne'er roughen'd by those cataracts and brakes
That humour interpos'd too often makes;
All this still legible in mem'ry's page,
And still to be so, to my latest age,
Adds joy to duty, makes me glad to pay 70
Such honours to thee as my numbers may;
Perhaps a frail memorial, but sincere,
Not scorn'd in heav'n, though little notic'd here.
Could time, his flight revers'd, restore the hours,
When, playing with thy vesture's tissued flow'rs,
The violet, the pink, and jessamine,
I prick'd them into paper with a pin,

35 sound] word *first in 1808*. 37 a] thy *first in 1808*. 40 disappointment] expectation *first in 1808*. 43 sorrows *1799*.

(And thou wast happier than myself the while,
Would'st softly speak, and stroke my head and smile)
Could those few pleasant hours again appear, 80
Might one wish bring them, would I wish them here?
I would not trust my heart—the dear delight
Seems so to be desir'd, perhaps I might.—
But no—what here we call our life is such,
So little to be lov'd, and thou so much,
That I should ill requite thee to constrain
Thy unbound spirit into bonds again.
 Thou, as a gallant bark from Albion's coast
(The storms all weather'd and the ocean cross'd)
Shoots into port at some well-haven'd isle, 90
Where spices breathe and brighter seasons smile,
There sits quiescent on the floods that show
Her beauteous form reflected clear below,
While airs impregnated with incense play
Around her, fanning light her streamers gay;
So thou, with sails how swift! hast reach'd the shore
"Where tempests never beat nor billows roar[1],"
And thy lov'd consort on the dang'rous tide
Of life, long since, has anchor'd at thy side.
But me, scarce hoping to attain that rest, 100
Always from port withheld, always distress'd—
Me howling winds drive devious, tempest toss'd,
Sails ript, seams op'ning wide, and compass lost,
And day by day some current's thwarting force
Sets me more distant from a prosp'rous course.
But oh the thought, that thou art safe, and he!
That thought is joy, arrive what may to me.
My boast is not that I deduce my birth
From loins enthron'd, and rulers of the earth;
But higher far my proud pretensions rise— 110
The son of parents pass'd into the skies.
And now, farewell—time, unrevok'd, has run
His wonted course, yet what I wish'd is done.
By contemplation's help, not sought in vain,
I seem t' have liv'd my childhood o'er again;
To have renew'd the joys that once were mine,
Without the sin of violating thine:
And, while the wings of fancy still are free,
And I can view this mimic shew of thee,
Time has but half succeeded in his theft— 120
Thyself remov'd, thy power to sooth me left.

[1] Garth [C.].

80 hours] days *first in 1808*. 99 at] by *first in 1808*.
102 winds] blasts *first in 1808*. 106 But] Yet *first in 1808*.

INSCRIPTION

FOR A STONE ERECTED AT THE SOWING OF A GROVE OF OAKS AT CHILLINGTON, THE SEAT OF T. GIFFORD, ESQ., 1790

[Written June, 1790. Published by Hayley, 1803.]

OTHER stones the æra tell,
When some feeble mortal fell:
I stand here to date the birth
Of these hardy sons of earth.
  Which shall longest brave the sky,
Storm and frost? these oaks or I?
Pass an age or two away,
I must moulder and decay,
But the years that crumble me
Shall invigorate the tree, 10
Spread the branch, dilate its size,
Lift its summit to the skies.
  Cherish honour, virtue, truth!
So shalt thou prolong thy youth;
Wanting these, however fast
Man be fixt, and form'd to last,
He is lifeless even now,
Stone at heart, and cannot grow.

ANOTHER

FOR A STONE ERECTED ON A SIMILAR OCCASION AT THE SAME PLACE IN THE FOLLOWING YEAR

[Written 1790. Published by Hayley, 1806.]

Reader! behold a monument
  That asks no sigh or tear,
Though it perpetuate th' event
  Of a great burial here. 4

TO MRS. KING

ON HER KIND PRESENT TO THE AUTHOR; A PATCH-WORK COUNTERPANE OF HER OWN MAKING

[Written Aug., 1790. Published by Hayley, 1803.]

THE Bard, if e'er he feel at all,
Must sure be quicken'd by a call
  Both on his heart and head,
To pay with tuneful thanks the care,
And kindness of a Lady fair,
  Who deigns to deck his bed. 6

11 the] its *1815*.

A bed like this, in ancient time,
On Ida's barren top sublime,
(As Homer's Epic shows)
Composed of sweetest vernal flow'rs,
Without the aid of sun or show'rs,
For Jove and Juno rose. 12

Less beautiful, however gay,
Is that, which in the scorching day
Receives the weary swain;
Who, laying his long scythe aside,
Sleeps on some bank, with daisies pied,
'Till rous'd to toil again. 18

What labours of the loom I see!
Looms numberless have groan'd for me:
Should ev'ry maiden come
To scramble for the patch, that bears
The impress of the robe she wears,
The bell would toll for some. 24

And O! what havoc would ensue!
This bright display of ev'ry hue
All in a moment fled!
As if a storm should strip the bow'rs,
Of all their tendrils, leaves and flowr's,
Each pocketing a shred. 30

Thanks then to ev'ry gentle fair
Who will not come to peck me bare
As bird of borrow'd feather;
And thanks to one, above them all,
The gentle Fair of Pertenhall,
Who put THE WHOLE TOGETHER! 36

STANZAS

ON THE LATE INDECENT LIBERTIES TAKEN WITH THE REMAINS OF THE GREAT MILTON

[Written Aug. (?), 1790. Published by Hayley, 1803.]

ME too, perchance, in future days,
The sculptur'd stone shall show,
With Paphian myrtle, or with bays
Parnassian, on my brow.

But I, before that season come,
  Escap'd from ev'ry care,
Shall reach my refuge in the tomb,
  And sleep securely there[1]. 8

So sang in Roman tone and style
  The youthful bard, ere long
Ordain'd to grace his native isle
  With her sublimest song.

Who then but must conceive disdain,
  Hearing the deed unblest
Of wretches who have dar'd profane
  His dread sepulchral rest? 16

Ill fare the hands that heav'd the stones
  Where Milton's ashes lay!
That trembled not to grasp his bones,
  And steal his dust away!

Oh! ill-requited bard! neglect
  Thy living worth repaid,
And blind idolatrous respect
  As much affronts thee dead. 24

IN MEMORY OF
THE LATE JOHN THORNTON, ESQ.

[Written Nov., 1790. Published by Hayley, 1803.]

POETS attempt the noblest task they can,
Praising the Author of all good in man,
And next commemorating worthies lost,
The dead, in whom that good abounded most.
  Thee, therefore, of commercial fame, but more
Fam'd for thy probity, from shore to shore;
Thee, THORNTON, worthy in some page to shine
As honest, and more eloquent than mine,
I mourn; or since thrice happy thou must be,
The world, no longer thy abode, not thee; 10
Thee to deplore were grief mispent indeed;
It were to weep, that goodness has its meed,
That there is bliss prepar'd in yonder sky,
And glory for the virtuous, when they die.
  What pleasure can the miser's fondled hoard,
Or spendthrift's prodigal excess afford,
Sweet, as the privilege of healing woe
Suffer'd by virtue combating below?

[1] Forsitan et nostros ducat de marmore vultus
Nectens aut Paphia myrti aut Parnasside lauri
Fronde comas—At ego secura pace quiescam.
MILTON [H.]

Stanzas—5 before] or ere *Hayley* (*1803*).

That privilege was thine; Heav'n gave thee means
To illumine with delight the saddest scenes, 20
Till thy appearance chas'd the gloom, forlorn
As midnight, and despairing of a morn.
Thou hadst an industry in doing good,
Restless as his, who toils and sweats for food.
Av'rice in thee was the desire of wealth
By rust unperishable, or by stealth.
And if the genuine worth of gold depend
On application to its noblest end,
Thine had a value in the scales of Heaven,
Surpassing all that mine or mint have given: 30
And tho' God made thee of a nature prone
To distribution boundless of thy own,
And still, by motives of religious force,
Impell'd thee more to that heroic course;
Yet was thy liberality discreet;
Nice in its choice, and of a temp'rate heat;
And, though in act unwearied, secret still,
As, in some solitude, the summer rill
Refreshes, where it winds, the faded green,
And cheers the drooping flow'rs—unheard, unseen.
Such was thy Charity; no sudden start, 41
After long sleep of passion in the heart,
But steadfast principle, and in its kind
Of close alliance with th' eternal mind;
Trac'd easily to its true source above,
To Him, whose works bespeak his nature, Love.
Thy bounties all were Christian, and I make
This record of thee for the Gospel's sake;
That the incredulous themselves may see
Its use and pow'r exemplified in thee. 50

THE MORALIZER CORRECTED

A TALE

[Written (?). Published 1795.]

A HERMIT (or if 'chance you hold
That title now too trite and old),
A man, once young, who lived retired
As hermit could have well desired,
His hours of study clos'd at last,
And finish'd his concise repast,
Stoppled his cruse, replac'd his book
Within its customary nook,
And, staff in hand, set forth to share
The sober cordial of sweet air, 10

30 have] had *1815*. 36 temper'd *1815*. 44 alliance with] relation to *1815*.

Like Isaac, with a mind applied
To serious thought at evening-tide.
Autumnal rains had made it chill,
And from the trees that fringed his hill
Shades slanting at the close of day
Chill'd more his else delightful way.
Distant a little mile he spied
A western bank's still sunny side,
And right toward the favour'd place
Proceeding with his nimblest pace, 20
In hope to bask a little yet,
Just reach'd it when the sun was set.
Your hermit, young and jovial sirs!
Learns something from whate'er occurs—
And hence, he said, my mind computes
The real worth of man's pursuits.
His object chosen, wealth or fame,
Or other sublunary game,
Imagination to his view
Presents it deck'd with ev'ry hue 30
That can seduce him not to spare
His pow'rs of best exertion there,
But youth, health, vigour, to expend
On so desirable an end.
Ere long, approach life's evening shades,
The glow that fancy gave it fades;
And, earn'd too late, it wants the grace
That first engag'd him in the chase.
True, answer'd an angelic guide,
Attendant at the senior's side— 40
But whether all the time it cost
To urge the fruitless chase be lost,
Must be decided by the worth
Of that which call'd his ardour forth.
Trifles pursued, whate'er th' event,
Must cause him shame or discontent;
A vicious object still is worse,
Successful there, he wins a curse;
But he, whom e'en in life's last stage
Endeavours laudable engage, 50
Is paid, at least in peace of mind,
And sense of having well design'd;
And if, ere he attain his end,
His sun precipitate descend,
A brighter prize than that he meant
Shall recompense his mere intent.
No virtuous wish can bear a date
Either too early or too late.

THE NEEDLESS ALARM

A TALE

[Written (?). Published 1795.]

THERE is a field through which I often pass,
Thick overspread with moss and silky grass,
Adjoining close to Kilwick's echoing wood,
Where oft the bitch-fox hides her hapless brood,
Reserv'd to solace many a neighb'ring squire,
That he may follow them through brake and briar,
Contusion hazarding of neck or spine,
Which rural gentlemen call sport divine.
A narrow brook, by rushy banks conceal'd,
Runs in a bottom, and divides the field; 10
Oaks intersperse it, that had once a head,
But now wear crests of oven-wood instead;
And where the land slopes to its wat'ry bourn,
Wide yawns a gulph beside a ragged thorn;
Bricks line the sides, but shiver'd long ago,
And horrid brambles intertwine below;
A hollow scoop'd, I judge in ancient time,
For baking earth, or burning rock to lime.
Not yet the hawthorn bore her berries red,
With which the fieldfare, wint'ry guest, is fed; 20
Nor autumn yet had brush'd from ev'ry spray,
With her chill hand, the mellow leaves away;
But corn was hous'd, and beans were in the stack,
Now, therefore, issued forth the spotted pack,
With tails high mounted, ears hung low, and throats
With a whole gamut fill'd of heav'nly notes,
For which, alas! my destiny severe,
Though ears she gave me two, gave me no ear.
The sun, accomplishing his early march,
His lamp now planted on heav'n's topmost arch, 30
When, exercise and air my only aim,
And heedless whither, to that field I came,
Ere yet with ruthless joy the happy hound
Told hill and dale that Reynard's track was found,
Or with the high-rais'd horn's melodious clang
All Kilwick[1] and all Dingle-derry[1] rang.
Sheep graz'd the field; some with soft bosom press'd
The herb as soft, while nibbling stray'd the rest;
Nor noise was heard but of the hasty brook,
Struggling, detain'd in many a petty nook. 40
All seem'd so peaceful, that from them convey'd
To me, their peace by kind contagion spread.

[1] Two woods belonging to John Throckmorton, Esq. [C.].

But when the huntsman, with distended cheek,
'Gan make his instrument of music speak,
And from within the wood that crash was heard,
Though not a hound from whom it burst appear'd,
The sheep recumbent, and the sheep that graz'd,
All huddling into phalanx, stood and gaz'd,
Admiring, terrified, the novel strain,
Then cours'd the field around, and cours'd it round again; 50
But, recollecting with a sudden thought,
That flight in circles urg'd advanc'd them nought,
They gather'd close around the old pit's brink,
And thought again—but knew not what to think.
The man to solitude accustom'd long
Perceives in ev'ry thing that lives a tongue;
Not animals alone, but shrubs and trees,
Have speech for him, and understood with ease;
After long drought, when rains abundant fall,
He hears the herbs and flow'rs rejoicing all; 60
Knows what the freshness of their hue implies,
How glad they catch the largess of the skies;
But, with precision nicer still, the mind
He scans of ev'ry loco-motive kind;
Birds of all feather, beasts of ev'ry name,
That serve mankind, or shun them, wild or tame;
The looks and gestures of their griefs and fears
Have, all, articulation in his ears;
He spells them true by intuition's light,
And needs no glossary to set him right. 70
This truth premis'd was needful as a text,
To win due credence to what follows next.
Awhile they mus'd; surveying ev'ry face,
Thou hadst suppos'd them of superior race;
Their periwigs of wool, and fears combin'd,
Stamp'd on each countenance such marks of mind,
That sage they seem'd, as lawyers o'er a doubt,
Which, puzzling long, at last they puzzle out;
Or academic tutors, teaching youths,
Sure ne'er to want them, mathematic truths; 80
When thus a mutton, statelier than the rest,
A ram, the ewes and wethers, sad, address'd:
Friends! we have liv'd too long. I never heard
Sounds such as these, so worthy to be fear'd.
Could I believe, that winds for ages pent
In earth's dark womb have found at last a vent,
And from their prison-house below arise,
With all these hideous howlings to the skies,

62 largess *first in 1803*: largeness *1795–1800*.

I could be much compos'd, nor should appear
For such a cause to feel the slightest fear. 90
Yourselves have seen, what time the thunders roll'd
All night, me resting quiet in the fold.
Or heard we that tremendous bray alone,
I could expound the melancholy tone;
Should deem it by our old companion made,
The ass; for he, we know, has lately stray'd,
And being lost, perhaps, and wand'ring wide,
Might be suppos'd to clamour for a guide.
But ah! those dreadful yells what soul can hear,
That owns a carcase, and not quake for fear? 100
Daemons produce them doubtless, brazen-claw'd
And fang'd with brass the daemons are abroad;
I hold it, therefore, wisest and most fit,
That, life to save, we leap into the pit.
  Him answer'd then his loving mate and true,
But more discreet than he, a Cambrian ewe.
  How? leap into the pit our life to save?
To save our life leap all into the grave?
For can we find it less? Contemplate first
The depth how awful! falling there we burst; 110
Or should the brambles, interpos'd, our fall
In part abate, that happiness were small;
For with a race like theirs no chance I see
Of peace or ease to creatures clad as we.
Meantime, noise kills not. Be it Dapple's bray,
Or be it not, or be it whose it may,
And rush those other sounds, that seem by tongues
Of daemons utter'd, from whatever lungs,
Sounds are but sounds, and till the cause appear,
We have at least commodious standing here; 120
Come, fiend, come, fury, giant, monster, blast
From earth or hell, we can but plunge at last.
  While thus she spake, I fainter heard the peals,
For Reynard, close attended at his heels,
By panting dog, tir'd man, and spatter'd horse,
Through mere good fortune, took a diff'rent course.
The flock grew calm again, and I, the road
Following that led me to my own abode,
Much wonder'd that the silly sheep had found
Such cause of terror in an empty sound, 130
So sweet to huntsman, gentleman, and hound.

MORAL

  Beware of desp'rate steps. The darkest day
  (Live till to-morrow) will have pass'd away.

133 Live] Left *1800* (*8vo*).

EPIGRAM

ON THE REFUSAL OF THE UNIVERSITY OF OXFORD TO SUBSCRIBE TO HIS TRANSLATION OF HOMER

[Written in letter to Mrs. Throckmorton, April 1, 1791. Published by Hayley, 1803.]

COULD Homer come himself, distress'd and poor,
And tune his harp at Rhedicina's door,
The rich old vixen would exclaim (I fear)
Begone! no tramper gets a farthing here. 4

THE FOUR AGES

(A BRIEF FRAGMENT OF AN EXTENSIVE PROJECTED POEM)

[Written May (?), 1791. Published by Hayley, 1803.]

"I COULD be well content, allow'd the use
Of past experience, and the wisdom glean'd
From worn-out follies, now acknowledg'd such,
To recommence life's trial, in the hope
Of fewer errors, on a second proof!"
Thus, while grey evening lull'd the wind, and call'd
Fresh odours from the shrubb'ry at my side,
Taking my lonely winding walk, I mus'd,
And held accustom'd conference with my heart;
When, from within it, thus a voice replied. 10
"Could'st thou in truth? and art thou taught at length
This wisdom, and but this, from all the past?
Is not the pardon of thy long arrear,
Time wasted, violated laws, abuse
Of talents, judgments, mercies, better far
Than opportunity vouchsaf'd to err
With less excuse, and haply, worse effect?"
I heard, and acquiesc'd: then to and fro
Oft pacing, as the mariner his deck,
My grav'lly bounds, from self to human kind 20
I pass'd, and next consider'd—what is man?
Knows he his origin?—can he ascend
By reminiscence to his earliest date?
Slept he in Adam? and in those from him
Through num'rous generations, till he found
At length his destin'd moment to be born?
Or was he not, till fashion'd in the womb?
Deep myst'ries both! which schoolmen much have toil'd
T' unriddle, and have left them myst'ries still.

It is an evil, incident to man, 30
And of the worst, that unexplor'd he leaves
Truths useful, and attainable with ease,
To search forbidden deeps, where myst'ry lies
Not to be solv'd, and useless if it might.
Myst'ries are food for angels; they digest
With ease, and find them nutriment; but man,
While yet he dwells below, must stoop to glean
His manna from the ground, or starve, and die.

. . . .

THE JUDGMENT OF THE POETS

[Written May, 1791. Published by Hayley, 1803.]

Two nymphs, both nearly of an age,
Of num'rous charms possess'd,
A warm dispute once chanc'd to wage,
Whose temper was the best.

The worth of each had been complete,
Had both alike been mild;
But one, although her smile was sweet,
Frown'd oft'ner than she smil'd, 8

And in her humour, when she frown'd,
Would raise her voice, and roar;
And shake with fury, to the ground,
The garland that she wore.

The other was of gentler cast,
From all such frenzy clear;
Her frowns were seldom known to last,
And never prov'd severe. 16

To poets of renown in song,
The nymphs referr'd the cause,
Who, strange to tell, all judg'd it wrong,
And gave misplac'd applause.

They gentle call'd, and kind, and soft,
The flippant, and the scold;
And though she chang'd her mood so oft,
That failing left untold. 24

No judges, sure, were e'er so mad,
Or so resolv'd to err;
In short, the charms her sister had
They lavish'd all on her.

Then thus the God, whom fondly they
Their great inspirer call,
Was heard, one genial summer's day,
To reprimand them all. 32

Since thus ye have combin'd, he said,
  My favourite nymph to slight,
Adorning May, that peevish maid!
  With June's undoubted right;

The minx shall, for your folly's sake,
  Still prove herself a shrew;
Shall make your scribbling fingers ache,
  And pinch your noses blue. 40

EPITAPH ON MRS. M. HIGGINS, OF WESTON

[Written 1791. Published by Hayley, 1803.]

LAURELS may flourish round the conqu'ror's tomb,
But happiest they, who win the world to come:
Believers have a silent field to fight,
And their exploits are veil'd from human sight.
They in some nook, where little known they dwell,
Kneel, pray in faith, and rout the hosts of hell;
Eternal triumphs crown their toils divine,
And all those triumphs, Mary, now are thine. 8

THE RETIRED CAT

[Written 1791. Published by Hayley, 1803.]

A POET'S cat, sedate and grave,
As poet well could wish to have,
Was much addicted to inquire
For nooks, to which she might retire,
And where, secure as mouse in chink,
She might repose, or sit and think.
I know not where she caught the trick—
Nature perhaps herself had cast her
In such a mould PHILOSOPHIQUE,
Or else she learn'd it of her master. 10
Sometimes ascending, debonair,
An apple-tree or lofty pear,
Lodg'd with convenience in the fork,
She watched the gard'ner at his work;
Sometimes her ease and solace sought
In an old empty wat'ring pot,
There wanting nothing, save a fan,
To seem some nymph in her sedan,
Apparell'd in exactest sort,
And ready to be borne to court. 20
  But love of change it seems has place
Not only in our wiser race;
Cats also feel as well as we
That passion's force, and so did she.

Her climbing, she began to find,
Expos'd her too much to the wind,
And the old utensil of tin
Was cold and comfortless within:
She therefore wish'd instead of those,
Some place of more serene repose, 30
Where neither cold might come, nor air
Too rudely wanton with her hair,
And sought it in the likeliest mode
Within her master's snug abode.
A draw'r,—it chanc'd, at bottom lin'd
With linen of the softest kind,
With such as merchants introduce
From India, for the ladies' use,—
A draw'r impending o'er the rest,
Half open in the topmost chest, 40
Of depth enough, and none to spare,
Invited her to slumber there.
Puss with delight beyond expression,
Survey'd the scene, and took possession.
Recumbent at her ease ere long,
And lull'd by her own hum-drum song,
She left the cares of life behind,
And slept as she would sleep her last,
When in came, housewifely inclin'd,
The chambermaid, and shut it fast, 50
By no malignity impell'd,
But all unconscious whom it held.
Awaken'd by the shock (cried puss)
Was ever cat attended thus!
The open draw'r was left, I see,
Merely to prove a nest for me,
For soon as I was well compos'd,
Then came the maid, and it was closed:
How smooth these 'kerchiefs, and how sweet,
O what a delicate retreat! 60
I will resign myself to rest
Till Sol, declining in the west,
Shall call to supper; when, no doubt,
Susan will come and let me out.
The evening came, the sun descended,
And puss remain'd still unattended.
The night roll'd tardily away,
(With her indeed 'twas never day)
The sprightly morn her course renew'd,
The evening gray again ensued, 70
And puss came into mind no more
Than if entomb'd the day before.

With hunger pinch'd, and pinch'd for room,
She now presag'd approaching doom,
Not slept a single wink, or purr'd,
Conscious of jeopardy incurr'd.
That night, by chance, the poet watching,
Heard an inexplicable scratching,
His noble heart went pit-a-pat,
And to himself he said—what's that? 80
He drew the curtain at his side,
And forth he peep'd, but nothing spied.
Yet, by his ear directed, guess'd
Something imprison'd in the chest,
And doubtful what, with prudent care,
Resolv'd it should continue there.
At length a voice, which well he knew,
A long and melancholy mew,
Saluting his poetic ears,
Consol'd him, and dispell'd his fears; 90
He left his bed, he trod the floor,
He 'gan in haste the draw'rs explore,
The lowest first, and without stop,
The rest in order to the top.
For 'tis a truth well known to most,
That whatsoever thing is lost,
We seek it, ere it come to light,
In ev'ry cranny but the right.
Forth skipp'd the cat; not now replete
As erst with airy self-conceit, 100
Nor in her own fond apprehension,
A theme for all the world's attention,
But modest, sober, cur'd of all
Her notions hyberbolical,
And wishing for a place of rest
Any thing rather than a chest:
Then stept the poet into bed,
With this reflexion in his head:

MORAL

Beware of too sublime a sense
Of your own worth and consequence! 110
The man who dreams himself so great,
And his importance of such weight,
That all around, in all that's done,
Must move and act for him alone,
Will learn, in school of tribulation,
The folly of his expectation.

YARDLEY OAK

[Written 1791. Published by Hayley, 1804. The MS. is in the Cowper Museum at Olney.]

SURVIVOR sole, and hardly such, of all
That once liv'd here thy brethren, at my birth
(Since which I number three-score winters past)
A shatter'd veteran, hollow-trunk'd perhaps
As now, and with excoriate forks deform,
Relicts of ages! Could a mind, imbued
With truth from heav'n, created thing adore,
I might with rev'rence kneel and worship thee.
  It seems idolatry with some excuse
When our fore-father Druids in their oaks 10
Imagin'd sanctity. The conscience yet
Unpurified by an authentic act
Of amnesty, the meed of blood divine,
Lov'd not the light, but gloomy into gloom
Of thickest shades, like Adam after taste
Of fruit proscrib'd, as to a refuge, fled.
  Thou wast a bauble once; a cup and ball,
Which babes might play with; and the thievish jay
Seeking her food, with ease might have purloin'd
The auburn nut that held thee, swallowing down
Thy yet close-folded latitude of boughs 21
And all thine embryo vastness, at a gulp.
But Fate thy growth decreed: autumnal rains
Beneath thy parent tree mellow'd the soil
Design'd thy cradle, and a skipping deer,
With pointed hoof dibbling the glebe, prepar'd
The soft receptacle in which secure
Thy rudiments should sleep the winter through.
  So Fancy dreams—Disprove it, if ye can,
Ye reas'ners broad awake, whose busy search 30
Of argument, employ'd too oft amiss,
Sifts half the pleasures of short life away.
  Thou fell'st mature, and in the loamy clod
Swelling, with vegetative force instinct
Didst burst thine egg, as theirs the fabled Twins
Now stars; two lobes, protruding, pair'd exact;
A leaf succeeded, and another leaf,
And all the elements thy puny growth
Fost'ring propitious, thou becam'st a twig.
  Who liv'd when thou wast such? Oh couldst
    thou speak, 40
As in Dodona once thy kindred trees
Oracular, I would not curious ask
The future, best unknown, but at thy mouth
Inquisitive, the less ambiguous past.

By thee I might correct, erroneous oft,
The clock of history, facts and events
Timing more punctual, unrecorded facts
Recov'ring, and misstated setting right—
Desp'rate attempt, till trees shall speak again!
Time made thee what thou wast—King of the woods; 50
And Time hath made thee what thou art—a cave
For owls to roost in. Once thy spreading boughs
O'erhung the champain; and the numerous flock
That graz'd it stood beneath that ample cope
Uncrowded, yet safe-shelter'd from the storm.
No flock frequents thee now. Thou hast outliv'd
Thy popularity and art become
(Unless verse rescue thee awhile) a thing
Forgotten, as the foliage of thy youth.
While thus through all the stages thou hast push'd
Of treeship, first a seedling hid in grass, 61
Then twig, then sapling, and, as century roll'd
Slow after century, a giant bulk
Of girth enormous, with moss-cushion'd root
Upheav'd above the soil, and sides imboss'd
With prominent wens globose, till at the last
The rottenness, which time is charg'd t' inflict
On other mighty ones, found also thee—
What exhibitions various hath the world
Witness'd of mutability in all 70
That we account most durable below!
Change is the diet, on which all subsist
Created changeable, and change at last
Destroys them.—Skies uncertain now the heat
Transmitting cloudless, and the solar beam
Now quenching in a boundless sea of clouds,—
Calm and alternate storm, moisture and drought,
Invigorate by turns the springs of life
In all that live, plant, animal, and man, 79
And in conclusion mar them. Nature's threads,
Fine passing thought, ev'n in her coarsest works,
Delight in agitation, yet sustain
The force, that agitates not unimpair'd,
But, worn by frequent impulse, to the cause
Of their best tone their dissolution owe.
Thought cannot spend itself, comparing still
The great and little of thy lot, thy growth
From almost nullity into a state

Between ll. 78 and 79 MS. has All-binding frost and all unbinding thaw *cancelled.*

Of matchless grandeur, and declension thence
Slow into such magnificent decay. 90
Time was, when, settling on thy leaf, a fly
Could shake thee to the root—and time has been
When tempests could not. At thy firmest age
Thou hadst within thy bole solid contents
That might have ribb'd the sides or plank'd the deck
Of some flagg'd admiral; and tortuous arms,
The ship-wright's darling treasure, didst present
To the four-quarter'd winds, robust and bold,
Warp'd into tough knee-timber [1], many a load.
But the axe spar'd thee; in those thriftier days
Oaks fell not, hewn by thousands, to supply 101
The bottomless demands of contest wag'd
For senatorial honours. Thus to Time
The task was left to whittle thee away
With his sly scythe, whose ever-nibbling edge
Noiseless, an atom and an atom more
Disjoining from the rest, has, unobserv'd,
Achiev'd a labour, which had, far and wide,
(By man perform'd) made all the forest ring.
  Embowell'd now, and of thy ancient self 110
Possessing nought but the scoop'd rind, that seems
An huge throat calling to the clouds for drink,
Which it would give in riv'lets to thy root,
Thou temptest none, but rather much forbid'st
The feller's toil, which thou couldst ill requite.
Yet is thy root sincere, sound as the rock,
A quarry of stout spurs and knotted fangs,
Which, crook'd into a thousand whimsies, clasp
The stubborn soil, and hold thee still erect.
  So stands a kingdom, whose foundations yet 120
Fail not, in virtue and in wisdom laid,
Though all the superstructure, by the tooth
Pulveriz'd of venality, a shell
Stands now, and semblance only of itself.
  Thine arms have left thee. Winds have rent them off
Long since, and rovers of the forest wild
With bow and shaft have burnt them. Some have left
A splinter'd stump bleach'd to a snowy white;
And some memorial none where once they grew.
Yet life still lingers in thee, and puts forth 130

[1] Knee-timber is found in the crooked arms of oak, which, by reason of their distortion, are easily adjusted to the angle formed where the deck and the ship-sides meet [H.].

95 or] and *Hayley*. 120 foundation . . . Fails *Hayley*.

Proof not contemptible of what she can,
Even where death predominates. The spring
Thee finds not less alive to her sweet force
Than yonder upstarts of the neighbour wood,
So much thy juniors, who their birth receiv'd
Half a millennium since the date of thine.
But since, although well qualified by age
To teach, no spirit dwells in thee, nor voice
May be expected from thee, seated here
On thy distorted root, with hearers none 140
Or prompter, save the scene, I will perform
Myself the oracle, and will discourse
In my own ear such matter as I may.
Thou, like myself, hast stage by stage attain'd
Life's wintry bourn; thou, after many years,
I after few; but few or many prove
A span in retrospect; for I can touch
With my least finger's end my own decease
And with extended thumb my natal hour,
And hadst thou also skill in measurement 150
As I, the past would seem as short to thee.
Evil and few—said Jacob—at an age
Thrice mine, and few and evil, I may think
The Prediluvian race, whose buxom youth
Endured two centuries, accounted theirs.
"Shortliv'd as foliage is the race of man.
The wind shakes down the leaves, the budding grove
Soon teems with others, and in spring they grow.
So pass mankind. One generation meets
Its destin'd period, and a new succeeds."[1] 160
Such was the tender but undue complaint
Of the Mæonian in old time; for who
Would drawl out centuries in tedious strife
Severe with mental and corporeal ill
And would not rather chuse a shorter race
To glory, a few decads here below?
One man alone, the Father of us all,
Drew not his life from woman; never gaz'd,
With mute unconsciousness of what he saw
On all around him; learn'd not by degrees, 170
Nor owed articulation to his ear;
But, moulded by his Maker into Man
At once, upstood intelligent, survey'd
All creatures, with precision understood

[1] The lines marked with inverted commas are borrowed from my own translation of Homer. Iliad 6, line 175 [C.].

133 Finds thee *Hayley*. 134 neighb'ring *Hayley*.

ll. 144–166 *crossed through in MS.; first printed by T. Wright in* Unpublished Poems of William Cowper, 1900. 148 fingers' *MS.*

Their purport, uses, properties, assign'd
To each his name significant, and, fill'd
With love and wisdom, render'd back to heav'n
In praise harmonious the first air he drew.
He was excus'd the penalties of dull
Minority. No tutor charg'd his hand 180
With the thought-tracing quill, or task'd his mind
With problems; history, not wanted yet,
Lean'd on her elbow, watching Time, whose course,
Eventful, should supply her with a theme;

* * * * * * * *

TO THE NIGHTINGALE
WHICH THE AUTHOR HEARD SING ON NEW-YEAR'S DAY, 1792

[Written Jan., 1792. Published by Hayley, 1803.]

WHENCE is it, that amaz'd I hear
  From yonder wither'd spray,
This foremost morn of all the year,
  The melody of May?

And why, since thousands would be proud
  Of such a favour shewn,
Am I selected from the crowd,
  To witness it alone? 8

Sing'st thou, sweet Philomel, to me,
  For that I also long
Have practis'd in the groves like thee,
  Though not like thee in song?

Or sing'st thou rather under force
  Of some divine command,
Commission'd to presage a course
  Of happier days at hand? 16

Thrice welcome then! for many a long
  And joyless year have I,
As thou to-day, put forth my song
  Beneath a wintry sky.

But thee no wintry skies can harm,
  Who only need'st to sing,
To make ev'n January charm,
  And ev'ry season Spring. 24

ll. 180–184 *originally written:*
Minority; no primer with his thumb
He soil'd, no grammar with his tears, but rose
Accomplish'd in the only tongue on earth
Taught then, the tongue in which he spake with God.

EPITAPH ON
A FREE BUT TAME REDBREAST

A FAVOURITE OF MISS SALLY HURDIS

[Written March, 1792. Published by Johnson, 1815.]

THESE are not dew-drops, these are tears,
  And tears by Sally shed
For absent Robin, who, she fears
  With too much cause, is dead.

One morn he came not to her hand
  As he was wont to come,
And, on her finger perch'd, to stand
  Picking his breakfast-crumb. 8

Alarm'd she call'd him, and perplext
  She sought him, but in vain,
That day he came not, nor the next,
  Nor ever came again.

She therefore rais'd him here a tomb,
  Though where he fell, or how,
None knows, so secret was his doom,
  Nor where he moulders now. 16

Had half a score of coxcombs died
  In social Robin's stead,
Poor Sally's tears had soon been dried,
  Or haply never shed.

But Bob was neither rudely bold
  Nor spiritlessly tame,
Nor was, like theirs, his bosom cold,
  But always in a flame. 24

SONNET

TO WILLIAM WILBERFORCE, ESQ.

[Written April, 1792. Printed in *The Northampton Mercury* in April 1792; published by Hayley, 1803.]

THY country, Wilberforce, with just disdain,
Hears thee, by cruel men and impious, call'd
Fanatic, for thy zeal to loose th' enthrall'd
From exile, public sale, and slav'ry's chain.
Friend of the poor, the wrong'd, the fetter-gall'd,
Fear not lest labour such as thine be vain!
Thou hast achiev'd a part; hast gain'd the ear
Of Britain's senate to thy glorious cause;
Hope smiles, joy springs, and tho' cold caution pause

And weave delay, the better hour is near, 10
That shall remunerate thy toils severe
By peace for Afric, fenc'd with British laws.
Enjoy what thou hast won, esteem and love
From all the just on earth, and all the blest above!

TO WARREN HASTINGS, ESQ.

BY AN OLD SCHOOL-FELLOW OF HIS AT WESTMINSTER

[Written May, 1792. Published by Hayley, 1803.]

HASTINGS! I knew thee young, and of a mind,
While young, humane, conversable, and kind,
Nor can I well believe thee, gentle THEN,
Now grown a villain, and the WORST of men.
But rather some suspect, who have oppress'd
And worried thee, as not themselves the BEST. 6

TO DR. AUSTIN, OF CECIL STREET, LONDON

[Written May, 1792. Published by Hayley, 1803.]

AUSTIN! accept a grateful verse from me!
The poet's treasure! no inglorious fee!
Lov'd by the Muses, thy ingenuous mind
Pleasing requital in a verse may find;
Verse oft has dash'd the scythe of Time aside,
Immortalizing names which else had died:
And oh! could I command the glitt'ring wealth,
With which sick kings are glad to purchase health;
Yet, if extensive fame, and sure to live,
Were in the power of verse like mine to give, 10
I would not recompense his art with less,
Who, giving Mary health, heals my distress.
Friend of my friend! I love thee, though unknown,
And boldly call thee, being his, my own.

TO WILLIAM HAYLEY, ESQ.

[Written June 2, 1792. Published by Johnson, 1815. There is a copy among the Ash MSS.]

HAYLEY, thy tenderness fraternal shown
In our first interview, delightful guest!
To Mary and me for her dear sake distress'd,
Such as it is has made my heart thy own,
Though heedless now of new engagements grown;
For threescore winters make a wintry breast,
And I had purpos'd ne'er to go in quest
Of Friendship more, except with God alone.

But thou hast won me; nor is God my foe,
Who, ere this last afflictive scene began, 10
Sent thee to mitigate the dreadful blow,
My brother, by whose sympathy I know
Thy true deserts infallibly to scan,
Not more t' admire the Bard than love the Man.

CATHARINA

THE SECOND PART

ON HER MARRIAGE TO GEORGE COURTENAY, Esq.

[Written June, 1792. Published by Hayley, 1803. There is a copy among the Ash MSS.]

BELIEVE it or not, as you choose,
 The doctrine is certainly true
That the future is known to the Muse,
 And poets are oracles too.

I did but express a desire
 To see Catharina at home
At the side of my friend George's fire,
 And lo! she is actually come. 8

Such prophecy some may despise,
 But the wish of a poet and friend
Perhaps is approv'd in the skies,
 And therefore attains to its end.

'Twas a wish that flew ardently forth
 From a bosom effectually warm'd
With the talents, the graces, and worth
 Of the person for whom it was form'd. 16

Maria[1] would leave us, I knew,
 To the grief and regret of us all;
But less to our grief, could we view
 Catharina the Queen of the Hall.

And therefore I wish'd as I did,
 And therefore this union of hands
Not a whisper was heard to forbid,
 But all cry Amen to the bands. 24

Since, therefore, I seem to incur
 No danger of wishing in vain
When making good wishes for her,
 I will e'en to my wishes again—

[1] Lady Throckmorton [H.].

9 And such *Hayley* (*1803*). 21 And ... wish'd] This led me to wish *MS. quoted by T. Wright.* 24 bands *A.*, *Hayley* (*1803*): bans *or* banns *Hayley* (*1812*), *Southey, and modern edd.*

With one I have made her a wife,
And now I will try with another,
Which I cannot suppress for my life—
How soon I can make her a mother. 32

LINES ADDRESSED TO DR. DARWIN

AUTHOR OF THE BOTANIC GARDEN

[Written June, 1792; for the first version of the poem see notes. Published 1800.]

Two poets[1], (poets by report
Not oft so well agree)
Sweet Harmonist of Flora's court!
Conspire to honour thee.

They best can judge a poet's worth,
Who oft themselves have known
The pangs of a poetic birth
By labours of their own. 8

We, therefore, pleas'd, extol thy song,
Though various, yet complete,
Rich in embellishment, as strong,
And learn'd, as it is sweet.

No envy mingles with our praise,
Though could our hearts repine
At any poet's happier lays,
They would, they must, at thine. 16

But we, in mutual bondage knit
Of friendship's closest tie,
Can gaze on even Darwin's wit
With an unjaundic'd eye;

And deem the bard, whoe'er he be,
And howsoever known,
Who would not twine a wreath for thee,
Unworthy of his own. 24

EPITAPH ON FOP

A DOG BELONGING TO LADY THROCKMORTON

[Written Aug., 1792. Published by Hayley, 1803.]

THOUGH once a puppy, and though Fop by name,
Here moulders one, whose bones some honour claim;
No sycophant, although of spaniel race!
And though no hound, a martyr to the chase!

[1] Alluding to the poem by Mr. Hayley, which accompanied this [1800].

Ye squirrels, rabbits, leverets, rejoice!
Your haunts no longer echo to his voice.
This record of his fate exulting view,
He died worn out with vain pursuit of you.
"Yes!" the indignant shade of Fop replies,
"And worn with vain pursuit, man also dies." 10

TO GEORGE ROMNEY, ESQ.

ON HIS PICTURE OF ME IN CRAYONS, DRAWN AT EARTHAM IN THE SIXTY-FIRST YEAR OF MY AGE, AND IN THE MONTHS OF AUGUST AND SEPTEMBER, 1792

[Written Oct., 1792. Published by Hayley, 1803.]

ROMNEY! expert infallibly to trace,
On chart or canvas, not the form alone,
And 'semblance, but, however faintly shown,
The mind's impression too on ev'ry face,
With strokes that time ought never to erase:
Thou hast so pencil'd mine, that though I own
The subject worthless, I have never known
The artist shining with superior grace.
But this I mark, that symptoms none of woe
In thy incomparable work appear: 10
Well! I am satisfied it should be so,
Since, on maturer thought, the cause is clear;
For in my looks what sorrow could'st thou see
When I was Hayley's guest, and sat to thee?

AN EPITAPH

[Written 1792. Published by Johnson, 1815.]

HERE lies one, who never drew
Blood himself, yet many slew;
Gave the gun its aim, and figure
Made in field, yet ne'er pull'd trigger.
Armed men have gladly made
Him their guide, and him obey'd;
At his signified desire,
Would advance, present, and fire—
Stout he was, and large of limb,
Scores have fled at sight of him; 10
And to all this fame he rose
Only following his nose.
Neptune was he call'd, not he
Who controls the boist'rous sea,

To George Romney—1 infallible *Hayley* (*1803*).

But of happier command,
Neptune of the furrow'd land;
And, your wonder vain to shorten,
Pointer to Sir John Throckmorton.

EPITAPH ON MR. CHESTER, OF CHICHELEY

[Written April, 1793. Published by Hayley, 1803.]

TEARS flow, and cease not, where the good man lies,
Till all who know him follow to the skies.
Tears therefore fall where CHESTER's ashes sleep;
Him wife, friends, brothers, children, servants, weep--
And justly--few shall ever him transcend
As husband, parent, brother, master, friend.

ON A PLANT OF VIRGIN'S-BOWER

DESIGNED TO COVER A GARDEN-SEAT

[Written May (?), 1793. Published by Johnson, 1815.]

THRIVE gentle plant! and weave a bow'r
For Mary and for me,
And deck with many a splendid flow'r
Thy foliage large and free.
Thou cam'st from Eartham, and wilt shade
(If truly I divine)
Some future day th' illustrious head
Of him who made thee mine. 8
Should Daphne show a jealous frown
And envy seize the bay,
Affirming none so fit to crown
Such honour'd brows as they,
Thy cause with zeal we shall defend,
And with convincing pow'r;
For why should not the Virgin's Friend
Be crown'd with Virgin's-bow'r? 16

TO MY COUSIN ANNE BODHAM

ON RECEIVING FROM HER A NETWORK PURSE MADE BY HERSELF

[Written May, 1793. Published by Hayley, 1803.]

MY gentle Anne, whom heretofore,
When I was young, and thou no more
Than plaything for a nurse,
I danced and fondled on my knee,
A kitten both in size and glee!
I thank thee for my purse.

Gold pays the worth of all things here;
But not of love:—that gem's too dear
For richest rogues to win it;
I, therefore, as a proof of love,
Esteem thy present far above
The best things kept within it. 12

INSCRIPTION

FOR AN HERMITAGE IN THE AUTHOR'S GARDEN

[Written May, 1793. Published by Hayley, 1803.]

THIS cabin, Mary, in my sight appears,
Built as it has been in our waning years,
A rest afforded to our weary feet,
Preliminary to—the last retreat. 4

INSCRIPTION FOR A MOSS-HOUSE IN THE SHRUBBERY AT WESTON

[Written 1793 (?). Published in *Cowper illustrated*, 1804.]

HERE, free from riot's hated noise,
Be mine, ye calmer, purer joys,
A book or friend bestows;
Far from the storms that shake the great,
Contentment's gale shall fan my seat,
And sweeten my repose. 6

SONNET TO MRS. UNWIN

[Written May, 1793. Published by Hayley, 1803.]

MARY! I want a lyre with other strings;
Such aid from Heaven as some have feign'd they drew!
An eloquence scarce given to mortals, new,
And undebas'd by praise of meaner things!
That, ere through age or woe I shed my wings,
I may record thy worth, with honour due,
In verse as musical as thou art true,—
Verse, that immortalizes whom it sings!
But thou hast little need: there is a book,
By seraphs writ with beams of heav'nly light, 10
On which the eyes of God not rarely look;
A chronicle of actions just and bright!
There all thy deeds, my faithful Mary, shine,
And since thou own'st that praise, I spare thee mine.

Sonnet to Mrs. Unwin—8 Verse] And *1815*.

TO JOHN JOHNSON

ON HIS PRESENTING ME WITH AN ANTIQUE BUST OF HOMER

[Written May 22, 1793. Published by Hayley, 1803. There is a copy among the Ash MSS.]

KINSMAN belov'd, and as a son, by me!
When I behold this fruit of thy regard,
The sculptur'd form of my old fav'rite bard,
I rev'rence feel for him, and love for thee.
Joy too and grief! much joy, that there should be
Wise men, and learn'd, who grudge not to reward
With some applause my bold attempt, and hard,
Which others scorn: critics by courtesy!
The grief is this, that sunk in Homer's mine
I lose my precious years, now soon to fail, 10
Handling his gold, which, howsoe'er it shine,
Proves dross, when balanc'd in the Christian scale.
Be wiser thou—like our fore-father DONNE,
Seek heav'nly wealth, and work for God alone.

TO A YOUNG FRIEND

ON HIS ARRIVING AT CAMBRIDGE WET, WHEN NO RAIN HAD FALLEN THERE

[Written May, 1793. Published by Hayley, 1803.]

IF Gideon's fleece, which drench'd with dew he found,
While moisture none refresh'd the herbs around,
Might fitly represent the Church, endow'd
With heav'nly gifts, to heathens not allow'd;
In pledge, perhaps, of favours from on high,
Thy locks were wet, when other locks were dry.
Heav'n grant us half the omen—may we see
Not drought on others, but much dew on thee! 8

A TALE[1]

[Written June, 1793. Published by Hayley, 1803.]

IN Scotland's realm, where trees are few,
Nor even shrubs abound;
But where, however bleak the view,
Some better things are found:—

[1] This tale is founded on an article of intelligence which the author found in the Buckinghamshire Herald, for Saturday, June 1, 1793, in the following words:

Glasgow, May 23.

"In a block, or pulley, near the head of the mast of a gabert, now lying at the Broomielaw, there is a chaffinch's nest and four eggs. The nest was built while the vessel lay at Greenock, and was followed hither by both birds. Though the block is occasionally lowered for the inspection of the curious, the birds have not forsaken the nest. The cock, however, visits the nest but seldom; while the hen never leaves it, but when she descends to the hull for food" [H.].

To a Friend—6 others' *1815*.

For husband there and wife may boast
  Their union undefil'd;
And false ones are as rare almost,
  As hedge-rows in the wild:— 8

In Scotland's realm, forlorn and bare,
  This hist'ry chanc'd of late,—
This hist'ry of a wedded pair,
  A chaffinch and his mate.

The spring drew near, each felt a breast
  With genial instinct fill'd;
They pair'd, and only wish'd a nest,
  But found not where to build. 16

The heaths uncover'd, and the moors,
  Except with snow and sleet;
Sea-beaten rocks and naked shores,
  Could yield them no retreat.

Long time a breeding place they sought,
  'Till both grew vex'd and tir'd;
At length a ship arriving brought
  The good so long desir'd. 24

A ship!—could such a restless thing,
  Afford them place of rest?
Or was the merchant charg'd to bring
  The homeless birds a nest?

Hush!—silent hearers profit most!—
  This racer of the sea
Prov'd kinder to them than the coast,
  It serv'd them with a tree. 32

But such a tree! 'twas shaven deal,
  The tree they call a mast;
And had a hollow with a wheel
  Through which the tackle pass'd.

Within that cavity aloft
  Their roofless home they fixt;
Form'd with materials neat and soft,
  Bents, wool, and feathers mixt. 40

Four iv'ry eggs soon pave its floor,
  With russet specks bedight;—
The vessel weighs—forsakes the shore,
  And lessens to the sight.

The mother-bird is gone to sea,
  As she had chang'd her kind;
But goes the mate? Far wiser he
  Is doubtless left behind. 48

15 only wish'd *Hayley*: would have built *1815*. 47 mate] male *1815*.

No !—soon as from ashore he saw
  The winged mansion move ;
He flew to reach it, by a law
  Of never-failing love !

Then perching at his consort's side
  Was briskly borne along ;
The billows and the blast defied,
  And cheer'd her with a song. 56

The seaman, with sincere delight,
  His feather'd shipmates eyes,
Scarce less exulting in the sight,
  Than when he tows a prize.

For seamen much believe in signs,
  And from a chance so new
Each some approaching good divines,
  And may his hopes be true ! 64

Hail ! honour'd land ! a desert, where
  Not even birds can hide ;
Yet parent of this loving pair,
  Whom nothing could divide :

And ye, who rather than resign
  Your matrimonial plan,
Were not afraid to plough the brine,
  In company with man ; 72

To whose lean country much disdain
  We English often show ;
Yet from a richer nothing gain
  But wantonness and woe ;

Be it your fortune, year by year,
  The same resource to prove ;
And may ye, sometimes landing here,
  Instruct us how to love ! 80

TO WILLIAM HAYLEY, ESQ.

IN REPLY TO HIS SOLICITATION TO WRITE WITH HIM IN A LITERARY WORK

[Written June 29, 1793, in letter to Hayley. Published by Hayley, 1803. There is a copy among the Ash MSS.]

DEAR architect of fine *Chateaux en l'air*,
Worthier to stand for ever, if they could,
Than any built with stone, or yet with wood

1 en l'air *A.*: in air *previous edd.* 3 with . . . with *A.*: of . . . of *previous edd.*

For back of royal elephant to bear!—
Oh for my youth again, that I might share,
Much to my own, tho' little to thy good,
With thee, not subject to the jealous mood,
A partnership of literary ware!
But I am bankrupt now, and doom'd henceforth
To drudge, in descant dry, on others' lays, 10
Bards, I acknowledge, of unequall'd worth,
But what is commentator's happiest praise?
That he has furnish'd lights for others' eyes,
Which they who need them use, and then despise.

ON A SPANIEL CALLED BEAU

KILLING A YOUNG BIRD

[Written July 15, 1793. Published by Hayley, 1803.]

A SPANIEL, Beau, that fares like you,
  Well-fed, and at his ease,
Should wiser be, than to pursue
  Each trifle that he sees.

But you have kill'd a tiny bird,
  Which flew not till to-day,
Against my orders, whom you heard
  Forbidding you the prey. 8

Nor did you kill, that you might eat,
  And ease a doggish pain,
For him, though chas'd with furious heat,
  You left where he was slain.

Nor was he of the thievish sort,
  Or one whom blood allures,
But innocent was all his sport,
  Whom you have torn for yours. 16

My dog! what remedy remains,
  Since, teach you all I can,
I see you, after all my pains,
  So much resemble man!

BEAU'S REPLY

[Written July, 1793. Published by Hayley, 1803.]

SIR! when I flew to seize the bird,
  In spite of your command,
A louder voice than yours I heard,
  And harder to withstand:

To Hayley—5 my . . . might *A.*: permission from the skies to *previous edd.* 13 others' *A.*: other *previous edd.*

You cried—Forbear!—but in my breast
A mightier cried—Proceed!
'Twas nature, Sir, whose strong behest
Impell'd me to the deed. 8

Yet much as nature I respect,
I ventur'd once to break
(As you perhaps may recollect)
Her precept, for your sake;

And when your linnet, on a day,
Passing his prison-door,
Had flutter'd all his strength away,
And panting press'd the floor, 16

Well knowing him a sacred thing,
Not destin'd to my tooth,
I only kiss'd his ruffled wing,
And lick'd the feathers smooth.

Let my obedience then excuse
My disobedience now,
Nor some reproof yourself refuse
From your aggriev'd Bow-wow! 24

If killing birds be such a crime,
(Which I can hardly see)
What think you, Sir, of killing Time
With verse address'd to me?

INSCRIPTION FOR A BUST OF HOMER

[Written in letters to Hayley, July 24 and Aug. 15, 1793. Published by Hayley, 1803.]

Εἰκόνα τίς ταύτην; κλυτὸν ἀνέρος οὔνομ' ὄλωλεν.
Οὔνομα δ' οὗτος ἀνὴρ ἄφθιτον αἰὲν ἔχει.

TRANSLATION

THE sculptor?—Nameless, though once dear to fame;
But this man bears an everlasting name.

ANSWER TO STANZAS ADDRESSED TO LADY HESKETH

BY MISS CATHARINE FANSHAWE

In returning a poem of Mr. Cowper's, lent to her on condition she should neither show it, nor take a copy.

[Written Aug., 1793. Published by Hayley, 1803. See note on pages 659–61.]

To be remember'd thus is fame,
And in the first degree;
And did the few like her the same,
The press might sleep for me.

20 the] his *Hayley* (*1806*).
Answer—4 sleep *1815*: rest *Hayley*.

So Homer, in the mem'ry stor'd
Of many a Grecian belle,
Was once preserv'd—a richer hoard,
But never lodg'd so well. 8

TO MARY

[Written in the autumn of 1793. Published by Hayley, 1803. There is a MS. copy in the Cowper Museum at Olney, from which the tenth verse was first printed by T. Wright in 1900.]

THE twentieth year is well-nigh past,
Since first our sky was overcast;
Ah would that this might be the last!
My Mary!

Thy spirits have a fainter flow,
I see thee daily weaker grow—
'Twas my distress that brought thee low,
My Mary! 8

Thy needles, once a shining store,
For my sake restless heretofore,
Now rust disus'd, and shine no more,
My Mary!

For though thou gladly wouldst fulfil
The same kind office for me still,
Thy sight now seconds not thy will,
My Mary! 16

But well thou play'd'st the housewife's part,
And all thy threads with magic art
Have wound themselves about this heart,
My Mary!

Thy indistinct expressions seem
Like language utter'd in a dream;
Yet me they charm, whate'er the theme,
My Mary! 24

Thy silver locks, once auburn bright,
Are still more lovely in my sight
Than golden beams of orient light,
My Mary!

For could I view nor them nor thee,
What sight worth seeing could I see?
The sun would rise in vain for me,
My Mary! 32

Partakers of thy sad decline,
Thy hands their little force resign;
Yet, gently prest, press gently mine,
My Mary!

On verses 3 and 4 see notes. 33 thy] the *MS.*

And then I feel that still I hold
A richer store ten thousandfold
Than misers fancy in their gold,
My Mary! 40

Such feebleness of limbs thou prov'st,
That now at every step thou mov'st
Upheld by two; yet still thou lov'st,
My Mary!

And still to love, though prest with ill,
In wintry age to feel no chill,
With me is to be lovely still,
My Mary! 48

But ah! by constant heed I know,
How oft the sadness that I show
Transforms thy smiles to looks of woe,
My Mary!

And should my future lot be cast
With much resemblance of the past,
Thy worn-out heart will break at last,
My Mary! 56

LINES WRITTEN ON A WINDOW-SHUTTER AT WESTON

[Written July 27, 1795. ll. 3-6 published in Corry's Life of Cowper, 1803.]

FAREWELL, dear scenes, for ever closed to me,
Oh, for what sorrows must I now exchange ye!
Me miserable! how could I escape
Infinite wrath and infinite despair!
Whom Death, Earth, Heaven, and Hell consigned to ruin,
Whose friend was God, but God swore not to aid me! 6

MONTES GLACIALES

IN OCEANO GERMANICO NATANTES

[In Norfolk MS. Written March 11, 1799. Published by Hayley, 1803.]

EN, quæ prodigia, ex oris allata remotis,
Oras adveniunt pavefacta per æquora nostras!
Non equidem priscæ sæclum rediisse videtur
Pyrrhæ, cum Proteus pecus altos visere montes
Et sylvas egit: sed tempora vix leviora
Adsunt, evulsi quando radicitus alti
In mare descendunt montes, fluctusque pererrant.

Lines—5 Whom] When *Corry*. Hell] All *Corry*.

Quid vero hoc monstri est magis et mirabile visu?
Splendentes video, ceu pulchro ex ære vel auro
Conflatos, rutilisque accinctos undique gemmis, 10
Bacca cærulea, et flammas imitante pyropo.
Ex oriente adsunt, ubi gazas optima tellus
Parturit omnigenas, quibus æva per omnia sumptu
Ingenti finxere sibi diademata reges?
Vix hoc crediderim. Non fallunt talia acutos
Mercatorum oculos: prius et quam littora Gangis
Liquissent, avidis gratissima præda fuissent.
Ortos unde putemus? An illos Vesvius atrox
Protulit, ignivomisve ejecit faucibus Ætna?
Luce micant propria, Phœbive, per aera purum 20
Nunc stimulantis equos, argentea tela retorquent?
Phœbi luce micant. Ventis et fluctibus altis
Appulsi, et rapidis subter currentibus undis,
Tandem non fallunt oculos. Capita alta videre est
Multa onerata nive, et canis conspersa pruinis.
Cætera sunt glacies. Procul hinc, ubi bruma fere
omnes
Contristat menses, portenta hæc horrida nobis
Illa strui voluit. Quoties de culmine summo
Clivorum fluerent in littora prona, solutæ
Sole, nives, propero tendentes in mare cursu, 30
Illa gelu fixit. Paulatim attollere sese
Mirum cœpit opus; glacieque ab origine rerum
In glaciem aggesta, sublimes vertice tandem
Æquavit montes non crescere nescia moles.
Sic immensa diu stetit, æternumque stetisset
Congeries, hominum neque vi neque mobilis arte,
Littora ni tandem declivia deseruisset,
Pondere victa suo. Dilabitur. Omnia circum
Antra et saxa gemunt, subito concussa fragore,
Dum ruit in pelagum, tanquam studiosa natandi,
Ingens tota strues. Sic Delos dicitur olim, 41
Insula, in Ægæo fluitasse erratica ponto.
Sed non ex glacie Delos; neque torpida Delum
Bruma inter rupes genuit nudum sterilemque.
Sed vestita herbis erat illa, ornataque nunquam
Decidua lauro; et Delum dilexit Apollo.
At vos, errones horrendi, et caligine digni
Cimmeria, Deus idem odit. Natalia vestra,
Nubibus involvens frontem, non ille tueri
Sustinuit. Patrium vos ergo requirite cælum! 50
Ite! Redite! Timete moras; ni, leniter austro
Spirante, et nitidas Phœbo jaculante sagittas
Hostili vobis, pereatis gurgite misti!

TRANSLATION
ON THE ICE ISLANDS
SEEN FLOATING IN THE GERMAN OCEAN

[In Norfolk MS., dated March 19, 1799. Published by Hayley, 1803.]

WHAT portents, from what distant region, ride,
Unseen till now in ours, th' astonish'd tide?
In ages past, old Proteus, with his droves
Of sea-calves, sought the mountains and the groves:
But now, descending whence of late they stood,
Themselves the mountains seem to rove the flood.
Dire times were they, full-charg'd with human woes;
And these, scarce less calamitous than those.
What view we now? More wondrous still! Behold!
Like burnish'd brass they shine, or beaten gold; 10
And all around the pearl's pure splendour show,
And all around the ruby's fiery glow.
Come they from India? where the burning earth,
All-bounteous, gives her richest treasures birth;
And where the costly gems, that beam around
The brows of mightiest potentates, are found?
No. Never such a countless dazzling store
Had left unseen the Ganges' peopled shore.
Rapacious hands, and ever-watchful eyes, 19
Should sooner far have mark'd and seiz'd the prize.
Whence sprang they then? Ejected have they come
From Ves'vius', or from Ætna's burning womb?
Thus shine they self-illum'd, or but display
The borrow'd splendours of a cloudless day?
With borrow'd beams they shine. The gales that breathe
Now land-ward, and the current's force beneath,
Have borne them nearer: and the nearer sight,
Advantag'd more, contemplates them aright.
Their lofty summits, crested high, they show,
With mingled sleet and long-incumbent snow. 30
The rest is ice. Far hence, where, most severe,
Bleak winter well-nigh saddens all the year,
Their infant growth began. He bade arise
Their uncouth forms, portentous in our eyes.
Oft as, dissolv'd by transient suns, the snow
Left the tall cliff, to join the flood below,
He caught and curdled, with a freezing blast,
The current, ere it reach'd the boundless waste.
By slow degrees uprose the wondrous pile,
And long-successive ages roll'd the while; 40
Till, ceaseless in its growth, it claim'd to stand
Tall as its rival mountains on the land.

Thus stood—and, unremovable by skill
Or force of man, had stood the structure still;
But that, tho' firmly fixt, supplanted yet
By pressure of its own enormous weight,
It left the shelving beach—and, with a sound
That shook the bellowing waves and rocks around,
Self-launch'd, and swiftly, to the briny wave,
As if instinct with strong desire to lave, 50
Down went the pond'rous mass. So bards of old,
How Delos swam th' Ægean deep, have told.
But not of ice was Delos. Delos bore
Herb, fruit, and flow'r. She, crown'd with laurel, wore,
E'en under wintry skies, a summer smile;
And Delos was Apollo's fav'rite isle.
But, horrid wand'rers of the deep, to you
He deems Cimmerian darkness only due.
Your hated birth he deign'd not to survey,
But, scornful, turn'd his glorious eyes away. 60
Hence! Seek your home; no longer rashly dare
The darts of Phœbus, and a softer air;
Lest ye regret, too late, your native coast,
In no congenial gulf for ever lost!

THE CASTAWAY

[Written March 20, 1799. Published by Hayley, 1803.]

OBSCUREST night involv'd the sky,
Th' Atlantic billows roar'd,
When such a destin'd wretch as I,
Wash'd headlong from on board,
Of friends, of hope, of all bereft,
His floating home for ever left. 6

No braver chief could Albion boast
Than he with whom he went,
Nor ever ship left Albion's coast,
With warmer wishes sent.
He lov'd them both, but both in vain,
Nor him beheld, nor her again. 12

Not long beneath the whelming brine,
Expert to swim, he lay;
Nor soon he felt his strength decline,
Or courage die away;
But wag'd with death a lasting strife,
Supported by despair of life. 18

61 no] nor *Hayley* (*1803*).

He shouted: nor his friends had fail'd
  To check the vessel's course,
But so the furious blast prevail'd,
  That, pitiless perforce,
They left their outcast mate behind,
And scudded still before the wind. 24

Some succour yet they could afford;
  And, such as storms allow,
The cask, the coop, the floated cord,
  Delay'd not to bestow.
But he (they knew) nor ship, nor shore,
Whate'er they gave, should visit more. 30

Nor, cruel as it seem'd, could he
  Their haste himself condemn,
Aware that flight, in such a sea,
  Alone could rescue them;
Yet bitter felt it still to die
Deserted, and his friends so nigh. 36

He long survives, who lives an hour
  In ocean, self-upheld;
And so long he, with unspent pow'r,
  His destiny repell'd;
And ever, as the minutes flew,
Entreated help, or cried—Adieu! 42

At length, his transient respite past,
  His comrades, who before
Had heard his voice in ev'ry blast,
  Could catch the sound no more.
For then, by toil subdued, he drank
The stifling wave, and then he sank. 48

No poet wept him: but the page
  Of narrative sincere,
That tells his name, his worth, his age,
  Is wet with Anson's tear.
And tears by bards or heroes shed
Alike immortalize the dead. 54

I therefore purpose not, or dream,
  Descanting on his fate,
To give the melancholy theme
  A more enduring date:
But misery still delights to trace
Its 'semblance in another's case. 60

No voice divine the storm allay'd,
  No light propitious shone;
When, snatch'd from all effectual aid,
  We perish'd, each alone:
But I beneath a rougher sea,
And whelm'd in deeper gulphs than he. 66

OLNEY HYMNS

[The sixty-seven Olney Hymns composed by Cowper were mostly written during 1771 and 1772; two, however (Nos. xlvi. and xlvii.), were apparently written in 1763, and one (No. xxxv.) in Jan. 1773, just before an attack of insanity. The remaining 281 hymns in the collection were written by Newton. The Hymns were published in one volume, divided into three books, in 1779, Cowper's hymns being distinguished from Newton's by the affixing of the letter C. The original numbers of the hymns are here placed in brackets at the head of each hymn.]

I. [Bk. i. iii.]

WALKING WITH GOD. *Gen.* v. 24

Oh! for a closer walk with God,
  A calm and heav'nly frame;
A light to shine upon the road
  That leads me to the Lamb!

Where is the blessedness I knew
  When first I saw the Lord?
Where is the soul-refreshing view
  Of Jesus, and his word? 8

What peaceful hours I once enjoy'd!
  How sweet their mem'ry still!
But they have left an aching void,
  The world can never fill.

Return, O holy Dove, return,
  Sweet messenger of rest;
I hate the sins that made thee mourn,
  And drove thee from my breast. 16

The dearest idol I have known,
  Whate'er that idol be;
Help me to tear it from thy throne,
  And worship only thee.

So shall my walk be close with God,
  Calm and serene my frame;
So purer light shall mark the road
  That leads me to the Lamb. 24

II. [Bk. i. vi.]

JEHOVAH-JIREH, The Lord will provide *Gen.* xxii. 14

The saints should never be dismay'd,
  Nor sink in hopeless fear;
For when they least expect his aid,
  The Saviour will appear.

This Abraham found, he rais'd the knife,
GOD saw, and said, "Forbear;
Yon ram shall yield his meaner life,
Behold the victim there." 8

Once David seem'd Saul's certain prey;
But hark! the foe's at hand[1],
Saul turns his arms another way,
To save th' invaded land.

When Jonah sunk beneath the wave
He thought to rise no more[2];
But GOD prepar'd a fish to save,
And bear him to the shore. 16

Blest proofs of pow'r and grace divine,
That meet us in his word!
May ev'ry deep-felt care of mine
Be trusted with the LORD.

Wait for his seasonable aid,
And tho' it tarry wait:
The promise may be long delay'd,
But cannot come too late. 24

III. [BK. I. xiv.]

JEHOVAH-ROPHI, I AM THE LORD THAT HEALETH THEE. *Exod.* XV.

HEAL us, EMMANUEL, here we are,
Waiting to feel thy touch;
Deep-wounded souls to thee repair,
And, Saviour, we are such.

Our faith is feeble, we confess,
We faintly trust thy word;
But wilt thou pity us the less?
Be that far from thee, LORD! 8

Remember him who once apply'd
With trembling for relief;
"Lord, I believe," with tears he cry'd[3],
"O help my unbelief."

She too, who touch'd thee in the press,
And healing virtue stole,
Was answer'd, "Daughter, go in peace[4],
Thy faith hath made thee whole." 16

[1] 1 Sam. xxiii. 27. [2] Jonah i. 17. [3] Mark ix. 24. [4] Mark v. 34. [*The references throughout come from the first edition.*]

Conceal'd amid the gath'ring throng,
She would have shunn'd thy view;
And if her faith was firm and strong,
Had strong misgivings too.

Like her, with hopes and fears, we come,
To touch thee if we may;
Oh! send us not despairing home,
Send none unheal'd away. 24

IV. [Bk. I. xvii.]

JEHOVAH-NISSI, The Lord my Banner
Exod. xvii. 15

By whom was David taught,
To aim the deadly blow,
When he Goliath fought,
And laid the Gittite low?
Nor sword nor spear the stripling took,
But chose a pebble from the brook. 6

'Twas Israel's God and King,
Who sent him to the fight;
Who gave him strength to sling,
And skill to aim aright.
Ye feeble saints, your strength endures,
Because young David's God is yours. 12

Who order'd Gideon forth,
To storm th' invaders' camp[1],
With arms of little worth,
A pitcher and a lamp?
The trumpets made his coming known,
And all the host was overthrown. 18

Oh! I have seen the day,
When with a single word,
God helping me to say,
My trust is in the Lord;
My soul has quell'd a thousand foes,
Fearless of all that could oppose. 24

But unbelief, self-will,
Self-righteousness and pride,
How often do they steal,
My weapon from my side?
Yet David's Lord, and Gideon's friend,
Will help his servant to the end. 30

[1] Judges vii. 20.

V. [Bk. i. xxii.]

JEHOVAH-SHALOM, The Lord send Peace

Judges vi. 24

Jesus, whose blood so freely stream'd
To satisfy the law's demand;
By thee from guilt and wrath redeem'd,
Before the Father's face I stand.

To reconcile offending man,
Make Justice drop her angry rod;
What creature could have form'd the plan,
Or who fulfil it but a God? 8

No drop remains of all the curse,
For wretches who deserv'd the whole;
No arrows dipt in wrath to pierce
The guilty, but returning soul.

Peace by such means so dearly bought,
What rebel could have hop'd to see?
Peace, by his injur'd sovereign wrought,
His Sov'reign fast'ned to a tree. 16

Now, Lord, thy feeble worm prepare!
For strife with earth and hell begins;
Confirm and gird me for the war;
They hate the soul that hates his sins.

Let them in horrid league agree!
They may assault, they may distress;
But cannot quench thy love to me,
Nor rob me of the Lord my peace. 24

VI. [Bk. i. lii.]

WISDOM. *Prov.* viii. 22–31

Ere God had built the mountains,
Or rais'd the fruitful hills;
Before he fill'd the fountains
That feed the running rills;
In me, from everlasting,
The wonderful I am
Found pleasures never wasting,
And Wisdom is my name. 8

When, like a tent to dwell in,
He spread the skies abroad;
And swath'd about the swelling
Of ocean's mighty flood;

V—Title] Jehovah-Shalem *1779*.

He wrought by weight and measure,
And I was with him then;
Myself the Father's pleasure,
And mine, the sons of men. 16

Thus wisdom's words discover
Thy glory and thy grace,
Thou everlasting lover
Of our unworthy race!
Thy gracious eye survey'd us
Ere stars were seen above;
In wisdom thou hast made us,
And died for us in love. 24

And couldst thou be delighted
With creatures such as we!
Who when we saw thee, slighted
And nail'd thee to a tree?
Unfathomable wonder,
And mystery divine!
The Voice that speaks in thunder,
Says, "Sinner I am thine!" 32

VII. [Bk. i. lv.]

VANITY OF THE WORLD

God gives his mercies to be spent;
Your hoard will do your soul no good:
Gold is a blessing only lent,
Repaid by giving others food.

The world's esteem is but a bribe,
To buy their peace you sell your own;
The slave of a vain-glorious tribe,
Who hate you while they make you known. 8

The joy that vain amusements give,
Oh! sad conclusion that it brings!
The honey of a crowded hive,
Defended by a thousand stings.

'Tis thus the world rewards the fools
That live upon her treach'rous smiles;
She leads them, blindfold, by her rules,
And ruins all whom she beguiles. 16

God knows the thousands who go down
From pleasure, into endless woe:
And with a long despairing grone
Blaspheme their Maker as they go.

O fearful thought! be timely wise;
Delight but in a Saviour's charms:
And God shall take you to the skies,
Embrac'd in everlasting arms. 24

VIII. [Bk. i. lviii.]

O LORD, I WILL PRAISE THEE. *Isa.* xii.

I will praise thee ev'ry day
Now thine anger's turn'd away!
Comfortable thoughts arise
From the bleeding sacrifice.

Here in the fair gospel field,
Wells of free salvation yield
Streams of life, a plenteous store,
And my soul shall thirst no more. 8

Jesus is become at length
My salvation and my strength;
And his praises shall prolong,
While I live, my pleasant song.

Praise ye, then, his glorious name,
Publish his exalted fame!
Still his worth your praise exceeds,
Excellent are all his deeds. 16

Raise again the joyful sound,
Let the nations roll it round!
Zion shout! for this is he,
God the Saviour dwells in thee!

IX. [Bk. i. lxiv.]

THE CONTRITE HEART. *Isa.* lvii. 15

The Lord will happiness divine
On contrite hearts bestow:
Then tell me, gracious God, is mine
A contrite heart, or no?

I hear, but seem to hear in vain,
Insensible as steel;
If ought is felt, 'tis only pain,
To find I cannot feel. 8

I sometimes think myself inclin'd
To love thee, if I could;
But often feel another mind,
Averse to all that's good.

My best desires are faint and few,
  I fain would strive for more;
But when I cry, "My strength renew,"
  Seem weaker than before. 16

Thy saints are comforted I know,
  And love thy house of pray'r;
I therefore go where others go,
  But find no comfort there.

Oh make this heart rejoice, or ache;
  Decide this doubt for me;
And if it be not broken, break,
  And heal it, if it be. 24

X. [Bk. i. lxv.]

THE FUTURE PEACE AND GLORY OF THE CHURCH. *Isa.* lx. 15–20

Hear what God the Lord hath spoken:—
O my people, faint and few;
Comfortless, afflicted, broken,
Fair abodes I build for you:
Thorns of heart-felt tribulation
Shall no more perplex your ways;
You shall name your walls Salvation,
And your gates shall all be Praise. 8

There, like streams that feed the garden,
Pleasures, without end, shall flow;
For the Lord, your faith rewarding,
All his bounty shall bestow;
Still in undisturb'd possession,
Peace and righteousness shall reign;
Never shall you feel oppression,
Hear the voice of war again. 16

Ye no more your suns descending,
Waning moons no more shall see;
But, your griefs for ever ending,
Find eternal noon in me:
God shall rise, and shining o'er you,
Change to day the gloom of night;
He, the Lord, shall be your glory,
God your everlasting light. 24

2 faint] weak *MS. letter of Newton, quoted by J. E. B. Mayor.*
5 Thorns] Themes *1779, 1781.*

XI. [Bk. i. lxvii.]

JEHOVAH OUR RIGHTEOUSNESS

Jer. xxiii. 6

My God, how perfect are thy ways!
But mine polluted are;
Sin twines itself about my praise,
And slides into my pray'r.

When I would speak what thou hast done
To save me from my sin,
I cannot make thy mercies known
But self-applause creeps in. 8

Divine desire, that holy flame
Thy grace creates in me;
Alas! impatience is its name,
When it returns to thee.

This heart, a fountain of vile thoughts,
How does it overflow?
While self upon the surface floats
Still bubbling from below. 16

Let others in the gaudy dress
Of fancied merit shine;
The Lord shall be my righteousness;
The Lord for ever mine.

XII. [Bk. i. lxviii.]

EPHRAIM REPENTING. *Jer.* xxxi. 18–20

My God! till I receiv'd thy stroke,
How like a beast was I!
So unaccustom'd to the yoke,
So backward to comply.

With grief my just reproach I bear,
Shame fills me at the thought;
How frequent my rebellions were!
What wickedness I wrought! 8

Thy merciful restraint I scorn'd,
And left the pleasant road;
Yet turn me, and I shall be turn'd,
Thou art the Lord my God.

Is Ephraim banish'd from my thoughts,
Or vile in my esteem?
No, saith the Lord, with all his faults,
I still remember him. 16

Is he a dear and pleasant child?
  Yes, dear and pleasant still;
Tho' sin his foolish heart beguil'd,
  And he withstood my will.

My sharp rebuke has laid him low,
  He seeks my face again;
My pity kindles at his woe,
  He shall not seek in vain. 24

XIII. [Bk. i. lxxi.]

THE COVENANT. *Ezek.* xxxvi. 25–28

The Lord proclaims his grace abroad!
Behold, I change your hearts of stone;
Each shall renounce his idol god,
And serve, henceforth, the Lord alone.

My grace, a flowing stream, proceeds
To wash your filthiness away;
Ye shall abhor your former deeds,
And learn my statutes to obey. 8

My truth the great design insures,
I give myself away to you;
You shall be mine, I will be yours,
Your God unalterably true.

Yet not unsought, or unimplor'd,
The plenteous grace shall I confer [1];
No—your whole hearts shall seek the Lord,
I'll put a praying spirit there. 16

From the first breath of life divine,
Down to the last expiring hour;
The gracious work shall all be mine,
Begun and ended in my pow'r.

XIV. [Bk. i. lxxii.]

JEHOVAH-SHAMMAH. *Ezek.* xlviii. 35

As birds their infant brood protect [2],
And spread their wings to shelter them;
Thus saith the Lord to his elect,
"So will I guard Jerusalem."

And what then is Jerusalem,
This darling object of his care?
Where is its worth in God's esteem?
Who built it? who inhabits there? 8

[1] Verse 37. [2] Isa. xxxi. 5.

JEHOVAH founded it in blood,
The blood of his incarnate Son;
There dwell the saints, once foes to GOD,
The sinners, whom he calls his own.

There, tho' besieg'd on ev'ry side,
Yet much belov'd and guarded well;
From age to age they have defy'd
The utmost force of earth and hell. 16

Let earth repent, and hell despair,
This city has a sure defence;
Her name is call'd, The LORD is there,
And who has pow'r to drive him thence?

XV. [BK. I. lxxix.]

PRAISE FOR THE FOUNTAIN OPENED

Zech. xiii. 1

THERE is a fountain fill'd with blood
Drawn from EMMANUEL'S veins;
And sinners, plung'd beneath that flood,
Lose all their guilty stains.

The dying thief rejoic'd to see
That fountain in his day;
And there have I, as vile as he,
Wash'd all my sins away. 8

Dear dying Lamb, thy precious blood
Shall never lose its pow'r;
Till all the ransom'd church of GOD
Be sav'd, to sin no more.

E'er since, by faith, I saw the stream
Thy flowing wounds supply;
Redeeming love has been my theme,
And shall be till I die. 16

Then in a nobler sweeter song
I'll sing thy power to save;
When this poor lisping stammering tongue
Lies silent in the grave.

LORD, I believe thou hast prepar'd
(Unworthy tho' I be)
For me a blood-bought free reward,
A golden harp for me! 24

'Tis strung, and tun'd, for endless years,
And form'd by pow'r divine;
To sound in GOD the Father's ears,
No other name but thine.

XVI. [Bk. i. lxxxv.]

THE SOWER. *Matt.* xiii. 3

Ye sons of earth prepare the plough,
Break up your fallow ground!
The Sower is gone forth to sow,
And scatter blessings round.

The seed that finds a stony soil,
Shoots forth a hasty blade;
But ill repays the sower's toil,
Soon wither'd, scorch'd, and dead. 8

The thorny ground is sure to baulk
All hopes of harvest there;
We find a tall and sickly stalk,
But not the fruitful ear.

The beaten path and high-way side
Receive the trust in vain;
The watchful birds the spoil divide,
And pick up all the grain. 16

But where the Lord of grace and pow'r
Has bless'd the happy field;
How plenteous is the golden store
The deep-wrought furrows yield!

Father of mercies, we have need
Of thy preparing grace;
Let the same hand that gives the seed,
Provide a fruitful place! 24

XVII. [Bk. i. xcvi.]

THE HOUSE OF PRAYER. *Mark* xi. 17

Thy mansion is the Christian's heart,
O Lord, thy dwelling-place secure!
Bid the unruly throng depart,
And leave the consecrated door.

Devoted as it is to thee,
A thievish swarm frequents the place;
They steal away my joys from me,
And rob my Saviour of his praise. 8

There too a sharp designing trade
Sin, Satan, and the world maintain;
Nor cease to press me, and persuade,
To part with ease and purchase pain.

I know them, and I hate their din,
Am weary of the bustling crowd;
But while their voice is heard within,
I cannot serve thee as I would. 16

Oh! for the joy thy presence gives,
What peace shall reign when thou art here!
Thy presence makes this den of thieves,
A calm delightful house of pray'r.

And if thou make thy temple shine,
Yet, self-abas'd, will I adore;
The gold and silver are not mine,
I give thee what was thine before. 24

XVIII. [Bk. I. cxviii.]

LOVEST THOU ME? *John* xxi. 16

Hark, my soul! it is the Lord;
'Tis thy Saviour, hear his word;
Jesus speaks, and speaks to thee;
"Say, poor sinner, lov'st thou me?

I deliver'd thee when bound,
And, when wounded, heal'd thy wound;
Sought thee wand'ring, set thee right,
Turn'd thy darkness into light. 8

Can a woman's tender care
Cease, towards the child she bare?
Yes, she may forgetful be,
Yet will I remember thee.

Mine is an unchanging love,
Higher than the heights above;
Deeper than the depths beneath,
Free and faithful, strong as death. 16

Thou shalt see my glory soon,
When the work of grace is done;
Partner of my throne shalt be;
Say, poor sinner, lov'st thou me?"

Lord, it is my chief complaint,
That my love is weak and faint;
Yet I love thee and adore,
Oh for grace to love thee more! 24

6 wounded] bleeding *first in 1797*.

XIX. [Bk. i. cxxxi.]

CONTENTMENT. *Phil.* iv. 11

Fierce passions discompose the mind,
As tempests vex the sea;
But calm content and peace we find,
When, Lord, we turn to thee.

In vain by reason and by rule,
We try to bend the will;
For none, but in the Saviour's school,
Can learn the heav'nly skill. 8

Since at his feet my soul has sat,
His gracious words to hear;
Contented with my present state,
I cast, on him, my care.

"Art thou a sinner, soul?" he said,
"Then how canst thou complain?
How light thy troubles here, if weigh'd
With everlasting pain! 16

If thou of murmuring wouldst be cur'd,
Compare thy griefs with mine;
Think what my love for thee endur'd,
And thou wilt not repine.

'Tis I appoint thy daily lot,
And I do all things well:
Thou soon shalt leave this wretched spot,
And rise with me to dwell. 24

In life my grace shall strength supply,
Proportion'd to thy day;
At death thou still shalt find me nigh,
To wipe thy tears away."

Thus I who once my wretched days
In vain repinings spent;
Taught in my Saviour's school of grace,
Have learn'd to be content. 32

XX. [Bk. i. cxxxii.]

OLD-TESTAMENT GOSPEL. *Heb.* iv. 2

Israel in ancient days,
Not only had a view
Of Sinai in a blaze,
But learn'd the gospel too:
The types and figures were a glass
In which they saw the Saviour's face. 6

The paschal sacrifice,
And blood-besprinkled door[1],
Seen with enlighten'd eyes,
And once apply'd with pow'r;
Would teach the need of other blood,
To reconcile an angry God. 12

The Lamb, the Dove, set forth
His perfect innocence[2],
Whose blood, of matchless worth,
Should be the soul's defence:
For he who can for sin atone,
Must have no failings of his own. 18

The scape-goat on his head[3]
The people's trespass bore,
And to the desart led,
Was to be seen no more:
In him, our Surety seem'd to say,
"Behold, I bear your sins away." 24

Dipt in his fellow's blood,
The living bird went free[4];
The type, well understood,
Express'd the sinner's plea;
Describ'd a guilty soul enlarg'd,
And by a Saviour's death discharg'd. 30

Jesus, I love to trace
Throughout the sacred page
The footsteps of thy grace,
The same in ev'ry age!
Oh grant that I may faithful be
To clearer light, vouchsaf'd to me! 36

XXI. [Bk. i. cxxxviii.]

SARDIS. *Rev.* iii. 1–6

"Write to Sardis, saith the Lord,
And write what he declares;
He whose Spirit, and whose word,
Upholds the seven stars:
All thy works and ways I search,
Find thy zeal and love decay'd;
Thou art call'd a living church,
But thou art cold and dead. 8

[1] Exod. xii. 13. [2] Lev. xii. 6. [3] Lev. xvi. 21. [4] Lev. xiv. 51-53.

Watch, remember, seek and strive,
Exert thy former pains;
Let thy timely care revive,
And strengthen what remains:
Cleanse thine heart, thy works amend,
Former times to mind recall;
Lest my sudden stroke descend,
And smite thee once for all. 16

Yet I number now, in thee,
A few that are upright;
These my Father's face shall see,
And walk with me in white:
When in judgment I appear,
They for mine shall be confess'd;
Let my faithful servants hear,
And woe be to the rest." 24

XXII. [Bk. ii. viii.]

PRAYER FOR A BLESSING

Bestow, dear Lord, upon our youth
The gift of saving grace;
And let the seed of sacred truth
Fall in a fruitful place.

Grace is a plant, where'er it grows,
Of pure and heav'nly root;
But fairest in the youngest shews,
And yields the sweetest fruit. 8

Ye careless ones, Oh hear betimes
The voice of sovereign love!
Your youth is stain'd with many crimes,
But mercy reigns above.

True, you are young, but there's a stone
Within the youngest breast;
Or half the crimes which you have done
Would rob you of your rest. 16

For you the public pray'r is made,
Oh join the public pray'r!
For you the secret tear is shed,
Oh shed yourselves a tear!

We pray that you may early prove
The Spirit's power to teach;
You cannot be too young to love
That Jesus whom we preach. 24

XXII-XXIV *are under the general heading,* "Hymns before annual sermons to young people on new-years' evenings."

XXIII. [Bk. II. xi.]

PLEADING FOR AND WITH YOUTH

Sin has undone our wretched race,
But Jesus has restor'd
And brought the sinner face to face
With his forgiving Lord.

This we repeat from year to year,
And press upon our youth;
Lord, give them an attentive ear,
Lord, save them by thy truth. 8

Blessings upon the rising race!
Make this an happy hour,
According to thy richest grace,
And thine almighty pow'r.

We feel for your unhappy state,
(May you regard it too)
And would awhile ourselves forget,
To pour out pray'r for you. 16

We see, tho' you perceive it not,
Th' approaching, awful doom;
O tremble at the solemn thought,
And flee the wrath to come!

Dear Saviour, let this new-born year
Spread an alarm abroad;
And cry, in ev'ry careless ear,
"Prepare to meet thy God!" 24

XXIV. [Bk. II. xii.]

PRAYER FOR CHILDREN

Gracious Lord, our children see,
By thy mercy we are free;
But shall these, alas! remain
Subjects still of Satan's reign?
Israel's young ones, when of old
Pharaoh threaten'd to withhold[1],
Then thy messenger said, "No;
Let the children also go." 8

When the angel of the Lord
Drawing forth his dreadful sword,
Slew, with an avenging hand,
All the first-born of the land[2]:

[1] Exod. x. 9. [2] Exod. xii. 12.

Then thy people's doors he pass'd,
Where the bloody sign was plac'd;
Hear us, now, upon our knees
Plead the blood of CHRIST for these! 16

LORD, we tremble, for we know
How the fierce malicious foe,
Wheeling round his watchful flight,
Keeps them ever in his sight:
Spread thy pinions, King of kings!
Hide them safe beneath thy wings;
Lest the rav'nous bird of prey
Stoop, and bear the brood away. 24

XXV. [BK. II. xxxviii.]

JEHOVAH-JESUS

MY song shall bless the LORD of all,
My praise shall climb to his abode;
Thee, Saviour, by that name I call,
The great Supreme, the mighty GOD.

Without beginning, or decline,
Object of faith, and not of sense;
Eternal ages saw him shine,
He shines eternal ages hence. 8

As much, when in the manger laid,
Almighty ruler of the sky;
As when the six days' works he made
Fill'd all the morning-stars with joy.

Of all the crowns JEHOVAH bears,
Salvation is his dearest claim;
That gracious sound well-pleas'd he hears,
And owns EMMANUEL for his name. 16

A cheerful confidence I feel,
My well-plac'd hopes with joy I see;
My bosom glows with heav'nly zeal,
To worship him who died for me.

As man, he pities my complaint,
His pow'r and truth are all divine;
He will not fail, he cannot faint,
Salvation's sure, and must be mine. 24

11 works] work *later editions.*

XXVI. [Bk. ii. xliv.]

ON OPENING A PLACE FOR SOCIAL PRAYER

Jesus, where'er thy people meet,
There they behold thy mercy-seat;
Where'er they seek thee thou art found,
And ev'ry place is hallow'd ground.

For thou, within no walls confin'd,
Inhabitest the humble mind;
Such ever bring thee, where they come,
And going, take thee to their home. 8

Dear Shepherd of thy chosen few!
Thy former mercies here renew;
Here, to our waiting hearts, proclaim
The sweetness of thy saving name.

Here may we prove the pow'r of pray'r,
To strengthen faith, and sweeten care;
To teach our faint desires to rise,
And bring all heav'n before our eyes. 16

Behold! at thy commanding word,
We stretch the curtain and the cord[1];
Come thou, and fill this wider space,
And help us with a large encrease.

Lord, we are few, but thou art near;
Nor short thine arm, nor deaf thine ear;
Oh rend the heav'ns, come quickly down,
And make a thousand hearts thine own! 24

XXVII. [Bk. ii. liii.]

WELCOME TO THE TABLE

This is the feast of heav'nly wine,
And God invites to sup;
The juices of the living vine
Were press'd, to fill the cup.

Oh, bless the Saviour, ye that eat,
With royal dainties fed;
Not heav'n affords a costlier treat,
For Jesus is the bread! 8

The vile, the lost, he calls to them,
Ye trembling souls appear!
The righteous, in their own esteem,
Have no acceptance here

[1] Isa. liv. 2.

20 help] bless *later editions.*

Approach ye poor, nor dare refuse
The banquet spread for you;
Dear Saviour, this is welcome news,
Then I may venture too. 16

If guilt and sin afford a plea,
And may obtain a place;
Surely the LORD will welcome me,
And I shall see his face!

XXVIII. [BK. II. lv.]

JESUS HASTING TO SUFFER

THE Saviour! what a noble flame
Was kindled in his breast,
When hasting to Jerusalem
He march'd before the rest!

Good-will to men, and zeal for God,
His ev'ry thought engross;
He longs to be baptiz'd with blood[1],
He pants to reach the cross. 8

With all his suff'rings full in view,
And woes, to us unknown,
Forth to the task his spirit flew,
'Twas love that urg'd him on.

LORD, we return thee what we can!
Our hearts shall sound abroad
Salvation, to the dying Man,
And to the rising GOD! 16

And while thy bleeding glories here
Engage our wond'ring eyes;
We learn our lighter cross to bear,
And hasten to the skies.

XXIX. [BK. II. lx.]

EXHORTATION TO PRAYER

WHAT various hindrances we meet
In coming to a mercy-seat!
Yet who that knows the worth of pray'r,
But wishes to be often there?

Pray'r makes the dark'ned cloud withdraw,
Pray'r climbs the ladder Jacob saw;
Gives exercise to faith and love,
Brings ev'ry blessing from above. 8

[1] Luke xii. 50.

Restraining pray'r, we cease to fight;
Pray'r makes the Christian's armour bright;
And Satan trembles, when he sees
The weakest saint upon his knees.

While Moses stood with arms spread wide,
Success was found on Israel's side[1];
But when thro' weariness they fail'd,
That moment Amalek prevail'd. 16

Have you no words! Ah, think again,
Words flow apace when you complain;
And fill your fellow-creature's ear
With the sad tale of all your care.

Were half the breath thus vainly spent,
To heav'n in supplication sent;
Your cheerful song would oft'ner be,
"Hear what the LORD has done for me!" 24

XXX. [Bk. II. lxii.]

THE LIGHT AND GLORY OF THE WORD

THE Spirit breathes upon the word,
And brings the truth to sight;
Precepts and promises afford
A sanctifying light.

A glory gilds the sacred page,
Majestic like the sun;
It gives a light to ev'ry age,
It gives, but borrows none. 8

The hand that gave it, still supplies
The gracious light and heat;
His truths upon the nations rise,
They rise, but never set.

Let everlasting thanks be thine!
For such a bright display,
As makes a world of darkness shine
With beams of heav'nly day. 16

My soul rejoices to pursue
The steps of him I love;
Till glory breaks upon my view
In brighter worlds above.

[1] Exod. xvii. 11.

XXX—19 breaks] break *Southey.*

XXXI. [Bk. ii. lxxiii.]

ON THE DEATH OF A MINISTER

His Master taken from his head,
Elisha saw him go;
And, in desponding accents said,
"Ah, what must Israel do?"

But he forgot the Lord, who lifts
The beggar to the throne;
Nor knew, that all Elijah's gifts
Would soon be made his own. 8

What! when a Paul has run his course,
Or when Apollos dies;
Is Israel left without resource?
And have we no supplies?

Yes, while the dear Redeemer lives,
We have a boundless store;
And shall be fed with what he gives,
Who lives for evermore. 16

XXXII. [Bk. iii. viii.]

THE SHINING LIGHT

My former hopes are fled,
My terror now begins;
I feel, alas! that I am dead
In trespasses and sins.

Ah, whither shall I fly?
I hear the thunder roar;
The law proclaims destruction nigh,
And vengeance at the door. 8

When I review my ways,
I dread impending doom;
But sure, a friendly whisper says,
"Flee from the wrath to come."

I see, or think I see,
A glimm'ring from afar;
A beam of day that shines for me,
To save me from despair. 16

Fore-runner of the sun [1],
It marks the Pilgrim's way;
I'll gaze upon it while I run
And watch the rising day.

[1] Ps. cxxx. 6.

XXXI—8 Should *A*. XXXII—1 fled] dead *1779*.

XXXIII. [Bk. iii. x.]

THE WAITING SOUL

Breathe from the gentle South, O Lord,
And cheer me from the North;
Blow on the treasures of thy word,
And call the spices forth!

I wish, thou know'st, to be resign'd,
And wait with patient hope;
But hope delay'd fatigues the mind,
And drinks the spirit up. 8

Help me to reach the distant goal,
Confirm my feeble knee;
Pity the sickness of a soul
That faints for love of thee.

Cold as I feel this heart of mine,
Yet since I *feel* it so—
It yields some hope of life divine
Within, however low. 16

I seem forsaken and alone,
I hear the lion roar;
And ev'ry door is shut but one,
And that is mercy's door.

There, till the dear Deliv'rer come,
I'll wait with humble pray'r;
And when he calls his exile home,
The Lord shall find me there. 24

XXXIV. [Bk. iii. xiii.]

SEEKING THE BELOVED

To those who know the Lord I speak,
Is my beloved near?
The bridegroom of my soul I seek,
Oh! when will he appear!

Tho' once a man of grief and shame,
Yet now he fills a throne;
And bears the greatest, sweetest name,
That earth or heav'n have known. 8

Grace flies before, and love attends
His steps where'er he goes;
Tho' none can see him but his friends,
And they were once his foes.

24 me] him *first in 1787.*

He speaks—obedient to his call
  Our warm affections move;
Did he but shine alike on all,
  Then all alike would love. 16

Then love in ev'ry heart would reign,
  And war would cease to roar;
And cruel, and blood-thirsty men,
  Would thirst for blood no more.

Such JESUS is, and such his grace,
  Oh may he shine on you[1]!
And tell him, when you see his face,
  I long to see him too. 24

XXXV. [BK. III. XV.]

LIGHT SHINING OUT OF DARKNESS

GOD moves in a mysterious way,
  His wonders to perform;
He plants his footsteps in the sea,
  And rides upon the storm.

Deep in unfathomable mines
  Of never failing skill;
He treasures up his bright designs,
  And works his sovereign will. 8

Ye fearful saints fresh courage take,
  The clouds ye so much dread
Are big with mercy, and shall break
  In blessings on your head.

Judge not the LORD by feeble sense,
  But trust him for his grace;
Behind a frowning providence,
  He hides a smiling face. 16

His purposes will ripen fast,
  Unfolding ev'ry hour;
The bud may have a bitter taste,
  But sweet will be the flow'r.

Blind unbelief is sure to err[2],
  And scan his work in vain;
GOD is his own interpreter,
  And he will make it plain. 24

[1] Song of Sol. v. 8. [2] John xiii. 7.

XXXV—20 sweet will be] wait to smell *MS. quoted by J. E. B. Mayor.*

XXXVI. [Bk. iii. xvi.]

WELCOME CROSS

'Tis my happiness below
Not to live without the cross;
But the Saviour's pow'r to know,
Sanctifying ev'ry loss:
Trials must and will befall;
But with humble faith to see
Love inscrib'd upon them all,
This is happiness to me. 8

God, in Israel, sows the seeds
Of affliction, pain, and toil;
These spring up, and choke the weeds
Which would else o'erspread the soil:
Trials make the promise sweet,
Trials give new life to pray'r;
Trials bring me to his feet,
Lay me low, and keep me there. 16

Did I meet no trials here,
No chastisement by the way;
Might I not, with reason, fear
I should prove a cast-away?
Bastards may escape the rod[1],
Sunk in earthly, vain delight;
But the true-born child of God,
Must not, would not, if he might. 24

XXXVII. [Bk. iii. xvii.]

AFFLICTIONS SANCTIFIED BY THE WORD

O how I love thy holy word,
Thy gracious covenant, O Lord!
It guides me in the peaceful way,
I think upon it all the day.

What are the mines of shining wealth,
The strength of youth, the bloom of health!
What are all joys compar'd with those
Thine everlasting word bestows! 8

Long unafflicted, undismay'd,
In pleasure's path secure I stray'd;
Thou mad'st me feel thy chast'ning rod[2],
And strait I turn'd unto my God.

[1] Heb. xii. 8. [2] Ps. cxix. 71.

15 bring me to] lay me at *MS. quoted by J. E. B. Mayor.*

What though it pierc'd my fainting heart,
I bless thine hand that caus'd the smart;
It taught my tears awhile to flow,
But sav'd me from eternal woe. 16

Oh! hadst thou left me unchastiz'd,
Thy precept I had still despis'd;
And *still* the snare in secret laid,
Had my unwary feet betray'd.

I love thee therefore O my God,
And breathe towards thy dear abode;
Where in thy presence fully blest,
Thy chosen saints for ever rest. 24

XXXVIII. [Bk. iii. xviii.]

TEMPTATION

The billows swell, the winds are high,
Clouds overcast my wintry sky;
Out of the depths to thee I call,
My fears are great, my strength is small.

O Lord, the pilot's part perform,
And guide and guard me thro' the storm;
Defend me from each threat'ning ill,
Control the waves, say, "Peace, be still." 8

Amidst the roaring of the sea,
My soul still hangs her hope on thee;
Thy constant love, thy faithful care,
Is all that saves me from despair.

Dangers of ev'ry shape and name
Attend the followers of the Lamb,
Who leave the world's deceitful shore,
And leave it to return no more. 16

Tho' tempest-toss'd and half a wreck,
My Saviour thro' the floods I seek;
Let neither winds nor stormy main,
Force back my shatter'd bark again.

XXXIX. [Bk. iii. xix.]

LOOKING UPWARDS IN A STORM

God of my life, to thee I call,
Afflicted at thy feet I fall[1];
When the great water-floods prevail,
Leave not my trembling heart to fail!

[1] Ps. lxix. 15.

XXXVII—18 precepts *Southey.*

Friend of the friendless, and the faint!
Where should I lodge my deep complaint?
Where but with thee, whose open door
Invites the helpless and the poor! 8

Did ever mourner plead with thee,
And thou refuse that mourner's plea?
Does not the word still fix'd remain,
That none shall seek thy face in vain?

That were a grief I could not bear,
Didst thou not hear and answer prayer;
But a pray'r-hearing, answ'ring GOD,
Supports me under ev'ry load. 16

Fair is the lot that's cast for me!
I have an advocate with thee;
They whom the world caresses most,
Have no such privilege to boast.

Poor tho' I am, despis'd, forgot[1],
Yet GOD, my GOD, forgets me not;
And he is safe and must succeed,
For whom the LORD vouchsafes to plead. 24

XL. [BK. III. XX.]

THE VALLEY OF THE SHADOW OF DEATH

MY soul is sad and much dismay'd;
See, LORD, what legions of my foes,
With fierce Apollyon at their head,
My heav'nly pilgrimage oppose!

See, from the ever-burning lake
How like a smoky cloud they rise!
With horrid blasts my soul they shake,
With storms of blasphemies and lies. 8

Their fiery arrows reach the mark[2],
My throbbing heart with anguish tear;
Each lights upon a kindred spark,
And finds abundant fuel there.

I hate the thought that wrongs the LORD;
Oh, I would drive it from my breast,
With thy own sharp two-edged sword,
Far as the east is from the west. 16

Come then, and chase the cruel host,
Heal the deep wounds I have receiv'd!
Nor let the pow'rs of darkness boast
That I am foil'd, and thou art griev'd!

[1] Ps. xl. 17. [2] Eph. vi. 16.

XLI. [Bk. iii. xxiii.]

PEACE AFTER A STORM

When darkness long has veil'd my mind,
And smiling day once more appears;
Then, my Redeemer, then I find
The folly of my doubts and fears.

Strait I upbraid my wandering heart,
And blush that I should ever be
Thus prone to act so base a part,
Or harbour one hard thought of thee! 8

Oh! let me then at length be taught
What I am still so slow to learn;
That God is love and changes not,
Nor knows the shadow of a turn:

Sweet truth, and easy to repeat!
But when my faith is sharply try'd,
I find myself a learner yet,
Unskilful, weak, and apt to slide. 16

But, O my Lord, one look from thee
Subdues the disobedient will;
Drives doubt and discontent away,
And thy rebellious worm is still.

Thou art as ready to forgive,
As I am ready to repine;
Thou, therefore, all the praise receive,
Be shame, and self-abhorrence, mine. 24

XLII. [Bk. iii. xxiv.]

MOURNING AND LONGING

The Saviour hides his face!
My spirit thirsts to prove
Renew'd supplies of pard'ning grace,
And never-fading love.

The favor'd souls who know
What glories shine in him,
Pant for his presence, as the roe
Pants for the living stream! 8

What trifles tease me now!
They swarm like summer flies,
They cleave to ev'ry thing I do,
And swim before my eyes.

How dull the sabbath day,
Without the sabbath's LORD!
How toilsome then to sing and pray,
And wait upon the word! 16

Of all the truths I hear
How few delight my taste!
I glean a berry here and there,
But mourn the vintage past.

Yet let me (as I ought)
Still hope to be supply'd;
No pleasure else is worth a thought,
Nor shall I be deny'd. 24

Tho' I am but a worm,
Unworthy of his care;
The LORD will my desire perform,
And grant me all my pray'r.

XLIII. [BK. III. XXVI.]

SELF-ACQUAINTANCE

DEAR LORD, accept a sinful heart,
Which of itself complains
And mourns, with much and frequent smart,
The evil it contains.

There fiery seeds of anger lurk,
Which often hurt my frame;
And wait but for the tempter's work,
To fan them to a flame. 8

Legality holds out a bribe
To purchase life from thee;
And discontent would fain prescribe
How thou shalt deal with me.

While unbelief withstands thy grace,
And puts the mercy by;
Presumption, with a brow of brass,
Says, "Give me, or I die." 16

How eager are my thoughts to roam
In quest of what they love!
But ah! when duty calls them home,
How heavily they move!

Oh, cleanse me in a Saviour's blood,
Transform me by thy pow'r,
And make me thy belov'd abode,
And let me rove no more. 24

XLIII—24 rove] roam *Southey.*

XLIV. [Bk. iii. xxviii.]

PRAYER FOR PATIENCE

Lord, who hast suffer'd all for me,
My peace and pardon to procure;
The lighter cross I bear for thee
Help me with patience to endure.

The storm of loud repining hush,
I would in humble silence mourn;
Why should th' unburnt, tho' burning bush,
Be angry as the crackling thorn? 8

Man should not faint at thy rebuke,
Like Joshua falling on his face[1],
When the curst thing that Achan took,
Brought Israel into just disgrace.

Perhaps some golden wedge suppress'd,
Some secret sin offends my God;
Perhaps that Babylonish vest
Self-righteousness, provokes the rod. 16

Ah! were I buffeted all day,
Mock'd, crown'd with thorns, and spit upon,
I yet should have no right to say,
My great distress is mine alone.

Let me not angrily declare
No pain was ever sharp like mine;
Nor murmur at the cross I bear,
But rather weep, rememb'ring thine. 24

XLV. [Bk. iii. xxix.]

SUBMISSION

O Lord, my best desire fulfil,
  And help me to resign
Life, health, and comfort to thy will,
  And make thy pleasure mine.

Why should I shrink at thy command,
  Whose love forbids my fears?
Or tremble at the gracious hand
  That wipes away my tears? 8

No, rather let me freely yield
  What most I prize to thee;
Who never hast a good withheld,
  Or wilt withhold from me.

[1] Joshua vii. 10, 11.

Thy favor, all my journey thro',
  Thou art engag'd to grant;
What else I want, or think I do,
  'Tis better still to want. 16

Wisdom and mercy guide my way,
  Shall I resist them both?
A poor blind creature of a day,
  And crush'd before the moth!

But ah! my inward spirit cries,
  Still bind me to thy sway;
Else the next cloud that vails my skies,
  Drives all these thoughts away. 24

XLVI. [Bk. iii. xliv.]

THE HAPPY CHANGE

How blest thy creature is, O God,
  When with a single eye,
He views the lustre of thy word,
  The day-spring from on high!

Thro' all the storms that veil the skies,
  And frown on earthly things;
The Sun of righteousness he eyes,
  With healing on his wings. 8

Struck by that light, the human heart[1],
  A barren soil no more;
Sends the sweet smell of grace abroad,
  Where serpents lurk'd before.

The soul, a dreary province once
  Of Satan's dark domain;
Feels a new empire form'd within,
  And owns a heav'nly reign. 16

The glorious orb, whose golden beams
  The fruitful year control;
Since first, obedient to thy word,
  He started from the goal;

Has cheer'd the nations, with the joys
  His orient rays impart;
But Jesus, 'tis thy light alone,
  Can shine upon the heart. 24

[1] Isa. xxxv. 7.

XLV—23 my] the *first in 1829*.

XLVII. [Bk. iii. xlv.]

RETIREMENT

Far from the world, O Lord, I flee,
From strife and tumult far;
From scenes, where Satan wages still
His most successful war.

The calm retreat, the silent shade,
With pray'r and praise agree;
And seem by thy sweet bounty made,
For those who follow thee. 8

There if thy Spirit touch the soul,
And grace her mean abode;
Oh with what peace, and joy, and love,
She communes with her God!

There like the nightingale she pours
Her solitary lays;
Nor asks a witness of her song,
Nor thirsts for human praise. 16

Author and Guardian of my life,
Sweet source of light divine;
And (all harmonious names in one)
My Saviour; thou art mine!

What thanks I owe thee, and what love
A boundless, endless store;
Shall echo thro' the realms above,
When time shall be no more. 24

XLVIII. [Bk. iii. xlvii.]

THE HIDDEN LIFE

To tell the Saviour all my wants,
How pleasing is the task!
Nor less to praise him when he grants
Beyond what I can ask.

My lab'ring spirit vainly seeks
To tell but half the joy;
With how much tenderness he speaks,
And helps me to reply. 8

Nor were it wise, nor should I choose
Such secrets to declare;
Like precious wines their taste they lose
Expos'd to open air.

But this with boldness I proclaim,
Nor care if thousands hear;
Sweet is the ointment of his name,
Not life is half so dear. 16

And can you frown, my former friends,
Who knew what once I was;
And blame the song that thus commends
The man who bore the cross?

Trust me, I draw the likeness true,
And not as fancy paints;
Such honour may he give to you,
For such have all his saints. 24

XLIX. [Bk. III. xlviii.]

JOY AND PEACE IN BELIEVING

Sometimes a light surprizes
The Christian while he sings;
It is the Lord who rises
With healing in his wings:
When comforts are declining,
He grants the soul again
A season of clear shining
To cheer it after rain. 8

In holy contemplation,
We sweetly then pursue
The theme of God's salvation,
And find it ever new:
Set free from present sorrow,
We cheerfully can say,
E'en let th' unknown to-morrow [1],
Bring with it what it may. 16

It can bring with it nothing
But he will bear us thro';
Who gives the lilies clothing
Will clothe his people too:
Beneath the spreading heavens,
No creature but is fed;
And he who feeds the ravens,
Will give his children bread. 24

Though vine, nor fig-tree neither [2],
Their wonted fruit should bear,
Tho' all the fields should wither,
Nor flocks, nor herds, be there:

[1] Matt. vi. 34. [2] Hab. iii. 17, 18.

25 Though] The *1779*. 26 should] shall *later editions*. 27 fields] field *first in 1787*.

Yet God the same abiding,
His praise shall tune my voice;
For while in him confiding,
I cannot but rejoice. 32

L. [Bk. iii. xlix.]

TRUE PLEASURES

Lord, my soul with pleasure springs,
When Jesus' name I hear;
And when God the Spirit brings
The word of promise near:
Beauties too, in holiness,
Still delighted I perceive;
Nor have words that can express
The joys thy precepts give. 8

Cloth'd in sanctity and grace,
How sweet it is to see
Those who love thee as they pass,
Or when they wait on thee:
Pleasant too, to sit and tell
What we owe to love divine;
Till our grateful bosoms swell,
And eyes begin to shine. 16

Those the comforts I possess,
Which God shall still increase[1];
All his ways are pleasantness,
And all his paths are peace:
Nothing Jesus did or spoke,
Henceforth let me ever slight;
For I love his easy yoke[2],
And find his burden light. 24

LI. [Bk. iii. l.]

THE CHRISTIAN

Honour and happiness unite
To make the Christian's name a praise;
How fair the scene, how clear the light,
That fills the remnant of his days!

A kingly character he bears,
No change his priestly office knows;
Unfading is the crown he wears,
His joys can never reach a close. 8

[1] Prov. iii. 17. [2] Matt. xi. 30.

Adorn'd with glory from on high,
Salvation shines upon his face;
His robe is of th' etherial dye,
His steps are dignity and grace.

Inferior honours he disdains,
Nor stoops to take applause from earth;
The King of kings himself, maintains
Th' expenses of his heav'nly birth. 16

The noblest creature seen below,
Ordain'd to fill a throne above;
GOD gives him all he can bestow,
His kingdom of eternal love!

My soul is ravish'd at the thought!
Methinks from earth I see him rise;
Angels congratulate his lot,
And shout him welcome to the skies! 24

LII. [BK. III. li.]

LIVELY HOPE, AND GRACIOUS FEAR

I WAS a groveling creature once,
And basely cleav'd to earth;
I wanted spirit to renounce
The clod that gave me birth.

But GOD has breath'd upon a worm,
And sent me, from above,
Wings, such as clothe an angel's form,
The wings of joy and love. 8

With these to Pisgah's top I fly,
And there delighted stand;
To view, beneath a shining sky,
The spacious promis'd land.

The LORD of all the vast domain,
Has promis'd it to me;
The length and breadth of all the plain,
As far as faith can see. 16

How glorious is my privilege!
To thee for help I call;
I stand upon a mountain's edge,
Oh save me, lest I fall!

Tho' much exalted in the LORD,
My strength is not my own;
Then let me tremble at his word,
And none shall cast me down. 24

LIII. [Bk. III. lvii.]

FOR THE POOR

When Hagar found the bottle spent[1],
  And wept o'er Ishmael;
A message from the Lord was sent
  To guide her to a well.

Should not Elijah's cake and cruse[2]
  Convince us at this day,
A gracious God will not refuse
  Provisions by the way? 8

His saints and servants shall be fed,
  The promise is secure;
"Bread shall be giv'n them," he has said,
  "Their water shall be sure[3]."

Repasts far richer they shall prove,
  Than all earth's dainties are;
'Tis sweet to taste a Saviour's love,
  Tho' in the meanest fare. 16

To Jesus then your trouble bring,
  Nor murmur at your lot;
While you are poor, and he is King,
  You shall not be forgot.

LIV. [Bk. III. lxi.]

MY SOUL THIRSTETH FOR GOD

I thirst, but not as once I did,
The vain delights of earth to share;
Thy wounds, Emmanuel, all forbid,
That I should seek my pleasures there.

It was the sight of thy dear cross,
First wean'd my soul from earthly things;
And taught me to esteem as dross,
The mirth of fools and pomp of kings. 8

I want that grace that springs from thee,
That quickens all things where it flows;
And makes a wretched thorn, like me,
Bloom as the myrtle, or the rose.

[1] Gen. xxi. 19. [2] 1 Kings xvii. 14. [3] Isa. xxxiii. 16.

LIII—3 A message from] An angel of *A*. 8 provision *A*. 11 he has *1779, 1781, A.*: as he *later edd.* 13 Repasts] Delights *A*. 17 troubles *A*. 19 While . . . and] Supply is sure while *A*.

Dear fountain of delight unknown!
No longer sink below the brim;
But overflow, and pour me down
A living, and life-giving stream! 16

For sure, of all the plants that share
The notice of thy Father's eye;
None proves less grateful to his care,
Or yields him meaner fruit than I.

LV. [Bk. iii. lxii.]

LOVE CONSTRAINING TO OBEDIENCE

No strength of Nature can suffice
To serve the Lord aright:
And what she has, she misapplies,
For want of clearer light.

How long beneath the law I lay
In bondage and distress!
I toil'd the precept to obey,
But toil'd without success. 8

Then to abstain from outward sin
Was more than I could do;
Now, if I feel its pow'r within,
I feel I hate it too.

Then all my servile works were done
A righteousness to raise;
Now, freely chosen in the Son,
I freely choose his ways. 16

What shall I do, was then the word,
That I may worthier grow?
What shall I render to the Lord?
Is my enquiry now.

To see the Law by Christ fulfill'd,
And hear his pard'ning voice;
Changes a slave into a child[1],
And duty into choice. 24

LVI. [Bk. iii. lxiii.]

THE HEART HEALED AND CHANGED BY MERCY

Sin enslav'd me many years,
And led me bound and blind;
Till at length a thousand fears
Came swarming o'er my mind.

[1] Rom. iii. 31.

LV—2 the *om. 1779.*

Where, I said in deep distress,
Will these sinful pleasures end?
How shall I secure my peace,
And make the LORD my friend? 8

Friends and ministers said much
The gospel to enforce;
But my blindness still was such,
I chose a legal course:
Much I fasted, watch'd and strove,
Scarce would shew my face abroad,
Fear'd, almost, to speak or move,
A stranger still to GOD. 16

Thus afraid to trust his grace,
Long time did I rebel;
Till, despairing of my case,
Down at his feet I fell:
Then my stubborn heart he broke,
And subdu'd me to his sway;
By a simple word he spoke,
"Thy sins are done away." 24

LVII. [BK. III. lxiv.]

HATRED OF SIN

HOLY LORD GOD! I love thy truth,
Nor dare thy least commandment slight·
Yet pierc'd by sin, the serpent's tooth,
I mourn the anguish of the bite.

But tho' the poison lurks within,
Hope bids me still with patience wait;
Till death shall set me free from sin,
Free from the only thing I hate. 8

Had I a throne above the rest,
Where angels and archangels dwell;
One sin, unslain, within my breast,
Would make that heav'n as dark as hell.

The pris'ner, sent to breathe fresh air,
And bless'd with liberty again,
Would mourn, were he condemn'd to wear
One link of all his former chain. 16

But oh! no foe invades the bliss,
When glory crowns the Christian's head;
One view of JESUS as he is,
Will strike all sin for ever dead.

LVIII. [Bk. III. lxviii.]

THE NEW CONVERT

THE new-born child of gospel-grace,
Like some fair tree when summer's nigh,
Beneath EMMANUEL'S shining face
Lifts up his blooming branch on high.

No fears he feels, he sees no foes,
No conflict yet his faith employs,
Nor has he learnt to whom he owes
The strength and peace his soul enjoys. 8

But sin soon darts its cruel sting,
And, comforts sinking day by day,
What seem'd his own, a self-fed spring,
Proves but a brook that glides away.

When Gideon arm'd his num'rous host,
The LORD soon made his numbers less;
And said, "lest Israel vainly boast[1],
My arm procur'd me this success." 16

Thus will he bring our spirits down,
And draw our ebbing comforts low;
That sav'd by grace, but not our own,
We may not claim the praise we owe.

LIX. [Bk. III. lxix.]

TRUE AND FALSE COMFORTS

O GOD, whose favourable eye
The sin-sick soul revives;
Holy and heav'nly is the joy
Thy shining presence gives.

Not such as hypocrites suppose,
Who with a graceless heart,
Taste not of thee, but drink a dose
Prepar'd by Satan's art. 8

Intoxicating joys are theirs,
Who while they boast their light,
And seem to soar above the stars,
Are plunging into night.

Lull'd in a soft and fatal sleep,
They sin, and yet rejoice;
Were they indeed the Saviour's sheep,
Would they not hear his voice? 16

[1] Judges vii. 2.

Be mine the comforts, that reclaim
The soul from Satan's pow'r;
That make me blush for what I am,
And hate my sin the more.

'Tis joy enough, my All in All,
At thy dear feet to lie;
Thou wilt not let me lower fall,
And none can higher fly. 24

LX. [Bk. III. lxxi.]

A LIVING AND A DEAD FAITH

The Lord receives his highest praise,
From humble minds and hearts sincere;
While all the loud professor says
Offends the righteous Judge's ear.

To walk as children of the day;
To mark the precepts' holy light;
To wage the warfare, watch and pray,
Shew who are pleasing in his sight. 8

Not words alone it cost the Lord,
To purchase pardon for his own;
Nor will a soul, by grace restor'd,
Return the Saviour words alone.

With golden bells, the priestly vest[1],
And rich pomegranates border'd round,
The need of holiness express'd,
And call'd for fruit, as well as sound. 16

Easy, indeed, it were to reach
A mansion in the courts above,
If swelling words, and fluent speech
Might serve, instead of faith and love.

But none shall gain the blissful place,
Or God's unclouded glory see;
Who talks of free and sov'reign grace,
Unless that grace has made *him* free. 24

LXI. [Bk. III. lxxii.]

ABUSE OF THE GOSPEL

Too many, Lord, abuse thy grace,
In this licentious day;
And while they boast they see thy face,
They turn their own away.

[1] Exod. xxviii. 33.

LX—6 precepts *1779*. LXI—*Entitled* Antinomians *in A*.

Thy Book displays a gracious light
  That can the blind restore;
But these are dazzled by the sight,
  And blinded still the more. 8

The pardon, such presume upon,
  They do not beg, but steal;
And when they plead it at thy throne,
  Oh, where's the Spirit's seal?

Was it for this, ye lawless tribe,
  The dear Redeemer bled;
Is this the grace the saints imbibe
  From CHRIST the living head? 16

Ah LORD, we know thy chosen few
  Are fed with heav'nly fare;
But these, the wretched husks they chew,
  Proclaim them what they are.

The liberty our hearts implore
  Is not to live in sin;
But still to wait at Wisdom's door,
  Till Mercy calls us in. 24

LXII. [Bk. III. lxxiii.]

THE NARROW WAY

WHAT thousands never knew the road!
What thousands hate it when 'tis known!
None but the chosen tribes of GOD,
Will seek or choose it for their own.

A thousand ways in ruin end,
One only leads to joys on high;
By that my willing steps ascend,
Pleas'd with a journey to the sky. 8

No more I ask, or hope to find,
Delight or happiness below;
Sorrow may well possess the mind
That feeds where thorns and thistles grow.

The joy that fades is not for me,
I seek immortal joys above;
There, glory without end shall be
The bright reward of faith and love. 16

Cleave to the world ye sordid worms,
Contented lick your native dust;
But GOD shall fight, with all his storms,
Against the idol of your trust.

LXI—12 Spirit's] Gospel *A*.

LXIII. [Bk. iii. lxxiv.]

DEPENDANCE

To keep the lamp alive
With oil we fill the bowl;
'Tis water makes the willow thrive,
And grace that feeds the soul.

The Lord's unsparing hand
Supplies the living stream;
It is not at our own command,
But still deriv'd from him. 8

Beware of Peter's word [1],
Nor confidently say,
"I never *will* deny thee, Lord,"
But "grant I never *may*."

Man's wisdom is to seek
His strength in God alone;
And e'en an angel would be weak,
Who trusted in his own. 16

Retreat beneath his wings,
And in his grace confide;
This more exalts the King of kings [2]
Than all your works beside.

In Jesus is our store,
Grace issues from his throne;
Whoever says, "I want no more,"
Confesses he has none. 24

LXIV. [Bk. iii. lxxv.]

NOT OF WORKS

Grace, triumphant in the throne,
Scorns a rival, reigns alone;
Come and bow beneath her sway,
Cast your idol works away:
Works of man, when made his plea,
Never shall accepted be;
Fruits of pride (vain-glorious worm)
Are the best he can perform. 8

Self, the god his soul adores,
Influences all his pow'rs;
Jesus is a slighted name,
Self-advancement all his aim:

[1] Matt. xxvi. 33. [2] John vi. 29.

But when God the Judge shall come,
To pronounce the final doom,
Then for rocks and hills to hide
All his works and all his pride! 16

Still the boasting heart replies,
What! the worthy and the wise,
Friends to temperance and peace,
Have not these a righteousness?
Banish ev'ry vain pretence
Built on human excellence;
Perish ev'ry thing in man,
But the grace that never can. 24

LXV. [Bk. iii. lxxx.]

PRAISE FOR FAITH

Of all the gifts thine hand bestows,
Thou Giver of all good!
Not heav'n itself a richer knows,
Than my Redeemer's blood.

Faith too, the blood-receiving grace,
From the same hand we gain;
Else, sweetly as it suits our case,
That gift had been in vain. 8

Till thou thy teaching pow'r apply,
Our hearts refuse to see;
And weak, as a distemper'd eye,
Shut out the view of thee.

Blind to the merits of thy Son,
What mis'ry we endure!
Yet fly that hand, from which alone
We could expect a cure. 16

We praise thee, and would praise thee more,
To thee our all we owe;
The precious Saviour, and the pow'r
That makes him precious too.

LXVI. [Bk. iii. lxxxi.]

GRACE AND PROVIDENCE

Almighty King! whose wond'rous hand,
Supports the weight of sea and land;
Whose grace is such a boundless store,
No heart shall break that sighs for more;

Thy Providence supplies my food,
And 'tis thy blessing makes it good;
My soul is nourish'd by thy word,
Let soul and body praise the LORD. 8

My streams of outward comfort came
From him, who built this earthly frame;
Whate'er I want his bounty gives,
By whom my soul for ever lives.

Either his hand preserves from pain,
Or, if I feel it, heals again;
From Satan's malice shields my breast,
Or overrules it for the best. 16

Forgive the song that falls so low
Beneath the gratitude I owe!
It means thy praise, however poor,
An angel's song can do no more.

LXVII. [Bk. III. lxxxiii.]

I WILL PRAISE THE LORD AT ALL TIMES

WINTER has a joy for me,
While the Saviour's charms I read,
Lowly, meek, from blemish free,
In the snow-drop's pensive head.

Spring returns, and brings along
Life-invigorating suns:
Hark! the turtle's plaintive song,
Seems to speak his dying grones! 8

Summer has a thousand charms,
All expressive of his worth;
'Tis his sun that lights and warms,
His the air that cools the earth.

What! has autumn left to say
Nothing, of a Saviour's grace?
Yes, the beams of milder day
Tell me of his smiling face. 16

Light appears with early dawn,
While the sun makes haste to rise,
See his bleeding beauties, drawn
On the blushes of the skies.

Ev'ning, with a silent pace,
Slowly moving in the west,
Shews an emblem of his grace,
Points to an eternal rest. 24

LONGING TO BE WITH CHRIST

[Not in the Olney Hymns. Hayley (1803) first printed verses 1–4 as a Fragment, which had been discovered in a book of Cowper's domestic accounts sent to him by Johnson. The Autobiography (1816) printed a slightly different version of verses 1, 2, and 4. Southey printed only the first two verses as Fragment of a Hymn; and the hymn was first given in its entirety by Grimshawe (1835), who says that he has been "enabled to authenticate it as the production of Cowper."]

To JESUS, the Crown of my Hope,
  My soul is in haste to be gone;
Oh bear me, ye cherubims, up,
  And waft me away to his throne!

My Saviour, whom absent I love,
  Whom not having seen I adore;
Whose name is exalted above
  All glory, dominion, and power; 8

Dissolve thou the bond, that detains
  My soul from her portion in thee,
And strike off the adamant chains,
  And make me eternally free.

When that happy æra begins,
  When array'd in thy beauty I shine,
Nor pierce any more, by my sins,
  The bosom on which I recline; 16

Oh then shall the veil be remov'd,
  And round me thy brightness be pour'd,
I shall meet him whom absent I lov'd,
  I shall see whom unseen I ador'd.

And then never more shall the fears,
  The trials, temptations, and woes,
Which darken this valley of tears,
  Intrude on my blissful repose; 24

Or, if yet remember'd above,
  Remembrance no sadness shall raise,
They will be but new signs of thy love,
  New themes for my wonder and praise.

Thus the strokes which from sin and from pain
  Shall set me eternally free,
Will but strengthen and rivet the chain,
  Which binds me, my Saviour, to thee. 32

5 Saviour] Jesus *1816*. 9 these bonds . . . detain *Grimshawe*. 11 Ah . . . this . . . chain *Grimshawe*. 14 beauty *Hayley*, *1816*: glories *Grimshawe*. 15 pierce] grieve *Grimshawe* (And pierce no *1816*).

HYMN

FOR THE USE OF THE SUNDAY SCHOOL AT OLNEY

[Written Aug., 1789. Published 1808.]

HEAR, LORD, the song of praise and pray'r,
  In Heav'n, thy dwelling place,
From infants made the public care,
  And taught to seek thy face!

Thanks for thy word, and for thy day;
  And grant us, we implore,
Never to waste in sinful play
  Thy holy sabbaths more. 8

Thanks that we hear,—but Oh, impart
  To each desires sincere,
That we may listen with our heart,
  And learn, as well as hear.

For if vain thoughts the minds engage
  Of older far than we,
What hope that, at our heedless age,
  Our minds should e'er be free? 16

Much hope, if thou our spirits take
  Under thy gracious sway,
Who canst the wisest wiser make,
  And babes as wise as they.

Wisdom and bliss thy word bestows,
  A sun that ne'er declines,
And be thy mercies show'r'd on *those*
  Who plac'd us where it shines. 24

5 thy day] this day *1808.*

[Title-page and dedication of Bull's edition.]

P O E M S

Translated from the French

OF

MADAME DE LA MOTHE GUION,

BY THE LATE

WILLIAM COWPER, Esq.

Author of the TASK.

TO WHICH ARE ADDED

SOME ORIGINAL POEMS

Of Mr. Cowper,

NOT INSERTED IN HIS WORKS.

NEWPORT-PAGNEL,
Printed and Sold by J. Wakefield;
sold also by
T. WILLIAMS, 10, STATIONERS' COURT, LONDON.
1801.
[*Entered at Stationer's Hall.*]

TO

THE REV. WILLIAM BULL,

THESE TRANSLATIONS

OF A FEW OF THE SPIRITUAL

SONGS

OF THE EXCELLENT

MADAME GUION,

MADE AT HIS EXPRESS DESIRE,

ARE DEDICATED,

BY HIS AFFECTIONATE FRIEND

AND SERVANT

WILLIAM COWPER.

July, 1782.

THE NATIVITY

POEME HEROIQUE.—Vol. 4, § 4.

[The translations from Madame Guion were written during the first six months of 1782, at the request of William Bull. They were first published by Bull in 1801, from a fair copy presented to him by Cowper (see notes at the end of the volume for Bull's preface). The Ash MSS. contain copies of all the translations except *Living Water*, and *Acquiescence of Pure Love*; but the readings of the 1801 edition, except where misprinted, must almost always be preferred to those of the MSS., which are all earlier drafts, many being full of interlineations and erasures. The most interesting verbal variants are given in the footnotes. A MS. of *Scenes Favourable to Meditation*, enclosed in a letter to Unwin, is in the British Museum.]

'Tis Folly all—let me no more be told
Of Parian porticos, and roofs of gold;
Delightful views of Nature dress'd by Art,
Enchant no longer this indiff'rent heart;
The Lord of all things, in his humble birth,
Makes mean the proud magnificence of Earth;
The straw, the manger, and the mould'ring wall,
Eclipse its lustre; and I scorn it all.
  Canals, and fountains, and delicious vales,
Green slopes, and plains whose plenty never fails;
Deep-rooted groves, whose heads sublimely rise, 11
Earth-born, and yet ambitious of the skies;
Th' abundant foliage of whose gloomy shades,
Vainly the sun in all its pow'r invades;
Where warbled airs of sprightly birds resound;
Whose verdure lives while winter scowls around;
Rocks, lofty mountains, caverns dark and deep,
And torrents raving down the rugged steep;
Smooth downs, whose fragrant herbs the spirits cheer;
Meads, crown'd with flow'rs; streams musical and clear, 20
Whose silver waters, and whose murmurs, join
Their artless charms, to make the scene divine;
The fruitful vineyard, and the furrow'd plain,
That seems a rolling sea of golden grain;
All, all have lost the charms they once possess'd;
An infant God reigns sov'reign in my breast;
From Bethl'em's bosom I no more will rove;
There dwells the Saviour, and there rests my love.
  Ye mightier rivers, that with sounding force
Urge down the valleys your impetuous course! 30

3 views... Art] scenes where nature vies with Art *A*. 6 proud] vain *A*. 12 Affect the clouds, and push into the skies *A*. 13 The plenteous *A*. 14 The sun, in all his pow'r, in vain invades *A*.

Winds, clouds, and lightnings! and ye waves, whose heads
Curl'd into monstrous forms, the seaman dreads!
Horrid abyss, where all experience fails,
Spread with the wreck of planks and shatter'd sails;
On whose broad back grim Death triumphant rides,
While havock floats on all thy swelling tides,
Thy shores a scene of ruin, strew'd around
With vessels bulged, and bodies of the drown'd!
Ye Fish, that sport beneath the boundless waves,
And rest, secure from man, in rocky caves; 40
Swift darting sharks, and whales of hideous size,
Whom all th' aquatic world with terror eyes!
Had I but Faith immoveable and true,
I might defy the fiercest storm, like you:
The world, a more disturb'd and boist'rous sea,
When Jesus shows a smile, affrights not me;
He hides me, and in vain the billows roar,
Break harmless at my feet, and leave the shore.
Thou azure vault, where, through the gloom of night,
Thick sown, we see such countless worlds of light!
Thou Moon, whose car, encompassing the skies, 51
Restores lost nature to our wondring eyes;
Again retiring, when the brighter Sun
Begins the course he seems in haste to run!
Behold *him* where he shines! His rapid rays,
Themselves unmeasur'd, measure all our days;
Nothing impedes the race he would pursue,
Nothing escapes his penetrating view,
A thousand lands confess his quick'ning heat,
And all he cheers, are fruitful, fair, and sweet. 60
Far from enjoying what these scenes disclose,
I feel the thorn, alas! but miss the rose;
Too well I know this aching heart requires
More solid good to fill its vast desires;
In vain they represent his matchless might
Who call'd them out of deep primaeval night;
Their form and beauty but augment my woe:
I seek the Giver of those charms they show;
Nor, him beside, throughout the world he made,
Lives there, in whom I trust for cure or aid. 70
Infinite God, thou great unrivall'd ONE!
Whose glory makes a blot of yonder sun;
Compar'd with thine, how dim his beauty seems,
How quench'd the radiance of his golden beams!

44 I might defy] My soul would brave *A*. 59 quick'ning] vital *A*. 66 out of deep] forth from black *A*.

Thou art my bliss, the light by which I move;
In thee alone dwells all that I can love;
All darkness flies when thou art pleas'd t' appear,
A sudden spring renews the fading year;
Where e'er I turn, I see thy power and grace
The watchful guardians of our heedless race; 80
Thy various creatures in one strain agree,
All, in all times and places, speak of thee;
Ev'n I, with trembling heart and stammering tongue,
Attempt thy praise, and join the gen'ral song.
Almighty Former of this wondrous plan,
Faintly reflected in thine image, Man,—
Holy and just,—the greatness of whose name
Fills and supports this universal frame,
Diffus'd throughout th' infinitude of space,
Who art thyself thine own vast dwelling-place; 90
Soul of our soul, whom yet no sense of ours
Discerns, eluding our most active pow'rs;
Encircling shades attend thine awful throne,
That veil thy face, and keep thee still unknown;
Unknown, though dwelling in our inmost part,
Lord of the thoughts, and Sov'reign of the heart!
Repeat the charming truth that never tires,
No God is like the God my soul desires;
He at whose voice heav'n trembles, even He,
Great as he is, knows how to stoop to me; 100
Lo! there He lies,—that smiling Infant said,
"Heav'n, Earth, and Sea, exist!"—and they obey'd.
Ev'n He whose Being swells beyond the skies,
Is born of woman, lives, and mourns, and dies;
Eternal and Immortal, seems to cast
That glory from his brows, and breathes his last.
Trivial and vain the works that man has wrought,
How do they shrink and vanish at the thought!
Sweet Solitude, and scene of my repose!
This rustic sight assuages all my woes— 110
That crib contains the Lord whom I adore;
And Earth's a shade, that I pursue no more.
He is my firm support, my rock, my tow'r,
I dwell secure beneath his shelt'ring pow'r,
And hold this mean retreat for ever dear,
For all I love, my soul's delight, is here.
I see th' Almighty swath'd in infant bands,
Tied helpless down, the Thunder-bearer's hands!
And in this shed that mystery discern, 119
Which Faith and Love, and they alone, can learn.

84 Attempt] Aim at *A*. 87 whose] thy *A*.

Ye tempests, spare the slumbers of your Lord!
Ye zephyrs, all your whisper'd sweets afford!
Confess the God that guides the rolling year;
Heav'n, do him homage; and thou Earth, revere!
Ye Shepherds, Monarchs, Sages, hither bring
Your hearts an off'ring, and adore your King!
Pure be those hearts, and rich in Faith and Love;
Join in his praise, th' harmonious worlds above;
To Bethl'em haste, rejoice in his repose,
And praise him there for all that he bestows! 130
Man, busy Man, alas! can ill afford
T' obey the summons, and attend the Lord;
Perverted reason revels and runs wild,
By glitt'ring shows of pomp and wealth beguil'd;
And, blind to genuine excellence and grace,
Finds not her Author in so mean a place.
Ye unbelieving! learn a wiser part,
Distrust your erring sense, and search your heart;
There, soon ye shall perceive a kindling flame
Glow for that Infant God from whom it came; 140
Resist not, quench not that divine desire,
Melt all your adamant in heavenly fire!
Not so will I requite thee, gentle Love!
Yielding and soft this heart shall ever prove;
And ev'ry heart beneath thy power should fall,
Glad to submit, could mine contain them all.
But I am poor, oblation I have none,
None for a Saviour, but Himself alone:
Whate'er I render thee, from thee it came;
And if I give my body to the flame, 150
My patience, love, and energy divine
Of heart and soul and spirit, all are thine.
Ah vain attempt, t' expunge the mighty score!
The more I pay, I owe thee still the more.
Upon my meanness, poverty, and guilt,
The trophy of thy glory shall be built;
My self-disdain shall be th' unshaken base,
And my deformity its fairest grace;
For destitute of Good and rich in Ill,
Must be my state and my description still. 160
And do I grieve at such a humbling lot?
Nay, but I cherish and enjoy the thought—
Vain pageantry and pomp of Earth, adieu!
I have no wish, no memory for you;

129, 130 rejoice in . . . there] that scene of his repose, There yield him thanks *A*. 136 Author] Sov'reign *A*. 145 ev'ry heart] all that are *A*. 150 give] yield *A*. 160 description] true picture *A*.

The more I feel my mis'ry, I adore
The sacred Inmate of my soul the more;
Rich in his Love, I feel my noblest pride
Spring from the sense of having nought beside.
  In thee I find wealth, comfort, virtue, might;
My wand'rings prove thy wisdom infinite; 170
All that I have, I give thee; and then see
All contrarieties unite in thee;
For thou hast join'd them, taking up our woe,
And pouring out thy bliss on worms below,
By filling with thy grace and love divine
A gulph of Evil in this heart of mine.
This is indeed to bid the valleys rise,
And the hills sink—'tis matching earth and skies!
I feel my weakness, thank thee, and deplore
An aching heart that throbs to thank thee more;
The more I love thee, I the more reprove 181
A soul so lifeless, and so slow to love;
Till, on a deluge of thy mercy toss'd,
I plunge into that sea, and there am lost.

GOD NEITHER KNOWN NOR LOVED BY THE WORLD

Vol. 2, Cantique 11

Ye Linnets, let us try, beneath this grove,
Which shall be loudest in our Maker's praise!
In quest of some forlorn retreat I rove,
For all the world is blind, and wanders from his ways.

That God alone should prop the sinking soul,
Fills them with rage against his empire now;
I traverse earth in vain from pole to pole,
To seek one simple heart, set free from all below. 8

They speak of Love, yet little feel its sway,
While in their bosoms many an idol lurks;
Their base desires well satisfied obey,
Leave the Creator's hand, and lean upon his works.

'Tis therefore I can dwell with man no more;
Your fellowship, ye warblers! suits me best:
Pure Love has lost its price, though priz'd of yore,
Profan'd by modern tongues, and slighted as a jest.

My God, who form'd you for his praise alone, 17
Beholds his purpose well fulfill'd in you:
Come, let us join the Choir before his throne,
Partaking in his praise with spirits just and true!

Title *om. A.* 2 our] his *A.* 20 just] pure *A.*

Yes, I will always love; and, as I ought,
Tune to the praise of Love my ceaseless voice;
Preferring Love too vast for human thought,
In spite of erring men, who cavil at my choice. 24

Why have I not a thousand thousand hearts,
Lord of my soul! that they might all be thine?
If thou approve—the zeal thy smile imparts,
How should it ever fail! Can such a fire decline?

Love, pure and holy, is a deathless fire;
Its object heav'nly, it must ever blaze:
Eternal Love a God must needs inspire,
When once he wins the heart, and fits it for his praise.

Self-love dismiss'd—'tis then we live indeed— 33
In her embrace, death, only death is found:
Come then, one noble effort, and succeed,
Cast off the chain of Self with which thy soul is
bound!

Oh! I would cry that all the world might hear,
Ye self-tormentors, love your God alone;
Let his unequall'd Excellence be dear,
Dear to your inmost souls, and make him all your
own! 40

They hear me not—alas! how fond to rove
In endless chase of Folly's specious lure!
'Tis here alone, beneath this shady grove,
I taste the sweets of Truth—here only am secure.

THE SWALLOW

VOL. 2, CANTIQUE 54

I AM fond of the Swallow—I learn from her flight,
Had I skill to improve it, a lesson of Love:
How seldom on earth do we see her alight!
She dwells in the skies, she is ever above.

It is on the wing that she takes her repose,
Suspended, and pois'd in the regions of air,
'Tis not in our fields that her sustenance grows,
It is wing'd like herself, 'tis ethereal fare. 8

She comes in the Spring, all the Summer she stays,
And dreading the cold, still follows the sun—
So, true to our Love, we should covet his rays,
And the place where he shines not, immediately shun.

39 unequall'd] unrivall'd *A*.

Our light should be Love, and our nourishment
pray'r;
It is dangerous food that we find upon earth:
The fruit of this world is beset with a snare,
In itself it is hurtful, as vile in its birth. 16

'Tis rarely, if ever, she settles below,
And only when building a nest for her young;
Were it not for her brood, she would never bestow
A thought upon any thing filthy as dung.

Let us leave it ourselves ('tis a mortal abode)
To bask ev'ry moment in infinite Love;
Let us fly the dark winter, and follow the road
That leads to the day-spring appearing above. 24

THE TRIUMPH OF HEAVENLY LOVE DESIRED

VOL. 2, CANTIQUE 236

AH! reign, wherever Man is found,
My Spouse, beloved and divine!
Then I am rich, and I abound,
When ev'ry human heart is thine.

A thousand sorrows pierce my soul,
To think that all are not thine own:
Ah! be ador'd from pole to pole;
Where is thy zeal? arise, be known! 8

All hearts are cold, in ev'ry place,
Yet earthly good with warmth pursue;
Dissolve them with a flash of grace,
Thaw these of ice, and give us new!

A FIGURATIVE DESCRIPTION OF THE PROCEDURE OF DIVINE LOVE

IN BRINGING A SOUL TO THE POINT OF SELF-RENUNCIATION AND ABSOLUTE ACQUIESCENCE

VOL. 2, CANTIQUE 110

'TWAS my purpose, on a day,
To embark and sail away;
As I climb'd the vessel's side,
Love was sporting in the tide;
"Come," he said—"ascend—make haste,
Launch into the boundless waste." 6

20 A] One *A*.
The Triumph—Title *om. A*. 2 beloved] Almighty *A*. 7 ador'd] beloved *A*. 9 cold] ice *A*.
A Figurative Description—Title] The proceedings of divine love in order to bring a soul . . . *A*.

Many mariners were there,
Having each his sep'rate care;
They that row'd us, held their eyes
Fixt upon the starry skies;
Others steer'd, or turn'd the sails
To receive the shifting gales. 12

Love, with pow'r divine supplied,
Suddenly my courage tried;
In a moment it was night,
Ship, and skies, were out of sight;
On the briny wave I lay,
Floating rushes all my stay. 18

Did I with resentment burn
At this unexpected turn?
Did I wish myself on shore,
Never to forsake it more?
No—"my soul," I cried, "be still;
If I must be lost, I will." 24

Next, he hasten'd to convey
Both my frail supports away;
Seiz'd my rushes; bade the waves
Yawn into a thousand graves:
Down I went, and sunk as lead,
Ocean closing o'er my head. 30

Still, however, life was safe;
And I saw him turn and laugh:
"Friend," he cried, "adieu! lie low,
While the wintry storms shall blow;
When the spring has calm'd the main,
You shall rise and float again." 36

Soon I saw him, with dismay,
Spread his plumes, and soar away;
Now I mark his rapid flight,
Now he leaves my aching sight;
He is gone whom I adore,
'Tis in vain to seek him more. 42

How I trembled then, and fear'd,
When my Love had disappear'd!
"Wilt thou leave me thus," I cried,
"Whelm'd beneath the rolling tide?"
Vain attempt to reach his ear!
Love was gone, and would not hear. 48

Ah! return, and love me still;
See me subject to thy will;
Frown with wrath, or smile with grace,
Only let me see thy face!
Evil I have none to fear,
All is good, if thou art near. 54

Yet he leaves me—cruel fate!
Leaves me in my lost estate—
Have I sinn'd? Oh say wherein;
Tell me, and forgive my sin!
King, and Lord, whom I adore,
Shall I see thy face no more? 60

Be not angry; I resign,
Henceforth, all my Will to thine;
I consent that thou depart,
Though thine absence breaks my heart;
Go then, and for ever too;
All is right that thou wilt do. 66

This was just what Love intended,
He was now no more offended;
Soon as I became a child,
Love return'd to me and smil'd:
Never strife shall more betide
'Twixt the Bridegroom and his Bride. 72

A CHILD OF GOD LONGING TO SEE HIM BELOVED

VOL. 2, CANTIQUE 144

THERE's not an Eccho round me,
  But I am glad should learn
How pure a fire has found me,
  The Love with which I burn.
For none attends with pleasure
  To what I would reveal;
They slight me out of measure,
  And laugh at all I feel. 8

The rocks receive less proudly
  The story of my flame;
When I approach, they loudly
  Reverberate my name.

64 break *A*.
Title] The desire of a new born soul to see God beloved ***A***.
10 story] tidings *A*.

I speak to them of sadness,
And comforts at a stand;
They bid me look for gladness,
And better days at hand. 16

Far from all habitation,
I heard a happy sound;
Big with the consolation
That I have often found;
I said, "my lot is sorrow,
My grief has no alloy;"
The rocks replied—"to-morrow,
To-morrow brings thee joy." 24

These sweet and secret tidings,
What bliss it is to hear!
For, spite of all my chidings,
My weakness and my fear,
No sooner I receive them,
Than I forget my pain,
And happy to believe them,
I love as much again. 32

I fly to scenes romantic,
Where never men resort;
For in an age so frantic,
Impiety is sport;
For riot and confusion,
They barter things above;
Condemning, as delusion,
The joy of perfect Love. 40

In this sequester'd corner
None hears what I express;
Deliver'd from the scorner,
What peace do I possess!
Beneath the boughs reclining,
Or roving o'er the wild,
I live, as undesigning,
And harmless as a child. 48

No troubles here surprise me,
I innocently play,
While providence supplies me,
And guards me all the day:
My dear and kind defender
Preserves me safely here,
From men of pomp and splendour,
Who fill a child with fear. 56

22 alloy *A.*: allay *Bull.* 24 thee] the *A.*

ASPIRATIONS OF THE SOUL AFTER GOD

Vol. 2, Cantique 95

My Spouse! in whose presence I live,
Sole object of all my desires,
Who know'st what a flame I conceive,
And canst easily double its fires;
How pleasant is all that I meet!
From fear of adversity free,
I find even sorrow made sweet,
Because 'tis assign'd me by Thee. 8

Transported I see thee display
Thy riches and glory divine;
I have only my life to repay,
Take what I would gladly resign.
Thy will is the treasure I seek,
For thou art as faithful as strong;
There let me, obedient and meek,
Repose myself all the day long. 16

My spirit and faculties fail;
Oh finish what Love has begun!
Destroy what is sinful and frail,
And dwell in the soul thou hast won!
Dear theme of my wonder and praise,
I cry, who is worthy as Thou!
I can only be silent and gaze;
'Tis all that is left to me now. 24

Oh glory, in which I am lost,
Too deep for the plummet of thought!
On an ocean of deity toss'd,
I am swallow'd, I sink into nought.
Yet lost and absorb'd as I seem,
I chaunt to the praise of my King;
And though overwhelm'd by the theme,
Am happy whenever I sing. 32

GRATITUDE AND LOVE TO GOD

Vol. 2, Cantique 96

All are indebted much to thee,
But I far more than all,
From many a deadly snare set free,
And rais'd from many a fall.
Overwhelm me, from above,
Daily, with thy boundless Love. 6

Aspirations—Title] A soul sick of Love *A*.
Gratitude—Title] Pure Love on a principle of gratitude *A*.
2 I far more] deeper I *A*.

What bonds of Gratitude I feel,
No language can declare;
Beneath th' oppressive weight I reel,
'Tis more than I can bear:
When shall I that blessing prove,
To return thee Love for Love? 12

Spirit of Charity, dispense
Thy grace to ev'ry heart;
Expell all other spirits thence,
Drive self from ev'ry part;
Charity divine, draw nigh,
Break the chains in which we lie! 18

All selfish souls, whate'er they feign,
Have still a slavish lot;
They boast of Liberty in vain,
Of Love, and feel it not.
He whose bosom glows with Thee,
He, and he alone, is free. 24

O blessedness, all bliss above,
When *thy* pure fires prevail!
Love only teaches what is Love;
All other lessons fail:
We learn its name, but not its pow'rs,
Experience only makes it ours. 30

HAPPY SOLITUDE—UNHAPPY MEN

VOL. 2, CANTIQUE 89

MY heart is easy, and my burthen light;
I smile, though sad, when thou art in my sight:
The more my woes in secret I deplore,
I taste thy goodness, and I love, the more.

There, while a solemn stillness reigns around,
Faith, Love, and Hope, within my soul abound;
And while the world suppose me lost in care,
The joys of angels, unperceiv'd, I share. 8

Thy creatures wrong thee, O thou sov'reign Good!
Thou art not lov'd, because not understood;
This grieves me most, that vain pursuits beguile
Ungrateful men, regardless of thy smile.

Frail beauty, and false honour, are ador'd;
While thee they scorn, and trifle with thy word;
Pass, unconcern'd, a Saviour's sorrows by;
And hunt their ruin, with a zeal to die. 16

Gratitude—12 repay *A*. 14 grace] self *A*. 23 bosom glows with] heart is warm'd by *A*.

LIVING WATER

VOL. 4, CANTIQUE 81

THE fountain in its source,
No drought of summer fears;
The farther it pursues its course,
The nobler it appears.

But shallow cisterns yield
A scanty, short supply;
The morning sees them amply fill'd,
At ev'ning they are dry. 8

TRUTH AND DIVINE LOVE REJECTED BY THE WORLD

VOL. 2, CANTIQUE 22

O LOVE, of pure and heav'nly birth!
O simple Truth, scarce known on earth!
Whom men resist with stubborn will;
And more perverse and daring still,
Smother and quench, with reas'nings vain,
While error and deception reign. 6

Whence comes it, that, your pow'r the same
As his on high, from whom you came,
Ye rarely find a list'ning ear,
Or heart that makes you welcome here?
—Because ye bring reproach and pain,
Where'er ye visit, in your train. 12

The world is proud, and cannot bear
The scorn and calumny ye share;
The praise of men the mark *they* mean,
They fly the place where *ye* are seen;
Pure Love, with scandal in the rear,
Suits not the vain; it costs too dear. 18

Then, let the price be what it may,
Though poor, I am prepar'd to pay;
Come shame, come sorrow; spite of tears,
Weakness, and heart-oppressing fears;
One soul, at least, shall not repine,
To give *you* room; come, reign in mine! 24

Title] Truth and pure Love rejected and accepted, by whom *A*. 3 resist] oppose *A*. 11, 12 ye . . . visit] reproach and grief and pain Are sure to follow *A*. 23 least *A*.: last *Bull*.

DIVINE JUSTICE AMIABLE

VOL. 2, CANTIQUE 119

THOU hast no lightnings, O thou Just!
Or I their force should know;
And if thou strike me into dust,
My soul approves the blow.

The heart, that values less its ease,
Than it adores thy ways;
In thine avenging anger, sees
A subject of its praise. 8

Pleas'd, I could lie conceal'd, and lost
In shades of central night;
Not to avoid thy wrath, thou know'st,
But lest I grieve thy sight.

Smite me, O thou whom I provoke!
And I will love thee still:
The well deserv'd and righteous stroke
Shall please me, though it kill. 16

Am I not worthy, to sustain
The worst thou canst devise;
And dare I seek thy throne again,
And meet thy sacred eyes?

Far from afflicting, thou art kind;
And in my saddest hours,
An unction of thy grace I find,
Pervading all my pow'rs. 24

Alas! thou spar'st me yet again;
And when thy wrath should move,
Too gentle to endure my pain,
Thou sooth'st me with thy Love.

I have no punishment to fear;
But Ah! that smile from thee,
Imparts a pang, far more severe
Than woe itself would be. 32

THE SOUL THAT LOVES GOD FINDS HIM EVERY WHERE

VOL. 2, CANTIQUE 108

OH thou, by long experience tried,
Near whom no grief can long abide;
My Love! how full of sweet content
I pass my years of banishment!

10 shades] caves *A*. 30 from thee] I see *A*.
The Soul—4 years of] long, long *A*.

All scenes alike engaging prove,
To souls impress'd with sacred love!
Where'er they dwell, they dwell in thee;
In heav'n, in earth, or on the sea. 8

To me remains nor place nor time;
My country is in ev'ry clime;
I can be calm and free from care
On any shore, since God is there.

While place we seek, or place we shun,
The soul finds happiness in none;
But with a God to guide our way,
'Tis equal joy to go or stay. 16

Could I be cast where thou art not,
That were indeed a dreadful lot;
But regions none remote I call,
Secure of finding God in all.

My country, Lord, art thou alone;
Nor other can I claim or own;
The point where all my wishes meet;
My Law, my Love; life's only sweet! 24

I hold by nothing here below;
Appoint my journey, and I go;
Though pierc'd by scorn, opprest by pride,
I feel thee good—feel nought beside.

No frowns of men can hurtful prove
To souls on fire with heav'nly Love;
Though men and devils both condemn,
No gloomy days arise for them. 32

Ah then! to his embrace repair;
My soul thou art no stranger there;
There Love divine shall be thy guard,
And peace and safety thy reward.

THE TESTIMONY OF DIVINE ADOPTION

VOL. 2, CANTIQUE 78

How happy are the new-born race,
Partakers of adopting grace;
How pure the bliss they share!
Hid from the world and all its eyes,
Within their heart the blessing lies,
And Conscience feels it there. 6

Title *om. A.* 3 joy *A.*

The moment we believe, 'tis ours;
And if we love with all our pow'rs
The God from whom it came,
And if we serve with hearts sincere,
'Tis still discernible and clear,
An undisputed claim. 12

But ah! if foul and wilful sin
Stain and dishonour us within,
Farewell the joy we knew;
Again the slaves of Nature's sway,
In lab'rinths of our own we stray,
Without a guide or clue. 18

The chaste and pure, who fear to grieve
The gracious Spirit they receive,
His work distinctly trace;
And strong in undissembling love,
Boldly assert, and clearly prove,
Their hearts his dwelling place 24

O messenger of dear delight,
Whose voice dispells the deepest night,
Sweet peace-proclaiming Dove!
With thee at hand to sooth our pains,
No wish unsatisfied remains,
No task, but that of Love. 30

'Tis Love unites what Sin divides;
The centre where all bliss resides;
To which the soul once brought,
Reclining on the first great Cause,
From his abounding sweetness draws
Peace passing human thought. 36

Sorrow foregoes its nature there,
And life assumes a tranquil air,
Divested of its woes;
There, sov'reign goodness sooths the breast,
Till then incapable of rest,
In sacred sure repose. 42

11 'Tis still discernible] It still is visible *A.* 31 unites] connects *A.*
37–39 There pain and sorrow lose their sting,
And toil becomes a trivial thing
Scarce worthy of a thought, *A.*

DIVINE LOVE ENDURES NO RIVAL

VOL. 2, CANTIQUE 155

LOVE is the Lord whom I obey,
Whose will transported I perform,
The centre of my rest, my stay,
Love all in all to me, myself a worm.

For uncreated charms I burn,
Oppress'd by slavish fear no more;
For one, in whom I may discern,
Ev'n when he frowns, a sweetness I adore. 8

He little loves him, who complains,
And finds him rig'rous and severe;
His heart is sordid, and he feigns,
Though loud in boasting of a soul sincere.

Love causes grief, but 'tis to move
And stimulate the slumb'ring mind;
And he has never tasted Love,
Who shuns a pang so graciously design'd. 16

Sweet is the cross, above all sweets,
To souls enamour'd with thy smiles;
The keenest woe life ever meets,
Love strips of all its terrors, and beguiles.

'Tis just, that God should not be dear,
Where Self engrosses all the thought,
And groans and murmurs make it clear,
Whatever else is lov'd, the Lord is not. 24

The love of Thee flows just as much
As that of ebbing Self subsides;
Our hearts, their scantiness is such,
Bear not the conflict of two rival tides.

Both cannot govern in one soul;
Then let self-love be dispossess'd;
The Love of God deserves the whole,
And will not dwell with so despis'd a guest. 32

SELF-DIFFIDENCE

VOL. 2, CANTIQUE 125

SOURCE of love, and light of day,
Tear me from myself away;
Ev'ry view and thought of mine,
Cast into the mould of thine;

Title] Love all in all *A*. 26 ebbing] sordid *A*.

Teach, Oh teach this faithless heart
A consistent, constant part;
Or, if it must live to grow
More rebellious, break it now! 8

Is it thus, that I requite
Grace and goodness infinite?
Ev'ry trace of ev'ry boon,
Cancell'd, and eras'd, so soon!
Can I grieve thee, whom I love;
Thee, in whom I live and move?
If my sorrow touch thee still,
Save me from so great an ill! 16

Oh! th' oppressive, irksome weight,
Felt in an uncertain state;
Comfort, peace, and rest, adieu,
Should I prove at last untrue!
Still I choose thee, follow still
Ev'ry notice of thy will;
But unstable, strangely weak,
Still let slip the good I seek. 24

Self-confiding wretch, I thought,
I could serve thee as I ought,
Win thee, and deserve to feel
All the Love thou canst reveal!
Trusting self, a bruised reed,
Is to be deceiv'd indeed:
Save me from this harm and loss,
Lest my gold turn all to dross! 32

Self is earthly—Faith alone
Makes an unseen world our own;
Faith relinquish'd, how we roam,
Feel our way, and leave our home!
Spurious gems our hopes entice,
While we scorn the pearl of price;
And preferring servant's pay,
Cast the children's bread away! 40

THE ACQUIESCENCE OF PURE LOVE

Vol. 2, Cantique 135

Love! if thy destin'd sacrifice am I,
Come, slay thy victim, and prepare thy fires;
Plung'd in thy depths of mercy, let me die
The death, which every soul that lives desires!

I watch my hours, and see them fleet away;
  The time is long, that I have languish'd here;
Yet all my thoughts thy purposes obey,
  With no reluctance, cheerful and sincere. 8

To me 'tis equal, whether Love ordain
  My life or death, appoint me pain or ease:
My soul perceives no real Ill in pain,
  In ease, or health, no real Good she sees.

One Good she covets, and that Good alone;
  To choose thy will, from selfish bias free;
And to prefer a cottage to a throne,
  And grief to comfort, if it pleases thee. 16

That we should bear the cross, is thy command,
  Die to the world, and live to self no more;
Suffer unmov'd beneath the rudest hand,
  As pleas'd when shipwreck'd as when safe on shore.

REPOSE IN GOD

VOL. 2, CANTIQUE 17

BLEST! who far from all mankind,
This world's shadows left behind,
Hears from heav'n a gentle strain
Whisp'ring Love, and loves again.

Blest! who free from self-esteem,
Dives into the Great Supreme,
All desire besides discards,
Joys inferior none regards. 8

Blest! who in thy bosom seeks
Rest that nothing earthly breaks,
Dead to self and worldly things,
Lost in thee, thou King of kings!

Ye that know my secret fire,
Softly speak and soon retire;
Favour my divine repose,
Spare the sleep a God bestows. 16

GLORY TO GOD ALONE

VOL. 2, CANTIQUE 15

OH lov'd! but not enough—though dearer far
Than self and its most lov'd enjoyments are;
None duly loves thee, but who, nobly free
From sensual objects, finds his all in thee.

Repose in God—Title *om. A.*
Glory—2 its . . . enjoyments] all the joys it covets *A.*

Glory of God! thou stranger here below,
Whom man nor knows, nor feels a wish to know;
Our Faith and Reason are both shock'd to find
Man in the post of honour—Thee behind. 8

Reason exclaims—"Let ev'ry creature fall,
"Asham'd, abas'd, before the Lord of all;"
And Faith, o'erwhelm'd with such a dazzling blaze,
Feebly describes the beauty she surveys.

Yet man, dim-sighted man, and rash as blind,
Deaf to the dictates of his better mind,
In frantic competition dares the skies,
And claims precedence of the only wise. **16**

Oh lost in vanity till once self-known!
Nothing is great, or good, but God alone;
When thou shalt stand before his awful face,
Then, at the last, thy pride shall know his place.

Glorious, Almighty, First, and without end!
When wilt thou melt the mountains, and descend?
When wilt thou shoot abroad thy conqu'ring rays,
And teach these atoms, thou hast made, thy praise?

Thy Glory is the sweetest heav'n I feel; 25
And if I seek it with too fierce a zeal,
Thy Love, triumphant o'er a selfish will,
Taught me the passion, and inspires it still.

My Reason, all my faculties, unite,
To make thy Glory their supreme delight;
Forbid it, Fountain of my brightest days,
That I should rob thee, and usurp thy praise! **32**

My soul! rest happy in thy low estate,
Nor hope, nor wish, to be esteem'd or great;
To take th' impression of a will divine,
Be that thy glory, and those riches thine.

Confess him rignteous in his just decrees,
Love what he loves, and let his pleasure please;
Die daily; from the touch of Sin recede; 39
Then thou hast crown'd him, and he reigns indeed.

7, 8 How are our faith, and reason shock'd to find
Man marching in the front, and God behind. *A*.
9 Reason exclaims aloud—let creatures fall *A*. 11 dazzling] boundless *A*. 12 But feebly speaks *A*. 20 at the last] then at least *A*. his] His *Bull*: its *A*.

SELF-LOVE AND TRUTH INCOMPATIBLE

Vol. 2, Cantique 21

From thorny wilds a Monster came,
That fill'd my soul with fear and shame;
The birds, forgetful of their mirth,
Droop'd at the sight, and fell to earth;
When thus a sage address'd mine ear,
Himself unconscious of a fear.
"Whence all this terror and surprise,
Distracted looks, and streaming eyes?
Far from the world and its affairs,
The joy it boasts, the pain it shares, 10
Surrender, without guile or art,
To God, an undivided heart;
The savage form, so fear'd before,
Shall scare your trembling soul no more;
For loathsome as the sight may be,
'Tis but the *Love-of-self* you see.
Fix all your Love on God alone,
Choose but His will, and hate your own;
No fear shall in your path be found,
The dreary waste shall bloom around, 20
And you, through all your happy days,
Shall bless his name, and sing his praise."
Oh lovely solitude, how sweet
The silence of this calm retreat!
Here Truth, the fair whom I pursue,
Gives all her beauty to my view;
The simple, unadorn'd display,
Charms every pain and fear away.
O Truth, whom millions proudly slight,
O Truth, my treasure and delight! 30
Accept this tribute to thy name,
And this poor heart, from which it came!

THE LOVE OF GOD THE END OF LIFE

Vol. 2, Cantique 165

Since life in sorrow must be spent,
So be it—I am well content,
And meekly wait my last remove,
Seeking only growth in Love.

Self-love—1 thorny] yonder *A*. 3 forgetful of] forgetting all *A*.
30 *A*.: *om*. *Bull*.

The Love of God—Title] Live to Love *A*.
1-3 Since we must sorrow, and why not?
For me I wish no gentler lot
But . . . *A*.

No bliss I seek, but to fulfil
In life, in death, thy lovely will;
No succours in my woes I want,
Save what thou art pleas'd to grant. 8

Our days are number'd, let us spare
Our anxious hearts a needless care:
'Tis thine, to number out our days;
Ours, to give them to thy praise.

Love is our only bus'ness here,
Love, simple, constant, and sincere;
O blessed days, thy servants see,
Spent, O Lord! in pleasing Thee. 16

LOVE FAITHFUL IN THE ABSENCE OF THE BELOVED

VOL. 4, CANTIQUE 49

IN vain ye woo me to your harmless joys,
Ye pleasant bow'rs, remote from strife and noise;
Your shades, the witnesses of many a vow,
Breath'd forth in happier days, are irksome now;
Denied that smile 'twas once my heav'n to see,
Such scenes, such pleasures, are all past with me. 6

In vain he leaves me, I shall love him still;
And though I mourn, not murmur at his will;
I have no cause—an object all divine
Might well grow weary of a soul like mine;
Yet pity me, great God! forlorn, alone,
Heartless and hopeless, Life and Love all gone. 12

LOVE PURE AND FERVENT

VOL. 4, CANTIQUE 31

JEALOUS, and with Love o'erflowing,
God demands a fervent heart;
Grace and bounty still bestowing,
Calls us to a grateful part.

Oh, then, with supreme affection,
His paternal Will regard!
If it cost us some dejection,
Ev'ry sigh has its reward. 8

The Love of God—7 succour *A*.
Love Faithful—Title *om. A*. 7 shall] will *A*.

Perfect Love has pow'r to soften
  Cares that might our peace destroy,
Nay, does more—transforms them often,
  Changing sorrow into joy.

Sov'reign Love appoints the measure,
  And the number of our pains;
And is pleas'd when we find pleasure
  In the trials he ordains. 16

THE ENTIRE SURRENDER

VOL. 4, CANTIQUE 77

PEACE has unveil'd her smiling face,
And woos thy soul to her embrace;
Enjoy'd with ease, if thou refrain
From earthly Love, else sought in vain;
She dwells with all who Truth prefer,
But seeks not them who seek not Her. 6

Yield to the Lord, with simple heart,
All that thou hast, and all thou art;
Renounce all strength but strength divine,
And peace shall be for ever thine:—
Behold the path which I have trod,
My path, 'till I go home to God. 12

THE PERFECT SACRIFICE

VOL. 4, CANTIQUE 74

I PLACE an off'ring at thy shrine,
  From taint and blemish clear,
Simple and pure in its design,
  Of all that I hold dear.

I yield thee back thy gifts again,
  Thy gifts which most I prize;
Desirous only to retain
  The notice of thine eyes. 8

But if, by thine ador'd decree,
  That blessing be denied,
Resign'd, and unreluctant, see
  My ev'ry wish subside.

Thy will in all things I approve;
  Exalted or cast down!
Thy will in ev'ry state I love,
  And even in thy frown. 16

The entire Surrender—1 smiling] lovely *A*. 6 them] those *A*.
The perfect Sacrifice—1 place . . . at] bring . . . to *A*.

GOD HIDES HIS PEOPLE

Vol. 4, Cantique 42

To lay the soul that loves him low,
  Becomes the Only-wise:
To hide beneath a veil of woe
  The children of the skies.

Man, though a worm, would yet be great;
  Though feeble, would seem strong;
Assumes an independent state,
  By sacrilege and wrong. 8

Strange the reverse, which, once abas'd,
  The haughty creature proves!
He feels his soul a barren waste,
  Nor dares affirm he loves.

Scorn'd by the thoughtless and the vain,
  To God he presses near;
Superior to the world's disdain,
  And happy in its sneer. 16

Oh welcome, in his heart he says,
  Humility and shame!
Farewell the wish for human praise,
  The music of a name!

But will not scandal mar the good
  That I might else perform?
And can God work it, if he would,
  By so despis'd a worm? 24

Ah, vainly anxious!—leave the Lord
  To rule thee, and dispose;
Sweet is the mandate of his word,
  And gracious all he does.

He draws from human littleness
  His grandeur and renown,
And gen'rous hearts with joy confess
  The triumph all his own. 32

Down then with self-exalting thoughts!
  Thy faith and hope employ
To welcome all that he allots,
  And suffer shame with joy.

No longer, then, thou wilt encroach
  On his eternal right;
And he shall smile at thy approach,
  And make thee his delight. 40

THE SECRETS OF DIVINE LOVE ARE TO BE KEPT

VOL. 3, CANTIQUE 48

SUN! stay thy course, this moment stay—
Suspend th' o'erflowing tide of day,
Divulge not such a Love as mine,
Ah! hide the mystery divine,
Lest man, who deems my glory shame,
Should learn the secret of my flame. 6

Oh night! propitious to my views,
Thy sable awning wide diffuse:
Conceal alike my joy and pain,
Nor draw thy curtain back again,
Though morning, by the tears she shows,
Seems to participate my woes. 12

Ye stars! whose faint and feeble fires
Express my languishing desires,
Whose slender beams pervade the skies
As silent as my secret sighs,
Those emanations of a soul
That darts her fires beyond the Pole; 18

Your rays, that scarce assist the sight,
That pierce, but not displace the night,
That shine indeed, but nothing show
Of all those various scenes below,
Bring no disturbance, rather prove
Incentives of a sacred Love. 24

Thou Moon! whose never-failing course
Bespeaks a providential force,
Go, tell the tidings of my flame
To him who calls the stars by name;
Whose absence kills, whose presence cheers;
Who blots, or brightens, all my years. 30

While, in the blue abyss of space,
Thine orb performs its rapid race;
Still whisper in his list'ning ears
The language of my sighs and tears;
Tell him, I seek him, far below,
Lost in a wilderness of woe. 36

Ye thought-composing, silent hours,
Diffusing peace o'er all my pow'rs;

Title . . . are to be kept] . . . not to be divulged *A*. 3 Fear to divulge this Love of mine *A*. 17 emanations *or* scintillations *A*. 18 her] its *A*.

Friends of the pensive! who conceal,
In darkest shades, the flame I feel;
To you I trust, and safely may,
The Love that wastes my strength away. 42

In sylvan scenes, and caverns rude,
I taste the sweets of solitude;
Retir'd indeed, but not alone,
I share them with a Spouse unknown,
Who hides me here, from envious eyes,
From all intrusion and surprise. 48

Imbow'ring shades, and dens profound!
Where echo rolls the voice around:
Mountains! whose elevated heads
A moist and misty veil o'erspreads;
Disclose a solitary Bride
To Him I love—to none beside. 54

Ye rills! that murm'ring all the way,
Among the polish'd pebbles stray;
Creep silently along the ground,
Lest, drawn by that harmonious sound,
Some wand'rer, whom I would not meet,
Should stumble on my lov'd retreat. 60

Enamel'd meads, and hillocks green,
And streams, that water all the scene!
Ye torrents, loud in distant ears!
Ye fountains, that receive my tears!
Ah! still conceal, with caution due,
A charge, I trust with none but you. 66

If when my pain and grief increase,
I seem t' enjoy the sweetest peace,
It is because I find so fair
The charming object of my care,
That I can sport, and pleasure, make
Of torment, suffer'd for his sake. 72

Ye meads and groves, unconscious things!
Ye know not whence my pleasure springs,
Ye know not, and ye cannot know,
The source from which my sorrows flow:
The dear sole Cause of all I feel,—
He knows, and understands them well. 78

Ye deserts! where the wild beasts rove,
Scenes sacred to my hours of love;

40 thickest *A*. 55 the] your *A*.

Ye forests! in whose shades I stray,
Benighted under burning day;
Ah! whisper not how blest am I,
Nor while I live, nor when I die. 84

Ye lambs! that sport beneath these shades,
And bound along the mossy glades:
Be taught a salutary fear,
And cease to bleat when I am near:
The wolf may hear your harmless cry,
Whom ye should dread, as much as I. 90

How calm, amid these scenes, my mind!
How perfect is the peace I find!
Oh hush, be still my ev'ry part,
My tongue, my pulse, my beating heart!
That Love, aspiring to its cause,
May suffer not a moment's pause. 96

Ye swift-finn'd nations, that abide
In seas, as fathomless as wide;
And unsuspicious of a snare,
Pursue at large your pleasures there:
Poor sportive fools! how soon does man
Your heedless ignorance trepan! 102

Away! dive deep into the brine,
Where never yet sunk plummet line;
Trust me, the vast Leviathan
Is merciful, compar'd with man;
Avoid his arts, forsake the beach,
And never play within his reach! 108

My soul her bondage ill endures;
I pant for liberty like yours;
I long for that immense Profound,
That knows no bottom, and no bound;
Lost in Infinity, to prove
Th' Incomprehensible of Love. 114

Ye birds! that lessen as ye fly,
And vanish in the distant sky;
To whom yon airy waste belongs,
Resounding with your cheerful songs;
Haste to escape from human sight;
Fear less the vulture, and the kite. 120

How blest, and how secure am I,
When quitting earth, I soar on high;

85 sport beneath] wander in *A*. 104 plummet] fathom *A*.

When lost, like you I disappear,
And float in a sublimer sphere!
Whence falling, within human view,
I am ensnar'd, and caught like you. 126

Omniscient God, whose notice deigns
To try the heart and search the reins;
Compassionate the num'rous woes,
I dare not, ev'n to thee, disclose;
Oh save me from the cruel hands
Of men, who fear not thy commands! 132

Love, all-subduing and divine,
Care for a creature truly thine;
Reign in a heart, dispos'd to own
No sov'reign, but thyself alone;
Cherish a Bride, who cannot rove,
Nor quit thee for a meaner Love! 138

THE VICISSITUDES EXPERIENCED IN THE CHRISTIAN LIFE

VOL. 3, CANTIQUE 69

I SUFFER fruitless anguish day by day,
Each moment, as it passes, marks my pain;
Scarce knowing whither, doubtfully I stray,
And see no end of all that I sustain.

The more I strive, the more I am withstood;
Anxiety encreasing ev'ry hour,
My spirit finds no rest, performs no good,
And nought remains of all my former pow'r. 8

My peace of heart is fled, I know not where;
My happy hours, like shadows, pass'd away;
Their sweet remembrance doubles all my care,
Night darker seems, succeeding such a day.

Dear faded joys, and impotent regret,
What profit is there in incessant tears?
Oh Thou, whom, once beheld, we ne'er forget,
Reveal thy Love, and banish all my fears! 16

Alas! he flies me—treats me as his foe,
Views not my sorrows, hears not when I plead;—
Woe such as mine, despis'd, neglected woe,
Unless it shorten life, is vain indeed.

2 marks] points *A*. 6 Anxiety] Fear, anxious fear *A*.
15 Come Thou, with all thy sacred charms, come yet *A*.

Pierc'd with a thousand wounds, I yet survive;
My pangs are keen, but no complaint transpires;
And while in terrors of thy wrath I live,
Hell seems to lose its less tremendous fires. 24

Has Hell a pain I would not gladly bear,
So thy severe displeasure might subside?
Hopeless of ease, I seem already There,
My life extinguish'd, and yet death denied.

Is this the joy so promis'd—this the love,
Th' unchanging love, so sworn in better days?
Ah dang'rous glories! shown me, but to prove
How lovely thou, and I how rash to gaze. 32

Why did I see them? had I still remain'd
Untaught, still ignorant how fair thou art,
My humbler wishes I had soon obtain'd,
Nor known the torments of a doubting heart.

Depriv'd of all, yet feeling no desires,
Whence then, I cry, the pangs that I sustain?
Dubious and uninform'd, my soul inquires,
Ought she to cherish, or shake off her pain. 40

Suff'ring I suffer not—sincerely love,
Yet feel no touch of that enliv'ning flame;
As chance inclines me, unconcern'd I move,
All times, and all events, to me the same.

I search my heart, and not a wish is there,
But burns with zeal that hated self may fall;
Such is the sad inquietude I share,
A sea of doubts, and self the source of all. 48

I ask not life, nor do I wish to die;
And if thine hand accomplish not my cure,
I would not purchase, with a single sigh,
A free discharge from all that I endure.

I groan in chains, yet want not a release;
Am sick, and know not the distemper'd part;
Am just as void of purpose, as of peace; 55
Have neither plan, nor fear, nor hope, nor heart.

27, 28 All is affliction, all is blank despair,
Life at its lowest ebb, yet death denied. *A.*
31 glories] beauties *A.* 34 Untaught, still] Stupid, and *A.*
39 Dubious] Anxious *A.* 41 sincerely] I truely *A.* 42 celestial *A.* 48 doubt *A.* 49 I neither wish for life nor yet for death, *A.*
50 thine hand] thyself *A.* 51 sigh] breath *A.* 53 Captive I groan *A.* 54 know . . . distemper'd] cannot find the ailing *A.*
55 Am just] I seem *A.*

My claim to life, though sought with earnest care,
No light, within me or without me, shows;
Once I had faith; but now, in self-despair
Find my chief cordial, and my best repose.

My soul is a forgotten thing, she sinks,
Sinks and is lost, without a wish to rise;
Feels an indiff'rence she abhors, and thinks
Her name eras'd forever from the skies. 64

Language affords not my distress a name,
Yet is it real and no sickly dream;
'Tis Love inflicts it; though to feel that flame,
Is all I know of happiness supreme.

When Love departs, a Chaos wide and vast
And dark as Hell, is open'd in the soul;
When Love returns, the gloomy scene is past,
No tempests shake her, and no fears control. 72

Then tell me, why these ages of delay?
O Love, all-excellent, once more appear;
Disperse the shades, and snatch me into day,
From this abyss of night, these floods of fear!

No—Love is angry, will not now endure
A sigh of mine, or suffer a complaint;
He smites me, wounds me, and withholds the cure;
Exhausts my pow'rs, and leaves me sick and faint.

He wounds, and hides the hand that gave the blow;
He flies, he re-appears, and wounds again— 82
Was ever heart that lov'd thee, treated so?
Yet I adore thee, though it seem in vain.

And wilt thou leave me, whom, when lost and blind,
Thou didst distinguish, and vouchsafe to choose,
Before thy laws were written in my mind,
While yet the world had all my thoughts and views? 88

Now leave me? when, enamour'd of thy laws,
I make thy glory my supreme delight;
Now blot me from thy register, and cause
A faithful soul to perish from thy sight?

57–68 *for MS. version see notes.* 72 Then neither tempests howl, nor billows roll *A.* 74 appear] draw nigh *A.* 75 shades] night *A.* 76 night . . . fear] darkness where I lie *A.* 77 not . . . endure] no longer hear *A.* 79 and . . . cure] is become severe *A.* 80 Makes me and leaves me weary, sick and faint *A.* 89 *Now*] What, *A.*

What can have caus'd the change that I deplore!
Is it to prove me, if my heart be true?
Permit me then, while prostrate I adore,
To draw, and place its picture in thy view. 96

'Tis thine without reserve, most simply thine;
So giv'n to thee, that it is not my own;
A willing Captive of thy grace divine;
And loves, and seeks thee, for thyself alone.

Pain cannot move it, danger cannot scare;
Pleasure, and wealth, in its esteem, are dust;
It loves thee, ev'n when least inclin'd to spare
Its tend'rest feelings, and avows thee just. 104

'Tis all thine own; my spirit is so too,
An undivided off'ring at thy shrine;
It seeks thy glory with no double view,
Thy glory, with no secret bent to mine.

Love, holy Love! and art thou not severe,
To slight me, thus devoted, and thus fixt?
Mine is an everlasting ardour, clear
From all self-bias, gen'rous and unmixt. 112

But I am silent, seeing what I see—
And fear, with cause, that I am self-deceiv'd;
Not ev'n my faith is from suspicion free,
And, that I love, seems not to be believ'd.

Live thou, and reign, forever, glorious Lord!
My last, least off'ring, I present thee now—
Renounce me, leave me, and be still ador'd!
Slay me, my God, and I applaud the blow. 120

WATCHING UNTO GOD IN THE NIGHT-SEASON

VOL. 3, CANTIQUE 71

SLEEP at last has fled these eyes,
Nor do I regret his flight,
More alert my spirits rise,
And my heart is free and light.

Nature silent all around,
Not a single witness near;
God, as soon as sought, is found;
And the flame of Love burns clear. 8

95 prostrate] humbly *A*. 97 without . . . most] explicitly and *A*. 98 So strictly that it is not now my own *A*. 105 all thine own] wholly thine *A*. 109 holy] sacred *A*. 118 least] last *A*. 120 Slay me, my God] Th' award is just *A*.

Interruption, all day long,
Checks the current of my joys;
Creatures press me with a throng,
And perplex me with their noise.

Undisturb'd I muse, all night,
On the first Eternal Fair;
Nothing there obstructs delight,
Love is renovated there. 16

Life, with its perpetual stir,
Proves a foe to Love and me;
Fresh entanglements occur—
Comes the night, and sets me free.

Never more, sweet sleep, suspend
My enjoyments always new:
Leave me to possess my Friend;
Other eyes and hearts subdue. 24

Hush the world, that I may wake
To the taste of pure delights;
Oh the pleasures I partake—
God the Partner of my nights!

David, for the self-same cause,
Night preferr'd to busy day;
Hearts, whom heav'nly beauty draws,
Wish the glaring sun away. 32

Sleep, Self-lovers, is for you—
Souls that love *celestial* know,
Fairer scenes by night can view,
Than the sun could ever show.

ON THE SAME

VOL. 3, CANTIQUE 72

SEASON of my purest pleasure,
  Sealer of observing eyes!
When, in larger freer measure,
  I can commune with the skies;
While, beneath thy shade extended,
  Weary man forgets his woes;
I, my daily trouble ended,
  Find, in Watching, my Repose. 8

12 perplex] distress *A*. 17 perpetual] busy *A*. 19 perplexities *A*. 30 bustling *A*. 32 glaring sun] hours of light *A*.

Silence all around prevailing,
  Nature hush'd in slumber sweet,
No rude noise mine ears assailing,
  Now my God and I can meet:
Universal nature slumbers,
  And my soul partakes the calm,
Breathes her ardour out in numbers,
  Plaintive song, or lofty psalm. 16

Now my passion, pure and holy,
  Shines, and burns, without restraint;
Which the day's fatigue, and folly,
  Caus'd to languish, dim and faint:
Charming hours of relaxation!
  How I dread th' ascending sun!
Surely, idle conversation
  Is an evil, match'd by none. 24

Worldly prate, and babble, hurt me;
  Unintelligible prove;
Neither teach me, nor divert me;
  I have ears for none but Love.
Me, they rude esteem, and foolish,
  Hearing my absurd replies;
I have neither art's fine polish,
  Nor the knowledge of the wise. 32

Simple souls, and unpolluted
  By conversing with the Great,
Have a mind and taste, ill suited
  To their dignity and state;
All their talking, reading, writing,
  Are but talents misapplied;
Infants' prattle I delight in,
  Nothing human choose beside. 40

'Tis the secret fear of sinning,
  Checks my tongue, or I should say,
When I see the night beginning,
  I am glad of parting day:
Love, this gentle admonition
  Whispers soft, within my breast;
"Choice befits not thy condition,
  Acquiescence suits thee best." 48

16 lofty] sprightly *A*.
21–24 How I love this peaceful season,
  How I dread th' ascending Sun,
For to me the world with reason
  Seems an evil match'd by none. *A*.
25 Its discourses grieve and hurt me *A*. 29 rude] coarse *A*.
31 arts' *Bull*: Arts *A*. 36 their dignity] formality *A*. 39 Infants *Bull*, *A*.

Henceforth, the repose and pleasure
 Night affords me, I resign;
And *thy* Will shall be the measure,
 Wisdom infinite! of mine:
Wishing, is but Inclination
 Quarrelling with thy decrees;
Wayward nature finds th' occasion,
 'Tis her folly and disease. 56

Night, with its sublime enjoyments,
 Now no longer will I choose;
Nor the day, with its employments,
 Irksome as they seem, refuse;
Lessons of a God's inspiring
 Neither time nor place impedes;
From our wishing and desiring,
 Our Unhappiness proceeds. 64

ON THE SAME

Vol. 3, Cantique 73

Night! how I love thy silent shades,
 My spirits they compose;
The bliss of heav'n my soul pervades,
 In spite of all my woes.

While sleep instills her poppy dews
 In ev'ry slumb'ring eye,
I watch, to meditate and muse,
 In blest tranquillity. 8

And when I feel a God immense
 Familiarly impart,
With ev'ry proof he can dispense,
 His favour to my heart,

My native meanness I lament,
 Though most divinely fill'd
With all th' ineffable content,
 That Deity can yield. 16

His purpose, and his course, he keeps;
 Treads all my reas'nings down;
Commands me out of Nature's deeps,
 And hides me in his own.

When in the dust, its proper place,
 Our pride of heart we lay;
'Tis then, a deluge of his grace
 Bears all our sins away. 24

55 Wayward nature] Nature always *A*. 61 a God's] the Lords *A*.

Thou, whom I serve, and whose I am,
  Whose influence from on high
Refines, and still refines my flame,
  And makes my fetters fly;

How wretched is the creature's state
  Who thwarts thy gracious pow'r;
Crush'd under sin's enormous weight,
  Increasing ev'ry hour! 32

The night, when pass'd entire with thee,
  How luminous and clear!
Then sleep has no delights for me,
  Lest *Thou* shouldst disappear.

My Saviour! occupy me still
  In this secure recess;
Let Reason slumber if she will,
  My joy shall not be less: 40

Let Reason slumber out the night;
  But if *Thou* deign to make
My soul th' abode of truth and light,
  Ah, keep my heart awake!

THE JOY OF THE CROSS

VOL. 3, CANTIQUE 97

LONG plung'd in sorrow, I resign
My soul to that dear hand of thine,
  Without reserve or fear;
That hand shall wipe my streaming eyes;
Or into smiles of glad surprise
  Transform the falling tear. 6

My sole possession is thy Love;
In earth beneath, or heav'n above,
  I have no other store;
And though with fervent suit I pray,
And importune thee night and day,
  I ask thee nothing more. 12

My rapid hours pursue the course
Prescrib'd them by love's sweetest force;
  And I, thy sov'reign Will,
Without a wish t' escape my doom;
Though still a suff'rer from the womb,
  And doom'd to suffer still. 18

29 creature's state] soul's estate *A*. 41 slumber out the] sleep the livelong *A*.

The Joy—13 the] their *A*. 14 Obedient to thy Love's sweet force *A*.

By thy command, where'er I stray,
Sorrow attends me all my way,
  A never-failing friend;
And if my suff'rings may augment
Thy praise, behold me well content—
  Let sorrow still attend! 24

It costs me no regret, that she,
Who follow'd Christ, should follow me;
  And though, where'er she goes,
Thorns spring spontaneous at her feet,
I love her, and extract a sweet
  From all my bitter woes. 30

Adieu! ye vain delights of earth;
Insipid sports, and childish mirth,
  I taste no sweets in you;
Unknown delights are in the Cross,
All joy beside, to me is dross;
  And Jesus thought so too. 36

The Cross! Oh ravishment and bliss—
How grateful ev'n its anguish is;
  Its bitterness, how sweet!
There ev'ry sense, and all the mind,
In all her faculties refin'd,
  Tastes happiness complete. 42

Souls once enabled to disdain
Base sublunary joys, maintain
  Their dignity secure;
The fever of desire is pass'd,
And Love has all its genuine taste,
  Is delicate and pure. 48

Self-love no grace in sorrow sees,
Consults her own peculiar ease;
  'Tis all the bliss she knows:
But nobler aims *true* Love employ;
In self-denial is her joy,
  In suff'ring her repose. 54

Sorrow, and Love, go side by side;
Nor height, nor depth, can e'er divide
  Their heav'n-appointed bands;
Those dear associates still are one,
Nor, till the race of life is run,
  Disjoin their wedded hands. 60

35 And all *A*. is] are *A*. 41 her] its *A*.

Jesus, avenger of our Fall,
Thou faithful Lover, above all
  The Cross has ever borne!
Oh tell me,—Life is in thy voice—
How much afflictions were thy choice,
  And sloth and ease thy scorn! 66

Thy choice, and mine, shall be the same;
Inspirer of that holy flame,
  Which must forever blaze!
To take the Cross, and follow thee,
Where love and duty lead, shall be
  My portion, and my praise. 72

JOY IN MARTYRDOM

VOL. 3, CANTIQUE 94

SWEET tenants of this grove!
  Who sing without design,
A song of artless love,
  In unison with mine;
These echoing shades return
  Full many a note of ours,
That wise ones cannot learn,
  With all their boasted pow'rs. 8

Oh thou! whose sacred charms
  These hearts so seldom love,
Although thy beauty warms
  And blesses all above;
How slow are human things
  To choose their happiest lot!
All-glorious King of Kings,
  Say, why we love thee not? 16

This heart, that cannot rest,
  Shall thine forever prove;
Though bleeding and distress'd,
  Yet joyful in thy Love:
'Tis happy, though it breaks
  Beneath thy chast'ning hand;
And speechless, yet it speaks
  What thou canst understand. 24

68 holy] deathless *A*. 69 must . . . blaze] thou inspir'st alone *A*. 72 portion . . . praise] pleasure . . . crown *A*.
Joy in Martyrdom—15 All-glorious] Ah tell me *A*.

SIMPLE TRUST

Vol. 3, Cantique 95

Still, still, without ceasing,
I feel it increasing,
This fervour of holy desire;
And often exclaim,
Let me die in the flame
Of a Love that can never expire! 6

Had I words to explain,
What *she* must sustain,
Who dies to the world and its ways;
How joy and affright,
Distress and delight,
Alternately chequer her days; 12

Thou, sweetly severe!
I would make thee appear,
In all thou art pleas'd to award,
Not more in the sweet,
Than the bitter I meet,
My tender and merciful Lord. 18

This Faith, in the dark
Pursuing its mark,
Through many sharp trials of Love,
Is the sorrowful waste,
That is to be pass'd,
In the way to the Canaan above. 24

THE NECESSITY OF SELF-ABASEMENT

Vol. 3, Cantique 92

Source of Love, my brighter Sun,
Thou alone my comfort art;
See my race is almost run;
Hast thou left this trembling heart?

In my youth, thy charming eyes
Drew me from the ways of men;
Then I drank unmingled joys;
Frown of thine, saw never *then*. 8

Spouse of Christ was then my name;
And, devoted all to thee,
Strangely jealous I became,
Jealous of this Self, in me.

Simple Trust—Title *om. A.*
The Necessity—2 alone my] my only *A.*

Thee to love, and none beside,
Was my darling, sole employ;
While alternately I died,
Now of grief, and now of joy. 16

Through the dark and silent night,
On thy radiant smiles I dwelt;
And to see the dawning light,
Was the keenest pain I felt.

Thou my gracious teacher wert;
And thine eye, so close applied,
While it watch'd thy pupil's heart,
Seem'd to look at none beside. 24

Conscious of no evil drift,
This, I cried, is Love indeed—
'Tis the Giver, not the Gift,
Whence the joys I feel proceed.

But soon humbled, and laid low,
Stript of all thou hadst conferr'd,
Nothing left, but Sin and woe,
I perceiv'd how I had err'd. 32

Oh, the vain conceit of man,
Dreaming of a good his own,
Arrogating all he can,
Though the Lord is good alone!

He, the graces Thou hast wrought,
Makes subservient to his pride;
Ignorant, that one such thought
Passes all his sin beside. 40

Such his folly—prov'd, at last,
By the loss of that repose
Self-complacence cannot taste,
Only Love divine bestows.

'Tis by this reproof severe,
And by this reproof alone,
His defects at last appear,
Man is to himself made known. 48

Learn, all Earth! that feeble Man,
Sprung from this terrestrial clod,
Nothing is, and nothing can;
Life, and pow'r, are all in God.

14 my darling] become my *A*. 24 look at none] watch no heart *A*. 40 sins *A*.

LOVE INCREASED BY SUFFERING

VOL. 3, CANTIQUE 98

"I LOVE the Lord," is still the strain
This heart delights to sing;
But I reply—your thoughts are vain,
Perhaps 'tis no such thing.

Before the power of Love divine,
Creation fades away;
Till only God is seen to shine
In all that we survey. 8

In gulphs of awful night we find
The God of our desires;
'Tis there he stamps the yielding mind,
And doubles all its fires.

Flames of encircling Love invest,
And pierce it sweetly through;
'Tis fill'd with sacred joy, yet press'd
With sacred sorrow too. 16

Ah Love! my heart is in the right—
Amidst a thousand woes,
To thee, its ever new delight,
And all its peace, it owes.

Fresh causes of distress occur,
Where'er I look, or move;
The comforts, I to all prefer,
Are solitude and love. 24

Nor exile I, nor prison fear;
Love makes my courage great;
I find a Saviour ev'ry where,
His grace, in ev'ry state.

Nor castle walls, nor dungeons deep,
Exclude his quick'ning beams;
There I can sit, and sing, and weep,
And dwell on heav'nly themes. 32

There, sorrow, for his sake, is found
A joy beyond compare;
There, no presumptuous thoughts abound,
No pride can enter there.

A Saviour doubles all my joys,
And sweetens all my pains,
His strength in my defence employs,
Consoles me, and sustains. 40

I fear no ill, resent no wrong;
  Nor feel a passion move,
When malice whets her sland'rous tongue;
  Such patience is in Love.

SCENES FAVOURABLE TO MEDITATION

VOL. 3, CANTIQUE 83

WILDS horrid and dark with o'ershadowing trees,
  Rocks that ivy and briars infold,
Scenes nature with dread and astonishment sees,
  But I with a pleasure untold,

Though awfully silent and shaggy and rude,
  I am charm'd with the peace ye afford,
Your shades are a temple where none will intrude,
  The abode of my Lover and Lord. 8

I am sick of thy splendour, O fountain of day,
  And here I am hid from its beams,
Here safely contemplate a brighter display
  Of the noblest and holiest themes.

Ye forests that yield me my sweetest repose,
  Where stillness and solitude reign,
To you I securely and boldly disclose
  The dear anguish of which I complain. 16

Here sweetly forgetting and wholly forgot
  By the world and its turbulent throng,
The birds and the streams lend me many a note
  That aids meditation and song.

Here wand'ring in scenes that are sacred to night,
  Love wears me and wastes me away,
And often the sun has spent much of his light,
  Ere yet I perceive it is day. 24

While a mantle of darkness invelopes the sphere,
  My sorrows are sadly rehears'd,
To me the dark hours are all equally dear,
  And the last is as sweet as the first.

Here I and the beasts of the desert agree,
  Mankind are the wolves that I fear,
They grudge me my natural right to be free,
  But nobody questions it here. 32

Title] The wonderfull contrarieties of the Christian Life *A*. 11 safely] freely *BM*. 20 aids] helps *A*. 22 wears . . . wastes *trs. BM*.

Though little is found in this dreary abode
  That appetite wishes to find,
My spirit is sooth'd by the presence of God,
  And appetite wholly resign'd.

Ye desolate scenes, to your solitude led,
  My life I in praises employ,
And scarce know the source of the tears that I shed,
  Proceed they from sorrow or joy. 40

There is nothing I seem to have skill to discern,
  I feel out my way in the dark,
Love reigns in my bosom, I constantly burn,
  Yet hardly distinguish the spark.

I live, yet I seem to myself to be dead,
  Such a riddle is not to be found,
I am nourish'd without knowing how I am fed,
  I have nothing and yet I abound. 48

Oh Love! who in darkness art pleas'd to abide,
  Though dimly yet surely I see,
That these contrarieties only reside
  In the soul that is chosen of thee.

Ah send me not back to the race of mankind,
  Perversely by folly beguil'd,
For where in the crowds I have left, shall I find
  The spirit and heart of a Child? 56

Here let me, though fixt in a desert, be free,
  A Little one whom they despise,
Though lost to the world, if in union with thee,
  Shall be holy and happy and wise.

33 is] be *BM.* 40 Proceed they from] Whether owing to *A.* 41 I am weak there is nothing I seem to discern *BM.* 44 the] a *BM.*, *A.* 45 yet I] and yet *BM.* 55 in the crowds] among all *BM.*, *A.*

TRANSLATIONS FROM THE LATIN CLASSICS

THE FIFTH SATIRE OF THE FIRST BOOK OF HORACE

A HUMOROUS DESCRIPTION OF THE AUTHOR'S JOURNEY FROM ROME TO BRUNDUSIUM

[Written 1757. Published 1759, in Duncombe's edition of Horace, vol. ii.]

'Twas a long journey lay before us,
When I and honest Heliodorus,
Who far in point of rhetoric
Surpasses every living Greek,
Each leaving our respective home,
Together sallied forth from Rome.
First at Aricia we alight,
And there refresh and pass the night.
Our entertainment? rather coarse
Than sumptuous, but I've met with worse. 10
Thence o'er the causeway soft and fair
To Appii Forum we repair.
But as this road is well supplied
(Temptation strong!) on either side
With inns commodious, snug, and warm,
We split the journey, and perform
In two days' time what's often done
By brisker travellers in one.
Here rather chusing not to sup
Than with bad water mix my cup, 20
After a warm debate, in spite
Of a provoking appetite,
I sturdily resolve at last
To balk it, and pronounce a fast,
And in a moody humour wait,
While my less dainty comrades bait.
Now o'er the spangled hemisphere
Diffus'd the starry train appear,
When there arose a desperate brawl;
The slaves and bargemen, one and all, 30
Rending their throats (have mercy on us!)
As if they were resolv'd to stun us.
"Steer the barge this way to the shore!"
"I tell you we'll admit no more!"

"Plague! will you never be content!"
Thus a whole hour at least is spent,
While they receive the several fares,
And kick the mule into his gears.
Happy, these difficulties past,
Could we have fall'n asleep at last! 40
But, what with humming, croaking, biting,
Gnats, frogs, and all their plagues uniting,
These tuneful natives of the lake
Conspir'd to keep us broad awake.
Besides, to make the concert full,
Two maudlin wights, exceeding dull,
The bargeman and a passenger,
Each in his turn essay'd an air
In honour of his absent fair.
At length the passenger, opprest 50
With wine, left off, and snor'd the rest.
The weary bargeman too gave o'er,
And hearing his companion snore,
Seiz'd the occasion, fix'd the barge,
Turn'd out his mule to graze at large,
And slept, forgetful of his charge.
  And now the sun, o'er eastern hill,
Discover'd that our barge stood still;
When one, whose anger vex'd him sore,
With malice fraught, leaps quick on shore, 60
Plucks up a stake; with many a thwack
Assails the mule and driver's back.
  Then slowly moving on, with pain,
At ten Feronia's stream we gain,
And in her pure and glassy wave
Our hands and faces gladly lave.
Climbing three miles, fair Anxur's height
We reach, with stony quarries white.
  While here, as was agreed, we wait,
Till, charg'd with business of the state, 70
Mæcenas and Cocceius come
(The messengers of peace) from Rome;
My eyes, by wat'ry humours blear
And sore, I with black balsam smear.
At length they join us, and with them
Our worthy friend Fonteius came;
A man of such complete desert,
Antony lov'd him at his heart.
  At Fundi we refus'd to bait,
And laugh'd at vain Aufidius' state; 80
A prætor now, a scribe before,
The purple-border'd robe he wore,
His slave the smoking censer bore.

Tir'd, at Muræna's we repose
At Formia, sup at Capito's.
With smiles the rising morn we greet;
At Sinuessa pleas'd to meet
With Plotius, Varius, and the bard
Whom Mantua first with wonder heard.
The world no purer spirits knows, 90
For none my heart more warmly glows.
Oh! what embraces we bestow'd,
And with what joy our breasts o'erflow'd!
Sure, while my sense is sound and clear,
Long as I live, I shall prefer
A gay, good-natur'd, easy friend,
To ev'ry blessing Heaven can send.
At a small village, the next night,
Near the Vulturnus, we alight;
Where, as employ'd on state affairs, 100
We were supplied by the purvey'rs
Frankly at once, and without hire,
With food for man and horse, and fire.
Capua next day betimes we reach,
Where Virgil and myself, who each
Labour'd with different maladies,
His such a stomach, mine such eyes,
As would not bear strong exercise,
In drowsy mood to sleep resort;
Mæcenas to the tennis-court. 110
Next at Cocceius' farm we're treated,
Above the Caudian tavern seated;
His kind and hospitable board
With choice of wholesome fare was stor'd.
Now, O ye Nine, inspire my lays!
To nobler themes my fancy raise!
Two combatants, who scorn to yield
The noisy, tongue-disputed field,
Sarmentus and Cicirrus, claim
A poet's tribute to their fame; 120
Cicirrus of true Oscian breed,
Sarmentus, who was never freed,
But ran away; we don't defame him;
His lady lives, and still may claim him.
Thus dignified, in hardy fray
These champions their keen wit display;
And first Sarmentus led the way.
"Thy locks," quoth he, "so rough and coarse,
Look like the mane of some wild horse."

114 fare] food *Hayley*. 125 hardy] harder *Hayley*.

We laugh. Cicirrus, undismay'd, 130
"Have at you!" cries, and shakes his head.
"'Tis well," Sarmentus says, "you've lost
That horn your forehead once could boast;
Since, maim'd and mangled as you are,
You seem to butt." A hideous scar
Improv'd, 'tis true, with double grace
The native horrors of his face.
Well, after much jocosely said
Of his grim front, so fiery red,
(For carbuncles had blotch'd it o'er, 140
As usual on Campania's shore)
"Give us," he cried, "since you're so big,
A sample of the Cyclops' jig!
Your shanks, methinks, no buskins ask,
Nor does your phyz require a mask."
To this Cicirrus: "In return,
Of you, Sir, now I fain would learn
When 'twas, no longer deem'd a slave,
Your chains you to the Lares gave?
For though a scrivener's right you claim, 150
Your lady's title is the same.
But what could make you run away,
Since, pygmy as you are, each day
A single pound of bread would quite
O'erpower your puny appetite?"
Thus jok'd the champions, while we laugh'd,
And many a cheerful bumper quaff'd.
To Beneventum next we steer,
Where our good host by over-care
In roasting thrushes lean as mice 160
Had almost fall'n a sacrifice.
The kitchen soon was all on fire,
And to the roof the flames aspire.
There might you see each man and master
Striving, amidst this sad disaster,
To save the supper—then they came
With speed enough to quench the flame.
From hence we first at distance see
Th' Apulian hills, well known to me,
Parch'd by the sultry western blast, 170
And which we never should have past,
Had not Trivicus, by the way,
Receiv'd us at the close of day.
But each was forc'd at entering here
To pay the tribute of a tear,
For more of smoke than fire was seen,
The hearth was pil'd with logs so green.

From hence in chaises we were carried
Miles twenty-four, and gladly tarried
At a small town, whose name my verse 180
(So barbarous is it!) can't rehearse.
Know it you may by many a sign;
Water is dearer far than wine;
There bread is deem'd such dainty fare,
That every prudent traveller
His wallet loads with many a crust;
For, at Canusium, you might just
As well attempt to gnaw a stone
As think to get one morsel down.
That too with scanty streams is fed: 190
Its founder was brave Diomed.
Good Varius (ah, that friends must part!)
Here left us all with aching heart.
At Rubi we arriv'd that day,
Well jaded by the length of way,
And sure poor mortals ne'er were wetter.
Next day, no weather could be better,
No roads so bad; we scarce could crawl
Along to fishy Barium's wall.
Th' Egnatians next, who by the rules 200
Of common-sense are knaves or fools,
Made all our sides with laughter heave,
Since we with them must needs believe
That incense in their temples burns,
And without fire to ashes turns.
To circumcision's bigots tell
Such tales! for me, I know full well,
That in high heaven, unmov'd by care,
The Gods eternal quiet share:
Nor can I deem their spleen the cause 210
Why fickle Nature breaks her laws.
Brundusium last we reach: and there
Stop short the Muse and Traveller.

THE NINTH SATIRE OF THE FIRST BOOK OF HORACE

ADAPTED TO THE PRESENT TIMES.

THE DESCRIPTION OF AN IMPERTINENT

[Written 1757. Published 1759, in Duncombe's edition of Horace, vol. ii.]

SAUNT'RING along the street one day,
On trifles musing by the way,
Up steps a free familiar wight;
(I scarcely knew the man by sight)

184 Their *Duncombe*. 189 one] a *Hayley*.

"Carlos," he cried, "your hand, my dear.
Gad, I rejoice to meet you here!
Pray Heaven I see you well!"—So, so;
E'en well enough, as times now go.
The same good wishes, sir, to you.
Finding he still pursu'd me close, 10
Sir, you have business, I suppose:
"My business, Sir, is quickly done,
'Tis but to make my merit known;
Sir, I have read"—O learned Sir,
You and your reading I revere.
Then, sweating with anxiety,
And sadly longing to get free,
Gods! how I scamper'd, scuffl'd for't,
Ran, halted, ran again, stopp'd short,
Beckon'd my boy, and pull'd him near, 20
And whisper'd—nothing in his ear.
Teaz'd with his loose unjointed chat,
"What street is this? Whose house is that?"
O Harlow! how I envied thee
Thy unabash'd effrontery,
Who dar'st a foe with freedom blame,
And call a coxcomb by his name!
When I return'd him answer none,
Obligingly the fool ran on,
"I see you're dismally distress'd, 30
Would give the world to be releas'd,
But, by your leave, Sir, I shall still
Stick to your skirts, do what you will.
Pray which way does your journey tend?"
O! 'tis a tedious way, my friend,
Across the Thames, the Lord knows where;
I would not trouble *you* so far.
"Well, I'm at leisure to attend you."
Are you? thought I, the De'il befriend you!
No ass with double panniers rack'd, 40
Oppress'd, o'erladen, broken-back'd,
E'er look'd a thousandth part so dull
As I, nor half so like a fool.
"Sir, I know little of myself,"
Proceeds the pert conceited elf,
"If Gray or Mason you will deem
Than me more worthy your esteem.
Poems I write by folios,
As fast as other men write prose.
Then I can sing so loud, so clear, 50
That Beard cannot with me compare.

15 reading] learning *Hayley*. 23 Whose] What *Hayley*.

In dancing too I all surpass,
Not Cooke can move with such a grace."
  Here I made shift, with much ado,
To interpose a word or two,—
Have you no parents, Sir? no friends,
Whose welfare on your own depends?
"Parents, relations, say you? No:
They're all dispos'd of long ago."
Happy to be no more perplex'd! 60
My fate too threatens, I go next.
Dispatch me, Sir, 'tis now too late,
Alas! to struggle with my fate!
Well, I'm convinc'd my time is come;
When young, a gipsy told my doom;
The beldam shook her palsied head,
As she perus'd my palm, and said,
"Of poison, pestilence, or war,
Gout, stone, defluxion, or catarrh,
You have no reason to beware. 70
Beware the coxcomb's idle prate,
Chiefly, my son, beware of that;
Be sure, when you behold him, fly
Out of all ear-shot, or you die!—"
  To Rufus' Hall we now drew near,
Where he was summon'd to appear,
Refute the charge the plaintiff brought,
Or suffer judgment by default.
"For Heav'n's sake, if you love me, wait
One moment! I'll attend you strait." 80
Glad of a plausible pretence—
Sir, I must beg you to dispense
With my attendance in the court.
My legs will surely suffer for't,—
"Nay, pr'ythee Carlos, stop awhile!"
Faith, Sir, in law I have no skill,
Besides, I have no time to spare,
I must be going you know where—
"Well, I protest, I'm doubtful now,
Whether to leave my suit or you!—" 90
Me, without scruple! I reply,
Me, by all means, Sir!—"No, not I!
Allons, Monsieur!" 'Twere vain, you know,
To strive with a victorious foe.
So I reluctantly obey,
And follow where he leads the way.
  "You and Newcastle are so close;
Still hand and glove, sir, I suppose?

80 attend] be with *Hayley*. 97, 99 Newcastle *Hayley*: *N——tle Duncombe.*

Newcastle (let me tell you, Sir,)
Has not his equal every where. 100
Well! There indeed your fortune's made!
Faith, Sir, you understand your trade.
Would you but give me your good word,
Just introduce me to my lord.
I should serve charmingly, by way
Of *second fiddle*, as they say:
What think you, Sir? 'twere a good jest;
'Slife! we should quickly scout the rest."
Sir, you mistake the matter far,
We have no *second fiddles* there. 110
Richer than I some folks may be;
More learned; but it hurts not me.
Friends though he has of different kind,
Each has his proper place assign'd.
"Strange matters these, alledg'd by you!"
Strange they may be, but they are true.
"Well, then, I vow, 'tis mighty clever;
Now I long ten times more than ever
To be advanc'd extremely near
One of his shining character." 120
Have but the will—there wants no more,
'Tis plain enough you have the pow'r.
His easy temper (that's the worst)
He knows, and so is shy at first.
But such a cavalier as you—
Lord, Sir, you'll quickly bring him to!
"Well, if I fail in my design,
Sir, it shall be no fault of mine;
If by the saucy servile tribe
Denied, what think you of a bribe? 130
Shut out to-day, not die with sorrow,
But try my luck again to-morrow.
Never attempt to visit him
But at the most convenient time,
Attend him on each *Levée* day,
And there my humble duty pay.
Labour, like this, our want supplies;
And they must stoop, who mean to rise."
While thus he wittily harangu'd,
For which you'll guess I wish'd him hang'd, 140
Campley, a friend of mine, came by,
Who knew his humour more than I.
We stop, salute, and—"Why so fast,
Friend Carlos? whither all this haste?"
Fir'd at the thoughts of a reprieve,
I pinch him, pull him, twitch his sleeve,

124 is so *Hayley*. 139 wittily] wittingly *Hayley*.

Nod, beckon, bite my lips, wink, pout,
Do every thing but speak plain out:
While he, sad dog, from the beginning,
Determin'd to mistake my meaning, 150
Instead of pitying my curse,
By jeering made it ten times worse.
Campley, what secret, pray, was that
You wanted to communicate?
"I recollect. But 'tis no matter;
Carlos! we'll talk of that herea'ter.
E'en let the secret rest; 'twill tell
Another time, Sir, just as well."
Was ever such a dismal day?
Unlucky cur! he steals away, 160
And leaves me, half bereft of life,
At mercy of the butcher's knife;
When, sudden, shouting from afar,
See his antagonist appear!
The bailiff seiz'd him, quick as thought,
"Ho! Mr. Scoundrel! are you caught!
Sir, you are witness to th' arrest.—"
Aye, marry, Sir, I'll do my best.
The mob huzzas; away they trudge,
Culprit and all, before the judge. 170
Meanwhile I, luckily enough,
(Thanks to Apollo) got clear off.

HORACE. BOOK I, ODE IX

Vides, ut alta stet nive candidum
Soracte; . . . . .

[Written 1757 (?). Published by Johnson, 1815.]

SEE'ST thou yon mountain laden with deep snow,
The groves beneath their fleecy burthen bow,
The streams congeal'd forget to flow;
Come, thaw the cold, and lay a cheerful pile
Of fuel on the hearth;
Broach the best cask, and make old Winter smile
With seasonable mirth. 7
This be our part—let heaven dispose the rest;
If Jove command, the winds shall sleep,
That now wage war upon the foamy deep,
And gentle gales spring from the balmy west.
E'en let us shift to-morrow as we may,
When to-morrow's past away,
We at least shall have to say,
We have liv'd another day;
Your auburn locks will soon be silver'd o'er, 16
Old age is at our heels, and youth returns no more.

HORACE. BOOK I, ODE XXXVIII

Persicos odi, puer, apparatus.

[Written (?). Published by Johnson, 1815.]

BOY, I hate their empty shows,
  Persian garlands I detest,
Bring not me the late-blown rose
  Ling'ring after all the rest:

Plainer myrtle pleases me
  Thus out-stretch'd beneath my vine,
Myrtle more becoming thee,
  Waiting with thy master's wine. 8

ANOTHER TRANSLATION OF THE SAME ODE

[Written (?). Published by Johnson, 1815.]

English Sapphics have been attempted, but with little success, because in our language we have no certain rules by which to determine the quantity. The following version was made merely in the way of experiment how far it might be possible to imitate a Latin Sapphic in English without any attention to that circumstance [J.].

BOY! I detest all Persian fopperies,
Fillet-bound garlands are to me disgusting,
Task not thyself with any search, I charge thee,
  Where latest roses linger;
Bring me alone (for thou wilt find that readily)
Plain myrtle. Myrtle neither will disparage
Thee occupied to serve me, or me drinking
  Beneath my vine's cool shelter. 8

HORACE. BOOK II, ODE XVI

Otium Divos rogat in patenti.

[Written (?). Published by Johnson, 1815.]

EASE is the weary merchant's pray'r,
  Who plows by night th' Ægean flood,
When neither moon nor stars appear,
  Or faintly glimmer through the cloud.

For ease the Mede with quiver grac'd,
  For ease the Thracian hero sighs,
Delightful ease all pant to taste,
  A blessing which no treasure buys. 8

For neither gold can lull to rest,
  Nor all a Consul's guard beat off
The tumults of a troubled breast,
  The cares that haunt a gilded roof.

Happy the man, whose table shows
  A few clean ounces of old plate;
No fear intrudes on his repose,
  No sordid wishes to be great. 16

Poor short-liv'd things, what plans we lay!
  Ah, why forsake our native home!
To distant climates speed away;
  For self sticks close where'er we roam!

Care follows hard; and soon o'ertakes
  The well-rigg'd ship, the warlike steed,
Her destin'd quarry ne'er forsakes,
  Not the wind flies with half her speed. 24

From anxious fears of future ill
  Guard well the cheerful, happy Now;
Gild ev'n your sorrows with a smile,
  No blessing is unmix'd below.

Thy neighing steeds and lowing herds,
  Thy num'rous flocks around thee graze,
And the best purple Tyre affords
  Thy robe magnificent displays. 32

On me indulgent Heav'n bestow'd
  A rural mansion, neat and small;
This Lyre;—and as for yonder crowd,
  The happiness to hate them all.

For the translation of Horace, Book II, Ode X. see p. 314 [Ed.].

VIRGIL'S ÆNEID

BOOK VIII, LINE 18

[Written (?). Published by Johnson, 1815.]

THUS Italy was mov'd—nor did the chief
Æneas in his mind less tumult feel.
On ev'ry side his anxious thought he turns,
Restless, unfixt, not knowing what to choose.
And as a cistern that in brim of brass
Confines the crystal flood, if chance the sun
Smite on it, or the moon's resplendent orb,
The quiv'ring light now flashes on the walls
Now leaps uncertain to the vaulted roof:
Such were the wav'ring motions of his mind. 10
'Twas night—and weary nature sunk to rest.
The birds, the bleating flocks, were heard no more.
At length, on the cold ground, beneath the damp
And dewy vault, fast by the river's brink,
The Father of his country sought repose.

When lo! among the spreading poplar boughs,
Forth from his pleasant stream, propitious rose
The god of Tiber: clear transparent gauze
Infolds his loins, his brows with reeds are crown'd:
And these his gracious words to sooth his care: 20
"Heav'n-born, who bring'st our kindred home again,
Rescued, and giv'st eternity to Troy,
Long have Laurentum and the Latian plains
Expected thee; behold thy fixt abode,
Fear not the threats of war, the storm is pass'd,
The gods appeas'd. For proof that what thou hear'st
Is no vain forgery or delusive dream,
Beneath the grove that borders my green bank,
A milk-white swine, with thirty milk-white young
Shall greet thy wond'ring eyes. Mark well the place;
For 'tis thy place of rest, there end thy toils: 31
There, twice ten years elaps'd, fair Alba's walls
Shall rise, fair Alba, by Ascanius' hand.
Thus shall it be—now listen, while I teach
The means t' accomplish these events at hand.
Th' Arcadians here, a race from Pallas sprung,
Following Evander's standard and his fate,
High on these mountains, a well-chosen spot,
Have built a city, for their Grandsire's sake
Named Pallanteum. These, perpetual war 40
Wage with the Latians: join'd in faithful league
And arms confed'rate, add them to your camp.
Myself between my winding banks, will speed
Your well-oar'd barks to stem th' opposing tide.
Rise, goddess-born, arise; and with the first
Declining stars, seek Juno in thy pray'r,
And vanquish all her wrath with suppliant vows.
When conquest crowns thee, then remember Me.
I am the Tiber, whose cærulean stream
Heav'n favours; I with copious flood divide 50
These grassy banks, and cleave the fruitful meads.
My mansion, This—and lofty cities crown
My fountain-head."—He spoke, and sought the deep,
And plung'd his form beneath the closing flood.
Æneas at the morning dawn awoke,
And rising, with uplifted eye beheld
The orient sun, then dipp'd his palms, and scoop'd
The brimming stream, and thus address'd the skies.
"Ye nymphs, Laurentian nymphs, who feed the source
Of many a stream, and thou, with thy blest flood,
O Tiber, hear, accept me, and afford, 61

At length afford, a shelter from my woes.
Where'er in secret cavern under ground
Thy waters sleep, where'er they spring to light,
Since thou hast pity for a wretch like me,
My off'rings and my vows shall wait thee still:
Great horned Father of Hesperian floods,
Be gracious now, and ratify thy word."
He said, and chose two gallies from his fleet,
Fits them with oars, and clothes the crew in arms.
When lo! astonishing and pleasing sight, 71
The milk-white dam, with her unspotted brood,
Lay stretch'd upon the bank, beneath the grove.
To thee, the pious Prince, Juno, to thee
Devotes them all, all on thine altar bleed.
That live-long night old Tiber smooth'd his flood,
And so restrain'd it, that it seem'd to stand
Motionless as a pool, or silent lake,
That not a billow might resist their oars.
With cheerful sound of exhortation soon 80
Their voyage they begin; the pitchy keel
Slides through the gentle deep, the quiet stream
Admires th' unwonted burthen that it bears,
Well polish'd arms, and vessels painted gay.
Beneath the shade of various trees, between
Th' umbrageous branches of the spreading groves,
They cut their liquid way, nor day, nor night
They slack their course, unwinding as they go
The long meanders of the peaceful tide.
The glowing sun was in meridian height, 90
When from afar they saw the humble walls,
And the few scatter'd cottages, which now
The Roman pow'r has equall'd with the clouds;
But such was then Evander's scant domain.
They steer to shore, and hasten to the town.
It chanc'd th' Arcadian monarch on that day,
Before the walls, beneath a shady grove,
Was celebrating high, in solemn feast,
Alcides and his tutelary gods.
Pallas, his son, was there, and there the chief 100
Of all his youth; with these, a worthy tribe,
His poor but venerable senate, burnt
Sweet incense, and their altars smok'd with blood.
Soon as they saw the towering masts approach,
Sliding between the trees, while the crew rest
Upon their silent oars, amaz'd they rose,
Not without fear, and all forsook the feast.
But Pallas undismay'd his jav'lin seiz'd,
Rush'd to the bank, and from a rising ground

Forbade them to disturb the sacred rites. 110
"Ye stranger youth! what prompts you to explore
This untried way? and whither do ye steer?
Whence, and who are ye? Bring ye peace or war?"
Æneas from his lofty deck holds forth
The peaceful olive branch, and thus replies:
"Trojans and enemies to the Latian state,
Whom they with unprovok'd hostilities
Have driv'n away, thou see'st. We seek Evander—
Say this—and say beside, the Trojan chiefs
Are come, and seek his friendship and his aid." 120
Pallas with wonder heard that awful name,
And "Whosoe'er thou art," he cried, "come forth;
Bear thine own tidings to my father's ear,
And be a welcome guest beneath our roof."
He said, and press'd the stranger to his breast:
Then led him from the river to the grove,
Where, courteous, thus Æneas greets the king:
"Best of the Grecian race, to whom I bow
(So wills my fortune) suppliant, and stretch forth
In sign of amity this peaceful branch, 130
I fear'd thee not, altho' I knew thee well
A Grecian leader, born in Arcady,
And kinsman of th' Atridæ. Me my virtue,
That means no wrong to thee—the Oracles,
Our kindred families allied of old,
And thy renown diffus'd thro' ev'ry land,
Have all conspir'd to bind in friendship to thee,
And send me not unwilling to thy shores.
Dardanus, author of the Trojan state,
(So say the Greeks) was fair Electra's son; 140
Electra boasted Atlas for her sire,
Whose shoulders high sustain th' æthereal orbs.
Your sire is Mercury, who Maia bore,
Sweet Maia, on Cyllene's hoary top.
Her, if we credit aught tradition old,
Atlas of yore, the selfsame Atlas, claim'd
His daughter. Thus united close in blood,
Thy race and ours one common sire confess.
With these credentials fraught, I would not send
Ambassadors with artful phrase to sound 150
And win thee by degrees—but came myself—
Me therefore, me thou see'st; my life the stake:
'Tis I, Æneas; who implore thine aid.
Should Daunia, that now aims the blow at thee,
Prevail to conquer *us*, nought then, they think,
Will hinder, but Hesperia must be theirs,
All theirs, from th' upper to the nether sea.

Take then our friendship, and return us thine.
We too have courage, we have noble minds,
And youth well tried, and exercis'd in arms." 160
Thus spoke Æneas—He with fixt regard
Survey'd him speaking, features, form and mien.
Then briefly thus—"Thou noblest of thy name,
How gladly do I take thee to my heart,
How gladly thus confess thee for a friend!
In thee I trace Anchises; his thy speech,
Thy voice, thy count'nance. For I well remember,
Many a day since, when Priam journey'd forth
To Salamis, to see the land where dwelt
Hesione, his sister, he push'd on 170
E'en to Arcadia's frozen bounds. 'Twas then
The bloom of youth was glowing on my cheek;
Much I admir'd the Trojan chiefs, and much
Their king, the son of great Laomedon,
But most Anchises, tow'ring o'er them all.
A youthful longing seiz'd me to accost
The hero, and embrace him; I drew near,
And gladly led him to the walls of Pheneus.
Departing, he distinguish'd me with gifts,
A costly quiver stor'd with Lycian darts, 180
A robe inwove with gold, with gold imboss'd,
Two bridles, those which Pallas uses now.
The friendly league thou hast solicited
I give thee therefore, and to-morrow, all
My chosen youth shall wait on your return.
Meanwhile, since thus in friendship ye are come,
Rejoice with us, and join to celebrate
These annual rites, which may not be delay'd,
And be at once familiar at our board."
He said, and bade replace the feast remov'd;
Himself upon a grassy bank dispos'd 191
The crew, but for Æneas order'd forth
A couch, spread with a lion's tawny shag,
And bad him share the honours of his throne.
Th' appointed youth with glad alacrity
Assist the lab'ring priest to load the board
With roasted entrails of the slaughter'd beeves,
Well-kneaded bread and mantling bowls. Well pleas'd
Æneas and the Trojan youth regale
On the huge length of a well-pastur'd chine. 200
Hunger appeas'd, and tables all despatch'd,
Thus spake Evander: "Superstition here,
In this our solemn feasting has no part.
No, Trojan friend, from utmost danger sav'd,

In gratitude this worship we renew.
Behold that rock which nods above the vale,
Those bulks of broken stone dispers'd around,
How desolate the shatter'd cave appears,
And what a ruin spreads th' incumber'd plain.
Within this pile, but far within, was once 210
The den of Cacus; dire his hateful form,
That shunn'd the day, half monster and half man.
Blood newly shed stream'd ever on the ground
Smoking, and many a visage pale and wan
Nail'd at his gate, hung hideous to the sight.
Vulcan begot the brute: vast was his size,
And from his throat he belch'd his father's fires.
But the day came that brought us what we wish'd,
Th' assistance and the presence of a God.
Flush'd with his vict'ry and the spoils he won 220
From triple-form'd Geryon, lately slain,
The great avenger Hercules appear'd.
Hither he drove his stately bulls, and pour'd
His herds along the vale. But the sly thief
Cacus, that nothing might escape his hand
Of villany or fraud, drove from the stalls
Four of the lordliest of his bulls, and four
The fairest of his heifers; by the tail
He dragg'd them to his den, that there conceal'd,
No footsteps might betray the dark abode. 230
And now, his herd with provender suffic'd,
Alcides would be gone: they as they went
Still bellowing loud, made the deep echoing woods
And distant hills resound: when hark! one ox,
Imprison'd close within the vast recess,
Lows in return, and frustrates all his hope.
Then fury seiz'd Alcides, and his breast
With indignation heav'd: grasping his club
Of knotted oak, swift to the mountain-top
He ran, he flew. Then first was Cacus seen 240
To tremble, and his eyes bespoke his fears.
Swift as an eastern blast he sought his den,
And dread increasing wing'd him as he went.
Drawn up in iron slings above the gate
A rock was hung enormous. Such his haste,
He burst the chains, and dropp'd it at the door,
Then grappled it with iron work within
Of bolts and bars by Vulcan's art contriv'd.
Scarce was he fast, when panting for revenge
Came Hercules; he gnash'd his teeth with rage,
And quick as lightning glanc'd his eyes around
In quest of entrance. Fiery red and stung 252

With indignation, thrice he wheel'd his course
About the mountain; thrice, but thrice in vain,
He strove to force the quarry at the gate,
And thrice sat down o'erwearied in the vale.
There stood a pointed rock, abrupt and rude
That high o'erlook'd the rest, close at the back
Of the fell monster's den, where birds obscene
Of ominous note resorted, choughs and daws. 260
This, as it lean'd obliquely to the left,
Threat'ning the stream below, he from the right
Push'd with his utmost strength, and to and fro
He shook the mass, loos'ning its lowest base;
Then shov'd it from its seat; down fell the pile;
Sky thunder'd at the fall; the banks give way,
Th' affrighted stream flows upward to his source.
Behold the kennel of the brute expos'd,
The gloomy vault laid open. So, if chance
Earth yawning to the centre should disclose 270
The mansions, the pale mansions of the dead,
Loath'd by the Gods, such would the gulph appear,
And the ghosts tremble at the sight of day.
The monster braying with unusual din
Within his hollow lair, and sore amaz'd
To see such sudden inroads of the light,
Alcides press'd him close with what at hand
Lay readiest, stumps of trees, and fragments huge
Of millstone size. He, (for escape was none)
Wond'rous to tell! forth from his gorge discharg'd
A smoky cloud, that darken'd all the den; 281
Wreath after wreath he vomited amain
The smoth'ring vapor, mixt with fiery sparks.
No sight could penetrate the veil obscure.
The hero, more provok'd, endur'd not this,
But, with a headlong leap, he rush'd to where
The thickest cloud envelop'd his abode.
There grasp'd he Cacus, spite of all his fires,
Till crush'd within his arms the monster shows
His bloodless throat, now dry with panting hard,
And his press'd eyeballs start. Soon he tears down
The barricade of rock, the dark abyss 292
Lies open; and th' imprison'd bulls, the theft
He had with oaths denied, are brought to light;
By th' heels the miscreant carcase is dragg'd forth,
His face, his eyes, all terrible, his breast
Beset with bristles, and his sooty jaws
Are view'd with wonder never to be cloy'd.
Hence the celebrity thou see'st, and hence

288 grasp *1815.*

This festal day.—Potitius first enjoin'd 300
Posterity these solemn rites, he first
With those who bear the great Pinarian name
To Hercules devoted, in the grove
This altar built, deem'd sacred in the highest
By us, and sacred ever to be deem'd.
Come then, my friends, and bind your youthful
brows
In praise of such deliv'rance, and hold forth
The brimming cup; your deities and ours
Are now the same: then drink, and freely too."
So saying, he twisted round his rev'rend locks 310
A variegated poplar wreath, and fill'd
His right hand with a consecrated bowl.
At once all pour libations on the board,
All offer pray'r. And now the radiant sphere
Of day descending, eventide drew near.
When first Potitius with the priests advanc'd,
Begirt with skins, and torches in their hands.
High piled with meats of sav'ry taste, they rang'd
The chargers, and renew'd the grateful feast.
Then came the Salii, crown'd with poplar too, 320
Circling the blazing altars; here the youth
Advanc'd, a choir harmonious, there were heard
The rev'rend seers responsive; praise they sung,
Much praise in honour of Alcides' deeds;
How first with infant gripe two serpents huge
He strangled, sent from Juno; next they sung
How Troja and Oechalia he destroy'd,
Fair cities both, and many a toilsome task
Beneath Eurystheus, (so his step-dame will'd)
Achiev'd victorious. "Thou, the cloud-born pair, 330
Hylæus fierce and Pholus, monstrous twins,
Thou slew'st the minotaur, the plague of Crete,
And the vast lion of the Nemean rock.
Thee Hell, and Cerberus, Hell's porter, fear'd,
Stretch'd in his den upon his half-gnaw'd bones.
Thee no abhorred form, not ev'n the vast
Typhœus could appal, tho' clad in arms.
Hail, true-born son of Jove, among the Gods
At length enroll'd, nor least illustrious thou,
Haste thee propitious, and approve our songs.—" 340
Thus hymn'd the chorus; above all they sing
The cave of Cacus, and the flames he breath'd.
The whole grove echoes, and the hills rebound.
The rites perform'd, all hasten to the town.
The king, bending with age, held as he went
Æneas, and his Pallas by the hand,

With much variety of pleasing talk
Short'ning the way. Æneas, with a smile,
Looks round him, charm'd with the delightful scene,
And many a question asks, and much he learns 350
Of heroes far renown'd in ancient times.
Then spake Evander: "These extensive groves
Were once inhabited by fauns and nymphs
Produc'd beneath their shades, and a rude race
Of men, the progeny uncouth of elms
And knotted oaks. They no refinement knew
Of laws or manners civiliz'd, to yoke
The steer, with forecast provident to store
The hoarded grain, or manage what they had,
But brows'd like beasts upon the leafy boughs, 360
Or fed voracious on their hunted prey.
An exile from Olympus, and expell'd
His native realm by thunder-bearing Jove,
First Saturn came. He from the mountains drew
This herd of men untractable and fierce,
And gave them laws: and call'd his hiding place,
This growth of forests, Latium. Such the peace
His land possess'd, the golden age was then,
So fam'd in story; till by slow degrees
Far other times, and of far diff'rent hue 370
Succeeded, thirst of gold and thirst of blood.
Then came Ausonian bands, and armed hosts
From Sicily, and Latium often chang'd
Her master and her name. At length arose
Kings, of whom Tybris of gigantic form
Was chief; and we Italians since have call'd
The river by his name; thus Albula
(So was the country call'd in ancient days)
Was quite forgot. Me from my native land
An exile, thro' the dang'rous ocean driv'n, 380
Resistless fortune and relentless fate
Placed where thou see'st me. Phœbus, and
The nymph Carmentis, with maternal care
Attendant on my wand'rings, fix'd me here."

[*Ten lines omitted.*]

He said, and shew'd him the Tarpeian rock,
And the rude spot, where now the capitol
Stands all magnificent and bright with gold,
Then overgrown with thorns. And yet ev'n then,
The swains beheld that sacred scene with awe;
The grove, the rock, inspir'd religious fear. 390
"This grove," he said, "that crowns the lofty top
Of this fair hill, some deity, we know,

Inhabits, but what deity we doubt.
Th' Arcadians speak of Jupiter himself,
That they have often seen him, shaking here
His gloomy Ægis, while the thunder-storms
Came rolling all around him. Turn thine eyes,
Behold that ruin; those dismantled walls,
Were once two towns, Ianiculum—
By Janus this, and that by Saturn built, 400
Saturnia." Such discourse brought them beneath
The roof of poor Evander; thence they saw,
Where now the proud and stately forum stands,
The grazing herds wide scatter'd o'er the field.
Soon as he enter'd—"Hercules," he said,
"Victorious Hercules, on this threshold trod,
These walls contain'd him, humble as they are.
Dare to despise magnificence, my friend,
Prove thy divine descent by worth divine,
Nor view with haughty scorn this mean abode."
So saying, he led Æneas by the hand, 411
And plac'd him on a cushion stuff'd with leaves,
Spread with the skin of a Lybistian bear.

[*The Episode of Venus and Vulcan omitted.*]

While thus in Lemnos Vulcan was employ'd,
Awaken'd by the gentle dawn of day,
And the shrill song of birds beneath the eaves
Of his low mansion, old Evander rose.
His tunic, and the sandals on his feet,
And his good sword well-girded to his side,
A panther's skin dependent from his left 420
And over his right shoulder thrown aslant,
Thus was he clad. Two mastiffs follow'd him,
His whole retinue and his nightly guard.

THE SALAD [1]

[In Norfolk MS., dated June 8, 21, 1799. Published by Hayley, 1803.]

THE winter-night now well-nigh worn away,
The wakeful cock proclaim'd approaching day,
When Simulus, poor tenant of a farm
Of narrowest limits, heard the shrill alarm,
Yawn'd, stretch'd his limbs, and anxious to provide
Against the pangs of hunger unsupplied,

[1] This singular poem, which the learned and judicious Heyne seems inclined to think a translation of Virgil's, from the Greek of Parthenius, was translated into English by Cowper, during his depressive malady, June 1799 [H.].

399 Were *Bailey:* Where *1815 and later edd.*

By slow degrees his tatter'd bed forsook,
And poking in the dark explor'd the nook,
Where embers slept with ashes heap'd around,
And with burnt fingers-ends the treasure found. 10
It chanc'd that from a brand beneath his nose,
Sure proof of latent fire, some smoke arose;
When trimming with a pin th' incrusted tow,
And stooping it toward the coals below,
He toils, with cheeks distended, to excite
The ling'ring flame, and gains at length a light.
With prudent heed he spreads his hand before
The quiv'ring lamp, and opes his gran'ry door.
Small was his stock, but taking for the day
A measur'd stint of twice eight pounds away, 20
With these his mill he seeks. A shelf at hand,
Fixt in the wall, affords his lamp a stand:
Then baring both his arms—a sleeveless coat
He girds, the rough exuviæ of a goat;
And with a rubber, for that use design'd,
Cleansing his mill within—begins to grind;
Each hand has its employ; lab'ring amain,
This turns the wince, while that supplies the grain.
The stone revolving rapidly, now glows,
And the bruis'd corn a mealy current flows; 30
While he, to make his heavy labour light,
Tasks oft his left hand to relieve his right;
And chants with rudest accent, to beguile
His ceaseless toil, as rude a strain the while.
And now, "Dame Cybale, come forth!" he cries;
But Cybale, still slumb'ring, nought replies.
From Afric she, the swain's sole serving-maid,
Whose face and form alike her birth betray'd.
With woolly locks, lips tumid, sable skin,
Wide bosom, udders flaccid, belly thin, 40
Legs slender, broad and most misshapen feet,
Chapp'd into chinks, and parch'd with solar heat.
Such, summon'd oft, she came; at his command
Fresh fuel heap'd, the sleeping embers fann'd,
And made in haste her simm'ring skillet steam,
Replenish'd newly from the neighbouring stream.
The labours of the mill perform'd, a sieve
The mingled flour and bran must next receive,
Which shaken oft, shoots Ceres through refin'd,
And better dress'd, her husks all left behind. 50
This done, at once, his future plain repast,
Unleaven'd, on a shaven board he cast,

28 winch *Hayley* (*1812*).

With tepid lymph first largely soak'd it all,
Then gather'd it with both hands to a ball,
And spreading it again with both hands wide,
With sprinkled salt the stiffen'd mass supplied;
At length, the stubborn substance, duly wrought,
Takes from his palms impress'd the shape it ought,
Becomes an orb—and quarter'd into shares,
The faithful mark of just division bears. 60
Last, on his hearth it finds convenient space,
For Cybale before had swept the place,
And there, with tiles and embers overspread,
She leaves it—reeking in its sultry bed.
Nor Simulus, while Vulcan thus, alone,
His part perform'd, proves heedless of his own,
But sedulous, not merely to subdue
His hunger, but to please his palate too,
Prepares more sav'ry food. His chimney-side
Could boast no gammon, salted well, and dried, 70
And hook'd behind him; but sufficient store
Of bundled annis, and a cheese it bore;
A broad round cheese, which, thro' its centre strung
With a tough broom-twig, in the corner hung;
The prudent hero therefore with address,
And quick dispatch, now seeks another mess.
Close to his cottage lay a garden-ground,
With reeds and osiers sparely girt around;
Small was the spot, but lib'ral to produce;
Nor wanted aught that serves a peasant's use, 80
And sometimes e'en the rich would borrow hence,
Although its tillage was his sole expense.
For oft, as from his toils abroad he ceas'd,
Home-bound by weather, or some stated feast,
His debt of culture here he duly paid,
And only left the plough, to wield the spade.
He knew to give each plant the soil it needs,
To drill the ground, and cover close the seeds;
And could with ease compel the wanton rill
To turn, and wind, obedient to his will. 90
There flourish'd star-wort, and the branching beet,
The sorrel acid, and the mallow sweet,
The skirret, and the leek's aspiring kind,
The noxious poppy—quencher of the mind!
Salubrious sequel of a sumptuous board,
The lettuce, and the long huge-bellied gourd;
But these (for none his appetite controll'd
With stricter sway) the thrifty rustic sold;
With broom-twigs neatly bound, each kind apart,
He bore them ever to the public mart; 100

Whence, laden still, but with a lighter load,
Of cash well earn'd, he took his homeward road,
Expending seldom, ere he quitted Rome,
His gains, in flesh-meat for a feast at home.
There, at no cost, on onions, rank and red,
Or the curl'd endive's bitter leaf, he fed:
On scallions slic'd, or with a sensual gust
On rockets—foul provocatives of lust!
Nor even shunn'd, with smarting gums to press
Nasturtium—pungent face-distorting mess! 110

Some such regale now also in his thought,
With hasty steps his garden-ground he sought;
There delving with his hands, he first displac'd
Four plants of garlick, large, and rooted fast,
The tender tops of parsley next he culls,
Then the old rue-bush shudders as he pulls,
And coriander last to these succeeds,
That hangs on slightest threads her trembling seeds.

Plac'd near his sprightly fire he now demands
The mortar at his sable servant's hands; 120
When stripping all his garlick first, he tore
Th' exterior coats, and cast them on the floor,
Then cast away with like contempt the skin,
Flimsier concealment of the cloves within.
These search'd, and perfect found, he one by one
Rinc'd, and dispos'd within the hollow stone.
Salt added, and a lump of salted cheese,
With his injected herbs he cover'd these,
And tucking with his left his tunic tight,
And seizing fast the pestle with his right, 130
The garlick bruising first he soon express'd,
And mix'd the various juices of the rest.
He grinds, and by degrees his herbs below
Lost in each other their own pow'rs forego,
And with the cheese in compound, to the sight
Nor wholly green appear, nor wholly white.
His nostrils oft the forceful fume resent,
He curs'd full oft his dinner for its scent,
Or with wry faces, wiping as he spoke
The trickling tears, cried "vengeance on the smoke!" 140
The work proceeds: not roughly turns he now
The pestle, but in circles smooth and slow,
With cautious hand that grudges what it spills,
Some drops of olive-oil he next instils;
Then vinegar with caution scarcely less,
And gath'ring to a ball the medley mess,

Last, with two fingers frugally applied,
Sweeps the small remnant from the mortar's side.
And thus complete in figure and in kind,
Obtains at length the Salad he design'd. 150
And now black Cybale before him stands,
The cake drawn newly glowing in her hands,
He glad receives it, chasing far away
All fears of famine, for the passing day;
His legs enclos'd in buskins, and his head
In its tough casque of leather, forth he led
And yok'd his steers, a dull obedient pair,
Then drove afield, and plung'd the pointed share.

TRANSLATION FROM OVID

TRIST. LIB. V. ELEG. XII

Scribis, ut oblectem.

[Written (?). Published by Johnson, 1815.]

YOU bid me write t' amuse the tedious hours,
And save from with'ring my poetic pow'rs.
Hard is the task, my friend, for verse should flow
From the free mind, not fetter'd down by woe;
Restless amidst unceasing tempests tost,
Whoe'er has cause for sorrow, I have most.
Would you bid Priam laugh, his sons all slain,
Or childless Niobe from tears refrain,
Join the gay dance, and lead the festive train?
Does grief or study most befit the mind, 10
To this remote, this barb'rous nook confin'd?
Could you impart to my unshaken breast
The fortitude by Socrates possess'd,
Soon would it sink beneath such woes as mine,
For what is human strength to wrath divine?
Wise as he was, and Heav'n pronounc'd him so,
My suff'rings would have laid that wisdom low.
Could I forget my country, thee and all,
And ev'n th' offence to which I owe my fall,
Yet fear alone would freeze the poet's vein, 20
While hostile troops swarm o'er the dreary plain.
Add that the fatal rust of long disuse
Unfits me for the service of the Muse.
Thistles and weeds are all we can expect
From the best soil impov'rish'd by neglect;
Unexercis'd and to his stall confin'd,
The fleetest racer would be left behind;
The best built bark that cleaves the wat'ry way,
Laid useless by, would moulder and decay—

No hope remains that time shall me restore, 30
Mean as I was, to what I was before.
Think how a series of desponding cares
Benumbs the genius, and its force impairs.
How oft, as now, on this devoted sheet,
My verse constrain'd to move with measur'd feet,
Reluctant and laborious limps along,
And proves itself a wretched exile's song.
What is it tunes the most melodious lays?
'Tis emulation and the thirst of praise,
A noble thirst, and not unknown to me, 40
While smoothly wafted on a calmer sea.
But can a wretch like Ovid pant for fame?
No, rather let the world forget my name.
Is it because that world approv'd my strain,
You prompt me to the same pursuit again?
No, let the Nine th' ungrateful truth excuse,
I charge my hopeless ruin on the Muse,
And, like Perillus, meet my just desert,
The victim of my own pernicious art.
Fool that I was to be so warn'd in vain, 50
And shipwreck'd once, to tempt the deep again.
Ill fares the bard in this unletter'd land,
None to consult, and none to understand.
The purest verse has no admirers here,
Their own rude language only suits their ear.
Rude as it is, at length familiar grown,
I learn it, and almost unlearn my own.—
Yet to say truth, ev'n here the Muse disdains
Confinement, and attempts her former strains,
But finds the strong desire is not the pow'r, 60
And what her taste condemns, the flames devour.
A part, perhaps, like this, escapes the doom,
And tho' unworthy, finds a friend at Rome;
But oh the cruel art, that could undo
Its vot'ry thus, would that could perish too!

TRANSLATIONS FROM VINCENT BOURNE

[Written, the first four, in 1780(?). Eight others, to which dates are affixed, come from the Norfolk MS., and are there so dated, together with 'An Ænigma', undated. The first four were published in 1782, the remainder by Hayley in 1803, except *On the Picture of a Sleeping Child*, which Croft published in 1825.]

THE GLOW-WORM

BENEATH the hedge, or near the stream,
  A worm is known to stray;
That shows by night a lucid beam,
  Which disappears by day.

Disputes have been, and still prevail,
  From whence his rays proceed;
Some give that honour to his tail,
  And others to his head. 8

But this is sure—the hand of might
  That kindles up the skies,
Gives *him* a modicum of light
  Proportion'd to his size.

Perhaps indulgent nature meant,
  By such a lamp bestow'd,
To bid the trav'ler, as he went,
  Be careful where he trod: 16

Nor crush a worm, whose useful light
  Might serve, however small,
To shew a stumbling stone by night,
  And save him from a fall.

Whate'er she meant, this truth divine
  Is legible and plain,
'Tis pow'r almighty bids him shine,
  Nor bids him shine in vain. 24

Ye proud and wealthy, let this theme
  Teach humbler thoughts to you,
Since such a reptile has its gem,
  And boasts its splendour too.

THE JACKDAW

THERE is a bird who, by his coat,
And by the hoarseness of his note,
  Might be suppos'd a crow;
A great frequenter of the church,
Where, bishop-like, he finds a perch,
  And dormitory too. 6

Above the steeple shines a plate,
That turns and turns, to indicate
From what point blows the weather.
Look up—your brains begin to swim,
'Tis in the clouds—that pleases him,
He chooses it the rather. 12

Fond of the speculative height,
Thither he wings his airy flight,
And thence securely sees
The bustle and the raree-show
That occupy mankind below,
Secure and at his ease. 18

You think, no doubt, he sits and muses
On future broken bones and bruises,
If he should chance to fall.
No; not a single thought like that
Employs his philosophic pate,
Or troubles it at all. 24

He sees, that this great roundabout—
The world, with all its motley rout,
Church, army, physic, law,
Its customs, and its bus'nesses,—
Is no concern at all of his,
And says—what says he?—Caw. 30

Thrice happy bird! I too have seen
Much of the vanities of men;
And, sick of having seen 'em,
Would cheerfully these limbs resign
For such a pair of wings as thine,
And such a head between 'em. 36

THE CRICKET

LITTLE inmate, full of mirth,
Chirping on my kitchen hearth,
Wheresoe'er be thine abode,
Always harbinger of good,
Pay me for thy warm retreat
With a song more soft and sweet;
In return thou shalt receive
Such a strain as I can give. 8

Thus thy praise shall be exprest,
Inoffensive, welcome guest!
While the rat is on the scout,
And the mouse with curious snout,

29 Is *1793–1800*: Are *1782–1788*.

With what vermin else infest
Ev'ry dish, and spoil the best;
Frisking thus before the fire,
Thou hast all thine heart's desire. 16

Though in voice and shape they be
Form'd as if akin to thee,
Thou surpassest, happier far,
Happiest grasshoppers that are;
Their's is but a summer's song,
Thine endures the winter long,
Unimpair'd and shrill and clear,
Melody throughout the year. 24

Neither night, nor dawn of day,
Puts a period to thy play;
Sing then—and extend thy span
Far beyond the date of man.
Wretched man, whose years are spent
In repining discontent,
Lives not, aged though he be,
Half a span, compar'd with thee. 32

THE PARROT

In painted plumes superbly drest,
A native of the gorgeous east,
  By many a billow tost;
Poll gains at length the British shore,
Part of the captain's precious store—
  A present to his toast. 6

Belinda's maids are soon preferr'd
To teach him now and then a word,
  As Poll can master it;
But 'tis her own important charge
To qualify him more at large,
  And make him quite a wit. 12

Sweet Poll! his doating mistress cries,
Sweet Poll! the mimic bird replies,
  And calls aloud for sack.
She next instructs him in the kiss;
'Tis now a little one, like Miss,
  And now a hearty smack. 18

At first he aims at what he hears;
And, list'ning close with both his ears,
  Just catches at the sound;
But soon articulates aloud,
Much to th' amusement of the crowd,
  And stuns the neighbours round. 24

A querulous old woman's voice
His hum'rous talent next employs—
He scolds and gives the lie.
And now he sings, and now is sick—
Here Sally, Susan, come, come quick;
Poor Poll is like to die! 30

Belinda and her bird! 'tis rare
To meet with such a well match'd pair,
The language and the tone,
Each character in ev'ry part
Sustain'd with so much grace and art,
And both in unison. 36

When children first begin to spell,
And stammer out a syllable,
We think them tedious creatures;
But difficulties soon abate,
When birds are to be taught to prate,
And women are the teachers. 42

ON THE PICTURE OF A SLEEPING CHILD

Sweet babe, whose image here express'd
Does thy peaceful slumbers show;
Guilt or fear, to break thy rest,
Never did thy spirit know.

Soothing slumbers, soft repose,
Such as mock the painter's skill,
Such as innocence bestows,
Harmless infant, lull thee still! 8

THE THRACIAN

Thracian parents, at his birth,
Mourn their babe with many a tear,
But with undissembled mirth
Place him breathless on his bier.

Greece and Rome, with equal scorn
"O the savages!" exclaim,
"Whether they rejoice or mourn,
Well entitled to the name!" 8

But the cause of this concern
And this pleasure, would they trace,
Even they might somewhat learn
From the savages of Thrace.

March 29-30 [1799].

RECIPROCAL KINDNESS THE PRIMARY LAW OF NATURE

Androcles from his injur'd lord, in dread
Of instant death, to Lybia's desert fled.
Tir'd with his toilsome flight, and parch'd with heat,
He spied, at length, a cavern's cool retreat.
But scarce had giv'n to rest his weary frame,
When, hugest of his kind, a lion came:
He roar'd approaching; but the savage din
To plaintive murmurs chang'd,—arriv'd within,
And with expressive looks, his lifted paw
Presenting, aid implor'd from whom he saw; 10
The fugitive, through terror at a stand,
Dar'd not awhile afford his trembling hand,
But bolder grown at length, inherent found
A pointed thorn, and drew it from the wound.
The cure was wrought; he wip'd the sanious blood,
And firm and free from pain the lion stood.
Again he seeks the wilds, and day by day
Regales his inmate with the parted prey:
Nor he disdains the dole, though unprepar'd,
Spread on the ground, and with a lion shar'd. 20
But thus to live—still lost, sequester'd still—
Scarce seem'd his lord's revenge an heavier ill.
Home, native home!—Oh might he but repair!
He must, he will, though death attends him there.
He goes, and doom'd to perish, on the sands
Of the full theatre unpitied stands!
When lo! the self-same lion from his cage
Flies to devour him, famish'd into rage.
He flies, but viewing in his purpos'd prey
The man, his healer, pauses on his way, 30
And soften'd by remembrance into sweet
And kind composure, crouches at his feet.
Mute with astonishment th' assembly gaze;
But why, ye Romans? Whence your mute amaze?
All this is nat'ral:—nature bade him rend
An enemy; she bids him spare a friend.

A MANUAL

MORE ANCIENT THAN THE ART OF PRINTING AND NOT TO BE FOUND IN ANY CATALOGUE

There is a book, which we may call
(Its excellence is such)
Alone a library, tho' small;
The ladies thumb it much.

15 flood *Hayley* (*1803*).

Words none, things num'rous it contains:
  And, things with words compar'd,
Who needs be told, that has his brains,
  Which merits most regard? 8

Ofttimes its leaves of scarlet hue
  A golden edging boast;
And open'd, it displays to view
  Twelve pages at the most.

Nor name, nor title, stamp'd behind,
  Adorns its outer part;
But all within 'tis richly lin'd,
  A magazine of art. 16

The whitest hands that secret hoard
  Oft visit; and the fair
Preserve it in their bosoms stor'd,
  As with a miser's care.

Thence implements of ev'ry size,
  And form'd for various use,
(They need but to consult their eyes)
  They readily produce. 24

The largest and the longest kind
  Possess the foremost page,
A sort most needed by the blind,
  Or nearly such from age.

The full-charg'd leaf, which next ensues,
  Presents in bright array
The smaller sort, which matrons use,
  Not quite so blind as they. 32

The third, the fourth, the fifth supply
  What their occasions ask,
Who with a more discerning eye
  Perform a nicer task.

But still with regular decrease
  From size to size they fall,
In ev'ry leaf grow less, and less;
  The last are least of all. 40

Oh! what a fund of genius, pent
  In narrow space, is here!
This volume's method and intent
  How luminous and clear!

It leaves no reader at a loss
  Or pos'd, whoever reads;
No commentator's tedious gloss,
  Nor even index needs. 48

Search Bodley's many thousands o'er!
  No book is treasur'd there,
Nor yet in Granta's num'rous store,
  That may with this compare.

No!—Rival none in either host
  Of this was ever seen,
Or that contents could justly boast,
  So brilliant and so keen. 56

April 3, 1799.

AN ÆNIGMA

A NEEDLE small, as small can be,
In bulk and use, surpasses me,
  Nor is my purchase dear;
For little, and almost for nought,
As many of my kind are bought
  As days are in the year. 6

Yet though but little use we boast,
And are procur'd at little cost,
  The labour is not light,
Nor few artificers it asks,
All skilful in their sev'ral tasks,
  To fashion us aright. 12

One fuses metal o'er the fire,
A second draws it into wire,
  The shears another plies,
Who clips in lengths the brazen thread
For him, who, chafing every shred,
  Gives all an equal size. 18

A fifth prepares, exact and round,
The knob, with which it must be crown'd;
  His follower makes it fast,
And with his mallet and his file
To shape the point, employs awhile
  The seventh and the last. 24

Now therefore, Œdipus! declare
What creature, wonderful and rare,
  A process, that obtains
Its purpose with so much ado,
At last produces!—Tell me true,
  And take me for your pains! 30

SPARROWS SELF-DOMESTICATED

IN TRINITY COLLEGE, CAMBRIDGE

None ever shar'd the social feast,
Or as an inmate, or a guest,
Beneath the celebrated dome,
Where once Sir Isaac had his home,
Who saw not (and with some delight
Perhaps he view'd the novel sight)
How num'rous, at the tables there,
The sparrows beg their daily fare.
For there, in ev'ry nook, and cell,
Where such a family may dwell, 10
Sure as the vernal season comes
Their nests they weave in hope of crumbs,
Which kindly giv'n, may serve with food
Convenient their unfeather'd brood;
And oft as with its summons clear
The warning bell salutes their ear,
Sagacious list'ners to the sound,
They flock from all the fields around,
To reach the hospitable hall,
None more attentive to the call. 20
Arriv'd, the pensionary band,
Hopping and chirping, close at hand,
Solicit what they soon receive,
The sprinkled, plenteous donative.
Thus is a multitude, though large,
Supported at a trivial charge;
A single doit would overpay
Th' expenditure of ev'ry day,
And who can grudge so small a grace
To suppliants, natives of the place? 30

April 7, 9 [1799].

FAMILIARITY DANGEROUS

As in her ancient mistress' lap,
The youthful tabby lay,
They gave each other many a tap,
Alike dispos'd to play.

But strife ensues. Puss waxes warm,
And with protruded claws
Ploughs all the length of Lydia's arm,
Mere wantonness the cause. 8

At once, resentful of the deed,
She shakes her to the ground
With many a threat, that she shall bleed
With still a deeper wound.

But, Lydia, bid thy fury rest!
  It was a venial stroke;
For she, that will with kittens jest,
  Should bear a kitten's joke. 16

April 10 [1799].

INVITATION TO THE REDBREAST

SWEET bird, whom the winter constrains—
  And seldom another it can—
To seek a retreat, while he reigns,
  In the well-shelter'd dwellings of man,
Who never canst seem to intrude,
  Tho' in all places equally free,
Come, oft as the season is rude!
  Thou art sure to be welcome to me. 8

At sight of the first feeble ray,
  That pierces the clouds of the east,
To inveigle thee every day
  My window shall show thee a feast;
For, taught by experience, I know
  Thee mindful of benefit long;
And that, thankful for all I bestow,
  Thou wilt pay me with many a song. 16

Then, soon as the swell of the buds
  Bespeaks the renewal of spring,
Fly hence, if thou wilt, to the woods,
  Or where it shall please thee to sing:
And shouldst thou, compell'd by a frost,
  Come again to my window or door,
Doubt not an affectionate host!
  Only pay, as thou pay'dst me before. 24

Thus music must needs be confest
  To flow from a fountain above;
Else how should it work, in the breast,
  Unchangeable friendship and love?
And who on the globe can be found,
  Save your generation and ours,
That can be delighted by sound,
  Or boast any musical pow'rs? 32

April 10 [1799].

STRADA'S NIGHTINGALE

THE shepherd touch'd his reed; sweet Philomel
  Essay'd, and oft essay'd to catch the strain,
And treasuring, as on her ear they fell,
  The numbers, echo'd note for note again.

5 canst *Hayley* (*1803*) : can *Hayley* (*later edd.*)

The peevish youth, who ne'er had found before
  A rival of his skill, indignant heard,
And soon (for various was his tuneful store)
  In loftier tones defied the simple bird. 8

She dar'd the task, and rising, as he rose,
  With all the force, that passion gives, inspir'd,
Return'd the sounds awhile, but in the close
  Exhausted fell, and at his feet expir'd.

Thus strength, not skill prevail'd. O fatal strife,
  By thee, poor songstress, playfully begun;
And O sad victory, which cost thy life,
  And he may wish, that he had never won! 16

April 14 [1799].

ODE ON THE DEATH OF A LADY

WHO LIVED ONE HUNDRED YEARS, AND DIED ON HER BIRTHDAY, 1728

ANCIENT dame, how wide and vast,
  To a race like ours appears,
Rounded to an orb at last,
  All thy multitude of years!

We, the herd of human kind,
  Frailer and of feebler pow'rs;
We, to narrow bounds confin'd,
  Soon exhaust the sum of ours. 8

Death's delicious banquet—we
  Perish even from the womb,
Swifter than a shadow flee,
  Nourish'd, but to feed the tomb.

Seeds of merciless disease
  Lurk in all that we enjoy;
Some, that waste us by degrees,
  Some, that suddenly destroy. 16

And if life o'erleap the bourn,
  Common to the sons of men;
What remains, but that we mourn,
  Dream, and doat, and drivel then?

Fast as moons can wax and wane,
  Sorrow comes; and while we groan,
Pant with anguish and complain,
  Half our years are fled and gone. 24

If a few, (to few 'tis giv'n)
  Ling'ring on this earthly stage,
Creep, and halt with steps unev'n,
  To the period of an age;

Wherefore live they, but to see
  Cunning, arrogance, and force;
Sights, lamented much by thee,
  Holding their accustom'd course? 32

Oft was seen, in ages past,
  All, that we with wonder view;
Often shall be to the last;
  Earth produces nothing new.

Thee we gratulate; content,
  Should propitious Heav'n design
Life for us, as calmly spent,
  Though but half the length of thine. 40

April 18, 1799.

THE CAUSE WON

Two neighbours furiously dispute;
A field, the subject of the suit.
Trivial the spot, yet such the rage,
With which the combatants engage,
'Twere hard to tell, who covets most
The prize—at whatsoever cost.
The pleadings swell. Words still suffice:
No single word but has its price:
No term but yields some fair pretence,
For novel and increas'd expense. 10
  Defendant thus becomes a name,
Which he, that bore it, may disclaim;
Since both, in one description blended,
Are plaintiffs—when the suit is ended.

April 21 [1799].

THE SILK WORM

THE beams of April, ere it goes,
A worm, scarce visible, disclose;
All winter long content to dwell
The tenant of his native shell.
The same prolific season gives
The sustenance, by which he lives,
The mulb'ry-leaf, a simple store,
That serves him—till he needs no more!
For, his dimensions once complete,
Thenceforth none ever sees him eat; 10
Tho', till his growing time be past,
Scarce ever is he seen to fast.
That hour arriv'd, his work begins.
He spins and weaves, and weaves and spins;
Till circle upon circle wound
Careless around him and around,

Conceals him with a veil, tho' slight,
Impervious to the keenest sight.
Thus self-inclos'd, as in a cask,
At length he finishes his task; 20
And, tho' a worm, when he was lost,
Or caterpillar at the most,
When next we see him, wings he wears,
And in papilio-pomp appears;
Becomes oviparous; supplies,
With future worms and future flies,
The next-ensuing year;—and dies!
Well were it for the world, if all
Who creep about this earthly ball,
Though shorter-liv'd than most he be, 30
Were useful in their kind as he.

THE INNOCENT THIEF

Not a flow'r can be found in the fields,
Or the spot that we till for our pleasure,
From the largest to least, but it yields
The bee, never-wearied, a treasure.

Scarce any she quits unexplor'd,
With a diligence truly exact;
Yet, steal what she may for her hoard,
Leaves evidence none of the fact. 8

Her lucrative task she pursues,
And pilfers with so much address,
That none of their odour they lose,
Nor charm by their beauty the less.

Not thus inoffensively preys
The canker-worm, in-dwelling foe!
His voracity not thus allays
The sparrow, the finch, or the crow. 16

The worm, more expensively fed,
The pride of the garden devours;
And birds peck the seed from the bed,
Still less to be spar'd than the flow'rs.

But she, with such delicate skill,
Her pillage so fits for her use,
That the chymist in vain with his still
Would labour the like to produce. 24

28-31 *om.* *Hayley* (*1803*).

Then grudge not her temperate meals,
Nor a benefit blame as a theft;
Since, stole she not all that she steals,
Neither honey nor wax would be left.

DENNER'S OLD WOMAN

In this mimic form of a matron in years,
How plainly the pencil of Denner appears!
The matron herself, in whose old age we see
Not a trace of decline, what a wonder is she!
No dimness of eye, and no cheek hanging low,
No wrinkle, or deep-furrow'd frown on the brow!
Her forehead indeed is here circled around
With locks, like the ribbon, with which they are bound;
While glossy and smooth, and as soft as the skin
Of a delicate peach, is the down of her chin; 10
But nothing unpleasant, or sad, or severe,
Or that indicates life in its winter—is here!
Yet all is express'd, with fidelity due,
Nor a pimple, or freckle, conceal'd from the view.
Many, fond of new sights, or who cherish a taste,
For the labours of art, to the spectacle haste;
The youths all agree, that could old age inspire
The passion of love, hers would kindle the fire,
And the matrons with pleasure confess, that they see
Ridiculous nothing or hideous in thee. 20
The nymphs for themselves scarcely hope a decline,
O wonderful woman! as placid as thine.
Strange magic of art! which the youth can engage
To peruse, half enamour'd, the features of age;
And force from the virgin a sigh of despair,
That she, when as old, shall be equally fair!
How great is the glory that Denner has gain'd,
Since Apelles not more for his Venus obtain'd!

THE TEARS OF A PAINTER

Apelles, hearing that his boy
Had just expir'd—his only joy!
Altho' the sight with anguish tore him,
Bade place his dear remains before him.
He seiz'd his brush, his colours spread;
And—"Oh! my child, accept"—he said,
"('Tis all that I can now bestow,)
This tribute of a father's woe!"
Then, faithful to the two-fold part,
Both of his feelings and his art, 10

He clos'd his eyes, with tender care,
And form'd at once a fellow pair.
His brow, with amber locks beset,
And lips he drew, not livid yet;
And shaded all, that he had done,
To the just image of his son.
  Thus far is well. But view again
The cause of thy paternal pain!
Thy melancholy task fulfil!
It needs the last, last touches still. 20
Again his pencil's pow'rs he tries,
For on his lips a smile he spies:
And still his cheek unfaded shows
The deepest damask of the rose.
Then, heedful to the finish'd whole,
With fondest eagerness he stole,
Till scarce himself distinctly knew
The cherub copied from the true.
  Now, painter, cease! Thy task is done.
Long lives this image of thy son; 30
Nor short-liv'd shall the glory prove,
Or of thy labour, or thy love.

THE MAZE

FROM right to left, and to and fro,
Caught in a labyrinth, you go,
And turn, and turn, and turn again,
To solve the myst'ry, but in vain.
Stand still, and breathe, and take from me
A clew, that soon shall set you free!
Not Ariadne, if you met her,
Herself could serve you with a better.
You enter'd easily—find where—
And make with ease your exit there! 10

NO SORROW PECULIAR TO THE SUFFERER

THE lover, in melodious verses,
His singular distress rehearses,
Still closing with a rueful cry,
"Was ever such a wretch as I?"
Yes! Thousands have endur'd before
All thy distress; some haply more.
Unnumber'd Corydons complain,
And Strephons, of the like disdain;

16 the] a *Hayley* (*1803*). 21 pow'r *Hayley* (*1803*).

And if thy Chloe be of steel;
Too deaf to hear, too hard to feel; 10
Not her alone that censure fits,
Nor thou alone hast lost thy wits.

THE SNAIL

To grass, or leaf, or fruit, or wall,
The snail sticks close, nor fears to fall,
As if he grew there, house and all
Together.

Within that house secure he hides,
When danger imminent betides
Of storm, or other harm besides
Of weather. 8

Give but his horns the slightest touch,
His self-collecting power is such,
He shrinks into his house, with much
Displeasure.

Where'er he dwells, he dwells alone,
Except himself has chattels none,
Well satisfied to be his own
Whole treasure. 16

Thus, hermit-like, his life he leads,
Nor partner of his banquet needs,
And if he meets one, only feeds
The faster.

Who seeks him must be worse than blind,
(He and his house are so combin'd)
If, finding it, he fails to find
Its master. 24

THE CANTAB

WITH two spurs or one; no great matter which,
Boots bought, or boots borrow'd, a whip or a switch,
Five shillings or less the hire of his beast,
Paid part into hand—you must wait for the rest.
Thus equipp'd Academicus climbs up his horse,
And out they both sally for better or worse;
His heart void of fear and as light as a feather,
And in violent haste to go—nor knowing whither;
Thro' the fields and the towns, see, he scampers along,
And is bark'd at, and laugh'd at by old and by young,

The Cantab—1 no *BM*: and no *Hayley*. 3 the *BM*: for the *Hayley*. 8 nor *BM*: not *Hayley*. 10 bark'd *BM*: look'd *Hayley*. (*Orig. line is* Adlatran´ catuli, multaque ridet anus.)

Till at length, overspent, and his sides smear'd with
blood, 11
Down tumbles his horse, man and all in the mud.
In a waggon or chaise shall he finish his route?
Oh scandalous fate! he must do it on foot.

Young gentlemen hear,—I am older than you,
The advice that I give I have prov'd to be true,
Wherever your journey may be, never doubt it,
The faster you ride, you're the longer about it.

TRANSLATION OF THE VERSES TO THE MEMORY OF DR. LLOYD,

SPOKEN AT THE WESTMINSTER ELECTION NEXT AFTER HIS DECEASE

[Written 1781. Published by Hayley, 1803. The original Latin verses were by Vincent.]

OUR good old friend is gone, gone to his rest;
Whose social converse was itself a feast.
O ye of riper years, who recollect
How once ye lov'd, and ey'd him with respect,
Both in the firmness of his better day,
While yet he rul'd you with a father's sway,
And when, impair'd by time, and glad to rest,
Yet still with looks in mild complacence drest,
He took his annual seat, and mingled here
His sprightly vein with yours—now drop a tear! 10
In morals blameless, as in manners meek,
He knew no wish, that he might blush to speak,
But, happy in whatever state below,
And richer than the rich in being so,
Obtain'd the hearts of all, and such a meed
At length from one[1] as made him rich indeed.
Hence then, ye titles, hence, not wanted here!
Go! garnish merit in a higher sphere,
The brows of those, whose more exalted lot
He could congratulate, but envied not! 20
Light lie the turf, good Senior, on thy breast;
And tranquil, as thy mind was, be thy rest.
Tho', living, thou hadst more desert than fame,
And not a stone now chronicles thy name!

[1] He was usher and under-master of Westminster near fifty years, and retired from his occupation when he was near seventy, with a handsome pension from the king [H.].

ANOTHER VERSION

[Written 1781. Published by Bruce, 1863, from MS. in British Museum.]

TH' old man, our amiable old man is gone—
Second in harmless pleasantry to none.
Ye, once his pupils, who with rev'rence just
View'd him, as all that were his pupils must,
Whether, his health yet firm, he gently strove
To rear and form you with a parent's love,
Or worn with age, and pleas'd to be at large,
He came still mindful of his former charge,
To smile on this glad circle ev'ry year,
And charm you with his humour, drop a tear. 10
Simplicity grac'd all his blameless life,
And he was kind, and gentle, hating strife.
Content was the best wealth he ever shar'd,
Though all men pay'd him love, and *one*, reward.
Ye titles! we have here no need of you,
Go, give the Great ones their eulogium due,
If Fortune more on others chose to shine,
'Twas not in Him to murmur or repine.
Placid old man! the turf upon thy breast,
May it lie lightly, sacred be thy rest; 20
Though, living, thou hadst none thy fame to spread,
Nor ev'n a stone to chronicle thee, dead.

TRANSLATION OF EPITAPH TO WILLIAM NORTHCOT

[Written July, 1780. Published by Hayley, 1804. The Latin epitaph was by Unwin.]

FAREWELL!—But not for ever, Hope replies;
Trace but his steps, and meet him in the skies!
There nothing shall renew our parting pain;
Thou shalt not wither, nor I weep, again. 4

ON THE SHORTNESS OF HUMAN LIFE

TRANSLATION FROM THE LATIN OF DR. JORTIN

[Written Jan., 1784. Published by Hayley, 1804. For Dr. Jortin's verses, see notes at the end of the volume.]

SUNS that set, and moons that wane,
Rise and are restor'd again.
Stars, that orient day subdues,
Night at her return renews.

Another Version—Heading in BM.: Translation of the Latin verses spoken in honour of the late Dr. Lloyd at the last Westminster Election, by W. C., who was two years under him while he was an usher, and had afterwards the happiness of his acquaintance. 1 aimable *BM.*

Herbs and flowers, the beauteous birth
Of the genial womb of earth,
Suffer but a transient death
From the winter's cruel breath.
Zephyr speaks; serener skies
Warm the glebe; and they arise. 10
We, alas! earth's haughty kings,
We, that promise mighty things,
Losing soon life's happy prime,
Droop and fade in little time.
Spring returns, but not our bloom,
Still 'tis winter in the tomb.

EPIGRAMS, TRANSLATED FROM THE LATIN OF OWEN

[Written Aug.—Dec., 1799. All published by Hayley, 1803.]

ON ONE IGNORANT AND ARROGANT

Thou mayst of double ign'rance boast,
Who know'st not that thou nothing know'st.

PRUDENT SIMPLICITY

That thou mayst injure no man, dove-like be,
And serpent-like, that none may injure thee!

TO A FRIEND IN DISTRESS

I wish thy lot, now bad, still worse, my friend!
For when at worst, they say, things always mend!

When little more than boy in age,
I deem'd myself almost a sage;
But now seem worthier to be stiled
For ignorance almost a child. 4

RETALIATION

The works of antient bards divine,
Aulus! thou scorn'st to read;
And should posterity read thine,
It would be strange indeed! 4

SUNSET AND SUNRISE

Contemplate, when the sun declines,
Thy death, with deep reflection!
And when again he rising shines,
The day of resurrection! 4

Sunset and Sunrise—3 he] his *Hayley* (*1812*).

TRANSLATIONS OF GREEK VERSES

[Written May—Dec., 1799, the first thirty-seven in the Norfolk MS. All published by Hayley, 1803.]

FROM THE GREEK OF JULIANUS

A SPARTAN, his companion slain,
Alone from battle fled,
His mother, kindling with disdain
That she had borne him, struck him dead;
For courage, and not birth alone,
In Sparta, testifies a son! 6

ON THE SAME, BY PALLADAS

A SPARTAN 'scaping from the fight,
His mother met him in his flight,
Upheld a faulchion to his breast,
And thus the fugitive address'd:
"Thou canst but live to blot with shame
Indelible thy mother's name,
While ev'ry breath that thou shalt draw,
Offends against thy country's law;
But, if thou perish by this hand,
Myself indeed throughout the land 10
To my dishonour shall be known
The mother still of such a son,
But Sparta will be safe and free,
And that shall serve to comfort me."

AN EPITAPH

MY name—my country—what are they to thee?
What—whether base or proud, my pedigree?
Perhaps I far surpass'd all other men—
Perhaps I fell below them all—what then?
Suffice it, stranger! that thou seest a tomb—
Thou know'st its use—it hides—no matter whom. 6

ANOTHER

TAKE to thy bosom, gentle earth, a swain
With much hard labour in thy service worn.
He set the vines, that clothe yon ample plain,
And he these olives, that the vale adorn.
He fill'd with grain the glebe, the rills he led,
Thro' this green herbage and those fruitful bow'rs;
Thou, therefore, earth! lie lightly on his head, 7
His hoary head, and deck his grave with flow'rs.

ANOTHER

Painter, this likeness is too strong,
And we shall mourn the dead too long.

ANOTHER

At three-score winters' end I died
A cheerless being, sole and sad,
The nuptial knot I never tied,
And wish my father never had. 4

BY CALLIMACHUS

At morn we placed on his funeral bier
Young Melanippus; and at even-tide,
Unable to sustain a loss so dear,
By her own hand his blooming sister died.
Thus Aristippus mourn'd his noble race,
Annihilated by a double blow,
Nor son could hope, nor daughter more t' embrace,
And all Cyrene sadden'd at his woe. 8

ON MILTIADES

Miltiades! thy valour best
(Although in every region known)
The men of Persia can attest,
Taught by thyself at Marathon. 4

ON AN INFANT

Bewail not much, my parents! me, the prey
Of ruthless Ades, and sepulcher'd here.
An infant, in my fifth scarce finish'd year,
He found all sportive, innocent, and gay,
Your young Callimachus; and if I knew
Not many joys, my griefs were also few. 6

ON A FOWLER, BY ISIDORUS

With reeds and bird-lime, from the desert air,
Eumelus gather'd free, though scanty, fare.
No lordly patron's hand he deign'd to kiss,
Nor lux'ry knew, save liberty, nor bliss.
Thrice thirty years he liv'd, and to his heirs
His reeds bequeath'd, his bird-lime, and his snares. 6

By Callimachus—1 plac'd . . . funereal *Norfolk MS.*, *Hayley* (*1812*).
On a Fowler—1, 6 reeds [καλάμοισιν] *Norfolk MS.*, seeds *Hayley*.

ON NIOBE

CHARON! receive a family on board
Itself sufficient for thy crazy yawl;
Apollo and Diana, for a word
By me too proudly spoken, slew us all. 4

ON A GOOD MAN

TRAV'LLER, regret not me; for thou shalt find,
Just cause of sorrow none in my decease,
Who, dying, childrens' children left behind,
And with one wife liv'd many a year in peace:
Three virtuous youths espous'd my daughters three,
And oft their infants in my bosom lay,
Nor saw I one of all deriv'd from me
Touch'd with disease, or torn by death away.
Their duteous hands my fun'ral rites bestow'd,
And me, by blameless manners fitted well 10
To seek it, sent to the serene abode
Where shades of pious men for ever dwell.

ON A MISER

THEY call thee rich—I deem thee poor,
Since if thou dar'st not use thy store,
But sav'st it only for thine heirs,
The treasure is not thine, but theirs. 4

ANOTHER

A MISER, traversing his house,
Espied, unusual there, a mouse,
And thus his uninvited guest,
Briskly inquisitive, address'd:
"Tell me, my dear, to what cause is it
I owe this unexpected visit?"
The mouse her host obliquely eyed,
And, smiling, pleasantly replied,
"Fear not, good fellow! for your hoard,
I come to lodge, and not to board." 10

ANOTHER

ART thou some individual of a kind
Long-liv'd by nature as the rook or hind?
Heap treasure, then, for if thy need be such,
Thou hast excuse, and scarce canst heap too much.
But man thou seem'st, clear therefore from thy breast
This lust of treasure—folly at the best!
For why shouldst thou go wasted to the tomb,
To fatten with thy spoils, thou know'st not whom? 8

ON HERMOCRATIA

Hermocratia nam'd—save only one,
Twice fifteen births I bore, and buried none;
For neither Phœbus pierc'd my thriving joys,
Nor Dian—she my girls, or he my boys.
But Dian rather, when my daughters lay
In parturition, chas'd their pangs away;
And all my sons, by Phœbus' bounty, shar'd
A vig'rous youth, by sickness unimpair'd.
Oh Niobe! far less prolific! see
Thy boast against Latona sham'd by me! 10

BY HERACLIDES

In Cnidus born, the consort I became
Of Euphron. Aretimias was my name.
His bed I shar'd, nor prov'd a barren bride,
But bore two children at a birth, and died.
One child I leave to solace and uphold
Euphron hereafter, when infirm and old;
And one, for his remembrance sake, I bear
To Pluto's realm, till he shall join me there. 8

ON FEMALE INCONSTANCY

Rich, thou hadst many lovers—poor, hast none,
So surely want extinguishes the flame,
And she, who call'd thee once her pretty one,
And her Adonis, now inquires thy name.

Where wast thou born, Sosicrates, and where
In what strange country can thy parents live,
Who seem'st, by thy complaints, not yet aware
That want's a crime no woman can forgive? 8

ON THE REED

I was of late a barren plant,
Useless, insignificant.
Nor fig, nor grape, nor apple bore,
A native of the marshy shore,
But gather'd for poetic use,
And plung'd into a sable juice,
Of which my modicum I sip,
With narrow mouth and slender lip,
At once, although by nature dumb,
All-eloquent I have become, 10
And speak with fluency untir'd,
As if by Phœbus' self inspir'd.

TO HEALTH

Eldest-born of pow'rs divine!
Blest Hygeia! be it mine
To enjoy what thou canst give,
And henceforth with thee to live:
For in pow'r if pleasure be,
Wealth, or num'rous progeny,
Or in amorous embrace,
Where no spy infests the place;
Or in aught that Heav'n bestows
To alleviate human woes, 10
When the wearied heart despairs,
Of a respite from its cares;
These and ev'ry true delight
Flourish only in thy sight;
And the sister Graces Three
Owe, themselves, their youth to thee,
Without whom we may possess
Much, but never happiness.

TO THE SWALLOW

Attic maid! with honey fed,
  Bear'st thou to thy callow brood
Yonder locust from the mead,
  Destin'd their delicious food?
Ye have kindred voices clear,
  Ye alike unfold the wing,
Migrate hither, sojourn here,
  Both attendant on the spring. 8
Ah for pity drop the prize;
  Let it not, with truth, be said
That a songster gasps and dies,
  That a songster may be fed.

ON THE GRASSHOPPER

Happy songster! perch'd above
On the summit of the grove,
Whom a dew-drop cheers to sing
With the freedom of a king;
From thy perch, survey the fields,
Where prolific nature yields
Nought that, willingly as she,
Man surrenders not to thee.
For hostility or hate
None thy pleasures can create. 10

Thee it satisfies to sing
Sweetly the return of Spring,
Herald of the genial hours,
Harming neither herbs nor flow'rs.
Therefore man thy voice attends
Gladly—thou and he are friends;
Nor thy never-ceasing strains
Phœbus or the Muse disdains
As too simple or too long,
For themselves inspire the song. 20
Earth-born, bloodless, undecaying,
Ever singing, sporting, playing,
What has nature else to show
Godlike in its kind as thou?

ON A BATH, BY PLATO

Did Cytherea to the skies
From this pellucid lymph arise?
Or was it Cytherea's touch,
When bathing here, that made it such? 4

ON PALLAS BATHING

FROM A HYMN OF CALLIMACHUS

Nor oils of balmy scent produce,
Nor mirror for Minerva's use,
Ye nymphs who lave her! she, array'd
In genuine beauty, scorns their aid.
Not even when they left the skies
To seek on Ida's head the prize
From Paris' hand, did Juno deign,
Or Pallas, in the crystal plain
Of Simois' stream her locks to trace,
Or in the mirror's polish'd face, 10
Though Venus oft with anxious care
Adjusted twice a single hair.

FROM MENANDER

Fond youth! who dream'st that hoarded gold
Is needful, not alone to pay
For all thy various items sold,
To serve the wants of ev'ry day;

Bread, vinegar, and oil, and meat,
For sav'ry viands season'd high;
But somewhat more important yet—
I tell thee what it cannot buy. 8

No treasure, hadst thou more amass'd
Than fame to Tantalus assign'd,
Would save thee from the tomb at last,
But thou must leave it all behind.

I give thee, therefore, counsel wise;
Confide not vainly in thy store,
However large—much less despise
Others comparatively poor! 16

But in thy more exalted state
A just and equal temper show,
That all who see thee rich and great
May deem thee worthy to be so.

ON LATE-ACQUIRED WEALTH

Poor in my youth, and in life's later scenes
Rich to no end, I curse my natal hour;
Who nought enjoy'd, while young, denied the means;
And nought, when old, enjoy'd, denied the pow'r. 4

ON FLATTERERS

No mischief worthier of our fear
In nature can be found,
Than friendship, in ostent sincere,
But hollow and unsound.
For lull'd into a dang'rous dream
We close infold a foe,
Who strikes, when most secure we seem,
Th' inevitable blow. 8

ON A TRUE FRIEND

Hast thou a friend? Thou hast indeed
A rich and large supply,
Treasure to serve your ev'ry need,
Well-manag'd, till you die. 4

ON INVALIDS

Far happier are the dead, methinks, than they
Who look for death, and fear it ev'ry day.

ON THE ASTROLOGERS

Th' Astrologers did all alike presage
My uncle's dying in extreme old age,
One only disagreed. But he was wise,
And spoke not till he heard the fun'ral cries. 4

ON AN OLD WOMAN

MYCILLA dyes her locks 'tis said,
But 'tis a foul aspersion;
She buys them black, they therefore need
No subsequent immersion. 4

TO DEMOSTHENIS

IT flatters and deceives thy view,
This mirror of ill-polish'd ore!
For were it just, and told thee true,
Thou would'st consult it never more. 4

ON A SIMILAR CHARACTER

YOU give your cheeks a rosy stain,
With washes dye your hair,
But paint and washes both are vain
To give a youthful air.

Those wrinkles mock your daily toil,
No labour will efface 'em,
You wear a mask of smoothest oil,
Yet still with ease we trace 'em. 8

An art so fruitless then forsake,
Which though you much excel in,
You never can contrive to make
Old Hecuba young Helen.

ON A BATTERED BEAUTY

HAIR, wax, rouge, honey, teeth, you buy,
A multifarious store!
A mask at once would all supply,
Nor would it cost you more. 4

ON AN UGLY FELLOW

BEWARE, my friend! of crystal brook
Or fountain, lest that hideous hook,
Thy nose, thou chance to see;
Narcissus' fate would then be thine,
And self-detested thou wouldst pine,
As self-enamour'd he. 6

ON A THIEF

WHEN Aulus, the nocturnal thief, made prize
Of Hermes, swift-wing'd envoy of the skies,
Hermes, Arcadia's king, the thief divine,
Who, when an infant, stole Apollo's kine,

And whom, as arbiter and overseer
Of our gymnastic sports we planted here,
Hermes! he cried, you meet no new disaster;
Ofttimes the pupil goes beyond his master. 8

ON ENVY

Pity, says the Theban Bard,
From my wishes I discard;
Envy! let me rather be,
Rather far, a theme for thee!
Pity to distress is shewn:
Envy to the great alone—
So the Theban—But to shine
Less conspicuous be mine!
I prefer the golden mean
Pomp and penury between; 10
For alarm and peril wait
Ever on the loftiest state,
And the lowest, to the end,
Obloquy and scorn attend.

ON PEDIGREE

FROM EPICHARMUS

My mother! if thou love me, name no more
My noble birth! Sounding at every breath
My noble birth, thou kill'st me. Thither fly,
As to their only refuge, all from whom
Nature withholds all good besides; they boast
Their noble birth, conduct us to the tombs
Of their forefathers, and from age to age
Ascending, trumpet their illustrious race:
But whom hast thou beheld, or canst thou name,
Deriv'd from no forefathers? Such a man 10
Lives not; for how could such be born at all?
And if it chance that, native of a land
Far distant, or in infancy depriv'd
Of all his kindred, one, who cannot trace
His origin, exist, why deem him sprung
From baser ancestry than theirs, who can?
My mother! he whom nature at his birth
Endow'd with virtuous qualities, although
An Æthiop and a slave, is nobly born.

BY PHILEMON

Oft we enhance our ills by discontent,
And give them bulk beyond what nature meant.

On Pedigree—7 forefather *Hayley* (*1812*).

A parent, brother, friend deceas'd, to cry—
"He's dead indeed, but he was born to die—"
Such temperate grief is suited to the size
And burthen of the loss; is just, and wise.
But to exclaim, "Ah! wherefore was I born,
"Thus to be left, for ever thus forlorn?"
Who thus laments his loss, invites distress,
And magnifies a woe that might be less, 10
Through dull despondence to his lot resign'd,
And leaving reason's remedy behind.

BY MOSCHUS

I SLEPT, when Venus enter'd: to my bed
A Cupid in her beauteous hand she led,
A bashful-seeming boy, and thus she said:
"Shepherd, receive my little one! I bring
An untaught love, whom thou must teach to sing."
She said, and left him. I suspecting nought
Many a sweet strain my subtle pupil taught,
How reed to reed Pan first with ozier bound,
How Pallas form'd the pipe of softest sound,
How Hermes gave the lute, and how the quire 10
Of Phœbus owe to Phœbus' self the lyre.
Such were my themes; my themes nought heeded he,
But ditties sang of am'rous sort to me,
The pangs that mortals and immortals prove
From Venus' influence, and the darts of love.
Thus was the teacher by the pupil taught;
His lessons I retain'd, and mine forgot.

TRANSLATION OF AN EPIGRAM OF HOMER

No title is prefixed to this piece, but it appears to be a translation of one of the Ἐπιγράμματα of Homer called Ὁ Κάμινος, or The Furnace. Herodotus, or whoever was the author of the Life of Homer ascribed to him, says: Certain potters, while they were busied in baking their ware, seeing Homer at a small distance, and having heard much said of his wisdom, called to him, and promised him a present of their commodity and of such other things as they could afford, if he would sing to them, when he sang as follows [Adapted from J.].

[Written Oct., 1790. Published by Johnson, 1815.]

PAY me my price, Potters! and I will sing.
Attend, O Pallas! and with lifted arm
Protect their oven; let the cups and all
The sacred vessels blacken well, and bak'd
With good success, yield them both fair renown
And profit, whether in the market sold
Or streets, and let no strife ensue between us.

But oh ye Potters! if with shameless front
Ye falsify your promise, then I leave
No mischief uninvok'd t' avenge the wrong. 10
Come Syntrips, Smaragus, Sabactes come,
And Asbetus, nor let your direst dread
Omodamus, delay! Fire seize your house,
May neither house nor vestibule escape,
May ye lament to see confusion mar
And mingle the whole labour of your hands,
And may a sound fill all your oven, such
As of a horse grinding his provender,
While all your pots and flagons bounce within.
Come hither also, daughter of the sun, 20
Circe the Sorceress, and with thy drugs
Poison themselves, and all that they have made!
Come also Chiron, with thy num'rous troop
Of Centaurs, as well those who died beneath
The club of Hercules, as who escap'd,
And stamp their crockery to dust; down fall
Their chimney; let them see it with their eyes
And howl to see the ruin of their art,
While I rejoice; and if a potter stoop
To peep into his furnace, may the fire 30
Flash in his face and scorch it, that all men
Observe, thenceforth, equity and good faith.

TRANSLATION OF PRIOR'S CHLOE AND EUPHELIA

[Written April, 1779. Published 1782. There is a MS. copy in the British Museum.]

MERCATOR, vigiles oculos ut fallere possit,
  Nomine sub ficto trans mare mittit opes;
Lene sonat liquidumque meis Euphelia chordis,
  Sed solam exoptant te, mea vota, Chlöe.
Ad speculum ornabat nitidos Euphelia crines,
  Cum dixit mea lux, heus, cane, sume lyram.
Namque lyram juxta positam cum carmine vidit,
  Suave quidem carmen, dulcisonamque lyram. 8

Fila lyræ vocemque paro. Suspiria surgunt,
  Et miscent numeris murmura mæsta meis,
Dumque tuæ memoro laudes, Euphelia, formæ,
  Tota anima interea pendet ab ore Chlöes.

Subrubet illa pudore, et contrahit altera frontem,
  Me torquet mea mens conscia, psallo, tremo;
Atque Cupidinea dixit Dea cincta corona,
  Heu! fallendi artem quam didicere parum. 16

4 Sed] At *BM.*

TRANSLATION OF DRYDEN'S POEM ON MILTON

[Written in letter to Unwin (MS. in British Museum), July, 1780. Published by Hayley, 1804.]

Tres tria, sed longe distantia sæcula, vates
  Ostentant, tribus e gentibus, eximios.
Græcia sublimem, cum majestate disertum
  Roma tulit, felix Anglia utrisque parem.
Partubus ex binis Natura exhausta coacta est,
  Tertius ut fieret, consociare duos. 6

TRANSLATION OF A SIMILE IN PARADISE LOST

[Written in letter to Unwin (MS. in British Museum), June 8, 1780. Published by Hayley, 1804.]

As when, from mountain tops, the dusky clouds
Ascending, &c.—(ii. 488.)

Quales aërii montis de vertice nubes
Cum surgunt, et jam Boreæ tumida ora quierunt,
Cælum hilares abdit spissa caligine vultus,
Nimbosumque nives aut imbres cogitat æther:
Tum si jucundo tandem sol prodeat ore,
Et croceo montes et pascua lumine tingat,
Gaudent omnia, aves mulcent concentibus agros,
Balatuque ovium colles vallesque resultant. 8

A SIMILE LATINISED

[Written April 27, 1782 (MS. in British Museum.) Published by Hayley, 1803.]

Sors adversa gerit stimulum, sed tendit et alas,
  Pungit api similis, sed velut ista fugit.

TRANSLATIONS FROM THE FABLES OF GAY

[Written Jan., 1800. In the Norfolk MS. Published by Hayley, 1803.]

LEPUS MULTIS AMICUS

Lusus amicitia est, uni nisi dedita, ceu fit,
  Simplice ni nexus fœdere, lusus amor.
Incerto genitore puer, non sæpe paternæ
  Tutamen novit, deliciasque domus:
Quique sibi fidos fore multos sperat, amicus
  Mirum est huic misero si ferat ullus opem.

A Simile in Paradise Lost—4 *om. Hayley and other edd.*

Comis erat mitisque, et nolle et velle paratus
  Cum quovis, Gaii more modoque, Lepus.
Ille quot in sylvis et quot spatiantur in agris
  Quadrupedes norat conciliare sibi. 10
Et quisque innocuo invitoque lacessere quenquam
  Labra tenus saltem fidus amicus erat.
Ortum sub lucis dum pressa cubilia linquit,
  Rorantes herbas, pabula sueta, petens,
Venatorum audit clangores pone sequentum,
  Fulmineumque sonum territus erro fugit.
Corda pavor pulsat, sursum sedet, erigit aures,
  Respicit, et sentit jam prope adesse necem.
Utque canes fallat late circumvagus, illuc
  Unde abiit, mira calliditate redit; 20
Viribus at fractis tandem se projicit ultro
  In media miserum semianimemque via.
Vix ibi stratus, equi sonitum pedis audit, et, O spe
  Quam læta adventu cor agitatur equi!
Dorsum (inquit) mihi, chare, tuum concede, tuoque
  Auxilio nares fallere vimque canum.
Me meus, ut nosti, pes prodit—fidus amicus
  Fert quodcunque lubens, nec grave sentit, onus.
Belle miselle lepuscule, (equus respondet) amara
  Omnia quæ tibi sunt, sunt et amara mihi. 30
Verum age—sume animos—multi, me pone, bonique
  Adveniunt, quorum sis cito salvus ope.
Proximus armenti dominus bos solicitatus
  Auxilium his verbis se dare posse negat.
Quando quadrupedum, quot vivunt, nullus amicum
  Me nescire potest usque fuisse tibi,
Libertate æquus, quam cedit amicus amico,
  Utar, et absque metu ne tibi displiceam;
Hinc me mandat amor. Juxta istum messis acervum
  Me mea, præ cunctis chara, juvenca manet; 40
Et quis non ultro quæcumque negotia linquit,
  Pareat ut dominæ, cum vocat ipsa, suæ?
Neu me crudelem dicas—discedo—sed hircus
  (Cujus ope effugias integer) hircus adest.
Febrem (ait hircus) habes. Heu sicca ut lumina languent!
  Utque caput collo deficiente jacet!
Hirsutum mihi tergum; et forsan læserit ægrum;
  Vellere eris melius fultus, ovisque venit.
Me mihi fecit onus natura, ovis inquit; anhelans
  Sustineo lanæ pondera tanta meæ; 50
Me nec velocem nec fortem jacto, solentque
  Nos etiam sævi dilacerare canes.

Ultimus accedit vitulus, vitulumque precatur
  Ut periturum alias ocyus eripiat.
Remne ego, respondet vitulus, suscepero tantam,
  Non depulsus adhuc ubere, natus heri?
Te quem maturi canibus validique relinquunt
  Incolumem potero reddere parvus ego?
Præterea tollens quem illi aversantur, amicis
  Forte parum videar consuluisse meis. 60
Ignoscas oro. Fidissima dissociantur
  Corda, et tale tibi sat liquet esse meum.
Ecce autem ad calces canis est! te quanta perempto
  Tristitia est nobis ingruitura!—Vale!

AVARUS ET PLUTUS

Icta fenestra Euri flatu stridebat, avarus
  Ex somno trepidus surgit, opumque memor.
Lata silenter humi ponit vestigia, quemque
  Respicit ad sonitum respiciensque tremit;
Angustissima quæque foramina lampade visit,
  Ad vectes, obices, fertque refertque manum.
Dein reserat crebris junctam compagibus arcam
  Exultansque omnes conspicit intus opes.
Sed tandem furiis ultricibus actus ob artes
  Queis sua res tenuis creverat in cumulum, 10
Contortis manibus nunc stat, nunc pectora pulsans
  Aurum execratur, perniciemque vocat;
O mihi, ait, misero mens quam tranquilla fuisset,
  Hoc celasset adhuc si modo terra malum!
Nunc autem virtus ipsa est venalis; et aurum
  Quid contra vitii tormina sæva valet?
O inimicum aurum! O homini infestissima pestis,
  Cui datur illecebras vincere posse tuas?
Aurum homines suasit contemnere quicquid honestum est,
  Et præter nomen nil retinere boni. 20
Aurum cuncta mali per terras semina sparsit;
  Aurum nocturnis furibus arma dedit.
Bella docet fortes, timidosque ad pessima ducit,
  Fœdifragas artes, multiplicesque dolos,
Nec vitii quicquam est quod non inveneris ortum
  Ex malesuada auri sacrilegaque fame.
Dixit, et ingemuit; Plutusque suum sibi numen
  Ante oculos, ira fervidus, ipse stetit.
Arcam clausit avarus, et ora horrentia rugis
  Ostendens, tremulum sic Deus increpuit. 30
Questibus his raucis mihi cur, stulte, obstrepis aures?
  Ista tui similis tristia quisque canit.

Commaculavi egone humanum genus, improbe? Culpa,
Dum rapis et captas omnia, culpa tua est.
Mene execrandum censes, quia tum pretiosa
Criminibus fiunt perniciosa tuis?
Virtutis specie, pulchro ceu pallio amictus
Quisque catus nebulo sordida facta tegit.
Atque suis manibus commissa potentia durum
Et dirum subito vergit ad imperium. 40
Hinc, nimium dum latro aurum detrudit in arcam,
Idem aurum latet in pectore pestis edax;
Nutrit avaritiam et fastum, suspendere adunco
Suadet naso inopes, et vitium omne docet.
Auri at larga probo si copia contigit, instar
Roris dilapsi ex æthere cuncta beat:
Tum, quasi numen inesset, alit, fovet, educat orbos,
Et viduas lacrymis ora rigare vetat.
Quo sua crimina jure auro derivet avarus
Aurum animae pretium qui cupit atque capit? 50
Lege pari gladium incuset sicarius atrox
Cæso homine, et ferrum judicet esse reum.

PAPILIO ET LIMAX

Qui subito ex imis rerum in fastigia surgit,
Nativas sordes, quicquid agatur, olet.

TRANSLATIONS OF THE LATIN AND ITALIAN POEMS OF MILTON

[Written Sept., 1791—Feb., 1792. Published by Hayley, 1808, in a handsome 4to volume illustrated by Flaxman, with Cowper's fragmentary commentary on *Paradise Lost*, for the benefit of Cowper's godson, W. C. Rose.]

COMPLIMENTARY PIECES TO MILTON

Well as the Author knows that the following testimonies are not so much *about* as *above* him, and that men of great ingenuity, as well as our friends, are apt, through abundant zeal, so to praise us as rather to draw their own likeness than ours, he was yet unwilling that the world should remain always ignorant of compositions, that do him so much honour; and especially because he has other friends, who have, with much importunity, solicited their publication. Aware that excessive commendation awakens envy, he would with both hands thrust it from him, preferring just so much of that dangerous tribute as may of right belong to him; but at the same time he cannot deny that he sets the highest value on the suffrages of judicious and distinguished persons.

THE NEAPOLITAN JOHN BAPTIST MANSO,

MARQUIS OF VILLA,

TO THE ENGLISHMAN JOHN MILTON

WHAT features, form, mien, manners, with a mind
Oh how intelligent! and how refined!
Were but thy piety from fault as free,
Thou wouldest no Angle [1] but an Angel be. 4

AN EPIGRAM

ADDRESSED TO THE ENGLISHMAN JOHN MILTON, A POET WORTHY OF THREE LAURELS, THE GRECIAN, LATIN, AND ETRUSCAN, BY JOHN SALSILLO OF ROME

MELES [2] and Mincio [3], both your urns depress,
Sebetus [4] boast henceforth thy Tasso less,
But let the Thames o'er-peer all floods, since he
For Milton famed shall, single, match the three. 4

TO JOHN MILTON

GREECE, sound thy Homer's, Rome, thy Virgil's name,
But England's Milton equals both in fame.

SELVAGGI.

[1] The reader perceives that the word Angle is essential, because the epigram turns upon it [C.].

[2] Meles is a river of Ionia, in the neighbourhood of Smyrna, whence Homer is called Melesigenes [C.].

[3] The Mincio watered the city of Mantua famous as the birthplace of Virgil [C.].

[4] Sebetus is now called the *Fiume della Maddalena*—it runs through Naples [C.].

AN ODE

ADDRESSED TO THE ILLUSTRIOUS ENGLISHMAN MR. JOHN MILTON, BY SIGNOR ANTONIO FRANCINI, GENTLEMAN OF FLORENCE

EXALT me, Clio, to the skies,
That I may form a starry crown
Beyond what Helicon supplies
In laureate garlands of renown;
To nobler worth be brighter glory giv'n, 5
And to a heav'nly mind a recompense from heav'n.

Time's wasteful hunger cannot prey
On everlasting high desert,
Nor can Oblivion steal away,
Its record graven on the heart;
Lodge but an arrow, Virtue, on the bow
That binds my lyre, and Death shall be a vanquish'd foe. 12

In Ocean's blazing flood enshrin'd
Whose vassal tide around her swells,
Albion from other realms disjoin'd
The prowess of the world excells,
She teems with heroes, that to glory rise, 17
With more than human force in our astonish'd eyes.

To Virtue, driv'n from other lands,
Their bosoms yield a safe retreat;
Her law alone their deed commands;
Her smiles they feel divinely sweet.
Confirm this record, Milton, gen'rous youth! 23
And by true virtue prove thy virtue's praise a truth.

Zeuxis, all energy and flame,
Set ardent forth in his career;
Urged to his task by Helen's fame
Resounding ever in his ear;
To make his image to her beauty true,
From the collected Fair each sov'reign charm he drew. 30

The bee with subtlest skill endued
Thus toils to earn her precious juice
From all the flow'ry myriads strew'd
O'er meadow and parterre, profuse;
Confed'rate voices one sweet air compound, 35
And various chords consent in one harmonious sound

An artist of celestial aim,
Thy genius, caught by moral grace,
With ardent emulation's flame
The steps of Virtue toil'd to trace,

Observ'd in ev'ry land who brightest shone,
And blending all their best, made perfect good thy
own. 42

From all, in Florence born, or taught
Our country's sweetest accent there,
Whose works, with learned labour wrought,
Immortal honours justly share,
Thou hast such treasure drawn of purest ore, 47
That not e'en Tuscan bards can boast a richer store.

Babel confus'd, and with her tow'rs
Unfinish'd spreading wide the plain,
Has serv'd but to evince thy pow'rs
With all her tongues confus'd in vain,
Since not alone thy England's purest phrase 53
But ev'ry polish'd realm thy various speech displays.

The secret things of heav'n and earth
By Nature, too reserv'd, conceal'd
From other minds of highest worth,
To thee are copiously reveal'd;
Thou know'st them clearly, and thy views attain
The utmost bounds prescrib'd to moral Truth's
domain. 60

Let Time no more his wing display,
And boast his ruinous career,
For virtue rescued from his sway
His injuries may cease to fear;
Since all events, that claim remembrance, find
A chronicle exact in thy capacious mind. 66

Give me, that I may praise thy song,
Thy lyre, by which alone I can,
Which, placing thee the stars among,
Already proves thee more than man;
And Thames shall seem Permessus, while his
stream,
Graced with a swan like thee, shall be my fav'rite
theme. 72

I, who beside the Arno strain
To match thy merit with my lays,
Learn, after many an effort vain,
T' admire thee rather than to praise,
And that by mute astonishment alone,
Not by the falt'ring tongue, thy worth may best be
shown. 78

TO MR. JOHN MILTON OF LONDON,

A youth eminent from his country and his virtues,

WHO in his travels has made himself acquainted with many nations, and in his studies, with all; that, like another Ulysses, he might learn all that all could teach him;

Skilful in many tongues, on whose lips languages now mute so live again, that the idioms of all are insufficient to his praise; happy acquisition by which he understands the universal admiration and applause his talents have excited;

Whose endowments of mind and person move us to wonder, but at the same time fix us immoveable; whose works prompt us to extol him, but by their beauty strike us mute;

In whose memory the whole world is treasured; in whose intellect, wisdom; in whose heart, the ardent desire of glory; and in whose mouth, eloquence. Who with Astronomy for his conductor, hears the music of the spheres; with Philosophy for his teacher, decyphers the handwriting of God, in those wonders of creation which proclaim his greatness; and with the most unwearied literary Industry for his associate,

Examines, restores, penetrates with ease the obscurities of antiquity, the desolations of ages, and the labyrinths of learning;

"But wherefore toil to reach these arduous heights?"

To him, in short, whose virtues the mouths of Fame are too few to celebrate, and whom astonishment forbids us to praise as he deserves, this tribute due to his merits, and the offering of reverence and affection, is paid by

CARLO DATI,
A PATRICIAN FLORENTINE,
This great man's servant, and this good man's friend[1].

[1] These complimentary pieces have been sufficiently censured by a great authority, but no very candid judge either of Milton or his panegyrists. He, however, must have a heart sadly indifferent to the glory of his country, who is not gratified by the thought that she may exult in a son whom, young as he was, the Learned of Italy thus contended to honour [C.].

ELEGIES

ELEGY I

TO CHARLES DEODATI

At length, my friend, the far-sent letters come,
Charged with thy kindness, to their destin'd home,
They come, at length, from Deva's Western side,
Where prone she seeks the salt Vergivian tide.
Trust me, my joy is great that thou shouldst be,
Though born of foreign race, yet born for me,
And that my sprightly friend, now free to roam,
Must seek again so soon his wonted home.
I well content, where Thames with refluent tide
My native city laves, meantime reside, 10
Nor zeal nor duty, now, my steps impell
To reedy Cam, and my forbidden cell.
Nor aught of pleasure in those fields have I,
That, to the musing bard, all shade deny.
'Tis time that I a pedant's threats disdain,
And fly from wrongs, my soul will ne'er sustain.
If peaceful days, in letter'd leisure spent,
Beneath my father's roof, be banishment,
Then call me banish'd, I will ne'er refuse
A name expressive of the lot I chuse. 20
I would, that, exiled to the Pontic shore,
Rome's hapless bard had suffer'd nothing more.
He then had equall'd even Homer's lays,
And Virgil! thou hadst won but second praise:
For here I woo the muse, with no controul;
And here my books—my life—absorb me whole.
Here too I visit, or to smile, or weep,
The winding theatre's majestic sweep;
The grave or gay colloquial scene recruits
My spirits, spent in learning's long pursuits; 30
Whether some senior shrewd, or spendthrift heir,
Suitor, or soldier, now unarm'd, be there,
Or some coif'd brooder o'er a ten years' cause,
Thunder the Norman gibb'rish of the laws.
The lacquey, there, oft dupes the wary sire,
And, artful, speeds th' enamour'd son's desire.
There, virgins oft, unconscious what they prove,
What love is, know not, yet, unknowing, love.
Or, if impassion'd Tragedy wield high
The bloody sceptre, give her locks to fly 40
Wild as the winds, and roll her haggard eye,
I gaze, and grieve, still cherishing my grief,
At times, e'en bitter tears yield sweet relief.

As when from bliss untasted torn away,
Some youth dies, hapless, on his bridal day,
Or when the ghost, sent back from shades below,
Fills the assassin's heart with vengeful woe,
When Troy, or Argos, the dire scene affords,
Or Creon's hall laments its guilty lords.
Nor always city-pent, or pent at home, 50
I dwell; but, when spring calls me forth to roam,
Expatiate in our proud suburban shades
Of branching elm, that never sun pervades.
Here many a virgin troop I may descry,
Like stars of mildest influence, gliding by.
Oh forms divine! Oh looks that might inspire
E'en Jove himself, grown old, with young desire!
Oft have I gazed on gem-surpassing eyes,
Outsparkling every star, that gilds the skies.
Necks whiter than the ivory arm bestow'd 60
By Jove on Pelops, or the milky road!
Bright locks, Love's golden snare! these falling low,
Those playing wanton o'er the graceful brow!
Cheeks too, more winning sweet than after show'r
Adonis turn'd to Flora's fav'rite flow'r!
Yield, heroines, yield, and ye who shar'd th' embrace
Of Jupiter in antient times, give place!
Give place, ye turban'd fair of Persia's coast!
And ye, not less renown'd, Assyria's boast!
Submit, ye nymphs of Greece! ye, once the bloom 70
Of Ilion! and all ye, of haughty Rome,
Who swept, of old, her theatres with trains
Redundant, and still live in classic strains!
To British damsels beauty's palm is due,
Aliens! to follow them is fame for you.
Oh city, founded by Dardanian hands,
Whose towering front the circling realm commands,
Too blest abode! no loveliness we see
In all the earth, but it abounds in thee.
The virgin multitude that daily meets, 80
Radiant with gold and beauty, in thy streets,
Outnumbers all her train, of starry fires,
With which Diana gilds thy lofty spires.
Fame says, that wafted hither by her doves,
With all her host of quiver-bearing loves,
Venus, preferring Paphian scenes no more,
Has fix'd her empire on thy nobler shore.
But lest the sightless boy inforce my stay,
I leave these happy walls, while yet I may.
Immortal Moly shall secure my heart 90
From all the sorc'ry of Circæan art,

And I will e'en repass Cam's reedy pools
To face once more the warfare of the schools.
Meantime accept this trifle! rhimes though few,
Yet such, as prove thy friend's remembrance true!

ELEGY II

ON THE DEATH OF THE UNIVERSITY BEADLE AT CAMBRIDGE

Composed by Milton in the seventeenth year of his age.

THEE, whose refulgent staff, and summons clear,
  Minerva's flock long time was wont t' obey,
Although thyself an herald, famous here,
  The last of heralds, Death, has snatch'd away.
He calls on all alike, nor even deigns
To spare the office, that himself sustains. 6

Thy locks were whiter than the plumes display'd
  By Leda's paramour in antient time,
But thou wast worthy ne'er to have decay'd,
  Or Æson-like to know a second prime,
Worthy, for whom some goddess should have won
New life, oft kneeling to Apollo's son. 12

Commission'd to convene, with hasty call,
  The gowned tribes, how graceful wouldst thou stand!
So stood Cyllenius erst in Priam's hall,
  Wing-footed messenger of Jove's command!
And so Eurybates, when he address'd
To Peleus' son Atrides' proud behest. 18

Dread queen of sepulchres! whose rig'rous laws
  And watchful eyes, run through the realms below,
Oh, oft too adverse to Minerva's cause!
  Too often to the muse not less a foe!
Chuse meaner marks, and with more equal aim
Pierce useless drones, earth's burthen, and its shame!

Flow, therefore, tears for him, from ev'ry eye, 25
  All ye disciples of the muses, weep!
Assembling, all, in robes of sable dye,
  Around his bier, lament his endless sleep!
And let complaining elegy rehearse,
In every school, her sweetest, saddest verse. 30

95 friends' *1808*.
Elegy II—9 was't *1808*. 18 Atrides *1808*.

ELEGY III
ON THE
DEATH OF THE BISHOP OF WINCHESTER

Composed in the Author's seventeenth year.

SILENT I sat, dejected, and alone,
Making, in thought, the public woes my own,
When, first, arose the image in my breast
Of England's sufferings by that scourge, the Pest!
How death, his fun'ral torch and scythe in hand,
Entering the lordliest mansions of the land,
Has laid the gem-illumin'd palace low,
And levell'd tribes of nobles, at a blow.
I, next, deplor'd the fam'd fraternal pair,
Too soon to ashes turn'd, and empty air! 10
The heroes next, whom snatch'd into the skies,
All Belgia saw, and follow'd with her sighs,
But thee far most I mourn'd, regretted most,
Winton's chief shepherd, and her worthiest boast!
Pour'd out in tears I thus complaining said:
"Death, next in pow'r to him, who rules the dead!
Is't not enough that all the woodlands yield
To thy fell force, and ev'ry verdant field;
That lilies, at one noisome blast of thine,
And ev'n the Cyprian queen's own roses, pine; 20
That oaks themselves, although the running rill
Suckle their roots, must wither at thy will;
That all the winged nations, even those,
Whose heav'n-directed flight the future shows,
And all the beasts, that in dark forests stray,
And all the herds of Proteus are thy prey.
Ah envious! arm'd with pow'rs so unconfin'd!
Why stain thy hands with blood of human kind?
Why take delight, with darts, that never roam,
To chase a heav'n-born spirit from her home?" 30
While thus I mourn'd, the star of evening stood,
Now newly ris'n above the western flood,
And Phœbus from his morning-goal again
Had reach'd the gulphs of the Iberian main.
I wish'd repose, and, on my couch reclin'd
Took early rest, to night and sleep resign'd.
When—Oh for words to paint what I beheld!
I seem'd to wander in a spacious field,
Where all the champaign glow'd with purple light
Like that of sun-rise on the mountain height; 40
Flow'rs over all the field, of ev'ry hue
That ever Iris wore, luxuriant grew.

9 paternal *1808*: fraternal *in notes.*

Nor Chloris, with whom am'rous Zephyrs play,
E'er dress'd Alcinous' garden half so gay.
A silver current, like the Tagus, roll'd
O'er golden sands, but sands of purer gold,
With dewy airs Favonius fann'd the flow'rs,
With airs awaken'd under rosy bow'rs.
Such, poets feign, irradiated all o'er
The sun's abode on India's utmost shore. 50
While I, that splendour, and the mingled shade
Of fruitful vines, with wonder fixt survey'd,
At once, with looks, that beam'd celestial grace,
The seer of Winton stood before my face.
His snowy vesture's hem descending low
His golden sandals swept, and pure as snow
New-fallen shone the mitre on his brow.
Where'er he trod a tremulous sweet sound
Of gladness shook the flow'ry scene around:
Attendant angels clap their starry wings, 60
The trumpet shakes the sky, all æther rings,
Each chaunts his welcome, folds him to his breast,
And thus a sweeter voice than all the rest:
"Ascend, my son! thy father's kingdom share!
My son! henceforth be free'd from ev'ry care!"
So spake the voice, and at its tender close
With psaltry's sound th' angelic band arose.
Then night retired, and chas'd by dawning day
The visionary bliss pass'd all away.
I mourn'd my banish'd sleep, with fond concern;
Frequent to me may dreams like this return! 71

ELEGY IV

TO HIS TUTOR, THOMAS YOUNG,

CHAPLAIN TO THE ENGLISH FACTORY AT HAMBURGH

Written in the Author's eighteenth year.

HENCE my epistle—skim the deep—fly o'er
Yon smooth expanse to the Teutonic shore!
Haste—lest a friend should grieve for thy delay—
And the Gods grant, that nothing thwart thy way!
I will myself invoke the king, who binds,
In his Sicanian echoing vault, the winds,
With Doris and her nymphs, and all the throng
Of azure gods, to speed thee safe along.
But rather, to insure thy happier haste,
Ascend Medea's chariot, if thou may'st; 10
Or that, whence young Triptolemus of yore
Descended, welcome on the Scythian shore.

The sands, that line the German coast, descried,
To opulent Hamburga turn aside!
So called, if legendary fame be true,
From Hama, whom a club-arm'd Cimbrian slew!
There lives, deep-learn'd and primitively just,
A faithful steward of his Christian trust,
My friend, and favorite inmate of my heart,
That now is forced to want its better part! 20
What mountains now, and seas, alas! how wide!
From me this other, dearer self divide,
Dear, as the sage renown'd for moral truth
To the prime spirit of the Attic youth!
Dear, as the Stagyrite to Ammon's son,
His pupil, who disdain'd the world he won!
Nor so did Chiron, or so Phœnix shine
In young Achilles' eyes, as he in mine.
First led by him thro' sweet Aonian shade,
Each sacred haunt of Pindus I survey'd; 30
And favor'd by the muse, whom I implor'd,
Thrice on my lip the hallow'd stream I pour'd.
But thrice the sun's resplendent chariot roll'd
To Aries, has new ting'd his fleece with gold,
And Chloris twice has dress'd the meadows gay,
And twice has summer parch'd their bloom away,
Since last delighted on his looks I hung,
Or my ear drank the music of his tongue:
Fly, therefore, and surpass the tempest's speed!
Aware thyself, that there is urgent need! 40
Him, entering, thou shalt haply seated see
Beside his spouse, his infants on his knee;
Or turning, page by page, with studious look,
Some bulky father, or God's holy book;
Or minist'ring (which is his weightiest care)
To Christ's assembled flock their heavenly fare.
Give him, whatever his employment be,
Such gratulation, as he claims from me!
And, with a down-cast eye, and carriage meek,
Addressing him, forget not thus to speak! 50
"If, compass'd round with arms thou canst attend
To verse, verse greets thee from a distant friend.
Long due, and late, I left the English shore;
But make me welcome for that cause the more:
Such from Ulysses, his chaste wife to cheer,
The slow epistle came, tho' late, sincere.
But wherefore this? why palliate I the deed,
For which the culprit's self could hardly plead?

19 innate *1808*.

Self-charged, and self-condemn'd, his proper part
He feels neglected, with an aching heart; 60
But thou forgive—delinquents, who confess
And pray forgiveness, merit anger less;
From timid foes the lion turns away,
Nor yawns upon or rends a crouching prey;
Even pike-wielding Thracians learn to spare,
Won by soft influence of a suppliant prayer;
And heav'n's dread thunderbolt arrested stands
By a cheap victim, and uplifted hands.
Long had he wish'd to write, but was withheld,
And writes at last, by love alone compell'd; 70
For fame, too often true, when she alarms,
Reports thy neighbouring-fields a scene of arms;
Thy city against fierce besiegers barr'd,
And all the Saxon chiefs for fight prepar'd.
Enyo wastes thy country wide around,
And saturates with blood the tainted ground;
Mars rests contented in his Thrace no more,
But goads his steeds to fields of German gore,
The ever verdant olive fades and dies,
And peace, the trumpet-hating goddess, flies, 80
Flies from that earth which justice long had
left,
And leaves the world of its last guard bereft.
Thus horror girds thee round. Meantime alone
Thou dwell'st, and helpless in a soil unknown;
Poor, and receiving from a foreign hand
The aid denied thee in thy native land.
Oh, ruthless country, and unfeeling more
Than thy own billow-beaten chalky shore!
Leav'st thou to foreign care the worthies, giv'n
By providence, to guide thy steps to Heav'n? 90
His ministers, commission'd to proclaim
Eternal blessings in a Saviour's name!
Ah then most worthy, with a soul unfed,
In Stygian night to lie for ever dead!
So once the venerable Tishbite stray'd
An exil'd fugitive from shade to shade,
When, flying Ahab, and his fury wife,
In lone Arabian wilds, he shelter'd life;
So, from Philippi, wander'd forth forlorn
Cilician Paul, with sounding scourges torn; 100
And Christ himself, so left, and trod no more,
The thankless Gergesenes' forbidden shore.
But thou take courage! strive against despair!
Quake not with dread, nor nourish anxious care!

102 Gergesene's *1808*, *text*: Gergesenes *notes*.

Grim war indeed on ev'ry side appears,
And thou art menac'd by a thousand spears;
Yet none shall drink thy blood, or shall offend
Ev'n the defenceless bosom of my friend.
For thee the Ægis of thy God shall hide,
Jehovah's self shall combat on thy side. 110
The same, who vanquish'd under Sion's tow'rs
At silent midnight, all Assyria's pow'rs;
The same who overthrew in ages past,
Damascus' sons that lay'd Samaria waste;
Their king he fill'd and them with fatal fears
By mimic sounds of clarions in their ears,
Of hoofs, and wheels, and neighings from afar,
Of clashing armour, and the din of war.
Thou, therefore, (as the most afflicted may)
Still hope, and triumph, o'er thy evil day! 120
Look forth, expecting happier times to come,
And to enjoy, once more, thy native home!

ELEGY V

ON THE APPROACH OF SPRING

Written in the Author's twentieth year.

TIME, never wand'ring from his annual round,
Bids Zephyr breathe the spring, and thaw the ground;
Bleak winter flies, new verdure clothes the plain,
And earth assumes her transient youth again.
Dream I, or also to the spring belong
Increase of genius, and new pow'rs of song?
Spring gives them, and, how strange soe'er it seems,
Impels me now to some harmonious themes.
Castalia's fountain, and the forked hill
By day, by night, my raptur'd fancy fill, 10
My bosom burns and heaves, I hear within
A sacred sound, that prompts me to begin.
Lo! Phœbus comes, with his bright hair he blends
The radiant laurel wreath; Phœbus descends;
I mount, and, undepress'd by cumb'rous clay,
Through cloudy regions win my easy way;
Rapt through poetic shadowy haunts I fly:
The shrines all open to my dauntless eye,
My spirit searches all the realms of light,
And no Tartarean gulphs elude my sight. 20
But this ecstatic trance—this glorious storm
Of inspiration—what will it perform?
Spring claims the verse, that with his influence glows,
And shall be paid with what himself bestows.

110 Jehova's *1808*.

Thou, veil'd with op'ning foliage, lead'st the throng
Of feather'd minstrels, Philomel! in song;
Let us, in concert, to the season sing,
Civic, and sylvan heralds of the spring!
With notes triumphant spring's approach declare!
To spring, ye Muses, annual tribute bear! 30
The Orient left, and Æthiopia's plains,
The Sun now northward turns his golden reins;
Night creeps not now; yet rules with gentle sway,
And drives her dusky horrors swift away;
Now less fatigued, on his ætherial plain
Bootes follows his celestial wain;
And now the radiant centinels above,
Less num'rous, watch around the courts of Jove,
For, with the night, force, ambush, slaughter fly,
And no gigantic guilt alarms the sky. 40
Now haply says some shepherd, while he views,
Recumbent on a rock, the redd'ning dews,
This night, this surely, Phœbus miss'd the fair,
Who stops his chariot by her am'rous care.
Cynthia, delighted by the morning's glow,
Speeds to the woodland, and resumes her bow;
Resigns her beams, and, glad to disappear,
Blesses his aid, who shortens her career.
Come—Phœbus cries—Aurora come—too late
Thou linger'st, slumb'ring, with thy wither'd mate!
Leave him, and to Hymettus' top repair! 51
Thy darling Cephalus expects thee there.
The goddess, with a blush, her love betrays,
But mounts, and driving rapidly, obeys.
Earth now desires thee, Phœbus! and t' engage
Thy warm embrace, casts off the guise of age;
Desires thee, and deserves; for who so sweet,
When her rich bosom courts thy genial heat?
Her breath imparts to ev'ry breeze that blows,
Arabia's harvest, and the Paphian rose. 60
Her lofty fronts she diadems around
With sacred pines, like Ops on Ida crown'd;
Her dewy locks, with various flow'rs new-blown,
She interweaves, various, and all her own,
For Proserpine, in such a wreath attired,
Tænarian Dis himself with love inspired.
Fear not, lest, cold and coy, the nymph refuse!
Herself, with all her sighing Zephyrs, sues;
Each courts thee, fanning soft his scented wing,
And all her groves with warbled wishes ring. 70

Nor, unendow'd and indigent, aspires
The am'rous Earth to engage thy warm desires,
But, rich in balmy drugs, assists thy claim,
Divine Physician! to that glorious name.
If splendid recompense, if gifts can move
Desire in thee (gifts often purchase love),
She offers all the wealth, her mountains hide,
And all that rests beneath the boundless tide.
How oft, when headlong from the heav'nly steep
She sees thee playing in the western deep, 80
How oft she cries—"Ah Phœbus! why repair
Thy wasted force, why seek refreshment there?
Can Tethys win thee? wherefore shouldst thou lave
A face so fair in her unpleasant wave?
Come, seek my green retreats, and rather chuse
To cool thy tresses in my chrystal dews,
The grassy turf shall yield thee sweeter rest;
Come, lay thy evening glories on my breast,
And breathing fresh, through many a humid rose,
Soft whispering airs shall lull thee to repose! 90
No fears I feel like Semele to die,
Nor let thy burning wheels approach too nigh,
For thou can'st govern them, here therefore rest,
And lay thy evening glories on my breast!"
Thus breathes the wanton Earth her am'rous flame,
And all her countless offspring feel the same;
For Cupid now through every region strays,
Bright'ning his faded fires with solar rays,
His new-strung bow sends forth a deadlier sound,
And his new-pointed shafts more deeply wound;
Nor Dian's self escapes him now untried, 101
Nor even Vesta at her altar-side;
His mother too repairs her beauty's wane,
And seems sprung newly from the deep again.
Exulting youths the Hymeneal sing,
With Hymen's name roofs, rocks, and vallies, ring;
He, new-attired, and by the season drest,
Proceeds, all fragrant, in his saffron vest.
Now, many a golden-cinctur'd virgin roves
To taste the pleasures of the fields and groves, 110
All wish, and each alike, some fav'rite youth
Hers, in the bonds of Hymeneal truth.
Now pipes the shepherd through his reeds again,
Nor Phillis wants a song, that suits the strain;
With songs the seaman hails the starry sphere,
And dolphins rise from the abyss to hear;

92 let] lest *Benham, perhaps rightly.*

Jove feels himself the season, sports again
With his fair spouse, and banquets all his train.
Now too the Satyrs, in the dusk of eve,
Their mazy dance through flowery meadows weave,
And neither god nor goat, but both in kind, 121
Sylvanus, wreath'd with cypress, skips behind.
The Dryads leave their hollow sylvan cells
To roam the banks, and solitary dells;
Pan riots now; and from his amorous chafe
Ceres and Cybele seem hardly safe,
And Faunus, all on fire to reach the prize,
In chase of some enticing Oread, flies;
She bounds before, but fears too swift a bound,
And hidden lies, but wishes to be found. 130
Our shades entice th' Immortals from above,
And some kind pow'r presides o'er every grove;
And long, ye pow'rs, o'er every grove preside,
For all is safe, and blest, where ye abide!
Return, O Jove! the age of gold restore—
Why choose to dwell, where storms and thunder
roar?
At least, thou, Phœbus! moderate thy speed!
Let not the vernal hours too swift proceed,
Command rough Winter back, nor yield the pole
Too soon to Night's encroaching, long controul! 140

ELEGY VI

TO CHARLES DEODATI

Who, while he spent his Christmas in the country, sent the Author a poetical epistle, in which he requested that his verses, if not so good as usual, might be excused on account of the many feasts, to which his friends invited him, and which would not allow him leisure to finish them, as he wished.

WITH no rich viands overcharg'd, I send
Health, which perchance you want, my pamper'd
friend;
But wherefore should thy muse tempt mine away
From what she loves, from darkness into day?
Art thou desirous to be told how well
I love thee, and in verse? verse cannot tell,
For verse has bounds, and must in measure move;
But neither bounds nor measure knows my love.
How pleasant, in thy lines describ'd, appear
December's harmless sports, and rural cheer! 10
French spirits kindling with cærulean fires,
And all such gambols, as the time inspires!
Think not that wine against good verse offends;
The Muse and Bacchus have been always friends,
Nor Phœbus blushes sometimes to be found
With ivy, rather than with laurel, crown'd.

The Nine themselves ofttimes have join'd the song,
And revels of the Bacchanalian throng;
Not even Ovid could in Scythian air
Sing sweetly—why? no vine would flourish there.
What in brief numbers sung Anacreon's muse? 21
Wine, and the rose, that sparkling wine bedews.
Pindar with Bacchus glows—his every line
Breathes the rich fragrance of inspiring wine,
While, with loud crash o'erturn'd, the chariot lies
And brown with dust the fiery courser flies.
The Roman lyrist steep'd in wine his lays
So sweet in Glycera's, and Chloe's praise.
Now too the plenteous feast, and mantling bowl
Nourish the vigour of thy sprightly soul; 30
The flowing goblet makes thy numbers flow,
And casks not wine alone, but verse, bestow.
Thus Phœbus favors, and the arts attend,
Whom Bacchus, and whom Ceres, both befriend.
What wonder then, thy verses are so sweet,
In which these triple powers so kindly meet.
The lute now also sounds, with gold in-wrought,
And touch'd, with flying fingers, nicely taught,
In tap'stried halls, high roof'd, the sprightly lyre
Directs the dancers of the virgin choir. 40
If dull repletion fright the Muse away,
Sights, gay as these, may more invite her stay;
And, trust me, while the iv'ry keys resound,
Fair damsels sport, and perfumes steam around,
Apollo's influence, like aethereal flame,
Shall animate, at once, thy glowing frame,
And all the Muse shall rush into thy breast,
By love and music's blended pow'rs possest.
For num'rous pow'rs light Elegy befriend,
Hear her sweet voice, and at her call attend; 50
Her, Bacchus, Ceres, Venus, all approve,
And, with his blushing mother, gentle Love.
Hence to such bards we grant the copious use
Of banquets, and the vine's delicious juice.
But they, who demi-gods, and heroes praise,
And feats perform'd in Jove's more youthful days,
Who now the counsels of high heaven explore,
Now shades, that echo the Cerberean roar,
Simply let these, like him of Samos live,
Let herbs to them a bloodless banquet give; 60
In beechen goblets let their bev'rage shine,
Cool from the chrystal spring, their sober wine!
Their youth should pass, in innocence, secure
From stain licentious, and in manners pure,

Pure as the priest, when rob'd in white he stands,
The fresh lustration ready in his hands.
Thus Linus liv'd, and thus, as poets write,
Tiresias, wiser for his loss of sight!
Thus exil'd Chalcas, thus the bard of Thrace,
Melodious tamer of the savage race! 70
Thus train'd by temp'rance, Homer led, of yore,
His chief of Ithaca from shore to shore,
Through magic Circe's monster-peopled reign,
And shoals insidious with the siren train;
And through the realms, where grizzly spectres dwell,
Whose tribes he fetter'd in a gory spell;
For these are sacred bards, and, from above,
Drink large infusions from the mind of Jove!
Would'st thou (perhaps 'tis hardly worth thine ear)
Would'st thou be told my occupation here? 80
The promised King of peace employs my pen,
Th' eternal cov'nant made for guilty men,
The new-born Deity with infant cries
Filling the sordid hovel, where he lies;
The hymning angels, and the herald star,
That led the Wise, who sought him from afar,
And idols on their own unhallow'd shore
Dash'd, at his birth, to be revered no more!
This theme on reeds of Albion I rehearse:
The dawn of that blest day inspired the verse; 90
Verse, that, reserv'd in secret, shall attend
Thy candid voice, my critic, and my friend!

ELEGY VII

Composed in the Author's nineteenth year.

As yet a stranger to the gentle fires,
That Amathusia's smiling queen inspires,
Not seldom I derided Cupid's darts,
And scorn'd his claim to rule all human hearts.
"Go, child," I said, "transfix the tim'rous dove!
An easy conquest suits an infant love;
Enslave the sparrow, for such prize shall be
Sufficient triumph to a chief like thee!
Why aim thy idle arms at human kind?
Thy shafts prevail not 'gainst the noble mind." 10
The Cyprian heard, and, kindling into ire,
(None kindles sooner) burn'd with double fire.
It was the spring, and newly risen day
Peep'd o'er the hamlets on the first of May;
My eyes too tender for the blaze of light,
Still sought the shelter of retiring night,
When Love approach'd, in painted plumes arrayed;
Th' insidious god his rattling darts betray'd,

Nor less his infant features, and the sly,
Sweet intimations of his threat'ning eye. 20
Such the Sigeian boy is seen above,
Filling the goblet for imperial Jove;
Such he, on whom the nymphs bestow'd their charms,
Hylas, who perish'd in a Naiad's arms.
Angry he seem'd, yet graceful in his ire,
And added threats, not destitute of fire.
"My power," he said, "by others' pain alone,
'Twere best to learn; now learn it by thy own!
With those, who feel my power, that power attest!
And in thy anguish be my sway confest! 30
I vanquish'd Phœbus, though returning vain
From his new triumph o'er the Python slain,
And, when he thinks on Daphne, even he
Will yield the prize of archery to me.
A dart less true the Parthian horseman sped,
Behind him kill'd, and conquer'd as he fled:
Less true th' expert Cydonian, and less true
The youth, whose shaft his latent Procris slew.
Vanquish'd by me see huge Orion bend,
By me Alcides, and Alcides' friend. 40
At me should Jove himself a bolt design,
His bosom first should bleed transfixt by mine.
But all thy doubts this shaft will best explain,
Nor shall it reach thee with a trivial pain;
Thy Muse, vain youth! shall not thy peace ensure,
Nor Phœbus' serpent yield thy wound a cure."
He spoke, and, waving a bright shaft in air,
Sought the warm bosom of the Cyprian fair.
That thus a child should bluster in my ear, 49
Provok'd my laughter, more than mov'd my fear.
I shunn'd not, therefore, public haunts, but stray'd
Careless in city, or suburban shade,
And passing, and repassing, nymphs, that mov'd
With grace divine, beheld where'er I rov'd.
Bright shone the vernal day, with double blaze,
As beauty gave new force to Phœbus' rays.
By no grave scruples check'd, I freely eyed
The dang'rous show, rash youth my only guide,
And many a look of many a fair unknown
Met full, unable to controul my own. 60
But one I mark'd (then peace forsook my breast)—
One—Oh how far superior to the rest!
What lovely features! such the Cyprian queen
Herself might wish, and Juno wish her mien.
The very nymph was she, whom when I dar'd
His arrows, Love had even then prepar'd!

27 others *1808.*

Nor was himself remote, nor unsupplied
With torch well-trimm'd and quiver at his side;
Now to her lips he clung, her eye-lids now,
Then settled on her cheeks, or on her brow. 70
And with a thousand wounds from ev'ry part
Pierced, and transpierced, my undefended heart.
A fever, new to me, of fierce desire
Now seiz'd my soul, and I was all on fire,
But she, the while, whom only I adore,
Was gone, and vanish'd, to appear no more.
In silent sadness I pursue my way;
I pause, I turn, proceed, yet wish to stay,
And while I follow her in thought, bemoan
With tears, my soul's delight so quickly flown. 80
When Jove had hurl'd him to the Lemnian coast,
So Vulcan sorrow'd for Olympus lost,
And so Oeclides, sinking into night,
From the deep gulf look'd up to distant light.
Wretch that I am, what hopes for me remain,
Who cannot cease to love, yet love in vain?
Oh could I once, once more behold the fair,
Speak to her, tell her, of the pangs I bear,
Perhaps she is not adamant, would show
Perhaps some pity at my tale of woe. 90
Oh inauspicious flame!—'tis mine to prove
A matchless instance of disastrous love.
Ah spare me, gentle pow'r!—If such thou be,
Let not thy deeds, and nature, disagree.
Spare me, and I will worship at no shrine
With vow and sacrifice, save only thine.
Now I revere thy fires, thy bow, thy darts:
Now own thee sov'reign of all human hearts.
Remove! no—grant me still this raging woe!
Sweet is the wretchedness, that lovers know: 100
But pierce hereafter (should I chance to see
One destin'd mine) at once both her, and me.

SUCH were the trophies, that, in earlier days,
By vanity seduc'd, I toil'd to raise,
Studious, yet indolent, and urg'd by youth,
That worst of teachers! from the ways of truth;
Till learning taught me, in his shady bow'r,
To quit love's servile yoke, and spurn his pow'r.
Then, on a sudden, the fierce flame suppress,
A frost continual settled on my breast, 110
Whence Cupid fears his flames extinct to see,
And Venus dreads a Diomede in me.

EPIGRAMS[1]

ON THE INVENTOR OF GUNS

PRAISE in old times the sage Prometheus won,
Who stole æthereal radiance from the sun;
But greater he, whose bold invention strove
To emulate the fiery bolts of Jove. 4

TO LEONORA SINGING AT ROME[2]

ANOTHER Leonora once inspir'd
Tasso, with fatal love to phrenzy fir'd,
But how much happier, liv'd he now, were he,
Pierc'd with whatever pangs for love of thee!
Since could he hear that heavenly voice of thine,
With Adriana's lute of sound divine,
Fiercer than Pentheus' tho' his eye might roll,
Or idiot apathy benumb his soul,
You still, with medicinal sounds, might cheer
His senses wandering in a blind career; 10
And sweetly breathing thro' his wounded breast,
Charm, with soul-soothing song, his thoughts to rest.

TO THE SAME

NAPLES, too credulous, ah! boast no more
The sweet-voic'd Siren buried on thy shore,
That, when Parthenope deceas'd, she gave
Her sacred dust to a Chalcidic grave,
For still she lives, but has exchang'd the hoarse
Pausilipo for Tiber's placid course,
Where, idol of all Rome, she now in chains,
Of magic song, both gods, and men, detains. 8

THE COTTAGER AND HIS LANDLORD

A FABLE

A peasant to his lord pay'd yearly court,
Presenting pippins, of so rich a sort
That he, displeas'd to have a part alone,
Remov'd the tree, that all might be his own.

[1] The Poems on the subject of the Gunpowder Treason I have not translated, both because the matter of them is unpleasant, and because they are written with an asperity, which, however it might be warranted in Milton's day, would be extremely unseasonable now [C.].

[2] I have translated only two of the three poetical compliments addressed to Leonora, as they appear to me far superior to what I have omitted [C.].

To the same—6 Pansilipo *1808, text*: Pausilipo *in notes.*

The tree, too old to travel, though before
So fruitful, wither'd, and would yield no more.
The 'squire, perceiving all his labour void,
Curs'd his own pains, so foolishly employ'd,
And "Oh," he cried, "that I had liv'd content
With tribute, small indeed, but kindly meant! 10
My av'rice has expensive prov'd to me,
Has cost me both my pippins, and my tree."

TO CHRISTINA, QUEEN OF SWEDEN

WITH CROMWELL'S PICTURE

CHRISTINA, maiden of heroic mien!
Star of the North! of northern stars the queen!
Behold what wrinkles I have earn'd, and how
The iron casque still chafes my vet'ran brow,
While following fate's dark footsteps, I fulfil
The dictates of a hardy people's will.
But soften'd, in thy sight, my looks appear,
Not to all Queens or Kings alike severe. 8

MISCELLANEOUS POEMS

ON THE DEATH OF THE VICE-CHANCELLOR

A PHYSICIAN

LEARN, ye nations of the earth,
The condition of your birth,
Now be taught your feeble state!
Know, that all must yield to fate!

If the mournful rover, Death,
Say but once—"resign your breath!"
Vainly of escape you dream,
You must pass the Stygian stream. 8

Could the stoutest overcome
Death's assault, and baffle doom,
Hercules had both withstood,
Undiseas'd by Nessus' blood.

Ne'er had Hector press'd the plain
By a trick of Pallas slain,
Nor the chief to Jove allied
By Achilles' phantom died. 16

Could enchantments life prolong,
Circe, sav'd by magic song,
Still had liv'd, and equal skill
Had preserv'd Medea still.

Dwelt in herbs, and drugs, a pow'r
To avert man's destin'd hour,
Learn'd Machaon should have known
Doubtless to avert his own. 24

Chiron had surviv'd the smart
Of the Hydra-tainted dart,
And Jove's bolt had been, with ease,
Foil'd by Asclepiades.

Thou too, sage! of whom forlorn
Helicon and Cirrha mourn,
Still had'st filled thy princely place,
Regent of the gowned race; 32

Had'st advanc'd to higher fame
Still, thy much-ennobled name,
Nor in Charon's skiff explor'd
The Tartarean gulph abhorr'd.

But resentful Proserpine,
Jealous of thy skill divine,
Snapping short thy vital thread
Thee too number'd with the dead. 40

Wise and good! untroubled be
The green turf, that covers thee!
Thence, in gay profusion, grow
All the sweetest flow'rs, that blow!

Pluto's consort bid thee rest!
Œacus pronounce thee blest!
To her home thy shade consign!
Make Elysium ever thine! 48

ON THE DEATH OF THE BISHOP OF ELY

Written in the Author's seventeenth year.

My lids with grief were tumid yet,
And still my sullied cheek was wet
With briny tears, profusely shed
For venerable Winton dead;
When Fame, whose tales of saddest sound
Alas! are ever truest found,
The news through all our cities spread
Of yet another mitred head
By ruthless fate to death consign'd,
Ely, the honour of his kind! 10
At once, a storm of passion heav'd
My boiling bosom, much I griev'd
But more I rag'd, at ev'ry breath
Devoting Death himself to death.

With less revenge did Naso teem,
When hated Ibis was his theme;
With less, Archilochus, denied
The lovely Greek, his promis'd bride.
  But lo! while thus I execrate,
Incens'd, the minister of fate, 20
Wond'rous accents, soft, yet clear,
Wafted on the gale I hear.
  "Ah, much deluded! lay aside
Thy threats, and anger misapplied!
Art not afraid with sounds like these
T' offend, where thou canst not appease?
Death is not (wherefore dream'st thou thus?)
The son of Night and Erebus:
Nor was of fell Erynnis born
On gulphs, where Chaos rules forlorn: 30
But sent from God; his presence leaves,
To gather home his ripen'd sheaves,
To call encumber'd souls away
From fleshly bonds to boundless day,
(As when the winged hours excite,
And summon forth the morning-light)
And each to convoy to her place
Before th' Eternal Father's face.
But not the Wicked—them, severe
Yet just, from all their pleasures here 40
He hurries to the realms below,
Terrific realms of penal woe!
Myself no sooner heard his call,
Than, scaping through my prison-wall,
I bade adieu to bolts and bars,
And soar'd, with angels, to the stars,
Like him of old, to whom 'twas giv'n
To mount, on fiery wheels, to Heav'n.
Bootes' waggon, slow with cold,
Appall'd me not; nor to behold 50
The sword, that vast Orion draws,
Or ev'n the Scorpion's horrid claws.
Beyond the Sun's bright orb I fly,
And, far beneath my feet, descry
Night's dread goddess, seen with awe,
Whom her winged dragons draw.
Thus, ever wond'ring at my speed,
Augmented still as I proceed,
I pass the planetary sphere,
The Milky Way—and now appear 60
Heav'n's chrystal battlements, her door
Of massy pearl, and em'rald floor.

But here I cease. For never can
The tongue of once a mortal man
In suitable description trace
The pleasures of that happy place;
Suffice it, that those joys divine
Are all, and all for ever, mine!"

NATURE UNIMPAIRED BY TIME

Ah, how the human mind wearies her self
With her own wand'rings, and, involv'd in gloom
Impenetrable, speculates amiss!
Measuring, in her folly, things divine
By human; laws inscrib'd on adamant
By laws of man's device, and counsels fixt
For ever, by the hours, that pass, and die.
How?—shall the face of nature then be plough'd
Into deep wrinkles, and shall years at last
On the great Parent fix a sterile curse? 10
Shall even she confess old age, and halt
And, palsy-smitten, shake her starry brows?
Shall foul Antiquity with rust and drought,
And Famine, vex the radiant worlds above?
Shall Time's unsated maw crave and ingulph
The very Heav'ns, that regulate his flight?
And was the Sire of all able to fence
His works, and to uphold the circling worlds,
But, through improvident and heedless haste,
Let slip th' occasion?—so then—all is lost— 20
And in some future evil hour, yon arch
Shall crumble, and come thund'ring down, the poles
Jar in collision, the Olympian king
Fall with his throne, and Pallas, holding forth
The terrors of the Gorgon shield in vain,
Shall rush to the abyss, like Vulcan hurl'd
Down into Lemnos, through the gate of Heav'n.
Thou also, with precipitated wheels,
Phœbus, thy own son's fall shalt imitate,
With hideous ruin shalt impress the deep 30
Suddenly, and the flood shall reek, and hiss,
At the extinction of the lamp of day.
Then too, shall Hæmus, cloven to his base,
Be shattered, and the huge Ceraunian hills,
Once weapons of Tartarean Dis, immers'd
In Erebus, shall fill himself with fear.
No. The Almighty Father surer lay'd
His deep foundations, and providing well

1 now *1808*.

For the event of all, the scales of Fate
Suspended, in just equipoise, and bade 40
His universal works, from age to age,
One tenour hold, perpetual, undisturb'd.
Hence the Prime mover wheels itself about
Continual, day by day, and with it bears
In social measure swift the heav'ns around.
Not tardier now is Saturn than of old,
Nor radiant less the burning casque of Mars.
Phœbus, his vigour unimpair'd, still shows
Th' effulgence of his youth, nor needs the god
A downward course, that he may warm the vales; 50
But, ever rich in influence, runs his road,
Sign after sign, through all the heav'nly zone.
Beautiful, as at first, ascends the star
From odorif'rous Ind, whose office is
To gather home betimes th' ethereal flock,
To pour them o'er the skies again at eve,
And to discriminate the night and day.
Still Cynthia's changeful horn waxes, and wanes,
Alternate, and with arms extended still,
She welcomes to her breast her brother's beams. 60
Nor have the elements deserted yet
Their functions: thunder with as loud a stroke
As erst, smites through the rocks, and scatters them.
The east still howls, still the relentless north
Invades the shudd'ring Scythian, still he breathes
The winter, and still rolls the storms along.
The king of ocean, with his wonted force,
Beats on Pelorus, o'er the deep is heard
The hoarse alarm of Triton's sounding shell,
Nor swim the monsters of th' Ægean sea 70
In shallows, or beneath diminish'd waves.
Thou too, thy antient vegetative power
Enjoy'st, O Earth! Narcissus still is sweet,
And, Phœbus! still thy favourite, and still
Thy fav'rite, Cytherea! both retain
Their beauty, nor the mountains, ore-enrich'd
For punishment of man, with purer gold
Teem'd ever, or with brighter gems the Deep.
Thus, in unbroken series, all proceeds;
And shall, till wide involving either pole, 80
And the immensity of yonder heav'n,
The final flames of destiny absorb
The world, consum'd in one enormous pyre!

46 Satan *1808*.

ON THE PLATONIC IDEA,

AS IT WAS UNDERSTOOD BY ARISTOTLE

YE sister pow'rs, who o'er the sacred groves
Preside, and thou, fair mother of them all,
Mnemosyne! and thou, who in thy grot
Immense reclin'd at leisure, hast in charge
The archives, and the ord'nances of Jove,
And dost record the festivals of heav'n,
Eternity!—Inform us who is He,
That great original by nature chos'n
To be the archetype of human kind,
Unchangeable, immortal, with the poles 10
Themselves coæval, one, yet ev'ry where,
An image of the god, who gave him being?
Twin-brother of the goddess born from Jove,
He dwells not in his father's mind, but, though
Of common nature with ourselves, exists
Apart, and occupies a local home.
Whether, companion of the stars, he spend
Eternal ages, roaming at his will
From sphere to sphere the tenfold heav'ns, or dwell
On the moon's side, that nearest neighbours earth;
Or torpid on the banks of Lethe sit 21
Among the multitude of souls ordain'd
To flesh and blood, or whether (as may chance)
That vast and giant model of our kind
In some far distant region of this globe
Sequester'd stalk, with lifted head on high
O'ertow'ring Atlas, on whose shoulders rest
The stars, terrific even to the gods.
Never the Theban seer, whose blindness prov'd
His best illumination, him beheld 30
In secret vision; never him the son
Of Pleione, amid the noiseless night
Descending, to the prophet-choir reveal'd;
Him never knew th' Assyrian priest, who yet
The ancestry of Ninus chronicles,
And Belus, and Osiris far-renown'd;
Nor even thrice great Hermes, although skill'd
So deep in myst'ry, to the worshippers
Of Isis show'd a prodigy like him.
And thou, who hast immortaliz'd the shades 40
Of Academus, if the schools receiv'd
This monster of the fancy first from thee,
Either recall at once the banish'd bards
To thy republic, or thyself evinc'd
A wilder fabulist, go also forth.

TO HIS FATHER

OH that Pieria's spring would thro' my breast
Pour its inspiring influence, and rush
No rill, but rather an o'erflowing flood!
That, for my venerable Father's sake
All meaner themes renounc'd, my muse, on wings
Of duty borne, might reach a loftier strain.
For thee, my Father! howsoe'er it please,
She frames this slender work, nor know I aught,
That may thy gifts more suitably requite;
Though to requite them suitably would ask 10
Returns much nobler, and surpassing far
The meagre stores of verbal gratitude:
But, such as I possess, I send thee all.
This page presents thee in their full amount
With thy son's treasures, and the sum is nought;
Nought, save the riches that from airy dream
In secret grottos, and in laurel bow'rs,
I have, by golden Clio's gift, acquir'd.
Verse is a work divine; despise not thou
Verse therefore, which evinces (nothing more) 20
Man's heav'nly source, and which, retaining still
Some scintillations of Promethean fire,
Bespeaks him animated from above.
The Gods love verse; th' infernal Pow'rs them selves
Confess the influence of verse, which stirs
The lowest deep, and binds in triple chains
Of adamant both Pluto and the Shades.
In verse the Delphic priestess, and the pale
Tremulous Sybil, make the future known,
And he who sacrifices, on the shrine 30
Hangs verse, both when he smites the threat'ning bull,
And when he spreads his reeking entrails wide
To scrutinize the Fates invelop'd there.
We too, ourselves, what time we seek again
Our native skies, and one eternal now
Shall be the only measure of our being,
Crown'd all with gold, and chaunting to the lyre
Harmonious verse, shall range the courts above,
And make the starry firmament resound.
And, even now, the fiery spirit pure 40
That wheels yon circling orbs, directs, himself,
Their mazy dance with melody of verse
Unutt'rable, immortal, hearing which
Huge Ophiuchus holds his hiss suppress'd,

Orion soften'd, drops his ardent blade,
And Atlas stands unconscious of his load.
Verse grac'd of old the feasts of kings, ere yet
Luxurious dainties, destin'd to the gulph
Immense of gluttony, were known, and ere
Lyæus delug'd yet the temp'rate board. 50
Then sat the bard a customary guest
To share the banquet, and, his length of locks
With beechen honours bound, propos'd in verse
The characters of heroes, and their deeds,
To imitation, sang of Chaos old,
Of nature's birth, of gods that crept in search
Of acorns fall'n, and of the thunder bolt
Not yet produc'd from Etna's fiery cave.
And what avails, at last, tune without voice,
Devoid of matter? Such may suit perhaps 60
The rural dance, but such was ne'er the song
Of Orpheus, whom the streams stood still to hear,
And the oaks follow'd. Not by chords alone
Well touch'd, but by resistless accents more
To sympathetic tears the ghosts themselves
He mov'd: these praises to his verse he owes.
  Nor thou persist, I pray thee, still to slight
The sacred Nine, and to imagine vain
And useless, pow'rs, by whom inspir'd, thyself
Art skilful to associate verse with airs 70
Harmonious, and to give the human voice
A thousand modulations, heir by right
Indisputable of Arion's fame.
Now say, what wonder is it, if a son
Of thine delight in verse, if so conjoin'd
In close affinity, we sympathize
In social arts, and kindred studies sweet?
Such distribution of himself to us
Was Phœbus' choice; thou hast thy gift, and I
Mine also, and between us we receive, 80
Father and son, the whole inspiring God.
  No! howsoe'er the semblance thou assume
Of hate, thou hatest not the gentle Muse,
My Father! for thou never bad'st me tread
The beaten path, and broad, that leads right on
To opulence, nor did'st condemn thy son
To the insipid clamours of the bar,
To laws voluminous, and ill observ'd;
But, wishing to enrich me more, to fill
My mind with treasure, led'st me far away 90
From city-din to deep retreats, to banks
And streams Aonian, and, with free consent,

Didst place me happy at Apollo's side.
I speak not now, on more important themes
Intent, of common benefits, and such
As nature bids, but of thy larger gifts
My Father! who, when I had open'd once
The stores of Roman rhetorick, and learn'd
The full-ton'd language of the eloquent Greeks,
Whose lofty music grac'd the lips of Jove, 100
Thyself didst counsel me to add the flow'rs,
That Gallia boasts, those too, with which the smooth
Italian his degen'rate speech adorns,
That witnesses his mixture with the Goth;
And Palestine's prophetic songs divine.
To sum the whole, whate'er the heav'n contains,
The earth beneath it, and the air between,
The rivers and the restless deep, may all
Prove intellectual gain to me, my wish
Concurring with thy will; science herself, 110
All cloud remov'd, inclines her beauteous head,
And offers me the lip, if, dull of heart,
I shrink not, and decline her gracious boon.
Go now, and gather dross, ye sordid minds,
That covet it; what could my Father more?
What more could Jove himself, unless he gave
His own abode, the heav'n, in which he reigns?
More eligible gifts than these were not
Apollo's to his son, had they been safe,
As they were insecure, who made the boy 120
The world's vice-luminary, bade him rule
The radiant chariot of the day, and bind
To his young brows his own all-dazzling wreath.
I therefore, although last and least, my place
Among the learned in the laurel grove
Will hold, and where the conqu'ror's ivy twines,
Henceforth exempt from the unletter'd throng
Profane, nor even to be seen by such.
Away, then, sleepless Care, Complaint away,
And, Envy, with thy "jealous leer malign!" 130
Nor let the monster Calumny shoot forth
Her venom'd tongue at me. Detested foes!
Ye all are impotent against my peace,
For I am privileg'd, and bear my breast
Safe, and too high, for your viperean wound.
But thou! my Father! since to render thanks
Equivalent, and to requite by deeds
Thy liberality, exceeds my power,
Suffice it, that I thus record thy gifts,
And bear them treasur'd in a grateful mind! 140

Ye too, the favourite pastime of my youth,
My voluntary numbers, if ye dare
To hope longevity, and to survive
Your master's funeral, not soon absorb'd
In the oblivious Lethæan gulph
Shall to futurity perhaps convey
This theme, and by these praises of my sire
Improve the Fathers of a distant age!

TO SALSILLUS,

A ROMAN POET, MUCH INDISPOSED

The original is written in a measure called *Scazon*, which signifies *limping*, and the measure is so denominated, because, though in other respects Iambic, it terminates with a Spondee, and has consequently a more tardy movement.

The reader will immediately see that this property of the Latin verse cannot be imitated in English [C.].

My halting Muse, that dragg'st by choice along
Thy slow, slow step, in melancholy song,
And lik'st that pace, expressive of thy cares,
Not less than Diopeia's sprightlier airs,
When, in the dance, she beats, with measur'd tread,
Heav'n's floor, in front of Juno's golden bed;
Salute Salsillus, who to verse divine
Prefers, with partial love, such lays as mine.
Thus writes that Milton then, who wafted o'er
From his own nest, on Albion's stormy shore, 10
Where Eurus, fiercest of th' Æolian band,
Sweeps, with ungovern'd rage, the blasted land,
Of late to more serene Ausonia came
To view her cities of illustrious name,
To prove, himself a witness of the truth,
How wise her elders, and how learn'd her youth.
Much good, Salsillus! and a body free
From all disease, that Milton asks for thee,
Who now endur'st the languor, and the pains,
That bile inflicts, diffus'd through all thy veins, 20
Relentless malady! not mov'd to spare
By thy sweet Roman voice, and Lesbian air!
Health, Hebe's sister, sent us from the skies,
And thou, Apollo, whom all sickness flies,
Pythius, or Pæan, or what name divine
Soe'er thou chuse, haste, heal a priest of thine!
Ye groves of Faunus, and ye hills, that melt
With vinous dews, where meek Evander dwelt!
If aught salubrious in your confines grow,
Strive which shall soonest heal your poet's woe, 30
That, render'd to the Muse he loves, again
He may enchant the meadows with his strain.

Numa, reclin'd in everlasting ease,
Amid the shade of dark embow'ring trees,
Viewing with eyes of unabated fire
His loved Ægeria, shall that strain admire:
So sooth'd, the tumid Tiber shall revere
The tombs of kings, nor desolate the year,
Shall curb his waters with a friendly rein, 39
And guide them harmless, till they meet the main.

TO GIOVANNI BATTISTA MANSO

MARQUIS OF VILLA

MILTON'S ACCOUNT OF MANSO

Giovanni Battista Manso, Marquis of Villa, is an Italian nobleman of the highest estimation among his countrymen, for genius, literature, and military accomplishments. To him Torquato Tasso addressed his Dialogues on Friendship, for he was much the friend of Tasso, who has also celebrated him among the other princes of his country, in his poem entitled, Gerusalemme Conquistata, book xx.

Fra cavalier magnanimi, e cortesi,
Risplende il Manso.

During the Author's stay at Naples, he received at the hands of the Marquis a thousand kind offices and civilities, and, desirous not to appear ungrateful, sent him this poem a short time before his departure from that city.

THESE verses also to thy praise the Nine,
Oh Manso! happy in that theme design,
For, Gallus and Mæcenas gone, they see
None such besides, or whom they love as thee,
And, if my verse may give the meed of fame,
Thine too shall prove an everlasting name.
Already such, it shines in Tasso's page
(For thou wast Tasso's friend) from age to age,
And, next, the Muse consign'd, (not unaware
How high the charge,) Marino to thy care, 10
Who, singing, to the nymphs, Adonis' praise,
Boasts thee the patron of his copious lays.
To thee alone the poet would entrust
His latest vows, to thee alone his dust;
And thou with punctual piety hast paid,
In labour'd brass, thy tribute to his shade.
Nor this contented thee—but lest the grave
Should aught absorb of their's, which thou could'st
save,
All future ages thou hast deign'd to teach
The life, lot, genius, character of each, 20
Eloquent as the Carian sage, who true
To his great theme, the life of Homer drew.

I, therefore, though a stranger youth, who come
Chill'd by rude blasts, that freeze my Northern
home,
Thee dear to Clio, confident proclaim,
And thine, for Phœbus' sake, a deathless name.
Nor thou, so kind, wilt view with scornful eye
A muse scarce rear'd beneath our sullen sky,
Who fears not, indiscreet as she is young,
To seek in Latium hearers of her song. 30
We too, where Thames with his unsullied waves
The tresses of the blue-hair'd Ocean laves,
Hear oft by night, or, slumb'ring, seem to hear,
O'er his wide stream, the swan's voice warbling clear,
And we could boast a Tityrus of yore,
Who trod, a welcome guest, your happy shore.
Yes—dreary as we own our Northern clime,
E'en we to Phœbus raise the polish'd rhyme,
We too serve Phœbus; Phœbus has receiv'd,
(If legends old may claim to be believ'd) 40
No sordid gifts from us, the golden ear,
The burnish'd apple, ruddiest of the year,
The fragrant crocus, and to grace his fane,
Fair damsels chosen from the Druid train;
Druids, our native bards in antient time,
Who gods and heroes prais'd in hallow'd rhyme!
Hence, often as the maids of Greece surround
Apollo's shrine with hymns of festive sound,
They name the virgins, who arriv'd of yore,
With British off'rings, on the Delian shore, 50
Loxo, from giant Corineus sprung,
Upis, on whose blest lips the future hung,
And Hecaerge, with the golden hair,
All deck'd with Pictish hues, and all with bosoms
bare.
Thou, therefore, happy sage, whatever clime
Shall ring with Tasso's praise in after-time,
Or with Marino's, shalt be known their friend,
And with an equal flight to fame ascend.
The world shall hear how Phœbus, and the Nine,
Were inmates once, and willing guests of thine. 60
Yet Phœbus, when of old constrain'd to roam
The earth, an exile from his heavenly home,
Enter'd, no willing guest, Admetus' door,
Though Hercules had ventur'd there before.
But gentle Chiron's cave was near, a scene
Of rural peace, cloth'd with perpetual green,
And thither, oft as respite he requir'd
From rustic clamours loud, the god retir'd.

There, many a time, on Peneus' bank reclin'd
At some oak's root, with ivy thick entwin'd, 70
Won by his hospitable friend's desire
He sooth'd his pains of exile with the lyre.
Then shook the hills, then trembled Peneus' shore,
Nor Oeta felt his load of forests more;
The upland elms descended to the plain,
And soften'd lynxes wonder'd at the strain.
Well may we think, O dear to all above!
Thy birth distinguish'd by the smile of Jove,
And that Apollo shed his kindliest pow'r,
And Maia's son, on that propitious hour, 80
Since only minds so born can comprehend
A poet's worth, or yield that worth a friend.
Hence, on thy yet unfaded cheek appears
The ling'ring freshness of thy greener years,
Hence, in thy front, and features, we admire
Nature unwither'd, and a mind entire.
Oh might so true a friend to me belong,
So skill'd to grace the votaries of song,
Should I recall hereafter into rhyme
The kings, and heroes of my native clime, 90
Arthur the chief, who even now prepares,
In subterraneous being, future wars,
With all his martial knights, to be restor'd,
Each to his seat, around the fed'ral board,
And Oh, if spirit fail me not, disperse
Our Saxon plund'rers, in triumphant verse!
Then, after all, when, with the past content,
A life I finish, not in silence spent,
Should he, kind mourner, o'er my death-bed bend,
I shall but need to say—"Be yet my friend!" 100
He, too, perhaps, shall bid the marble breathe
To honour me, and with the graceful wreath,
Or of Parnassus, or the Paphian isle,
Shall bind my brows,—but I shall rest the while.
Then also, if the fruits of Faith endure,
And Virtue's promis'd recompense be sure,
Borne to those seats, to which the blest aspire
By purity of soul, and virtuous fire,
These rites, as Fate permits, I shall survey
With eyes illumin'd by celestial day, 110
And, ev'ry cloud from my pure spirit driv'n,
Joy in the bright beatitude of Heav'n!

107 Borne] Born *1808*.

ON THE DEATH OF DAMON

THE ARGUMENT

Thyrsis and Damon, shepherds and neighbours, had always pursued the same studies, and had, from their earliest days, been united in the closest friendship. Thyrsis, while travelling for improvement, received intelligence of the death of Damon, and, after a time, returning and finding it true, deplores himself, and his solitary condition, in this poem.

By Damon is to be understood Charles Deodati, connected with the Italian city of Lucca by his father's side, in other respects an Englishman; a youth of uncommon genius, erudition, and virtue.

YE nymphs of Himera (for ye have shed
Erewhile for Daphnis, and for Hylas dead,
And over Bion's long-lamented bier,
The fruitless meed of many a sacred tear)
Now, through the villas lav'd by Thames, rehearse
The woes of Thyrsis in Sicilian verse,
What sighs he heav'd, and how with groans profound
He made the woods, and hollow rocks, resound,
Young Damon dead; nor even ceas'd to pour
His lonely sorrows at the midnight hour. 10
The green wheat twice had nodded in the ear,
And golden harvest twice enrich'd the year,
Since Damon's lips had gasp'd for vital air
The last, last time, nor Thyrsis yet was there;
For he, enamour'd of the Muse, remain'd
In Tuscan Fiorenza long detain'd,
But, stor'd at length with all, he wish'd to learn,
For his flock's sake now hasted to return,
And when the shepherd had resum'd his seat
At the elm's root, within his old retreat, 20
Then 'twas his lot, then, all his loss to know,
And, from his burthen'd heart, he vented thus his woe.
"Go, seek your home, my lambs; my thoughts are due
To other cares, than those of feeding you.
Alas! what deities shall I suppose
In heav'n, or earth, concern'd for human woes,
Since, Oh my Damon! their severe decree
So soon condemns me to regret of thee!
Depart'st thou thus, thy virtues unrepaid
With fame and honour, like a vulgar shade? 30
Let him forbid it, whose bright rod controuls,
And sep'rates sordid from illustrious souls,
Drive far the rabble, and to thee assign
A happier lot, with spirits worthy thine!

Go, seek your home, my lambs; my thoughts are due
To other cares, than those of feeding you.
Whate'er befall, unless by cruel chance
The wolf first give me a forbidding glance,
Thou shalt not moulder undeplor'd, but long
Thy praise shall dwell on ev'ry shepherd's tongue;
To Daphnis first they shall delight to pay, 41
And, after him, to thee the votive lay,
While Pales shall the flocks, and pastures, love,
Or Faunus to frequent the field, or grove;
At least, if antient piety and truth,
With all the learned labours of thy youth,
May serve thee aught, or to have left behind
A sorrowing friend, and of the tuneful kind.
Go, seek your home, my lambs; my thoughts are due
To other cares, than those of feeding you. 50
Yes, Damon! such thy sure reward shall be;
But ah, what doom awaits unhappy me?
Who, now, my pains and perils shall divide,
As thou wast wont, for ever at my side,
Both when the rugged frost annoy'd our feet,
And when the herbage all was parch'd with heat;
Whether the grim wolf's ravage to prevent,
Or the huge lion's, arm'd with darts we went?
Whose converse, now, shall calm my stormy day,
With charming song, who now beguile my way? 60
Go, seek your home, my lambs; my thoughts are due
To other cares, than those of feeding you.
In whom shall I confide? Whose counsel find
A balmy med'cine for my troubled mind?
Or whose discourse, with innocent delight,
Shall fill me now, and cheat the wint'ry night,
While hisses on my hearth the pulpy pear,
And black'ning chesnuts start and crackle there,
While storms abroad the dreary meadows whelm,
And the wind thunders thro' the neighb'ring elm. 70
Go, seek your home, my lambs; my thoughts are due
To other cares, than those of feeding you.
Or who, when summer suns their summit reach,
And Pan sleeps hidden by the shelt'ring beech,
When shepherds disappear, nymphs seek the sedge,
And the stretch'd rustic snores beneath the hedge,
Who then shall render me thy pleasant vein
Of Attic wit, thy jests, thy smiles, again?

Go, seek your home, my lambs; my thoughts are due
To other cares, than those of feeding you. 80
Where glens and vales are thickest overgrown
With tangled boughs, I wander now alone,
Till night descend, while blust'ring wind and show'r
Beat on my temples through the shatter'd bow'r.
Go, seek your home, my lambs; my thoughts are due
To other cares, than those of feeding you.
Alas! what rampant weeds now shame my fields,
And what a mildew'd crop the furrow yields!
My rambling vines, unwedded to the trees,
Bear shrivell'd grapes, my myrtles fail to please, 90
Nor please me more my flocks; they, slighted, turn
Their unavailing looks on me, and mourn.
Go, seek your home, my lambs; my thoughts are due
To other cares, than those of feeding you.
Ægon invites me to the hazel grove,
Amyntas, on the river's bank to rove,
And young Alphesibœus to a seat
Where branching elms exclude the mid-day heat.
'Here fountains spring—here mossy hillocks rise;'
'Here Zephyr whispers, and the stream replies.'—
Thus each persuades, but, deaf to ev'ry call, 101
I gain the thickets, and escape them all.
Go, seek your home, my lambs; my thoughts are due
To other cares, than those of feeding you.
Then Mopsus said, (the same who reads so well
The voice of birds, and what the stars foretell,
For he by chance had noticed my return)
'What means thy sullen mood, this deep concern?
Ah Thyrsis! thou art either craz'd with love,
Or some sinister influence from above; 110
Dull Saturn's influence oft the shepherds rue;
His leaden shaft oblique has pierc'd thee through.'
Go, go, my lambs, unpastur'd as ye are,
My thoughts are all now due to other care.
The nymphs amaz'd, my melancholy see,
And 'Thyrsis!' cry—'what will become of thee?
What would'st thou, Thyrsis? such should not appear
The brow of youth, stern, gloomy, and severe;
Brisk youth should laugh, and love—ah shun the fate
Of those, twice wretched mopes! who love too late!'
Go, go, my lambs, unpastur'd as ye are, 121
My thoughts are all now due to other care.

Ægle with Hyas came, to sooth my pain,
And Baucis' daughter, Dryope the vain,
Fair Dryope, for voice and finger neat
Known far and near, and for her self-conceit;
Chloris too came, whose cottage on the lands,
That skirt the Idumanian current, stands;
But all in vain they came, and but to see
Kind words, and comfortable, lost on me. 130
Go, go, my lambs, unpastur'd as ye are,
My thoughts are all now due to other care.
Ah blest indiff'rence of the playful herd,
None by his fellow chosen, or preferr'd!
No bonds of amity the flocks enthrall,
But each associates, and is pleas'd with all;
So graze the dappled deer in num'rous droves,
And all his kind alike the zebra loves;
The same law governs, where the billows roar,
And Proteus' shoals o'erspread the desert shore;
The sparrow, meanest of the feather'd race, 141
His fit companion finds in ev'ry place,
With whom he picks the grain, that suits him best,
Flirts here and there, and late returns to rest,
And whom if chance the falcon make his prey,
Or hedger with his well aim'd arrow slay,
For no such loss the gay survivor grieves;
New love he seeks, and new delight receives.
We only, an obdurate kind, rejoice,
Scorning all others, in a single choice, 150
We scarce in thousands meet one kindred mind,
And if the long-sought good at last we find,
When least we fear it, Death our treasure steals,
And gives our heart a wound, that nothing heals.
Go, go, my lambs, unpastur'd as ye are,
My thoughts are all now due to other care.
Ah, what delusion lur'd me from my flocks,
To traverse Alpine snows, and rugged rocks!
What need so great had I to visit Rome,
Now sunk in ruins, and herself a tomb? 160
Or, had she flourish'd still as when, of old,
For her sake Tityrus forsook his fold,
What need so great had I t' incur a pause
Of thy sweet intercourse for such a cause,
For such a cause to place the roaring sea,
Rocks, mountains, woods, between my friend and me?
Else, had I grasp'd thy feeble hand, compos'd
Thy decent limbs, thy drooping eye-lids clos'd,
And, at the last, had said—'Farewell—ascend—
Nor even in the skies forget thy friend!' 170

Go, go, my lambs, untended homeward fare,
My thoughts are all now due to other care.
Although well-pleas'd, ye tuneful Tuscan swains!
My mind the mem'ry of your worth retains,
Yet not your worth can teach me less to mourn
My Damon lost.—He too was Tuscan born,
Born in your Lucca, city of renown!
And wit possess'd, and genius, like your own.
Oh how elate was I, when stretch'd beside
The murm'ring course of Arno's breezy tide, 180
Beneath the poplar grove I pass'd my hours,
Now cropping myrtles, and now vernal flow'rs,
And hearing, as I lay at ease along,
Your swains contending for the prize of song!
I also dar'd attempt (and, as it seems,
Not much displeas'd attempting) various themes,
For even I can presents boast from you,
The shepherd's pipe, and ozier basket too,
And Dati, and Francini, both have made
My name familiar to the beechen shade, 190
And they are learn'd, and each in ev'ry place
Renown'd for song, and both of Lydian race.
Go, go, my lambs, untended homeward fare,
My thoughts are all now due to other care.
While bright the dewy grass with moon-beams shone,
And I stood hurdling in my kids alone,
How often have I said (but thou had'st found
Ere then thy dark cold lodgment under ground)
Now Damon sings, or springes sets for hares,
Or wicker work for various use prepares! 200
How oft, indulging fancy, have I plann'd
New scenes of pleasure, that I hop'd at hand,
Call'd thee abroad as I was wont, and cried—
What hoa! my friend—come, lay thy task aside,
Haste, let us forth together, and beguile
The heat, beneath yon whisp'ring shades awhile,
Or on the margin stray of Colne's clear flood,
Or where Cassibelan's grey turrets stood!
There thou shalt cull me simples, and shalt teach
Thy friend the name, and healing pow'rs of each,
From the tall blue-bell to the dwarfish weed, 211
What the dry land, and what the marshes breed,
For all their kinds alike to thee are known,
And the whole art of Galen is thy own.
Ah, perish Galen's art, and wither'd be
The useless herbs, that gave not health to thee!
Twelve evenings since, as in poetic dream
I meditating sat some statelier theme,

The reeds no sooner touch'd my lip, though new,
And unassay'd before, than wide they flew, 220
Bursting their waxen bands, nor could sustain
The deep-ton'd music of the solemn strain;
And I am vain perhaps, but I will tell
How proud a theme I chose—ye groves farewell!
Go, go, my lambs, untended homeward fare,
My thoughts are all now due to other care.
Of Brutus, Dardan chief, my song shall be,
How with his barks he plough'd the British sea,
First from Rutupia's tow'ring headland seen,
And of his consort's reign, fair Imogen; 230
Of Brennus and Belinus, brothers bold,
And of Arviragus, and how of old
Our hardy sires th' Armorican controll'd,
And of the wife of Gorlois, who, surpris'd
By Uther, in her husband's form disguis'd,
(Such was the force of Merlin's art) became
Pregnant with Arthur of heroic fame.
These themes I now revolve—and Oh—if Fate
Proportion to these themes my lengthen'd date,
Adieu my shepherd's reed—yon pine-tree bough
Shall be thy future home, there dangle thou 241
Forgotten and disus'd, unless ere long
Thou change thy Latian for a British song;
A British?—even so—the pow'rs of man
Are bounded; little is the most he can;
And it shall well suffice me, and shall be
Fame, and proud recompence enough for me,
If Usa, golden-hair'd, my verse may learn,
If Alain bending o'er his chrystal urn,
Swift-whirling Abra, Trent's o'ershadow'd stream,
Thames, lovelier far than all in my esteem, 251
Tamar's ore-tinctur'd flood, and, after these,
The wave-worn shores of utmost Orcades.
Go, go, my lambs, untended homeward fare,
My thoughts are all now due to other care.
All this I kept in leaves of laurel-rind
Enfolded safe, and for thy view design'd;
This, and a gift from Manso's hand beside,
(Manso, not least his native city's pride)
Two cups, that radiant as their giver shone, 260
Adorn'd by sculpture with a double zone.
The spring was graven there; here slowly wind
The Red-sea shores with groves of spices lin'd;
Her plumes of various hues amid the boughs
The sacred, solitary Phœnix shows,

224 chose] chuse *1808*.

And watchful of the dawn, reverts her head,
To see Aurora leave her wat'ry bed.
—In other part, th' expansive vault above,
And there too, even there, the God of love;
With quiver arm'd he mounts, his torch displays
A vivid light, his gem-tipt arrows blaze, 271
Around, his bright and fiery eyes he rolls,
Nor aims at vulgar minds, or little souls,
Nor deigns one look below, but aiming high
Sends every arrow to the lofty sky,
Hence forms divine, and minds immortal, learn
The pow'r of Cupid, and enamour'd burn.
Thou also Damon (neither need I fear
That hope delusive) thou art also there;
For whither should simplicity like thine 280
Retire, where else such spotless virtue shine?
Thou dwell'st not (thought profane) in shades below,
Nor tears suit thee—cease then my tears to flow,
Away with grief! on Damon ill-bestow'd!
Who, pure himself, has found a pure abode,
Has pass'd the show'ry arch, henceforth resides
With saints and heroes, and from flowing tides
Quaffs copious immortality, and joy,
With hallow'd lips!—Oh! blest without alloy,
And now enrich'd with all, that faith can claim, 290
Look down, entreated by whatever name,
If Damon please thee most (that rural sound
Shall oft with echoes fill the groves around)
Or if Deodatus, by which alone
In those etherial mansions thou art known.
Thy blush was maiden, and thy youth the taste
Of wedded bliss knew never, pure and chaste,
The honours, therefore, by divine decree
The lot of virgin worth, are given to thee;
Thy brows encircled with a radiant band, 300
And the green palm-branch waving in thy hand,
Thou in immortal nuptials shalt rejoice,
And join with seraphs thy according voice,
Where rapture reigns, and the ecstatic lyre
Guides the blest orgies of the blazing quire."

294 Diodatus *1808.*

AN ODE ADDRESSED TO MR. JOHN ROUSE,

LIBRARIAN, OF THE UNIVERSITY OF OXFORD

ON A LOST VOLUME OF MY POEMS, WHICH HE DESIRED ME TO REPLACE, THAT HE MIGHT ADD THEM TO MY OTHER WORKS DEPOSITED IN THE LIBRARY

This Ode is rendered without rhime, that it might more adequately represent the original, which, as Milton himself informs us, is of no certain measure. It may possibly for this reason disappoint the reader, though it cost the writer more labour than the translation of any other piece in the whole collection [C.].

STROPHE

My two-fold book! single in show,
But double in contents,
Neat, but not curiously adorn'd,
Which, in his early youth,
A poet gave, no lofty one in truth,
Although an earnest wooer of the Muse—
Say while in cool Ausonian shades
Or British wilds he roam'd,
Striking by turns his native lyre,
By turns the Daunian lute, 10
And stepp'd almost in air,—

ANTISTROPHE

Say, little book, what furtive hand
Thee from thy fellow-books convey'd,
What time, at the repeated suit
Of my most learned friend,
I sent thee forth, an honour'd traveller,
From our great city to the source of Thames,
Cærulian sire!
Where rise the fountains, and the raptures ring,
Of the Aonian choir, 20
Durable as yonder spheres,
And through the endless lapse of years
Secure to be admir'd?

STROPHE II

Now what God, or Demigod
For Britain's antient Genius mov'd
(If our afflicted land
Have expiated at length the guilty sloth
Of her degen'rate sons)
Shall terminate our impious feuds,
And discipline, with hallow'd voice, recall? 30
Recall the Muses too,
Driv'n from their antient seats

In Albion, and well nigh from Albion's shore,
And with keen Phœbean shafts
Piercing th' unseemly birds,
Whose talons menace us,
Shall drive the Harpy race from Helicon afar?

ANTISTROPHE

But thou, my book, though thou hast stray'd,
Whether by treach'ry lost,
Or indolent neglect, thy bearer's fault, 40
From all thy kindred books,
To some dark cell, or cave forlorn,
Where thou endur'st, perhaps,
The chafing of some hard untutor'd hand,
Be comforted—
For lo! again the splendid hope appears
That thou may'st yet escape
The gulphs of Lethe, and on oary wings
Mount to the everlasting courts of Jove!

STROPHE III

Since Rouse desires thee, and complains 50
That, though by promise his,
Thou yet appear'st not in thy place
Among the literary noble stores,
Giv'n to his care,
But, absent, leav'st his numbers incomplete:
He, therefore, guardian vigilant
Of that unperishing wealth,
Calls thee to the interior shrine, his charge,
Where he intends a richer treasure far
Than Iön kept (Iön, Erectheus' son 60
Illustrious, of the fair Creüsa born)
In the resplendent temple of his God,
Tripods of gold, and Delphic gifts divine.

ANTISTROPHE

Haste, then, to the pleasant groves,
The Muses' fav'rite haunt;
Resume thy station in Apollo's dome,
Dearer to him
Than Delos, or the fork'd Parnassian hill!
Exulting go,
Since now a splendid lot is also thine, 70
And thou art sought by my propitious friend;
For there thou shalt be read
With authors of exalted note,
The antient glorious lights of Greece and Rome.

EPODE

Ye, then, my works, no longer vain,
And worthless deem'd by me!
Whate'er this steril genius has produc'd
Expect, at last, the rage of envy spent,
An unmolested happy home,
Gift of kind Hermes, and my watchful friend,
Where never flippant tongue profane 81
Shall entrance find,
And whence the coarse unletter'd multitude
Shall babble far remote.
Perhaps some future distant age,
Less ting'd with prejudice, and better taught,
Shall furnish minds of pow'r
To judge more equally.
Then, malice silenced in the tomb,
Cooler heads and sounder hearts, 90
Thanks to Rouse, if aught of praise
I merit, shall with candour weigh the claim.

A TRANSLATION OF THE ITALIAN POEMS

SONNET

FAIR Lady! whose harmonious name the Rhine,
Through all his grassy vale, delights to hear,
Base were indeed the wretch, who could forbear
To love a spirit elegant as thine,
That manifests a sweetness all divine,
Nor knows a thousand winning acts to spare,
And graces, which Love's bow and arrows are,
Temp'ring thy virtues to a softer shine.
When gracefully thou speak'st, or singest gay,
Such strains, as might the senseless forest move,
Ah then—turn each his eyes, and ears, away, 11
Who feels himself unworthy of thy love!
Grace can alone preserve him, ere the dart
Of fond desire yet reach his inmost heart.

SONNET

As on a hill-top rude, when closing day
Imbrowns the scene, some past'ral maiden fair
Waters a lovely foreign plant with care,
Borne from its native genial airs away,
That scarcely can its tender bud display,

So, on my tongue these accents, new, and rare,
Are flow'rs exotic, which Love waters there.
While thus, O sweetly scornful! I essay
Thy praise, in verse to British ears unknown,
And Thames exchange for Arno's fair domain; 10
So Love has will'd, and ofttimes Love has shown
That what he wills, he never wills in vain.
Oh that this hard and steril breast might be,
To Him, who plants from Heav'n, a soil as free!

CANZONE

THEY mock my toil—the nymphs and am'rous swains—
"And whence this fond attempt to write," they cry,
"Love songs in language, that thou little know'st?
How dar'st thou risk to sing these foreign strains?
Say truly. Find'st not oft thy purpose cross'd,
And that thy fairest flow'rs here fade and die?"
Then with pretence of admiration high—
"Thee other shores expect, and other tides,
Rivers, on whose grassy sides
Her deathless laurel leaf, with which to bind 10
Thy flowing locks, already Fame provides;
Why then this burthen, better far declin'd?"
Speak, Muse! for me.—The fair one said, who guides
My willing heart, and all my fancy's flights,
"This is the language, in which Love delights."

SONNET

TO CHARLES DIODATI

CHARLES—and I say it wond'ring—thou must know
That I, who once assum'd a scornful air,
And scoff'd at love, am fallen in his snare,
(Full many an upright man has fallen so)
Yet think me not thus dazzled by the flow
Of golden locks, or damask cheek; more rare
The heart-felt beauties of my foreign fair;
A mien majestic, with dark brows, that show
The tranquil lustre of a lofty mind;
Words exquisite, of idioms more than one, 10
And song, whose fascinating pow'r might bind,
And from her sphere draw down the lab'ring Moon,
With such fire-darting eyes, that should I fill
My ears with wax, she would inchant me still.

SONNET

Lady! It cannot be, but that thine eyes
Must be my sun, such radiance they display,
And strike me ev'n as Phœbus him, whose way
Through horrid Lybia's sandy desert lies.
Meantime, on that side steamy vapours rise
Where most I suffer. Of what kind are they,
New as to me they are, I cannot say,
But deem them, in the lover's language—sighs.
Some, though with pain, my bosom close conceals,
Which, if in part escaping thence, they tend 10
To soften thine, thy coldness soon congeals.
While others to my tearful eyes ascend,
Whence my sad nights in show'rs are ever drown'd,
Till my Aurora comes, her brow with roses bound.

SONNET

Enamour'd, artless, young, on foreign ground,
Uncertain whither from myself to fly,
To thee, dear Lady, with an humble sigh
Let me devote my heart, which I have found
By certain proofs, not few, intrepid, sound,
Good, and addicted to conceptions high:
When tempests shake the world, and fire the sky,
It rests in adamant self-wrapt around,
As safe from envy, and from outrage rude,
From hopes and fears, that vulgar minds abuse,
As fond of genius, and fixt fortitude, 11
Of the resounding lyre, and every Muse.
Weak you will find it in one only part,
Now pierc'd by Love's immedicable dart.

APPENDIX OF JUVENILE, FRAGMENTARY AND IMPROMPTU VERSE

ON LOYALTY

[Written 1754. Published by T. Wright in *Unpublished Poems of Cowper*, 1900; the letters and words enclosed within brackets are missing in the MS., and were supplied by Mr. Wright.]

Cum tot sustineant reges et tanta, neque ulla
  Parte voluptati deliciisque vacent:
Cum varios capiti affigat diadema dolores,
  Bellorumque premant sollicitentque minae:
Cur queritur populus? cur caeco murmure mussat?
  Inque suum insane vim meditatur herum,
Qui vigil excubias agit usque et ⟨sustinet⟩ usque
  Imperii, populus ne qua laboret, onus?
Hoc Satanæ scelus est nec Dæmone dignius ul⟨lum⟩,
  Nam primum in Satanæ pectore crime⟨n erat⟩. 10
Præmia quin date digna viro verusque sequatur
  Collata in gentem commoda gentis amor.
Illum jure colant populi, tueantur amante⟨s⟩;
  Ille colit populos, ille tuetur, amat.
Tu vero (si talis erit) quicunque verendum
  Execrare caput Principis, Eia! tace;
Nec quia rara fides regi fert præmia, demens
  Immeritum regem quem venerere putes;
Ipse tibi plaudas, quae laus est optima: laudem
  Externam ingenuis est meruisse satis. 20

LETTER IN VERSE

[Written Oct. 10, 1755, to Hill. Published first here, as written, from MS. in possession of Canon Cowper Johnson.]

If I write not to you
As I gladly would do
To a Man of your Mettle & Sense,
'Tis a Fault I must own
For which I'll attone
When I take my Departure from hence. 6

To tell you ye Truth,
I'm a queer kind of Youth
And I care not if all ye world knows it;
Whether Sloven, or Beau,
In Square, Alley, or Row,
At Whitehall, in ye court, or ye closet. 12

Having written thus much
In honest high Dutch,

I must now take a nobler still up:
Give my Fancy, a prick,
My Invention, a flick,
And my Genius a pretty smart Fillip. 18

For tho Bus'ness in hand
You are to understand,
Is indeed neither trifling nor small:
But wch you may transact
If your scull is not crackt
As well as ye best of them all. 24

And so may your *Dear Wife*
Be ye joy of your Life,
And of all our brave troops ye Commandress,
As you shall convey
What herein I say
To ye very fair Lady, my Laundress. 30

That to Town I shall trot
(No I Lie, I shall not,
For to Town I shall jog in ye stage)
On October ye Twentieth,
For my Father consenteth
To make me ye Flower of ye Age. 36

So bid her prepare
Every Table & Chair,
And warm well my Bed by ye Fire,
And if this be not done
I shall break her Back bone
As sure as I ever come nigh her. 42

I am Jovial & Merry,
Have writ till I'm weary,
Am become, with a great deal of Talking, hoarse:
So farewell—sweet Lad!
Is all I shall add,
Except— 48
y^rs^ obed^ly^ *stalking Horse.*

W. Cowper.

G. Berk:
Octb^r^ 10th 1755.

IN A LETTER TO C. P. ESQ.

ILL WITH THE RHEUMATISM

[Written (?). Published by Croft, 1825.]

GRANT me the muse, ye Gods! whose humble flight
Seeks not the mountain-top's pernicious height;
Who can the tall Parnassian cliff forsake,
To visit oft the still Lethean lake;

2 height *Southey*: heights *1825*.

Now her slow pinions brush the silent shore,
Now gently skim the unwrinkled waters o'er;
There dips her downy plumes, there upward flies,
And sheds soft slumbers in her votary's eyes. 8

IN A LETTER TO THE SAME

IN IMITATION OF SHAKESPEARE

[Written (?). Published by Croft, 1825.]

TRUST me, the meed of praise, dealt thriftily
From the nice scale of judgment, honours more
Than does the lavish and o'erbearing tide
Of profuse courtesy: not all the gems
Of India's richest soil at random spread
O'er the gay vesture of some glittering dame
Give such alluring vantage to the person,
As the scant lustre of a few, with choice
And comely guise of ornament disposed. 9

A THUNDER STORM

[Written 1768 (?). Published in T. Wright's *Life of Cowper*, 1892.]

THE Sky begins to lower and thick'ning Clouds
Portend a speedy storm, the Vocal tribes
No longer Sonnets sing; all, *all* are mute;
The Beasts forbear to graze and seek the shade:
Yon herd of Swine—see, see how fast they run;
'Tis said they see the Wind—
A solemn and awful silence now prevails,
Save when the breeze the Thunder's harbinger
Just rustles through the Grove: on ev'ry brow
A dark despondence reigns, and hark! it comes;
I heard the sudden roar,—my Soul, be calm, 11
Look up and view its progress, be serene,
Calm and collected, as becomes a Man.
Again it roars—and now the Lightning flies;
Not faster flies the timid Hare from Hounds;
Nor from the victor flies the vanquish'd Foe,
Than Trav'llers seek for Shelter; e'en my Dog
Cow'rs at my feet and looks up for protection.
And now 'tis dreadful truly—Heav'n and Earth,
How hard it rains! the Atmosphere's on fire! 20
Chaos presides! Confusion quite surrounds me!
Yet, yet again the broad expanded glare
Of vivid Lightning flashes o'er the Plain
Leaving a sulph'rous stench; Heav'ns what a Peal!

In a Letter to C. P.—7 there] thence *Southey*. 8 in] on *Southey*.

Still; still it roars incessant! What to this
The din of armies on the hostile Plain?
An Atom to a Mountain.—
See the sky opens—shuts—and forky fires
Dart oblique to the Earth; and o'er my Head
Tempest rides forward on the Whirlwind's wing:
Still the Almighty flashes for his Spear; 31
His Chariot wheels most awfully resound:
Well! be it so, my Soul; consoling thought!
He is thy maker and, I trust, thy friend;
Then wherefore tremble, wherefore shudder thus?
No, I will cease to fear, tho' even now
The Ear of Nature feels so strong a Shock
As scarce before it felt: yet as a Man,
A Christian Man, I shudder now no more.
When God in Thunder spoke from Sinai's mount,
Israel approach'd with Awe; if Moses then 41
Could mediate for the People, and avert
The great Jehovah's anger, sure his Son,
The fam'd Immanuel, the Prince of Peace,
Can ransom from his wrath and reconcile.
But oh! my Soul how poor a Portrait this!
How weak the Colours and how faint th' Idea,
Of what one day thou must be a Spectator!
Oh! bright and blessed morning to the Just!
Oh! Day of doom, of infinite distress, 50
To those who unprepar'd Messiah meet;
When thron'd in Clouds, surrounded by the Host
Of Heav'n, worshipping, the Judge descends:
Consummate Triumph. Hark! the Trumpet sounds,
The Breath of Michael blows th' Amazing blast;
The Dead arise, the Living all are Chang'd,
And Adam's family appear before Him.
Amid that throng, in that Assembly vast,
Must thou, my soul, appear and there receive
A Plaudit glorious or Silence sad: 60
Sink deep in Thought, Oh, deeper, deeper still:
May it ne'er be forgotten, on my Couch
Be it my dreaming subject; when awake,
Oh! be it still remember'd: for its worth
What tongue can speak, or any language tell?
Then from this hour deep on my heart engraved
Be all my duty needful; Ha! that blaze,
That Shock tremendous that appals me thus
Says I am not prepar'd—but I submit;
No more will I rebel against thy sway 70
Nor dispute thy dominion, Gracious God!
My sins shall suffer, and by Grace divine

I will forsake them all and trust alone
For true felicity, for pleasure high,
To Thee: who only can true pleasure give.
The Storm abates—less too the Thunder roars,
The Vault of Heav'n grows brighter, and the Sun
Strives to Emerge from yonder dusky Cloud;
More faint the flashes grow—and distant fly;
Nature resumes her charms, and from the Grove
Musick again is heard: the Warblers there 81
Attempt a feeble strain: The Dog Star now
Throws his warm beams around the weeping Scene;
Salubrious Zephyrs gently fan the Air:
Love, Life, and Joy return by due degrees
And Harmony once more revisits Earth.

RIDDLE

[Written July, 1780 (MS. in the British Museum). First six lines published by Hayley, 1803; afterwards in *The Gentleman's Magazine*, Dec. 1806.]

I AM just two and two, I am warm, I am cold,
And the parent of numbers that cannot be told.
I am lawful, unlawful—a duty, a fault,
I am often sold dear, good for nothing when bought.
An extraordinary boon, and a matter of course,
And yielded with pleasure—when taken by force.
Alike the delight of the poor and the rich,
Tho' the vulgar is apt to present me his breech. 8

TOM RABAN

[Written in letter to Newton, Aug. 31, 1780. Published by Southey, 1836.]

THE curate and churchwarden,
And eke exciseman too,
Have treated poor Tom Raban
As if he was a Jew.

For they have sent him packing,
No more in church to work,
Whatever may be lacking;
As if he was a Turk. 8

Thus carry they the farce on,
Which is great cause of grief,
Until that Page the parson
Turn over a new leaf.

Thus sings the muse, and though her fav'rite cue
Is fiction, yet her song is sometimes true.

[Written 1781 (?). Published from the copy among the Ash MSS. in *Unpublished Poems of Cowper*, 1900.]

METHINKS I see thee decently array'd
In long flowed nightgown of stuff-damask made;
Thy cassock underneath it closely braced
With surcingle about thy mod'rate waist;
Thy morning wig, grown tawny to the view,
Though once a grizzle, and thy square-toed shoe.
The day was, when the sacerdotal race
Esteem'd their proper habit no disgrace,
Or rather when the garb their order wears
Was not disgrac'd as now, by being theirs. 10
I speak of prigs—

IMPROMPTU ON READING THE CHAPTER ON POLYGAMY, IN MR. MADAN'S THELYPHTHORA

[Written 1780. Published in *The Gentleman's Magazine*, Dec. 1780.]

IF John marries Mary, and Mary alone,
'Tis a very good match between Mary and John.
But if John weds a score, oh, what claws and what scratches!
It can't be a match—'tis a bundle of *matches.*

ON MADAN'S ANSWER TO NEWTON'S COMMENTS ON THELYPHTHORA

[Written May 13, 1781. Published by Southey, 1836.]

M. QUARRELS with N., for M. wrote a book
And N. did not like it, which M. could not brook,
So he call'd him a bigot, a wrangler, a monk,
With as many hard names as would line a good trunk,
And set up his back, and claw'd like a cat,
But N. liked it never the better for that.
Now N. had a wife, and he wanted but one,
Which stuck in M.'s stomach as cross as a bone.
It has always been reckon'd a just cause of strife
For a man to make free with another man's wife;
But the strife is the strangest that ever was known,
If a man must be scolded for loving his own. 12

ON A REVIEW CONDEMNING THELYPHTHORA

[Written Oct. (?), 1780. Published by Southey, 1836.]

I HAVE read the Review; it is learned and wise,
Clear, candid, and witty—Thelyphthora dies.

"*Methinks I see*"—7 The *1900* : Thy *A.* 11 *not in 1900.*

ON THE HIGH PRICE OF FISH

[Written to Mrs. Newton, Aug., 1781. Published by Johnson, 1824.]

COCOA-NUT naught,
Fish too dear,
None must be bought
For us that are here;
No lobster on earth,
That ever I saw,
To me would be worth
Sixpence a claw. 8
So, dear Madam, wait
Till fish can be got
At a reas'nable rate,
Whether lobster or not;
Till the French and the Dutch
Have quitted the seas,
And then send as much
And as oft as you please. 16

TO MRS. NEWTON.

[Written Sept. 16, 1781. Published by Johnson, 1824.]

A NOBLE theme demands a noble verse,
In such I thank you for your fine oys*ters*.
The barrel was magnificently large,
But being sent to Olney at free charge,
Was not inserted in the driver's list,
And therefore overlook'd, forgot, or miss'd;
For when the messenger whom we dispatch'd
Enquir'd for oysters, Hob his noddle scratch'd;
Denying that his waggon or his wain
Did any such commodity contain. 10
In consequence of which, your welcome boon
Did not arrive till yesterday at noon;
In consequence of which some chanced to die,
And some, though very sweet, were very dry.
Now Madam says, (and what she says must still
Deserve attention, say she what she will,)
That what we call the Diligence, be-case
It goes to London with a swifter pace,
Would better suit the carriage of your gift,
Returning downward with a pace as swift; 20
And therefore recommends it with this aim—
To save at least three days,—the price the same;
For though it will not carry or convey
For less than twelve pence, send whate'er you may,
For oysters bred upon the salt sea shore,
Pack'd in a barrel, they will charge no more.

News have I none that I can deign to write,
Save that it rain'd prodigiously last night:
And that ourselves were, at the seventh hour,
Caught in the first beginning of the show'r; 30
But walking, running, and with much ado,
Got home—just time enough to be wet through.
Yet both are well, and, wond'rous to be told,
Soused as we were, we yet have caught no cold;
And wishing just the same good hap to you,
We say, good Madam, and good Sir, Adieu!

[Written in letter to Newton, Feb., 1782. Published by Southey, 1836.]

LET Banister now lend his aid
To furnish shoes for the Baker,
Who has put down a pump, with a lamp on its head,
For the use of the said Shoe-maker.

AGAINST INTERESTED LOVE

[Written 1782. Published from the copy among the Ash MSS. in *Unpublished Poems of Cowper*, 1900.]

WHO does not blush when charged with selfish views?
Man boasts for man a principle of Love,
But each with God a diff'rent course pursues,
Short interest is the spring by which they move.

Oh blindness of our mean and stupid race!
The selfish and the sordid we despise,
And yet the Love of God incurs disgrace,
While Love to man is sounded to the skies. 8

How speaks the world? in Friendship's sacred cause
A gen'rous service is its own reward—
A maxim all have stamp'd with their applause.

* * * * * * *

FRAGMENT

[Written (?). Published first here from the copy among the Ash MSS.]

HE came to him in the extasy of pray'r,
And pour'd his spirit in an angel, when
He led him by the hand into a room,
A sacred room, and made him sit and hear
How wonderful the lot design'd for him. 5

[Written in letter to Unwin, Jan. 3, 1784. Published by Southey, 1836.]

ONE parson, one poet, one belman, one crier,
And the poor poet is our only 'squire.

9, 10 *re-written in A. thus:*
How speaks the world, my dear and valued friend,
My recompense is found in serving you.

LINES

WRITTEN ON A PAGE OF THE MONTHLY REVIEW, WHICH HAD SPOKEN OF MR. NEWTON'S OPINIONS AS CANT

[Written 1784. Published in *The Record*, Feb., 1867.]

THESE critics, who to faith no quarter grant,
But call it mere hypocrisy and cant
To make a just acknowledgment of praise,
And thanks to God for governing our ways,
Approve Confucius more, and Zoroaster,
Than Christ's own servant, or that servant's
Master. 6

IMPROMPTU

ON WRITING A LETTER WITHOUT HAVING ANYTHING TO SAY

[Written in letter to Unwin, 1786 (?) (MS. in British Museum). Published by Hayley, 1804.]

So have I seen the maids in vain
Tumble and teaze a tangled skein;
They bite the lip, they scratch the head,
And cry "the deuce is in the thread,"
They torture it, and jerk it round,
Till the right end at last is found,
Then wind and wind and wind away,
And what was work is changed to play. 8

LINES AFTER THE MANNER OF HOMER,

DESCRIPTIVE OF THE OPENING OF A HAMPER

[Written in letter to Rose, Oct. 4, 1789. Published by Hayley, 1803.]

THE straw-stuff'd hamper with his ruthless steel
He open'd, cutting sheer th' inserted cords
Which bound the lid and lip secure. Forth came
The rustling package first, bright straw of wheat,
Or oats, or barley; next a bottle green,
Throat-full, clear spirits the contents, distill'd
Drop after drop odorous, by the art
Of the fair mother of his friend—the Rose. 8

[Written in letter to Bagot, Feb. 26, 1791. Published by Hayley, 1803.]

IT is a maxim of much weight,
Worth conning o'er and o'er—
He, who has Homer to translate,
Had need do nothing more.

LINES

WRITTEN FOR INSERTION IN A COLLECTION OF HANDWRITINGS AND SIGNATURES MADE BY MISS PATTY, SISTER OF HANNAH MORE

[Written March 6, 1792. Published by Johnson, 1815. See notes at the end of the volume.]

In vain to live from age to age
  While modern bards endeavour,
I write my name in Patty's page
  And gain my point for ever.

TO A YOUNG LADY WHO STOLE A PEN FROM THE PRINCE OF WALES'S STANDISH

[Written in letter to Mrs. King, March 8, 1792. Published by Southey, 1836. There is a copy among the Ash MSS.]

Sweet nymph, who art, it seems, accused
  Of stealing George's pen,
Use it thyself, and having used,
  E'en give it him again.

The Plume of his that has one scrap
  Of thy good sense express'd,
Will be a Feather in his cap
  Worth more than all his Crest. 8

ON A MISTAKE IN HIS TRANSLATION OF HOMER

[Written in letter to Hill, April 15, 1792. Published by Johnson, 1824.]

Cowper had sinn'd with some excuse,
  If, bound in rhyming tethers,
He had committed this abuse
  Of changing ewes for wethers;

But, male for female is a trope,
  Or rather bold misnomer,
That would have startled even Pope,
  When he translated Homer. 8

[Written in letter to Hayley, May 9, 1792. Published by T. Wright in *Letters of Cowper*, 1904.]

Away goes Sussex William with his pack
Of Buckingamian acres at his back,
And, as he trudges off with Weston, feels
The gentle Ouse cascading at his heels;

Then, Buckshire William lifting in his turn,
Beneath one arm Ouse gathers and his urn,
Beneath the other Eartham and her swain,
And back to Weston, Weston bears again. 8

TO SIR JOHN FENN

[Written in letter to Johnson, May 20, 1792. Published from the copy among the Ash MSS. in *Unpublished Poems of Cowper*, 1900.]

Two omens seem propitious to my fame,
Your spouse embalms my verse, and you my name;
A name, which, all self-flatt'ry far apart,
Belongs to one who ven'rates in his heart
The wise and good, and therefore, of the few
Known by those titles, Sir, both yours and you. 6

ON THURLOW

[Written in letter to Hayley, July 4, 1792. Published by T. Wright in *Letters of Cowper*, 1904.]

The Chancellor once was a tree full of fruit,
A tree in the summer and fann'd by the south,
He was great at the top and moist at the root,
And the good things he bore would drop into your mouth.

But since that his Lordship has quitted his place,
Steriles numerandus est arbores inter,
And *now* to solicit his favour and grace
Is searching your boughs for plums in the winter.

ON HIS PORTRAIT

[Written in letter to Hayley, July 15, 1792. Published by Hayley, 1803.]

Abbot is painting me so true,
That (trust me) you would stare,
And hardly know, at the first view,
If I were here, or there.

ON HIS APPROACHING VISIT TO HAYLEY

[Written in letter to Hayley, July 29, 1792. Published by Hayley, 1803.]

Through floods and flames to your retreat
I win my desp'rate way,
And when we meet, if e'er we meet,
Will echo your huzza!

ON HAYLEY'S PORTRAIT

[Written in letter to Hayley, Nov. 25, 1792. Published by T. Wright in *Letters of Cowper*, 1904.]

ACHILLES and Hector and Homer and all
When your face appears shall come down from the
 wall,
And mine, theme of many an angry remark,
Shall then hide its pick-pocket looks in the dark.

ON RECEIVING HAYLEY'S PICTURE

[Written Dec. (?), 1792. Published by Johnson, 1815. There is a copy among the Ash MSS.]

IN language warm as could be breath'd or penn'd,
Thy picture speaks th' original my friend;
Not by those looks that indicate thy mind—
They only speak thee friend of all mankind:
Expression here more soothing still I see,
That friend of *all* a partial friend to *me*. 6

THANKS FOR A GIFT OF PHEASANTS

[Written in letter to Johnson, Jan. 31, 1793. Published by Johnson, 1824.]

IN Copeman's ear this truth let Echo tell,—
"Immortal bards like mortal pheasants well:"
And when his clerkship's out, I wish him herds
Of golden clients for his golden birds.

[Written in letter to Lady Hesketh, Feb. 10, 1793. Published by Hayley, 1803.]

MY pens are all split, and my ink-glass is dry;
Neither wit, common sense, nor ideas have I.

[Written in letter to Lady Hesketh, March, 1793. Published in *Unpublished Poems of Cowper*, 1900.]

AN epigram is but a feeble thing
With straw in tail, stuck there by way of sting.

[Written in letter to Hayley, July 7, 1793. Published by Hayley, 1803.]

AH brother Poet ! send me of your shade,
And bid the zephyrs hasten to my aid !
Or, like a worm unearth'd at noon, I go
Dispatch'd by sunshine, to the shades below.

EPIGRAMS ON HIS GARDEN SHED

[Written July 24 and Aug. 15, 1793. Published by Hayley, 1803.]

I

BEWARE of building! I intended
Rough logs and thatch, and thus it ended.

II

Instead of a pound or two, spending a mint
Must serve me at least, I believe, with a hint,
That building and building a man may be driven
At last out of doors, and have no house to live in.

ON A LETTER OF MISS FANSHAWE

[Written in letter to Lady Hesketh, Aug. 29, 1793. Published by Hayley, 1803.]

HER pen drops eloquence as sweet
As any muse's tongue can speak;
Nor need a scribe like her regret
Her want of Latin or of Greek.

TO GRAVINA,

ON HIS TRANSLATING THE AUTHOR'S SONG ON A ROSE INTO ITALIAN VERSE

[Written Aug., 1793. Published by Hayley, 1803.]

MY Rose, Gravina, blooms anew,
And, steep'd not now in rain,
But in Castalian streams by you,
Will never fade again.

ON FLAXMAN'S PENELOPE

[Written Sept., 1793. Published by Hayley, 1803.]

THE suitors sinn'd, but with a fair excuse,
Whom all this elegance might well seduce;
Nor can our censure on the husband fall,
Who, for a wife so lovely, slew them all.

ON RECEIVING HEYNE'S VIRGIL FROM HAYLEY

[Written Oct., 1793. Published by Johnson, 1815.]

I SHOULD have deem'd it once an effort vain
To sweeten more sweet Maro's matchless strain,
But from that error now behold me free,
Since I receiv'd him as a gift from Thee.

NOTES

PREFACE TO THE FIRST VOLUME

[This was written and even printed for issue with the first edition of Cowper's first volume in 1782; but at the earnest request of Johnson the publisher it was omitted from the first edition and not inserted until the fifth edition in 1793, when it could no longer injure the well-established sale of Cowper's Poems. Some copies of the first edition containing it are extant.]

WHEN an Author, by appearing in print, requests an audience of the Public, and is upon the point of speaking for himself, whoever presumes to step before him with a preface, and to say, "Nay, but hear me first," should have something worthy of attention to offer, or he will be justly deemed officious and impertinent. The judicious reader has probably, upon other occasions, been beforehand with me in this reflection: and I am not very willing it should now be applied to me, however I may seem to expose myself to the danger of it. But the thought of having my own name perpetuated in connexion with the name in the title page is so pleasing and flattering to the feelings of my heart, that I am content to risk something for the gratification.

This Preface is not designed to commend the Poems to which it is prefixed. My testimony would be insufficient for those who are not qualified to judge properly for themselves, and unnecessary to those who are. Besides, the reasons which render it improper and unseemly for a man to celebrate his own performances, or those of his nearest relatives, will have some influence in suppressing much of what he might otherwise wish to say in favour of a *friend*, when that friend is indeed an *alter idem*, and excites almost the same emotions of sensibility and affection as he feels for himself.

It is very probable these Poems may come into the hands of some persons, in whom the sight of the Author's name will awaken a recollection of incidents and scenes which, through length of time, they had almost forgotten. They will be reminded of *one*, who was once the companion of their chosen hours, and who set out with them in early life, in the paths which lead to literary honours, to influence and affluence, with equal prospects of success. But he was suddenly and powerfully withdrawn from those pursuits, and he left them without regret; yet not till he had sufficient opportunity of counting the cost, and of knowing the value of what he gave up. If happiness could have been found in classical attainments, in an elegant taste, in the exertions of wit, fancy, and genius, and in the esteem and converse of such persons as in these respects were most congenial with himself, he would have been happy. But he was not—He wondered (as thousands in a similar situation still do) that he should continue dissatisfied, with all the means apparently conducive to satisfaction within his reach—But in due time the cause of his disappointment was discovered to him—He had lived without God in the world. In a memorable hour, the wisdom which is from above visited his heart. Then he felt himself a wanderer, and then he found a guide. Upon this change of views, a change of plan and conduct followed of course. When he saw the *busy* and the *gay* world in its true light, he left it with as little reluctance as a prisoner, when called to liberty, leaves his dungeon. Not that he became a Cynic or an Ascetic—A heart filled with love to God, will assuredly breathe benevolence to men. But the turn of his temper inclining him to rural life, he indulged it, and the providence of God evidently preparing his way and marking out his retreat, he retired into the country. By these steps the good hand of God, unknown to me, was providing for me one of the principal blessings of my life; a friend and a counsellor, in whose company for almost seven years, though we were seldom seven successive waking hours separated, I always found new pleasure. A friend, who was not only a comfort to myself, but a blessing to the affectionate poor people, among whom I then lived.

Some time after inclination had thus removed him from the hurry and bustle of life, he was still more secluded by a long indisposition, and my pleasure was succeeded by a proportionable degree of anxiety and concern. But a hope, that the God whom he served would support him under his affliction, and at length vouchsafe him a happy deliverance, never forsook me. The desirable crisis, I trust, is now nearly approaching. The dawn, the presage of returning day, is already arrived. He is again enabled to resume his pen, and some of the first fruits of his recovery are here presented to the public. In his principal subjects, the same acumen which distinguished him in the early period of life, is happily employed in illustrating and enforcing the truths of which he received such deep and unalterable impressions in his maturer years. His satire, if it may be called so, is benevolent, (like the operations of the skilful and humane surgeon, who wounds only to heal) dictated by a just regard for the honour of God, an indignant grief excited by the profligacy of the age, and a tender compassion for the souls of men.

His favourite topics are least insisted on in the piece entitled Table Talk; which therefore, with some regard to the prevailing taste, and that those who are governed by it may not be discouraged at the very threshold from proceeding farther, is placed first. In most of the larger Poems which follow, his leading design is more explicitly avowed and pursued. He aims to communicate his own perceptions of the truth, beauty, and influence of the religion of the Bible.—A religion which, however discredited by the misconduct of many who have not renounced the Christian name, proves itself, when rightly understood, and cordially embraced, to be the grand *desideratum*, which alone can relieve the mind of man from painful and unavoidable anxieties, inspire it with stable peace and solid hope, and furnish those motives and prospects which, in the present state of things, are absolutely necessary to produce a conduct worthy of a rational creature, distinguished by a vastness of capacity, which no assemblage of earthly good can satisfy, and by a principle and pre-intimation of immortality.

At a time when hypothesis and conjecture in philosophy are so justly exploded, and little is considered as deserving the name of knowledge, which will not stand the test of experiment, the very use of the term *experimental*, in religious concernments, is by too many unhappily rejected with disgust. But we well know, that they who affect to despise the inward feelings which religious persons speak of, and to treat them as enthusiasm and folly, have inward feelings of their own, which, though they would, they cannot suppress. We have been too long in the secret ourselves to account the proud, the ambitious, or the voluptuous, happy. We must lose the remembrance of what we once were, before we can believe, that a man is satisfied with himself, merely because he endeavours to appear so. A smile upon the face is often but a mask worn occasionally and in company, to prevent, if possible, a suspicion of what at the same time is passing in the heart. We know that there are people, who seldom smile when they are alone, who therefore are glad to hide themselves in a throng from the violence of their own reflections; and who, while by their looks and their language they wish to persuade us they are happy, would be glad to change their conditions with a dog. But in defiance of all their efforts, they continue to think, forebode, and tremble. This we know, for it has been our own state, and therefore we know how to commiserate it in others. From this state the Bible relieved us—When we were led to read it with attention, we found *ourselves* described.—We learnt the causes of our inquietude—we were directed to a method of relief—we tried, and we were not disappointed.

Deus nobis hæc otia fecit.

We are now certain that the gospel of Christ is the power of God unto salvation, to every one that believeth. It has reconciled us to God, and to ourselves, to our duty, and our situation. It is the balm and cordial of the present life, and a sovereign antidote against the fear of death.

Sed hactenus hæc. Some smaller pieces upon less important subjects close the volume. Not one of them I believe was written with a view to publication, but I was unwilling they should be omitted.

JOHN NEWTON.

CHARLES SQUARE, HOXTON,
February 18, 1782.

TABLE TALK

PAGE **1**. A fragment containing the first 28 lines is among the Ash MSS.; in l. 15 it has a variant, 'sound both heart and root' for 'of unshaken root.'

3 115. Thus, free from censure (overaw'd by fear)] All early editions omit the brackets, which Southey first inserted. Though not absolutely necessary, they make the sense of the line at once apparent.

5 201. Briton's *1782–1793*: Britain's *1794–1800*. Britain occurs as late as the 1722 edition of Camden's Britannia, meaning 'Briton'; but it is probably a misprint in these editions of Cowper.

7 276. Courage, in arms] I have inserted the comma.
298. *1800* wrongly inserts a comma after 'grant'.
301. Too] To *1800*.

8 365, 6. Southey punctuates with a comma after 'bay' and a semicolon after 'perplex'd' against all the early editions; he thus gets an easier sense, but breaks the couplet contrary to Cowper's usual practice.

11 488. borne] born *1793–1800*.

12 562. chose;] chose, *1782*, *1786*, *1798*¹.

13 583. paddoc] paddock *first in 1803*.

14 619. lumber] lumber'd *1800*.

15 689. muses' *1793–1800*: muses *1782–1788*: Muse's *Southey*.

16 710, 11. *1782*, *1786* punctuate with commas after 'goal' and 'roll'; *1793-1800* with semicolon after 'goal', comma after 'roll', inserting also a comma after 'Or'.
753. delight, *1782–1786*: delight; *1787*, *1788*: delight *1793–1800*.

PROGRESS OF ERROR

18 27. fatalist's] fatalists *all early editions.*
37. conscience] conscious *1800.*
28 491. hair-brain'd] hare-brain'd *1782–1787.*
29 536. *1782–1788* place the comma after 'child', *1793–1800* after 'contradiction'; the punctuation of the earlier editions, to which *1803* returns, is clearly right.

TRUTH

33 125. grows *1782–1788, 1803*: grows; *1793–1800.* The semicolon blunts the point of the couplet.
35 197. obligations] obligation's *1798*², *1800.*
36 231. despise ;] despise. *all early editions.*
37 282. as] has *1786.*
40 417. passions] passion's *1800.*
433. libertine profess'd, *1782–1788, 1803*: libertine, profess'd *1793–1800.*
42 528, 9. All early editions and Southey punctuate with a full point after 'sought'; *1793–1800* further obscure the sense by placing a comma after 'still'.

EXPOSTULATION

52 390–413. Instead of these lines the following were originally written and printed:

Hast thou admitted with a blind, fond trust,
The lie that burn'd thy father's bones to dust,
That first adjudg'd them heretics, then sent
Their souls to Heav'n, and curs'd them as they went?
The lie that Scripture strips of its disguise,
And execrates above all other lies,
The lie that claps a lock on mercy's plan,
And gives the key to yon infirm old man,
Who once insconc'd in apostolic chair
Is deified, and sits omniscient there;
The lie that knows no kindred, owns no friend
But him that makes its progress his chief end,
That having spilt much blood, makes that a boast,
And canonizes him that sheds the most?
Away with charity that sooths a lie,
And thrusts the truth with scorn and anger by;
Shame on the candour and the gracious smile
Bestow'd on them that light the martyrs pile,
While insolent disdain in frowns express'd,
Attends the tenets that endur'd that test:
Grant them the rights of men, and while they cease
To vex the peace of others, grant them peace,
But trusting bigots whose false zeal has made
Treach'ry their duty, thou art self-betray'd.

Thinking that they were too strongly expressed and

would give grave offence, Cowper cancelled them and substituted the lines which stand in the text. Some copies of the first edition are extant containing the original lines, either uncancelled or together with the substituted passage on a cancel leaf.

53 466. borne] born *1793–1800*.

HOPE

64 207. devotes] dovotes *1800*.

66 301. (Oh cast them from thee !)] The brackets were first added in *1793*.

68 385. divines] devines *1800*.

73 627. None of the early editions punctuate rightly. *1782*, *1786* place a comma after 'wall', but a full point after 'spare'; *1787–1803* place a semicolon after 'wall' and a full point or mark of exclamation after 'spare'. Southey punctuated, 'And smite the untemper'd wall, 'tis death to spare,'.

CHARITY

76 motto. Quo *1798*[1]: Qua *rest*.

84 366. Th' o'erflowing] The o'erflowing *1800*.

87 526. Scrib.] Scrib *first in 1803*. There is no reason for omitting the mark of abbreviation.

CONVERSATION

93 167. at the bottom barb'rous still and rude; *1793–1798*, *1800*: at the bottom, barb'rous still and rude, *1782–1788*: at the bottom barb'rous still and rude, *1799*, *1803*.

100 474. polite ;] polite. *all early editions*.

103 642. speed,] All early editions omit the comma, thus obscuring the sense of the passage.

104 664. And] And, *1793–1800*.

108 862. reelings,] All early editions omit the comma.

RETIREMENT

112 121. amidst] amid *1782–1793*.

123 633. he proves, *1782*, *1786*: *1787–1803* wrongly omit the comma.

THE TASK

Book I—**132** 136. stile] style *1798*[2], *1800*.

134 239. scite] All early editions have this curious form of 'site'.

143 633 note. Omai *1785*, *1786*, *1798*[1], *1803*: Omia *rest*. All editions read 'Omai' in the Argument of the book. That various forms of the name were current is shown by the following extract from Miss Burney's *Early Diary* (Sept. 1, 1774: ed. 1889, vol. i. p. 311): "the capital friend and favourite of Omai, or Omiah, or Omy, or Jack, for my brother says he is called by all those names on board".

145 743. ordinance] ordonance *1785*: ordonnance *1786-1788*.

748. hassocks] hassocs *1793-1800*.

754. borne *1785-1788*, *1798*[1], *1803*: born *rest*.

Book II—**147** 53. the] th' *1800* (*8vo*).

150 190. homogeneal] homogenial *1798*[2], *1800*.

160 651. feed] feel *1799*.

Book III—**169** 222. works *1785*, *1786*: works, *1787-1800*.

169 224. *him*] him *1785-1788*.

174 495. fog] fogg *1800* (*8vo*).

Book IV—**182** 1, 4. The punctuation in the text is that of *1793-1800*. *1785* punctuates thus: 'Hark! 'tis the twanging horn! o'er yonder bridge . . . . . reflected bright,' with which *1786-1788* agree, except that they place a semicolon instead of a comma after 'bright' and *1787*, *1788* add a comma after 'bridge'.

Book V—**217** 820. new-created] new created *1798*[2], *1800* (*8vo*).

Book VI—**226** 317. beach] beech *1785*, *1786*.

TIROCINIUM

245 128. The colon after 'man' is in *1798*[1] alone of the early editions; the rest have a full point.

131. borne] born *1793-1800*.

248 271. Or if, by nature sober,] *1785-1788*, *1803* have no comma after 'if'; *1793-1800*, trying to make the meaning more obvious, reduce the passage to nonsense by placing a comma after 'Or'. I have inserted the comma after 'if', to make misunderstanding impossible.

252 455. abhorrence] ahhorrence *1800* (*8vo*).

MISCELLANEOUS POEMS

The preface prefixed by Croft to his edition of the early poems of Cowper (1825) is as follows:

As it may be expected to mention the lady to whom the following Poems are addressed, it may not be deemed improper, at the same time, to notice the circumstances which occasioned them. The Life of Cowper having been already written, it is not necessary to repeat what his biographers have so ably done; but if there is any thing relative to this great genius, which could not be known at the time when his Life was published, it will not be amiss to mention the same, as every act of Cowper cannot but be interesting. The lady to whom these Poems are addressed, under the name of Delia, was the second daughter of Ashley Cowper, son of the Judge, and nephew of Lord Chancellor Cowper. This lady (Miss Theodora Jane Cowper) was first cousin to the Poet, the son of the Reverend Doctor Cowper, Rector of Great Berkhamstead, and brother to Ashley Cowper. The Poet formed an early attachment for his cousin Theodora, an accomplished woman, with an elegant person, and possessing a superior understanding.

With such qualities, it is no wonder that he conceived a strong affection for her; and the lady, sensible of her cousin's amiable disposition, regarded him with equal affection. But, unfortunately, her father, from an idea that the union of persons so nearly related was improper, refused to accede to the wishes of his daughter and nephew; and as the former, from a strong sense of filial duty, would not consent to unite herself to her cousin without the approbation of her father, the happiness they had promised to themselves was altogether prevented.

But, though frustrated in their wishes, they did not cease to love, nor occasionally to meet. At this time these Poems were addressed to her on whose affections the Poet had placed all his happiness, still indulging the hope of possessing the object of his love. But it proved, alas! otherwise, as appears by the poem in which he speaks so feelingly of his separation from her: after which, it was their fate never to meet again.

In consequence of this disappointment, and other circumstances, he gave up his professional pursuits, and retired into the country, with a depression of spirits which continued at times to affect this amiable person to the end of his life.

To the credit of the lady, she remained constant to him on whom she had placed her affections. Neither time nor absence could diminish her attachment. She preserved with the greatest care, for many years, these pleasing memorials of the beloved author; when, for reasons known only to herself, she sent them in a sealed packet to a lady (her particular friend,) with directions not to be opened till after her decease. This took place on the twenty-second of last October, and her friend having died a short time previous to that event, her executors sent the packet to me with other articles, according to the directions of that lady.

The Poems, though not equal to his later productions, yet appeared to me to possess the sweet muse of this delightful Poet, in no small degree. Nevertheless, on first reading them, much as I know any productions of Cowper would gratify his many admirers, yet I did not feel disposed to make them public, fearing that my partiality might lead me to set a value upon them beyond their merit; and, knowing they could not add to his reputation, I was fearful of doing any thing to diminish the high character his poetry had so justly acquired. Not wishing, however, to deprive the public of any thing so interesting, and yet dreading to do any thing to lessen the fame of this admired Poet, I resolved to take the opinion of those whose judgment was superior to mine, and so necessary to guide me in a point of this delicate nature. Under this impression, I placed them in the hands of some friends highly distinguished for talents and judgment.

Sanctioned by such authority, I shall feel most happy in having it in my power to gratify the admirers of Cowper with these his early productions, trusting they will afford as much delight to their readers, as they have to

Your obedient servant,

J. C.

264 *Psalm cxxxvii.* Some modern editors unnecessarily entitle this 'Translation of Psalm cxxxvii'. Croft and Southey head it as in the text.

271 '*Delia, th' unkindest girl on earth*' 13. Bruce's reading 'Yes' is not necessary; 'Yet' refers back to and meets the objection anticipated in ll. 9, 10 ('however odd it may appear to say'). Possibly we should place a dash after 'dear', and another after 'prey' instead of the full point, thus making ll. 9–12 parenthetical; but such a parenthesis would be an unusual complication in the simple structure of Cowper's juvenile poems.

275 28. Then] Canon Benham perhaps rightly reads 'There'.

276 *Ode* 1. Thou *Southey*: The *Croft*.

5. warblings *Southey*: waters *Croft*.

With great reluctance I have adopted the two emendations proposed by Southey; 'undulating warblings' is an almost intolerable expression, but 'water' cannot refer to the sounds of a lyre, and it is clear that the first verse is intended as an invocation to the lyre, not as a statement about the Hebrus. I thought of retaining Croft's readings and including ll. 5, 6 in brackets; they would then be a feeble and untrue parenthetical reflection on the river. But the brackets make little or no improvement in the sense of the verse and complicate its structure.

279 26. set] It is quite possible that Cowper wrote 'sat;' cp. what may be a similar confusion in *The Dog and the Water-Lily* l. 23 (p. 383), where all early editions read 'sat' instead of the more usual 'set'.

284 16. The reading of all previous editions 'safer' yields little or no meaning; 'suffer' is so slight an alteration, and makes such good sense, that I have not hesitated to put it into the text on my own authority.

288 *Ode.* This is printed exactly as it appeared in the *St. James' Magazine*, with three exceptions: l. 12 a comma is omitted after 'words', l. 24 'fancy' is given an initial capital, l. 71 Southey's emendation 'wreath' is adopted for the misprint 'wreathe'. Southey and later editors somewhat blunted the point of the Ode, such as it is, by neglecting the intentional abuse of capitals (see ll. 32, 47, 52); and some misprints such as 'mouldering' for 'smould'ring' (l. 56), have crept in. The evidence for Cowper's authorship is that in his only authenticated contribution to the magazine, a *Dissertation on the Modern Ode*, signed W.C., he promised a specimen Ode; and in the next number this Ode appeared, signed however L. Southey, followed by later editors, considered this sufficient proof that the Ode was Cowper's; Mr. Bailey, however, rejects it.

297 *The Pine-Apple and the Bee.* There is another MS. copy of this in the possession of Canon Cowper Johnson, containing the following variations: 7 Urg'd] Push'd. 9 still] all. 10 only pervious] pervious only.

On the Promotion of Thurlow. There is a MS. copy in the possession of Canon Cowper Johnson, containing only one variation: 14 sprang] sprung.

299 *Yearly Distress.* This was printed in the *General Evening Post* in 1783, but I have been unable to collate this version. In l. 7 *1800, 1803* read 'sithe' for 'scythe'; in 21 they have a comma after 'all.'

309 *Love of the World Reproved.* The version printed in *The Gentleman's Magazine* supplies the following variants: 2 abstain from] beware of. 4 follower or friend. 13 And] So. 15 straight arose] therefore rose. 32 and] or.

317 *Anti-Thelyphthora.* The text reproduces the edition of 1781, our only authority, but the 'e' of a few preterite forms in -ed has been elided in conformity with the rest, and the following small alterations have been made: 127 founders'] founders *1781.* 129 few :] few, *1781.* 169 To horse !] To horse *1781.* Southey and modern editors, perhaps rightly, make the speech which begins at l. 99 end at l. 122: but I follow the indications of *1781*, which has ending quotation marks after l. 118, though it has no beginning marks in l. 99.

324 *Sir Joshua Reynolds.* 4, 5. The text follows the punctuation of the MS.; *1824* punctuates with no comma after 'away' and a comma after 'Futurity.'

325 *Heroism.* Cowper originally entitled this 'Aetna.'

329 *Friendship.* Cowper wrote this poem for insertion in his first volume, but omitted it at his publisher's request. The version printed by Hayley is as follows:

WHAT virtue can we name, or grace,
But men unqualified and base,
    Will boast it their possession?
Profusion apes the noble part
Of liberality of heart;
    And dullness of discretion.

But as the gem of richest cost
Is ever counterfeited most;

So always imitation
Employs the utmost skill she can
To counterfeit the faithful man,
The friend of long duration.

Some will pronounce me too severe,
But long experience speaks me clear,
Therefore, that censure scorning,
I will proceed to mark the shelves,
On which so many dash themselves,
And give the simple warning.

Youth, unadmonish'd by a guide,
Will trust to any fair outside :—
An error soon corrected!
For who, but learns, with riper years,
That man, when smoothest he appears,
Is most to be suspected?

But here again a danger lies;
Lest, thus deluded by our eyes,
And taking trash for treasure,
We should, when undeceiv'd, conclude
Friendship imaginary good,
A mere Utopian pleasure.

An acquisition rather rare
Is yet no subject of despair;
Nor should it seem distressful,
If either on forbidden ground,
Or, where it was not to be found,
We sought it unsuccessful.

No friendship will abide the test,
That stands on sordid interest
And mean self-love erected;
Nor such, as may awhile subsist
'Twixt sensualist and sensualist,
For vicious ends connected.

Who hopes a friend, should have a heart
Himself, well furnish'd for the part,
And ready on occasion
To show the virtue that he seeks;
For 'tis an union, that bespeaks
A just reciprocation.

A fretful temper will divide
The closest knot that may be tied,
By ceaseless sharp corrosion:
A temper passionate and fierce
May suddenly your joys disperse
At one immense explosion.

In vain the talkative unite
With hope of permanent delight:
The secret just committed
They drop through mere desire to prate,
Forgetting its important weight,
And by themselves outwitted.

How bright soe'er the prospect seems,
All thoughts of friendship are but dreams,
If envy chance to creep in.
An envious man, if you succeed,
May prove a dang'rous foe indeed,
But not a friend worth keeping.

As envy pines at good possess'd,
So jealousy looks forth distress'd,
On good, that seems approaching;
And, if success his steps attend,
Discerns a rival in a friend,
And hates him for encroaching.

Hence authors of illustrious name,
Unless belied by common fame,
Are sadly prone to quarrel;
To deem the wit a friend displays
So much of loss to their own praise,
And pluck each other's laurel.

A man renowned for repartee,
Will seldom scruple to make free
With friendship's finest feeling,
Will thrust a dagger at your breast,
And tell you, 'twas a special jest,
By way of balm for healing.

Beware of tatlers! keep your ear
Close stopt against the tales they bear.
Fruits of their own invention!
The separation of chief friends
Is what their kindness most intends;
Their sport is your dissension.

Friendship that wantonly admits
A joco-serious play of wits
In brilliant altercation,
Is union such as indicates,
Like hand-in-hand insurance-plates,
Danger of conflagration.

Some fickle creatures boast a soul
True as the needle to the pole;

Yet shifting, like the weather,
The needle's constancy forego
For any novelty, and show
Its variations rather.

Insensibility makes some
Unseasonably deaf and dumb,
When most you need their pity.
'Tis waiting, till the tears shall fall
From Gog and Magog in Guildhall,
Those playthings of the City.

The great and small but rarely meet
On terms of amity complete :
Th' attempt would scarce be madder,
Should any, from the bottom, hope
At one huge stride, to reach the top
Of an erected ladder.

Courtier and patriot cannot mix
Their het'rogeneous politics
Without an effervescence,
Such as of salts with lemon-juice,
But which is rarely known t' induce,
Like that, a coalescence.

Religion should extinguish strife,
And make a calm of human life :
But even those, who differ
Only on topics left at large,
How fiercely will they meet and charge !
No combatants are stiffer.

To prove, alas ! my main intent,
Needs no great cost of argument,
No cutting and contriving.
Seeking a real friend we seem
T' adopt the chymist's golden dream
With still less hope of thriving.

Then judge before you choose your man,
As circumspectly as you can,
And, having made election,
See that no disrespect of yours,
Such, as a friend but ill endures,
Enfeeble his affection.

It is not timber, lead, and stone,
An architect requires alone,
To finish a great building ;
The palace were but half complete,
Could he by any chance forget
The carving and the gilding.

As similarity of mind,
Or something not to be defin'd,
First rivets our attention;
So manners decent and polite,
The same we practis'd at first sight,
Must save it from declension.

The man who hails you Tom or Jack,
And proves by thumping on your back
His sense of your great merit,
Is such a friend, that one had need
Be very much his friend indeed,
To pardon, or to bear it.

Some friends make this their prudent plan—
"Say little, and hear all you can!"
Safe policy, but hateful!
So barren sands imbibe the show'r,
But render neither fruit nor flow'r,
Unpleasant, and ungrateful.

They whisper trivial things, and small;
But to communicate at all
Things serious, deem improper.
Their fæculence and froth they show,
But keep their best contents below,
Just like a simm'ring copper.

These samples (for alas! at last
These are but samples, and a taste
Of evils, yet unmention'd)
May prove the task, a task indeed,
In which 'tis much, if we succeed,
However well-intention'd.

Pursue the theme, and you shall find
A disciplin'd and furnish'd mind
To be at least expedient,
And, after summing all the rest,
Religion ruling in the breast
A principal ingredient.

True friendship has in short a grace
More than terrestrial in its face,
That proves it Heav'n-descended:
Man's love of woman not so pure,
Nor when sincerest, so secure,
To last till life is ended.

337 *To Miss Creuzé.* The undated letter to Unwin in which this occurs is shown by internal evidence to belong to Oct. or Nov., 1780. Cowper is still much excited by *Thelyphthora* (published 1780), and mentions a review of it which has begun to appear in the October (1780) number of the *Monthly Review*, and which he has not seen until the letter is finished; he gives his opinion of the review in a rhyming postscript (see p. 629). Southey misplaced the letter among the letters of 1786, but noticed his mistake in time to add a note of the true date in his analytical table of contents. Mr. Wright did not see Southey's correction and places the letter in 1786. It may be worth while to point out that the letter immediately following this in the bound MS. volume, dated Dec. 24, 1780, occurs twice in the editions of Southey and Mr. Wright; once, dated, in its proper place (Southey iv. 54, Wright i. 249); again, undated, among the letters of 1786 (Southey vi. 4, Wright iii. 84).

342 *The Distressed Travellers.* The two letters from Cowper of Aug. 12 and Aug. 27, 1782, to Lady Austen and Unwin, make the date of this poem almost certain. (See Wright, *Letters of Cowper* ii. 6–9). The letter of Aug. 12 begins with the poem, 'To watch the storms, and hear the sky' (p. 341).

344 *Royal George.* The MS. in the British Museum (from which Hayley probably printed), is written in three six-line stanzas. The six-line stanza looks cumbrous in print; but the division into three twelve-line stanzas both adheres more closely to the MS. and displays the triple division of the poem far more clearly than the nine four-line verses into which all editors, following Hayley, have divided it. It was obviously with intention that Cowper closed each of the three stanzas with a recital of the most appalling incident of the disaster—the loss of eight hundred men; and the effect of this threefold iteration is lost if the poem is printed in four-line verses.

346 *John Gilpin.* The variant readings from the MS. and the first edition (*Public Advertiser* (*PA.*)) are as follows: (where no authority for the variant is given, it is in both the MS. and the first edition) 22 doth] does 28 both] so *PA.* 42 folks *PA.* 51 head] face 56 trouble him] grieve him still 59 screaming came down stairs] scream'd into his ears 67 that] which 69 a . . . ear] two . . . ears 71 And . . . a] He . . . one 85 he cried] did cry 88 and] or 93 His] The in that sort] had before 94 Had] Been been before] in this kind

95, 96 Affrighted fled and as he flew
Left all the world behind.

PA. prints 97–100 before 93–96. 128 they] he 131 all might see the bottle-necks] still the bottlenecks were left 132 Still] Both 149 yet] ah 159 Friend's *PA.* 161 amaz'd] surpriz'd 162 neighbour in such trim] friend in such a trim 165 your] the 166 Make haste and tell me all 172 guise] strains 182 flow'd] droop'd 190 upon] about 194 all the world would] folks would gape and

197 So, turning] Then speaking 201 speech] word 205 he] if 206 Had] He 213 Mistress Gilpin, . . . saw] Gilpin's wife, . . . had seen
221–224 The youth did ride, and soon they met,
He tried to stop John's horse,
By seizing fast the flowing rein,
But only made things worse.
225 But,] For 227 He thereby frighted Gilpin's horse 232 lumb'ring] lumber 239 And all and each] So they and all 240 Did join] Soon join'd 241 And now] But all 243 The toll-men] The men still 247 had] first 251 doth] does

Three verses of an intended sequel to *John Gilpin* were found in Cowper's handwriting among Mrs. Unwin's papers; they were first printed in 1827, in Hone's *Table Book* (see vol. II. pp. 79, 80). They are as follows:

Then Mrs. Gilpin sweetly said
Unto her children three,
'I'll clamber o'er this style so high,
And you climb after me.'

But having climb'd unto the top,
She could no further go,
But sate, to every passer by,
A spectacle and show:

Who said 'Your spouse and you this day
Both show your horsemanship,
And if you stay till he comes back,
Your horse will need no whip.'

353 *Epitaph on a Hare.* Cowper's prose description of his hares was reprinted from *The Gentleman's Magazine* for June, 1784,—with the omission of the introductory remarks and a few other words—in the 1800 edition of his poems. This fact, and the charm of the description, must be my excuses for giving it here:

In the year 1774, being much indisposed both in mind and body, incapable of diverting myself either with company or books, and yet in a condition that made some diversion necessary, I was glad of any thing that would engage my attention without fatiguing it. The children of a neighbour of mine had a leveret given them for a plaything; it was at that time about three months old. Understanding better how to tease the poor creature than to feed it, and soon becoming weary of their charge, they readily consented that their father, who saw it pining and growing leaner every day, should offer it to my acceptance. I was willing enough to take the prisoner under my protection, perceiving that in the management of such an animal, and in the attempt to tame it, I should find just that sort of employment which my case required. It was soon known among the neighbours that I was pleased with the present, and the consequence was, that in a short time I had as many leverets offered to me as would have stocked a paddock. I undertook the care of three, which it is necessary that I should here distinguish by the names I gave them—Puss, Tiney, and Bess. Notwithstanding the two feminine appellatives, I must inform you that they were all males. Immediately commencing carpenter, I built them houses to sleep in; each had a separate apartment, so contrived that their ordure would pass through the bottom of it; an earthen pan placed under each received whatsoever fell, which being duly emptied and washed, they were thus kept perfectly sweet and clean. In the day time they had the range of a hall, and at night retired each to his own bed, never intruding into that of another.

Puss grew presently familiar, would leap into my lap, raise himself upon his hinder feet, and bite the hair from my temples. He would suffer me to take him up and to carry him about in my arms, and has more than once fallen fast asleep upon my knee. He was ill three days, during which time I nursed him, kept him apart from his fellows that they might not molest him, (for, like many other wild animals, they persecute one of their own species that is sick,) and by constant care and trying him with a variety of herbs, restored him to perfect health. No creature could be more grateful than my patient after his recovery; a sentiment which he most significantly expressed, by licking my hand, first the back of it, then the palm, then every finger separately, then between all the fingers, as if anxious to leave no part of it unsaluted; a ceremony which he never performed but once again upon a similar occasion. Finding him extremely tractable, I made it my custom to carry him always after breakfast into the garden, where he hid himself generally under the leaves of a cucumber vine, sleeping or chewing the cud till evening; in the leaves also of that vine he found a favourite repast. I had not long habituated him to this taste of liberty, before he began to be impatient for the return of the time when he might enjoy it. He would invite me to the garden by drumming upon my knee, and by a look of such expression as it was not possible to misinterpret. If this rhetoric did not immediately succeed, he would take the skirt of my coat between his teeth, and pull at it with all his force. Thus Puss might be said to be perfectly tamed, the shyness of his nature was done away, and on the whole it was visible, by many symptoms which I have not room to enumerate, that he was happier in human society than when shut up with his natural companions.

Not so Tiney ; upon him the kindest treatment had not the least effect. He too was sick, and in his sickness had an equal share of my attention ; but if, after his recovery, I took the liberty to stroke him, he would grunt, strike with his fore feet, spring forward and bite : he was, however, very entertaining in his way ; even his surliness was matter of mirth, and in his play he preserved such an air of gravity, and performed his feats with such a solemnity of manner, that in him too I had an agreeable companion.

Bess, who died soon after he was full grown, and whose death was occasioned by his being turned into his box, which had been washed, while it was yet damp, was a hare of great humour and drollery. Puss was tamed by gentle usage ; Tiney was not to be tamed at all ; and Bess had a courage and confidence that made him tame from the beginning. I always admitted them into the parlour after supper, when the carpet affording their feet a firm hold, they would frisk, and bound, and play a thousand gambols, in which Bess, being remarkably strong and fearless, was always superior to the rest, and proved himself the Vestris of the party. One evening the cat being in the room, had the hardiness to pat Bess upon the cheek, an indignity which he resented by drumming upon her back with such violence, that the cat was happy to escape from under his paws and hide herself.

I describe these animals as having each a character of his own. Such they were in fact, and their countenances were so expressive of that character, that, when I looked only on the face of either, I immediately knew which it was. It is said, that a shepherd, however numerous his flock, soon becomes so familiar with their features, that he can by that indication only distinguish each from all the rest, and yet to a common observer the difference is hardly perceptible. I doubt not that the same discrimination in the cast of countenances would be discoverable in hares, and am persuaded that among a thousand of them no two could be found exactly similar ; a circumstance little suspected by those who have not had opportunity to observe it. These creatures have a singular sagacity in discovering the minutest alteration that is made in the place to which they are accustomed, and instantly apply their nose to the examination of a new object. A small hole being burnt in the carpet, it was mended with a patch, and that patch in a moment underwent the strictest scrutiny. They seem too to be very much directed by the smell in the choice of their favourites: to some persons, though they saw them daily, they could never be reconciled, and would even scream when they attempted to touch them; but a miller coming in engaged their affections at once; his powdered coat had charms that were irresistible. It is no wonder that my intimate acquaintance with these specimens of the kind has taught me to hold the sportsman's amusement in abhorrence; he little knows what amiable creatures he persecutes, of what gratitude they are capable, how cheerful they are in their spirits, what enjoyment they have of life, and that impressed as they seem with a peculiar dread of man, it is only because man gives them peculiar cause for it.

That I may not be tedious, I will just give a short summary of those articles of diet that suit them best.

I take it to be a general opinion that they graze, but it is an erroneous one, at least grass is not their staple; they seem rather to use it medicinally, soon quitting it for leaves of almost any kind. Sow-thistle, dent-de-lion, and lettuce, are their favourite vegetables, especially the last. I discovered by accident that fine white sand is in great estimation with them; I suppose as a digestive. It happened that I was cleaning a bird-cage when the hares were with me; I placed a pot filled with such sand upon the floor, which being at once directed to by a strong instinct, they devoured voraciously; since that time I have generally taken care to see them well supplied with it. They account green corn a delicacy, both blade and stalk, but the ear they seldom eat; straw of any kind, especially wheat-straw, is another of their dainties; they will feed greedily upon oats, but if furnished with clean straw, never want them; it serves them also for a bed, and, if shaken up daily, will be kept sweet and dry for a considerable time. They do not indeed require aromatic herbs, but will eat a small quantity of them with great relish, and are particularly fond of the plant called musk. They seem to resemble sheep in this, that, if their pasture be too succulent, they are very subject to the rot; to prevent which, I always made bread their principal nourishment, and filling a pan with it cut into small squares, placed it every evening in their chambers, for they feed only at evening and in the night. During the winter, when vegetables were not to be got, I mingled this mess of bread with shreds of carrot, adding to it the rind of apples cut extremely thin; for though they are fond of the paring, the apple itself disgusts them. These however not being a sufficient substitute for the juice of summer herbs, they must at this time be supplied with water; but so placed, that they cannot overset it into their beds. I must not omit, that occasionally they are much pleased with twigs of hawthorn, and of the common briar, eating even the very wood, when it is of considerable thickness.

Bess, I have said, died young; Tiney lived to be nine years old, and died at last, I have reason to think, of some hurt in his loins by a fall. Puss is still living, and has just completed his tenth year, discovering no signs of decay, nor even of age, except that he is grown more discreet and less frolicksome than he was. I cannot conclude, without observing that I have lately introduced a dog to his acquaintance, a spaniel that had never seen a hare to a hare that had never seen a spaniel. I did it with great caution, but there was no real need of it. Puss discovered no token of fear, nor Marquis the least symptom of hostility. There is therefore, it should seem, no natural antipathy between dog and hare, but the pursuit of the one occasions the flight of the other, and the dog pursues because he is trained to it; they eat bread at the same time out of the same hand, and are in all respects sociable and friendly.

I should not do complete justice to my subject, did I not add, that they have no ill scent belonging to them; that they are indefatigably nice in keeping themselves clean, for which purpose nature has furnished them with a brush under each foot; and that they are never infested by any vermin.—May 28, 1784.

Memorandum found among Mr. Cowper's papers.

Tuesday, March 9, 1786.

This day died poor Puss, aged eleven years eleven months. She died between twelve and one at noon, of mere old age, and apparently without pain.

362 *The Poplar-Field.* 17–20. Modern editors have not noticed that the note in *1803* is probably wrong, as my critical note points out.

372 *Negro's Complaint.* 30. 'Matches' of *1800* and later editions doubtless refers to some form of torture, perhaps the tying of lighted pieces of tow between the fingers (see N.E.D. s.v. Match *sb.*[2]); it can hardly be a misprint for the earlier reading 'fetters.

375 *Pity for poor Africans.* This was first printed in *The Northampton Mercury* for Aug. 9, 1788, with the following variants: 1 purchase] traffic 18 is] was 29 speak] talk 31 you shall have] we'll give you 33 spoke] ceas'd 36 behind] behind them 39 take] have.

376 *Epigram.* The date of first printing is May 12, 1792. Probably therefore, in strict chronology, this is here out of order; but its subject makes this position, immediately after the other poems about slavery, suitable enough.

377 *Gratitude.* Southey's version (vol. ii. pp. 300, 301) is as follows:

BENEFACTIONS

A POEM IN SHENSTONE'S MANNER

Addressed to my dear Coz, April 14, 1788.

THIS cap that so stately appears
  With ribbon-bound tassel on high,
Which seems by the crest that it rears
  Ambitious of brushing the sky;
This cap to my Harriet I owe;
  She gave it, and gave me beside
A ribbon, worn out long ago,
  With which in its youth it was tied.

This chair that I press at my ease,
  With tresses of steeds that were black
Well cover'd, and wadded to please
  The sitter, both bottom and back;
Thick-studded with bordering nails,
  Smooth-headed and gilded and bright,
As Vesper, who when the day fails,
  Adorns the dark forehead of Night:

These carpets, so soft to the foot,
  Caledonia's traffic and pride,
(Oh spare them, ye Knights of the Boot,
  Dirt-splash'd in a cross-country ride!)
This table and mirror within,
  Secure from collision and dust,
At which I oft shave cheek and chin,
  And periwig nicely adjust:

This moveable structure of shelves,
  Contrived both for splendour and use,
And charged with octavoes and twelves,
  The gayest I had to produce;
Where flaming in scarlet and gold
  My poems enchanted I view,
And hope in due time to behold
  My Iliad and Odyssey too:

This china that decks the alcove,
  Which mortals have named a beaufette,
But what the Gods call it above
  Has ne'er been revealed to us yet:

These curtains that keep the room warm
  Or cool, as the season demands;
Those stoves which for figure and form
  Seem the labour of Mulciber's hands:

That range, from which many a mess
  Comes smoking the stomach to cheer;
That tub,—(you might bathe in a less,)
  Where malt is transform'd into beer:
These painted and unpainted chairs,
  Those cushion'd, these curiously framed;
Yon bedding and bed above stairs,
  With other things not to be named:

These items endear my abode,
  Disposing me oft to reflect
By whom they were kindly bestowed,
  Whom here I impatient expect.
But, hush! She a parent attends,
  Whose dial-hand points to eleven,
Who, oldest and dearest of friends,
  Waits only a passage to Heaven.

Then willingly want her awhile,
  And, sweeping the chords of your lyre,
The gloom of her absence beguile
  As now, with poetical fire.
'Tis yours, for true glory athirst,
  In high-flying ditty to rise
On feathers renown'd from the first
  For bearing a goose to the skies.

383 *Dog and Water-Lily.* 23. set] Cp. note on p. 279, l. 26.

403 62. largess] Probably Cowper wrote 'largeness', as printed by the early editions, but the N. E. D. gives no instance of a parallel use.

413 144–166. These lines may have been crossed out by Cowper himself, but it is at least equally probable that Hayley omitted them, exercising his editorial discretion. They are not markedly inferior to the rest of the fragment, though the transition to Adam in l. 167 is abrupt.

415 *Sonnet.* The variations in *The Northampton Mercury* (April 21, 1792), where the Sonnet first appeared with a letter from Cowper, are as follows: 1 Thy country] I praise thee with just] and with 2 Hears] Hear 5 wrong'd] scourg'd 7 gain'd] won 9 pause] draws 10 And weave] Delay 11 thy toils] all thy pains 12 for] to

13, 14 Then let them scoff—two prizes thou hast won—
  Freedom for Captives, and thy God's—WELL DONE.

417 *Catharina.* 24. I retain 'bands', as Cowper wrote it in the copy preserved among the Ash MSS., and the copy from which Hayley printed appears to have had it also. 'Bands' must be understood not as equivalent to 'banns,' but as meaning an agreement or binding promise. See N. E. D. s. v. Band *sb.*[1] 10.

418 *To Dr. Darwin.* This was sent to Hayley in a letter dated June 10, 1792, for his criticism; the first version differed from the poem as published in the following passages: 8 labours of] bringing forth. Between ll. 8 and 9 came this stanza:

The verse that kindles meets a fire,
  A kindred fire in them,
The numbers live, that they admire,
  And die, that they condemn.

9, 10 Live thou—well pleas'd alike, thy song
  With that award we greet,

16 At whose so soon as thine? 24 Unworthy] Scarce worthy.

Hayley's copy of verses is criticized by Cowper in a letter of June 23, 1792 (*Letters*, ed. Wright, iv. p. 240), and the last verse as there printed is by Cowper:

Two social bards who roamed that way
  Learned all, and all they learned
Were charged by Nature to convey
  To whom it most concerned.

421 *Inscription for a Moss-House.* This first appeared in *Cowper illustrated*, &c. (see p. xxiii), 1804; afterwards in Grimshawe's edition. There seems no reason to doubt its genuineness, though Grimshawe's unsupported authority would be of little value; he printed as Cowper's the *Sonnet to a Young Lady on her Birthday*, which Cowper expressly disowned.

426 *Answer to Stanzas.* By the kind offices of Mr. Falconer Madan I am now able to give, from the *Times Literary Supplement* of Jan. 3, 1924, both (*a*) the Stanzas by Miss Catherine Fanshawe and (*b*) the 'poem of Mr. Cowper's,' then for the first time printed from the MS. Common Place Book which belonged to the Hon. Mrs. Maitland, a daughter of Judith Madan (*née* Cowper), and is now in the possession of her descendants.

What wonder, if my wavering hand
  Had dared to disobey,
When Hesketh gave a harsh command,
  And Cowper led astray?

Then take this tempting gift of thine,
  By pen uncopied yet;
But canst thou Memory confine,
  Or teach me to forget?

More lasting than the touch of art
The characters remain,
When written by a feeling heart
On tablets of the brain.

THE POEM.

To Lady Hesketh from Wm Cowper of Olney, on her great Freindship in visiting him at that place, & Removing him from thence to a neat & comfortable habitation Furnish'd at her own expence.

[*Mrs. Maitland's note: then follows:—*]

To my dearest Cousin
on
her removal of us
from
Silver End, to
Weston.

1.

WHO gave me grassy Lawns for miry ways,
These silent shades for dull and noisy streets,
For Rustics who can only gape & gaze,
Good neighbourhood with all its social sweets?

2.

Whe took me from my dwelling old and drear
As Prisons or inclosures of the dead,
By vermin haunted, sinking ev'ry year,
And threat'ning downfall on its Tenant's head?

3.

Plac'd me, when least I hop'd so fair a change,
In this neat Mansion furnish'd by her care,
And gave me for yon marshy flats, to range
These pleasant heights, and breathe this purer air?

4.

No patron prais'd 'till his relenting hands
Forgot their gripe, no poem-pamper'd Peer,
But lib'ral as the show'rs on thirsty lands
And true as Day-Spring, *Harriot* has been *here*.

5.

She stoop'd from yon great city, from the sight
Of proud Hyde-Park was happy to descend
Wing'd with Benevolence, into the night
Of infant-throng'd, thief-harb'ring *Silver End*.

6.

She took me thence, and my departure shap'd
From scenes of filth, to Weston's verdant scene;
So by an Angel's conduct *Lot* escap'd
From *Sodom's* fires to *Zoar* fresh and green.

7.

Sweet Cousin! with whom so oft at early day,
While many a homely lass lay slumb'ring still,
Chearful & happy I was wont to stray
Through *Ducal Bedford's* fields to *Primrose-Hill.*

8.

I little thought that Pleasures dead so long
Should yet revive, that I should hear again
The once familiar music of that tongue
So oft employ'd to mitigate my pain.

9.

And would'st thou now, that after many a year
With sadness of the deepest gloom o'ercast,
The evening of my life should open clear,
And *Mary* taste, and I, some ease at last?

10.

Come then—frequent what thou hast made so fair,
Thy Converse add to all thy gifts beside,
Else thou shalt leave the want we least can bear,
Still, after all thy kindness, unsupplied.

427 *To Mary.* The MS. copy contains the following cancelled version of ll. 9–16:

Thy needles, once a shining store,
Discernible by thee no more,
Rust in disuse, their service o'er,
My Mary!

But thy ingenious work remains,
Nor small the profit it obtains
Since thou esteemst my pleasure gains
My Mary!

428 *Lines.* I have placed these lines here, among the few and mournful poems of Cowper's last years, rather than in the Appendix, because their biographical interest is thus more clearly displayed.

433 *Olney Hymns.* The text is that of the first edition, with the exceptions noted; a few obvious errors of punctuation and quotation-marks have been silently corrected. To complete the list of words misprinted in the first edition should be added: p. 435 IV. 12 God] God's. p. 471 LX. 11 will] with. p. 472 LXI. 6 That] Than.

The MS. readings given on Professor Mayor's authority are taken from an unfinished series of articles which appeared in *Notes and Queries*, 10th series, vol. ii.

477 *Hymn for Sunday School.* This first appeared in *The Northampton Mercury* for Aug. 7, 1790, with a few variants: 1 song] voice 3 infants] children 14 elder 23 mercy. In line 5 it reads 'thy day' rightly. Had I seen this version earlier I should have been inclined to adopt its readings in the text, though the *1808* version may be equally authentic, being printed from another manuscript copy, slightly altered according to Cowper's wont.

479 *Translations from Madame Guion.* Bull's preface is as follows:

It seems needless, if not impertinent, in an obscure individual, to say any thing in praise of the Author of the Task. It is of more consequence to inform the reader of the circumstances that have led to this publication. About twenty years ago a very dear and venerable friend[1] introduced me to the truly great and amiable Mr. Cowper. This gave rise to a friendship which increased with every repeated interview, and for several years I had the pleasure of spending an afternoon with him every week. At length this delightful intercourse was terminated, by his removal to a distant situation, and the painful approaches of that event which dissolves every social connexion.

One day amusing myself with the poetical works of the celebrated Madame Guion, I was struck with the peculiar beauty of some of her poems, as well as edified with the piety and devotion of which they are strongly expressive. I mentioned them to Mr. C.; and partly to amuse a solitary hour, partly to keep in exercise the genius of this incomparable man, I requested him to put a few of the poems into an english dress. Afterward, during my absence upon a journey, I received a letter, in which Mr. C. says, 'I have but little leisure, strange as it may seem. That little I devoted for a month after your departure to the translation of Madame Guion. I have made fair copies of all the pieces I have produced on this last occasion, and will put them into your hands when we meet. They are yours to serve as you please, you may take and leave as you like, for my purpose is already served. They have amused me and I have no further demand upon them.' On my return, Mr. C. presented me with these translations, to which he added the Letter to a Protestant Lady in France, and the Poem on Friendship.

[1] The Rev. John Newton, Rector of St. Mary Woolnoth, London.

The idea of printing them was afterwards suggested to Mr. C.; and he gave his full consent, intending to revise them before I should send them to press. Various circumstances prevented him from doing this; and the poems would probably have still remained unpublished, if it had not been found that several copies of them had already got abroad. The Editor therefore had reason to believe, that they would otherwise have made their appearance in a state far less correct than if printed from the original Manuscript. Nor can he imagine that even in their present form, they will, on the whole, tend to diminish the well-deserved reputation of their excellent Author.

To infer that the peculiarities of Madame Guion's theological sentiments, were adopted either by Mr. C. or by the Editor, would be almost as absurd as to suppose the inimitable Translator of Homer to have been a pagan. He reverenced her piety, admired her genius, and judged that several of her poems would be read with pleasure and edification by serious and candid persons.

I have taken the liberty to add the Stanzas subjoined to the Bills of Mortality, which had been published a few years past at Northampton; and the Epitaph[1], which had appeared in a periodical publication. They sufficiently mark the genius of their Author, correspond with the other parts of this small volume, and have not before been printed in a uniform manner with his poems.

NEWPORT-PAGNEL, *William Bull.*
6th June, 1801.

508 Instead of ll. 57–68 *A.* has the following:

ASK ye my souls opinion of her state,
She answers, of her state she nothing knows—
Time was she lived by Faith, but finds of late
In self-forgetfullness her best repose.

She either floats at random, or she sinks
By her own weight, without a wish to rise,
Feels an Indifference worse than death, and thinks
Her name erased for ever from the skies.

Language affords not my distress a name,
Yet is it real and no transient dream,—
I know but this that where Loves sacred flame
Is kindled, there is Happiness supreme.

9 *uncancelled variant:*
I cannot even give my woes a name,
11, 12 *uncancelled variants:*
Tis Love inflicts it, whose seraphic flame
Felt in the soul is happiness supreme.

[1] On Hamilton. [Ed.]

521 *Fifth Satire of First Book of Horace.* In this and the next translation Hayley's alterations of the first edition —they cannot be called emendations—have descended through Southey to almost all modern editors. None of the alterations are necessary,—even 'Their' in l. 184, p. 525, is quite a possible reading, though 'There' is probably right,—several are mischievous.

I have not thought it necessary to disfigure the text with the innumerable italics and capitals of the first edition.

523 84, 85 The punctuation of the first edition is right here; the Latin is:

In Mamurrarum lassi deinde urbe manemus,
Murena præbente domum, Capitone culinam.

Hayley and modern editors wrongly read:

Tir'd, at Muræna's we repose;
At Formia sup at Capito's.

546 The Latin originals of the first four translations from Vincent Bourne were printed in *1800* (vol. I. Appendix) and *1803*. Lack of space prevents me from printing them here, as well as most of the other fairly accessible originals translated by Cowper. Hayley printed the Latin originals of the translations that he first published, from *The Thracian* (p. 549) to *The Cantab* (p. 560). The first edition of Vincent Bourne's Latin verses was published in 1734; the latest reprint is that of 1840, edited by Mitford.

561 Vincent's Latin verses, printed by Hayley, are as follows:

ABIIT senex. Periit senex amabilis,
  Quo non fuit jucundior.
Lugete vos, ætas quibus maturior
  Senem colendum prœstitit;
Seu quando, viribus valentioribus
  Firmoque fretus pectore,
Florentiori vos juventute excolens
  Cura fovebat patria,
Seu quando, fractus, jamque donatus rude,
  Vultu sed usque blandulo,
Miscere gaudebat suas facetias
  His annuis leporibus!
Vixit probus, puraque simplex indole,
  Blandisque comis moribus,
Et dives æqua mente, charus omnibus,
  Unius auctus munere.
Ite, tituli! Meritis beatioribus
  Aptate laudes debitas!
Nec invidebat ille, si quibus favens
  Fortuna plus arriserat.
Placide senex, levi quiescas cespite,
  Etsi superbum nec vivo tibi
Decus sit inditum, nec mortuo
  Lapis notatus nomine!

562 *Epitaph.* I give Unwin's Latin epitaph, published by Hayley:

Care, vale! Sed non æternum, care, valeto!
  Namque iterum tecum, sim modo dignus, ero:
Tum nihil amplexus poterit divellere nostros,
  Nec tu marcesces, nec lacrymabor ego.

On the Shortness of Human Life. Cowper enclosed Dr. Jortin's original verses in a letter to Newton, prefaced by six lines of doggerel; I give both below, as printed by Hayley:

THE late Dr. Jortin
Had the good fortune,
To write these verses
Upon tombs and hearses;
Which I, being jingleish,
Have done into English.

IN BREVITATEM VITÆ SPATII HOMINIBUS CONCESSI

HEI mihi! Lege rata sol occidit atque resurgit,
Lunaque mutatæ reparat dispendia formæ,
Astraque, purpurei telis extincta diei,
Rursus nocte vigent. Humiles telluris alumni
Graminis herba virens, et florum picta propago,
Quos crudelis hyems lethali tabe peredit,
Cum zephyri vox blanda vocat, rediitque sereni
Temperies anni, fœcundo e cespite surgunt.
Nos domini rerum, nos, magna et pulchra minati,
Cum breve ver vitæ robustaque transiit ætas,
Deficimus; nec nos ordo revolubilis auras
Reddit in ætherias, tumuli neque claustra resolvit.

563 *Epigrams, translated from the Latin of Owen.* In this fourth edition I am able, through the kindness of Mr. Falconer Madan, to give the following twelve hitherto unprinted epigrams from Bodleian MS. Autogr. d. 21, ff. 191–2, with the manuscript readings in those already printed.

ON A LITIGIOUS DEBTOR

You pay your lawyer more than was my due—
Oh what a knave and what a fool are you!

ON A NEW-CREATED NOBLE

Of a long line, my Lord, you well may brag,
Whose Mother spun, whose Father cast the drag.
['well may' is corrected from 'justly']

VERSE AND PROSE

Why swifter far than Prose do verses run?
Verses have num'rous feet, and Prose has none.

COMFORT FOR WALKERS

Ne'er did Triptolemus in his chariot rise,
Nor Castor mount on horse-back to the skies.
On foot the strait way may be safely trod,
But studs and wheels demand a spacious road.

TO ERASMUS

Thy praise of Folly so well writ
Proves not thy folly, but thy wit.

ON HIS CANDID & UNCANDID READERS

My Good are excellent, the candid say,
And e'en my Worst too good to cast away.
Th' uncandid deem Indifferent e'en my Best,
And without mercy censure all the rest.

ON THE PRODIGAL AND THE COVETOUS

Misers distribute nothing while they live,
And Spendthrifts when they die have nought to give.

CHEAP AND DEAR

Though Vice be common, we pay dear for Vice,
While Virtue, rare, is yet of little price.

ON THE SALT SEA

Salt begets thirst; then well may rivers be,
Salt as it is, all swallowed by the sea.

THE EVILS OF BAD EXAMPLE

Princes and Parents, sinning, must atone
For the example, not the crime alone.
The son still follows where the father leads,
And in her mother's steps the daughter treads;
Unchaste, if she be such; for seldom wild
And wanton mother owns a prudent child.
Ye Parents! give your offspring, then, to read
Their Duty plainly in your word and deed,
Since virtuous habits at an early day
Acquir'd, no time can ever steal away.

[In l. 6 'prudent' is a correction from 'virtuous', and in l. 8 'offspring' is a correction from 'child'.]

PHILAUTOS

Philautos loves himself alone,
Himself alone admires;
But save himself beholder none
With love of Him inspires.

[Line 3 originally ran 'But none except himself alone', and is corrected.]

TO LADY M. N. HIS PATRONESS

Praise to deserve yet never to desire
Is such high praise that none can merit higher
And this I give Thee with no base design
To flatter Thee for it is justly thine.

The same manuscript contains (besides two, or perhaps three, from the Greek, for which see notes to pp. 572, 573) the six printed on p. 563 with the following variant:

Sunset and Sunrise. Ll. 3, 4:

And when again in East he shines
Thy day of resurrection.

564 *Translations of Greek Verses.* I have not followed Hayley's order, which is quite arbitrary; no order is wholly satisfactory, but I have attempted to group the poems more or less according to subjects. The titles all come from Hayley.

571 *To Demosthenis.* Modern editors follow Southey in printing 'To Demosthenes'.

572 *By Philemon.* In the Bodleian MS. Autogr. d. 21, f. 191ʳ, l. 4, *For* indeed, *read* alas!

573 *By Moschus.* In the same MS. line 2 was corrected from 'An infant Cupid by his hand she led' and line 3 from 'He, bashful, eyed the ground...'. l. 9. *For* softest *read* softer.

In addition to these the Bodleian MS. has the following fragment from an unidentified original:

Nor this contented thee—thou, bent to save
All that of each could perish, from the grave,
In lasting records hast vouchsafed to trace
For each, his lot, his talents, manners, race.

575 *Simile in Paradise Lost.* 4. Hayley doubtless omitted this line because of its false concord; but if the scrap is printed it should be printed as Cowper wrote it. This applies too to the last two lines of *A Riddle* (p. 628.) This 'suppressed passage' at least supplies evidence that Cowper was not a first-rate Latin scholar; the other that he was not afraid of a broad joke even in a letter to Newton.

Translations from the *Fables of Gay.* In addition to the three published by Hayley in 1803, the Norfolk MS. includes:

PHILOSOPHUS ET PHASIANI

DILUCULO surgit Sapiens, et per juga nigra
 Quercubus, et raro trita rubeta pede,
Dum nemus altum avium resonat concentibus, aures
 Oblectandi ergo, difficile urget iter.
Alter ut ales opus suspendit, suscipit alter
 Œmulus, et renovat continuatque modos.
Sed quocunque pedem fert Aduena, territus illinc
 Se raptat volucer quisque, chorusque silet;
Argutâ Turdi dant signum voce timoris,
 Lusciniis monstrum est, attonitaeque vident,
Nec minus oderunt Animalia caetera, nec se
 Segnius in celerem prœripuere fugam.
† Cur Animal Hominem fugiunt alia omnia? formam †
 An odisse magis rere, magisne genus?
Haec animi trutinâ dubii dum volvit et errat,
 Vix minùs incertos accipit aure sonos;
Accedit pedetentim ubi densis Ales in umbris
 Stridebat, fluvio ex Phaside nomen habens;
Progenie gaudens multâ quâ cincta sedebat
 Consilium monitrix hoc dabat alma suis.

Ne migrate in agros. Vos hic violentia nulla
Chara mihi soboles! insidiæve manent.
Accipitrem milvumque cavete; cavete sed, oro!
Tetrum animal Hominem, pejus utrisque magis.
Solum Hominem fas est ingratum dicere; solum
Nulla ad amicitiam quem benefacta movent.
Arcet ei frigus, pulchris et vestibus ornat
Quam variè tinctum! tonsile vellus ovis.
Sic amicitur Homo, tractamque in turpe macellum
Dulcibus ex pratis, illico cœdit ovem.
Quæ per odoratas volitant examina valles,
Ingentique ferunt mella labore domum,
Sulphure supposito plenis alvearibus, ille
Enecat, inclusas ut sibi sumat opes.
Nudatus plumis quas grates accipit Anser
Cujus Homo scivit scibile quicquid ope?
Plumæ opus est Juveni ut secretum narret Amorem,
Mercatoris opes crescere Pluma facit;
Ille tamen cæsâ crudeliter Ansere, plumas
Evellit flammis, ustulat, assat, edit.
Ergo Hominem fugite, atque exosum semper habete,
Sic vobis aberit mors, aberitque diù.
Namque sibi utilibus qui nescit parcere, sævis
Ille coquis certe vos verubusque dabit.

579 *Translations of Milton.* The text is that of the first edition (*1808*), with the exceptions noted. I have altered the punctuation only where it is clearly wrong. At the end of the first edition are eighty-four pages of 'notes from various authors,' those not attributed by initials to Hayley, Warton, or others, being Cowper's. These are for the most part explanations of a few of the numerous classical allusions, obviously written down by Cowper at haphazard when he had the intention of completing a thorough annotation later. One note, however, on ll. 4-6 of the last Sonnet (p. 623) is worth repeating, as a pendant to Cowper's reference to Bentley (p. 582, *note*): 'It has ever been thought difficult for an author to speak gracefully of himself, especially in commendation; but Milton, who was gifted with powers to overcome difficulties of every kind, is eminently happy in this particular. He has spoken frequently of himself both in verse and prose, and he continually shows, that he thought highly of his own endowments; but if he praises himself, he does it with that dignified frankness and simplicity of conscious truth, which render even egotism respectable and delightful: whether he describes the fervent and tender emotions of his juvenile fancy, or delineates his situation in the decline of life, when he had to struggle with calamity and peril, the more insight he affords us into his own sentiments and feelings, the more reason we find both to love, and to revere him.'

592 92. 'let' is the reading of the first edition, text and notes; if it stands it must be governed by 'to' in l. 91.

621 In the third edition I included the following translations of two Greek poems by Milton, from Brit. Mus. Add. MS. 30801, ff. 61, 62, first printed by Mr. John Bailey in his edition of Cowper, 1905. I was indebted to him for the reference.

THE PHILOSOPHER AND THE KING

A Philosopher, included in the same sentence of condemnation with several guilty persons among whom he had been apprehended, sent the following lines, composed suddenly in the moment when be was going to death, to a certain King who had ignorantly condemned him.

Know this, O King! that if thou shalt destroy
Me, no man's enemy and who have liv'd
Obedient to the Laws, thou may'st with ease
Strike off a wise man's head, but, taught the truth
Hereafter, shalt with vain regret deplore
Thy city's loss of one, her chief support.

ON THE ENGRAVER OF HIS POURTRAIT

Look on myself, and thou shalt own at once
This Copy of me taken by a Dunce;
My Friends, who gaze and guess not whom ye see,
Laugh. Would ye think it? He intended me!

[The version printed by Mr. Bailey from Add. MS. 30801 is there interlined with a second version in another ink. Neither version is crossed out, but the first, third, and fourth lines of Mr. Bailey's version are underlined. That the following is Cowper's later version is shown by the omission indicated below in the third line, which is left to be supplied from the earlier-written version.]

Survey my Features—you will own it clear
That little skill has been exerted here
[My Friends,] who know me not here smile to see
How ill the model and the work agree.

633 *Lines.* Cowper took great pains over this trifle, and produced several versions before he and his friends were satisfied. An earlier version ran:

In vain to live from age to age
We modern bards endeavour;
But write in Patty's book one page,
You gain your point for ever.

In W. Roberts's *Memoirs of Hannah More* (ed. 2, 1834, ii. 282) is a letter from Cowper to Newton in 1791 with the following version, marked by Newton: 'Exemplar verum. Witness J. N.'

In vain to live from age to age,
We modern bards endeavour,
In Patty's book I wrote one page,
And gained my point for ever.

On April 23, 1923, the MS. of the following Sonnet was sold at Sotheby's.

A SONNET

Addressed to Mr. Phillips Printer now in confinem^t at Leicester

PHILLIPS ! the suff'rer less by law than pow'r,
Though prison'd in an adamantine hold,
May bear a heart as free and uncontroul'd
In his dark cell, as in a summer's bow'r.

[1]The sly accuser—He, who in an hour
When all suspicion slept, like Him of old
Eve's Tempter, wreath'd in many an artful fold
Conceal'd his drift with purpose to devour—
He is the pris'ner, and those ribs within
That hoop his sorry vitals round about
Dwells one, who never shall compassion win
Feel what he may, 'till Judgment call him out.

Thou then less deeply at thy wrongs repine,
Scorn is his meed, commiseration thine.

Written by the Poet Cowper, about the year 1793. Given to Mrs. Howard of Corby, by Lady Throckmorton, July 29, 1823.

The Phillips to whom this sonnet is addressed was Sir Richard Phillips, author, bookseller, and publisher, who was sentenced to 18 Months imprisonment in Leicester Gaol for selling Paine's 'Rights of Man.'

In the Norfolk MS. is the following hitherto unpublished and apparently original poem :

THE GRIEF OF AN HEIR

The Rich man's Heir, his father's spirit fled,
How mourns the stripling, with what rites, the Dead ?
Haste—bid the sexton toll two hours the bell,
That all may know it for my father's knell.
Tie up the knocker. Darken ev'ry room
With half-closed shutters. Sorrow loves a gloom.
To deepen the funereal silence more
With tip-toe step, ye lacqueys ! tread the floor.
Let each be measur'd for his suit of woe ;
A sad event demands as sad a show.
Within, without, wheels, harness, box and all
Black be my carriage ; sable as the pall.

[1] I forget his name, but he purchased the book insidiously that he might inform against the culprit. [W.C.]

Th' emblazon'd coat of my paternal race
Fix in my mansion's front, its proper place;
And, hung with sables, let the pulpit prove,
Itself, my deep regret, my filial love.
 Ah specious counterfeit! Thy sorrow, dress'd
In all this solemn pomp is all a jest;
Earth has no joy that can thy joys exceed,
And, could we doubt them, we were fools indeed.

April 20, 1799.

In this fourth edition I am enabled, once more through the kindness of Mr. Falconer Madan, to include the following seven poems, six of which were for the first time printed in 1931, while the seventh is from a rare printed broadside and anonymous. They are derived from two sources:

1. A quarto volume containing 251 pages, purchased in 1925 by the Bodleian Library, and comprising collections and notes relating to William Cowper, made by John Bruce, F.S.A. (1802–69), who edited the Aldine edition of Cowper's *Works* in 1865. This is now Bodl. MS. Eng. Misc. d. 135, and referred to as *Bodleian MS.*

2. A folio volume of 321 leaves, containing a large number of manuscript and printed pieces (chiefly in verse). It is in effect a miscellaneous scrap-book, probably first formed by the Rev. Martin Madan (author of *Thelyphthora*: 1726–90), with additions to about 1810 by members of the Madan family, and now owned by F. Madan, of Oxford. The Madan and Cowper families were related by at least three marriages in the eighteenth century. It is referred to as *Madan MS.*

I

ON THE JOY UNIVERSALLY EXPRESS'D ON THE KING'S HAPPY ESCAPE FROM ASSASSINATION

By Wm Cowper Esq.

The Cloud that frowns on what we prize
 Endears it but the more
It gains new lustre in our eyes
 When once the Storm is o'er.

Since George escap'd the mad design
 That threaten'd us with Night
The Royal Virtues seem to shine
 With more resplendent light.

So when the dread Eclipse is gone
 The happy Persians gaze
Upon their Deity the Sun
 And give him double Praise.

[*Madan MS.*, p. 61. The date of the poem is perhaps July 1777. The ascription to Cowper is an addition, not much later.]

II
CUM RATIONE INSANIRE

I AM a Caledonian born
  And in the British Senate
Have sounded oft Sedition's horn
  "For vary weal I ken it".

When London blazed then I was warm,
  Association-drunk,
And hoped in that illustrious storm
  Britannia should have sunk.

Two themes I chose, Popery one,
  Prerogative the other,
And Tag and Rag by canting won
  And Bob-tail and his brother.

Tried and acquitted (none can tell
  On what sufficient reason)
On other projects soon I fell,
  Still hank'ring after treason.

I raved and bawl'd with such a noise
  As we're in Homer told
Ulysses made, as big a voice
  As a man's head could hold.[1]

And all to show how well inclin'd
  I stood to ev'ry measure
In Congress plann'd—To ease my mind—
  And for my own good pleasure.

Fam'd d'Adhemar I worried next
  For popular diversion,
And Royal Antoinitta vex'd
  With libellous aspersion.

The Pris'ners too in Newgate all
  To mutiny exciting
I taught them on their knees to fall
  With pray'rs of my inditing.

Convict at last, I fled the Land,
  And set my patriot shoulder
To help the Dutchman to withstand
  And shove out the Stadtholder.

But thence expell'd, I took it ill,
  Renounced my own Baptismal,
And with long beard made longer still
  My length of visage dismal.

No Christian then—I'm now a Jew,
  And as my last good work
Hope yet to prove the Koran true,
  And die a turban'd Turk.

These and a thousand pranks beside
  Of similar complexion
Prove me at all points qualified
  For Akerman's protection.

[1] Ὅσον κεφαλὴ χάδε φωτός.

You call me mad, but, if you dare,
E'en turn me loose and try
Who best deserves that blame to bear,
You, my good friend, or I.

[*Bodleian MS.*, fol. 47: from Cowper's Entry Book of his Poems.
The Ulysses reference is to *Iliad* xi. 462. Adhemar was the fashionable Comte d'Adhémar, living in London in 1785; Antoinitta is, no doubt, Marie Antoinette. Akerman was Keeper of Newgate at this time.]

III

A

GOOD SONG

TUNE. "How happy could I be with either."

HERE 's a health to honest JOHN BULL,
When he 's gone we shan't find such another;
And with hearts and with glasses brim full,
Here 's a health to OLD ENGLAND his mother.

She gave him a good education,
Bade him keep to his church and his KING;
Be loyal and true to the Nation,
And then go be merry and sing.

Now *John* is a good humoured fellow,
Industrious, honest, and brave;
Not afraid of his *betters* when mellow,
For *betters* he knows he must have.

For there must be fine lords and fine ladies,
There must be some *little* and *great*;
Their wealth the supply of the trade is,
Our hands the support of their state.

Some are born for the court and the city,
And some for the village and cot;
But oh! 'twere a dolorous ditty,
If all became equal in lot.

If our ships have no pilots to steer,
What wou'd 'come of poor Jack in the shrouds?
Or our troops no commanders to fear,
They'd soon be arm'd robbers in crouds.

Then the plough and ⟨the⟩[1] loom must stand still,
If they made of us *gentlemen* all;
Or all clodhoppers; then who wou'd fill
The parliament, pulpit, and hall?

"Rights of Man" make a very fine sound,
"Equal Riches" a plausible tale;
But whose labour wou'd then till the ground?
All wou'd drink, but who'd brew the best ale?

When half naked, half starv'd in the street,
We were wand'ring about *sans culottes*,
Wou'd *equality* go fetch us meat?
Or wou'd *liberty* lengthen our coats?[2]

1 *the* added in manuscript. 2 *coat?* altered in manuscript to *coats?*

That knaves are for levelling no wonder,
'Tis easy to guess at their views;
'Tis *they* who get all by their plunder,
'Tis *they* who have nothing to lose.

Then away with such nonsense and stuff,
Full of treason, confusion and blood;
Ev'ry BRITON has freedom enough
To be *happy* as long as he's *good.*

To be rul'd by a merciful KING,
To be guarded by juries and laws;
And when our work's finished to sing—
This, this is true liberty's cause.

Then holloo boys! holloo boys! ever;
For just such a nation are[1] *we*;
'Tis our pleasure; O may it cease never![2]
'Tis our pride,[3] to be *loyal* and *free.*

[*printer's ornament.*]

[A printed sheet in the *Madan MS.*, p. 58. "By W. Cowper Esq." is added in manuscript.]

IV

TRANSLATION
by
W^m.Cowper Esqr

THY counsel sage, Maria fair,
Persuades me to be free;
And, free that I may still remain—
I bid adieu to thee!

[*Madan MS.* Cowper's "Maria" is usually Mrs. Throckmorton.]

V

THE SCHOLAR AT HIS WITS' END

A TALE

IN days when the learned, as old stories tell,
Were famous for raising his Highness of Hell,
A Scholar, with pot-hooks and hangers all bloody,
Succeeded, and conjur'd him into his study.
Now, though to excite him cost labour and pain,
It costs twice as much to lay him again,
And ne'er can be done, unless you can give
His De'ilship a task that he cannot atchieve.
So the Scholar enjoin'd him whatever he thought
Would puzzle him most, but he puzzled him not.
There was nothing so difficult, nothing so nice
But he did it, and show'd it him done in a trice.
At length said the Scholar (and look'd less aghast
For he surely believed he had hit it at last)

[1] *as* altered in manuscript to *are.*
[2] comma altered in manuscript to !.
[3] comma added in manuscript.

Go—fetch me a thing hard enough to defie
All force of impression, whatever we try.
Then he brought him a flint, but that would not do—
Then a bridling old maiden, but she yielded too—
Then he stood at a plunge, and feared he must go
Back again to his dreary apartment below,
But suddenly starting, as one just awake
From a nap that he had not intended to take
"Oh how"—he exclaim'd—"could I be such a dunce!
"I have it—I'll furnish you with it at once."
So he went, and return'd twice as soon as before
With the heart of a plump Overseer of the Poor.
"Alas!" quoth the Student, with sorrowful face,
"I give up the point, 'tis a desperate case—
"I never shall lay thee, and woe to the art
"That taught me to raise thee, say I, from my heart,
"'Tis the thing in the world that I wish'd thee to miss,
"For thy own is not half so obdurate as This."

[*Bodleian MS.* From a copy in Cowper's handwriting in his Entry Book of his Poems, vol. I, p. 110.]

VI

PSALM 114th

"by Willm Cowper Esq."

1

WHEN Israel by Jehovah call'd
From Ægypt's hostile plain,
Pour'd forth in numbers as the Sand
And sought the adjacent main:

2

Then God descended from on high
To lead the favour'd Race
To rule o'er Jacob, & his Name
In Judah's Tribe to place.

3

The Sea at their approach allarm'd
In wild amazement fled
And Jordans flood was driven back
Within it's fountain head.

4

The Mountains from their basis shook
Confess'd the Parent God!
With sudden throws like Rams they skipp'd
And broken, fell abroad.

5

The little Hills by the same power
Were from their Center torn
Like Lambs resistless they gave way
In Tumult wild, upborn.

6

Ye Waves what strange amazement, say,
Seiz'd on you that you fled?
Thou Jordan too! on Israels march,
Why driven to thy Head?

7

Ye Mountains whence this sudden fright
That shook you from your base?
And whence, ye little Hills, your flight
From Israels chosen Race?

8

Tremble thou Earth! It's God who comes,
Whose Presence fills thy Coast.
Tremble thou Earth! Jehovah leads,
And guards the mighty Host!

That God who by his awfull Word,
Commands the Stream to flow
From flinty Rocks; & pouring thence,
To form the Lake below.

[*Madan MS.*, p. 140.]

VII

A HYMN

FOR A CHILD THAT HAS UNGODLY PARENTS

How happy are those Little ones
Whose parents fear the Lord,
And shew their daughters and their sons
The treasures of his Word!

Instructed, not at school alone,
But at their home beside,
With quicker pace they travel on,
And never want a guide.

I know that scripture tells me true,
There is a place of woe
(My parents! I am pain'd for you)
To which the careless go.

O Lord, who causest Babes to see,
And lead'st the ancient blind,
Their case, who being gave to me,
Sits heavy on my mind.

Must we and shall we, when the date
Of this short life is o'er
Be fixt in such a diff'rent state,
And meet in love no more?

Forbid it, Lord! and change a pray'r
In trembling hope preferr'd,
To praise and thanks for saving care
And supplication heard.

[*Bodleian MS.*, fol. 51, from Cowper's Entry Book of his Poems.]

INDEX OF FIRST LINES

SET IN GREAT BRITAIN AT THE UNIVERSITY PRESS, OXFORD
AND PRINTED BY THE CAMELOT PRESS LTD. SOUTHAMPTON